Ukraine
Over the Edge

Ukraine Over the Edge

*Russia, the West
and the "New Cold War"*

GORDON M. HAHN

McFarland & Company, Inc., Publishers
Jefferson, North Carolina

LIBRARY OF CONGRESS CATALOGUING-IN-PUBLICATION DATA

Names: Hahn, Gordon M., author.
Title: Ukraine over the edge : Russia, the West and the "new Cold War" /
Gordon M. Hahn.
Other titles: Russia, the West and the "new Cold War"
Description: Jefferson, North Carolina : McFarland & Company, Inc.,
Publishers, 2018 | Includes bibliographical references and index.
Identifiers: LCCN 2017040555 | ISBN 9781476669014
(softcover : acid free paper) ∞
Subjects: LCSH: Ukraine Conflict, 2014– | Ukraine—Politics and
government—1991– | Ukraine—History—1991– | Geopolitics—Ukraine. |
Ukraine—Foreign relations—Russia (Federation) | Russia
(Federation)—Foreign relations—Ukraine. | United States—Foreign
relations—Ukraine. | Ukraine—Foreign relations—United States. |
Ukraine—Foreign relations—European Union countries. |
European Union countries—Foreign relations—Ukraine.
Classification: LCC DK508.846 .H38 2018 | DDC 947.7086—dc23
LC record available at https://lccn.loc.gov/2017040555

BRITISH LIBRARY CATALOGUING DATA ARE AVAILABLE

ISBN (print) 978-1-4766-6901-4
ISBN (ebook) 978-1-4766-2875-2

Front cover photograph of Ukrainian flag on the barricade
at Hrushevskogo street in Kiev, 2014 © 2018 AndreyKrav/iStock

Printed in the United States of America

*McFarland & Company, Inc., Publishers
Box 611, Jefferson, North Carolina 28640
www.mcfarlandpub.com*

To the memory
of my late loving wife,
Marina Markovna Stegantseva-Hahn
(April 1, 1966–June 23, 2015)

Table of Contents

"They sow the wind and reap the whirlwind.
The stalk has no head; it will produce no flour.
Were it to yield grain, foreigners would swallow it up."—Hosea 8:7

Preface

As I read, listened and watched Western sources on the events surrounding the mass demonstrations on central square in Kiev during winter 2013–2014, a sense of *déjà vu* became undeniable. Having studied the nature of terrorism in Russia's North Caucasus, the causes and course of the August 2008 Georgian-Russian war, and other events involving Russia, I had seen a pattern of misrepresentation of these events by most Western, especially American, media, academia and government sources. There was a clear sense that this pattern was being repeated with regard to the events on the Maidan. Hence, I decided to investigate matters for myself and have come to a distinctly different conclusion regarding them than that imparted to the Western public.

Two years after the Maidan "revolution of dignity," it was already clear that the Western-backed overthrow of Ukrainian President Viktor Yanukovich was not entirely a revolution and was ultimately in vain regardless of how one conceptualizes the events surrounding the fall-winter 2013–2014 demonstrations and violence on Kiev's Maidan. The movement was based intially on middle class opposition to corruption and soft authoritarianism and support for European integration. Ultimately, the nascent pro-democratic revolution was hijacked by neofascist elements that infiltrated the Maidan protests, overthrew the government, and then were themselves superseded by several key oligarchs, who always have thrived under the post–Soviet *ancien regime*. Thus, corruption and criminality have increased rather than decreased, European integration has stalled, and authoritarianism is not just in the corridors of power but on the streets under the yoke of roaming bands of neofascist groups seeking to foment a second, truly "national revolution."

Despite the all-too-numerous adepts of democratization and democratic "transition," this is not the first, nor is it likely to be the last time when the West has misunderstood processes it has hoped for, encouraged, and often funded and helped to organize. The "Arab Spring" is only the most recent set of cases in point. Predictably, that spring's various revolutions became an Islamist winter spread across parts of the Middle East and North Africa, except in Egypt—where a counterrevolution returned the *status quo ante*.

Similarly, in 1991 the adepts of democratic transitions or "transitology" got it wrong. Few post–Soviet states became democracies because the "democratic revolution" that overthrew the reformist late Soviet regime of Mikhail Gorbachev's *perestroika* was assumed to be a "revolution from below" led by societal opposition forces bent on living in a democracy. This was true in the Baltic republics, but in most cases the elements of democratic revolution from below were subsumed by a mix of less civil state bureaucrat–led revolutions from above and nationalist-led revolutions from below. In Russia, the revolution was largely one led from above by the Russian President Boris Yeltsin and the Russian state apparatus against the partially reformed but crumbling central Soviet state and regime. In Central Asia and elsewhere, there was simply a change of signboards, rebranding for still very authoritarian regimes. The partial exception is Kyrgyzstan's tulip revolutions and counterrevolutions, which also had strong elements from above. Thus, it is no surprise that both Ukraine's 2004 Orange revolution, as I noted at the time, and the 2013–2014 Maidan "revolution of dignity," as I predicted, proved to be something less than the democratic revolutions "transitologists" hailed.

In addition to elements of revolution from below, the Maidan revolt also has elements of revolution from above led by some state officials and state-tied oligarchs. Moreover, the revolution from below was under considerable influence from national chauvinist, ultranationalist, and neofascist groups. The Maidan ultranationalist-oligarchic regime now has little popular support and few accomplishments in democratization, and is little different from the previous, except for a marked increase in western Ukrainian neofascism (both in the corridors of power and on the streets) and a near catastrophic economy. Revolutions are indeed unwieldly things, not very manageable once unleashed.

The international geopolitical consequences have been even more deleterious. A deepening Russian-Western confrontation over Ukraine risks recreating a bipolar "world split apart," with Russia more inclined than ever to forge alliances with regimes opposed to American and Western power.

This book is dedicated to clarifying these events and their consequences, something that is imperative given the misleading government and media characterizations of them. This study is based on Western, Ukrainian and Russian sources, including media reports, reliable primary and secondary Internet sources, and official documents of governments and international organizations. They show Maidan's quasi-revolution was driven by international geopolitics, supporting counterposed Western and Russian "civilizationist" beliefs, and deep divisions within Ukrainian society itself, not a wellspring of widespread aspiration to Western-style democracy.

1

A World Split Apart
Geopolitical and Civilizationalist Sources

The causes of the contemporary Ukrainian conflict are both geopolitical-civilizational and Ukrainian domestic. It is certainly true that, as one analyst notes, "geopolitics teaches that subjective inclinations do not erase historical patterns."[1] However, structural causes, such as geography, and their reflection in historical patterns do not pre-determine political outcomes, but significantly shape them. They provide a structure of constraints, which might be overcome or exacerbated by political contingency—the actions of political actors and historical accident. This is especially true if strategic cultures, ideas, attitudes and beliefs of actors accept the geopolitical approach's explanatory and analytical power for understanding international relations.

The Geopolitical Schism

The father of geopolitical theory, Halford J. Mackinder, designated the European-Eurasian continent the "World Island" and Russia and central Eurasia as the World Island's "Pivot Area" or "Heartland." Mackinder's formula was: "Who rules East Europe commands the Heartland: Who rules the Heartland commands the World-Island: Who rules the World-Island commands the world." Traditional geostrategic thinking in lieu of other factors tends to dictate that great powers will endeavor to rule Eastern Europe in order to command Russia, the World Island, and thus the world. In this conceptualization, the U.S. in the post–Cold War world was bound to carry out a foreign policy that first and foremost prevented a revival or survival of Russian influence in Eastern Europe which would enable Moscow to check Western hegemony over the Eurasian landmass and thus globally.

Less theoretical considerations can help us understand how theory actually plays out in contemporary international politics. If the heartland is controlled by a massive central Eurasian power like Russia, then Russia has gone a long way towards controlling the World Island–Eurasia. Thus, Russia's geographic position both exposes it to potentially multiple external threats and offers opportunities for asserting its interests and even inflicting its power and control over some or all of the heartland's peripheries: Europe, Asia, and the Middle East. This complicates the political and economic lives of the countries or empires in these regions as well as any outside powers that seek control of the "World Ocean." Thus, oceanic powers seek dominon over the World Island. They include

3

naval powers on the World Island's edges, such as Great Britain, or from across the Atlantic or Pacific, in the Americas, such as the U.S. If an outside power seeks or establishes a foothold on the world island, it will confront resistance from the heartland power, usually Russia. This, according to classical geopolitical thought, is the foundation of the tussle for Europe and Eurasia between Moscow and Washington today.

Various factors might mitigate the salience of this tectonic: the relative strength or weakness of contending powers, state ideologies, cultural and/or civilizational characteristics and differences, trade patterns, synergies between markets, etc. For example, if America and Russia were status quo powers adhering to democracy and markets, and Europe was not, a Russian-American alliance countering Europe would be more likely to occur. If trade synergies cemented strong Russian-European bonds, both might act to limit American efforts in Europe. The hard reality of geography determines the shape and dynamics of these tendencies in international relations, but the geostrategic structure and dynamics do not predetermine outcomes in international affairs given the other noted factors: power correlation, economic interests, and ideology. In the contemporary world, the structure faced the post–Cold War West with a choice in attempting to access the heartland: either seek a *modus vivendi* with the USSR's successor as the heartland's hegemon—Russia—or contest Russia's status as such.

There is no doubt that Mackinder's ideas influence geostrategic thinking the world over, no more so than in Washington. The introduction to a 1996 U.S. National Defense University (NDU) republication of Mackinder's 1919 study "The Geographical Pivot of History" notes: "In the 1950s Mackinder's influence declined as the Western strategy of containment of the Soviet Union came to dominate political and military planning. Since the end of the Cold War, however, as regional strategic concerns have replaced those of the global bipolar confrontation of the twin superpowers, the relevance of Mackinder's study is once again apparent."[2] The NDU republication makes no bones about who are the contenders with whom the U.S. must compete to "rule" East Europe and command the World Island: "Prescient in its anticipation of German resurgence, and of later superpower status of the Soviet Union, it was little heeded at the time…. His immediate warning concerned the potential resurgence of Germany after World War I. Recognizing that Russia could pose little danger for the near term, he nonetheless reasoned that the postwar peace required a buffer between the two great historical 'organizers' to prevent the ascendance of either to challenge the powers of the littoral nations, which he called the inner and outer crescents."[3]

Mackinder's "inner and outer crescents" equated with Yale University professor Nicholas Spykman's "Rimland." Writing during World War II, Spykman amended Mackinder with his "Rimland theory": "Who controls the Rimland rules Eurasia, who rules Eurasia controls the destinies of the world."[4] Eurasia's periphery around Russia formed the outer edges of Eurasia from the European "peninsula" in the west to the Islamic south to the Asian southeast. The geostrategic question is which way to look at this dynamic. If one controls or partners with a powerful enough organizer of the heartland (Russia), then one can command the periphery and thus the world. By contrast, one can control the Eurasian peripheries or "crescents" and hope to parlay that into control of the heartland. Each strategy approach dictates rather different policies, especially towards Russia.

In accordance with the first approach, former CIA analyst and Stratfor director George Friedman, an adherent of the geopolitical approach influential in American thinking, stated explicitly in 2010: "While the United States can welcome a powerful Turkey, the same can't be said for a powerful Russia, particularly not one allied with Germany. The single greatest American fear should not be China or al Qaeda. It is the amalgamation of the European Peninsula's technology with Russia's natural resources. That would create a power that could challenge American primacy. That was what the 20th century was all about."[5] Of course, the 20th century was dominated by the Cold War waged in Washington and Moscow, but the Cold War was not about who commanded the World Island. It was a global conflict between the international, totalitarian communist movement and Western-oriented democratic capitalism.

Another influential Mackinderite is former U.S. presidential National Security advisor and Polish émigré' Zbigniew Brzezinski. Referring to Russia as "The Black Hole" in his study *The Grand Chessboard: American Primacy and Its Geostrategic Imperatives*, he called for a "comprehensive and integrated Eurasian geostrategy" as the cornerstone of American foreign policy:

> American foreign policy must remain concerned with the geopolitical dimension and must employ its influence in Eurasia in a manner that creates a stable continental equilibrium, with the United States as the political arbiter.
>
> Eurasia is thus the chessboard on which the struggle for global primacy continues to be played, and that the struggle involves geostrategy—the strategic management of geopolitical interests.... Adolf Hitler and Joseph Stalin, agreed explicitly (in the secret negotiations of November 1940) that America should be excluded from Eurasia. Each realized that the injection of American power into Eurasia would preclude his ambitions regarding global domination. Each shared the assumption that Eurasia is the center of the world. A half century later, the issue has been redefined: will America's primacy in Eurasia endure, and to what ends might it be applied?
>
> The ultimate objective of American foreign policy should be benign and visionary: to shape a truly cooperative global community, in keeping with long-range trends and with the fundamental interests of humankind. *But in the meantime, it is imperative that no Eurasian challenger emerges, capable of dominating Eurasia and thus also of challenging America* [my emphasis].[6]

It is obvious in this rendering that not just Hitler and Stalin, but also Brzezinski himself, were channeling Mackinder. Similarly to Friedman, Brzezinski saw the *modus vivendi* between Germany and Soviet Russia to join in organizing Eurasia was intended to limit American power. Brezinski proposes a countering "great game" in the same Eurasia writ large based on a similar Mackinderian hypothesis: a power dominating Eurasia, the World Island, will challenge America's "command of the world" or hegemony.

Brzezinski's Mackinderian orientation becomes clearer when we examine the specifics of his analysis. Brzezinski divided his "Eurasian chessboard" into four regions: the West (Europe as a whole), the middle space (the former USSR), the South (Turkey, the Levant, the Arabian Peninsula, and South and Central Asia), and the East (Japan, China and the rest of Southeast Asia). Crucially, he warned if "America's primacy in Eurasia" is not to shrink "dramatically," then U.S. geostrategy must prevent an outcome whereby "the middle space rebuffs the West, becomes an assertive single entity, and either gains control over the South or forms an alliance with the major Eastern actor."[7] Since Russian control over the entire South is a near impossibility and reasonably excluded in any foreseeable future, then the goal of Brzezinski's U.S. geostrategy should be to prevent Moscow from both organizing the post–Soviet states and forming an alliance with the major Eastern actor, clearly China. Again the Mackinderian theory focuses American foreign policy on limiting and, depending on circumstances, weakening Russian influence and power in its own region and along its borders.

In terms of policies to implement this strategy, Brzezinski proposed gradual, simultaneous, and "integrally connected" processes of EU and NATO expansion. Rather than Europe's expansion beginning in the east with Russia, it should proceed from the west, thereby excluding Russia and bringing in countries largely antagonistic towards Russia—Poland, the Czech Republic, and the Baltic states. For Brzezinski, if an increasingly geographically larger EU must base its security on continued alliance with America, "then it follows that its geopolitically most exposed sector, Central Europe, cannot be demonstratively excluded" from NATO. He delineates a "historic timetable" for NATO's expansion: admission of the "first" new Central European members by 1999; the beginning of accession talks and admission by 2005 for the Baltic states and Romania; eligibility for the Balkan states at about the same time; possible accession by Sweden and Finland; and somewhere between 2005 and 2010 the beginning of "serious negotiations" for Ukraine with both the EU and NATO. Except for the last two stages, Brzezinski's timetable played out approximately as advised. The logic was to build "the critical core of Europe's security running" from France (actually the U.S.) in the west through Ukraine in the east, thereby ending at Russia's border. For Brzezinski there were two "vital geopolitical pivots" in Eurasia—Azerbaijan and Ukraine.[8] Generals on Arbat Square would, should and surely did logically ask: "Security from whom?"

In Western policymaking circles, Friedman, Brzezinski, and other Mackinderites are considerably influential. Friedman's views are not atypical of thinking in the intelligence and military departments. Brzezinski has both family members and like-minded political minions ensconced across Washington in government, think tanks, and media. Brzezinski can determine across a large network whether scholars and analysts get hired, get published or receive grants for their work. In this way, their brand of Russia-targeted geopolitical thought undergirds much of the thinking in Washington, Brussels, and other Western capitols. Their message is clear: Russia cannot be allowed to be powerful and "organize" the World Island.

Brzezinski's preferred course was not just driven by the objective implications of Mackinderian geopolitical analyses. His Polish anti–Russianness surely informed his approach. It is no conincidence that the same flaws extant across the former USSR were only applied to Russia as criteria for consideration as a partner by Brzezinski: "Russia was just too backward and too devastated by Communist rule to be a viable democratic partner of the United States."[9] The Central and East European lobbies surely echoed Brzezinski's bias in the ears of policymakers and in media. The existing institutions and strategic culture of many in the West led in the same direction, producing a traditional "19th-century approach," even an 18th-century approach, to the heartland challenge tied to a policy—NATO expansion. To many in Moscow (and elsewhere), this appeared to be a return of Cold War containment rather than an enjoinment or partnership with a post–Cold War, democratizing Russian power.

The Mackinderian strain in American geostrategic thinking helped produce, and largely predetermined, a dynamic that led to what many now in the wake of the Ukrainian crisis and civil war refer to as a "new Cold War." But the geostrategic thinking in which Mackinder, Friedman, and those Western policymaking circles engage is also what Western and Russian critics of Russian foreign policy accuse Moscow of deploying—"19th-century thinking." Since both sides engage in "19th-century thinking," they helped bring about in East Europe an early 20th century–like crisis like that which sparked World War I. This includes the development of a system of competing alliances even if still in embryonic form. Late 2014 and 2015 were marked by a deepening and expansion of several multinational organizations that Moscow has worked hard to build as a counterweight to NATO and the EU: the Eurasian Economic Union, BRICS, and the increasingly security-oriented Shanghai Cooperation Organization (SCO).

Alternative Geostrategy?

Despite Russia's lack of capacity to "organize Eurasia" at the Cold War's end, it became the target of a 19th-century–style and Cold War–style policy—alliance building. But geopolitical theory and geostrategic concepts can be applied variously and produce a range of specific policy prescriptions. This is where contingency can trump structural constraints and produce outcomes different from those favored by the structure of geostrategics and geopolitical strategizing. Indeed, both Mackinder and his 21st-century reincarnation, Freidman, proposed an alternative to an alliance-bifurcated World Island of the kind experienced in Cold War 1.0. Mackinder proposed, in the words of the NDU introduction, "a buffer between the two great historical 'organizers' to prevent the ascendance of either to challenge the powers of the littoral nations."[10] In 2010, Friedman resurrected interwar Polish dictator Pilsudski's idea of an "Intermarium"—consisting of Poland, Slovakia, Hungary, Romania and perhaps Bulgaria—as "this generation's alliance." The Intermarium's benefit is to the countries caught between NATO expansion and Russia's opposition, since "it blocks the Russians, splits them from the Germans and gently limits Turkey's encroachment in southeastern Europe." "[A] U.S.–backed Poland guarding the North European Plain, with Slovakia, Hungary and Romania guarding the Carpathian approaches, would prevent what the United States should fear the most: an alliance between Russia and Germany plus Western Europe." Friedman regards NATO to be doomed and correctly, in my view, realizes it is a bureaucracy seeking perpetuity after it has served its purpose.[11]

The Intermarium becomes possible only if NATO dissolves, since all prospective Intermarium members are NATO members. The Intermarium's time may also have passed, despite its being praised by former Polish President Lech Kaczyński, present Polish President Andrzei Duda, and some Ukrainians.[12] In the early to mid–1990s it might have been a potential solution to the problem of NATO expansion and Russia's then moderate opposition to it. Depending on how it was implemented and what relationship it developed with NATO, Russia, and Russia's immediate neighbors, the Intermarium could have helped avoid the present Ukrainian and Western-Russian crises. A NATO-Intermarium alliance would reiterate the problem, including western Ukraine's attraction, eastern Ukraine's repulsion, and Russian opposition. After all, part of the geostrategic calculus of East Europe is the northern plain's historical usage as an invasion route running both ways, but mostly east. Teutonic, Livonian, Polish-Lithuanian, Napoleonic, and German Nazi armies have made the march through them into Russia. Thus, it was ironic when, during the Ukrainian crisis, an American general argued on a U.S. television channel in 2014 the importance of Ukraine for U.S. national security based on the region's convenient geography for a Russian invasion of Europe. Good invasion routes run both ways.

Moscow is no less inured to the subtleties and vicissitudes of foreign policy discussions in Washington, than Washington is to those in Moscow. Russians are familiar with contemporary policy prescriptions by influential actors and the theories that inform them, including Mackinder, Friedman, and Brzezinski. Moreover, there are Russian counterparts to them and their geostrategic thinking. At the time and since, Brzezinski's *The Grand Chessboard*, published in a Russian translation in 1998, was widely discussed in Russia. The influential daily *Nezavisimaya gazeta* published a long, detailed review noting that Brzezinski's work is "little different from the works of other American specialists." Add to this the tendency of many Russians to regard any pronouncement from a Washington think tank scholar to be that of the U.S. government (no less one who was once a high-ranking U.S. official), and Brzezinksi's views are perceived from Moscow as having even greater weight. The reviewer takes some umbrage to the use of the term "black hole" in reference to his country and to Brzezinski's "unkind tone," though he acknowledges it is somewhat justified. He sums up Brzezinski's view:

> Therefore, the Russian "black hole," in Brzezinski's opinion should be either marginalized, reduced to a minimum … or destroyed by way of the further breakup of our country into easily manageable and controllable principalities or as the result of the creation in it of a responsible and ruling regime according to Western standards. Anything else will be unacceptable and will be considered a source of danger and a target of various forms and methods of coercion. And for now the West and the U.S. in particular should do everything to create along Russia's periphery a kind of sphere of security: in Central and Eastern Europe by way of NATO's expansion; in the Balkans by way of filling the power vaccum with NATO forces; in the Caucasus and Caspian region by the efforts of Turkey; and in Central Asia by the collective efforts of the West and Japan.[13]

The reviewer then discusses a number of questions Brzezinksi's prescriptions raise and issues what is perhaps a veiled or objectively logical warning:

> [H]ow is it planned to introduce this order [in Eurasia]: By organizing some kond of European-wide process with corresponding negotiations or will it be introduced by force not necessarily through war but nevertheless by way of coercion? [I]f such an order is actually created, what are the guarantees of its survival and who will provide those guarantees and over what period of time?
> Force can do a lot, but it is necessary to know when, how, and with what goal it will be used. Besides this, the laws of nature and social relations are well-known. Against every force there is an equal and opposing counteraction. Even if force introduces order, there are always sufficient elements which come forward against any order and so too in society where there are always opposition elements coming forward against any system. Is the U.S. prepared to struggle against these elements until eternity, or, as occurred in Somalia will they board their people on ships and sail to blessed America on the first major losses? … The book is written as if the "chess game" on the "board" of Eurasia is already over or is just about to come to the end. But we who live in this part of the world know that it is far from completion, and there will absolutely be unexpected turns and to present the wreath to the victor is still just a bit early.[14]

Russian intellectual resistance to the geostrategic approach of NATO and EU expansion was already emerging. From its different geopolitical perspective, Moscow counters using the same theory precisely in order to remain the decisive power in the heartland.

"Mackinder-skis": Russia's Neo-Eurasianist Geostrategic Thinking

At the height of the Cold War, the Soviet Communist Party general secretary issued his "new political thinking" as a way of de-escalating if not ending the Cold War. In the post–Cold War era, "neo–Eurasianist" geostrategic thought in various variations replaced both old communist and new political thinking, taking up the geopolitical challenge posed by Western geostrategy and policies such as NATO expansion. By the post–Soviet period, neo–Eurasianists were intimately familiar with Mackinder, Brzezinski and other

Western geostrategists and turned geopolitical logic against them in support of an alternative to Russia's Western integration and westernization. In the 19th century, Eurasianism emerged as an attempt to overcome the philosophical and political rift among the Russian intelligentsia between pro-reform Westernizers and pro-tsarist Slavophiles. Eurasianism was less geopolitical than philosophical, historiological and culturological, envisaging a unique civilization rather than geostrategy. Russia's role, Eurasianists argued, was not to imitate Western liberalism and democracy or to reject it out of hand on the basis of Russian "specificity." Russia's unique and missionary role was to gather together from Eurasia's rich civilizational diversity a "third way" consistent with the culture and traditions of Orthodoxy and Russia, as the most modern of Eurasia's civilizations, but incorporating the best from East and West.

Post-Soviet neo–Eurasianism became, however, very much geopolitical and geostrategic, rooting the original 19th-century vintage on the ground in Eurasia as an alternative geopolitical space, political-historical project and, as discussed below, mega-civilization needing protection from the West and capable of integrating much of the non–West. Neo-Eurasian geopolitical thought thus facilitates Western Russophobes' stereotypes concerning Russian "zapadnophobia," just as Western geostrategicians' analysis confirms the fears of Russian, indeed Eurasianist, Americanophobes.

Alexander Panarin's 1998 study, *History's Revenge*, is one of the first syntheses of anti–Western and Russian nationalist political thought formulated into a Eurasianist geopolitical and geostrategic response to American hegemony and globalization.[15] Panarin, who died in 2003, was a well-established scholar: a professor at Moscow State University (MGU), founder of the Sub-Department of Political Science in MGU's Philosophy Department, and a specialist on American and French conservatism.[16] One of his first major publications was the book *Orthodox Christian Civilization*.[17] Panarin's anti–Westernism, and indeed that of much of contemporary neo–Eurasianism, is mostly anti–American, conceptualized in many of the terms of the postmodern Left's critique of globalization. America, according to this view, is both subjectively (self-servingly) and objectively the purveyor of destructive globalization. American-driven globalization is leading the world down a cataclysmic road of unsustainable development, the destruction of national cultures and non–Western civilizations at the hands of the consumer culture, and ultimately the death of the ecology and thus mankind. The only hope is to divide the West by slicing off Europe from the U.S.–led Atlantic juggernaut. Points of leverage in this strategy are the romantic and resurgent Germans of Central Europe and perhaps the fraternal Slavs of Eastern Europe. The other approach is to rally the non–West against Atlantic civilization. Points of leverage are Russia's syncreticism, Chinese economic power, and Indian and Persian mysticism.[18]

Panarin's Eurasianist geostrategy reflects not just traits portrayed in stereotypes of Russia's anti-Western geostrategic culture but incorporates messianistic and promethean strains and substrains from the depths of Russian political and strategic culture. Panarin's neo–Eurasianism resents the encroachment of American power and the press of globalization, in neo–Mackinderian terms. In his view, Eurasia's stability and global survival are impossible without Russia. It is uniquely poised to offer and organize an alternative civilization to the allegedly reckless techno-economic imperative of American-led globalization threatening the global ecology. Russia is destined by geography and history not just to organize central Eurasia (the former Soviet republics), but is assigned the promethean task of organizing China, India, Iran and the Islamic world against the West.[19]

Russia's historical and spatial sensibility regarding Eurasia's development and organization, respectively, imparts "the great historical task of Russian civilization—the capacity to form large interethnic syntheses—… its answer to the challenge of the plains of the Eurasian space."[20]

Panarin sees three main theaters of Russian geopolitical strategy in Eurasia and expresses them in precisely Mackinderian terms. The Eastern scenario holds that the impossibility of China's integration into the West, and the post–Cold War failure to so integrate Russia, give impetus to a Sino-Russian "union"—"a partner in the heartland"— creating a line of differentiation in Eurasia corresponding to "the classic geopolitical dichotomy of 'heartland-rimland.'" A more "radical" version of this counterpoint to Atlanticism would include India. India's accession to the heartland partnership or Eurasian "union" would be driven by the ostensible existential threat to the global ecology and mankind's multicultural diversity posed from globalized industrialization and consumerism. In Panarin's reading, Indian civilization does not tolerate hierarchy or destruction of nature. The "Hindu-Buddhist tradition" treasures even the "smallest insect" as "irreplaceable and an ultimate value" equivalent to "the other constituent parts of the Great Living Cosmos." This civilizational value might become a central thesis for a Eurasia-driven "new reformation," according to Panarin. India's accession to the Eurasian project would bring about "a new bipolar structure of the world," which would include on one side the West and the Muslim world and on the other—India, China and Russia. Iran's integration into the project is to be based not just on Tehran's and Moscow's mutual suspicions of Turkish expansionism into the Middle East, the Caucasus, and Central Asia but also on ancient cultural "reforms" enacted by the ancient Zarathustrians supposedly still retained in Iran's "cultural memory."[21]

Panarin also posits a less convincing Central European scenario. In his telling, Russia's double-headed eagle implies a Western option, but one centered on Germany and German-dominated Central Europe, not "Atlantism." Central Europe's emergence as a separate if not yet wholly autonomous entity is a potential reaction to Europe's enforced uniformity and geopolitical dependence under the American hegemon. The possible reconstruction and consolidation of Germany's and Central Europe's geopolitical (and cultural) independence would turn Germany away from "Americanism" and Atlantism to the Eurasian "continental idea." "Germany's identity as a continental country that is part of the Eurasian heartland" has "large geopolitical potential." Therefore, Germany faces a dilemma: "[W]hether to build the heartland *together with* Russia, or Russia will build it with China in an *alternative* form" [Panarin's emphases]. At times, Panarin echoes the Intermarium idea, with "[t]he new phenomenon of Central Europe crystallizing around Germany" dismantling both the "Atlantic system" and the "previous system of Eastern Europe and the Eurasian bloc once controlled by the USSR."[22]

Least convincing of all is Panarin's discussion of the southern, essentially Islamic scenario. Oddly, Iran is not raised as an anchor for a Russian geostrategy for Eurasia's southern "rim." Instead, almost the entire discussion centers around the prospects of an alliance with the Muslim south—with no distinction made between Shiia and Sunni Islam—and relations with Central Asia. The traditionalist religious core of the Russian Christian Orthodox and Islamic civilizations forms the basis for Panarin's relative optimism about an alliance.[23]

The work of the philosopher, political scientist, and geostrategist Alexander Dugin represents probably the most sophisticated if exotic face of radical contemporary Russian geopolitical neo–Eurasianism. A prolific writer and lecturer, Dugin's worldview, according to Sheffield, is "highly syncretic" and constantly evolving.[24] His politics, however, are an eclectic mix of neo–Eurasianism (discussed below), explicit Russian imperialism, and anti–Westernism. He has been a leader in several totalitarian movements, including occupying top posts in the National Bolshevik Party and later his own Eurasian Party. Dugin is a representative of the younger generation of geopolitical theorists and strategists, which has had a tense relationship with some among the older generation of the same due to the former's increased radicalism and, some would say, para-scientific work. Unlike Panarin's work, Dugin's is not accepted as scholarly by Russian academics.[25] Thus, Dugin's influence should not be overstated—he is not the Kremlin's gray cardinal or Putin's advisor. In the 1990s and early 2000s he was an advisor to successive chairmen of the State Duma. In the late 2000s he became a columnist for two major Russian newspapers: *Izvestiya* and *Komsomol'skaya Pravda*.[26] Dugin briefly headed a Sub-Department of the International Relations Department at MGU until summer 2014, when he was fired for harshly criticizing Putin's Ukraine policy, which he viewed as passive.[27] Dugin's writings have on occasion degenerated into anti–Semitism, such as in his 2000 article "Krestovyi pokhod Solntsa" (Crusade of the Sun), in which he rants against "Jewish dictatorship" and "the eschatological ghost of world Jewry that undoubtedly stands at the center of the 'new world order.'"[28]

Regarding Dugin's influence, Shenfield puts it well: "[I]t is not insignificant." His geopolitical writings do have some influence within the *siloviki* (military, intelligence, security, and law enforcement organs).[29] Shenfield's work and Dugin's numerous publications (in particular, *The Geopolitics of the Post-Modern* and *The Basics of Geopolitics*) and video lectures, demonstrate that Dugin's "geopolitical model" is based on Mackinder and Karl Haushofer, who elaborated on the theory in Weimar and Nazi Germany and emphasized "the imperative of Russo-German solidarity against the Anglo-American adversary."[30] In his 2002 book, *Yevraziiskii put' kak natsional'naya ideya* (*The Eurasian Path as National Idea*), Dugin proposed, like Panarin, that Russia's national mission is to accept its role as the "last bastion" of resistance to Western expansion by developing Eurasia's alternative self-identification.[31]

Mackinderian geopolitical thinking like that of Panarin and Dugin began to penetrate some corridors of power in Russia during the very first post–Soviet years. Thus, in order to demonstrate in *The Grand Chessboard* the radical Russian nationalist strain of Eurasianist thought, Brzezinski quotes the first post–Soviet Russian President Boris Yeltsin's vice-president, Aleksandr Rutskoi, "channeling" Mackinder: "[I]t is apparent from looking at our country's geopolitical situation that Russia represents the only bridge between Asia and Europe. Whoever becomes the master of this space will become the master of the world."[32]

Mackinder's geographical approach highlights one likely structural factor in "East-West" relations. History tends to support the relevance though hardly any predeterminism of the globe's geographic structure on geopolitics and geostrategy. In Hegelian and Marxist terms, geography can be seen as the base or part of the base that forms economic and political systemic, institutional, and ideational (cultural-civilizational) superstructures in international relations. One can question the explanatory power of geography as a determinant or predeterminant of international geopolitics. But one cannot deny its effect once reified by belief into geopolitical theory.

To the extent to which policymakers on either side of the Atlantic or elsewhere buy into the tenets of geopolitical theory as laid down by Mackinder, Friedman, Brzezinski, Panarin and Dugin, geostrategic thought and its civilizationalist hypotheses will shape international geopolitics. To the extent that geography shapes global politics and Mackinder's geographical analysis informs the views of influential figures on either side or both sides of the "World Ocean," geography can be said to help form geopolitically oriented civilizationalist national self-identities and even multinational institutional strategic cultures. Those civilizational ideas and strategic cultures—along with political and economic systems, other cultural and civilizational values, state and private institutions—in turn influence policymaking. In many ways, geography and Mackinder's geopolitical and geostrategic analysis helped fashion civilizationalist thought in Russia and the West.

The Civilizational Schism

Samuel P. Huntington's seminal study, *The Clash of Civilizations*, published first as an article in America's prestigious *Foreign Affairs* and later as a book, argued that conflict not between states but civilizations would play the lead role in 21st-century global politics. He argued that civilizations emerged from religions and that the world was devided into seven or eight major civilizations: Western, Slavic-Orthodox, Confucian, Japanese, Islamic, Hindu, Latin American, and "possibly" African.[33] Huntington's geography of the fault lines between two of those civilizations, the West and the Orthodox Christain, coincides precisely with Mackinder's political geography:

> The fault lines between civilizations are replacing the political and ideological boundaries of the Cold War as the flash points for crisis and bloodshed. The Cold War began when the Iron Curtain divided Europe politically and ideologically. The Cold War ended with the end of the Iron Curtain. As the ideological division of Europe has disappeared, the cultural division of Europe between Western Christianity, on the one hand, and Orthodox Christianity and Islam, on the other, has reemerged. The most significant dividing line in Europe, as William Wallace has suggested, may well be the eastern boundary of Western Christianity in the year 1500. This line runs along what are now the boundaries between Finland and Russia and between the Baltic states and Russia, cuts through Belarus and Ukraine separating the more Catholic western Ukraine from Orthodox eastern Ukraine, swings westward separating Transylvania from the rest of Romania, and then goes through Yugoslavia almost exactly along the line now separating Croatia and Slovenia from the rest of Yugoslavia. In the Balkans this line, of course, coincides with the historic boundary between the Hapsburg and Ottoman empires. The peoples to the north and west of this line are Protestant or Catholic; they shared the common experiences of European history—feudalism, the Renaissance, the Reformation, the Enlightenment, the French Revolution, the Industrial Revolution; they are generally economically better off than the peoples to the east; and they may now look forward to increasing involvement in a common European economy and to the consolidation of democratic political systems. The peoples to the east and south of this line are Orthodox or Muslim; they historically belonged to the Ottoman or Tsarist empires and were only lightly touched by the shaping events in the rest of Europe; they are generally less advanced economically; they seem much less likely to develop stable democratic political systems. The Velvet Curtain of culture has replaced the Iron Curtain of ideology as the most significant dividing line in Europe. As the events in Yugoslavia show, it is not only a line of difference; it is also at times a line of bloody conflict.[34]

Thus, civilizations are cultures writ large and should be viewed not just as the ideational expression of geographical structure but also as reinforcing and reifying geopolitical fault lines established by geography (structural constraint) and history (the result of actors acting in the world with political contingency).

The Neo-Eurasianists: Civilizational Thought in Russia

Until the late 19th and early 20th centuries, Russian civilizational and to a certain extent geopolitical thought were divided between Westernizers and Slavophiles (with both later cross-cut by socialists). The former argued that Russia's destiny was Europe. However much Russia had been influenced by Russian Orthodoxy, the Mongol yoke, and the late scientific and cultural renaissance of the Silver Age, its fate lay in Europe. Russia, therefore, should and eventually would adopt Western-style political, economic and social institutions over time. Slavophiles saw a *sui generis* Russian and Slavic world, where Eastern Orthodox spirituality replaced materialism (whether capitalist or socialist) and mechanistic rationality. Spiritual collectivity—*sobornost'*—trumped individualism and competititon. The collapse of Russian autocracy and the rise of Bolshevik communism forced considerable rethinking within the Russian intelligentsia now in exile in the West. For a good portion of the Russian émigré intelligentsia in the West, familiarity bred dissent if not contempt.

In the 1920s, therefore, a new trend emerged in response to the dilemma created by rejection of Western political thought, the collapse of the Russian Imperial autocracy, and the pan-Slavism that had led Russia into the trap of World War I and fatally undermined the Tsarist regime and Russian state. Slavic unity and Russian imperial autocracy were replaced by a more expansive vision—Eurasianism. The Eurasianists rejected pan-Slavism and ethnic Russian nationalism of the kind espoused by the Black Hundreds.

Early Eurasianism's most seminal works belong perhaps to philologist and linguist Prince Nikolai S. Trubetskoi: "Iskhod k Vostoku" (Exit to the East) and "Yevraziistvo: Opyt sistematicheskogo izlozheniya" (Eurasianism: The Experience of a Systematic Explication).[35] Trubetskoi's civilizationalist vision begins where Huntington's does: religion is the "basis of ideology" and "creates and defines culture," which taken together define a civilization.[36] According to Trubetskoi, Russia is Eurasia's core, and Orthodox Christianity is Russia's core. Therefore, Russian Orthodox Christianity comprises the Eurasian project's core. Orthodoxy is the "foundation" of Russia's "way of life," its "specific attitude towards nature and the world," and "idea of the transformation of the world." For Trubetskoi, Orthodoxy will be the basis of a prospective broader Eurasian ideology, amended and supplemented by Asian religious thought—Islam, Confucianism, Buddhism, and Hinduism. These religions, especially Buddhism, have an affinity with Orthodoxy's "mystical contemplativeness," so "distant" from Protestantism and more so Catholicism.[37]

Like Slavophiles, Trubetskoi views Peter the Great's westernizing reforms as a deviation from the true Eastern Orthodox roots of "Russia-Eurasia." Imperial Russia was also diverted from its Eurasian-Asian destiny because of its wars with Islamic khanates (Kazan, Astrakhan, Crimea), which unnaturally allied it with Europe. These twin "Europeanizations," in Trubetskoi's view, led to the Westernizer-Slavophile split and Russia's Western-rooted socialist revolution, which only Eurasianism can overcome. Eurasians are ethnically closer to the Tatars' ethnic predecessors, the Bolgars, who hailed from central Eurasia and adopted Islam. Contrary to many of the later Eurasianists, Trubetskoi argued that Russian culture was neither European nor Asian and should not attempt to formulate a synthesis with them. Rather, Russian culture was "between [them], a Eurasian culture, and should resist them." Thus, Trubetskoi does not argue in favor of a grand Eurasian project stretching from south and southeast Asia to Central Europe. Rather, he is focused on Russia's proper civilizational identity.[38]

For Trubetskoi, the Eurasian "psychological makeup" or national character, contrary to the European, tends towards "an awareness of the limitations of socio-political life and of its connection with nature" (a higher value and truer source of happiness), "a continental sweep" (of Eurasia), "the Russian breadth [of spirit]," a consciousness of the "conditionality of its historically established forms," and "a continental self-identification in limitedness." To the European, this looks like a lack of national patriotism. Yet the Eurasian is rooted in "an indestructible self-confidence" and "ancient nomadic instinct"—not external forms. He values tradition like a Turk but "hates its despotic limits like his close relative—the Iranian." He feels at home in Asia, not in Europe. His future demands putting an end to Peter the Great's "tactical and necessary turn to Europe" and making an "organic turn to Asia."[39]

Trubetskoi claims that Russian-Eurasian *symfoniya* (organic unity) and *sobornost'* (collective spirituality) form the basis for Eurasia's "true unity," in contradistinction to the chimera of European unity. He finds precedents for Eurasian unity in Genghis Khan's Mongol empire, which posed the "historical task" of uniting Eurasia politically and laid the foundation of a political system. Moscow inherited this task and the Mongols' "cultural-political legacy." In the post–Petrine Imperial system the "Russian-Eurasian idea" was left dormant and even distorted. Writing as the Soviet communist experiment was gaining steam, Trubetskoi believed that "Russia-Eurasia" would survive the "criminal experiments" conducted by Peter and various successive "ultra–Europeans." After these catastrophic forays into Europeanism, it would not be shaken and weakened, but rather renewed and full of pent-up strength for another attempt to build a Eurasian civilization.[40] Ultimately, Trubetskoi displays the same schism that had plagued Russian thought since Peter. He recommended a political system for Eurasia based on the original soviets (destroyed by Bolshevik dictatorship)—either a democratic federative or a renewed monarchical system.[41]

Early Eurasianism's perhaps most sophisticated thinker was another émigré, Pyotr N. Savitskii. As an ethnographer, Savitskii saw Eurasia possessing an organic unity created by the interaction between the dictates of steppe topography, on the one hand, and cultural and civilizational input by all its ethnic groups—Russians, Mongols, Bolgars (predecessors of the Tatars), other Turkic peoples, among others—on the other hand. Ideologically, Marxism-Leninism would be replaced by an "Orthodox Eurasian-Russian" ideology, and the Communist Party dictatorship by a Eurasianist Party dictatorship. He proposed an assembly of Eurasia's peoples in which each ethnic group received seats proportional to "its cultural capacity." Savitskii's vision had totalitarian and fascist elements, but was proposed as an alternative to communism and fascism.[42]

In 1945, Savitskii was arrested in Prague by the Red Army and sent to a labor camp where he met the young historian, Lev Gumilev, son of the famous Petersburg (Leningrad) poets Nikolai Gumilev and Anna Akhmatova. Gumilev became Savitskii's pupil, and both were rehabilitated in 1956 as part of CPSU General Secretary Nikita Khruschev's de-Stalinization policies. Savitskii returned to Prague, dying there in 1968. Gumilev took the Eurasianist baton from Savitskii and spread the idea among some of the Soviet elite, with adherents in such high places as the CPSU Central Committee, the Soviet Foreign Ministry, and the General Staff.[43] During *perestroika*, Gumilev's work enjoyed a revival among the public, with large print-runs of his books and his complete works or a large portion of them available in Russian bookstores.[44]

Like Savitskii, Gumilev applied detailed knowledge of Eurasia's history and ethnography to the study of Eurasia as integral entity or civilization and the proselytization of the Eurasian idea. For Gumilev, neither space, time nor geography primarily drive the course of history. To be sure, geography and landscape were important. Historically, settled Europe was set apart from nomadic Eurasia, defined by life on the steppe. But more important for him were ethnic groups or nationalities: "[H]istory is created within the framework of ethnic groups (nationalities or 'ethnoses') interacting with each other, for each historical fact is an achievement in the life of a concrete nationality." Each nationality and national and civilizational identity group (super-ethnos) is "a collective of people who contrasts itself from all other similar collectives, proceeding not just from a conscious calculation but from a feeling of complimentarity—a subconscious sense of mutual sympathy and commonality of people which defines the contrast 'we'—'they' and the division into 'ours' and 'others.'"[45] Gumilev's ethnographic work was supplemented by mystical writings on esoteric ideas such as the "noosphere" and the "ethnos" or ethnic group as a bio-cosmic entity, presaging Dugin's mysticism. Each ethnos is a living being traversing a human-like life cycle, and peaking in mid-life in a burst of creative, developmental energy—"*passionarnost.*" In the peak period of a nation, *passionarnost* is the "engine" of cultural formation. Its "steering wheel" is its "ethnic tradition" derived from the ethnic character and material culture developed in response to the space occupied by the particular nation. The idea of Eurasia as a separate civilization was based in part on the idea that ethnoses with similar cultural traits could form a super-ethnos—a civilization.[46]

In his more grounded works, Gumilev sought to demonstrate the Russian nationality's ability to interact, mix, and network culturally and ethnically with Eurasia's other ethnic groups as the key element in Eurasian civilization's "ethnogenesis." The Russians first brought Orthodoxy along the ravines of Eurasia's natural topography—the river systems of European Russia and Siberia. Muscovy reached *passionarnost* in the 13th to 15th centuries, marked by Ivan III's "gathering in of the Russian lands" in the late 15th and early 16th centuries. Muscovy's expansion west, south and east in the 16th to 20th centuries evidenced its high *passionarnost.* Gumilev acknowledges that Moscovite Russia borrowed from Kievan Rus the religious tradition of Eastern Orthodoxy—the core tradition of Russian-Eurasian civilization—which "allowed Russia to have its say in the history of Eurasia." Like Trubetskoi, however, Gumilev found Russia-Eurasia's source in Muscovite, not Kievan Rus: "Moscow did not continue the traditions of Kiev as did Novgorod. It destroyed the traditions of popular assembly (*veche*), freedom, as well as internecine conflict among the princes. Instead, it replaced these with other norms of conduct borrowed from the Mongols—the system of strict discipline, ethnic tolerance, and deep religiosity." These three Mongol qualities, for Gumilev, are Eurasia's distinguishing civilizational traits. At the same time, however, he emphasized that each of Eurasia's "ethnoses"—Russians, Mongols, Tatars and other Turkish nationalities, among others—"rendered a powerful influence on the course of the overall super-ethnos's ethnogenesis."[47]

Gumilev saw three civilizations "resisting" or impinging upon Russia-Eurasia: "Catholic Europe in the west; China in the far east, and the Muslim world in the south." Therefore, like his Eurasianist predecessors, he envisaged a smaller Eurasia than his neo-Eurasianist successors; one confined to approximately the territory of the late Imperial Russia and the Soviet Union and not destined to unite the heartland and rimland from China to Central Europe. Eurasia's peoples developed a unique "political culture" and "vision of the paths and goals of development." They "built a common statehood proceeding from the principle of the priority of the *rights of each people* to a self-defined way of life" [Gumilev's emphasis]. In the 20th century, the Soviet leadership "rejected this healthy policy traditional for [the] country and began to be led by European principles, trying to make everyone the same." Thus, Gumilev rejected integration of Russia into the West. Although he acknowledged it is healthy to study and borrow some elements of foreign and European practice, he concluded that "the price of the integration of Russia with Western Europe in any case will mean a full rejection of native traditions and ensuing assimilation." Ultimately, Gumilev is skeptical of rationalist assumptions about the "basis" of interethnic relations, which for him lies "beyond the limits of the sphere of the conscious—it is in emotions: sympathies and antipathies, loves and hatreds."[48]

Eurasianist thought (as republication of Trubetskoi's and other Eurasianists' works in post–Soviet Russia demonstrate) experienced a neo–Eurasianist revival in the late *perestroika* years and especially during the post–Soviet period, and neo–Eurasianist ideas would infiltrate some corridors of Russian power. Reiterating the 19th- and 20th-century Eurasianists' experience, 21st-century neo–Eurasianists responded to the challenge of Russia's failed engagement with the West and "Westernism" (*zapadnichestvo*). Again Panarin and Dugin are the most prominent examples of contemporary neo–Eurasianist thought. That these Mackinder-influenced geostrategists are also Eurasianist-civilizationist ideologists is itself a reflection of geography's function as both the base and structural cause reified in the ideational, cultural, and ultimately civilizationalist components of the contingent superstructure. In Russian thought, the Eurasianist civilizational perspective at the ideational level is a key intervening variable between the structural cause of geography, on the one hand, and ideology and policymaking, on the other, just as Huntington's civilizationalist approach bridged geography and Mackinder's geopolitical analysis with Western ideology and policy.

Delving into Savitskii, Trubetskoi and Gumilev, today's neo–Eurasianists are constantly reworking and propagating a Russo-centric alternative to the post–Cold War Western civilizational model based on neoliberal economics, an open information society, and political and military interventionism outside the transatlantic community of democracies. Neo-Eurasianists' alternative civilizational models are barely revamped ideologically, but significantly broadened in their geographic aspirations from those of the original Eurasianists. Panarin states explicitly that the West "not only did not accept [Russia] into the 'European home' but tried to block and isolate her within the post–Soviet space using anti–Russian sentiments." This is no concern, however, because "the main creative success of Russian (rossiiskaya) civilization is the capacity to form large interethnic syntheses; this was its response to the challenge of steppe plains expanse."[49] In this way, neo–Eurasianists, more consistently than their forebears, envision a Russian messianic destiny in the formation of a super-ethnos or civilization encompassing not just the Eurasian heartland, but potentially its rimland from Southeast Asia to the Muslim south to Central Europe. As a first step, Russia must pursue "the reintegration of the post–Soviet space on the basis of a new formative idea." Panarin's ostensibly inclusive model of civilizational diversity is designed to counter Western-dominated, homogenizing globalization and "the barbarism manifested by the so-called 'clash of civilizations.'" For Panarin, Russia can be both the East's modernizer and the West's reformer. Eurasia's European and Slavic cultural roots make it the logical bridge through which a more spiritual and sustainable form of global development can be synthesized in less developed Eurasia and offered to Europe as an alternative to his predicted America-induced global, environmental self-holocaust.[50] In short, similar to other influential nativist Russian thinkers in the past, such as Fyodor Dostoevskii and Vladimir Solovyov, neo–Eurasianists believe Russia will save the world.

This more expansive quasi-global neo–Eurasianism is aspirational rather than materially or spiritually predetermined. Panarin has doubts about what will be the final destination of Slavdom, Eastern Europe, and Central Europe. Caught between Germany and Russia, they are destined for second-tier status at best in the west; this is explicitly stated with regard to those regions' Slavic states. Supposedly, the Slavs and the Eastern and Central European regions are "objectively interested in the existence of a Russian geopolitical alternative. With a strong Russia the status of Slavdom in Central Europe in any case will be higher and more acceptable than with a weak Russia."[51] But implicit in his analysis is that for the Slavic states today Russia is a secondary consideration compared to their aspirations to be be fully European. Only in this latter context does Russia become important, and only as a lever they can use to strengthen their positions in the EU, NATO, and the West writ large. The best Russia can hope for is an Intermarium that would render Slavs one step removed from Europe and its institutions. However, this would not solve the problems of Slavdom's separation from Russia and of Eastern and Central Europe having become a geopolitical barrier delimiting the neo–Eurasianist project.

Ideologically, like their Eurasianist forebears and Huntingtonian contemporaries, neo–Eurasianists emphasize religion's central role in civilization-formation. Neo–Eurasianism is centered on traditional religions, especially Russian Orthodox civilization's unique affinity with the mysticism of Eurasia's other major religions—Islam, Confucianism, Buddhism, and Hinduism. According to Panarin, Russia's messianic role is to "propose to the peoples of Eurasia a new, powerful, superenergetic synthesis" based on "people's conservatism" and "civilizational diversity."[52] The fundamental tenet of the Russian-Eurasian "mission of people's conservatism" is "socio-cultural conservatism," the goal of which is to preserve Eurasia's and the world's traditional cultures, religious mysticisms, and ethnic and "civilizational diversity and pluralism" from Western-framed globalization, cultural homogenization, and the left-liberal intelligentsia's attraction to mass, urban, "semi-bohemianism" (*polubogema*) and "consumer hedonism." Thus, orthodox Eurasia will give birth to a "new historical paradigm of mankind."[53]

Ultimately, for Panarin, despite its present dire economic condition, Russia can leap over the stage of advanced industrialism to a higher developmental stage based on clean technology. It will lead Eurasia and the world into a new post-industrial, eco-cultural, multi-civilizational world that rejects the anti-cultural "technologism," consumerism, and homogeneity of the "soulless" American worldview which threatens nature and national cultures. Indeed, much of Russian Eurasianism and neo–Eurasianism rejects what is viewed as the West's overreliance on the rationality of the physical and social (especially market economic) sciences, technology, and technocracy.

Dugin, advancing Panarin, proposes an apocalyptic confrontation between good and evil: between Atlanticism's "mercantile, individualistic, materialist, and cosmopolitan outlook" and Eurasia's and Russia's "spirituality, ideocracy, collectivism, authority, hierarchy, and tradition."[54] In a 2014 article "Eurasia in the Net War," Dugin gave an exhaustive list of cultural antipodes dividing Eurasia and the West in Mackinderian terms: "[E]ither we are on the side of the civilization of the Land, or we are on the side of the civilization of the Ocean. The Land is Tradition, Faith (for ethnic Russians—Orthodox Christianity),

Empire, the people, the sacred, history, the family and ethics. The Ocean is modernization, trade, technology, liberal democracy, capitalism, parliamentarianism, individualism,
materialism, and gender politics. Two mutually exclusive value complexes."[55] In *Yevraziiskii put' kak natsional'naya ideya* (The Eurasian Way as a National Idea), he posited Russia's messianic role: "[O]nly Russia in the future can become the main pole and haven
for the planetary resistance and rallying point of all the world's forces which insist on
their own special path and their own special cultural, national, state, and historical 'I.'"[56]
Dugin's imaginative, mystical, sometimes irrational side envisions the Atlanticist-
Eurasianist tectonic in "realms lying well beyond the reach of empirical investigation,"
including mysticism, myth, and apocalypticism.[57] In his *Misterii Yevrazii* (Mysteries of
Eurasia), he asserts that there was once an island Arctic paradise, "Hyperborea," from
which a pure Aryan race, the Russians' ancestors, moved into Eurasia.[58]

In sum, Russia's leading neo–Eurasianist thinkers believe in the emergence of a neo-
traditional spirituality that communes with nature and God and, in Hegelian terms, will
be the new antithesis to the techno-globalization thesis, producing a new civilization
and a new level of civilization. Yet, despite Russian Eurasianist discourse's frequent
emphasis on the equality of Eurasia's peoples and cultures, Russia remains for many
Eurasianists today "first among equals," allegedly possessing what Dostoevsky called Russian "universalism"—a cultural affinity and ability to partner with other civilizations that
is benign and beneficial for the partnered group.

At times, we see more benign neo–Eurasianist ideas in Russian officials' public statements. In August 2015, Russian Foreign Minister Sergei Lavrov echoed Panarin on the
need to resist ostensible Western efforts to impose globally a homogenous set of state
and societal standards under the rubric of democratization:

> We see attempts to preserve [Western] domination artificially, including by pressuring other coun-
> tries and using sanctions and even military force, in violation of international law and the UN Char-
> ter. This is adding an element of chaos to international relations, turning entire regions and countries
> into pockets of terrorism, violent extremism and many other negative things, which we see happen-
> ing, unfortunately, over much of the Middle East and North Africa.
>
>   We firmly believe that the only practical formula for settling these issues has nothing to do with
> military interference or any other way of forcing a certain mode of behaviour, which may seem right
> to the enforcer, on others, but that this formula is based on respect for the right of nations to per-
> sonal identity and the diversity of the modern world. Both in nature and in society, diversity is the
> key to prosperity and progress.[59]

Thus, in the terminology of contemporary international relations systems theory,
Eurasianism's insistence on the importance of an autonomous Russian-Eurasian civilization counterposing the West fits hand-in-glove with the idea—one especially favored in
the foreign policy practice of Moscow and Beijing—of replacing the American- and
Western-dominated, unipolar international system formed after the collapse of the Cold
War's bipolar structure with a multipolar structure in which Eurasia constitutes one of
the system's several pillars.

Russia's emphasis on multipolarity as the emerging, proper "democratic" structure
for the international system began with Yevgenii Primakov's appointment as Russian
Foreign Minister in the late 1990s, well before Vladimir Putin's reign. So it is difficult to
disentangle multipolarism and neo–Eurasianism within the latter's world view and that
of other top foreign policy officials. Similarly, there is little separation in geographical
terms to separate ideas such as the "post–Soviet space," the former Soviet Union, and so

on from geographic Eurasia, and efforts to unite the post–Soviet/Eurasian geographical space economically and/or politically predate Putin, including: the Commonwealth of Independent States (1991), the Collective Security Treaty Organization (1992), and the Eurasian Union. The last was first proposed in 1994 by Kazakhstan President Nursultan Nazarabaev. He is an adherent of moderate neo–Eurasianist views with an emphasis on the Turkic peoples' role in uniting Eurasia in league with Russia. He even opened the state-run Lev Gumilev University in Alma Ata in the 1990s.

Putin's speeches and writings display neither systematic nor pronounced Eurasianist thinking. Putin has never used the word "Eurasianism." He sometimes refers to some of the basic elements of neo–Eurasianism, such as the importance of Christian Orthodoxy for Russian culture, and the idea of geographic Eurasia and even Eurasian civilization. But these do not amount to neo–Eurasianist thinking. Such elements were present and in many ways were default positions with communism's collapse and the post–Soviet turn from Western democracy and the free market after the failures in Russian domestic reforms and Russian-Western relations. There is no evidence that radical neo–Eurasianists like Dugin have convinced Putin to recreate the Russian or Soviet empire or some new Eurasian empire. When Dugin was afforded the opportunity to tell the world that he had the Russian president's ear and influenced his ideas, he refused to do so.[60] When Putin references philosophers and ideologists, he never mentions Eurasianists or neo–Eurasianists.[61]

Even Putin's programmatic article for the 2012 presidential campaign on his plan to create a Eurasian Economic Union (EEU) on the basis of the Customs Union and the Eurasian Economic Space includes nothing Eurasianist or neo–Eurasianist. He did not mention the Eurasian idea or any related Eurasian or even Russian culture or civilization and expresses none of the traditional antagonism towards the West displayed by neo–Eurasianists. Rather, Putin described the EEU's purpose and goals purely in economic terms, both as an engine for Eurasian economic development and competitiveness under a "free trade zone," and as a bridge to other key pillars of the global economic system, in particular the European Union: "The Eurasian union will be built on universal integrative principles as an inseparable part of Big Europe." Putin envisages the EEU as a mechanism for creating a cooperative but still competitive multipolar international trade and economic system—part of an overall multipolar international system—with the EEU functioning as one of the system's key centers of power. He writes:

[A]n economically logical and balanced system of partnership between the Eurasian Union and the EU is capable of creating the real conditions for changing the geopolitical and geo-economic configuration of the entire continent, and would have an undoubted positive global impact....

In our view, the solution could be the elaboration of common approaches "at the grassroots level," as they say. At first, within the existing regional structures—the EU, NAFTA, APEC, ASEAN, and others—and then, by means of dialog between them. It is precisely from such integrative "bricks" that a world economy of a more stable character could be formed.

For example, the two biggest associations on our continent—the European Union and the Eurasian Union now being formed—basing their collaboration on the rules of free trade and the compatibility of systems of regulation, are objectively capable, including through relations with third countries and regional structures, of extending these principles to the entire area—from the Atlantic to the Pacific. To an area that will be harmonious in its economic nature, but polycentric from the point of view of specific mechanisms and executive decisions. It will then be logical to begin a constructive dialog on the principles of collaboration with the states of the Asia-Pacific Region, North America, and other regions.[62]

In August 2015, Despite the "new cold war" induced by the Ukrainian crisis, his foreign minister echoed Putin regarding EEU's potential role as an economic and trade bridge between the Asian Pacific and the EU: "[T]he Eurasian Economic Union has the potential to become a link between the integration processes in the Asia Pacific region and what our colleagues in Europe to the west of the Eurasian Economic Union are working on."[63] In sum, we can call Putin's neo–Eurasianism "practical economic neo–Eurasianism," having nothing to do with traditional idealistic, mystical, or imperialistic neo–Eurasianism.

Neo-Eurasianism and Ukraine

If Russia's advantage is a unique universalism—an ability to connect with other ethnicities and religions—then it should be a *fait accompli* to keep the Ukrainian Orthodox Christian element of Slavdom in the Russia-Eurasia orbit. The "loss" of so many other Slavic peoples to the West—Poles, Czechs, Slovaks, even Serbs and Montenegrins—is a blow to the Eurasian idea. In this light it would begin to resemble a myth rather than a potential or kinetic reality. What do Eurasianists and neo–Eurasianists say regarding the Ukrainian question, so pivotal for western Eurasia?

The original early 20th-century Eurasianists did not comment directly on Ukraine's or the Ukrainians' place within Russia and Eurasia. However, from their descriptions of the geography and civilizational identity of Eurasia, it is clear that they regarded Ukraine to be an organic part of the Russian empire and Eurasia, with the possible exception of western Ukraine's largely Uniate Catholic Galicia. Geographically, the key feature of the Eurasian idea is the steppe. Isaev notes if one is to "go into the nuances," not simply reducing Eurasia's geographic borders to those of the Russian Empire, then the "unbroken steppe unites and permeates [Eurasia] from west to east."[64] This would include all of present-day Ukraine, which extends up to and includes the Carpathian Mountains' southwest and northern ridges, beyond which lies Ukraine's borders with Hungary and Romania. Steppe lands continue further west to the north and south of the Carpathians, into Poland and Serbia in the north and southeastern Romania in the south. Ideationally and civilizationally, in the narrower strictly Orthodox Christian Eurasian framework based on Eurasianism's Huntingtonian-like reliance on religion as the source of civilizations, the lands dominated by Romanians, Hungarians, and perhaps even the Uniate Catholic Galicians would be excluded from the Eurasian concept. But the largely Russian Orthodox (and atheistic), ethnic Russian and Russian-speaking eastern and mixed Russian-Ukrainian central Ukraine up to the Dnepr River, including Kiev, would be regarded as Eurasia.

Gumilev clearly saw Ukraine as belonging to Russia-Eurasia. He noted that in the early 17th century, after Moscovite Rus had recovered from the Time of Troubles, Polish incursions and Cossack marauding, it extended its domain to the Volga, Urals, and western Siberian regions. Moscow formed special military units of nomadic peoples—the "lower force," as they were called. Fighting without pay, they helped the second tsar of the Romanov dynasty, Aleksei Mikhailovich, "liberate Ukraine from Poland and so saved her from destruction."[65] Gumilev had in mind the destruction of Ukraine's and the Cossacks' Orthodox Christian identity rather than physical genocide. He emphasized the importance of "the process of the ethnic integration into the Russian super-ethnos" of the Don Cossacks that resulted from their effort—with Moscow's assistance in 1642—to seize the Black Sea port of Azov from the Ottoman Turks.[66] Azov's nearby city of Mariupol became a pivotal battleground in the 2014–2015 civil war waged between western and eastern Ukraine, principally between Galicia and the Donbass.

Panarin foresaw the conflict between eastern and western Ukraine, with each being of a different culture. Western "Right Bank" Ukraine's politics are rooted in the Galician "Lvovshchina" (rule of Galicia) and "culture of the [Roman Catholic] Church"—"humanitarians who address values and 'profane national holies.'" Left Bank politics are dominated by industrial Kharkov and the Donbass, the "owners and commanders of production," and their "culture of the Industrial Enterprise." Panarin rightly perceived that the gap between these cultures was being exacerbated by the tussle for Ukraine between Western and Russian-Eurasian civilizations:

> The foreign conqueror [the United States representing the West as a whole], the foot of which had never before stepped into Eurasia, decided to subject the continent to an unheard of experiment. Their main goal is to split the local peoples in the spirit of the principle "divide and rule." ... This is not simply about creating conflict between national interests. This is about counterposing the chosen and the unchosen, the civilized ones and the barbarians, those worthy of "a common human future" and contemptible untouchables. The artificial dilemma of acceptance or rejection in the European home is served by the racist segregation. The opponent is trying very hard to whisper in the ears of the elite of the new post–Soviet states that precisely they and not their neighbors could be worthy of acceptance into the "club of the chosen," naturally, on definite conditions. They whispered into the ears of the Russian ruling Westernizers that acceptance of "their" Russia into the European home will happen on the condition that there occurs a decisive rejection of the imperial legacy and Russia throws off the weight of Asianism and cleaned from these harmful racial admixtures of the type stands before a high European commission. They "confidentially" reported to Ukraine in turn that only decisive resistance to the former "older brother" (who is in no way a brother but rather a Central Asian landowner with impermissibly high admixture of Asian-Tatar blood) will create the European democratic image for the country and secure its recognition in the European home.[67]

Thus, Panarin's civilizationalist approach, like Huntington's, finds the divide between the West and Orthodox Eurasia running through central Ukraine.

The same is true for Dugin, who sees an inevitable clash between the Western and Eurasian civilizations inexorably splitting Ukraine in two. In his "Eurasia in the Net War," Dugin asserts: "According to Eurasian geopolitics either Ukraine will be together with the Atlanticists (and then its eastern part and south will be chipped off), or it will be with Russia (then westernizers will rise up in revolt)."[68] As I discuss in the next chapter, the threat of a Ukrainian split along these fault lines was real. Both Eurasianists and Atlanticists incorporate the myths and resulting realities into their theory and practice, creating an unstable geopolitical faultline.

Ukraine and Public Opinion in "Putin's Russia"

Western observers often use the term "Putin's Russia." However, an equally operative dynamic is "Russia's Putin." Putin's economic Eurasianism is as much a product of the late Soviet and post–Soviet Russian experience as is the Russian public. To a considerable extent, he reflects Russians' political, economic, social, cultural, and civilizational preferences. Beyond Russian nationalist and neo–Eurasianist theorists and opinion makers, what place have Ukraine and its tectonic schisms held in post–Soviet Russian popular political culture?

The Russian public clearly sees Ukraine or parts thereof as part of a broader ethnic Russian or Slavic culture. Although there is survey data on Russians' self-identity as a

Eurasian and/or European country, as noted above, there is little or no reliable data on average Russians' views regarding Ukrainians' relationship to any Eurasian civilization. Opinion surveys show a majority of Russians considering Ukrainians to be a "fraternal people," brothers to Russians. Thus, in 1998, nearly two years before Putin's rise to the presidency, 89 percent of Russians fully or mostly supported the idea of a "Slavic Union" including Russia, Ukraine and Belarus.[69]

Russian-dominated Ukrainian regions and historical legacies play a role here. However, a distinction is made between the mostly Orthodox Christian, ethnic Russian and russophone population of Crimea and Donbass (Donetsk and Lugansk/Luhansk) and the more ethnic Ukrainian and Uniate Catholic central and especially western Ukraine. Thus, in opinion surveys since the 1990s, Russians have supported Crimea's reunification with Russia. In May 1998, for example, 77 percent supported Crimea's return to Russia (in 2002, 80 percent; in 2008, 85 percent; in March 2014, 79 percent).[70] A majority of Russians looks upon the Donbass population more favorably than that of the rest of Ukraine. In 2014, 80 percent expressed a good or very good attitude towards Donbassians; in 2015, 79 percent. By contrast, only 53 and 55 percent viewed central and western Ukrainians favorably or very favorably.[71] Russians have expressed unequivocal support for the Donbass rebels and various kinds of Russian support for them, but reject Donbass's annexation, preferring an independent Donbass state (41 percent) or Donbass's autonomy within Ukraine (21 percent) rather than Russian annexation (15 percent) and Donbass non-autonomous status within Ukraine (7 percent).[72] Still, even at the height of the 2014 Ukrainian crisis, 63 percent of Russians retained a very favorable (13 percent) or favorable (50 percent) attitude towards citizens of Ukraine as a whole, down albeit from 81 percent in 2006 and 75 percent in 2009.[73]

In 1994, Russians in similar numbers—70 percent—supported defending the 25 million ethnic Russians living in other post–Soviet states,[74] the largest diaspora being located in Ukraine, particularly in its southern and eastern regions, most of all Crimea and Donbass. Putin generally reflected Russian public opinion. In 1994—that is, during his democratic period, when Putin was still St. Petersburg Mayor Anatolii Sobchak's deputy mayor for international relations—he warned a group of foreign Russia experts about the 25 million ethnic Russians left abroad after the Soviet collapse: "For us, their fate is a question of war and peace." A decade later, as Russia's president Putin made a similar point more softly in reaction to the 2004 Orange Revolution: "We want to avoid a split between east and west in Ukraine. The Russians in Ukraine deserve a safe future. We cannot go back to the Russian Empire. Even if we wanted to—it would be impossible.... We are not against change in the post–Soviet space. But we want to make sure that those changes do not end in chaos."[75]

So for both Russia's Putin and Putin's Russia there are gradations of affinity with Ukraine as a Slavic people with a long Russian history. The closest affinity is between Russians and Ukraine's ethnic Russians and Russian speakers and the territories in which they dominate. Russians relate to the remainder of Ukrainians and the central and western Ukrainian territories with a slightly lesser sense of ethno-national and cultural affinity. More importantly, for both East and West the real or imagined geostrategic and civilizational fault line that separates Europe in the west of the World Island from Orthodox-led Eurasia in the east runs through Ukraine. At the same time, post–Soviet Ukraine's real and imagined schism has carried with it a tectonic of tension, conflict and potential violence about which Putin and many others warned.

2

The Historical Roots
of Ukraine's Schism

Noting that Russia was the most important of the "torn" countries, split by nationalities representing different civilizations, Huntington's initial article did not discuss Ukraine as a torn country, though he did discuss the Western-Slavic Orthodox divide running through it.[1] When pointing to the potential conflict around Ukraine, Huntington missed the potential conflict *inside* Ukraine, between the Western civilizational element in western Ukraine and the pro–Russian element in the east and south. He also noted but downplayed the potential for conflict between Ukraine and Russia, expecting their ostensibly common Orthodox and Slavic roots to preclude conflict:

> In 1991 and 1992 many people were alarmed by the possibility of violent conflict between Russia and Ukraine over territory, particularly Crimea, the Black Sea fleet, nuclear weapons and economic issues. If civilization is what counts, however, the likelihood of violence between Ukrainians and Russians should be low. They are two Slavic, primarily Orthodox peoples who have had close relationships with each other for centuries. As of early 1993, despite all the reasons for conflict, the leaders of the two countries were effectively negotiating and defusing the issues between the two countries. While there has been serious fighting between Muslims and Christians elsewhere in the former Soviet Union and much tension and some fighting between Western and Orthodox Christians in the Baltic states, there has been virtually no violence between Russians and Ukrainians.[2]

Ukraine's ethnic, religious, regional, social, and historical complexities, while perhaps not reaching the level of more multifarious Russia, are more robust than Huntington and other Westerners understand. Post-Soviet Ukraine's ethnic, religious, economic, and regional structure would require as much political sensitivity and leadership in order to avoid conflict and craft a new national and civic identity as is required in Russia. There are at least five important tectonic rifts challenging the Ukrainian state's political stability and territorial integrity: ethnonational, religious, regional, socioeconomic, and historical.

The Ukraine State's Russian Roots

It can be argued that all states' territorial configurations are in one way or another "accidental"—the result of disparate historical forces, themselves the results of accidents of history. If the argument is to be made, it is perhaps most easily done by examining the history of the places and peoples that contemporary Ukraine comprises. This not the place for an exhaustive history of what is now the territory of Ukraine or of all the various incarnations that can be regarded as a Ukrainian state. Nor is it suitable for a detailed review of competing Russian and Ukrainian claims on various aspects of the territory's various state and imperial experiences and legacies. However, a brief discussion of these issues is necessary and demonstrates that Ukraine's existence and form are functions of Russian imperial expansion and Soviet communist foreign and domestic policies as they are a product of episodic resistance to them.

Kievan Rus

There were several states and quasi-state or semi-autonomous entities that can be argued were Ukrainian, with the first being Kievan Rus (882–1240). A fundamental problem lies in the competing claims made by Ukrainians and Russians to the legacy of ancient Kiev. Kievan Rus was consolidated as a unified political entity with the accession to the throne of the city-state by Oleh (Oleg) in 882, and then disappeared with the Mongol conquest in 1240. At its height, medieval Kiev encompassed a very different and much larger territory than that of contemporary Ukraine. Similarly bound in the north by Lithuanians, in the west by Poles, in the southwest by the Transcarpathian Mountains and Hungarians, and in the south by Turks, it included areas to Kiev's northeast extending into the Eurasian steppe's northwestern areas. Encompassing the Novgorod principality as far as Ladoga in the north and ancient Vladimir and Suzdal in the east, it subsumed, on and off, other "Russias" of the day that would make up historical Russia for centuries, including to the present day. Thus, Kievan Rus was deeply intertwined with the "other Russias," and there was no substantial ethnonational or linguistic differentiation between the Russians in Kiev, Suzdal, Rostov, Novgorod or Ladoga.[3]

Galicia and Volhynia

Some historians regard the small principalities of Galicia and Volhynia to be Kiev's successors as "Ukrainian" state formations after the Mongol conquest, absorbing and preserving "much of the Kievan heritage" and preventing the "absorption of West Ukrainian lands by Poland."[4] Poland's seizure of Lvov (Lviv) in 1349 put an end to the Galician and Volhynian independence. Most of present-day western and western-central Ukraine remained part of the Polish-Lithuanian Commonwealth until the mid–17th century. During this period much of the Ukrainian elite converted from Orthodoxy to Catholicism, facilitating cultural Polonization. Ukrainians became divided between Russian Orthodox and Greek or Uniate Catholics, who retained Orthodox rituals and liturgy but whose allegiance remained to the Pope in Rome, thereby "laying the foundation for the many sharp distinctions that eventually developed between East and West Ukrainians."[5]

Cossack Ukraine: Rise and Ruin

By the late 16th century, the much-depopulated area around the Dnepr River became the next locus of Ukrainian development if not quasi-statehood. Already the area was being referred to as "*Ukraina*,"[6] emerging to challenge the terms "*Malorossiya*" and "*Malorus*" traditional at the time. "*Ukraina*" won the struggle to name and thus imagine the emerging regional entity and people by the late 19th century when Ukrainian national identity solidified.[7] The terminological uncertainty reflects the national and political uncertainty fostered by the Orthodox, often pro–Russian but turbulent and anarchic

Cossack tradition that emerged after the Polish-Lithuanian Commonwealth. That tradition would dominate the far western Eurasian steppe—the "wild steppe" of the Don and Dnepr river basins—until the area's incorporation into the Russian Empire in the 18th century and the gradual taming of the Cossack tradition by St. Petersburg and Moscow in the coming centuries of modernization.

Nearly two centuries earlier, at the turn of the 16th-17th centuries, Ukrainians in support of, or sometimes in parallel with, the Polish-Lithuanian Commonwealth were undermining Russian statehood. During Muscovite Russia's "*smutnoe vremno*" or Time of Troubles, the Poles schemed with unruly Ukrainian and Russian Cossacks and competing groups of Russian boyars to seize the Muscovite throne and deliver the "Third Rome" to Warsaw and thus expand Catholicism east.[8]

When Russia managed to reestablish its crumbling statehood with the founding of the Romanov dynasty in 1613, Ukrainians under Cossack leadership were turning against the commonwealth. The Cossack era—the first formation of a separate identity in the region independent of Poland, Russia and Turkey—saw a warrior *ethos* and *ethnos* of "Cossack-frontiersman" emerge to help Polish and Russian elements fend off Tatar and Turkish advances from the south into the Dnepr River basin and limit the region's Polonization and "religionational and socioeconomic oppression of the Polish *szlachta*" (landowning aristocracy). The Cossacks in this period moved to the head of this quasi–Ukrainian society and continued to provide leadership over the next few centuries. Although there was a Cossack movement in the Don River Basin in Russia and somewhat similar groups in other Eastern European countries, nowhere did these groups' role become as central as in Ukraine. Thus, the Cossacks became a central myth and source of national identity for Ukraine as well as Russia. Because of Cossack assertion, Ukrainians recoalesced around ancient Kiev to regenerate their Orthodox Christian roots, after the Polonization and Catholicization they (and Belorussians as well) experienced.[9]

After a series of failed Cossack-led insurrections against Polish rule in 1625 and 1638, the Zaporozhian Cossack Bohdan Khmelnytsky (1595–1657) led the Great Revolt of 1648. His estate seized by a Polish magnate, his son killed, and his wife abducted, "Khmel," as he was called, became the leader or "Hetman" of the Zaporozhian Sich, a semi-autonomous Cossack entity at various times under Polish-Lithuanian, Ottoman Turkish, and Russian tutelage. Forging an alliance with the Crimean Tatars, who were also experiencing great tensions with the Poles, Khmelnytsky raised the Sich in revolt. He achieved repeated military victories, inspiring as many as 100,000 Ukrainians on both the Right and Left Banks of the Dnepr to join the cause. In 1649 the exhausted Tatars forced Khmelnytsky to sue for peace. The Treaty of Zboriv (Zborov) secured autonomous Ukrainian rule in the Sich areas in and around Kiev, Bratslav, and Chernigiv (Chernigov). The revolt also inaugurated the Ukrainian tendency towards intense anti–Polish and anti–Semitic feeling, as the previously oppressed Ukrainian lords and peasants took brutal revenge on their Polish and Jewish overlords.[10]

The post–Zboriv Zaparozhian "Ukraine" retained the socioeconomic problem of serfdom—a time bomb planted under Cossackdom. The Cossack elite secured its freedom, but the bulk of peasants did not. When the Poles attempted to retake Zaporozhia in 1651, forcing the Bela Tserkva Treaty, Cossacks had to settle for a reduction in the number of free men on the commonwealth registry from 40,000 to 20,000 and an autonomy limited to Kiev and its environs. These arrangements allowed the Polish *szlachta* to return to Cossack areas and re-enserf the peasants. The prospect of widespread Polish servitude drove many Cossacks to flee across the border into Russia, leading to the formation of "Sloboda Ukraine" centered on Kharkov (Kharkiv), Russia. When Polish-Cossack fighting resumed, Khmelnytsky decided he needed a foreign ally to prolong the revolt, but the Crimean khan was interested only in using the Cossacks for an assault on Russia.[11]

Ukrainian and Russian historians diverge in their emphases on the Cossacks' turn to Russia. Platonov notes that in 1651 Khmelnytsky appealed to Tsar Aleksei Mikhailovich "to take Little Russia (Malorossiya) under your wing," but Moscow was indecisive about incorporating this Polish province and entering a war with Poland. Instead, Tsar Aleksei used diplomatic channels in order to try to protect Ukraine, but to no avail. At the same time, Khmelnytsky sought to make the Ukrainian "Hetmanate" a vassal of the Ottoman Porte alongside the Crimean Khanate, Moldavia, and Wallachia. Therefore, in 1653 the "*Zemskii sobor*" or Land Assembly convened and approved Malorossiya's accession to Russia. The Pereiaslav agreement stipulated 60,000 Ukrainian Cossacks on the Russian register and autonomy in social relations and government for Malorossiya. Also, the Hetman was given the right to his own foreign relations, except with the Poles and Turks.[12]

In 1654, only after internal opposition to submission to the predominantly Muslim Porte pushed him, the Hetman turned north to the "much more popular candidate"— the Slavic and Orthodox "Tsar of all the Russias."[13] On January 18, 1654, Khmelnytsky called an assembly of the Cossack elite, which decided to accept tsarist rule over the Sich and Ukraine under the Pereiaslav agreement. Subtelny describes the decision as a pro–Orthodoxy choice: "On that day, drummers summoned the populace to the town square where the hetman spoke about Ukraine's need for an overlord, presented the four candidates for such a position—the Polish king, the Tatar khan, the Ottoman sultan, and the Muscovite tsar—and declared that the Orthodox tsar was best suited for the role. Pleased that the choice had fallen on an Orthodox ruler, the crowd responded favorably to the hetman's speech."[14] Subsequently, Muscovite ambassadors traveled Ukraine receiving the loyalty oaths to Tsar Aleksei from 117 towns and 127,000 Ukrainians.[15] From the perspective of today, it seems perhaps ironic that it was Ukrainian history's "greatest military and political leader," according all Ukrainian and other scholars,[16] who initiated Ukraine's integration into the emerging Russian Empire under the Pereiaslav agreement.[17]

It needs emphasizing that while eastern Ukraine came under Russian tutelage, Galicia and Volhynia remained under Polish control, despite an attempt by Khmelnytsky to forge an alliance with invading Swedish forces in order to reclaim western Ukrainian lands. This division of what became Ukrainian territory contributed to today's east-west, Russian-Greek Orthodox, Westernized-Russified schisms. Although Russia's war with Sweden and peace accord with Poland under the 1656 Treaty of Vilnius created tensions with Khmelnytsky, he soon died in Cyhyryn in September 1657.

The Partitions

After Khmelnytsky, Ukrainian Cossack lands devolved into internecine warfare— Ukraine's own Time of Troubles often referred to as the "Ruin"—caused by disagreement within the Cossack elite over whether or not to reverse the decision to seek Russian protection and turn to another great power. Additional conlict erupted between the Cossack elite and the peasants over the latter's servitude now to Cossack landowners, as opposed to the previous Polish and Jewish overlords. Instead of solidifying political self-determination and creating a society of free Cossack farmers, the anarchic steppe people turned on each other, leading to the Cossack lands' territorial fragmentation and full subjugation to Moscow. In an attempt to escape Moscow's tutelage, new Hetman Ivan Vyhovsky signed in 1658 the Hadiach Treaty with Poland-Lithuania. Kiev, Bratislav, and Chernigiv would have formed the third pillar of the commonwealth on an equal footing, with internal political self-determination for all three. However, the treaty was never implemented, and Moscow invaded in league with Polish and Tatar allies. Although Russian forces were routed and Moscow was under threat of counterattack by Vyhovsky, internal dissent between pro–Moscow and pro–Polish Cossack leaders forced Vyhovsky's resignation.

Moscow was able to dictate the terms of a new Pereialsav agreement in 1659 under which Russia was allowed to station troops not just in Kiev but in each major town, and the election of the Ukrainian hetman was subject to confirmation by the tsar. Moreover, the Cossacks were allowed no independent foreign relations. The 1660 Polish-Russian war was fought over Ukraine. The Cossacks on the Right Bank (west of the Dnepr), led by hetman Yurii Khmelnytsky, son of the great Bohdan, backed a return to the commonwealth. On the Russian-controlled Left Bank (east of the Dnepr), Cossacks elected Yakiv Somko their hetman. The schism heralded in the Ruin. Dejected by the *de facto* partition of Malorossiya, Khmelnytsky resigned and entered a monastery. Successor Pavlo Teteria led the Cossacks in an ill-fated invasion of the Left Bank with the Poles. Upon returning to the Left Bank, the Polish army brutally crushed Cossack insurrections that broke out against the returning Polish *szlachta,* and opened up Bohdan Khmelnytsky's grave and scattered its contents to the wind. This meant a final break with the Poles.

In 1667, the Russians and Poles signed the Treaty of Andrusovo formalizing their partition of Ukraine and hoping the Cossacks would function as a buffer from the Crimean Tatar Khanate. With little choice remaining, new Ukrainian hetman Petro Doroshenko revived the Cossacks' alliance with the Porte. Together with the Turks, he attacked the Poles in Galicia and Volhynia and won some autonomy for the Right Bank from the Poles. Doroshenko then crossed the Dnepr to the Left Bank and declared himself hetman of a reunited Cossack land. The Tatars and Poles appointed a rival hetman against Doroshenko, who was forced to the Right Bank and a fight against the Poles, allowing Moscow to retake control over the Left Bank. Doroshenko's star, already in decline, fell rapidly as Cossacks became disillusioned by their alliance with infidel Turks. This reached an apogee in 1675 when Moscow attacked the Ottomans at the Cyhyryn fortress, once Khmelnytsky's capitol. Doroshenko was now in the position of fighting for Muslims against Orthodox Christian Left Bank Cossacks and Russians. Surrendering, Doroshenko was exiled by Moscow. The Turks dragged the younger Khmelnytsky out of the monastery and declared him hetman, but his repeated failures led the Turks to execute him in 1681. The same year the Russians and Turks (with the Crimean Tatars) concluded the Treaty of Bakhchesarai, under which Russia's ownership of the Left Bank and the Muslim parties' hold on Crimea and a small portion of the neighboring Black Sea coast was codified for twenty years.[18]

In 1686, Poland and Russia signed another treaty dividing the Cossack lands anew. The Left Bank, the Zaporozhiya Sich lands, and Sloboda Ukraine (the area west of the Left Bank and Kiev and east of Poltava centered on present-day Kharkiv) came under the Tsar's rule. East of the Dnepr, the Poles regained control, holding the Right Bank and the non–Cossack, *szlachta*-dominated regions of Galicia, Volhynia, and Polissia. Ironically, Khmelnytsky's liberation of the Cossacks from Polish-Lithuanian tutelage had culminated in the Ruin and Russian-Polish partition of Ukrianian/Cossack lands. It would take nearly three centuries for a united Ukrainian entity, independent or otherwise, to emerge again.[19]

Crucially, the Moscow-controlled territories became "the center of Ukrainian political, cultural, and economic life," shifting from western Galicia and Volhynia. The region retained near-total political autonomy internally, becoming a refuge for the free Cossack tradition on the open wild steppe. The "Hetmanate," as it came to be called, developed its own political administration and semi-republican form of government. When Peter the Great began to impinge on the Hetmanate's autonomy during the Great Northern War against Sweden and refused to provide military assistance to the Cossacks after Sweden's Polish allies moved on the Left Bank, hetman Ivan Mazepa (1687–1709) and a 3,000-strong Cossack force defected to the Swedes. The Russians' victory at Poltava in June 1709 forced Mazepa and Sweden's King Charles XII to flee to Ottoman-controlled Moldavia, where Mazepa died on September 21. The Russian victory ended Left Bank Ukrainians' attempts to separate from Russia for some two centuries.

On the Right Bank an atomized, perhaps unconscious political revolt resembling the Chechen *begovaya kultura*, or raiding culture, dominated the mid–18th century (1734–1768). This kind of free Cossack "social banditry" reflected ethnic and social resentment and manifested itself in marauding by small- to medium-scale bands of robbers or *haidamaki* (*hajdamaky*), Turkish for robbers. *Haidamaki* had no clear political agenda and focused on stealing and destroying the Polish *szlachta*'s holdings. Cossack frustration climaxed in 1768. *Haidamaki* joined a larger and more concerted uprising of free Cossacks led by Maxym Zaliznyak and Ivan Honta (Gonta) that escalated to mass violence against Poles and Jews.

After Peter the Great, relatively weak Russian emperors refrained from dismantling the Hetmanate, needing stability and support for conquering the Ottomans and returning Constantinople to Orthodox Christian and Russian control. The final blow to Hetmanate autonomy was dealt by Catherine the Great. In 1775 she ordered Russian troops to seize the Zaporozhian Sich, the nucleus and symbol of Cossack freedom. The Sich's territory was surrounded in an enormous military operation that caught the usual battle-hearty if unruly and often drunk Cossacks off guard. The Zaporozhians surrendered without a fight. Their last *koshevoi* (ataman elected by all Cossack settlements), Pyotr Kal'nishevskiy, was arrested on June 4, 1775 and condemned to a life sentence in Russia's Arctic prison at the Solovetskii Monastery in 1776. Despite a pardon from Tsar Alexander I in 1801, the 110-year old ataman chose to serve out his term, dying two years later at the age of 112 among the dank, cold stones of Solovetsk.[20] From 1781, under Empress Catherine's administrative centralization scheme, the Hetmanate was officially abolished and subordinated directly to Imperial administration. Russian dragoon regiments replaced the Cossack army's "hosts" and "hundreds," and Russification policies were instituted in culture and education.[21]

By 1795 Austria, Prussia, and Russia had completed the last of three partitions of the Poland-Lithuanian Commonwealth, and Russia received 62 percent of its territory and 45 percent of its population, including all of the Right Bank. Austria took Galicia and Bukovina. With Russia's incorporation of the Crimean khanate into the empire in 1783, most of what is today central, eastern, and southern Ukraine came under Russian rule.

Imperial Rule and the Rise of Ukrainian Nationalism

The different imperial systems experienced by Greek or Uniate Orthodox Ukrainians in Austria-Hungary and the predominantly Russian Orthodox and Cossack Ukrainians in Russia prolonged and deepened the cultural schism between eastern and western Ukrainians. Despite attempts to assimilate the "Little Russians" (*Malorossy*—Russia's eastern Ukrainians), as Russians and many Ukrainians referred to Ukrainians, Cossack traditions continued among them. But the predominant peasant class was entrenched in serfdom as Catherine the Great and her successors expanded the institution to all Russia and newly controlled territories. By contrast, the western Ukrainians of Austria-Hungary had no Cossack tradition and either mimicked the Polish *szlachta* and became landowners or, with serfdom out of practice in the West, became shopowners, more urbanized and embourgoised than their largely enserfed peasant counterparts.

Modern Ukrainian national self-awareness and identity solidified in the 19th century as the Austrian and Russian Empires underwent intense intellectual ferment. Especially in Russia, where the regime was harsher, somewhat less tolerant of ethno-national differences, and inclined to regard the *Malorossy* as essentially Russians, a separate Ukrainian national identity and nationalist sentiment developed somewhat more rapidly. The Russians' "otherness" was driven home by occasional attempts to re-convert Greek Catholics back to Orthodoxy. The Poles' several uprisings against Russian rule were increasingly accompanied by some attempts to rally the Ukrainians to their side. The Galicians' and Volhynians' historical experience with the Poles, however, engendered little enthusiasm for such an alliance. Poles dominated the region's center, Lviv, and Ukrainians retained considerable resentment towards them and the significant Jewish minority. By and large, the Polish revolts, though they occurred in western Ukrainians' regions, did not involve Ukrainians, reflecting, in Subtelny's words, "how vague and emasculated the political significance of Ukraine and Ukrainians had become in the Russian Empire."[22] This political insignificance was a consequence of demoralization, malaise, even decline in Ukrainian self-identity and ethnonational mobilization as a result of recent failures to achieve autonomous quasi-statehood. The only manifestation of a Malorossiyan/Ukrainian national movement in the first half of the 19th century, the Brotherhood of Saints Cyril and Methodius, was uncovered and destroyed in 1847. National leaders in the second half of the century, such as poet Taras Shevchenko and historian Mykola Kostomarov, were predominantly concerned with greater political freedoms, cultural rights, and economic well-being for Ukraine's peasants rather than statehood. Kostomarov proposed a federation to resolve the problem of Ukrainian self-determination and saw Ukraine as being one of six historical Russian nationalities.[23]

The rise of more radical ideologies and the growth of nationalism Europe-wide, World War I, the Romanov dynasty's collapse, and the Russian civil war produced more radical political projects among eastern Ukrainians. Some saw in the chaos another opportunity to carve out of history an independent Ukrainian state.

War, Revolution and the Ukrainian State in the 20th Century

The 20th century would bring three wars and two revolutions to Ukraine, as part of the Russian Empire and then the Soviet Union. These catastrophes were visited on Ukraine and Ukrainians in three epochal periods: (1) World War I, the revolution and civil war; (2) Soviet rule and World War II; and (3) the late 1980s' and early 1990s' anti–Soviet revolutionary regime transformation. This chapter focuses on the first two periods, leaving the last for later chapters.

Except for the Bolsheviks, early 20th-century Russia's radical opposition parties rejected any form of political self-determination, not to mention those parties supporting the Tsarist regime. Vladimir Lenin's support for national self-determination in the Bolshevik program was purely a tactical maneuver to win over ethnic minorities during the revolution's destructive phase. His notion of self-determination did not include state independence. While he supported "the freedom of secession," he asserted immediately thereafter: "Separation is not our scheme." He supported the formation of large states, opposing the "idiotic system of petty states," and envisaged the merging of nations and minorities' assimilation and adoption of the Russian language. After seizing power, the right to national self-determination could be watered down or jettisoned altogether during the revolution's "constructive phase."[24]

With the February 1917 revolution, the local government in Kiev declared an Executive Committee of the Soviet of Combined Public Organizations to run the city and outlying regions in the crisis. Simultaneously, Ukrainian democrats and socialists in Kiev declared a Central Rada. Soon, the Rada radicalized with the arrival to Kiev of leaders like Ukrainian nationalist historian Mikhail Hrushevskii, radical socialists and nationalists, and soldiers from the front. Hrushevskii was elected the Central Rada's president. But the Rada did not request or demand state independence from Alexander Kerensky's new Provisional Government in Petrograd. Rather, in early June, it sent a note to the government demanding Ukrainian autonomy within a democratic Russia, creation of a Ukrainian territorial-administrative unit fashioned from twelve provinces with predominantly ethnic Ukrainian populations, and formation of a Ukrainian army. After the note's rejection, the Ukrainian Central Rada declared it was now the sovereign power over Ukraine (but would not separate from Russia) and proceeded to form legislative and executive governmental bodies. A Kerensky-led delegation arrived in Kiev on June 28, and agreement was reached on a process whereby the Rada would prepare a set of proposals on the "questions of the national political organization of the Ukraine" for consideration by an All-Russian Constituent Assembly to be elected and convene in spring 1918.[25]

July 1917 elections to the new city councils in Ukraine showed that pro–Ukrainian parties were supported by less than a fifth of the urban electorate; they received a mere 20 percent in Kiev. This lack of support may have led to the Provisional Government's rejection in August of the Rada's draft Ukrainian constitution. Dismayed by the negotiations' course, the Rada's General Secretary Volodomir Vinnichenko left for Kiev before new talks ended, and the Provisional Government issued a "Temporary Instruction" for Vinnichenko's Ukrainian government that reduced it to a mere administrative appendage of the central government, sharply limiting the Rada's powers, especially its control over the Ukrainian "army." Although the Instruction constricted Ukraine's autonomy, it "represented an important step forward in the development of Russian federalism," according to Russia historian Richard Pipes, marking "the first time in history a Russian government … had ceded a part of its authority to an organ of self-rule formed along national-territorial lines."[26]

However, these were revolutionary times, and the more radical Ukrainian nationalists and socialists, specifically the Bolsheviks, were able to join forces through Lenin's insistence on the principle of national self-determination during the revolutionary struggle. In early August 1917, the Bolsheviks joined the Central Rada but rejected joining the more important Small Rada, a standing parliament of sorts set up by the Central Rada, created back in July. The Bolsheviks remained divided between those who opposed and those who supported utilizing Ukrainian nationalism in the revolutionary struggle. With their October coup in Petrograd, the Bolsheviks made league with Ukrainian nationalists in hopes of repeating their comrades' success in Kiev and joined the Small Rada. The nationalist Radas and the Bolsheviks agreed to cooperate in: (1) preventing the use of the railroads by troops headed to Petrograd to overturn the Bolshevik coup; (2) mutual assistance in the event pro–Provisional Government or pro–Tsarist forces moved on either the Radas or the Bolsheviks; and (3) the Radas' abstention from any expression of opposition to the coup. A day later, October 26, the revolutionary Committee of the Central Rada adopted a resolution opposing the Bolshevik revolt in Petrograd, and the Bolsheviks abandoned the Small Rada. Nevertheless, when the pro-government Kievan Staff government's forces surrounded the Bolsheviks as they prepared a coup in Kiev, the Ukrainian nationalists fulfilled their agreement with the Bolsheviks, blocking the Staff forces' efforts to destroy Red units. Outside Kiev, the local soviets seized power in Kiev province, Kherson, Odessa, Yekaterinoslav, and Chernigiv. In other places, Ukrainian socialists—the Ukrainian Social Democratic Party (USD) and the Ukrainian Socialist Revolutionary Party (USR)—joined the Bolshevik-majority revolutionary committees and helped them seize power. Many in the USD and USR, such as Ukrainian Minister of War Simon Petliura, were also nationalists. In short, the Ukrainian nationalists—perhaps thinking the Reds would fail—and Ukrainian and Russian socialists coalesced in support of Bolshevik coups both in Petrograd and Ukraine.[27]

By winter, the nationalists and Bolsheviks had fallen out with each other. On behalf of the Radas, the General Secretariat declared it was taking power on November 3. Both the Secretariat and Central Rada maintained that Ukraine would remain part of Russia. They also began to seek out an alliance with moderate socialists to remove the Bolsheviks from power and found a Russian federation. Towards that goal, the Rada refused recognition of the Bolsheviks' government, the Council of People's Commissars, and convened a conference of nationalities in November. By December the socialist-dominated but not Bolshevik-dominated Kiev (City) Soviet and other city soviets—except for the key industrial center of Kharkiv and rural areas—had recognized the authority of the Secretariat and Rada. Without a final break between Ukraine's Bolsheviks and the Rada government, the Kiev (City) Soviet assisted the Kiev Bolshevik Committee in convening an All-Ukrainian Congress of Soviets in December. Lenin's continued support for "the principle" of Ukrainian and other minorities' self-determination was pivotal in glossing over the fundamental clash of interests between the nationalists and the Bolsheviks.[28]

In Ukraine's southeast, the Don Cossacks under Ataman Kaledin formed common cause with the pro–Tsarist White Army, founding a Don Cossack Republic. At the same time, Ukrainian War Minister Simon Petliura called on Ukrainians serving in the disintegrating Russian Army to fall in behind him. From spring, Ukrainians at the World War I front were forming Ukrainian units in the hope that they might fight later for Ukraine's independence given the opportunities afforded by revolutionary upheaval. Although his orders were countermanded by the General Army Headquarters, they boded as ill for the Reds as for the Whites' hopes of maintaining the ranks of a united armed force needed now to fight both the Axis and the civil war. The final stroke was the

Central Rada's arrest of the leading Bolsheviks of the Kiev City Soviet and the expulsion of Red militia units after word was received that Bolsheviks were plotting another coup by the soviets against the Secretariat and Radas. On November 22, 1917, the Central Rada issued its "Third Universal," declaring the Secretariat and Rada the only legitimate governing bodies in an independent Ukrainian Republic. Their Ukraine encompassed nine ethnic Ukrainian-dominated governates (*gubernii*): Kiev, Chernigiv (Chernigov), Kharkiv (Kharkov), Kherson, Podolsk, Poltava, Tavriya (without Crimea[29]), Volyn, and Yekaterinoslav. The Ukrainian Republic left for future resolution the issue of the predominantly Ukrainian counties (uezdy) in the Russian governates of Kholmsk (to the west of the Ukrainian Republic in Polish Russia), Kursk, and Voronezh, as well as "other mixed population counties" to the east. Moreover, it did not claim the Don Cossack Host Province (Oblast' Donskogo Voisko), though some mixed counties in the Don Cossack east might be in play.[30] This roughly corresponds to post–2014 Ukraine, minus its western provinces taken from Poland for the USSR and its Ukrainian SSR by Joseph Stalin after World War II.

Ukraine's Bolsheviks retreated to Kharkiv and declared a Kharkiv Soviet Republic. In Petrograd, Lenin ordered the Red Army to prepare an attack on the Don Cossacks and, if necessary, on Kiev. Simultaneously, the Bolsheviks attempted coups through the local soviets in many cities during December and January, succeeding in all but one— Kiev. Before the army forces and Kharkiv Reds were able to reach Kiev, the Ukrainian General Secretariat issued a declaration of independence. At least hypothetically, for the first time since Khmelnytsky an independent Ukrainian entity existed. *De facto*, it survived one month. *De jure*, the Central Rada's Ukrainian nationalists retained some claim to sovereignty through most of April by way of the German army and the Central Powers, with which the Rada signed a peace treaty on February 9, 1918. It soon became clear that the Ukrainian government lacked the capacity to harness "Europe's food basket" to help feed German and Austrian soldiers as the Powers had hoped. On April 28, as the Rada prepared to adopt a new Ukrainian constitution, German forces seized the assembly hall and disbanded the parliament.[31] This would not be the last effort by Ukrainian nationalists of the revolutionary era to found a Ukrainian state. The countryside was home to some 300,000 soldiers back home from the front, who had sat out the early phase of the revolution centered in the cities and towns and were available to any force that could rally them to its side.

In the old government's place, the Germans established a puppet administration headed by Hetman Pavlo Skoropadskii, a former Tsarist officer and commander of the Free Cossack detachments loyal to the fallen Rada government. Meanwhile, the Ukrainian Bolsheviks, now organized under the new Ukrainian Communist Party (UCP) subordinated to the Russian Communist Party (RCP) by Lenin, began preparing an uprising. The German occupiers played into the communists' hands by brutally extracting food from the peasants. For the first time, large numbers of Ukrainian peasants sided with the Bolsheviks, and some of the old nationalists even renewed their cooperation with them. But their August 1918 uprising failed miserably. In October, Moscow, in the person of the RCP's Central Committee (CC) chaired by Lenin, ordered Ukrainian detachments left over from the uprising to deploy against the White Army in the North Caucasus. As the world war came to its end in November, Skoropadskii's Hetmanate appeared more vulnerable, forced to fend for itself.[32]

Anarchy now seized Ukraine. Marauding bands of peasants and thieves roamed the countryside pillaging, murdering, targeting Jews in pogroms, and seeking to make the most of their "freedom" before either the Hetman or the Whites re-established Tsarist agrarian laws. On November 14 the Hetman created a new Cabinet dominated by monarchists that adopted the Federation Act, which committed Ukraine to membership in a post–Bolshevik state. This act alienated Ukraine's peasants, the nationalist portion of the elite, and socialists simultaneously. The united opposition appealed for a general insurrection, issued radical land decrees to attract peasants, and established a new governing body, the Directory, led by two rivals: the socialist-oriented Vinnichenko and the nationalist-oriented Petliura. Significantly, the Directory also signed an agreement with a new Ukrainian government in Galicia just formed in disintegrating Austria-Hungary, thereby asserting a united Ukrainian state. The Directory's forces of peasant partisans marched into Kiev on December 14, 1918, and Skoropadskii resigned. Instead of uniting against General Denikin's White forces, who opposed Ukrainian separatism and Bolshevik communism, the nationalists and especially the communists, still differing over the national question, could not forge a united front. The communist "leftists" and Stalin, who opposed playing with the "principle" of national self-determination and had organized the failed August uprising, secretly established a Ukrainian underground soviet over the border in Russia's Kursk. The "rightists," led by Lenin, urged patience. On November 28, Nationalities Commissar Stalin ordered Kursk to put its plan in action, and military operations were mobilized against the Directory. Throughout early winter, Ukrainian and Russian peasants, already tired of the Directory and susceptible to communist slogans of "land to the peasants" and "national self-determination," gave up pillaging and pogroms and joined the communists' march on Kharkiv, then Kiev. On February 6, 1919, the Red Army reentered Kiev.[33] The Red and White armies battled across Ukraine for another year. The Red triumph culminated in the evacuation of tens of thousands by ship from Crimea, which the RCP would retain for the USSR's Russian Federation, not the Ukrainian SSR, for several decades.

Thus, the last independent Ukrainian entities to exist before the rise of today's Ukraine after the 1991 Soviet collapse were the essentially nascent Ukrainian state formations of the Russian revolutionary and civil war period. They arose as the result of the fall of the Tsarist regime and the resulting plague of two simultaneous wars: World War I and the civil war. Ukrainian nationalists' efforts to fashion an independent state, while often admirable and courageous, were secondary and ultimately proved insufficient to make good on the opportunity chaos brought. Leading Ukrainian historians, such as Subtelny and John Reshetar, acknowledge that the main cause of the Ukrainian nationalist movement's failure was neither the Secretariat's nor Central Rada's inadequacies but rather "underdevelopment" of the movement.[34] Regardless, the first viable modern project for the achievement of independent Ukrainian statehood was dead. Given the cruel totalitarian and hyper-centralized order now poised to consolidate its hold across the Eurasian steppe from the Dnepr to the Pacific, the quest for Ukrainian statehood could only be resurrected first in the interwar years outside the confines of the Soviet Union.

The Ukrainian Soviet Socialist Republic (Ukraine SSR) was established with the Soviet constitution's "ratification" by the Second All-Union Congress of Soviets on January 31, 1924. The Ukraine SSR encompassed a large portion of Ukraine as understood by Ukrainians in recent decades, minus Galicia and Volhynia. Although the NEP (New Economic Program) years were a period in which "national communism" survived and could put forward various schemes of autonomy for "union republics" such as Ukraine, Stalin's tightening grip on power with the first five-year plans and collectivization of agriculture soon yielded campaigns targeting "national deviationists" in Ukraine and across the USSR. The centralization, ideologization, and "sovietization" of culture and education dealt a final blow to any possibility for public articulation of notions such as extra-territorial and territorial national cultural autonomy, no less political autonomy.

Over the decades, however, Soviet communism did redefine the notion of Ukrainian territory by reconfiguring, indeed expanding the Ukraine SSR. This was often done with an eye toward the reality of continuing Ukrainian national feeling, however circumscribed its expression had to be, given the ambitious Soviet goal of creating a new Soviet man and proletarian culture to replace ethnic identities and national cultures. Soviet-era border changes made to the Ukraine SSR redounded to the benefit of the territory under post–Soviet Ukraine's sovereignty. After the adoption of the Soviet constitution and new adminstrative-territorial structures for both the USSR and Ukraine SSR, the 1920s saw a series of territorial exchanges between the Ukraine SSR and the Russian Federation (the Russian Socialist Federative Soviet Republic or RSFSR) in 1925 and 1928. These exchanges amounted overall to little real change in the Ukraine SSR's territory, except for the somewhat significant though not major transfers from Ukraine to Russia of the cities Taganrog and Shakhty in 1925.[35]

The interwar period and especially the Soviet experience added much more territory. By virtue of the fact that they involved the unification of the western Ukrainian lands with the Ukraine SSR, these "border changes" or annexations contributed to today's divide within the Ukrainian state. Territorially, contemporary Ukraine is in significant part the work of Joseph Stalin. The territories Stalin seized and attached to the Ukraine SSR before and after World War II were far more substantial than the internal territorial exchanges of the 1920s. The August 23, 1939 Nazi-Soviet (Molotov-Ribbentrop) Pact allowed the Red Army to enter Poland from the east and seize eastern Poland: almost all of the West Ukrainian lands, including the Galicia-Volhynia territories. More western Ukrainian-populated lands came under German and Hungarian control before Galicia-Volhynia were temporarily removed from Soviet control after the Nazi invasion of the USSR. However, with the Red Army's reconquest and march further west at the end of the war, Stalin was able to dictate the USSR's postwar borders with Poland, Hungary and Romania and incorporate all even partially Ukrainian-populated lands into the Ukraine SSR. This vast territory included all of eastern Poland's West Ukrainian provinces: Lviv (Lvov), Lutsk, Rivne (Rovne), Ternopil' (Ternopol'), Ivano-Frankivsk (Ivan-Frankovsk), Chernivtsy (Chernovtsy), and Uzhgorod, with its significant Hungarian minority. Also included was the Black Sea coastline area formerly belonging to Romania and located west of Odessa. This area has comprised the southern half of Soviet and post–Soviet Ukraine's Odessa Province (Oblast'). Thus, Stalin's annexations of territories from Poland, Hungary and Romania make up 7.5 of present-day Ukraine's 26 provinces, or about 15 percent of its territory.[36]

Ukraine's domain over Crimea was similarly Soviet in origin and therefore problematic and vulnerable to delegitimization. No independent Ukrainian entity ever gained sovereignty over Crimea until the Soviet regime under its Ukrainian-born CPSU General Secretary, Nikita Khruschev, transferred the peninsula—the Crimean Autonomous Soviet Socialist Republic (ASSR)—from the RSFSR to the Ukraine SSR in 1954. Catherine the Great first won Crimea for the Russian Empire in a war with the Ottoman Empire in the 18th century. Tsarist Russia fought another war to preserve its Crimean holding against an alliance of Western empires and the Ottoman Turks in the real first world war, the early 1850s' Crimean War. Ukrainians and Ukrainian Cossacks played roles in both wars for the Crimea, but the peninsula for more than two centuries was Russian, not Ukrainian territory. There is a dispute over whether the Central Rada's briefly declared Ukrainian Republic included Crimea within its territorial claims. There is another dispute over whether Khruschev's transfer of Crimea to Ukraine was legal in that it allegedly was formulated in violation of Soviet constitutional procedure. Regardless, the transfer of Crimea added another 5 percent to Ukraine's present territorial expanse.

In sum, the Soviet Union and Stalin made much of both the Ukraine SSR and what we now call post–Soviet, independent Ukraine, adding some 20 percent of its current territory. It is important to stress that the Ukraine SSR exited the USSR fully intact to become the state it is today. However, the cobbled-together territory of the Ukraine SSR made for a complex ethno-national, linguistic, religious, and regional construction unprecedented for this region that would prove a challenge to hold together in new revolutionary times as it had been so many times before in the region's troubled history.

Stalin's mass collectivization of all agricultural life and the resulting Great Famine of 1930–33—or "Holodomor," as Ukrainians call it—destroyed the Ukrainian peasantry. In Ukraine alone, the famine starved several million to death. But as elsewhere in the USSR, the famine was a result of the regime's collectivization policy of confiscating not just feed grain but the seed grain needed for planting the next year's crop, and not of any nationalities policy pursuing genocide in general, or that of Ukrainians in particular. Neither collectivization nor confiscation targeted the Ukrainian peasantry alone. The famine simply had its greatest impact in Ukraine because of the region's large agricultural sector. Western historians emphasize that Stalin's goal was the destruction of the "kulak class" as the carrier of ethnic nationalism and that the famine also devastated the Black Soil and Volga regions of Russia and parts of Central Asia. The West's perhaps supreme historian of the period, Robert Conquest, concluded that the first goal of the terror-famine was to destroy the "kulak" class and complete the overall peasant class's collectivization on state farms. In Ukraine, the destruction of Ukrainian nationalism—not the Ukrainian nation—was a secondary goal, and ethnic Ukrainian communists helped to implement the famine in Ukraine, as other native communists did in Central Asia and the Volga region.[37]

The Rise of Nationalism in Western Ukraine

As noted above, Western Ukraine or Galicia writ large and surrounding areas were located in the Austro-Hungarian Empire and its successor states, most of all Poland in the interwar period. In contrast to their counterparts in the totalitarian USSR, the Galician Ukrainian nationalist movement had political space to develop in autocratic but relatively free Austria-Hungary, and much more so in the fledgling, democratic nation-states of early interwar Poland, Czechoslovakia, Romania, and Hungary. Ukrainian nationalists came under increasing harassment and persecution as these Eastern European countries, except for Czechoslovakia, devolved into growing ultranationalism and quasi-fascism. But sufficient political space and organizational development put Ukrainian nationalists there in a position to attempt achieving Ukrainian statehood in the interstices created in the region by the great conflagration of World War II. Encouraged by, but the only major nationality left out, of the region's new nation-state order based on the principle of national self-determination, 7 million Western Ukrainians, most of whom lived in Poland, produced a new nationalist movement. It would be tainted, however, by its ultranationalism and cooperation with the German Nazis in the Holocaust.

Ukrainian-Polish conflict had become a central feature of Ukrainian nationalism. After Poland's defeat of the Red Army's attempt to export communist revolution to Europe through Galicia in 1919, the Western Powers temporarily recognized Warsaw's jurisdiction over the region in 1923. This came on condition that Poland granted Galicia administrative and cultural autonomy. Galicians already had resisted Polish authority, boycotting the 1921 census and 1922 *sejm* or parliamentary elections. Then Warsaw failed to abide by the condition that it grant Galicia autonomy, sparking ethnonational mobilization among Ukrainians. Ukrainian-language schools created under the Hapsburgs were "systematically eliminated," with 2,048 of 2,400 closed in Eastern Galicia by 1937. Some Ukrainians turned to "lone wolf" sabotage and assassinations of Polish officials.[38] Despite growing Polish nationalism and authoritarianism in the wake of Marshal Joseph Pilsudski's 1926 military coup civic space remained in which Ukrainians could self-organize their new nationalist movement.

The new movement's core was the Organization of Ukrainian Nationalists (OUN), led by Stepan Bandera and based largely in Polish Galicia. OUN was founded in 1929 as a revolutionary nationalist organization; much of its leadership spent time in Nazi Germany, and the group held up the notion of an ethnically pure Ukrainian nation. The OUN emerged out of the "integral nationalism" movement—a reaction to the failure in establishing an independent Ukrainian state during the opportune upheavals in the revolutionary period of 1917–20. Integral nationalism was not an integrated system of ideas but a collection of basic concepts intended to "incite people" to revolutionary action. Pro-Ukrainian historian Orest Subtelny notes Ukrainian integral nationalism "clearly contained elements of fascism and totalitarianism," proposing "revolutionary action, radical solutions, and the creation of a new breed of 'super' Ukrainians." It resembled the agrarian fascism of the Romanian Iron Guard, the Croatian Ustashi, and the Hungarian Arrow Cross. A key element was similar to a component of Russian nationalist thought frequently attributed to the Russian Orthodox Church and emphasized by Westerners— *sobornist'* (in Russian *sobornost'*). *Sobornist'* in Ukrainian ultranationalist thought, both in the interwar period and today, signifies national collectivism: the nation's cause supercedes individual rights and interests.[39]

On the eve of the war, the OUN included some 20,000 members, with sympathizers numbering many times more. Its members carried out hundreds of sabotage acts, dozens of "expropriations" of government moneys, and over 60 successful or attempted assassinations, including that of Polish Interior Minister Bronislaw Pieracki in 1934. The entire leadership of the OUN's home base in Galicia was arrested in response to the Pieracki assassination, including its future pre-eminent leader Stepan Bandera. Bandera and his OUN associates were predisposed to "a violent, heroic type of resistance," which by the eve of the war had reached a fever pitch of "fanaticism," according to Subtelny.[40] In 1939, as the war began, the OUN split between its mostly Germany-based older generation of the 1917–1920 struggle for independence and the younger Galicia-based wing, the members of which came to OUN in the 1930s. The former, the OUN-M or Melnykites, was led by Andrei Melnyk, who supported close ties with Germany alone. The "young radicals" or OUN-B or OUN-R (revolutionary) were led by "the dynamic, strong-willed"

Bandera, who recently had been released from a Polish prison. Bandera supported the creation of a military underground and developing contacts not just with the Nazis but the Western powers as well.[41] Bandera and the Banderites are the leading light of today's ultranationalists—including those of the deceptively named ultranationalist Freedom (Svoboda) Party, led by notorious anti–Semite and Russophobe Oleg Tyagnibok, and the neofascist Right Sector led by Dmitro Yarosh—who would lead the February 2014 revolutionary takeover of power. Bandera's family roots and blood sink deep into the soil of Galicia and its metropole, Lviv (Lvov), the wellspring of historical and contemporary Ukrainian nationalism, ultranationalism, neofascism and the attendant Bandera legend.

Ukraine in World War II

Under the secret protocols of the Soviet-Nazi or Molotov-Ribbentrop Pact, Soviet troops seized Galicia and all of western Ukraine, what was then eastern Poland, in September 1939. Like many OUN members and thousands of western Ukrainians, Bandera's grandfather Andrei, a Uniate Catholic priest and a founding member of the 1918 self-declared Western Ukrainian National Republic, was executed by the NKVD. He was accused of having close ties to the OUN, which he denied during interrogation, confessing he only sympathized with the organization and was simply a Christian scholar.[42] The Soviets initially supported Ukrainization in education and culture, but Ukrainian and all other political parties except for the communists were forced to disband. Tens of thousands, including many OUN members and supporters, fled to German-occupied Poland. Soviet policy shifted in 1940 and repressions against Ukrainians and Poles ensued in force, including deportation of 400,000 Ukrainians from Galicia alone. Western Ukrainians remaining in Soviet-occupied areas were left with one political force to protect them— the ultranationalist OUN. Since Jews were disproportionate in numbers among the Communists who backed the Soviet takeover, Ukrainians' (and Poles') already strong anti–Semitism intensified. OUN leaders' ideological tracts contained the anti–Semitic elements extant among interwar Europe's ultranationalist and neofascist groups.[43] The historical irony for Ukraine was that the Soviet incorporation of Galicia into the USSR meant that it was the Soviet dictator Stalin who united all Ukrainians inside a single state entity for the first time in centuries.

Ukrainians in the eastern parts of German-occupied Poland—called the "General Government," run by Hans Frank—immediately began cooperating with the Nazis in so-called self-help committees staffed mostly by OUN members and supporters from Galicia who fled from the Red Army. The committees were coordinated by the Ukrainian Central Committee (UCC), which the OUN used to raise national consciousness, expanding Ukrainians' educational, publishing, and youth group infrastructure, despite German warnings that the committees should refrain from political activity. After the German invasion of the USSR on June 21, 1941, the UCC extended its work to Galicia.[44]

With the Nazi invasion of the USSR, Ukrainian nationalists turned the tables on the communists in Galicia and eastern Ukraine. But not before the retreating Soviets massacred several tens of thousands of Ukrainian prisoners en masse in Lviv, Sambir, Stanislavyiv, Rivne, Lutsk, and Volhynia during the week of June 21–28, 1941. Many in Galicia, in particular the OUN, turned to Hitler's Nazis as a vehicle for attaining Ukrainian independence, or at least avoiding Stalin and communism, submitting to the devil they did not know. Subtelny accurately describes the Nazi-OUN relationship in German-occupied Ukraine as "tenuous," with each side maneuvering to use it "for its own, often contradictory purposes."[45] But both parties had in common racism, a cult of violence, and an interest in, and no compunction about, slaughtering Poles, Jews, and communists.

OUN discourse was ultranationalistic, often racist and violent, with Poles and Jews being the objects of its ire. As Per A. Rudling demonstrates, the Nazis and OUN had much in common: "The OUN shared the fascist attributes of antiliberalism, anticonservatism, and anticommunism, an armed party, totalitarianism, anti–Semitism, Fuhrerprinzip (the Fuhrer principle), and an adoption of fascist greetings." OUN leaders stressed to the German Nazi leadership that they shared the Nazi worldview and goal of a fascist Europe.[46] The author of the most detailed study of the OUN, Franziska Bruder, concluded that the OUN is "a classic representative of a nationalist movement with fascist characteristics that appeared in East-Central Europe."[47] OUN literature held that interracial marriages should be banned and that "Ukrainians are those who are blood of our blood and bone of our bone. Only Ukrainians have the right to Ukrainian lands, Ukrainian names, and Ukrainian ideas." Anti-Semitism was significant in OUN publications. The OUN's most influential ideologist, Dmytro Dontsov, translated the writings of Mussolini, Hitler, Goebbels, Rosenberg and Franco and wrote anti–Semitic articles for publication in the OUN's *Visnyk* and other journals.[48] In 1938, Volodomyr Martynets, the editor of the OUN's main ideological organ *Razbudova Natsii* (Awakening of the Nation), wrote:

> How to deal with the Jews? We have over two million of them in Ukraine.... Should we allow them to continue to abuse the Ukrainian national organism? Assimilate them? Take them in? Amalgamate them? Get rid of them from Ukraine? How? Expel them? Where? It is neither that easy to expel 2 million people, nor get rid of them altogether. Nobody wants them; everybody is only happy to get rid of them. In practice, other than the Spaniards, no single European Christian nation has been able to solve the Jewish problem in a fully satisfactory way. Various methiods have been used, and not a single one of them has solved the issue.[49]

That the OUN's preference for violence would hold sway in any final solution to the "Jewish problem" was evident throughout OUN texts of the 1930s. One frequent icon of the OUN was the violent *haidamaki* and the 1768 uprising: "When this new, great day [of national revolution] arrives, we will have no mercy. There will be no cease-fire, the Pereiaslavl or Hadiack peace treaties will not be repeated. A new Zalizniak, a new Gonta will come. There will be no mercy, neither for the big, nor for the small, and the bard will sing: 'And father slaughtered son.'" The OUN's 1935 military instructions demanded that "a fighter should not hesitate to kill his father, brother, or best friend if he gets such an order." In 1936 Bandera himself indicated the scale of atrocities he thought would be needed to protect the Ukrainian nation from its enemies and achieve statehood: "The OUN values the life of its members, values it highly; but—our idea in our understanding is so grand, that when we talk about its realization, not single individuals, nor hundreds, but millions of victims have to be sacrificed in order to realize it." Thus, the OUN supported the Nazis' plans for European conquest.[50]

Not surprisingly, then, Bandera and the OUN collaborated with, then broke from, but again collaborated with the Nazis. At the war's beginning, Bandera received Nazi funding to carry out sabotage attacks in the USSR as Nazi forces advanced across Poland and the Soviet Union. Under Nazi cover, the OUN declared an independent state in Lviv on June 30, 1941 and appointed Bandera's deputy and close associate, Yaroslav Stetsko, as its premier.[51] The OUN's declaration sparked a rift between the Banderites and the Nazis in 1941, but not before the OUN carried out pogroms in July. With "above average brutality" compared with their Nazi colleagues, OUN members slaughtered 5,000 of Lviv's Jews, demonstrating the extent of the OUN's sympathy for Nazi anti–Semitism.[52]

Subtelny, like many other Ukrainian historians, apologizes for the OUN and other Ukrainians' participation in the Jewish holocaust, claiming "Ukrainian participation in the massacres was neither extensive nor decisive."[53] In fact, the OUN's deep, premeditated involvement is clear. On June 25, 1941, Stetsko informed Bandera that he "was setting up a militia that will help remove the Jews and protect the population," and instructions to OUN fighters urged "the liquidation of undesirable Polish, Muscovite, and Jewish activists, especially supporters of Bolshevik-Muscovite imperialism. Destroy the officer staff, shoot the Muscovites, Jews, NKVD men, the political instructors, and all who want war and our death." Eventually, pogroms spread beyond Lviv and were led by the Stetsko government's "Nachtigall Battalion" led by the notorious Ukrainian anti–Semite Roman Shukhevych. Deaths reached at least 13,000.[54]

Despite their demonstration of solidarity with Nazi anti–Semitism, Bandera and the entire OUN-B leadership were arrested days after their June 30 declaration of independence and sent to a concentration camp. This and the Nazi-approved formation of Ukrainian "expeditionary groups" to follow the Nazi army into Ukrainian lands and organize the rear led to OUN-B assassinations of OUN-M officials and mutual recriminations made to Nazi officials. As the OUN-M sought to replace the OUN-B and engaged in increasingly overt political activity, the Nazis turned on the Ukrainian nationalists. In September, the Gestapo executed the leaders of the expeditionary committees, and in November over forty members of the OUN-M were executed. The Nazi government then instituted a brutal policy against suspect Ukrainians and divided Ukraine between governates in Poland and Ukraine, with other parts distributed to Hungarian or Romanian occupational regimes.[55]

During the OUN leadership's internment, OUN elements continued to wage war on Jews, Poles, and "*moskals*" (a derogatory Ukrainian term for "Muscovites"). The central role was played by Waffen SS's volunteer "Galician Division" (GC) death squads, characterized even by Subtelny as "the most important case of Ukrainian collaboration with Hitler's regime on the organizational level." Eager to slaughter Jews and other ethnic enemies and hoping to parlay the volunteer GC into an army that in future could fight for an independent Ukrainian state, over 82,000 OUN members and sympathizers answered the call, and 13,000 were eventually brought into the GC's ranks. The GC and other OUN-manned units were responsible for at least 47,000–79,000 Jewish deaths.[56] Most notably, in several days in late September 1941 on the outskirts of Kiev at a ravine near Babi Yar, nearly 34,000 Jews were executed by Nazi Einsatzgruppen mobile death squads with assistance from the Ukrainian auxiliary police dominated by OUN members.[57] Subordinated auxiliary police units were the standard instrument with which the Einsatzgruppen recruited locals to assist them in their dirty work. The auxiliary police searched for, detained, transported, and sometimes assisted the Germans in the execution of Jews and other "alien" groups.[58] Also, OUN sympathizers and other Ukrainians participated— sometimes with real enthusiasm—in detaining and transporting Ukraine's 2 million Jews to Nazi Jewish ghettos and killing about 850,000 of those in 180 large concentration camps located in Ukraine.[59]

As German occupation continued, a partisan movement emerged in western

Ukraine. Combining the Taras-Bulba Borovets' partisans, the "Polissian Sich" formed in late 1941, and elements of the Petlurist Ukrainian National republic government-in-exile, the Ukrainian Insurgent or Partisan Army (*Ukrainska Povstanska Armiya*), or UPA, was born. In 1942 members of both OUNs established partisan units in Volhynia, and by the end of the year the Banderite wing of Volhynia partisans decided to form a Ukrainian army. Gradually building up its forces, the OUN was boosted by the Nazis' release of the OUN leadership in early 1944. Usurping the UPA name, the Banderite OUN-UPA forced units of the original UPA and Melnykite OUN into the new OUN-UPA, killed many of the original UPA's leaders and others who refused to subordinate to the OUN-B, and appointed the notorious Shukhevych as UPA commander. The disasters at Stalingrad and Kursk and the beginning of the Red Army's march west forced the Nazis to give the Ukrainian ultranationalists more freedom to organize militarily and politically. The OUN-UPA's new political organ, the Ukrainian Supreme Liberation Council, called on the USSR's national minorities to rebel against Moscow, signaling a shift in OUN fascism's ethnic targeting from Jews to *moskals*.[60]

Nazi Germany freed Bandera and the OUN leadership, hoping his Ukrainian partisans could help stop the advance of the Soviet army from eastern into western Ukraine. Bandera was able to set up a headquarters in Berlin and manage Nazi training of Ukrainian insurgents. Many had already served in the occupation's police and done the Nazis' dirty work. The OUN-UPA leadership was now dominated by Nazi-trained commanders. It expanded and disciplined the UPA's ranks by terror and forced recruitment, led by its special service shock troops, the *Sluzhba Bezpeki* (Security Service) or SB. However, the Nazis' clearly declining prospects prompted a shift in the OUN's preference regarding a protector, and contacts with and hopes for backing from Western powers motivated a change in OUN rhetoric, even as the OUN-UPA slaughter of Poles and Jews mounted in the homeland. In this period, some OUN-UPA units accepted a Jew here or there to counter a shortage of medical personnel; however, these Jews were executed when the Red Army approached.[61]

In spring 1943 the interim OUN-B leader Mykola Lebed' ordered an ethnic cleansing of Ukrainian territory targeting all ethnic minorities. Although Poles and after them the Jews bore the brunt of the OUN-UPA spear, mass extermination also aimed to liquidate Czechs, Hungarians, Armenians, and others. In 1943, the OUN-UPA's SB in Volhynia issued orders to "physically exterminate Jews who were hiding in the villages." Jews who escaped the ghettos were captured and executed on the spot by OUN-UPA forces. A strategy of luring Jews out of their hiding places in order to execute them was adopted. This phase of murdering Jews culminated in early 1944 and reached "only" several thousand, given that almost all of Ukraine's Jews had been slaughtered or were in labor camps already. By March 1944 the OUN-UPA was reporting to the Nazi SS on its successes in exterminating Jews and Poles. The OUN-UPA chaplain, Father Ivan Hrymokh (Grymokh), assured the Nazis any claim that the Banderites viewed the Reich as an enemy was "mistaken," and that they would not have engaged in subversive activity if in 1941 the Reich had granted Ukraine protectorate status. Hrymokh stressed that even when opposing the Reich, the OUN-B "was maintaining the rules not to attack German interests and aim all its forces toward the preparation for a decisive struggle against the Muscovites." OUN-UPA songs hailed the slaughtering: "We slaughtered the Jews, we'll slaughter the Poles, old and young, everyone; we'll slaughter the Poles, we'll build Ukraine." Thus, from mid–1943 through most of 1944, OUN-UPA and the OUN's security service carried out widespread, brutal massacres of Poles across Galicia and Volhynia that left 60,000–88,700 dead. Ukrainians claim Poles began the massacres in 1942 and continued them in 1944–45 in areas west of the San River.[62] However, Ukrainians cannot point to any documentation of Polish murders on such a scale or so carefully organized and ideologically justified like that detailing the scale and premeditated nature of OUN crimes perpetrated in Galicia and Volhynia.

In some cases, Ukrainians participated in Nazi war crimes against Russians, Jews and other minorities because they were communists, no less than because they were non–Ukrainian. As the Nazis swept east, Ukrainian CPSU members and sympathizers also felt fascism's wrath. Therefore, in the five major pro–Soviet partisan units in late-war Ukraine, 46 percent of the fighters were ethnic Ukrainians, while Ukraine's overall population was 80 percent Ukrainian.[63] The Germans occasionally executed Ukrainian nationalists in the Donbass, but overall the OUN had a small following in southeastern Ukraine. The limited OUN following developed in the region by way of the relaxation of antinationalist (as in antireligious) policy granted by Stalin as the war began, the German occupation of the region, and the import of OUN forces as a result. The southern port city of Mariupol became a relative OUN stronghold in the region. Nevertheless, the OUN's influence was still minimal even under the German occupation and erased completely when the Red Army moved back into the region in 1943. The Galician dialect of OUN members was barely decipherable in Russified Donbass, where Ukrainian speakers often denied speaking Ukrainian, claiming they spoke a local language. Indeed, many spoke a peculiar mix of Russian and Ukrainian. The difficulty of communication made conversion rare. Some Russians joined the OUN but remained suspicious of its extremist ideology. Some favored a Soviet Ukraine "without Germans and Bolsheviks."[64]

The Donbass and some other regions in central and southeastern Ukraine largely rejoiced with the Red Army's return. OUN emissaries and sympathizers in Donbass and elsewhere in southeastern as well as central Ukraine, especially those who collaborated with the German occupation regime, were subject to repressions carried out by the NKVD and supported by the bulk of underground and returning pro–Soviet locals. Mass repressions in the postwar years were significant. The number of false accusations is unknown, but 21,412 people were tried as German traitors and spies in the first seven months of 1946. Almost all were imprisoned—most to ten years—and 2 percent of those tried were executed.[65]

But western Ukraine was a completely different story. Whereas elsewhere in Ukraine there was little and usually no resistance to the return of Soviet power, OUN-UPA nationalists of western Ukraine mounted a partisan campaign from the forests of Galicia and Volhynia until the mid–1950s. With the Wehrmacht's withdrawal and the Soviet rear weakened by the offensive into Europe and towards Berlin, battalion-sized units of OUN-UPA partisans took control of large areas in western Ukraine and took on MVD and NKVD special units, as too many Ukrainians in the Red Army were in reality, or were suspected of being, reluctant to fight the Ukrainian partisans. In 1944–45 pitched battles took place between the somewhat dispersed 30–40,000 OUN-UPA partisans and Soviet force concentrations numbering sometimes as many as 30,000 troops. After the Nazi surrender in May 1945, the Soviets were able to step up operations against the partisans. Hundreds of special operations were carried out to root out straggling units. As the partisans retreated into the Transcarpathian Mountains, there were mass arrests and executions across western Ukraine. Tens of thousands of OUN members and sympathizers had openly collaborated with the Nazis. In order to deprive them of their support base, the NKVD blockaded and depopulated areas of Galicia, Volhynia, and the Transcarpathian foothills, deporting families and sometimes entire villages of OUN-UPA members. As many as 500,000 may have been deported to Siberia in 1946–49. Suffering heavy losses, the OUN-UPA decided to return to an insurgent strategy, avoiding large frontal engagements and breaking its forces into smaller units, but by 1948 most units had disbanded. Establishing "loose, sporadic contacts with the British and American secret services," the OUN-UPA turned to a strategy of propaganda, sabotage, terror, and assassinating Soviet officials. With Shukhevych's death in a skirmish near Lviv in March 1950, the OUN and UPA soon ceased to exist.[66] With their dissolution, Soviet power was consolidated.

Postwar Ukraine SSR

In addition to Cossack and Russian Ukraine, the postwar Ukraine SSR now encompassed formerly Polish, Austrian, and Hungarian Ukraine. Western Ukraine's subjugation was further consolidated by the Greek Catholic Church's liquidation; its entire hierarchy was arrested and exiled to Siberia by 1946 for the collaboration of some clergy with the Nazis. The entire western Ukrainian peasant class was herded onto collective farms, repeating the fate of eastern Ukrainians and others in the 1930s—minus the famine.[67]

Ukraine fared significantly better under Stalin's successors. Nikita Khrushchev, a native Ukrainian, handed Crimea to Ukraine in 1956, completing the process of modern Ukraine's formation and laying a time bomb under the "stateness" and territorial integrity of post–Soviet Ukraine, Russo-Ukrainian relations, and Russo-Western relations. By the time of Khrushchev's successor, Leonid Brezhnev, born in Ukraine of parents of Russian and Ukrainian ethnicity, Ukrainians became the USSR's unofficial second nationality. The CPSU instituted a policy of appointing Slavs—mostly Russian, then Ukrainians, and some Belorussians—as second secretaries to watch over native first secretaries in the non–Slavic union republics, autonomous republics, and other so-called "autonomous" formations. In the early Brezhnev years, Ukraine SSR's CPSU branch, the Ukrainian Communist Party (UCP), was given some leeway in nationality policy, reviving some of Ukraine's traditional cultural legacy. This was curtailed when UCP First Secretary Pyotr/Petro Shelest was replaced in 1972 by the more Moscow-loyal Volodomyr Shcherbytskiy. However, some Ukrainian cultural traditions gradually re-emerged before the major revival under the *perestroika* era's political and cultural liberalization. Ironically, Ukraine, forged territorially and institutionally under Soviet power, would ring the USSR's death knell in December 1991. In turn, the Soviet collapse would usher in a "time of troubles" across much of the former USSR, providing an opening for the West's political, military, economic, cultural and overall "civilizational" expansion.

3

Western Expansionism
Operationalizing the Geopolitical and Civilizational Divide

Introduction

The two previous chapters detailed the lay of the land—geopolitically, stratego-culturally, and ideationally—"east" (Russia) and west; that is, the ideational structure or environment in which post–Cold War Russia, Ukraine, and the West were operating as they made policy decisions. The remaining chapters deal with the operationalization of some of the contingencies or potential future courses resulting from decisions and policies. Decisions and policies are the contingent or more immediate causes of the Ukrainian crisis. By contingent causes I mean causes not built into the environment (structure) within which actors make decisions. Structure shapes but does not predetermine decisions or policy; hence their contingency. The next two chapters examine the contingent causes at the international level that operationalized further contingent causes at both the international and domestic Ukrainian level: NATO expansion, EU expansion, and Western democracy-promotion policy.

NATO Expansion

The most crucial contingent cause of the present Russo-West and Ukrainian crises is NATO expansion without the inclusion of Russia. From its outset, post–Soviet Russia was a *potential* threat to its neighbors and the West, especially if not integrated into the West. That potential, however, needed to be actualized to become an actual or kinetic threat. Potential's actualization was contingent on policies—whether Western or Russian—that isolated and/or alienated Russia from the West. The expansion of Western institutions, especially NATO—world history's most powerful military-political bloc—to Russia's borders without Russia's inclusion in the bloc gradually actualized the Russian threat. Moreover, NATO expansion without Russia institutionalized and reinforced the geopolitical and civilizational divides Mackinderians, Huntingtonians, and neo–Eurasianists on both sides of the Atlantic perceived.

There were several aspects of the 1993–95 discussion, the 1995 decision and 1997 implementation of the first round of NATO expansion that brought Poland, the Czech Republic and Hungary into the military alliance which altered the Soviet-American and

Russian-American early post–Cold War honeymoon. First, the decison to expand NATO eastward broke the trust and the implied if not explicit promise not to so expand and thus take advantage of the Warsaw Pact's dissolution. Second, the U.S. policy made no extra effort to entice Russia into NATO commensurate with the country's great-power status. To the contrary, policymakers appear to have discouraged, if not outright rejected Russian overtures. Third, NATO enlargement shifted the correlation of forces in Russian domestic politics from support for, to opposition against Westernization and democratization. Fourth, NATO expansion undermined Russian national security vis-à-vis NATO. This not only further alienated the Russian power ministries or *siloviki* from the West and Russia's pro–Western leadership, it humiliated Russia's proud military and national security establishment. This was all the more so since NATO's more forward-leaning configuration required adjustments to Russian force structure, defense procurement, and military and national security doctrines, many of which Moscow was in no position to carry out because of the dire economic depression into which the collapse of the USSR had plunged the country.

Broken Promise—Broken Trust

The West had given at a minimum the impression during talks on Germany's reunification in early 1990 that it was promising Moscow that NATO at the least for some time would not take in any new members besides reunified Germany or take advantage of the disappearance of the Warsaw Pact in any way.[1] Western diplomats' language in discussions with Soviet officials, moreover, resembled full-fledged promises not to expand NATO beyond Germany, and it is no surprise the Soviets perceived it that way. For all intents and purposes, there was a *de facto* promise not to expand NATO after united Germany's incorporation into the Atlantic alliance. The sum of the discussions at the time makes this clear.

On November 9, 1990, for example, U.S. Secretary of State James Baker told Soviet President Mikhail Gorbachev in the Kremlin's St. Catherine Hall that NATO would not expand beyond reunified Germany "one inch in the eastern direction" even if NATO maintained its presence in Germany after reunification. He added: "We think that consultations and discussions within the framework of the mechanism 'Two Plus Four' should give a guarantee that the unification of Germany will not lead to the spreading of the military organization NATO to the East."[2] Baker now claims he never made any such promise. However, West German Foreign Minister Hans-Dietrich Genscher's chief of staff, Frank Elbe, has written that when he met with Baker on February 2, 1990, the two agreed that there was to be no NATO expansion to the East, and this would be communicated to the Soviets to facilitate their acceptance of reunified Germany's entrance into the alliance.[3] In his 1995 memoir, Gorbachev remembers Baker asking him: "Assuming that [German] reunification takes place, what is preferable for you: a united Germany outside NATO, fully independent without American troops, or a united Germany preserving ties to NATO but under a guarantee that NATO jurisdiction and troops will not spread to the east from today's position?" Gorbachev says that although he did not commit to either of these at that time, "the latter part of Baker's phrases became the nucleus of the formula on the basis of which compromise on Germany's military-political status was later reached."[4]

According to declassified German documents, on February 10, 1990, FRG Foreign

Minister Genscher told his Soviet counterpart Eduard Shevardnadze: "We are aware that NATO membership for a unified Germany raises complicated questions. For us, however, one thing is certain: NATO will not expand to the east."[5] Videos of Genscher's and Baker's 1990 statements to the press promising NATO would not expand beyond Germany are readily available.[6] However, weeks later, Baker was claiming he already was getting signals that "Central European countries wanted to join NATO," to which Genscher responded that they "should not touch this at this point." The exchange seems to suggest that Genscher, at least, did not necessarily see the commitment not to expand NATO as a permanent or one encompassing the east outside the GDR.[7] Although some, perhaps all of these pledges came in discussions of a possible NATO expansion to the former GDR's territory as part of the FRG after reunification, the assumption at the time was that expansion beyond the GDR was unthinkable. Since Western and Soviet leaders were agreeing that a unified Germany could join NATO, the promises not to expand to the east had to mean not to do so anywhere beyond the GDR.

In other discussions, explicit pledges appear to have been made not to expand NATO beyond the GDR. The late former Russian Foreign Minister (January 1996–September 1998), Prime Minister (September 1998–September 1999), and *perestroika*-era Politburo and Presidential Council member Yevgenii Primakov quotes Russian Foreign Affairs Ministry archival documents from various meetings, showing Baker, German Chancellor Helmut Kohl, British Prime Minister John Major, and French President Francois Mitterand all telling Gorbachev in February and March 1990 that former Soviet bloc countries of Eastern Europe would not become NATO members. British Foreign Minister Douglas Hurd told Soviet Foreign Minister Alexander Bessmertnykh in March that there "were no plans" to expand NATO beyond united Germany.[8] What seems clear is that there was at least a joint assumption and informal agreement that NATO would not expand to the east beyond the GDR.

Many Russians, including Primakov,[9] would later harshly criticize Gorbachev with justification (and hindsight's advantage) for failing to codify this in a signed agreement. Claiming this was possible, none of them can produce evidence they proposed this to Gorbachev or his inner circle. These were heady days of rapprochement and hopes for peace in a "common European home" from Paris to Vladivostok. Some would say they were days of naiveté soon trumped by cynicism. In memoirs, Gorbachev's closest advisor, Georgii Shakhnazarov, lamented the Warsaw Pact's dissolution without "achieving the liquidation of NATO." He added: "This is just a question of time. One should not regret the end of the military blocs. They are Europe's yesterday. In [Europe], security should, of course, be built on a rational, collective basis."[10]

The increasingly cynical realism of Russian foreign policy as successive rounds of NATO expanded to Russia's borders, as well as the hyper-cynicism of much of Putin's foreign policy at present, have their roots in Russian disenchantment that resulted from NATO expansion. The idealistic and naïve Russians of the democratic *perestroika* generation learned a harsh lesson from the partner they hoped for in the United States. The lone superpower, increasingly hubristic hegemon, and "victor in the Cold War"—the United States—demonstrated that Russian national security, even domestic stability, placed a distant second when it came to not just America's maintenance of its position as world leader, but also the unlimited enhancement of U.S. power globally and to boot within Russia's traditional sphere of influence.

NATO Without Russia

American hubris was communicated to Moscow in no uncertain terms by Assistant Secretary of State Richard Holbrooke, whom President Barack Obama dubbed "one of the giants of American foreign policy" after the former's passing in 2010.[11] At a Washington conference in 1997, Russia's Ambassador to the U.S. Yuli Vorontsov reported how Holbrooke and other U.S. officials repeatedly and sometimes abruptly rejected queries regarding Russia's possible entry into NATO:

> When the decision was originally floated, I came to the State Department and had a long talk with the then assistant secretary of state, Mr. Holbrooke. I said, "Have you thought about Russia while you were putting forward this idea of enlargement of NATO?" And his answer was very honest. He said, "No, not at all; you have nothing to do with that." "Aha," I said, "that is very interesting, and what about an invitation for Russia to join the enlarged NATO?" He said, "Anybody but Russia! No." That was a nice beginning of our conversations about enlargement of NATO in the State Department and later on in the corridors of power in Washington. And from all quarters I received that kind of answer: "Anyone but Russia. Not you!"[12]

The essential problem was that Russia's inordinate power relative to NATO members and prospective members, except for the United States, made it an undesirable candidate. Its accession would tip the balance in favor of Europe as opposed to the U.S., and Russia could become the leader of the more powerful European pillar. On this background, neither NATO's Partnership for Peace Program (PPP) nor the NATO-Russia Council could overcome the growing Russian-Western tensions created by NATO expansion without Russia. The PPP fostered cooperation with all states wishing such, including Russia, but also all the former Soviet republics—now independent states—along Russia's periphery, institutionalizing what looked from Moscow like Cold War containment policy 2.0. The NATO-Russia Council was a mere talking shop, gave Russia no voice in NATO matters, and had a charter NATO soon violated (see below). What was needed was an effort to at least forestall outright NATO expansion by only offering a halfway house to prospective members, including Russia, such as an associate membership in the form perhaps of a more robust PPP concept. This could have included a NATO-Associate Members' council modeled on the NATO-Russia Council: a special security relationship based on a much closer military-to-military relationship between Russia and the U.S., including frequent, substantial maneuvers and exchanges of personnel. This might have assuaged Moscow's security concerns and its offended pride at being lumped in together with weaker, former colonial minions under associate status. Together, these measures could have been the first step towards merging NATO into the OSCE, with the latter becoming the alliance's political arm for conflict resolution and decisionmaking regarding any use of military force across the European-Eurasian landmass.

Instead, a different path was chosen: NATO expansion without Russia. Once begun, it could only end at Russia's borders unless stopped by active Russian resistance by military and/or other means. Brzezinski alluded to the internal "geographical" logic that drives NATO and EU expansion to Russia's borders by noting: "If the European Union is to become a geographically larger community—with a more-integrated Franco-German leading core and less-integrated outer layers—and if such a Europe is to base its security on a continued alliance with America, then it follows that its geographically most exposed sector, Central Europe, cannot be demonstratively excluded from partaking in the sense of security that the rest of Europe enjoys through the transatlantic alliance."[13] Thus, once

Central Europe was brought into NATO, Europe's "geographically most exposed sector" would become those countries still "excluded from partaking in the sense of security" provided by NATO membership located directly east, northeast and/or southeast of the Central or Eastern European countires just brought in. Each time new countries are brought in from the "exposed sector" to the NATO zone of security, different countries farther east fall into the new "geographically most exposed sector" and need to be brought into the security zone, and so on until all the countries between Russia's borders and the Atlantic, Baltic, and Black Seas belonged to NATO. Brzezinski's and the West's fundamental error in thinking was in emphasizing Europe's "geographically most exposed sector" rather than forecasting Europe's most geopolitically and geostrategically exposed sector, which was southeastern and southern Europe, given the rise of radical Islam and the security, immigration, and resulting cultural and economic threats emanating from the rise of jihadism in the Middle East and North Africa. As of this writing, the failure to see this emerging threat, combined with the alienation of Moscow through NATO expansion and the rise of Russia-friendly China, has created openings for the global jihad, and thus a dangerous world not only for American leadership but for American homeland security.

The American rejection delivered by Holbrooke, combined with Russian political and strategic culture's strong, even central value of "honor" historically in Russia's relations with the West, could only damage relations.[14] If this slight to Russian honor did not damage U.S.-Russian and Western-Russian relations irretrievably, then the objective effect on the Russian strategic calculus and culture, as well as its domestic political scene, would. Understanding this, some, including the present author, opposed NATO expansion without Russia, warning that it would function as a self-fulfilling prophecy, recreating the very enemy we had fought to defeat during the Cold War and that had been a point of conflict in Europe for centuries. More importantly, a group of more than 40 leading foreign policy practitioners and experts, including Bill Bradley, Sam Nunn, Gary Hart, Paul Nitze, and Robert McNamara, sent an open letter in 1997 to President Clinton expressing the view that NATO expansion was unnecessary given the lack of an external threat from Russia and the fact that expansion might unnecessarily harm Russian-Western relations.[15] The architect of U.S. Cold War containment policy, George Kennan, said the following in 1998 about the risks of NATO expansion:

> I think it is the beginning of a new cold war. I think the Russians will gradually react quite adversely and it will affect their policies. I think it is a tragic mistake. There was no reason for this whatsoever. No one was threatening anybody else. This expansion would make the Founding Fathers of this country turn over in their graves. We have signed up to protect a whole series of countries, even though we have neither the resources nor the intention to do so in any serious way. [NATO expansion] was simply a light-hearted action by a Senate that has no real interest in foreign affairs.[16]

Confounding Russia's Tentative "Transition"

Given Russia's historical ambivalence if not suspicion and distrust of the West, the tenuousness of post–Soviet Russia's young democracy and pro–Western orientation, and the primary geostrategic importance of its consolidation for European and international security, NATO expansion proved a pivotal, grave mistake. Even Brzezinski acknowledged already in 1997 "the progressive weakening of the political position of the westernizers in the Kremlin," which resulted, he mistakenly claimed, from delaying the declaration of NATO expansion past 1993 and, more perceptively, from failing to offer Russia "a special cooperative relationship between Russia and NATO."[17] As documented at the time, NATO expansion indeed upset the correlation of power between pro-democratic, pro–Western and anti-democratic, anti–Western political groups and economic interests inside Russia in favor of the latter.[18] Russia's historical ambivalence toward the West and its latent inclination to seek its own Slavophilic "third way" are deeply rooted in her political culture. The liberal democratic strain, though stronger than it had ever been, was still not strong enough to ensure a smooth consolidation of democracy and the market. Thus, additional pressures imposed on the transition—for example, those that might emanate from the international environment—were likely to be decisive in the success of Russia's full democratic capitalist transformation: the "straw that breaks the camel's back." Due to such considerations, NATO Secretary General Manfred Worner said publicly in June 1991 that granting NATO membership to former Warsaw Pact members "would be a serious obstacle to reaching mutual understanding with the Soviet Union."[19] This admonition remained true for post-communist Russia.

It was clear from the late 1980s that transition to, and consolidation of democracy and market capitalism would be difficult in Russia and the other former Soviet republics. The institutional and cultural legacy of Russian and Soviet history meant that the impetus behind post–Soviet Russia's initial turn to democracy and the West was tentative. Russian political culture has traditionally been at best leery of democracy as a viable political system for a vast, multinational country such as Russia and suspicious of Western intentions even during times of growing comity like the *perestroika* and early post-*perestroika* periods. The cultural legacy of Soviet ideology and the Cold War, which strengthened suspicion of the West, was only partially mitigated by Gorbachev's *rapprochement* with the West and the collapse of the Soviet regime and state. The complexities of Russia's multiple transition—economic, political, and cultural—were among the most daunting of the post-communist cases. The cultural preconditions for civil society and free market activity—interpersonal trust, life satisfaction and commitment to democratic institutions—though taking root, remained weak. While pro–American sentiment and the Western vector was strong in the USSR and Russia during the Gorbachev and early Yeltsin years, it was susceptible to a reversion to anti–Westernism in response to any negative impulses, real or perceived, emanating from the West.

Moreover, the West's failure to understand the nature of what had happened during the Soviet collapse led to an overestimation of the tenuous hold democratization had on Moscow, not to mention on the rest of Russia and most parts of the USSR at the time. The teleological assumptions that lay behind the transition model and "transitology," so popular in American academic circles at the time, compounded this problem. The consequent unrealistic expectations led inevitably to disappointment and hysterical calls in the West for vigilance in the face of supposed resurgent Russian totalitarianism and imperialism. These are the fruits of the grand misunderstanding of the nature of Russia's transformation from Soviet totalitarian rule, misconceptualized variously as a "peaceful revolution" from below, a "transition to democracy," state "collapse," or breakup of an empire. Although aspects of all of these were present in the Soviet/Russian transformation, the most fundamental mode of the transformation was one I characterized as "revolution from above."[20]

The 1990s Soviet/Russian revolution was neither a peaceful revolution from below, like Czechoslovakia's "velvet revolution," nor a negotiated transition to democracy, like that in Poland and Hungary. Nor was it violent revolution from below, like the 1905 and 1917 Russian revolutions against tsarist autocracy, and the Chinese Revolution, won by political movements organized in councils (soviets) of workers, peasants and soldiers rooted in society and independent from the state. The Soviet/Russian regime transformation was primarily a bureaucrat-led and state-based revolution from above. Reform-minded Party and especially Russian state bureaucrats used state institutions and bodies to undermine the party-state and totalitarian remnants of the regime already being modestly democratized by Soviet leader Mikhail Gorbachev. Led by Boris Yeltsin, elected chairman of the new RSFSR Congress of People's Deputies in June 1990, opportunistic Soviet Communist Party (CPSU) and state *apparatchiks*, who defected from the reform camp led by Gorbachev, were most instrumental in overthrowing the communist regime, not the Soviet people, peoples or society. In mid–1990, Soviet Party bureaucrats and younger members of its *nomenklatura* ruling class won control over the core "republic" in the Soviet Union—the Russian Soviet Federated Socialist Republic (RSFSR)—and proceeded to carry out a creeping bureaucratic revolution against the central Soviet party-state machine. Their weapons were RSFSR state institutions, parliamentary laws, presidential decrees and administrative orders, not the marches, strikes, bombs and bullets of revolutions from below.

The RSFSR Supreme Soviet declared Russia sovereign in June 1990, establishing the supremacy of RSFSR law over USSR law on Russian territory. Russian law then transferred all property, financial and natural resources on RSFSR territory from USSR to RSFSR jurisdiction. The Russian Central Bank and new quasi-commercial Russian banks destroyed the Soviet centralized financial and banking systems. By winter, Russia outlawed at all levels combining the posts of Communist Party first secretary and chairman of the soviets semi-democratized by Gorbachev and took the first steps to establishing its own presidential, KGB and military institutions. Upon election as Russian president in July 1991, Yeltsin decreed the removal of Party organizations from all state institutions and enterprises in Russia. During the failed August 1991 hard-line coup, Yeltsin placed under RSFSR control all USSR institutions, including the KGB and military. When the coup failed, the Party was banned, effectively abolishing the old regime. With the Party gone, Russia easily abolished or expropriated the Soviet state, ministry by ministry. With the regime and state apparatus gone, there was little reason for the republics to maintain the Union. The USSR was tossed into history's dustbin. Throughout this entire period the masses were rarely and then only tactically mobilized to defend Russia's revolutionaries from above (as in February–March and August 1991), not to overthrow the remnants of the partocratic regime. This explains the limited extent of social revolution and the lack of violence during the fall of the Soviet regime. In sum, the revolution from above, as opposed to the nascent revolution from below, was decisive in bringing down the *ancien regime*, and it in fact prevented the democratic movement below from achieving administrative power.

Thus, revolution from above also explains much of the troubled development of democracy and the market in post–Soviet Russia (and many other former Soviet republics). In the wake of the opportunistic apparatchiks' seizure of power, many of their more hard-line former colleagues, as well as the only half-reformed institutions of the Soviet state, were incorporated into the new regime. The co-optation of Party and state apparatchiks and entire political and economic institutions and structures by the revolutionary Russian regime left the *nomenklatura* in power with its limited understanding of, and weak commitment to building political and economic institutions based on democracy and the rule of law. This explains why the new regime would implement policies at odds with the ideology of much of Russia's democratic movement. Moreover, a good part of the "new" elite represented economic interests formed under the old regime or during its death throes, so the "new" Russian state was rendered deeply penetrated by old and new economic oligarchs. Thus, state institutions remained significantly divided politically, diminishing the cohesion needed for concerted revolutionary economic transformation. This helped produce the undemocratic, uneconomical insider "*nomenklatura* privatization" and cemented the relationship between corrupt bureaucrats and criminalized semi-private and private financial-industrial groups. The expropriation of the old regime's structures also prolonged old operating procedures, preserving the massive bureaucracy's strong role in the economy. The result was a weak Russian state unable to defend either its interests or those of society from the preferences of bureaucrats and oligarchs, and an inefficient state that does too many things and does them all poorly. The Putin administration has sought to restore the state's strength and autonomy vis-à-vis not only the oligarchs but society as well, co-opting and demobilizing elites and society in order to weaken political opposition.

The revolution from above was distinct from the nascent, but more amorphous and weak revolutionary movement below. The limited mobilization of the masses, while it may have helped avert the violence associated with revolution, also stunted the development of civil society, especially the formation of political parties and trade unions that defend societal interests. Moreover, even Boris Yeltsin and the leaders of Russia's leading democratic parties, not to mention Russia as a whole, lacked the cultural prerequisites for democracy: social trust, traditions of compromise, and a rejection of totalitarian methods. Thus, Russian society and its democratic elements in particular have been too weak and divided to encourage the state to concentrate on the development of a civil polity and economy. The consequence of these limitations in Russia's revolution was an unstable, corrupt, cleptocratic, oligarchic, and almost anarchic quasi-democracy and market.[21] Putin has sought to eliminate the market's anarchy by in effect nationalizing strategic sectors of the economy, arresting some criminalized oligarchs and co-opting those who agreed to play by the Kremlin's new rules, which under the more vigorous Putin and his team were sure to be enforced.

If Russia's revolution had been properly understood, there would have been more realism regarding the prospects for even mid-term progress toward the consolidation of democracy and the market. Because of the limited nature of elite and institutional change during the revolution from above, the institutionalization of democracy and the market should have been understood as a decades-long process, greatly dependent on generational change and the slow grind of socioeconomic development and differentiation (formation of a large middle class), cultural transformation, and nonviolent institutional change.[22]

Moreover, not only was Russia's transformation into a market democracy a tenuous proposition, but so too was its integration into the West. Any shift in the balance of Russian perceptions would prove decisive for its future direction. The economic difficulties experienced by the average Russian citizen quickly discredited democracy and capitalism. The revolution properly understood might have prompted Western leaders to maximize economic assistance to Moscow. The West provided no economic assistance to Gorbachev as the Soviet economy crashed in 1989, undermining his reform leadership. Little assistance arrived before 1994, leaving the Russian people to struggle through a depression far worse than the Ameerican depression of the 1930s for two full years, undermining Yeltsin's democrats. Moreover, a disproportionate level of economic assistance was delivered to the Eastern European post-communist states, and later other states of the former USSR, as compared to that delivered to Russia.[23] Then the West backed a hastily implemented, poorly conceived, disastrous and broadly unpopular privatization and economic reform program that left the general public out and enriched the old "red" enterprise directors and a young generation of unscrupulous "new Russian" bandits and oligarchs.[24]

Russian perceptions were particularly vulnerable to the slightest sense on the Russians' part that there was a weak or no commitment in the West and, most importantly, from the United States to integrate Russia into the western community and acquiesce in the protection of at least some basic Russian interests. Given Russia's rather tentative and tenuous turn towards democracy and the West, the expansion of NATO and, to a lesser extent, the EU east without including Russia played a pivotal role in its turn from the West and democracy. This development tipped the scale of the former Soviet elite's perceptions in favor of growing distrust of Western, especially U.S. intentions.

The impetus for NATO expansion came immediately, just as the Warsaw Pact and USSR were dissolving. As early as its July 1990 summit—more than a year before the USSR's collapse—NATO began "outlining proposals for developing cooperation with the countries of Central and Eastern Europe."[25] In February 1991, Poland, Hungary, and Czechoslovakia (divided later that year into the Czech Republic and Slovakia) formed the Visegrád Group to press jointly for European integration, including accession to both the EU and NATO through military and other reforms that would bring their countries in line with NATO standards. Initial NATO reaction to these former Warsaw Pact countries' initiative was restrained, even negative. However, in the wake of the failed August 1991 coup in Moscow, when infighting in Moscow between Soviet President Gorbachev, Russian President Boris Yeltsin, and the union republics was at its peak, NATO held its 12th summit in Rome in November. The Rome Summit agreed to a series of market and democratization reforms in the Visegrád states—with NATO participation on issues such as reform of their militaries and civil-military relations—to lead to NATO accession.

By August 1993 the Clinton administration and NATO were already discussing alliance enlargement. By fall 1994 the administration had "reached a broad agreement on the need to press ahead, forcefully, with NATO enlargement." For some time, the Yeltsin administration had been warning of a growing public backlash against the U.S. and NATO and had turned to a policy of demonstrating some resistance to NATO expansion rather than accepting it passively. The first open break over NATO came on December 1, 1994, when Russian Foreign Minister Kozyrev traveled to Brussels to sign a Partnership for Peace agreement with the alliance but instead refused to sign in protest of a NATO communiqué released earlier that day proclaiming a policy of NATO expansion. On December 5, Yeltsin protested against attempts "from a single capitol" (that is, Washington) to decide "the destinies of whole continents and the world community as a whole" and warned this was pushing Europe "into a cold peace."[26] That Yeltsin sounded precisely like his successor would after a decade of NATO expansion demonstrates that the worsening of U.S.-Russian relations has more to do with that expansion than with Putin's arrival to power. Russia's sometimes seeming acceptance of NATO expansion had more to do with Russians' traditional sense of honor and ability to hunker down in winter, regroup, and exact revenge like a wounded bear.

The other Visegrád members were invited to join NATO at its 1997 Madrid summit, but Slovakia was excluded because of what some NATO member-states regarded as limited democratic change there. In May 1997, as Moscow and Brussels were finalizing the agreement on the NATO-Russian Founding Act, President Yeltsin, not unlike his successor, warned that he would "revise" Moscow's relations with the alliance if it "starts admitting" states of the former Soviet Union. Yeltsin also proposed establishing joint Russian-Western security guarantees to the Baltic states instead of NATO membership.[27] Nevertheless, NATO's July 1997 Madrid summit signaled in no uncertain terms that the military alliance was eager to accept post–Soviet states into NATO. Its final communiqué referred to the Baltic states as "aspiring members" and described their "progress achieved towards greater stability and cooperation."[28]

Moreover, the summit included a "distinctive partnership" agreement with Ukraine building on Kiev's participation in the PPP, thereby opening up a direct bilateral special relationship between the military alliance and Russia's most important neighbor. The "Charter on a Distinctive Partnership between the North Atlantic Treaty Organization and Ukraine" stipulated the parties were "looking forward … to deepen the process of integration with the full range of European and Euro-Atlantic structures."[29] This was a clear reference to Ukraine's eventual membership in both NATO and the EU. At a September 2007 meeting of Central and Eastern European leaders in Vilnius, Russian Prime Minister Viktor Chernomyrdin proposed a series of security guarantees and confidence-building measures if the Baltic states would refrain from joining NATO.[30]

Coit Blacker noted at the time the pressures exerted on Russia's all too vulnerable revolution from above:

[A]s the years passed and Russia's economic and social crises deepened, the government found itself increasingly on the defensive across a broad range of policy issues, foreign as well as domestic. Especially difficult to defend against was the charge notwithstanding Western economic and financial resistance, the United States and its principal allies were content to let Russia deteriorate…. Opponents of the regime also charged—and not without cause—that in placing such a high premium on cooperation with the West, Russia had become inexcusably lax in the defense of many of its historical interests…. As Russia's domestic crises deepened, so too did the now-palpable sense of national humiliation and exploitation.[31]

The rhetorical initiation and official adoption of NATO expansion as official policy—combined with Moscow's December 1994 intervention into Chechnya in the face of growing militant and criminal influence in the breakaway republic—had three immediate effects. It led to the first chill in the "cold peace" in Russian-Western relations since the end of the Cold War, sparked the neo–Eurasianist revival within the foreign policy and general intellectual elite, and prompted a search for an alternative to Moscow's early post–Soviet reliance on relations with the West and hope for a "common European home."

The First Yugoslav War: The "First Swallow" of Russian-Western Conflict

A harbinger of the potential for NATO's intervention at Western-Orthodox fault lines to produce conflict in conditions of Russian weakness to the detriment of Moscow's interests came with Yugoslavia's post-communist breakup and wars in the 1990s. In the first phase of the Yugoslav demise, Western civilization's key players and Russia backed different sides in accordance with Huntingtonian and Eurasian/neo–Eurasian religio-civilizational logic. In convincing an EU majority to intervene, the Roman Catholic Pope and then Germany displayed unprecedented diplomatic and geostrategic initiative in granting state recognition to Catholic Slovenia and Croatia (and later Muslim Bosnia-Herzogovina). After some wavering, the United States followed suit in spring 1992. War quickly ensued as the former Yugoslav communist turned Serbian ultranationalist leader Slobodan Milosevich moved his army into Croatia and Bosnia. Eventually, Croatia received substantial arms supplies from Western and pro–Western Central European countries, as did Bosnia-Herzogovinia, which also received arms and volunteers, sometimes jihadi-oriented fighters, from some Mulsim countries.

Yeltsin mildly countered by criticizing Western actions against Yugoslavia and issuing rhetoric morally supportive of the Orthodox Serbs. However, he repeatedly gave in to demands from Washington and Brussels that he toe the line in UN votes on resolutions detrimental to Moscow's Serbian ally. For those willing to open their eyes that Western support for opponents of Russian allies could lead to Western-Russian tension and conflict, a sign of things to come would be seen in Russian conservative and nationalist parties' harsh attacks on Yeltsin for failing to stand up for Russia's fellow Orthodox Slavs. Some among these elements went to fight alongside Serbian forces and may have secured Russian arms supplies for them.

Weak at home in the face of a rising communist and nationalist "red-brown" coalition and a collapsing economy, Yeltsin made several compromises with the Clinton administration at key junctures, shocking Russia's Serbian allies. In May 1992, Russia voted in the UN in favor of sanctions against Milosevich (while the Chinese did not). Despite broad opposition to such a vote in the Russian Foreign Ministry, pro–Western foreign minister Kozyrev delivered the ministry's overall institutional support for the vote.[32]

In the end, the first Yugoslav war brought all three breakaway provinces their state independence after several years of war, sanctions, no-fly zones, diplomacy, and a UN peacekeeping operation. In early 1993 Russia supported the Vance-Owens peace plan, which was to include establishing a no-fly zone, but it opposed a French plan to institute it before final agreement on the peace plan by all parties. Moscow ultimately agreed to the no-fly zone but won removal of a clause granting the enforcing U.S. Air Force the authority to hit targets on the ground. President Yeltsin was maneuvered into this less independent position by virtue of Foreign Minister Kozyrev's bureaucratic "dirty tricks," dissembling and withholding of information from the Russian president. Ultimately, the U.S. and NATO violated the UN resolution and hit land targets anyway. When the U.S. sought to level new sanctions against Serbia at the April 1993 Vancouver summit, Assistant Secretary of State Strobe Talbott informed Russia's ambassador to the U.S. Vladimir Lukin that Moscow would need to announce its support for more sanctions if it expected any further economic assistance from the West. Yeltsin ordered Russia's UN delegation to abstain in the April 18 Security Council vote.[33]

This came at the height of Russia's post–Soviet great depression and a mounting challenge from the red-brown coalition; that challenge had already forced Yeltsin to hand power over the economy from liberals like Prime Minister Yegor Gaidar to centrists like Viktor Chernomyrdin in autumn 1992 and in foreign policy a few short years later. Despite sarcastically calling the abstention "an Easter present for Orthodox Serbs," a then generally pro–Western Russian diplomat later emphasized that religious and ethnic solidarity were not the motives of those who sought a more independent policy. If Russian diplomacy could not instill a more balanced approach to the Yugoslav conflict, then it would seek to wrest more benefits for Moscow. It found a post–Cold War mechanism for settling the myriad of emerging post-communist and other interethnic conflicts on something other than an "American" framework.[34]

The Kosovo Watershed

The Yugoslav wars' second phase—this time in Kosovo—occurring simultaneously with another tremor of NATO expansion added to the polarizing dynamic. NATO enlargement's first round was consummated in March 1999, when Poland, Hungary, and the Czech Republic officially entered NATO. Twelve days later, NATO planes began a 78-day bombing campaign targeting Russia's Serbian ally, ostensibly in order to protect ethnic Albanians from alleged plans by Serbian President Milosevich to carry out "ethnic cleansing" in Kosovo to hold it within Belgrade's fold. Kosovo was an almost entirely Muslim ethnic Albanian-populated province in the Serbian portion of what was left of the Federal Republic of Yugoslavia, consisting of Serbia and Montenegro. The Kosovar separatist movement and the Kosovo Liberation Army (KLA) had waged a mounting, violent and sometimes terrorist campaign since the early 1990s in an effort to forge an independent state or, being almost entirely populated by Muslim ethnic Albainians, to unify with Albania in a Greater Albania. NATO military intervention in March 1999 on the KLA's behalf involved a massive air campaign against the Serbian army and the Yugoslav capitol, Belgrade. In contrast to the first Yugoslav war, Washington and Brussels abandoned diplomatic niceties with the now gravely ailing Russian president. This time NATO's intervention was carried out without any UN mandate or any invitation from Belgrade, in clear violation of international law. Thus, it was the West in March 1999 in Serbia—and not Russia a decade later in Georgia, or in March 2014 in Crimea—which dared to violate the post–World War II order, overturning Yalta.

NATO's Operation Allied Force air campaign, involving 13 countries' militaries,[35] targeted Yugoslavian military, intelligence, and government installations and included 37,465 sorties attacking over 900 targets. However, collateral damage and misidentified targets inflicted significant Serbian civilian casualties.[36] Estimates range from Human Rights Watch's confirmation of at least 489 to 528 killed, to U.S. Vice Chairman of the Joint Chiefs of Staff General Joseph W. Ralston's "less than 1,500 dead," to Yugoslav estimates of 2,000–10,000 killed as a result of Operation Allied Force. In addition, NATO action wounded several thousand more civilians. Moreover, Human Rights Watch documented 7 to 12 incidents of NATO forces (specifically U.S. and British fighter planes) using illegal, banned cluster bombs, leading to the deaths of tens if not one hundred or more civilians and wounding even more. The most serious of these incidents, which occurred on May 7 in an urban area in Nis, killed 14 civilians and injured 28. In April NATO forces hit a passenger train near Nis, killing 15 and wounding 44. By June 10, the day it halted, NATO's campaign had also forced over 200,000 members of the Serbian minority in Kosovo to flee their homeland and destroyed or damaged more than 300 schools and libraries, more than 20 hospitals, and thousands of other buildings.[37]

With NATO's bombing of Moscow's Serbian ally, the Visegrád states' entry into NATO days earlier, and the spectre of the upcoming April NATO summit in Washington, at which more enlargement plans were set to be adopted, a new low in post–Cold War Russian-Western relations had come. The bloc's now violent encroachment on Russia's sphere of influence was galling Moscow. Thus, at the news of the commencement of the

NATO bombing, Yevgenii Primakov, now Russia's prime minister, promptly ordered his plane en route to the U.S. over the Atlantic to be turned around and flown back to Moscow, scuttling a series of high-level meetings and sending a firm signal of Moscow's displeasure with NATO actions. The symbolism of this watershed moment in post–Soviet Russian foreign policy could not have been starker. Not just Primakov's plane had reversed its course heading west over the Atlantic; Russia's foreign policy trajectory would now firmly be redirected east to Eurasia writ large and other vectors.

Primakov's attitude reflected not just the majority of the Russian elite's disgust with the illegal NATO bombing; across the political spectrum, Russian society was unanimous in its condemnation of the attacks. In a 1999 opinion survey conducted by the All-Russian Center for Public Opinion Research (VTsIOM), 99 percent of respondents said NATO had no right to bomb Yugoslavia without a mandate from the UN.[38] Another 1999 survey showed that 67 percent of respondents were "outraged" by the bombing campaign. Another 17 percent were "concerned by the strengthening of the influence of NATO and its claims to the role of the world's gendarme." Another 7 percent "regretted" the bombing, and 3 percent were shaken.[39] In a March 1999 VTsIOM survey, in which respondents were asked whether they thought the ultimate goal of the U.S. and NATO role in the Yugoslav conflict was to locate a military base and troops in Kosovo or to stop the bloodletting of Albanians, 81 percent answered that the goal was the former, 19 percent responded it was the latter.[40]

In the West, in particular at NATO headquarters, there was complete refusal to recognize, care, or publicly admit to the damage Operation Allied Force had inflicted on Russian public opinion. An early 2000 NATO-commissioned study by the Head of the Georgian Foreign Ministry's NATO Division, Vasili Siharulidze, citing another 1999 VTsIOM opinion survey with responses similar to those cited herein, simply wrote off the Russian public's outrage to propaganda: "Old soviet propaganda machinery was employed to highlight ongoing events in Yugoslav republic [*sic*] and therefore to justify position [*sic*] of the government in this regard. It has affected public opinion appropriately."[41] It should be noted that in 1999, Russian mass media, including national television, was still completely free.

As NATO bombs continued to rain down on Serbia, NATO convened a summit in Washington on April 23–24 and announced the ushering in of a second round of expansion. The summit issued guidelines or "Membership Action Plans" (MAPs) to nine countries: three more former Warsaw Pact countries (Albania, Bulgaria, and Romania); three new countries formed from one former Warsaw Pact state (Slovakia from the former Czechoslovakia) and from embattled Yugoslavia (Slovenia and Macedonia); and the three former Soviet Baltic republics extremely antagonistic towards Russia (Estonia, Latvia, and Lithuania). In May 2000, these countries along with with Croatia founded the Vilnius Group to coordinate their lobbying for NATO membership. Seven members of the Vilnius Group—the three Baltic states, Bulgaria, Romania, Slovakia and former Yugoslavia's Slovenia—were invited into NATO at its 2002 summit held in the new member-state of the Czech Republic, underscoring the rolling juggernaut that had become NATO expansion. Russia was particularly upset by the both the plans and actual 2004 accession of the Baltic states.[42] Not only did expansion to these countries bring NATO to Russia's very border, but their elites and populations were (and are) extremely antagonistic in their attitudes towards Russia, intensifying the anti–Russian semtiment within the bloc, and their policies often openly discriminated against ethnic Russians. Lithuania's accession was particularly troublesome; it meant NATO territory now cut off Russia's exclave of

Kaliningrad Oblast' (formerly Konigsberg, and ceded to the USSR after World War II) from the "mainland."

The cruelest blow from the Kosovo saga for Russia—one that would have long-lasting influence on Russian actions in the Georgian and Ukrainian crises—was Washington's and the West's violation of the UN resolution that ended the conflict and established the UN Interim Administration Mission (UNMIK). UN Resolution 1244, adopted on June 10, 1999, put Kosovo under UNMIK administration and UN peacekeepers' protection. The resolution affirmed three times the "principle" of, and "the commitment of Member States" of the UN to, "the sovereignty and territorial integrity of the Federal Republic of Yugoslavia." Under its mandate, Kosovo was to be granted self-government and autonomy, not state independence from now rump Yugoslavia.[43]

Rather than preserving Yugoslavia's territorial integrity, however, the Kosovars used the UNMIK protectorate not just to establish broad autonomy from Belgrade but to prepare for full state independence. The KLA intimidated the remaining ethnic Serbs, destroyed many of Kosovo's Orthodox churches, and consolidated various illegal smuggling syndicates and networks abroad before repeating its 1990 declaration of independence on February 17, 2008. Kosovo's parliament acted in defiance of both Belgrade and Resolution 1244. Rather than honoring 1244, the next day Washington recognized Kosovo's state independence.[44] Moreover, the International Court of Justice ruled in July 2010 that the Kosovar declaration of independence was legal. In September 2012, the Western-led UNMIK handed over administration to Prishtina, recognizing *de facto* Kosovo's independence. Western countries led the way in recognizing Kosovo's independence; 108 UN member-states and Taiwan would recognize it. This further alienated Moscow from "rules of the game" established by, and now frequently being violated by, the UN when international law conflicted with its interest.

In addition to violations of international law by bombing Yugoslavia and granting Kosovo independence, the West also violated the NATO-Russian Founding Act (NRFA) upon which the NATO-Russian Council was established. Devised in Washington and Brussels as a way to mollify Moscow as NATO expanded, the founding act was essentially a charter for NATO-Russian relations attached to the NATO-Russian Council. However, much like the council, which amounted to little more than a talking shop providing Russia with no influence whatsoever on the future course of the ever-approaching military bloc, the founding act was a dead letter in a unipolar geopolitical world, where the West made the rules or broke them as it thought fit, able to ignore a seemingly weak Russia's interests. The Act committed NATO and Russia to refrain "from the threat or use force against each other as well as against any other state, its sovereignty, territorial integrity or political independence in any manner inconsistent with the United Nations Charter and with the Declaration of Principles Guiding Relations between Participating States contained in the Helsinki Final Act." The NRFA also pledged both parties to maintain "respect for sovereignty, independence and territorial integrity of all states and their inherent right to choose the means to ensure their own security, the inviolability of borders and peoples' right of self-determination as enshrined in the Helsinki Final Act and other OSCE documents."[45] NATO's willful act of carrying out a major military operation in defiance of the UN's rejection of a resolution approving such an intervention, and the UN's and the West's violation of UN Resolution 1244, clearly constituted failure to refrain from the use of force and to respect the inviolability of borders, respectively. These violations of international law—occurring long before any Russian violations—undermined simultaneously the principle of state sovereignty and ensured that a resurgent Russia would have little compunction from refraining from the same when its national security interests were threatened in Georgia and Ukraine.

Finally, despite the fact that war crimes were committed on all sides during the first Yugoslav war, only Serbia's Milosevich would end up in the dock at the Hague, reducing both Moscow's trust in international institutions further and the likelihood that future inter-ethnic wars could be settled by diplomacy rather than military force. Moreover, with Milosevich in the dock, Russia's pro–Western leadership had proven itself incapable of protecting not just its allies' interests but their lives.

Aside from Primakov's aerial turnaround over the Atlantic, Moscow now responded with the only other act of resistance to a decade of humiliating Western *diktats*. The so-called "march to Prishtina" occurred on June 11, 1999, when Russian forces carrying out a UN peacekeeping mission in Bosnia in the wake of the first Yugoslav war redeployed into Serbia at Prishtina International Airport unilaterally in order to establish a separate mission under Russian command. The Russians rejected subordination to a NATO command and sought to set up a peacekeeping operation to protect Serbian-populated northern Kosovo and perhaps carve out a separate Serbian enclave. A column of some thirty Russian armored vehicles with 250 Russian troops took up positions at the airport ahead of the planned arrival of NATO troops.

Informed of the Russian move, American NATO KFOR commander, General Wesley Clark, ordered British and French paratroopers to be helicoptered in to seize the airport from the Russians. Staff officers and the French government were concerned that Serbian forces might fire on the helicopters or the Serbian government might pull out of the cease-fire agreement and peacekeeping arrangements set out in UN Resolution 1244. Since national governments had the right to withdraw their own forces under the SFOR (Bosnian peacekeeping force) and KFOR missions, the French government pulled their battalion out. The British paratroopers stood by in helicopters through the night. On June 12, British and Norwegian troops approached the Russian-occupied airport and took up positions opposite the Russians. British General Michael Jackson flew to Prishtina and met with Russian commander, General Viktor Zavarzin. In the wreckage of airport's terminal, Jackson shared a flask of whiskey with the Russian general, breaking some of the ice. General Clark feared Russian troops might be flown in, even though NATO controlled the airspace.

On the morning of June 13, Clark went to Jackson's HQ at Skopje and ordered that the airport runway be blocked. Jackson argued that the Russians posed no threat, since they were cut off from any possible reinforcement by air. Moreover, the Russians' support had been crucial in securing Belgrade's agreement to the peace deal. Russian support had been a vital part of getting a peace agreement, and a confrontation—or worse, any military engagement—could scuttle the deal. Nevertheless, Clark continued to order the runway blocked, but Jackson refused, telling him: "I'm not going to start the Third World War for you."[46] Clark's order to block the runways was never carried out. But British forces set up a perimeter around the airport, and the U.S. convinced Serbia's eastern neighbors to close their airspace to Russian transport. Negotiations ongoing throughout the confrontation ultimately satisfied the Russian demand that Russian peacekeepers would be only under Russian command. However, NATO rejected their demand for a separate peacekeeping zone. Instead, it was agreed that Russian troops would deploy throughout Kosovo under separate Russian command.

If nothing else, the march demonstrated that there were limits to Moscow's patience and servility, at least among the *siloviki*, in the face of the repeated slights—Clinton's "shit in your face"—to Russian national honor and pride inflicted by Washington and Brussels through NATO. As Jeffrey Mankoff has written: "What the conflict in the Balkans seemingly proved was that even under a committed internationalist like Clinton, the United States would not hesitate to act outside the framework of international law or the United Nations if doing so were deemed to be in the United States' national interest. This resort to unilateral application of military power (against a close Russian ally, no less) was evidence to many in Russia that, notwithstanding the end of the Cold War, international politics continued to be based on national interest and power rather than on multilateral cooperation or the international legality embodied in the United Nations."[47] With this harsh lesson learned, the Russia of the 2000s under Putin would assert more strongly its right to a major role in the resolution of key international security issues and would step up efforts to build not necessarily an anti–Western alliance, but a multipolar world, or at least an alternative counterbalancing pole in the international system's structure.

It is possible that if NATO had not been regenerated as the sole security architecture in Europe without Russia, the resulting greater reliance on Russian leverage in Belgrade would have avoided the Yugoslav wars, especially over Kosovo. This was a real alternative path because during the first Yugoslav war, there were examples of Russian cooperation with the West and episodes when Russian mediation produced compromise. Russian peacekeeping forces operated cooperatively alongside Western forces in the SFOR peacekeeping operation in Bosnia-Herzogovina. The NATO-Russia Founding Act referred to "the positive experience of working together in Bosnia and Herzogovina" as a reason and model for future NATO-Russian cooperation, including joint peacekeeping and "the establishment of Combined Joint Task Forces."[48]

An example of Russia's cooperation in Bosnia and Herzogonia occurred in February 1994 after NATO began bombing Yugoslavian targets on the ground in violation of the UN no-fly resolution. Some 70 people were killed and hundreds injured on February 5 at a market in Sarajevo, allegedly by the Serbs, but actually by the Bosnians, as a later investigation determined. In response, NATO, which had never carried out a military operation in its history, issued an ultimatum to the Serbs demanding under threat of NATO air strikes that they withdraw all their heavy weapopns from the approaches to Sarajevo. On the morning of February 6, Russian Deputy Foreign Minister Anatolii Adamishin devised a scheme to convince the Serbs to withdraw the weapons, proposing that the offer be made by the Russians separately from a NATO ultimatum, to which the honor-riven Serbs would be loath to succumb. Foreign Minister Kozyrev approved and presented the idea to Yeltsin, who phoned Milosevich and made the request. Yeltsin then redeployed 400 Russian peacekeepers, based in Croatia as part of a UN peacekeeping mission, to the area around Sarajevo to control and monitor the Serbs and shield them from a Bosnian counterattack, if not NATO air strikes. The Russian move helped defuse the situation around Sarajevo, as both the Serbs and Bosnians withdrew or handed over their heavy weapons to NATO. According to Adamishin, the Russian move was praised by the Europeans but not the Americans. On February 8, NATO began its first military operation, bombing ground targets with air strikes and destroying four Yugoslav jet fighters.[49] Thus, real potential for NATO-Russian cooperation was undermined by Western actions—especially NATO's Operation Allied Force—and Russia's subsequent experience in Bosnia and Kosovo.

The Yugoslav wars and continuing expansion of NATO created a strong majority against NATO in Russian public opinion. By March 1999, 69 percent of Russians, according to a VTsIOM opinion survey, felt to one degree or another that Russia had something to fear in countries joining NATO; only 31 percent did not think so.[50] By June 1999, VTsIOM found that 73 percent of Russian citizens had a negative view of NATO, and only 27 percent a positive view.[51] When in the same month newly inaugurated President Putin said it was possible Russia might join NATO in the future, he went sharply against the grain of Russian public opinion. A VTsIOM poll found that only 30 percent of respondents approved of Putin's statement, 31 percent expressed bewilderment, 21 percent outrage, and 19 percent indifference.[52] This turns the favored Western expression "Putin's Russia" on its head. What the West was and still is dealing with is Russia's Putin or, alternatively, NATO expansion's Russia.

Indeed, the succeeding U.S. administration saw a temporary improvement in relations with Moscow. It is well-known that Putin was the first national leader to call U.S. President George W. Bush and express his condolences after the 9/11 terrorist attacks and support for the war on terrorism—that is, against the global jihadi revolutionary movement or jihadism. Russia (and Putin himself, first as FSB chief and then as prime minister) had been battling a mix of homegrown radical Chechen ultranationalists and other Chechen, North Caucasus, and foreign and Al Qa'ida-sponsored jihadists under the so-called Chechen Republic of Ichkeriya since the mid–1990s. By October 2000, the majority Russian view that Russia had something to fear from countries entering NATO had lost ground, with only 61 percent now thinking there was something to fear, compared with 69 percent in March.[53] This could have been a consequence of Putin's statement that Russia could join NATO someday and/or views about the specific countries being considered for entry to NATO at that time. President Bush perhaps more famously—or infamously—summed up a burgeoning if fleeting trust between Moscow and Washington, when he said at the leaders' first summit in June 2001 that he had looked into Putin's soul and had seen that it was good.

The honeymoon was brief. No one in the West picked up on Putin's mention of Russia's possible entry into NATO, and the last realistic chance for achieving the central international security task at the Cold War's end—Russia's integration with the West—was lost. Washington's first subsequent action affecting Russian national security came in June 2002 when the Bush administration announced its withdrawal from the Anti-Ballistic Missile (ABM) Treaty. Again, Russia could muster little in the way of resistance. Russian Foreign Minister Igor Ivanov expressed Russia's regret but emphasized that it was "now a *fait accompli*." Moscow would seek "to minimize the adverse consequences."[54] It announced Russia would no longer be bound by nuclear missile and warhead limits established by the START II offensive arms reduction treaty. This was largely symbolic, since START II had never come into force and was superseded by the May 2002 Strategic Offensive Reduction Treaty. The certainty of no imminent national missile defense system deployment and Putin's desire to consolidate good relations with Washington likely muted the response. But arms control was the ultimate Cold War issue. With the Cold War's end, it was no longer so central to U.S.-Russian relations. It had been supplanted a decade earlier by NATO expansion. The subsequent connection, perceived and real, between it, democracy promotion and color revolutions in Russia's Eurasian sphere of influence would now define the tone and direction of relations between Washington and Moscow.

Discussion of the third round of NATO expansion began in the early 2000s on the background of NATO operations in Afghanistan, beginning in 2001, and then Iraq, beginning in 2003. These "out-of-area" operations occurred in two countries directly bordering the former Soviet Union. They impinged on Moscow's sphere of influence in two sensitive areas. Iraq is located just south of the Caucasus, bordering on Russia's North Caucasus, where the Chechen Republic of Ichkeriya was increasingly jihadized and allied with Afghanistan-based Al Qa'ida (AQ). Moreover, Sadaam Hussein's fall led to Russia's loss of hundreds of millions of dollars in oil contracts. Afghanistan bordered former Soviet Central Asia, which, with the exclusion of Kazakhstan, consists of four weak states with limited military capability and highly vulnerable to state failure. Many, including in Moscow, argued that NATO was doing Russia's national security work in Afghanistan, and therefore it was in Moscow's interests to support the Afghan operations. Indeed, Moscow eventually did so by opening up the so-called Northern Supply Route, running supplies through Russia and Central Asia to Western forces. But the intervention posed grave risks for Russia over which Moscow had no control. It had no role in the decision to invade Afghanistan and no influence on the conduct of the war or of Western nation-building and democratization efforts that could, more easily than not, destabilize an unprepared, backward Afghan society. Moscow's security interests could easily be damaged by a failed Western intervention in Iraq as well, since it could and did stir up a hornets' nest of jihadism. Just years after the Kosovo debacle, Washington and Brussels were carrying out vast air-, land- and sea-based operations all along the Russia's "soft underbelly." These operations underscored the growing geographical scope of NATO interventionism and the strategic salience for Moscow of the Eurasian Rimland. Russia's contingency planning had just become more expensive and complicated.

Sparks at the Rimland:
NATO Moves to Russia's Border

In late June 2004, as NATO operations in Afghanistan and Iraq intensified, the three Baltic states—along with Bulgaria, Romania, Slovakia and former Yugoslavia's Slovenia—officially acceded to NATO, bringing the military alliance to Russia's border for the first time. Moscow was presumably placated by the joint NATO-Russian military counterterrorism exercise "Kaliningrad 2004" held two weeks earlier. Meanwhile, Russia's southern flank, already destabilized by risky NATO operations, had become even more turbulent when in November 2003 a controversy over election results in formerly Soviet Georgia led to the seizure of power, or "Rose revolution," by an opposition coalition largely antagonistic to Moscow led by Mikheil Saakashvili. Then the 2005 "Orange revolution" in Ukraine brought an anti–Russian regime to power in Kiev. The fact that the Rose and Orange "revolutions" were bookends to the Baltic states' accession to NATO, and were followed just a few years later with a NATO summit statement declaring that both Georgia and Ukraine would someday be NATO members, could only reinforce the association in Russian minds between democracy promotion and regime change, on the one hand, and NATO (and EU) expansion, on the other. As detailed further below, Washington and Brussels persistently tightened relations with, and boosted support for, the Rose and Orange regimes and the Georgian and Ukrainian militaries.

At NATO'S April 2008 Bucharest Summit, the trans–Atlantic allies declared that both Georgia and Ukraine would become NATO members at some future date, provided they meet all necessary requirements.[55] A small scandal emerged from the summit, as reports circulated that Putin, who attended part of the summit, had told President Bush: "You do understand, George, that Ukraine is not even a state. What is Ukraine? A part of its territories is Eastern Europe, but a part, a significant [part] was given as a gift from us." He also reportedly threatened that if Georgia and Ukraine sought NATO membership, Russia would recognize the independence of Abkhaziya and South Ossetiya and annex Crimea and southeastern Ukraine (Novorossiya). The only documentation provided by the Russian daily *Kommersant* reporting the statement was an unidentified "source in the delegation of one of the NATO countries."[56] Putin's alleged statements were then broadcast across the globle as evidence of Russian belligerence and expansionism.

Most likely, Putin never said these things and the claim was a "strategic communications" propaganda operation carried out by then Polish Foreign Minister and former Polish Deputy Defense Minister Radoslaw (Radek) Sikorski. He was likely *Kommersant*'s "source in the delegation of one of the NATO countries."[57] Neither Bush nor any other meeting attendee has reported Putin made these comments. Moreover, in October 2014 the very same Sikorski was caught red-handed making up statements he alleged Putin made about the very same Ukraine. In a *Politico* article, Sikorski was quoted claiming that in a meeting with Polish President Donald Tusk, Putin had proposed Poland and Russia divide Ukraine between themselves. It is revealing that in his 2014 false statement, Sikorski repeats his claim about Putin's words to Bush in 2008, noting that Putin "went on to say that Ukraine is an artificial country."[58] Soon Sikorski's alleged Putin interlocutor, former Polish Prime Minister Donald Tusk, denied that any such exchange ever occurred with Putin, and Sikorski was forced by his party to retract his words at a public press conference.[59] Months earlier, Sikorski had been a leading candidate for the position of NATO Secretary General; his *faux pas* scuttled that candidacy. It is likely that both in 2008 and 2014 Sikorski was carrying out an operation to discredit Putin and heighten urgency regarding Georgia's and Ukraine's entries to NATO. This demonstrates how expanding NATO to Poland and other former Soviet bloc states before bringing in Russia put the former in a position to harden NATO's position on Russia and further expansion and otherwise spoil Russian-Western relations. Putting aside history, Ukraine's membership in NATO would create a useful buffer for its western neighbors.

Moscow's Red Line

Moscow had signaled several times previously that it would react robustly to Georgian and/or Ukrainian accession to NATO. In June 2006, as a wave of demonstrations swept Crimea protesting the port call by the U.S. cargo vessel in *Feodosia* (as part of a NATO-Ukrainian military exercise, "Sea Breeze 2006," seen as a sign of Ukraine's move towards NATO membership), Russian Foreign Minister Sergei Lavrov stated that Georgian and/or Ukrainian membership in NATO would spark a "colossal shift" in global geopolitics. At the same time, Russia's State Duma issued a statement to Ukraine's Supreme Rada (*Verkhovna Rada*) expressing its "extremely negative attitude towards such plans," noting: "Ukraine's joining NATO contradicts the agreement on friendship, cooperation and partnership between Russia and Ukraine dating from 1997 that states the strategic nature of Russian-Ukrainian relations."[60]

However, the clearest message was delivered on February 10, 2007, when a confident, cantankerous and feisty Putin took the podium at the annual Munich Conference on Security Policy. He delivered a blistering rejection of American hegemony or "unipolarity" and NATO's advancing encroachment on Russia's borders. On unipolarity, he noted:

> More and more we are witness to the flouting of the basic principles of international law. Above all the rights of one state are overtaking separate norms, indeed the entire system of [international] law. The United States is overstepping its national borders in every field: in economics, in politics, even in the humanitarian sphere.... And this, of course, is very dangerous.
>
> ... Russia is a country with a history that spans more than a thousand years and has practically always used the privilege to carry out an independent foreign policy. We are not going to change this tradition today.[61]

With Kosovo and Iraq in mind, Putin decried the use of force by NATO or others without a UN mandate:

> I do not understand what was said quite recently by our colleague, the minister of defense of Italy, or he expressed imprecisely. I, in any case, heard that the use of force can only be considered legitimate, if the decision was taken in NATO, or the European Union, or the UN. If he really thinks that, then we have very different points of view. Or I misheard. The use of force may be considered legitimate only if the decision is taken on the basis and within in the framework of the UN. It is not necessary to replace the United Nations with NATO and the European Union.[62]

Putin was particularly clear regarding Moscow's decade-long disappointment over the West's broken promises that NATO would not be expanded beyond reunited Germany and that Russia's choice in favor of democracy would result in a "common European home" from Vancouver to Vladivostok:

> I think that the process of NATO enlargement has no relation to modernization of the alliance itself or guaranteeing security in Europe. On the contrary, it represents a serious provoking factor that reduces the level of mutual trust. And we have the justified right to ask candidly: Against whom is this expansion intended? And what happended to those assurances that were given by our Western partners after the dissolution of the Warsaw Pact? Where are these statements now? No one even remembers them. But I will permit myself to recall in this hall what was said. I would like to offer a citation from a speech of the General Secretary of NATO, Mr. Manfred Woerner, in Brussels on May 17, 1990: "The very fact that we are prepared not to deploy NATO troops beyond the territory of the FRG gives the Soviet Union a firm guarantee of security." Where are these guarantees?
>
> The stones and cement blocks of the Berlin Wall long ago have been dispersed as souvenirs. But it is impossible to forget that its fall became possible thanks to the historic choice in particular of our people—the people of Russia—the choice in favor of democracy, freedom, openness and sincere partnership with all the members of the European family
>
> Now they are trying to bind us with new lines of division and walls—perhaps virtual, but nevertheless dividing and cutting up our common continent. Will we again need long years, even decades and the changeover of several generations of politicians in order to "tear down" and dismantle these new walls?[63]

Putin also addressed NATO's decision not to ratify new conventional force limits on flank deployments abroad in Europe under the Conventional Forces in Europe (CFE) treaty until Moscow removed troops from Georgia and Moldova left over from the Soviet era. He emphasized that while Russian forces were being withdrawn from Georgia, NATO was moving its bases east. With regard to Moldova, he noted that the remnants of Russia's 14th Army there were guarding arms depots, and that he was continuously discussing the withdrawal technicalities with NATO General Secretary Xavier Solana. This, he contrasted with NATO's recent establishment of advance bases in the NATO member-states of Bulgaria and Romania, noting: "It turns out that NATO is moving its advance bases to our state borders, and we, strictly observing the [CFE] treaty, are not reacting to these moves."[64]

Putin's démarche was a function of resurgent Russian economic and thus geopolitical power. By summer 2007, Russia was in the midst of a global diplomatic and military-political offensive:

- A diplomatic offensive across the Middle East and Asia that included hints of forming a natural gas cartel.
- President Vladimir Putin's moves to withdraw from the Treaty on Conventional Armed Forces in Europe.
- The resumption of long-range strategic bomber flights that would patrol areas bordering European and U.S. airspace.
- An announcement to expand the navy's global presence, including basing once again some of its forces in the Mediterranean Sea.
- The militarization of the Shanghai Cooperation Organization, which includes Russia, China, Kazakhstan, Kyrgyzstan, Tajikistan and Uzbekistan as members, and Iran, India, Pakistan and Mongolia as observers.
- Moscow's surprise expedition to the Arctic to gather scientific evidence to support a legal territorial claim to the Lomonosov Ridge.

This offensive reflected, and had further implications for, the cooling in Russian-Western relations, but it was perceived in Washington solely as an open challenge to U.S. hegemony. Russia was back as a global player, no longer a starry-eyed admirer of the West.

A third round of NATO expansion was confirmed at the contentious and pivotal April 2008 Bucharest summit, held in a new member-state (Romania). NATO invited Croatia (of former Yugoslavia) and Albania to join NATO. They acceded officially just prior to the 2009 Strasbourg-Kehl summit with little opposition from Russia. The lack of overt Russian disagreement with this third round of expansion had more to do with Moscow's more global foreign policy and pivot to China and Asia and a focus on preventing any further expansion into former Soviet republics in a fourth round. Putin drew a line in the sand at the Munich conference and backed it up with his strong response and, some would say, overreaction to Georgia's August 2008 invasion of South Ossetiya (SO). As I demonstrate in the next chapter, American revolutionism and democracy-promotion and the West's increasingly close relationship with Georgian President Saakashvili encouraged the unstable leader to make war, sparking Russia's counterincursion. NATO's promise to Georgia and Ukraine of future alliance membership encouraged Saakashvili to risk war with Russia. Before a discussion of that war, the EU's role in deepening the East-West divide must be considered.

EU Expansion

EU expansion marked an additional, if secondary encroachment on Russian interests. Primarily economic and financial in nature, agreements between the EU and prospective members have included a military component. Brzezinski lays out the geopolitical, civilizational, and ultimately American power-maximizing nature of Western thinking about the symbiotic nature of NATO and EU enlargement:

> The essential point regarding NATO expansion is that it is a process integrally connected with Europe's own expansion....
> ... Ultimately at stake in this effort is America's long-range role in Europe. A new Europe is still

taking shape, and if that new Europe is to remain geopolitically a part of the "Euro-Atlantic" space, the expansion of NATO is essential. Indeed, a comprehensive U.S. policy for Eurasia as a whole will not be possible if the effort to widen NATO, having been launched by the United States, stalls and falters. That failure would discredit American leadership; it would shatter the concept of an expanding Europe; it would demoralize the Central Europeans; and it could reignite currently dormant or dying Russian geopolitical aspirations in Central Europe. For the West, it would be a self-inflicted wound that would morally damage tht prospects for a truly European pillar in any eventual Eurasian security architecture; and for America, it would thus be not only a regional defeat but a global defeat as well.

   The bottom line guiding the progressive expansion of Europe has to be the proposition that no power outside of the existing transatlantic system has the right to veto the participation of any quali fied European state in the European system—and hence also its transatlantic security system—and that no qualified European state should be excluded *a priori* from eventual membership in either the EU or NATO.[65]

Other influential proponents of NATO expansion openly noted that EU expansion is crucial for the former.[66] The connection was institutionalized in the EU's 2007 Lisbon "Treaty on Reform," requiring states joining the EU to bring their defense policies in line with NATO policy.

   Consistent with this new Atlantic policy, EU and NATO enlargement have gone hand-in-hand. Thus, as of this writing, both the EU and NATO each had 28 member-states; their memberships are almost identical. The United States, Canada, and Albania are the only NATO member-states that are not EU members, but Albania will soon be an EU member. Cyprus, Malta, and Sweden are the only EU members that are not NATO member-states.[67] When it comes to the post–Soviet and post-communist states of East and Central Europe, the EU has been NATO's Trojan horse. Once any of these states started the EU accession process by signing an EU association agreement, it took on average 8 and a half years before it acceded to NATO (see Table 1).

Table 1. Key Dates in Post-Communist States' Accession Processes to EU and NATO

	EU AA Signed	EU AA in Force	EU Member	NATO
Albania	June 12, 2006	April 1, 2009	—	April 1, 2009
Bulgaria	March 8, 1993	February 1, 1995	January 1, 2007	March 29, 2004
Croatia	October 29, 2001	February 1, 2005	July 1, 2013	April 1, 2009
Czech Rep.	October 4, 1993	February 1, 1995	May 1, 2004	March 12, 1999
Estonia	June 12, 1995	February 1, 1998	May 1, 2004	March 29, 2004
Hungary	December 16, 1991	February 1, 1994	May 1, 2004	March 12, 1999
Latvia	June 12, 1995	February 1, 1998	May 1, 2004	March 29, 2004
Lithuania	June 12, 1995	February 1, 1998	May 1, 2004	March 29, 2004
Poland	December 16, 1991	February 1, 1994	May 1, 2004	March 12, 1999
Romania	February 1, 1993	February 1, 1995	January 1, 2007	March 29, 2004
Slovakia	October 4, 1993	February 1, 1995	May 1, 2004	March 29, 2004
Slovenia	June 10, 1996	February 1, 1999	May 1, 2004	March 29, 2004

It has taken five years and eight months on average to accede to NATO after EU association agreements have come into force, which usually occurs a few years after signing. In each post–Soviet/post-communist case, accession to NATO preceded EU accession. As noted above, these organizations made no great secret of the interrelationship between EU and NATO accession processes. For example, the previously noted "Charter on a Distinctive Partnership between the North Atlantic Treaty Organization and Ukraine" stipulated the parties were "looking forward to" Ukraine's "integration with the full range of European and Euro-Atlantic structures."[68] This phrasing was a not-so-veiled reference to Ukraine's eventual membership accession processes to both the EU and NATO. Indeed, the new Ukrainian Maidan regime signed an EU association agreement in 2015. Later that year Ukrainian President Petro Poroshenko stated that Ukraine would fulfill all the criteria for NATO membership in 6 to 8 years. A U.S. official, apparently in a greater hurry, said this is expected by the year 2020.[69]

In addition to the NATO Trojan horse element of EU expansion, the inclusion of post-communist and especially post–Soviet states in the EU would have a deleterious effect on Russia's trade and economy. Their accession of these economies to the EU would have profound consequences for Moscow by accelerating their reorientation away from Moscow and erecting new trade and other economic barriers with Russia, damaging the Russian economy. EU rules, policies and standards would complicate Russian access to these states' markets, and EU goods would flood the Russian market unless Moscow erected barriers against them, limiting Russia's integration into the European economy.

Indeed, another EU policy, the Eastern Partnership Program (EPP), proposed by two of Russia's historical nemeses, Poland and Sweden, "showed that the fight for post–Soviet space was moving to a new, more active phase," as one analyst correctly notes.[70] With the EPP, the EU began isolating Russia's economy from those of prospective EU members. Launched in 2008, the EPP was established to strengthen EU relationships with Ukraine, Belarus, Moldova, Armenia, Azerbaijan, and Georgia—that is, all the former Soviet republics still outside the EU and NATO, except Russia and the Central Asian states. An EU advisor and well-connected activist for NATO and EU expansion noted publicly in 2015: "Let's not pretend: the European Union's Eastern Partnership clearly excludes Russia." The program had "become the de facto dividing line between Russia and 'not Russia.'" He acknowledged that the EPP was designed to "push back" against "those who favor a 'Russia first' policy" regarding EU integration of Eastern Europe. He cautioned that "the EU should think less about winning the EPP countries away from Russia, and more about instituting lasting economic and political reforms" and "not punish countries that choose closer association with the Eurasian Union."[71] Not surprisingly, Russian Foreign Minister Lavrov agreed with this assessment: "The EU's Eastern Partnership programme is designed to bind the so-called focus states tightly to itself, shutting down the possibility of co-operation with Russia."[72] That the EPP was in fact a mechanism helping to isolate Russia and expand the EU (and thus NATO as well) was underscored by the fact that a November 2013 EPP summit in Vilnius would spark the Ukrainian crisis (see Chapter 4).

One should not overstate the impact of EU enlargement relative to that of NATO expansion proper on Russia's alienation from democracy, capitalism, and the West. If there were no NATO expansion, Moscow would have tolerated EU expansion despite the damage it does to its economy. In February 1997, then Russian Foreign Minister Primakov expressed Moscow's "positive" attitude towards the Baltic states' possible entry into the EU.[73] But neither Primakov nor any others among the Russian elite or public have ever viewed NATO expansion positively.

More importantly, NATO expansion in effect "militarized" or "securitized"—that is, added a vital national military/security component to EU expansion and democracy promotion, not just in perception but in reality. Thus, in 1998 Garnett admitted, albeit vaguely, that there are "security implications" from EU accession of the Balts—and by implication, other post–Soviet and post-communist states—"both within the terms of the European Union itself" and by way of "direct links between the core members of the Union and NATO."[74]

Atlantic Expansion's Impact
on Russian Thought, Politics and Policy

Atlantic (NATO and EU) institutional and operational (Yugoslavia, Iraq, Afghanistan, color revolutions) expansion had a profound impact on Russian elite and public opinion, politics and policy. Among the elite, neo–Eurasianist and Russian nationalist views became much more prevalent. It is no coincidence that ultranationalist, Eurasianist Russian geostrategists such as Panarin, Dugin, and many others emerged circa 1997–98—in the wake of the decision to expand NATO to Poland, the Czech Republic, and Hungary. Public opinion reflected a significant decline in positive views regarding the West, especially the U.S. and NATO. Most importantly, Russian foreign policy began to reflect Primakov's and now Vladimir Putin's moderate, practical neo–Eurasianism and a growing distrust of Western policy and the intent and growing capacity that stood behind it.

Ideological Transformation

To such thinkers as Panarin, Dugin and their allies, NATO and EU enlargement seemed, with some good reason, the manifestation and institutionalization of the fundamental Mackinderian geopolitical dynamic: the Atlantic "oceanic" states were attempting to control the heartland and "command the world." For many liberals, these policies undermined their political position and hope for democratization. To the extent reality seemed to reflect neo–Eurasianist postulates, neo–Eurasianism became the new ideological fashion. Thus, according to a student of Alexander Panarin's at Moscow State University in the early 1990s, the then young professor's lectures expressed support for liberal democracy and market economics. Panarin's political orientation changed "at the end of the 1990s," and Panarin began to designate his ideas as "late Eurasianism" (*pozdnee evraziistvo*).[75]

The anti–Western, anti–American, and geostrategic imperative for Russian foreign policy to dominate the World Island began to be reflected in the Russian culture, relayed to the public in books, journalism, and electronic media, including the Internet. In May 2002, literary scholar Lyudmilla Saraskina lamented: "[I]t was not after September 11, 2001 but rather after April 11, 1999—the same Easter Sunday when NATO bombs, painted with the blasphemous inscription 'Happy Easter,' brought down fire upon Belgrade—that the picture of the world and the methods of globalization announced themselves in full measure." Saraskina was speaking at the award ceremony of the annual Solzhenitsyn Literary Prize for literature, sponsored by the great Russian writer and Soviet dissident Alexander Solzhenitsyn. Once a hero of the West exiled from his country for his courageous battle against the Soviet system, Solzhenitsyn himself sought a moderate, non–Western "third way" for Russia that would avoid the excesses of capitalism while burying communism. He called Panarin's 2000 work *Iskushenia globalizmom* (*Tempted by Globalism*) "a just cry of desperation, a passionate warning about a critical danger, the mobilization of minds, and the moment's pain."[76]

A new picture of the West, if not the world, had emerged in Russian eyes, and it depicted a geopolitical landscape shaped by Washington and the West against the Eurasian heartland and Russian civilization. The West had taken advantage of Russia's post–Soviet "time of troubles," and more Russians were intent on resistance, if not revenge. One literary example is Mikhail Yurev's futuristic novel, *Tret'ya Imperiya* (*The Third Empire*), published in 2006. A Russian nationalists' or Eurasianists' ultimate fantasy, it envisages not just Russia's reconquering of the Russian and Soviet imperial spaces, but the conquest of the entire World Island—all of Western Europe, including the United Kingdom. The rest of the world is divided into states, empires or federations that either are friendly towards Russia (the "Heavenly Republic" of China, which has conquered all of Southeast Asia and Japan) or under its control (the American Federation, encompassing all of the Americas, North and South). Russia defeats the U.S. by way of a nuclear attack, as a result of which U.S. President "Bush III" surrenders to Russian leader "Gavrill the Great."[77] Growing elite fascination with traditional Eurasianist and neo–Eurasianist thought throughout the late 1990s and 2000s gradually reshaped public opinion. By December 2001, according to Russia's VTsIOM polling agency, 71 percent of Russians agreed with the statement, "Russia belongs to the special 'Eurasian' or Orthodox civilization, and therefore cannot follow the Western path of development." Only 13 percent considered Russia a part of Western civilization.[78]

Accordingly, NATO's reputation among Russians deteriorated with each round of expansion, and especially the bombing of Serbia. For example, in April 1996, a VTsIOM poll found that 55 percent of survey respondents opposed NATO membership for the Baltic states, Ukraine and "other" former Soviet republics now independent states, while 19 percent approved and 26 percent were indifferent.[79] As the Yugloslav crisis deepened, the West began discussing NATO intervention in the war, and NATO prepared to accept the Visegrád three into the alliance at its April 1997 summit, Russians responded in a repeat VTsIOM poll. Now 61 percent were opposed, 17 percent were for, and 21 percent were indifferent.[80] One month later, as NATO bombs fell on Yugoslavia, a VTsIOM survey showed 64 percent were now opposed, 19 percent were for, and 17 percent were indifferent.[81] By the time Putin had come to power, a 2001 survey showed a strong majority of Russians, 75 percent, were increasingly convinced that NATO was subordinated to the American national interest rather than those of all its members (25 percent).[82]

As the number of accessions to NATO and MAPs for the NATO accession process grew throughout the 2000s, Russians developed an overwhelmingly negative attitude towards NATO. According to VTsIOM opinion surveys, between November 2001 and November 2011, most of what positive sentiment towards NATO (and by extension the U.S. and the West) remained among Russians from the 1990s had dissipated. In November 2001 and November 2011 VTsIOM polls, respondents were asked to choose among Russian policy options in relation to NATO; 16 percent and 4 percent, respectively, supported an effort to join the alliance; 36 and 43 percent chose trying to improve relations with it; and 16 and 29 percent supported formation of an alternative alliance.[83] Polls show that from 2005 to 2009 the percentage of Russians supporting the creation of a counteralliance had more than doubled from 16 to 39 percent, and the proportion who supported cooperation with NATO dropped from 52 to 33 percent.[84] The portion of Russians who saw NATO as a Russian national security threat doubled from "only" 21 percent of respondents in 2003 to 41 percent by 2009.[85] In 2009–2011 approximately 60 percent of Russians, with marginal variation (59–62 percent), considered NATO expansion to the east as a threat to Russian national security.[86]

In a 2011 opinion poll, VTsIOM allowed respondents up to three answers regarding NATO's purpose. Of the six most frequently chosen answers, at least three were negative and one was distinctly neutral in their attitude towards the alliance. The most neutral assessment—that NATO's mission is to defend its members' interests—was chosen by 28 percent. Less neutral though not necessarily largely negative was another response receiving 28 percent: the alliance's mission is to advance American interests. This response's assessment depends on the proportion of those who see the advancement of American interests as detrimental, favorable or neutral for Russian interests. More negatively, 24 percent thought NATO's mission is to "carry out aggressive military actions against other countries." Also, 20 percent thought NATO "has lost its mission and remains just a leftover from the 'Cold War,'" and 17 percent thought the alliance's purpose is "to restrain the interests of great powers such as Russia and China." Finally, 19 percent saw a NATO mission to be "fighting international terrorism."[87] This should be seen as a positive assessment, given Russia's struggle with the global jihadi revolutionary terrorist organization, the Caucasus Emirate.[88] The August 2008 Ossetiyan war was followed by a sharp downturn in Russians' attitude towards NATO. For example, the percentage of VTsIOM survey respondents supporting efforts to cooperate with NATO fell from 53 in 2007 to 33 in 2009.[89] However, after three years of the Medvedev-Obama "reset," the percentage favoring cooperation with NATO had rebounded by 2011 to 43 percent, only to be driven down by events in Libya and Ukraine, as addressed below.[90]

Although the percentage of Russians with a negative attitude towards the U.S. has stayed steady overall during the post–Soviet period—at approximately 30 percent—negative attitudes have spiked much higher, often doubling following NATO-driven conflicts like the first round of expansion in 1997, and in 2008 with the expansion to the Baltic states and the Georgian-Ossetiyan August war. While anti–American attitudes were held by roughly 30–40 percent of Russians through 1993, that figure doubled later in the decade in reaction to the expansion of NATO into Eastern Europe, the NATO bombing of Bosnian Serbs in 1994, and the NATO bombing of Serbia in 1999.[91] To some extent, the rise of anti–American feeling in the mid–1990s was a pendular reaction to Russians' naive idealization of the United States between 1989 and 1992. With the USSR's downfall, many urban Russians vaguely hoped their country could magically become prosperous like the United States, and they expected massive financial aid as a reward for the overthrow of the "evil empire." But when no Marshall Plan for Russia materialized, NATO expansion ensued, and economic reforms pushed by American advisers brought widespread hardship, many became disillusioned and embittered. Specific Western policies and actions often produced spikes in anti–American and anti–Western sentiment.[92] In early 2002, anti–Americanism became more pronounced, partly because many believed Russians were victimized by unfair judging and scapegoating at the Salt Lake City Olympic Games. However, anger over the Salt Lake scandals soon faded, and anti–American sentiment returned suspicion of NATO expansion and believe U.S. leaders seek to subordinate Russia to American interests instead of pursuing a mutually beneficial partnership. By May 2002, the ROMIR agency found only 29 percent of Russians considered the U.S. "friendly," 28 percent thought it "neutral," and 40 percent characterized it as "hostile."[93] After nearly a decade of NATO expansion, conflict with the West, and an increasingly rich anti–American menu of media offerings, the results are predictable. In a December 2006 VTsIOM survey, 30 percent named the

United States as the main threat to Russia's national security, with China second at 17 percent.[94]

The percentage of Russians with a negative attitude towards the U.S. spiked sharply in 2008 with the expansion to the Baltic states and the Georgian-Ossetiyan August war. VTsIOM's September 2008 survey found 65 percent of respondents with a negative attitude. Subsequent VTsIOM polls in 2009–2013 found negative attitudes towards the U.S. among Russians ranging from a low of 27 percent in May 2010 to a high of 33 percent in June 2009.[95] On the eve of the Ukrainian crisis in 2013, 11 percent and 10 percent of Russians chose as the greatest threats to their well-being among some twenty possible answers a Western-sponsored color revolution and a war with Western countries, respectively.[96] Russian attitudes and policies do not develop in a vacuum. When significant percentages of Russians say that the U.S. and/or NATO pose a threat to Russia, that should be understood as a response to U.S. and NATO policies, residual sentiment from Russia's history of military invasions from the West, and the emotional tribulations Russians have undergone over the last decades, rather than as a manifestation of inherent cultural xenophobia.

Political Transformations

In terms of Russia's domestic political battles, NATO expansion early on had at least four immediate effects that would help to confound democratization and Westernization in conditions of revolution from above. First, it undercut the authority of pro–Western Russian democrats. Second, it strengthened the hand of anti–Western Russian hardliners. Third, it radicalized and mobilized the *siloviki* (power ministries or organs of coercion) against Westernization. Fourth, it damaged Russia's overall economic security and drove Russia's crucial defense industry into less lucrative markets in non-democratic and anti–Western states.[97]

UNDERCUTTING PRO-WESTERNERS

By 1996 tensions in Moscow intensified, as it became clear NATO expansion was inevitable and would not include Russia. Already in January, President Boris Yeltsin fired his Western-oriented foreign minister, Andrei Kozyrev, who had long claimed such expansion would never occur, and if it did, would not affect Russian national security. Kozyrev had been Russia's foreign minister since October 1990 under the still Soviet-era RSFSR before the USSR's 1991 collapse and during the heyday of the late Soviet and early post–Soviet era Russian-American romance. That over, the so-called "party of war"— led by First Deputy Premier Oleg Soskovets, with close ties to the military-industrial complex, and Aleksandr Korzhakov, Yeltsin's hardline chief of security—used NATO expansion to convince Yeltsin to turn away from Kozyrev and later Yegor Gaidar and Anatolii Chubais, all three of whom took pro–American stances and discounted the likelihood of NATO expansion. The moderate, pro-democratic daily *Nezavisimaya Gazeta* carried an opinion piece in April 1997 that underscored this point: "We will recall how five years ago the entrance of Poland and the Baltics into NATO seemed a 'comic chimera' to several radical democratic analysts. And what about today?" Elementary knowledge of politics tells us that, all else being equal, as a threat—real or perceived—grows, so do the prospects of those who warned about, predicted, or at least did not downplay the threat.

Kozyrev's successor on Arbat Square became the centrist Soviet-era politican Yevgenii Primakov, a specialist in Arab politics. Primakov gradually ushered in a "multipolar" policy, explicitly intended to counterbalance American power, especially in the post–Soviet region. He immediately began moving towards a Eurasia-centric foreign policy model and stressed the benefits of close relations with "Third World" states as an alternative to close cooperation with the West. In a world of realpolitik where the prospects for a close Russian-American partnership seemed to have all but disappeared, Primakov and Russian foreign policy elites moved to counter the unipolar world dominated by the American hegemon, lobbying globally for a multipolar world. Russia's new strategy was to play off Western and "Asian" interests—Chinese versus American, Arab and Islamic versus American, ASEAN versus EU—in order to increase Russia's influence on the world stage and garner cards that could be traded with the West in pursuit of Russian interests there. The reduced importance to the West of its relationship with Russia, represented by NATO expansion, induced Russia to diminish the importance it placed on relations with the West, especially the U.S. In this new world, the Kozyrevs and pro–Western democrats were expendable, their authority inside Russia irrevocably damaged. As successive rounds of NATO expansion proceeded, democrats became more excluded from foreign policy decision-making and influence, and the turn to non–Western countries in security and foreign trade matters transformed from a playing card to be parlayed in the West into a habit and growing reliance on a network of non–Western relations.

President Bill Clinton, with his keen political instincts, was well aware of this new dynamic already in early 1996, but the *fait accompli* that was now NATO expansion offered little in the way of meeting the Russian democrats' political needs. Clinton's Undersecretary of State, Strobe Talbott, gives us a sense of how much Clinton was concerned about the extent to which Washington had been "taking advantage" of Moscow's weakness in pushing NATO enlargement without Russia, and about the tensions the full-court press by Washington and Brussels was creating between President Yeltsin's liberal camp and the hard-line opposition. In a private exchange during the April 1996 Moscow summit, Clinton acknowledged:

> We haven't played everything brilliantly with these people; we haven't figured out how to say yes to them in a way that balances off how much and how often we want them to say yes to us. We keep telling Ol' Boris, "Okay, now here's what you've got to do next—here's some more shit in your face." And that makes it real hard for him, given what he's up against and who he's dealing with…. We've got to remember that Yeltsin can't do more with us than his own traffic will bear…. I've got some domestic politics of my own—stuff I can't do that I'd like to do, stuff I've got to do that I'd like not to. But he's got a much harder deal than I do.[98]

Talbott evidences Yeltsin's domestic burden, referencing interactions with the Russian side. He describes then Prime Minister Viktor Chernomyrdin's grabbing him by the arm, and "with a note of abject desperation" he had never heard from any politician in such a high position, beseeching Talbott: "I beg you, please, please make sure that we solve this problem together! Don't just ram something down our throat!" The next day, Primakov told Talbott that NATO enlargement was "a life-or-death issue on the political Olympus!"[99]

STRENGTHENING HARD-LINERS

The hard-line opposition, with some support from radicalizing centrists, were galvanized by NATO's march east. NATO expansion intensified Russian chauvinism among hard-line, anti–Western communist and nationalist opposition forces. It converted some moderate and ambivalent nationalists, conservatives and social democratic "centrists," into the hard-liners' allies, undermining Western-oriented democratic parties. This trend even prompted the Clinton administration to delay announcing its decision to consider the admission of new members to NATO until after the 1996 Russian presidential elections so as to protect Yeltsin from a hard-line backlash.[100]

In February 1997, deputies from the opposition "Power to the People" faction (*Narodovlastie*) in the Russian Federal Assembly's lower house, the State Duma, organized an "Anti-NATO" association of some 240 of the body's 450 deputies. By July it had grown to 260, reflecting growing alarm among centrist deputies. The anti–NATO Duma majority would become permanent (if noninstitutionalized) in later convocations of the Russian parliament and would complicate ratification of the START II nuclear weapons reduction treaty, chemical weapons agreements, the Open Skies agreement, and other important arms control, nonproliferation and confidence-building measures. The leading organizers of the early, official anti–NATO caucus were, for the most part, members of the communist-nationalist opposition, particularly the Communist Party of the Russian Federation (KPRF) and *Narodovlastie*. But there were also many representatives of Prime Minister Chernomyrdin's centrist "Our Home is Russia" (*Nash Dom–Rossiya*) party (NDR) and the independent or nonparty deputies elected in single mandate districts and standing autonomously in the Duma. The Anti-NATO Commission, created in the State Duma in April at the association's behest, included, besides five KPRF deputies, several deputies from *Narodovlastie* and the less extremist Agrarian Party, two NDR deputies, and one from the centrist "Russia's Regions." This indicated broad "center-right" opposition to NATO expansion, as well as the potential for additional co-optation of centrists in the future. Many of the non–KPRF deputies or future candidates like them would form the core of Putin's United Russia party in the 2000s.

Moreover, the anti–NATO caucus and commission provided an institutional and resource base for hard-liners to push their anti–Western agenda. In future electoral campaigns, depending on the details of NATO's expansion, anti–NATO sentiment would prove a useful wedge issue for undermining support for Westernization. Before any of the Russian-NATO international disputes or conflicts in Yugoslavia, Georgia, and Ukraine, half of post–Soviet Russia's population opposed NATO expansion. In April 1996 and February 1997, 47 percent and 50 percent of respondents, respectively, were opposed, and only 19 percent approved NATO's expansion to the countries of the former Warsaw Pact—Poland, Hungary, the Czech Republic and "others."[101] Therefore, over the mid- to long term, there was a political base upon which anti–Western forces would exploit NATO expansion at the polls. This, in turn, created potential for either the coming to power of anti–Western communist-nationalist forces or the hardening of a centrist Russian regime's stance toward the West. The first possibility was writ large in Yeltsin's September 19 statement in Orel, in which he stated that the U.S. had too much influence in Europe. The second emerged behind Putin.

Hardening of other Russian political forces was made clear in a report made to the Anti-NATO Commission offering a rather chilling vision of an alternative future should NATO expansion continue unabated. The report, delivered by Chairman of the Duma's Committee of Geopolitics Aleksei Mitrofanov, a leading member of Vladimir Zhirinovskii's Liberal Democratic Party (LDP) at the time, called for Russian foreign policy to pursue a "revolution" in the international system based on a national and ethnic ethos, rather than on "class struggle," a system informed by a quasi–Eurasianist geostrategic doctrine of "Russian national egoism." The collapse of the Cold War's bipolar structure, in Mitrofanov's view, gave birth to a new historical epoch: one of "partitioning of the world." According to Mitrofanov:

> It has now become absolutely obvious that matters are proceeding toward the isolation of Russia from Europe; the creation around its perimeter of a quarantine belt made up of unfriendly states united in military blocs with the United States of America and their closest allies; our country's further weakening; the development of centrifugal tendencies (inside Russia); and its final break-up with the formation, on its debris, of 10–15 satellite countries fighting amongst themselves and, as a whole, dependent on foreign sovereigns.

The remedy, according to Mitrofanov, is to correct "the blind pro–American orientation" which "carried an overt, provocative character under Kozyrev and has not changed but is being disguised" under Primakov's "Eurasian orientation."

Radicals like Mitrofanov saw even Eurasianist policies as insufficiently anti–Western. For Mitrofanov (and other such radicals and many Eurasianists), Russian foreign policy's premise should be that the United States is Russia's "main opponent," followed by Great Britain, Turkey and NATO. Specifically, Mitrofanov suggested that Russia must actively counter the role designated by Washington and Brussels for Ukraine, which is to be the cornerstone of containment in the west. An American and NATO *carte blanche* supposedly appoints Turkey to be the "regional superpower" that should contain Russia from the south. All the "pitiful and unnatural" attempts to negotiate Russia's participation in "hostile" NATO should be ceased, in Mitrofanov's view. Instead, the State Duma must "officially and juridically define NATO as a hostile military-political bloc" and issue "a renunciation of all agreements defining and supporting post-war borders in Europe as well as Asia." This will regard "in first order Poland and [NATO's] other new members."[102]

While such views were rare at the time, NATO expansion helped to make them mainstream through the popularization of neo–Eurasianism. At the time, however, NATO expansion "merely" galvanized and energized the red-brown united opposition (which excluded Mitrofanov's LDPR and the KPRF) and depolarized its relationship with many in Russia's centrist parties, including Chernomyrdin's NDR. The former trend was reflected not only by the "Anti-NATO" deputies. In 1997, communist party (KPRF) leader Gennadii Zyuganov, who nearly defeated Yeltsin in the 1996 presidential election, demanded Duma hearings on national security and military reform during the autumn session, as a prelude to any vote on START II. The communists' call for these hearings just as the budget was being negotiated signaled their intention to use NATO expansion in order to demand increased defense appropriations, cozy up to the *siloviki*, and play on longstanding tensions in Russia's civil-military relations. The government issued a statement that the General Staff not take NATO expansion into account in defense planning, indicative of the civilian leadership's desire to limit the defense budget and target most defense spending on arms production and military pay, highlighting the political rift between the liberal government and the still hard-line *siloviki*. The government's statement was at odds with the draft national security "concept" and even with a September 17, 1997 statement by Ivan Rybkin, Russia's centrist Russian Security Council secretary. Both the concept and Rybkin's statement affirmed that national security policy should include, among possible threats to Russia, "the preservation or creation by major powers and their alliances of powerful groupings of armed forces"—a clear reference to NATO expansion.[103]

Hardening the Siloviki, Straining Civil-Siloviki Relations

On the background of battles over the national security budget and military reform, NATO expansion could only harden Russia's *siloviki* and complicate civil-*siloviki* relations already strained since the Soviet collapse. The USSR's *siloviki*, after all, were brought into the post–Soviet Russian regime virtually unreformed in accordance with the noted tendency inherent in revolutions from above. Even without this, the different corporate insterests and functions between the *siloviki* and civilian leaderships created a dynamic of potential conflict. Even more than foreign policymakers, military and security policymakers are contingency planners, designing force structures and operational capabilities for as many possibilities as far into the future as budget allocations will allow. Regardless of regime type, foreign and national security policymaking is and should be built not on the intentions of foreign powers, but on their capabilities. Intentions, stated or real, are difficult to read and fluid; capabilities, less so. Thus, *siloviki* in any country tend to approach policy and especially contingency planning through the lens of capabilities.

NATO's more forward-leaning configuration required adjustments to Russian force structure, defense procurement, and overall military and national security doctrines. Many of these Moscow was in no position to carry out because of the dire economic depression into which the Soviet collapse had plunged the country. In light of the capabilities dictum, robust action should have been no surprise, and should not have been regarded as "imperialistic." Looking at the implications of NATO expansion from the perspective of a Russian national security or military planner—even imagining one who is not a hard-liner, but a moderate military professional—one would have to conclude that the capabilities of NATO vis-à-vis Russia would grow as the bloc expanded in Russia's direction, thus increasing the capabilities arrayed against and the potential threat posed to Russia. Indeed, as expansion was being set in motion, U.S. Defense Department and NATO officials openly acknowledged the enhanced capability an enlarged NATO would garner compared with the status quo. In a July 1997 congressional hearing on U.S. NATO policy, U.S. Under Secretary of Defense Walter Slocombe emphasized the added capacity an expanded alliance would possess:

[T]here can be no question that if we had to meet such a threat, and it is not impossible that we will, we could do so more effectively and less expensively in an expanded alliance than in a Europe still divided along cold war lines. In such a circumstance, the added manpower, military capability, political support, and strategic depth afforded by NATO enlargement would amply justify whatever additional costs there would be in having additional members in the alliance. Perhaps the most important point to be made about the costs of enlargement is there would be greater costs and risks to not enlarging. If we fail to seize this historic opportunity to help integrate, consolidate, and stabilize Central and Eastern Europe, we would risk a much higher price later. The most efficient and cost-effective way to guarantee stability in Europe is to do so collectively through NATO. Alliances save money. Collective defense is both cheaper and stronger than purely national defense, and it carries many fewer political risks.[104]

The correlation of forces would change, perhaps drastically, to the detriment of Russia's already compromised post–Soviet security, weakened by technological backwardness, economic decline, and the growing jihadi threat. Alexei Arbatov, deputy chairman of the Russian State Duma's Defense Committee and the leading national security expert of the liberal Yabloko Party, told an audience at the U.S. Army War College that after the first phase of NATO enlargement, the ratio for conventional ground and air forces would change from a 2.5:1 NATO advantage over Russia to a 4:1 advantage.[105]

Thus, Russian military planning responses to NATO expansion immediately appeared. In a July 1997 interview, Colonel-General Vladimir Yakovlev, commander of the Strategic Missile Force, noted one effect of NATO's post-expansion capabilities on Russia's security:

> [N]ow that NATO is moving eastward it will have the ability to use most of its tactical aircraft to deliver strikes at our facilities. Moreover, they will be able to spend more time in our deployment areas, which will increase their combat load. There is no direct threat of this now, but the Strategic Missile Force is doing research designed to increase the viability of launching sites and command stations. This is done as part of the work to ensure high combat readiness and effectiveness.[106]

Such responses, however, had to be undertaken at a time when the civilian leadership, having imposed on the army a new defense minister, was implementing a reform eliminating the Air Defense Forces as a separate branch of the military and cutting overall manpower and expenditures sharply.

Arbatov, as well as a small coterie of reformist officers, needed to convince the rest of Russia's conservative security and military policy community that they should embark on an unsettling and costly military reform in a more threatening international and domestic political environment created in part by NATO expansion. In a *New York Times* editorial at the time, Arbatov wrote that expansion was already making military reform and arms control more difficult to sell.[107] The elite of the decaying Russian military, so badly in need of reform, was highly politicized precisely because of insufficient financing—which produced a half-year of wage arrears, lack of housing for officers and their families, crumbling equipment, and a rising suicide rate. The additional pressure of military reform and further budget and staff cuts, in tandem with NATO expansion, actually scuttled Russian military reform for a decade to come and further alienated the *siloviki* from potential Western partners.

This dynamic was reflected when a supporter of the Yeltsin-Chernomyrdin administration, General Lev Rokhlin, denounced President Yeltsin for intentionally destroying the military. Rokhlin, a leading member of the centrist NDR and reportedly well-respected in the military, was expelled from the party, but maintained chairmanship of the Duma's Defense Committee. He then organized a new military opposition movement that included the most sinister of former and active-duty military and KGB officers in the country: Vladimir Kryuchkov, leader of the failed August 1991 armed coup and former USSR KGB chairman; Vladislav Achalov, former USSR first deputy defense minister (a leading participant in the August 1991 coup and the October 1993 uprising); Leonid Shebarshin, former head of the USSR KGB Intelligence Department; and Stanislav Terekhov, the ultranationalist Officers' Union chairman (veteran of the October 1993 uprising who committed suicide in July 1997). In an appeal to President Yeltsin, whom Rokhlin hoped his movement could impeach, Rokhlin tied NATO expansion to a demand for increased expenditures on Russia's strategic nuclear deterrent. Rokhlin's movement held its founding congress in Moscow on September 20 with more than 2,000 delegates in attendance, representing 62 regions of Russia. Both the KPRF and 1996 presidential candidate Aleksandr Lebed offered to cooperate with the new movement, while Rokhlin agreed to support the KPRF during the national security hearings. Thus, NATO expansion was already paving the way for a more hard-line leadership to emerge.

ALIENATING ECONOMIC INTERESTS

In addition to mobilizing and unifying various hardline and centrist political groups, NATO expansion began to damage important Russia economic interests that would then turn to and strengthen anti–NATO, anti-democracy, and anti–Western causes. Premier among them was the powerful defense industry lobby. The option or prospect of joining NATO changed calculations on weapons markets. American and other Western arms became more attractive to many countries and would become obligatory to new NATO members because of the bloc's interoperability standards. Initially, when NATO expansion was still in some doubt, the interests of Russian weapons producers did not suffer. In June 1993, Hungary accepted Russian MiG-29s as partial payment for Russia's hard currency debt to Hungary. This mitigated somewhat the U.S. sponsorship of the Hungarian military air control system's modernization. But when Russians attempted the same with the Czech Republic, they were rejected due to Prague's concerns about remaining dependent upon Russian-made weapons at a time when they were planning to join NATO. This might have been avoided had a more cooperative security relationship with Russia been achieved prior to or in place of expansion. Under some form of NATO associate membership or alternative European security institution, such as the OSCE, issues such as the non-interoperability of Russian weaponry could have been resolved. For example, Germany managed to make 24 MiG-29s, incorporated from the former East German air force, interoperable with NATO forces.

As it turned out, NATO expanded, and Russia would be gradually expelled from all of Central and Eastern Europe's arms markets. This was a heavy blow to an already crippled Russian economy. Russia had no other manufacturing sector capable of competing on international markets, and the boom in oil, gas, and other commodity exports was only just beginning and still tenuous. In 1997, more efficient organization and subordination to the state and federal budget were only a gleam in Putin's eye, or at least his doctoral dissertation. In order to preserve its defense industrial base, Moscow now had no choice but to rely exclusively on weapons sales to non-democracies and anti–Western states. Consequently, Russia's overall relations with these countries deepened. Since almost all of them, with the exception of major Russian weapons purchaser India, were authoritarian or totalitarian states, Russia was in effect making a small pivot to the nondemocratic world, with all the attendant cultural, political, and other influences that might have. The trends detailed above would intensify by the time Western discussions of a second round of expansion began, bringing NATO to Russia's borders for the first time.

At this time, neo–Eurasianism began to produce various political movements and organizations; for example, the Eurasian Party headed by the above-mentioned Dugin. Eurasianist organizations' greater ethnic and religious inclusiveness, compared with Russian nationalist organizations, somewhat masked the movement's intolerance and authoritarian orientation. Several political and ideological trends contributed to the coalescence of this quasi-inclusive strain of neo–Eurasianism. Neo-Eurasianist thought was becoming influential in post–Soviet Tatar and Kazakhstani political thought. Many Tatar intellectuals argue that the origins of the Russian nation and state are as much or nearly as much Tatar as they are Russian. They invoke the Tatar-Mongol "yoke" and partial "Tatarization" of Russian society and state before Ivan Grozny's liberation of Russia, which culminated in his capture of the Kazan Khanate in 1522. The special "sovereign" and "associated" status won for Tatarstan in the 1990s by President Mintimer Shaimiev—amounting, according to some, to a confederal relationship—seemed to institutionalize Tatars' sense of their special role in Russian history. Such a policy was supported by those, including Shaimiev and his top aide Rafael Khakimov, who were seeking to consolidate a delicate balance within the republic between Tatars and Russians and between Muslims and Orthodox.[108] This policy of inclusion coincides with some Eurasianists' contention that Russia's stability and future great power status can and should be achieved by taking the lead in bringing Eurasia's numerous ethnicities, confessions, and civilizations closer together as a counter to globalization.

This inclusivist strain in neo–Eurasianism is reflected in the membership of Dugin's Eurasian Party. It has been joined by various Russian Muslim thought leaders over the years, including by the supreme mufti of Russia and the European countries of the CIS and chairman of the Central Muslim Religious Board, Talgat Tadjuddin, and the controversial publicist Dzhemal Gaidar. The Central Muslim Religious Board's entire leadership and an overwhelming majority of its members joined the Eurasia Party. Thus, NATO expansion helped defeat military reform for years, radicalized and mobilized the *siloviki* against democratization and Westernization, and paved the way for a potentially more hard-line leadership to emerge in the 2000s.

NATO's Lybia Intervention and Putin's Return

Yet another downturn in Russian-Western relations and Russians' views of NATO came with the alliance's likely violation of the March 17, 2011 UN Resolution 1973 authorizing the implementation of a no-fly zone in the Libyan civil war. The Libya intervention came in the wake of one of the first "Arab Spring" revolutions and an ensuing civil war between the Muammar al Qadhafi regime and various opposition forces. Resolution 1973 imposed a no-fly zone over Libya and authorized member states to take all necessary measures to protect civilians and civilian-populated areas under attack or threat of attack. The push for the resolution and the intervention's implementation would create a pivot point in Russian politics. The adoption of Resolution 1973 was facilitated by Moscow, and the decision not to block its passage sparked a dispute between then Prime Minister Putin and President Dmitrii Medvedev, Putin's more liberal counterpart in the so-called "ruling tandem" of 2008–2012. The dispute appears to have convinced Putin to return to the Kremlin for a third presidential term, depriving Medvedev of a second presidential term and ensuring a failure of the "reset" in Russian-American relations initiated by the Barack Obama administration.

In March 2011, Medvedev decided not to use Russia's veto as a permanent member of the UN's Security Council to block the U.S.–backed resolution establishing the Libyan no-fly zone. Russia's abstention allowed the resolution to pass. Putin came out calling into question Medvedev's decision to abstain, calling the resolution "defective" and resembling a "medieval call for a crusade," and invoking the "U.S. policy" of unilateral military intervention in Yugosloavia as a similar case.[109] Medvedev hastily called a press conference to respond. Donning a fighter pilot's jacket outside his Gorky presidential residence, he blamed Qadhafi for the intervention, defended the resolution, but was critical of its implementation on the ground. Medvedev seemed to counter Putin's remark when he emphasized: "I think we need to be very careful in our choice of wordings. It is inadmissible to say anything that could lead to a clash of civilisations, talk of "crusades" and so on. This is unacceptable."[110]

There were other cases of disagreement between Putin and Medvedev, and considerable differences in policy and style between their respective presidencies. Ignored in the Western media, Medvedev's presidency saw a marked political "thaw," with a series of liberalizing reforms. Police and anti-corruption reforms led to better performance in these areas, according to international watchdog organzations' rankings and opinion surveys. State officials allowed mass demonstrations to occur more frequently, and state television became more accessible to opposition figures. New laws freed NGOs from much of the state interference they had suffered during Putin's presidencies. After the December 2011 Duma elections and resulting mass protests in Moscow and other cities, Medvedev issued a series of major electoral reforms making it easier for opposition parties to form, register and run candidates. The March 2012 presidential election included unprecedented measures to prevent voter fraud, making it the cleanest since the Yeltsin era. Putin's rollback of most of these reforms, except the party and electoral reforms, created new tension with the West.[111]

It is possible that matters inside the tandem were never as simple and stable as observers have portrayed them. Typically, Medvedev was seen as Putin's loyal puppet, holding his presidential chair warm until 2012. Putin's September 2011 decision to run for a third term has been interpreted by almost all Russia observers as an inevitable pre-planned "castling." This hypothesis—and it is nothing more and often driven by political bias and false assumption—is a problematic one. It is just as likely that the rise of the "Arab Springs" and the Qadhafi regime's demise in particular drove Putin's decision, which was not pre-determined from the outset. NATO bombing, led by the Europeans rather than Americans, commenced in March 2011 and continued into October. In September, as the bombing had become more overtly interventionist on the rebel side, Putin and Medvedev announced the decision that Putin would run for the presidency in the March 2012 presidential election. On, or days before October 20, jets bombed a convoy spiriting Qadhafi away from rebel fighters, facilitating his capture and death at their hands.[112] Qadhafi had followed Milosevic into the twilight on the wings of NATO bombers, and Medvedev's position on Libya was proven to be mistaken in the eyes of many Russians, most notably Putin's.

As Putin's dissertation at St. Petersburg State University suggests, he deploys a management style emphasizing strategic and tactical flexibility and maneuverability, leaving the maximal room for change of strategic direction in response to changes in the political environment. Accordingly, it is not in Putin's character to set a major move in stone four years ahead of time. One should recall the long delay in announcing the Kremlin's presidential candidate through much of 2012 and the panic it sowed within the elite. The delay was a result of Putin's indecision, not inevitability. It is just as likely that Putin designated Medvedev to run in 2008 and hoped gradual reforms would allow both a rapprochement between regime and state and his departure from politics in a term or two. However, Putin's plan to gradually unleash Medvedev and liberalization was confounded by Medvedev's growing desire for an independent political identity, his corresponding pursuit of his own political agenda, and, most of all, a series of developments that in Putin's estimation seemed to bode ill should Medvedev remain in the presidency, in particular his understudy's "mistaken" decision to abstain on Resolution 1973.

Both the lateness of Putin's decision and Medvedev's growing independence and liberalism were evident in April 2011 during the latter's trip to China. Medvedev said in an interview on Chinese state television: "I do not rule out the possibility of running for a second term in the presidential elections. The decision will be taken very shortly." For the first time, Medvedev seemed to suggest that the decision on whether or not he would run might be solely his own and not taken within the tandem. He did note: "I and Vladmir Putin have the single task so that in ten to twenty years Russia will be one of the strongest and most powerful states in the world." But he added: "We, perhaps, see the methods and ways of attaining this flowering differently, but this is democracy and this is competition."[113] The differences in policy between the two presidents are a reflection of their philosophical differences and at the time were already beginning to form factions within the elite. The gap between the two principals and their respective factions would likely have grown had Medvedev remained in the Kremlin for a second term, a development that ultimately could lead to the Putin regime's fall.

In Putin's view, Medvedev's growing independence and reformism, the rise of the protest sentiment beginning in December 2009, and United Russia's declining poll numbers at the time risked the most negative outcome that both Putin and Medvedev sought to avoid—regime transformation by revolutionary rather than evolutionary or, as political scientists discuss it, "transitional" regime change. Medvedev's liberal response to the protest movement was not Putin's preference, as he would demonstrate when he was back in the Kremlin. Medvedev proposed and eventually signed into law a series of reforms before Putin's inauguration. They included: (1) elimination of the requirement that political parties gather signatures to run in parliamentary election at the federal, regional, city, and district level (the signature-vetting process had been used to keep some opposition parties and candidates from running in elections); (2) a sharp reduction in the number of signatures needed to register presidential candidates for parties (from 1 million to 100,000) and independents (from 2 million to 300,000); and (3) a sharp reduction in the number of members that a party needs to be registered and a streamlining of the signature and registration process (from 45,000 to 500). In addition, a reform of the method of appointing senators was adopted, tying it to the new, "filtered" election of governors. It cannot be overlooked that some of these reforms were introduced against Putin's will. Thus, Putin likely stood behind the watering down of one of the key December reforms: the gubernatorial election reform proposed by Medvedev did not include any qualifications or "filters" of the kind forced into the draft legislation when passed in spring. Indeed, the tandem again openly disagreed, with Medvedev saying there would be no filters and Putin arguing that it would be good to consider them.[114] Putin's first year back in the presidency saw the repeal of some other Medvedev reforms, though none of the other December 2011 reforms.

Aside from the rhetorical differences between Medvedev and Putin at the time of Russia's March 2011 abstention on the Libya resolution, there is other evidence that Medvedev's decision on the issue was taken independently and opposed by elements within the Kremlin. Sources inside the Kremlin have stated that the decision mobilized and sparked indignation within the traditionalist camp as Putin was making his final decision on who should run for the presidency, driving his decision to return.[115] Medvedev's decision, the ensuing Medvedev-Putin public disagreement, the subsequent Western bombing of Libyan forces, and Qadhafi's bloody demise could only pique Putin's and the traditionalists' anti–Western angst and their doubts about Medvedev. More importantly, the bombing and Qadhafi's extrajudicial demise meant the resounding defeat in Moscow for Medvedev's more Western-oriented policy that emphasized more cooperation with the U.S. and the West.

The Libyan debacle, Putin's return to the presidency, and the ensuing chaos created in Libya could have been avoided. The Citizens' Commission on Benghazi (CCB)—founded in September 2013 and including among its members former U.S. Congressman Peter Hoekstra and numerous former CIA and military officers—concluded that Libyan leader Muammar Qadhafi had communicated to the U.S. his willingness to resign and depart from Libya and that the U.S. facilitated the delivery of arms to Libyan rebels tied to Al Qa'ida (AQ). Based on interviews with sources in U.S. intelligence agencies and the military, their investigation concluded that the U.S. ignored Libyan leader Muammar Qadhafi's call for a truce, and that he had expressed a readiness to abdicate shortly after the 2011 Libyan revolt began, but was ignored or rebuffed by U.S. officials. It also concluded that the Obama administration had facilitated the delivery of weapons and military support to Libyan rebels from from the radical Islamist group, the Muslim Brotherhood (MB), who were linked to AQ, including its cell that undertook the Benghazi consulate attack that killed U.S. ambassador Christopher Stevens and three CIA operatives.[116]

The Libyan debacle was a single episode within the larger challenge to Russian national security posed by the "Arab Spring," and was a final straw for Putin, who now regarded Medvedev unfit for the challenges to come. The "Arab Spring"—part of what is really a revolutionary situation across much of the Islamic world, in which a global Islamist revolutionary movement and a global jihadi revolutionary alliance are growing—was properly of grave concern to Putin. For all his occasional boorishness and heavy-handedness, Putin had a better handle on the nature of the "Arab Spring" than did U.S. policymakers, who were blinded by the chimera of Arab democratic revolutions. This same dynamic was playing out in Syria, as of this writing.

Thus, the return of Putin—less democratic and pro–Western than Medvedev—was a direct consequence of another unilateral NATO action that went contrary to promises made to, and the national interests of, Russia. Moreover, this NATO action followed Western support for "color revolutions" across the Arab world, sowing chaos and the rise of the Islamic State and other global jihadi revolutionary groups threatening Russian national security through networks created between these groups and Russia's own jihadi group, the Caucasus Emirate.[117]

NATO's bombing of Libya also led to another downturn in Russian attitudes towards NATO, and by default the West and the United States as well. As noted above, in November 2001 and November 2011 VTsIOM polls, when respondents were asked to choose among Russian policy options in relation to NATO, 16 and 29 percent supported formation of an alternative alliance, respectively.[118] Polls also showed that from 2005 to 2009 the percentage of Russians supporting the creation of a counteralliance had more than doubled from 16 to 39 percent, and the proportions who supported seeking cooperation with NATO dropped from 52 to 33 percent.[119] Also, in June, during the NATO bombing of Libya, VTsIOM gave respondents a binary choice between supporting or opposing the creation of a military bloc to counter NATO. Some two-thirds of respondents able to decide favored forming such a bloc.[120]

Policy Transformation

As detailed in the previous chapter, neo–Eurasionism grew in influence within the Russian foreign policy elite during the late 1990s but there was no widespread or official adoption of neo–Eurasianist views at that time or later. However, Foreign Minister Primakov's counsel that Russia avoid overreliance on efforts to create the "common European home" and focus on building a multipolar international system to contain Western ambitions was taken to heart early on. Already under Yeltsin, the building blocks of what became Putin's own multipolar focus and economic quasi–Eurasianism were being put in place.

The Rise of Russian Multipolarism

The Clinton Administration's August 1993 decision to proceed forward with NATO enlargement spawned changes in more than thinking and rhetoric such as Yeltsin's 1994 warning of a "cold peace." The unilateralism of Washington and Brussels, reflected by NATO expansion, induced a quick shift in Moscow's foreign policy conduct. The Yeltsin-Kozyrev foreign policy team made its first pivot to Asia, most notably to China and Iran in September 1994. As Western talk of proceeding with NATO expansion was in high gear, Chinese President Jiang Zemin visited Moscow, and a Sino-Russian "constructive partnership" was declared.

After the poor showing of the pro–Kremlin party, *Nash Dom–Rossiya* (Our Home is Russia), in the December 1995 Duma elections, Yeltsin was even more bound to change policy, replacing Kozyrev and appointing Primakov at Russia's foreign ministry (MID) the next month. One of Primakov's first acts as foreign minister was to call a meeting on NATO expansion. Aware that some of the top officials at MID were very much opposed to NATO expansion but had remained in the minority, Primakov's arrival signaled change. There is no doubt about Russian bureaucrats' ability to sense and shift with changing political winds. According to Primakov, the meeting saw just one official defend what Primakov called in his memoir the "ostrich-like" position of accepting NATO expansion and seeking ways to develop cooperation with the alliance.[121] With Yeltsin's imprimatur, Primakov ushered in a more balanced, non–Eurocentric foreign policy favoring closer relations with China, India, the Islamic world, even Japan, as well as other states of Eurasia. The larger goal was to build a multipolar structure in the international system in order to counter Western, in particular American, hegemony.

In April 1996, relations with China graduated to a "strategic partnership" with Yeltsin's visit to Beijing. Primakov traveled there in November, and Chinese Premier Li Peng spent three days in Moscow in 1996. An April 1997 Sino-Russian summit issued a joint statement characterizing the international relations as unduly multipolar and opposing any country's efforts to "monopolize international affairs." At a press appearance with President Zemin, Yeltsin again presaged his Kremlin successor by quipping: "[S]omeone is longing for a unipolar world. He wants to decide things for himself."[122] Sino-Russian counter-containment had been launched.

The new multipolarism also involved seeking replacement clients for its weapons' producers, since it was becoming clear that Russia's military industry was locked out of the weapons markets of present and future NATO members, many of which had previously purchased Soviet weapons. Russia's sale of weapons to the West's Iranian nemesis reached a new level in January 1995, when Moscow sold two Kilo-class attack submarines to Tehran. This agreement led to a more far-reaching and potentially catastrophic agreement with Iran's mullahs, when Russia's Atomic Energy Ministry (MinAtom) signed a long-term cooperation agreement with Tehran to build at least one 1000-megawatt, light-water nuclear reactor and two smaller 440-megawatt reactors. The approximately $1 billion contract opened the possibility that Iran's intensely anti–American rogue regime could acquire nuclear weapons, destabilizing the entire Middle East and perhaps much more. Eventually, Iran was able to parlay the received technology and know-how into constructing its own enrichment and reprocessing facilities. This would force the West to institute sanctions in the 2000s and by 2015 enter into a nuclear deal brokered by Moscow that ostensibly will dismantle these aspects of Iran's nuclear program and any potential for it to acquire nuclear weapons, assuming Tehran honors all aspects of the deal.

At the same time, Primakov pursued deeper ties with India, and a revival of Russo-Japanese relations frozen since 1992 when Yeltsin suddenly canceled a long-scheduled trip to Tokyo. He also intensified diplomacy with the former Soviet republics of the largely dormant Commonwealth of Independent States (CIS). In these and other ways, Moscow has been responding to NATO expansion and other Western policies to which it objects—the ABM withdrawal and American national missile defense plans, as just two examples—impressing upon the West that Russia remains a global power not to be threatened in its western borderlands. If it so chooses, Moscow can wreak havoc against Western interests and security—a hidden cost of NATO expansion. Putin would impart even greater vigor to building a multipolar international order and countering American hegemony.

The Formation of Putin's Foreign Policy

As can be seen from the earlier discussion, contemporary neo–Eurasianism is a unique, exotic, even ethereal blend of ideologies, historico-philosophies, and certain anti–Western strains taken from Russia's political and strategic cultures. The radical versions described above have not translated into radical policies under Yeltsin's successor. Instead, Putin has adopted some elements of neo–Eurasianism that have seeped into Russian policymaking circles over the last two decades. He has done so gradually as he has refined his own geopolitical and, especially, geoeconomic strategy, in response to international and domestic challenges. This has initially produced a more practical, economic multilateralaism and neo–Eurasianism. However, as tensions with the West have increased since the 2008 Georgian-Ossetian war and the global jihadi revolutionary movement has become a key domestic, regional and global security challenge, some of Putin's multilateral projects have seen a growing "securitization."

Putin is a Russian patriot with moderate nationalist tendencies in foreign affairs and statist ones domestically; his chief goal is a secure and strong Russia. Domestically speaking, Putin is neither a democrat nor a dictator. He is a statist, authoritarian-inclined "hybrid regime" ruler. His highest value is neither the sovereignty of the people over the state nor his personal power over the state and people. His strong inclination is to preserve order, stability and security. This leads him to err on the authoritarian side. Putin rejects totalitarianism and lofty ideology and is neither repelled nor impressed by democracy or authoritarianism. He sees himself as the exception to the rule among Russian officials: an enlightened Russian who knows what is in the Russian state's and people's interest and how to realize their fullest potential.

Given his formative political experiences with *perestroika*'s reforms and the Soviet collapse, Putin is likely to err on the side of authoritarian and anti–Western measures in order to protect his power and system and maximize Russian power rather than accept Western tutelage. However, the liberalization under his hand-picked inter-regent, Medvedev, from 2008 to 2012 shows that Putin is not averse to changes in course or democratic development, as long as stability is not threatened as a result. This suggests that Putin adopts authoritarian methods not because he sees them as inherently superior or

conducive to Russian culture, but because they seem to serve the goal of a modern, globally competitive Russia.

In foreign policy, Putin sees Russia as the leading power in central Eurasia. His
vision and goal is Russia as a global power—the core of one pole in a multipolar international system. Russia should strengthen and expand upon its own Eurasian sphere of
influence in order to construct a multipolar order. These goals require a modern competitive economy, and a population largely satisfied with life in Russia because they enjoy
moderate-to-high levels of socioeconomic well-being and political, civil and human
rights—hence, the Customs Union and then more ambitiously the Eurasian Economic
Union (EEU), the Shanghai Cooperation Organization (SCO), and the BRICS association,
bringing together Russia, Brazil, China, India, and South Africa. Putin does not seek
restoration of the USSR or any imperial project. Such claims derive from delusions, paranoia, and/or well-compensated stratcomm. Actions that have been perceived as aggressive
and expansionist in the West, such as those in Georgia in 2008, were defensive in nature.
Overall, he is a rational actor, but when provoked and especially when he perceives he
has been betrayed, he tends to overreact, pushing the envelope of possible responses.

His minimum goal is to ensure Russia's status as a regional power, one of several
great powers in Eurasia writ large, and the indispensable country for any other pursuing
a presence in central Eurasia—the former USSR. There is no sure-fire Russian strategy
for achieving this goal other than that established by Primakov before Putin's rise to
power. The "Primakov doctrine" is the pursuit of a multipolar world through a "multi-
vector" or multidirectional foreign policy that takes seriously the Russian state emblem
of the double-headed eagle looking both east and west. Putin continued and developed
Primakov's line; he did not invent it. The robustness of the Sino-Russian strategic partnership and more broad "Asian pivot" are Putin's work, but also a logical extension of
Primakov's "multipolarism" made necessary as Russo-Western tensions mount.

Putin has elaborated considerably on the Primakov doctrine and developed effective,
flexible strategies for deepening Russia's presence in every region of the world. Years
before the crisis in Russian-Western relations around Ukraine, Putin was implementing
what Russian political scientist Dmitry Trenin recommended in 2015 as a "diversified"
Asian (non–Western) pivot: one not just towards China but all of Asia. In fact, Russian
foreign policy under Putin for years had been making a "diversified non–Western pivot"
encompassing all non–Western states, including the "Orient" writ large (Asian east and
Islamic south), as well as Africa and Latin America—hence BRICS. Over time, he broadened his horizons in building a network of relationships that Russia can use to develop
its economy, grow its political influence, and political-militarily protect these vital interests and its national security. His multilateral or "multi-vectoral" strategy has geographical
multidirectional and functionally multidimensional aspects and growth potential.

Initially, Putin focused on both developing relations east and west and building a
Eurasian and global energy export infrastructure to finance Russia's economic growth
and military might. By his second term, he began focusing on building multilateral organizational networks, concentrating most of Russia's diplomatic resources on the enlargement and development of three international organizations extending geographically in
concentric circles farther and farther from the homeland in order to spread Russian influence: the EEU for inner or central Eurasia; SCO for Eurasia writ large; and BRICS globally.
These projects filled gaps created by the stagnation and ineffectiveness of previous efforts
to consolidate the post–Soviet space around Russia: the CIS and the Collective Security

Treaty Organization (CSTO). Each had lost rather than gained members and institutional vigor during the 1990s, partly as a result of NATO and EU expansion, as well as often clumsy, sometimes heavy-handed Russian policies.

Putin's practical, economic Eurasianism was evident early on in a series of policies. Following through on his dissertation, Putin sought to harness the profits of Russia's export commodities—especially oil, natural gas and other energy resources—to fuel the Russian state's and society's modernization. In foreign policy, therefore, Putin focused on energy transportation trade and development and on creating Eurasia-wide energy transportation infrastructures: the policy to extend Russian energy exports and pipelines to the east (including China), to the south, and to the West; the policy of developing "North-South" and "East-West" transport networks; and the effort to integrate post–Soviet Central Asian, Caucasian, and European post–Soviet (and perhaps other) states into a Eurasian Economic Union and a Eurasian Energy Community. The strategy is aimed at making Russia the energy, transport and, ultimately, the economic hub of Eurasia.

The Eurasian Economic Union (EEU) is Putin's variation on the failed CIS and his multipolar strategy for the Eurasian region within the larger global multipolar strategy. It has much less to do with imperialistic Eurasianist geostrategic thought than with an economic development strategy for Russia and Eurasia in which the EEU becomes a counterweight to the European Union and Russia becomes the transportation, trade and overall economic hub for this mega-region. It is also intended to function as a bridge between the Asian-Pacific region and Europe. Russia's geographic comparative advantages make this a sound strategy.

The EEU emerged from the Russian-Belarus Customs Union, then the Russian-Belarus-Kazakhstan Customs Union, which removed customs barriers between its member-states. After Kazakhstan President Nursultan Nazarbaev first broached the idea of a Eurasian common market in a 1994 speech in Moscow, the first agreements on creating a common market modeled on the EU were signed in 1995 by Russia, Belarus, and Kazakhstan and later by Kyrgyzstan and Tajikistan, but progress remained slow through the 1990s. Under Putin the integration process was accelerating by the mid–2000s. The process intensified especially in response to the EU's 2009 EPP initiative, as the Russia-West struggle for the post–Soviet space came to a head.

After nearly two decades of talks, preliminary treaties and agreements, and various preliminary organizational incarnations, Russia, Belarus, and Kazakhstan finally signed a treaty officially establishing the EEU on May 29, 2014. Armenia acceded in January 2015, and Kyrgyzstan acceded in May. As of this writing, Tajikistan is in talks on joining the EEU. Ukraine was an original signatory to the predecessor "Treaty on a Single Economic Space" (SES), along with Russia, Belarus, and Kazakhstan. Signed in 2003 and ratified in 2004, the SES's institutionalization process stalled after Kiev's Orange revolution in 2005. The EEU operates through supranational and intergovernmental institutions and provides for the free movement of goods, capital, services and people. That the EEU has nothing to do with empire-building or "recreating the Soviet Union," and everything to do with developing trade links across the Eurasian continent and beyond, becomes clear if one looks at the numerous EEU free trade zone agreements being concluded with countries far outside the former USSR and central Eurasia.[123]

The second key international organizational project Putin has aggressively promoted, the Shanghai Cooperation Organization (SCO), geographically covers most of central, eastern and southern Eurasia (Southeast, Central and South Asia).[124] Putin energetically pursued expanding and upgrading SCO in order to achieve economic integration and political and military cooperation in the region and limit Western penetration. The political goal of resisting Western-backed regime change and humanitarian intervention policies was stated at the first Putin-era Shanghai Five summit held in Dudhanbe, Tajikistan, in 2000, at which the parties pledged to "oppose intervention in other countries' internal affairs on the pretexts of 'humanitarianism' and 'protecting human rights'; and support the efforts of one another in safeguarding the five countries' national independence, sovereignty, territorial integrity, and social stability."[125] The 2001 Shanghai Five summit issued a declaration founding SCO and bringing in Uzbekistan as its sixth member. SCO now encompassed 60 percent of Eurasia's landmass and more than 50 percent of the world's population. By the end of Putin's second presidential term, SCO had initiated more than twenty large-scale energy, transportation and telecommunications projects and had routinized itself institutionally, holding regular meetings of member-states' security, military, defense, foreign affairs, economic, cultural, banking and other officials. SCO also has established relations with the UN, EU, CIS, the Association of Southeast Asian Nations (ASEAN), and the Organization of Islamic Cooperation.

By early 2015, SCO had not just six full members, but six observing members (Afghanistan, Belarus, Iran, India, Mongolia and Pakistan), and two dialogue partners (NATO member Turkey and Sri Lanka). From 2012, Armenia, Azerbaijan, Bangladesh, Nepal, Sri Lanka, and Syria had applied for observer status, and Egypt, Maldives, and Ukraine had applied for dialogue partner status. SCO's July 2015 summit—hosted by Russia in Ufa, the capitol of the Volga-Urals republic of Bashkortostan, simultaneously with the BRICS summit—marked a global "pivot" to Eurasia. Several states located outside post–Soviet Eurasia—in Greater Eurasia or Eurasia writ large—deepened their involvement with SCO. In Eurasia's east, former SCO observer members India and Pakistan were approved to become full members. Cambodia and Nepal became dialogue partners. Westward, observer Iran agreed to become a full member in future, and Belarus took observer status. Also, Azerbaijan and Armenia became dialogue partners. Given SCO's growing role in Eurasian security issues, we can expect that the multinational organization could become a forum for settling the Azeri-Armenian frozen conflict over Nagorno-Karabagh and containing tensions in Indo-Pakistani relations.

SCO's significance for Sino-Russian relations cannot be overstated and was vividly demonstrated in June 2012, when Putin took his first foreign visit outside of the former USSR since his May inauguration to China and an SCO summit. Although disagreement over pricing again stalled a long-awaited Sino-Russian agreement on LNG—reached at the next summit and called "the deal of the century"—Putin's meetings with Premier Hu Jintao yielded what he called ten "crucial" commercial agreements on economic cooperation. In addition, Putin backed stepping up military cooperation, and Hu supported increasing cooperation in high technology research and development.[126] Putin was effusive about Sino-Russian relations, saying they had reached "new heights," trust between the two powers was "especially high," and China is a "good friend" and "a good partner on the world stage."[127] Trade with China continued to climb on the back of 40 percent rises year on year for the last two years and projections that the goal of $100 billion trade turnover by 2015 would be reached earlier.

As relations with NATO irretrievably soured and southern Eurasia increasingly became threatened by the Arab winter and the global jihadist and Islamist revolutionary movements, Putin increasingly supported SCO's gradual "securitization," which now includes a counterterrorism center, a rapid reaction force, and frequent military maneuvers. Indeed, Russia and China stood together blocking UN resolutions that mandated a Western-Sunni humanitarian intervention in Syria, an SCO observer member applicant since August 2015. SCO's July 2015 Ufa summit focused on cooperation on four often interconnected security issues: counterterrorism, extremism, border security, and drug trafficking. The SCO is potentially the most far-reaching joint Sino-Russian-led international organization; its competitor in this regard is BRICS.

BRICS—with a member country on each non–Western continent—is a strategic achievement and perhaps Putin's most innovative. Although BRICS is increasingly Sino-centric, it was Putin who proposed the BRICS idea, and he has persistently pursued its geographical and functional expansion. The organization is positioning itself as the foundation for an alternative global financial and trading system to that presently dominated by the U.S., EU, IMF, World Bank and other players. Russia pursues a series of interrelated long-term strategic geopolitical and economic goals through its participation in BRICS. In March 2014, Putin emphasized the goal of transforming BRICS "from a forum for dialogue into a fully formatted mechanism for strategic interaction." Russia's "Concept for the Participation of the Russian Federation in the Association 'BRICS,'" approved by President Putin in February 2013, lays out Russia's vision for BRICS and its future cooperation with the association. BRICS's importance in the structure of Russian foreign policy is reflected in the Concept: "The creation of BRICS, initiated by the Russian Federation in 2006, was one of the more significant geopolitical events of the beginning of the new century. This association was able in a short time to become a major factor in world politics."[128] Although the veracity of the last assertion is dubious, Moscow hopes this will be the case.

Russia has at least eight strategic political and economic goals it pursues through BRICS. Russia's first and most fundamental strategic purpose for BRICS is as a mechanism for Russia to maximize and project globally Russian economic and political influence and power. The association creates opportunities for Russia to develop economic and political partnerships with global reach, strengthening Russia's global presence through "non-institutionalized" global "management" and "network diplomacy" based on cooperation with the world's key regional powers in Asia (China and India), Africa (South Africa), and South America (Brazil) placed on each continent (excluding Europe and North America—i.e., the West) and in numerous international associations and organizations. These goals drove Moscow's initiative for BRICS, expanding BRIC by way of South Africa's inclusion, creating BRICS. Second, by including only non–Western powers from across the globe's continents, BRICS facilitates Russia's geostrategic goals of creating a multipolar world. The importance of the geostrategic goal of pluralizing the international system's structure through multipolarity is mentioned numerous times in both Russia's BRICS Concept and Foreign Policy Concept.[129] The third strategic goal is to undermine the international system's monopolarity under "American hegemony" as well as U.S. and its allies' efforts to delegitimize Russian domestic and foreign policy. Fourth, Moscow seeks to strengthen stability by using BRICS to buttress the principles of state sovereignty, territorial integrity, and noninterference in the internal affairs of states in response to what it interprets as Western efforts in support of separatism and regime change. Fifth, BRICS is a PR vehicle for projecting an image of a new Russia as a normal country to the East, West, North, and South. Russia seeks to strengthen and expand its "linguistic, cultural and informational" presence and influence around the world in service of the ends mentioned above and below.[130]

In addition, there are three economic goals. The first is to utilize complimentary aspects of the members' economies to promote trade and development in Russia and other member-states. Second, Moscow seeks to marshal BRICS to push for reforms of the international currency and financial systems so they become more broad-based, stable, and effective from Moscow's perspective. The Kremlin might even view BRICS institutions such as the association's Development Bank, agreed upon by the members at the March 2013 Fifth Summit in Durban, as a potential future competitor of the World Bank and International Monetary Fund (IMF) for bolstering the international system's multi-polarization. Third, Russia seeks to leverage its participation in BRICS in order to develop "privileged bilateral relations" between the association's member-states, in particular Russia's economic, trade and investment ties with each other BRICS member. As in politics, BRICS helps Russia overcome its relative economic isolation from the West. Like the Customs Union, the EEU and SCO, BRICS is a mechanism for the pursuit of trade partnerships and overall economic growth and development independent of the West and its demands regarding human, civil and political rights. As a result of pairing NATO expansion with democracy-promotion and regime change policy, Moscow increasingly views such demands as a Western mechanism for limiting Russia's economic and political potential and preventing Russia's re-emergence as a great power.[131]

In pursuing its strategic political and economic goals, Moscow also promotes BRICS's and its member-states' role in other international and regional organizations—most importantly, the UN. Russia's BRICS Concept proposes that after agreeing on joint policy positions, BRICS members will also introduce resolutions to the General Assembly and UN specialized bodies and institutions in order to strengthen the role of international law in global affairs. It also proposes expanding the UN Security Council's membership, presumably to include those BRICS members without a seat on the Council: Brazil, India, and South Africa. This is to be done while preserving the permanent members' prerogatives, including their veto power. Putin appears to believe that in this way Russia and its BRICS partners in the UN and Security Council can block Western preferences for regime change, unilateral and coercive resolution of conflicts, arbitrary interpretation of UN Statutes and Security Council resolutions, and politicization of human rights issues. A similar approach is to be taken in the WTO, the G8, the G20, the Asian-Pacific Economic Community (APEC), and other international fora.[132]

The BRICS project is also very much, though far from exclusively, focused on Eurasia as far as Russia and China are concerned. At the 7th BRICS summit, the organization's Development Bank officially opened with $50 billion in start-up capital and potential to garner $400 billion in capital. Funds will target member-states' infrastructure development, including China's New Silk Road in southern Eurasia. The summit saw Russia's Direct Investment Fund (RDIF) and BRICS member-states' foreign investment body, including the Silk Road Fund and India's Infrastructure Development Finance Company, sign agreements on cooperation.[133] Russia simultaneously joined the new Chinese-founded Asian Infrastructure Investment Bank (AIIB). The BRICS bank, AIIB, and the Sino-Russian partnership's other new financial institutions are focused on China's New Silk Road that will link Greater Eurasia through a network of air, rail, road, river, and ocean transportation hubs and connections. These will compliment Eurasian intracontinental and global intercontinental energy production and transportation networks.

Indeed, China recently changed the path of its efforts to establish a New Silk Road so that it will pass through Russia as well as numerous other states in southern Greater Eurasia. Thus, Russia will also benefit from the infrastructure development projects through contracts with countries from across Eurasia, the BRICS states and partners, and EEC FTZs.[134]

Politico-militarily, BRICS and especially SCO are set to fill the security gap in Afghanistan created by the West's withdrawal from the conflict. Afghanistan has become an SCO observer-member, and in Ufa both BRICS and SCO called on the Taliban to disarm, accept the present Afghan regime as legitimate, and cut ties to global jihadi revolutionary groups like Al Qa'ida, the Islamic State, and the Caucasus Emirate. Like Moscow, Beijing is interested in a successful Kabulization and ultimately a resolution of the conflict because of the potential threat to Xingjiang from the Uighur jihadi group, the Islamic Movement of Turkestan, and energy and other economic interests both in Central and South Asia, such as the 900-mile-long Turkmenistan-Afghanistan-Pakistan-India (TAPI) gas pipeline.[135]

Moscow brought all its international networking projects together when it convened a join EEC-SCO-BRICS meeting on July 9, 2015. One breakthrough was that Moscow and Beijing agreed to set up a working group to discuss ways to integrate the EEU and the New Silk Road under the auspices of SCO. With the last being increasingly "securitized" in recent years, this scale of Eurasian economic integration opens the potential for more robust Eurasian economic, political and military infrastructures that would overshadow the largely decorative G-8 and G-20 and challenge NATO, the EU, and TTP.

It is no coincidence that the geography of almost all of Putin's multilateral multipolarity-building projects coincide with the logic of neo–Eurasianism, Mackinder's geopolitics, and Huntington's civilizational analysis—the EEU and SCO, especially.[136] It appears reasonable to conclude that geography and civilizationist thinking are structuring post–Cold War politics and strategy in post-communist Eurasia writ large. To the extent geography and geopolitics were not enough to limit contingency in any significant way, their determinative impact is magnified by the ideational factors of Huntingtonian and Eurasian civilizationalism (and American revolutionism). Moreover, the strategic cultures on both sides of the Atlantic imbibed the teachings of Mackinder's geopolitics and Huntington's and Eurasianism's civilizationalist thinking. On both sides of the Atlantic—and the Dnepr—key policy players and opinion makers bought into the mutual exclusivity between Europe and Russia, the West and Eurasia, and Orthodox and non–Orthodox Christianity. This produced policies on the international level that would increasingly constrain the two main geopolitical contestants' choices and eventually those of their geopolitical and civilizational allies on the ground in places like Georgia and, more tragically, in Ukraine.

4

Democracy Promotion
The Dual-Use Technology of Color Revolutions

Introduction

As NATO enlargement proceeded ever eastward, it was often accompanied not just by EU expansion but by Western democracy-promotion activity, and often resulted in regime changes, or, as they came to be called, "color revolutions"—rose, orange, white ribbon, etc. Although democracy-promotion's goal was not necessarily revolution, it certainly demanded regime transformation, which has many modes ranging from violent revolutionary change to peaceful, barely conflictual imposed transitions. The problem arises in the inability of democracy-promotion's adepts to control the modality of regime transformation once they have induced a political crisis. Once processes of political organization, mobilization, articulation, demonstration, and protest are put in play, there is no telling what kind of transformation, revolutionary or transitional, will develop. Potential regime transformational situations sometimes explode into dramatic revolutionary overthrows of regimes. In other cases, negotiations between regime and opposition elements pave a smooth transition to democracy. This is the "dual-use" nature of the political technology of democracy-promotion.

The Dual-Use Democracy-Promotion

Democracy-promotion (DP) is an ambiguous, risky and even provocative political technology. It can be benign, occurring unintentionally through democratic values' and practices' spontaneous diffusion, emulation, cross-fertilization and "contagion," with no intentional foreign involvement. Such processes are really self-democratization rather than foreign-influenced "democracy-promotion," however. Typically, DP *per se* is intentional, originates from abroad, and involves clients within the target state interested in the democratization of their country. One definition is "all overt and voluntary activities adopted, supported, and (directly or indirectly) implemented by (public or private) foreign actors explicitly designed to contribute to the political liberalization of autocratic regimes, democratization of autocratic regimes, or consolidation of democracy in specific recipient countries."[1]

The definition itself reveals DP's potential problems. First, the implementation of DP programs by "public" foreign actors means implementation by foreign states. Since states are in competition in the international system, it is quite natural for the government of a target state subjected to one or more DP programs to be circumsuspect about the activities of foreign entities on its territory. In particular, in one way or another, to one degree or another, a foreign state or multinational organization might use DP intentionally or unintentionally either for its own benefit or to the target state government's detriment. Not long ago the *U.S. Marine Corps University Journal* published an article examining DP's "international dimension," which in addition to "coercive" and "intrusive" measures in support of creating democratic regimes in authoritarian states, also discussed more benign "prodemocratic public diplomacy." Author Alessandra Pinna noted that this form of DP is "combined action of government agencies and private partners" that seeks to "influence opinion and mobilize the public in ways that support interests and policies of foreign states" within the target state. Its "essence" is "strategic communication," which is modern-speak for propaganda that "aims to capture the hearts and minds of the general public in recipient countries."[2] "Capturing the hearts and minds of the general public" in "recipient countries" is also an important task in the conduct of politics by military means.

Depending on how one defines terms, at least one of the three possible goals pursued by DP's public diplomacy and stratcomm—"political liberalization," "democratization," and "consolidation of democracy"—requires a regime change or transformation. By definition, democratization of an autocratic (or authoritarian) regime (form of rule) means a change from a nondemocratic form of rule to a democratic one. Even if one argues that DP programs are focused on process rather than ultimate outcome, another problem arises. The path and outcome of any regime transformation process is often unpredictable. This is all the more so since, as Pinna notes, DP seeks to fundamentally transform all the institutions of state and society: the constitution, legal system, police forces, and bureaucracy. Political society's political parties are transformed through the training of party leaders and practitioners who choose leaders, recruit candidates, manage campaigns, and make policies. PD programs also work with the target state's civil society, including private voluntary organizations, nongovernmental organizations (NGOs), interest groups and professional associations, and independent media.[3]

Once liberalization or democratization processes begin, there is little to no control over where the transformation of the institutions, political societies and civil societies of states targeted by such programs will lead. The vector is all the more uncontrollable if the object of PD is to create a political crisis. In her *Marine Corps University Journal* article, Pinna acknowledges that this is the DP process: "Because political parties participate in elections to acquire ruling incumbents, *international actors tend to assist prodemocratic parties to bring about a crisis* in the authoritarian regime and to encourage a democratic transition" (my emphasis).[4]

In sum, DP is a dual- or multiple-use political technology intended to bring about regime change by any one of several modalities of regime transformation and tactics. The latter are to be determined by the locals, providing Washington, Brussels and others—intentionally or unintentionally—a convenient plausible deniability of intent to foment regime change. DP programs seek or can seek to create or otherwise result in a political crisis that leads to a regime transformation. Like the political crises that can produce regime change, the mode of regime transformation that ultimately develops— if one does, and the crisis does not lead to a crackdown, authoritarian restoration, or civil war—is uncontrollable. There is no guarantee of an orderly, peaceful "democratic transition" that Pinna and other DP practioners assume. The "democratic transition" is but one of many modes of regime transformation. Some forms of regime change are benign and inspiring; others are malign and horrifically violent. In this way, DP is an imprecise, risky and indeed dangerous "dual-use" political technology for the "recipient" country.

Types of Regime Transformation

Any particular country's form of rule can be transformed by one of several modalities, each having different potential to end in democracy, authoritarianism (including totalitarianism), or a hybrid of these two basic regime types. Historically, however, there are two basic kinds of internally driven regime change: revolution and transition.[5] Within these two basic types there are four domestically driven ways for an authoritarian regime to become democratic (and vice versa in theory): revolution from below, revolution from above, pacted transition, and imposed transition. As a general proposition, transitions are more likely to produce democratic outcomes than are revolutions.

Revolutions from below, for example, are led by elements within society. They are familiar to us all and are burned into our memories by images of peaceful or violent crowds seizing power against the will of the old regime and its ruling groups. France beginning in the late 18th century, Russia and China in the early and mid–20th century, Romania, the Czech Republic, and the Philippines in the late 20th century, and Egypt, Libya, and Syria in the early 21st century are just a few examples. The overthrow of the *ancien regime* from below can be peaceful, as in Czechoslovakia in 1989 and the Phillippines in the 1990s, or it can be violent as it was in France in the 18th century, Russia and China during the first half of the 20th century, and Iran in in the late 20th century. Violent revolutions from below rarely produce democracy. Peaceful ones often do. In revolutions from below—whether peaceful or violent—opposition forces are rooted in society and arrayed against the present forms of rule, state organization, elite behavior, and state-society relations. Opposition forces seize power from the streets, eschewing, destroying and replacing the old order's institutions.

Revolutions from above, on the other hand, are led by state actors, who take control of some state institutions illegally or legally and then use them against other state actors illegally or extraconstitutionally in order to dismantle some of the old order's institutions, replacing them with new ones in an effort to enact a new form of rule. Whether military-led (as in Meiji Japan, Ataturk's Turkey, or Nasser's Egypt, among others) or civilian-led (as in Boris Yeltsin's Russian revolution from above against the USSR's reforming communist system), revolutions from above tend to produce authoritarian or weak, tentatively democratic outcomes. By leaving some of the old institutions and power-holders in place, revolutions from above weaken any original democratic impulse. This appears to be especially true in more coercive military-led revolutions from above, such as those in Turkey and Egypt. Even in the peaceful Russian/Soviet civilian-led case of the 1990s, the initial impulse towards democracy was followed by the violent October 1993 revolt in Moscow, and then stagnation and backsliding to a predominantly authoritarian, if still hybrid system.

In contrast to revolutions, transitions are more reliable producers of democracy, in large part because they use the old order's institutions as a vehicle for gradually but fully replacing them. There are two basic kinds of transitional regime transformations:

imposed and pacted (negotiated) transitions. Imposed transitions occur when the ruling elite gradually reforms the regime, with few or no negotiations with, and little input from, opposition groups. Eventually, the regime ruling group allows the opposition to take power by winning a mostly free and fair election. This transitional mode may be less reliable in that it can be aborted or experience backsliding because there is no opposing force to restrain regime elements that might get cold feet. Imposed transitions seem to be more frequent in countries with single-party dominant, soft authoritarian regimes like Russia's system today. Among previous examples are the democratic transitions overseen by Taiwan's Kuomintang or Nationalist Party, South Korea's Democratic Justice Party, and Mexico's Institutional Revolutionary Party (PRI) in the 1990s.

A pacted transition occurs when the old regime's elite negotiates a process with societal opposition forces for the gradual replacement or radical reform of existing state institutions. The pacting process may include both implicit and explicit negotiations. There are numerous examples of this type of transition, stretching from Latin America to Eastern Europe to Southeast Asia. Classic examples are Poland's and Hungary's transitions from communism to democracy and the Spanish transition from Francoism.

Contingency in Revolutionary Situations and Transformational Paths

The balance between a transitional versus a revolutionary regime transformation is highly contingent. Reform periods can proceed for years with both transition and revolution remaining viable transformational modalities. Transitions and revolutions have two important points of congruence: (1) the onset of state reforms or decay because of structural crisis or institutional decay (background causes) and (2) regime splits (intermediate causes). As in most transitions to democracy and revolutions from below, revolutions from above begin with reforms that are intended to address a regime's macro-structural crisis, systemic disequilibrium or a less threatening pre-crisis decline in institutional or economic performance.[6] Change in the international environment, foreign threats, values and regime legitimacy, political institutions, or economic organization in one combination or another constitute the structural contradictions that give an impetus toward the reorganization of power.[7]

More often than not, institutional reorganization and reform bring unintended consequences, including fracturing the regime's institutional and political unity. The new mixture of institutions and practices that emerges from abrupt reforms is much more difficult to control than the original therapy that created it.[8] States and their institutions or "organizational configurations, along with their overall patterns of activity, affect political culture, encourage some kinds of group formation and collective political actions (but not others), and make possible the raising of certain political issues (and not others)." These configurations intentionally and unintentionally influence and change political groups' formation, capacities, and ideas and the demands of various sectors of society.[9]

The kinds of unsuccessful institutional reform that devolve into revolutionary and transitional regime changes have been found to produce a regime split. The split of the regime is the most important intermediate cause in a regime's ultimate demise, whether by transition or revolution.[10] The post-structural model of democratic transition holds that, in response to a crisis or a pre-crisis situation, regime soft-liners decide on a policy response, typically beginning with some form of economic or political liberalization program (the extension of civil political liberties and toleration of opposition). This decision provokes a regime split between hard-liners, who want to preserve the status quo, and soft-liners who understand the need to re-establish equilibrium between the regime's performance and the requirements for stability. Once the split has occurred, soft-liners, seeking to strengthen their hand vis-à-vis the hard-liners, endeavor to win allies among moderates in society and the opposition in an attempt to exclude extremists from the political game, whether they be of the regime or opposition. Eventually, soft-liners are confronted with a choice. They can turn the liberalization process back and join hard-liners in re-establishing the *status quo ante*, or they can engage a full democratization of the liberalized authoritarian order, either from above in an imposed transition, or through a negotiated transition. In the latter case, a transition "pact" with moderate elements of the opposition establishes democratic procedures and a consensus about the rules for the contestation and assumption of power.[11] The negotiating of a pact is typically conducted among elites and the leaders of the most powerful factions contending for power.[12] In imposed transitions to democracy, regime soft-liners maintain control over the democratization process and submit to the uncertainty of elections only after a longer period during which they pave the way for themselves and their supporters to make a smooth transfer to the new democratic system with as little damage as possible being done to their vital interests.[13]

However, regime soft-liners, who initially might back an imposed or pacted transition from authoritarian rule, may also defect from the regime if political disunity leads to growing institutional decay, incohesion and incapacity. Opportunists who defect from the regime to the opposition in an attempt to accelerate reforms, to force a negotiated transition to democracy, or even to overthrow the regime, may opt for establishing a power base by taking over or creating one or more state organizations or institutions. The powers, jurisdiction and resources of this structure may already be sufficient or may be enhanced to such a degree that alternative (dual or multiple) sovereignty is established, thereby creating a revolutionary situation. A revolutionary situation is conceptualized with regard to ultimate outcome. It is both potentially revolutionary and transitional. It consists of the institutionalization or organization of dual or multiple sovereignty supporting credible competing claims on the authority to rule over the same territory by an opposition of significant and somewhat comparable strength in human, financial, and institutional resources to those of the ruling regime it seeks to replace.

Even in a revolutionary situation, there are alternative outcomes ranging from authoritarian restoration, to the freezing of within-system reform, to transition, and finally to revolution. Revolutionary transformation to a new regime is contingent on the configuration of constraints on the range of choices available to political actors, particularly the institutional environment and the structure of political strategic action ("intentional" constraints[14]), but also the continuation or deepening of the structural crisis that initially sparked reform. If reform resolves the structural crisis, the regime avoids both transition and revolution. If not, then the coexistence and interaction of the macro-structural crisis and institutional and intentional constraints will sooner or later bring some mode of regime change. (This "interacting constraints theory" of revolution is discussed in more detail below.) If reform produces a relatively balanced regime split, then an imposed transition and the maintenance of, or return to, the authoritarian status quo are unlikely. The regime is simply too weak to impose its will. If a transition cannot be negotiated because of a burdensome configuration of interacting institutional, political (intentional), and macro-structural constraints on the range of choices available to key strategic actors, then the only regime change modes remaining are revolutionary ones. If transition is not possible and the revolutionary situation is built on the opposition's establishment of a credible alternative sovereignty institutionalized autonomously within society, then the revolutionary destruction of the *ancien regime* is likely to come from below, in society. If a moderates' dilemma is combined with a weak society and a weak regime, then the development of either a revolution from below or a transition pact is problematic. If in the ensuing deadlock an alternative sovereignty is institutionalized within one or more state institution by opportunistic bureaucrats and officials defecting from the regime, then the political takeover and revolution are likely to come from above, within the state.

As unintended consequences and various constraints mount—as occurred in the Soviet case—transitions are confounded, and revolutionary paths become more likely. Processes of revolution from above and below as well as a negotiated transition coexisted in the USSR after 1987, and both remained possible outcomes in 1991. Gorbachev's *perestroika* 1.0 began as a modest reform to save, not to destroy, the Soviet regime, but as happens so often with reforms, unintended consequences intervened. Gorbachev decided to continue and radicalize rather than terminate reforms as the unintended consequences mounted. Those consequences interacted increasingly to constrain his options. The enormous institutional, political, economic, and foreign policy difficulties inherent in conducting reforms after a long period of the most totalitarian form of rule compounded those constraints until reform and imposed transitional regime transformation were ultimately confounded. The result was a three-way regime split, intersecting the state and society, and a regime transformational mode of revolution from above. Nascent revolutions—one developing from above inside the state and another from below nascent in the numerous nationalist and/or democratic opposition movements—developed and coexisted for a year or more before revolution from above prevailed. Contingency in regime transformational situations is demonstrated by the fact that Russia's revolution from above went through several pacting episodes and appeared on the verge of a successful transition pact agreement between Soviet President Gorbachev, Russian President Yeltsin, and the leaders of 8 of the 14 Soviet Union republics in August 1991. But hardline communists intervened, undertaking a failed coup and leading to full regime and state collapse.[15]

The Contingency of Democratic Outcome

With the exception of imposed transition, each transformational mode needs a strong opposition movement (democratic under an authoritarian regime), especially in the post-takeover regime/state-building and consolidation stage. Therefore, if a revolution from below is to produce a democratic outcome, a strong, united democratic opposition movement is needed. Otherwise, during the destructive phase, more extremist elements are likely to destroy the old regime through violent means, which historically has not led to democracy in many cases. Radicals also might undermine democracy-building and consolidation in the revolution's constructive phase. Democrats may risk an alliance with radicals (socialist, communist, fascist or others) in order to gather the critical mass to remove the old order, but they do so at the peril of a democratic outcome.

Following revolutions from below, the regime change mode that most needs a strong, united democratic opposition is the "pacted" or negotiated transition. In this case the opposition needs to be strong enough to force a key regime ruling group of soft-liners to negotiate a transition pact outlining the path to, and design of, the aspired democracy. An alliance of strong, united democratic forces and pro-democracy elements within the regime groups with whom they negotiate ensures a strong democratic core that can isolate both regime and opposition radicals during the transition process of state and/or constitutional design and defeat them in successive elections needed to consolidate the institutions, culture and habits of democracy.

Revolutions from above, being largely state-based in both the destructive and constructive phases of the regime transformation, require less societal mobilization than revolutions from below and pacted transitions. Nevertheless, a significant opposition movement with a substantial democratic component is needed on occasion as an ally for pressuring the regime hard-liners to abstain from reactionary actions to combat the efforts by the softline revolutionaries from above to dismantle the old order and bring in the new. The threat of revolution can be held out to intimidate potential putschists seeking to restore the old system. After the seizure of power, the revolutionaries above are likely to try to demobilize the societal opposition in the nascent revolution from below with which they had allied during the destructive phase in coming to power. The revolutionaries above might also co-opt former hard-line or fence-sitting regime elements in order to shore up their power base and obviate the need for support from the societal and democratic revolutionaries. In this way, they are likely to quash the prospects for democratization in the short to mid-term at the least. This is why a more robust united democratic opposition is more requisite for a democratic outcome in revolutions from above than in imposed transitions.[16]

All four types of regime transformation need a strong democratic movement after the old regime has been removed. Thus, it is more the absence of a united and strong democratic movement since the mid–1990s than the authoritarian nature of President Vladimir Putin and his inner circle that has plagued Russia's democratic development in recent years. Indeed, when mass opposition demonstrations emerged in December 2011 after many regarded the results of the Duma elections to be fraudulent, the Kremlin immediately offered a series of far-reaching reforms.[17]

Democracy Promotion and the Dangers of Revolutionism

Despite the contingency and unpredictability of regime transformational processes, a kind of "revolutionism"—an almost blind faith in the positive, democratizing nature of revolutions—infused the American foreign policy community after the fall of communism. We Americans have a distinctively different historical experience with revolution and its outcome than that of most other peoples. Our revolution wrought successful democratic, capitalist, and state-building experiments, with rather limited intra-statal bloodshed compared with other revolutions from below. American revolutionism is shared through the French experience by Europe. The French model's guillotines and dictatorial Directory should strike a note of caution in American hearts regarding the universality of the revolution as a value.

Democracy promotion poses the danger of wittingly or unwittingly fomenting revolution and violence. No matter how peaceful and seemingly justified they are intended or seem to be, revolutions increase the likelihood of violence and state collapse precip-itously. The tactic of clandestinely supporting opposition groups, instigating crises and colored revolutions, is based on the faulty assumption that democratization at the fastest pace possible—writ large in democratic color revolutionism—is the best solution to all problems, in all places, at all times. It is an especially risky proposition to support the massing of thousands on the central squares of national capitals where the regimes that rule are by definition, and in the democracy-promoters' own views, undemocratic or not sufficiently democratic, and thus often irresponsible, even dismissive as regards human life. The Washington DP consensus constantly reminds us that "dictatorial regimes" are more likely to use force. The use of force under such circumstances can be reciprocated multiply, escalating to civil war. The spark—a push, a punch, a knife cut or gunshot—can be ignited by any one of the thousands assembled. Demonstrations convened in a heated political atmosphere of electoral politics and high levels of distrust or in a revo-lutionary situation are prone to violent turns. This is true regardless of the many lectures and lessons on methods of civil disobedience organized by Western NGOs under their democracy promotion efforts. Thus, revolutionism and revolution, democratic or oth-erwise, as political values drive a dangerous paradigm that deprives DP of proper caution and mechanisms for preventing violence.

The demise of communism—America's arch-enemy in the Cold War—often by way of revolution reinforced American revolutionism. That several communist regimes—those in Czechoslavakia and Hungary, for instance—fell not as a result of violent or peaceful revolution, but rather through a pacted transition, has not been sufficiently reflected in our hagiography of communism's demise.

Revolutions and State Collapse

From statues of Dzerzhinskii to Saddam Hussein, as in 1989 Central and Eastern Europe and in 1991 Moscow, so too in Iraq and Egypt, the toppling of the *ancien regime*'s idols became an icon of U.S. and Western media reporting in the post–Cold War era. These topplings are a metaphor for the contingency that regime changers refuse to acknowledge. They are a revolutionary image underscoring lawlessness, anarchy, and unconstitutionality. Where the statues and regimes once stood, there are left only empty spaces and vacuums of power that need to be filled. No one can guarantee who will fill such voids. Once the political game moves outside legality and constitutionality, all bets are off; anything can happen. If the first casualty of war is the truth, then the first casualty of revolution is legality.

The risk of violence is magnified when revolutionary situations arise in states with multi-communal (multiethnic and/or multi-confessional) populations, ethno-national administrative-territorial subdivisions, and sovereignty or separatist issues. This is par-ticularly problematic for the territorial integrity of multicommunal states like Ukraine. When such states undergo revolutionary forms of regime transformation, they are highly vulnerable to break up. Revolutions often consume not just the old regime but the country and people over which it ruled. As the ideological and administrative centers implode, politics polarize and institutions dissolve into hyper-dysfunction and the breakup of the state. Therefore, if the first casualty of revolution is legality, then in multi-national states the second is "stateness": weakness of state institutions and integrity results. Intensifica-tion of inter-communal conflict often leads to destabilization of the state's territorial integrity, even failing or failed/collapsed states which can end in communalist (interethnic and/or inter-confessional) wars and separatism. The breakdown of institutionalized politics and revolutionary dual/multiple power in the metropole or central capital often sparks separatism in minority-dominated regions. Imposed and negotiated transitions under the full or partial control of the old elite, respectively, are able to weather the storm against stateness leveled by revolution and to maintain territorial integrity.

For example, in the 1990–91 Russian revolution from above, Yeltsin weakened thoroughly the USSR's Communist Party and state apparati. Gorbachev had begun to separate the two apparati as he semi-democratized the country in 1989–1990, and the Soviet Union saw a series of separatist movements and inter-ethnic conflicts emerge. But it was Yeltsin's efforts to fully separate the Party from the state inside the Russian Federation and support politically some of the separatist movements in the 14 union republics before and after his frontal attack on the Union state during and after the failed August 1991 coup, that led to the fall of the Soviet regime and state. The implosion in Moscow, and the death blow it dealt to Gorbachev's attempt to negotiate a transition to democracy and a new federative, truncated version of the USSR caused by the failed coup, sparked full collapse of the USSR along the administrative-territorial borders of the 14 ethno-national union republics and Russia. The process did not stop there. Six autonomous republics broke away from several of the former union republics, now independent "post–Soviet" states: Abkhaziya, Ajariya, and South Ossetiya from Georgia; Nagorno-Karabakh from Azerbajan; Transdniestr from Moldova; and the Chechen half of Checheno-Ingushetiya from Russia. Outside the USSR, similar outcomes—state collapse—occurred in communist Czeckoslovakia in 1989 and in communist Yugoslavia in the 1990s.[18] A seemingly contrary dynamic in revolutionary modes of regime transformation is rare: reunification rather than dissolution. A prominent example is Germany's reunification after the 1989 peaceful revolution from below in East Germany.[19]

State collapse during revolutionary breakdowns is most often the result of the breakdown of administration and institutionalized politics and the emergence of revolutionary dual power in the central capital first and in the periphery later. These processes in turn are prone to spark separatism in minority-dominated regions. The pivotal role of revolutionary, as opposed to transitional modes of regime transformation in state breakups is demonstrated by the contrasting results of two late Soviet-era referenda on maintaining the Soviet Union. The first asked voters to approve or disapprove preservation of the Soviet Union on the basis of a new Union Treaty—the imminent signing of which sparked the August 1991 coup. The draft treaty included constitutional changes for a transition to democracy—a transition pact—rather than consummation of Yeltsin's revolution from above. This first referendum was held in March 1991—before the August coup and the cascading state collapse through that autumn's second round of negotiations on the Union Treaty—and 71.48 percent of Ukrainians voted in favor of preserving the Union. The second referendum was held in December—after the failed August coup and the consummation of Yeltsin's revolution from above through autumn—and 90.3 percent of Ukrainians voted against Ukraine's remaining in the Union and for Ukrainian independence, including 54 percent in Crimea and 57 percent in Sevastopol.

Ironically, Ukraine—which put the last nail in the coffin of the USSR in December 1991—would suffer a similar fate as a consequence of its own post–Soviet revolutionary upheavals, with Crimea and Sevastopol leading the way back to Russia. By the second decade of the 21st century, those encouraging regime change in places like Ukraine should have been aware of the grave risk that revolution can end in separatism and civil war, given the record of the Soviet and communist demise.

History's Revenge–Communalist Revival in the Post-Soviet Space

Ultranationalism's and irredentism's rise across much of the post–Soviet region is the revenge of history, a reaction to seven decades of Soviet attempts to negate nations and national identity. It would find perhaps its ultimate crisis in Ukraine. Although nationalism was not the main cause of the Soviet collapse, it played no small role. Opposing forces fighting for power in Moscow sought to use nationalist aspirations for sovereignty within, and sometimes outright independence from, the USSR to weaken their competitors and win allies in the periphery. Nationalism reared its head early in the *perestroika* era. Moderates among nationalists made justifiable claims; radicals were more ambitious. One of the first political demonstrations came in 1986 when a group of Crimean Tatars demonstrated on Red Square for their people's "rehabilitation" from the "charges" that Stalin used as a pretext to deport them from the peninsula in 1944. Ironically and perhaps significantly, rehabilitation was only granted by Russian President Vladimir Putin in an effort to assuage the Tatars' dissatisfaction with his reunification of Crimea with Russia during the Ukrainian crisis.

Since the collapse of communism in Eastern Europe and the Soviet Union, the post–Soviet region has seen an almost continuous series of wars driven by revivalist nationalism, ultranationalism, even neofascism. The present Ukrainian crisis and slow-burning Russian-Ukrainian civil war are part and parcel of this pulling of the post–Soviet thread. By 1992 the revival of national identity and an accompanying rise in ultranationalism during the USSR's last years had brought war to all three of the former Soviet "union republics" in the South Caucasus—Armenia, Azerbaijan, and Georgia. Azerbaijan and Armenia went to war over the Nagorno-Karabakh autonomous republic, an Armenian-dominated enclave entirely embedded within neighboring Azerbaijan. Azeri anti–Armenian pogroms in Sumgait in 1988 and in Azerbaijan's capital of Baku in 1990 preceded the 1992–94 war. A resulting cold war or hot truce is frequently punctuated by sometimes fatal cross-border skirmishes and shootings. Negotiations long ago stalled, and renewal of the war remains a real option for both sides.

In Georgia, the political ascension of ultranationalist Zviad Gamsakhurdia from 1988 to his death in 1992 brought a series of additional interethnic clashes and ultimately small wars to the region. Gamsakhurdia and his allies used crude racist rhetoric against Georgia's ethnic minorities, created armed militias to intimidate and attack them, and stripped their eponymous oblasts (regions or provinces)—Abkhaziya, Ajariya, and South Ossetiya—of their autonomous status at a time when Georgia was seeking independence from Moscow. Running on an ultranationalist platform ("Georgia for the Georgians"), Gamsakhurdia and his party won the Georgian presidency with 86 percent of the vote in 1991 and a majority in parliament in 1990, with most Ossetiyans, Abkhazians and Ajarians boycotting the elections. Gamsakhurdia's dictatorial tendencies soon alienated his supporters, and he was run out of Tbilisi and killed in 1992. By then Georgian-Abkhaz tensions were too high, and Gamsakhurdia's successor, former Soviet Foreign Minister Eduard Shevardnadze, reneged on a late agreement between Gamsakhurdia and the Abkhaz in which a new Abkhaz parliament with a majority of seats set aside for ethnic

Abkhazians would be elected, sparking the 1992–93 Georgian-Abkhaz war. It left 10,000 dead and 20,000 wounded.

A smaller, very brief war or set of skirmishes with South Ossetiya left nearly 1,000 killed and some 2,000 wounded. By the mid–1990s, all three Georgian autonomies became *de facto* independent and remained so until 2005, when Ajariya was brought back under Georgian control. Abkhaziya and South Ossetiya strengthened their *de facto* independence in the wake of yet another Georgian conflict—the August 2008 South Ossetiyan war. Georgia lost the war, which was caused by democratic nationalist Georgian President Mikheil Saakashvili's attempts to revive Gamsakhurdia's ultranationalism in moderate form and seize South Ossetiya by force. Russia and a handful of other states recognized Abkhazia's and South Ossetiya's state independence. Other nationalist post–Soviet wars include the 1992 Ingushetiyan-North Ossetiyan and Moldovan-Transdniestr wars.

Religious communalism has combined with ethno-nationalism at times to fuel post–Soviet conflicts. Religious difference was a second driver behind ethnic difference in the conflicts between Orthodox Christian Georgia and the largely Muslim Abkhaz and between the Orthodox Christian Ossetiyans and Muslim Ingush. A better case in point is the 1992–1997 Tajikistan civil war. The revolutionary coalition, the United Tajik Opposition, included not only Tajik national and democratic elements but also Islamic, even Islamist elements, in the form of the Islamic Rebirth Party (IRP). Some, especially Uzbek IRP members like Juma Namagani and Tadir Uldashev, shifted to outright jihadism and terrorism. They founded the radical Islamic Movement of Uzbekistan, which left for Afghanistan after the Tajik war and carried out numerous terrorist attacks in Uzbekistan, Tajikistan, and Kyrgyzstan, as well as in the AfPak area. IMU splinter groups and emulators have carried out terrorist attacks since then in these republics and Kazakhstan.

In many contexts, Islamism and its violent brother jihadism function as surrogates for ultranationalism. In some, the former evolve from the latter, as was the case in post–Soviet Russia's two Chechen wars. The radical Chechen separatist movement emerged in the early 1990s, declaring independence from Russia for the "Chechen Republic of Ichkeriya" (ChRI) in 1991. By 1997, during the inter-war period, Al Qa'ida-tied Arabs from Afghanistan and elsewhere had infiltrated the ChRI and established training and indoctrination camps in Chechnya. In July 1999 their local and foreign forces led an invasion of Dagestan, kicking off the second post–Soviet Chechen war. The defeat of the ChRI on the traditional battlefield strengthened the hand of the AQ jihadists and an increasing number of local ones from across the North Caucasus. They came to dominate the ChRI by late 2002. In October 2007 the fully global jihadist-oriented "Caucasus Emirate" was declared; it continues to function to this day, despite hundreds of its mujahedin leaving to fight in Syria, Iraq and elsewhere under the banners of AQ, the Islamic State and other groups.[20]

The post–Soviet communalist wars alone have come at high cost. A general estimate of the number of killed and wounded in the post–Soviet nationalist and sometimes religious wars (the second Chechen war, in part, and the Caucasus Emirate) is more than half a million casualties—196,000 killed and 376,000 wounded—in addition to millions of displaced refugees (see Table 1). Thousands more casualties have occurred as a result of various inter-ethnic riots and pogroms—such as those victimizing Uzbeks in Kyrgyzstan, Armenians, Azeris, Meskhetiyan Turks, and others in the late USSR and post–Soviet space.

Table 1. Post-Soviet Wars and Attendant Casualty Figures, 1990–2013

War	Killed	Wounded
Armenian-Azeri Nagorno-Karabakh War	15,000	25,000
Georgian-Abkhaz War	10,000	20,000
Tajikistan Civil War	65,000	120,000
Georgia-South Ossetiya War 1992–93	1,000	2,000
Ingushetia-North Ossetia War	500	800
Moldovan-Transdniestr War	1,000	2,000
First Chechen-Russian War	50,000	100,000
Second Chechen-Russian War	50,000	100,000
Caucasus Emirate Insurgency	3,500	6,000
Georgian-South Ossetia War, August 2008	400	1,000

The post–Cold War communalist revival is also occurring outside both the post–Soviet space and ethno-nationalist framework.[21] But this, especially its occurrence in the developed West, only underscores the risks of fomenting political instability. Rather than recognizing the dangers of revolution and encouraging reform and transitional regime change, the U.S. and the West opted to deploy the dual-use technology of democracy promotion, mobilizing oppositions and accepting the possibility of a revolutionary regime change.

The Color Revolutions

Increasingly, "dual-use" DP political technologies came to produce not transitions but potential and kinetic messy "color revolutions" closer and closer to Moscow's doorstep. The West, in particular the U.S. under programs and funding of the Agency for International Development (USAID), funded—sometimes intentionally, sometimes not—revolutionary elements. The USAID has a long record of regime-change promotion going back to the Cold War, which casts a long shadow of doubt over its claims of humanitarian assistance and supporting DP and economic development. Ironically, USAID was active in helping authoritarian regimes in Latin America and Southeast Asia from falling victim to revolutions organized by communists funded in Moscow. USAID funded the CIA's Office of Public Safety (OPS), which was shut down in 1974 after evidence emerged in congressional hearings that it was involved in teaching torture techniques in its police, military, and intelligence training programs.

As the new Ukrainian regime began its "anti-terrorist" operation against the anti–Maidan, pro-autonomy and pro-independence movement in the Donbass in April 2014, revelations emerged that in 2010 USAID was carrying out clandestine operations that were explicitly pursuing regime change in Cuba. USAID financed and ran a clandestine effort to set up "ZunZuneo," a Cuban Twitter social media project, involving a messaging network that could reach hundreds of thousands of Cubans, aimed at undermining Cuba's communist government.[22] The ZunZuneo project demonstrates that during the color revolution era, USAID was involved in explicit regime change operations and used tactics that would be repeated in Ukraine. Therefore, USAID's DP techonology might have been less ambiguous and "dual-use," and more clandestine regime-change oriented, in the post–Soviet color revolutions, including in Ukraine. We do know that Facebook, Twitter and other social networking and messaging systems were ubiquitous in Tunisia in 2010, Egypt in 2011 and Kiev in 2013–14, and that they received USAID funding.

Some of the color revolutionary elements funded by USAID and its conduit organizations across the globe were initially, or at least during the revolution would become, allied with radicals, including communalist elements, whether ultranationalists in Tbilisi, neofascists in Ukraine, or Islamists in Afghanistan, Egypt, and Syria. As color revolutions spread eastward, across Eurasia, first in Belgrade, then Tbilisi, Bishkek and Kiev, Moscow became more concerned. There was a growing sense and eventually clear evidence that Washington and Brussels were encouraging regime transformation, if not revolution itself.

Serbia's Otpor: The First Post-Communist "Color Revolution"

The first color revolution came in Serbia, Russia's traditional Slavic ally. Serbian president Slobodan Milosevic had been weakened politically by the economic costs of the Yugoslav wars and his failure—in the face of NATO bombings and Western sanctions—to preserve control over the cradle of Serbian culture known to Serbs as Metokhiya, but transformed into Albanian-populated "Kosovo" under the communist regime of Josif Tito. The October 2000 revolution that overthrew Milosevic was led by the Democratic Opposition of Serbia (DOS). DOS was led and largely created by the pro-democracy organization "Otpor," which received substantial financial and practical assistance through DP programs run by USAID and "private" institutions funded by USAID and other U.S. government agencies, such as the National Endowment for Democracy (NED), the U.S. Democratic Party's National Democratic Institute (NDI), and the U.S. Republican Party's International Republican Institute (IRI).[23]

American officials made no bones about wishing to help democratic forces to overthrow Milosevic. The prospects for, and the $100 million devoted to, this goal were discussed openly by administration officials and U.S. senators, including then Senator Joseph Biden, at a U.S. Senate hearing on July 29, 1999.[24] DOS received more than $30 million to "purchase cell phones and computers" for its leadership, "recruit and train an army of 20,000 election monitors," and fashion "a sophisticated marketing campaign with posters, badges and T-shirts."[25] USAID Assistant Administrator Donald L. Pressley admitted that several hundred thousand dollars went to Otpor directly for similar purposes. The IRI's Daniel Calingaert acknowledged that his institute gave an unspecified portion of $1.8 million to Otpor and that he met with its representatives seven to ten times beginning in October 1999.[26] The IRI also organized seminars for Otpor members on how to organize nonviolent resistance and strikes, communicate with symbols, overcome fear, and undermine the authority of a dictatorial regime.[27] The seminars were taught by retired U.S. Army Colonel Robert Helvey, who introduced Otpor to the nonviolent revolutionology of the radical American academic Gene Sharp, author of *From Dictatorship to Democracy* (a book published in 1993 in Thailand, originally for Burmese dissidents).[28]

U.S.–funded consultants played a crucial role behind the scenes in virtually every facet of Otpor's actions by running tracking polls, training thousands of opposition activists, and helping to organize a politically pivotal parallel vote count. U.S. taxpayers paid for 5,000 cans of spray paint used by Otpor activists to inscribe anti–Milosevic graffiti on walls across Serbia and for 2.5 million stickers with the words "He's Finished," which became the revolution's slogan.[29] Serbia continues to claim it does not aspire to NATO membership; NATO's bombing in 1999 is still fresh in the memory. However, an

EU-Serbian Stabilization and Association Agreement entered into force in 2013, and Belgrade agreed in January 2015 to develop cooperation with NATO through an Individual Partnership Action Plan.

All of the information presented above on the U.S. government's sponsorship of the Otpor revolution was published in Western open sources, most of it in the first year of Vladimir Putin's first presidential term. Some was published in the first year of his second term. In between, a color revolution would occur for the first time in a country on Russia's border.

Georgia's Rose "Revolution" and NATO's Georgian Gambit

Georgia's so-called "Rose Revolution" of 2003 was really not a revolution. It did not involve a fundamental transformation of regime type from authoritarianism or totalitarianism to democracy (or vice versa). Rather, it was an intra-elite revolt in which one portion of the elite was able to overpower another with limited popular mobilization independent of elite agitation and little to no use of violence, institutional destruction or replacement, or change of elites. Under former Soviet Politburo member and *perestroika*-era Soviet foreign minister Eduard Shevardnadze, Georgia had been a weak, unconsolidated democracy. But the Shevardnadze regime was more democratic than authoritarian, with freedom of speech, information, and assembly, and usually more-or-less free and fair if corrupt elections. Corruption was massive across all spheres of life and showed itself in robust fashion in the 2003 election vote counting, helping to spark the Rose revolt. But the fuel for the revolt came from Belgrade.

In the wake of Milosevic's overthrow, the Serbian capital had become home to the Center for Applied NonViolent Action and Strategies (CANVAS), which lent a helping hand and, some would say, inspired and organized the Rose "revolution." Run by Otpor members and other young Serbs whose formative political experience was the student uprising against Milosevic, CANVAS adapted its methodology for application in over 50 countries, including color revolutions, it acknowledged, against "some of the worst governments in the world … in Georgia, Ukraine, Syria-occupied Lebanon, the Maldives, and … Egypt."[30] CANVAS's strategy consists of four pillars: (1) overcome citizens' passivity, fatalism, and fear in countries lacking a history of effective opposition; (2) nonviolent struggle; (3) winning over young people and the middle class to the opposition; and (4) at least neutralizing if not converting the security forces. Amassing large concentrations of people in marches and demonstration is not necessary at the outset and should be reserved for when the opposition has won majority support.[31] Agitation and propaganda should precede large actions and make use of leaflets, banners, sit-ins, boycotts, picketing, music, and even funerals.[32] Although CANVAS/Otpor activists "cannot carry revolution in their suitcases," their strategies "can greatly increase the chance that when there is a moment that shakes a dictatorship, the opposition will be able to take advantage of it," as one favorable journalistic review of the group notes.[33] CANVAS itself acknowledges all this openly, but claims that it relies solely on private funding. But nowhere on its Web site does it indicate the specific private sources of its funding, eschewing the very transparency its DP teachings demand of "the worst governments."[34]

Within months of Milosevic's demise, Otpor began to get feelers from democracy activists in other countries. Slobodan Djinovic, one of Otpor's founders, soon began traveling to Belarus, meeting secretly with a student movement that was quickly infiltrated by police and collapsed. In 2002, Djinovic and other former Otpor leaders began visiting Tbilisi and hosting in Serbia members of a then obscure Georgian movement "Kmara" ("Enough!").[35] Djinovic later told the BBC he had been working with Kmara in Tbilisi in the months before the Rose revolt. In spring 2003, Kmara activists, on funds provided by George Soros's Open Society Foundation (OSF), visited Otpor, by now rebranded as CANVAS. Kaha Lomaia, director of Georgia's OSF branch at the time, says Kmara played a crucial role in the Rose revolt and that Georgia's OSF gave an unidentified portion of $350,000 election support funding to Kmara. According to the BBC, the U.S. invested nearly $2.4 million in Georgia's election system, but Mr. Lomaia insists no U.S. money was spent on Kmara.[36] Thus, modeling itself on Otpor and schooled by its USAID/CANVAS adepts Helvey and Sharp, Kmara spread Otpor's tactics and networked together a multi-party opposition movement. It began the original demonstration protesting alleged fraud in the parliamentary elections, and thousands rallied to its side. Eventually, Mikheil Saakashvili, Nino Burjanadze and several other Georgian party leaders led a Kmara-generated crowd, storming and occupying parliament and overthrowing Shevardnadze in the November 2003 Rose "revolution."[37]

Like most subsequent color revolutions in the post–Soviet space—including Kiev's "Orange Revolution," Kyrgyzstan's 2005 "Tulip Revolution," and 2010 "anti–Tulip Revolution"—the Rose "revolution" was not a society-led revolution from below. Rather, it was an internal elite affair involving a struggle for power among competing governmental factions. CANVAS's "people power" was used by various factions in these color "revolutions" to seize power, after which they tended to demobilize the societal opposition and isolate the activists. Therefore, Tbilisi's Rose revolt resulted in little to no major overturn in Georgia's social, economic or political institutions. In January 2004 the anti–Russian democratic nationalist Saakashvili won the presidential election with a curiously high 96 percent of the votes. Although Saakashvili pushed through some reforms, the only real successes came in the economy and against police corruption. Overall corruption remained rampant. As opposition grew, the regime became aggressive and sometimes violent in dealing with demonstrations. At the same time, the Rose regime's leaders, especially Saakashvili, were intensely anti–Russian and nationalistic, harking back to the quasi-fascism of the late Zviad Gamsakhurdia, whose reputation Saakashvili sought to rehabilitate.

A writer and professor of linguistics, Gamsakhurdia rose to power on the wave of anti–Soviet nationalism that swept through Georgia and much of the USSR during Gorbachev's *perestroika*. In 1990, Georgia declared its independence and elected the ultra-nationalist Gamsakhurdia as president. One of his first acts was to repeal South Ossetiya's and Abkhaziya's status as autonomous republics. South Ossetiya (SO) is mountainous, like much of the Caucasus, with a small population of some 60,000. The majority is ethnic Ossetiyan, speaks a Farsi-related language, and is overwhelmingly Orthodox Christian, like Russians and Georgians. About a quarter of the population was ethnic Georgian, and about 10 percent were Russian. SO lies across the Russian border from North Ossetiya (NO), and during *perestroika* some Ossetiyans in both republics began to support an independent united Ossetiya. Others have supported a united Ossetiya that is a constituent member of the Russian Federation. Very few supported Georgian rule, fearing SO would increasingly be populated by ethnic Georgians, and thus begin to encourage NO's separation from Russia.

In 1989, ethnic Georgians began to direct violence against Ossetiyans and other ethnic minorities like the Abkhaziyans, as both groups began to demand return of their autonomous status. The Georgian violence was encouraged by Gamsakhurdia, who backed the formation of violent ultranationalist paramilitary groups such as Tengiz Kitovani's National Guard and Jaba Ioselani's notorious *Mkhedrioni* (The Horsemen), who attacked minorities and made violent raids into the autonomous republics. The violence forced the Soviet leadership to deploy troops to the region to stop the bloodletting. In April 1989 Soviet troops cracked down on a Georgian demonstration in the capitol of Tbilisi, killing 16 and wounding more than a hundred more. This intensified Georgian nationalism, and ethnic violence continued. Gamsakhurdia, his ministers, and Mkhedrioni militias unleashed a wave of oppression, violence and calls for genocide against the Ossetiyans, Abkhaziyans, and Ajariyans.[38]

By 1991 South Ossetiya's leaders announced plans to secede from Georgia and become like Georgia, a Soviet Socialist Republic (SSR), perhaps to be united with the Russia's NO in Gorbachev's would-be revamped Union of SSRs under his proposed Union Treaty. In response, Gamsakhurdia sent police units into SO's capitol of Tskhinvali, and they ransacked the city. Ossetiyans responded by firing on Georgian villages, and Ossetiyans in other Georgian cities were driven out of their homes either in panic or because of intimidation by Georgian militia. SO's demand for independence became non-negotiable. With the collapse of the USSR, President Gamsakhurdia sent Georgian troops into Abkhaziya, which also had declared its independence. Calls for genocide against the Abkhaz by top Georgian officials intermeshed with the Georgian commanding officers' declarations that prisoners would not be taken.[39] In an April 1993 interview with *Le Monde Diplomatique*, Georgian Minister of War Georgi Khaindrava warned that Georgian forces "can easily and completely destroy the genetic stock" of the Abkhaz nation.[40] When Georgian forces invaded Abkhaziya, they destroyed the Abkhaz National Library in Sukhumi, which held much of the documentary record of Abkhaziyans' history and that of the region's ancient Greek communities.[41]

The West had a very benign view of Gamsakhurdia's ultranationalism, and as usual it was defined by the chimera of a Jeffersonian democrat. In its June 1991 issue, *The Economist* cast Gamsakhurdia in mixed but at times glowing terms: "[I]n the case of Zviad Gamsakhurdia, just elected president of the southern republic of Georgia, joy is not unalloyed. Mr Gamsakhurdia has all the credentials to be a Soviet Vaclav Havel. A brave and uncompromising anti-communist, he spent years in jail. He is chairman of the Georgian branch of Helsinki Watch, which is committed to the defence of human rights."[42] It would also have an all too simplified view of Saakashvili.

Gamsakhurdia's invasion of Abkhaziya in 1992 was not repeated in South Ossetiya, though skirmishes and violence frequently broke out. Gamsakhurdia was ultimately rejected in 1992 by the Georgians themselves, overthrown in a coup, and hunted down and killed, bringing Shevardnadze back to stabilize the increasingly failing state. After the 1992–1994 Abkhaz war, Abkhaziya under Russia's protection became a *de facto* independent state—a breakaway republic—in a so-called "frozen conflict." Russia, Georgia, and the Ossetiyans established a joint peacekeeping force under the auspices of the Commonwealth of Independent States (CIS). Conflict between Tbilisi, on the one hand, and Tskhinvali and Sukhumi, on the other, remained frozen, but negotiations repeatedly failed. Occasional sniper, machine gun and artillery exchanges occurred on and off for over a decade.

Matters changed after the Rose Revolution's overthrow of Shevardnadze. During his presidential campaign, Saakashvili vowed to reintegrate the breakaway republics with Georgia by any means and began to rehabilitate the image of Gamsakhurdia. Shevard- nadze had let the frozen conflicts remain frozen and attempted to return the breakaway republics through negotiations, which invariably went nowhere. Saakashvili targeted breakaway and *de facto* independent Abkhaziya and Ajariya with coups in 2003 and 2004, respectively. The latter succeeded, bringing Ajariya back into the Georgian fold. Simul- taneously, exchanges of fire between Georgian and SO forces became more frequent. Saakashvili's often heated rhetoric and failure to reject the use of force, as well as repeated provocations by Ossetiyans and Russians, raised tensions precipitously. In May 2004 Tbilisi refused to recognise parliamentary elections held in SO. Three months later, clashes erupted between Georgian and South Ossetiyan soldiers along the cease-fire line.

In 2005, Saakashvili ordered his Defense Ministry to draw up plans for an invasion of Abkhaziya and South Ossetiya, according to his former defense minister, Irakli Okru- ashvili.[43] This might explain Saakashvili's repeated refusal in the context of the ongoing conflict resolution talks to sign a "no use of force" agreement proposed by Russia, SO and Abkhazia, committing the parties to resolve the "frozen conflict" only by political means. Also, South Ossetiya rejected a Georgian offer of autonomy within Georgia. In January 2006, Saakashvili, offering no evidence, accused Moscow of setting off an explo- sion on the main Russian Gazprom pipeline transporting natural gas to Georgia. He then accepted gas supply from Iran to replace Russian supply, despite a U.S.–led international embargo against energy purchases from Tehran. A month later, Georgia's parliament voted unanimously for international peacekeepers to replace Russian peacekeeping forces in SO. In response, SO and Abkhaziya signed a mutual defense agreement in the event of a Georgian military démarche, and in November SO held a referendum reaffirming its 1992 referendum asserting its independence from Georgia. The West rejected the legality of the vote, but Russia called for respecting its results. Moscow then began to issue Russian passports to the breakaway republics' residents in order to provide social welfare to their population after Saakashvili cut off all welfare, pension and other public programs to residents of the breakaway republics. Thus, on the eve of stepped-up efforts to bring Georgia into NATO discussed below, relations between Georgia and its two remaining breakaway regions had been completely severed. As a result, they turned to Russia both for national and social security, transforming these disputes even more than they had been into Russian-Georgian disputes on the international level as much as they were Ossetiyan-Georgian or Abkhaziyan-Georgian conflicts on the intra-state level.

Georgia's relations with NATO at the Cold War's end began as it did for the other post–Soviet states, including Russia. It joined the North Atlantic Cooperation Council in 1992 and the Partnership for Peace Program (PPP) in 1994. After the "Rose Revolution," however, dialogue and cooperation deepened, signaling Washington's, Brussels,' and Tbil- isi's intent that Georgia join NATO. As a result, NATO and the American military became deeply involved with Saakashvili's military and national security structures.

In 2004 the U.S. military instituted a series of military assistance programs for the Georgian army for 2004–2005 to build on the $64 million Georgian Train and Equip Program (GTEP) offered by the U.S. government to Georgia in order to create and train four 600-man light infantry battalions and one mechanized armor company. The GTEP, which lasted from October 2002 to April 2004, was ostensibly designed to deal with the presence of Chechen Republic of Ichkeriya terrorists hiding out in Georgia's

Pankisi Gorge.[44] The follow-up programs maintained support to the GTEP graduate infantry units and would assist the Georgian Defense Ministry with the reforms and the reorganization necessary to institutionalize U.S. and Western military standards—in other words, to prepare the Georgian military for Georgia's entry into NATO. The American military assistance also provided equipment and advanced training for the GTEP-trained troops and for their officers, and established, trained and equipped new support units within the Georgian army's 11th Brigade. In 2005 the U.S. carried out several programs with the Georgian Defense Ministry, including the Foreign Military Financing Program (FMFP), the International Military Education and Training Program (IMETP), and the Joint Contact Team Program (JCTP), as well as other programs funded by the U.S. Departments of Defense and State. The IMETP provided professional military courses and training in the United States and other overseas facilities to hundreds of Georgian military and civilian defense personnel. The FMFP funded a program in which U.S. military consultants worked out of offices located at the Ministry of Defense, General Staff and 11th Brigade.

In August 2004, the U.S. officer in charge of implementing all of these programs explained their ultimate goal: "These military experts work to restructure and reform the Ministry of Defense and General Staff, as well as implement NATO compatible structures, systems and doctrine, since Georgia is considered one of the real candidates for joining NATO." Just nine months after the Rose revolution, U.S. military officers were already publicly touting the goal of Georgia's membership in NATO and carrying out multimillion-dollar programs to ensure that it happened.[45] This tight Georgian-American military relationship cemented the political relationship, with both deepening throughout the mid–2000s.

Domestically, lost in all the talk of "Georgian democracy" and Saakashvili as "the beacon of democracy in the former USSR" was Saakashvili's increasingly authoritarian bent: banning of opposition demonstrations, less than free and fair presidential and parliamentary elections in 2007 and 2008 (according to OSCE reports), acquisition of presidential power to appoint the capital's mayor and regional governors, closing down an opposition television station, and the mysterious death of its owner and leading opposition figure Badri Patsarkhashishvili, among other developments. Aside from police and anti-corruption reforms, Saakashvili's regime was beginning to look like Putin's, who was roundly condemned in the West for similar developments, but who was allowing or supporting Medvedev's increasingly liberalized approach to governance at the time. By the eve of Saakashvili's invasion of SO, his legitimacy had waned considerably and was declining further; the beacon of democracy was dimming rapidly.

Both the January 2008 presidential and May 2008 parliamentary elections were badly marred by election irregularities, including faulty vote counting, falsification, intimidation, and vote buying. Reports by the pro-democracy, anti–Putin Russian newspaper *Novaya gazeta* on the corruption in both elections were ignored by Western governments and media.[46] An OSCE report on the parliamentary election stated that 22 percent of its monitors characterized the vote counting process as bad or very bad.[47] A report on the presidential election assessed it was "in essence consistent with most OSCE and Council of Europe commitments and standards," but also revealed "significant challenges which need to be addressed urgently."[48] Nevertheless, President Saakashvili was barely re-elected in the first round with only 53.7 percent of the vote; this compared with 96 percent in 2004. Moreover, he responded to the opposition's demonstrations and refusal to recognize the results of the earlier election with a temporary ban on demonstrations and the closing of mass media outlets. Shevardnadze's administration had never engaged in efforts to limit democracy; the image created by the nomenclature of the "Rose Revolution" had wilted away.

Fourteen months later, NATO'S Bucharest Summit resolved that both Georgia and Ukraine would become NATO members at some point in the future. The U.S. and NATO were enticing Tbilisi into NATO against Russia's wishes and training the Georgian army under circumstances in which Georgia had a grave sovereignty dispute with peoples who were seeking independence for homelands that straddled the Russo-Georgian border, and whom Moscow had undertaken to protect from Georgia's "little imperialism." The West was becoming party to this country's complicated post–Soviet national-territorial conflict, without understanding it or being prepared to use force to protect Georgia in the event a conflict with Russia and its Ossetiyan and Abkhaz allies broke out. Meanwhile, Saakashvili perceived a different message from Western actions: the U.S. and NATO were behind him and just might intervene to protect Georgia in any confrontation he could portray as, or make, grave enough. U.S. Secretary of State Condoleezza Rice claims to have warned the "impulsive," "capricious," and "emotional" Saakashvili against "letting the Russians provoke him."[49] This was too little, too late.

SAAKASHVILI'S WAR

Contrary to the claims of Saakashvili, Washington and Brussels, it was not Russia that initiated the August 2008 Georgian-Ossetiyan war, but rather the "impulsive, capricious, and emotional" Saakashvili. For the year prior to the war, tensions had been high, with repeated violations of a tenuous cease-fire committed by all sides; the Russians declaring special relations with both breakaway republics, and without notice to Tbilisi, sending troops into Abkhaziya to repair the Abkhaz railroad; the Georgians moving troops and equipment into both conflict zones; and both sides' forces occasionally opening fire on the other sides' villages. In early 2008 Saakashvili did offer an olive branch in the form of proposed plan for internal autonomy for the republics, but the Georgians also continued to escalate tensions as their forces continued to break the cease-fire agreement by placing heavy artillery in the conflict zone.

Spring and summer 2008 saw both the Georgian and Ossetiyans gradually step up the frequency and intensity of military operations from occasional tit-for-tat rifle fire to sniper attacks, mine detonations, and sporadic artillery shots. Many of the major jumps in escalation were undertaken by the Georgians.[50] In early August, in the wake of Georgia's July military exercises with NATO, Saakashvili moved his troops and artillery into position to invade the SO capital Tskhinval (in Ossetiyan, Tskhinvali in Georgian). Meanwhile, Georgian snipers were firing at Ossetiyan villages during joint NATO-Georgian military exercises in the week leading up to his attack.[51] Georgian forces renewed lower-intensity military operations around Tskhinvali on August 1, including moving into position for the offensive.[52] On the evening of August 7, 2008, the impulsive and now emboldened Saakashvili ordered his army to unleash a ground invasion of SO, which followed a massive, indiscriminate, fourteen-hour Georgian artillery barrage on Tskhinvali with inaccurate GRAD missile launchers, killing tens if not hundreds of civilians and 19 Russian peacekeeping troops and destroying much of the city.[53] In response, Russian troops still in place after military exercises in the North Caucasus Military District, and likely informed by intelligence assets (overhead and over the border) of an impending Georgian attack, quickly streamed through the Roki Tunnel and needed little more than a day to force the Georgians to withdraw from Tskhinvali and into a general retreat.

With all of its technical means and a proposal from Moscow to convene a UN Security Council session to stop the war as matters escalated on the eve of Saakashvili's invasion, one wonders: (1) why the Bush administration failed to exercise pressure on Tbilisi in the days and hours leading up to Saakashvili's attack; (2) why the U.S. administration did not call for a UN Security Council session to short-circuit the crisis; and (3) whether others in the Bush administration, such as the very hawkish anti–Russian Vice-President Richard Cheney, might have delivered a somewhat different message through back channels than Rice's and then hoped to convince the malleable Bush to take military measures to counter Moscow. We now know that during an August 11 White House meeting of the "principals," Cheney and others in the administration engaged in what Rice later called "loose talk," and others say there was "some consideration of limited military options to stem the Russian advance," including "bombardment and sealing of the Roki Tunnel as well as other surgical tasks to reduce Russian military pressure on the Georgian government."[54] Such a course would likely have prompted a Russian response. A cycle of escalation could have then been parlayed by Cheney and Saakashvili to escalate and force a quagmire, negotiatons, and mitigation, or even the full removal of the price Moscow hoped to exact from Saakashvili as a result of his démarche. Even without a back-channel wink and a nod, the closeness of the Georgian-American military and political relationship encouraged Saakashvili's brinksmanship in South Ossetiya in summer 2008.

As his troops were digging more guns, mortars and cannons into position, Saakashvili addressed the world in the early evening of August 7 and announced he was implementing a unilateral "cease-fire." Hours later, Saakashvili again addressed the world, claiming he had decided to "restore the constitutional order," making no reference to any Russian invading force on Georgian territory of the kind he would allege days later had forced his decision to strike. Saakashvili also stated: "We have been in constant contacts with the leadership of the local Russian peacekeeping forces. Several hours ago, they told us that they have completely lost control over the actions of the separatists....We are in constant contact with the leadership of the Russian Ministry of Foreign Affairs, and the Ministry tells us Russia is trying to stop the separatists from engaging in armed action, but without any success."[55] Days later, Saakashvili seemed to forget about his order to "restore the constitutional order" and was now claiming he ordered the attacks in response to reports the Russians were invading through the Roki Tunnel connecting North and South Ossetiya. This was part of a wide-ranging propaganda or "strategic communications" operation filled with falsehoods reported by Western media as truth.[56]

The war ended with a total of some 1,000 killed and several thousand wounded, distributed approximately evenly between the Georgian and Ossetiyan-Georgian sides. Russia also sent forces into Abkhaziya fearing a second stage in Saakashvili's gambit would target that breakaway republic. On August 26, 2008, Moscow recognized the state independence of both SO and Abkhaziya, returning the West's "favor" of recognizing Kosovo's independence six months prior.

Over a year after the war, an exhaustive EU investigation confirmed that Saakashvili, not the Russians, started the war.[57] Moscow was not innocent in the making of the war, but was less responsible than Saakashvili, the South Ossetiyans, and perhaps even NATO and the West. The history of the Georgian "frozen conflict" and the Ossetiyan war is much more complicated than the party line of "Russian aggression" against Georgia.

Indeed, the EU report acknowledged the multicausal nature of the war—typical of wars and other major political outcomes—blaming Georgia, SO, Russia, and the West to varying degrees:

> This Report shows that any explanation of the origins of the conflict cannot focus solely on the artillery attack on Tskhinvali in the night of 7/8 August and on what then developed into the questionable Georgian offensive in South Ossetia and the Russian military action. The evaluation also has to cover the run-up to the war during the years before and the mounting tensions in the months and weeks immediately preceding the outbreak of hostilities. It must also take into account years of provocations, mutual accusations, military and political threats and acts of violence both inside and outside the conflict zone. It has to consider, too, the impact of a great power's coercive politics and diplomacy against a small and insubordinate neighbour, together with the small neighbour's penchant for overplaying its hand and acting in the heat of the moment without careful consideration of the final outcome, not to mention its fear that it might permanently lose important parts of its territory through creeping annexation. We also notice with regret an erosion of the respect of established principles of international law such as territorial integrity, and at the same time an increased willingness on all sides to accept the use of force as a means to reach one's political goals and to act unilaterally instead of seeking a negotiated solution, as difficult and cumbersome as such a negotiation process might be.[58]

The report was careful to stress the importance of both Georgian and Ossetiyan violations of the Dargomys ceasefire and peacekeeping agreement and escalations of violence, as well as the Georgian and Russian violations of international law and human rights in the 1990s and early to mid–2000s which made war more likely. It also noted the violations of international law and human rights by all sides during the war, the U.S. and other Western or pro–Western powers' role in aggravating the tense environment in the region, and international organizations' failure to more aggressively pursue a resolution of Georgia's long-frozen conflicts.[59]

The report finds that there was no genocide, contrary to hyperbolic Russian claims. However, the Georgians' conduct of the war, which other reports and numerous YouTube videos make clear was in violation of all standards of the law of war, suggests that they might have been prepared to engage in genocide. Saakashvili's massive, indiscriminate bombing of Tskhinvali suggests the same, but Russian forces intervened before the Georgians had any chance to carry one out. Continued indiscriminate bombing of Tskhinvali and a subsequent successful occupation of South Ossetiya (and perhaps Abkhaziya) and resulting partisan warfare would have led to massive Ossetiyan (and Abkhaziyan) casualties. Though perhaps short of preventing a genocide, the Russian intervention was consistent with a legal humanitarian intervention, saving perhaps many thousands of civilian lives.

The EU report also condemned Russia for recognizing the state independence of SO and Abkhazia, thereby eroding the principle of state sovereignty in international law.[60] However, given the history of Georgian oppression and violence against Ossetiyans—now extended by Georgia's August 2008 aggression—Russia could not help but leave troops in SO and Abkhaziya. For the Ossetiyans' protection and its own authority and influence in the Caucasus, Russia needed to ensure that Georgia would not be in a position to repeat Saakashvili's démarche. The "declarations of 'independence'" at which Washington and commentators scoffed were not as fictive as thought or claimed. Sukhumi is unlikely to submit to any Russian attempt to impose its rule over Abkhaziya. However, Ossetiyans, including those in SO, have always been inclined towards reunification with North Ossetiya in Russia. Historically the Orthodox Christian Ossetiyans have sought

Russian protection—as once did Georgia—against the North Caucasus and Turkish (Ottoman) Muslims. After Gamsakhurdia's discriminatory and brutal treatment of the Ossetiyans, the SO's desire for Moscow's protection was heightened.

In terms of legality, if the international community has established in international law and even condoned humanitarian military interventions without a UN mandate in the past, as occurred in Bosnia and Kosovo, respectively, then Russia has as much of a legal basis or lack thereof as other powers or UN member-states for engaging in such military interventions. The applicability and appropriateness of any particular humanitarian intervention should be addressed on the merits of the case. The fact that Russia opposed the American humanitarian intervention in Bosnia and Kosovo does not disqualify Moscow from intervening in other cases. Similarly, the rejection of Russia's possession of any right to intervene in South Ossetiya does not disqualify a country making such a rejection from engaging in a humanitarian intervention. The EU report's authors did not condemn the West's recognition of Kosovo's independence, despite stipulations in UN Resolution 1244 regarding the preservation of Yugoslavia's territorial integrity and state sovereignty, and despite the U.S. and NATO intervention's lacking any UN mandate. The West had asserted a basic post–Cold War rule that borders in Europe would never again be changed by force, and international law also rejected the redrawing borders by force. The rule and law held until the West ignored them in violating UN Resolution 1244 on Yugoslavia/Serbia. The West used 1244's Kosovo peacekeeping mandate, in effect, to occupy Kosovo and then support its independence. It justified this on the basis of Yugolsavia's use of force against Kosovo. Russia's recognition of the independence of South Ossetiya and Abkhaziya rested on the same argument—Georgia's aggression against Abkhaziya and SO.[61] This makes "international law" a veritable fiction. It cannot or at times will not be enforced, and some states, in particular great powers, are free to use it for political reasons when the law can be read to be on their side. When this is the case, it opens up the possibility that a majority of states can be rallied to back one side in a conflict in order to isolate and punish other powers that might seek to go it alone. The West, in particular the U.S., did so in Kosovo, perhaps to some good overall effect. Russia did so in Georgia, also perhaps with some good effect, but without a supporting majority of nations. While each side scored points geopolitically, international law and security suffered in the balance.

Moscow's Calculus for Intervention

Putting aside legality, Russia's national security would have been severely undermined had it stood by passively and let Saakashvili have his way in Ossetiya and Abkhaziya, given its own Ossetiyan and several Abkhaz-related (Circassian) nationalities just over the border. As in Ukraine six years later, there was a two-tier structure to the Georgian crisis. At the international level, the geopolitical contest between Russia and the West over NATO expansion and conflicting spheres of influence was being played out on the ground in Georgia. Aside from the insult and humiliation of having Western powers ignore Russia's preferences on NATO expansion, Yugoslavia, Kosovo, missile defense, nuclear arms control, Jackson-Vanik, and much else, such Western actions were having a negative impact on Russia's national security situation. The West's move toward offering Georgia and Ukraine NATO membership brought the geopolitical contest to a boiling point for Russia.

Ukraine's prospective NATO membership meant significantly weakening Russia's defense capabilities and would require building a new base for its Black Sea Fleet based in Ukraine's Sevastopol. Georgia's and Ukraine's membership together would reduce Russia's prospects of defending itself against the alliance. To this one can add the U.S. bases in Central Asia and the planned placement of a U.S. anti-missile defense system in the Czech Republic and Poland, which rejected meaningful Russian participation in or monitoring of the installations, further aggravating Moscow's sense of betrayal, isolation, and vulnerability. The prospect of NATO military installations in Georgia at some point in the future, the West's willingness to arm and verbally support an unstable Saakashvili with his intentions to reintegrate SO and Abkhaziya and refusal to reject the use of force, and these regions' proximity to Russia's still jihad-plagued North Caucasus represented a catastrophic security scenario from Moscow's point of view. A Georgian dagger was pointed at Moscow's soft underbelly. At the same time, Georgia's potential entry into NATO gave Russia a stake in the maintenance of Georgia's frozen conflicts, since NATO custom required incoming members be free of border disputes or secessionist issues. Russia's protection of SO and Abkhaziya worked to block Tbilisi's entry into NATO. Moscow also regarded Western support for Kosovo's secession from Serbia (declared the previous spring) and Western rejection of separatist aspirations for Georgia's Abkhaz and Russia's traditional ally in the Caucasus, the Ossetiyans, as an intolerable double standard.

The geostrategic context in which Georgia was boiling over was not the kind that contributes to stability and negotiations. Ethnic and sovereignty conflicts are more likely to explode into violence when imbedded in a larger international contest between great powers that intervene in the dispute and adopt the opposing local parties as proxies, making them pawns in their larger game. This was true on both sides on the Georgian-Ossetiyan conflict, with the West backing Georgia and Russia supporting the Ossetiyans and Abkhaz.

In contrast with faraway Europe and the U.S., for Moscow there was great potential for destabilization of the Caucasus region both within and adjacent to Russia's borders as a result of Saakashvili's decision. SO and Abkhaziya are populated by nationalities with close ethnic kin just across the border in Russia. For the South Ossetiyans, there are the Ossetiyans of Russia's North Caucasus republic of North Ossetiya. For the Abkhaz, there are the ethnic Muslim Circassian groups—the Kabardins, Cherkess, and Adygs—in Russia's republics of Kabardino-Balkariya, Karachaevo-Cherkessiya, and Adygea, respectively. This means Russia has a most vital, even an existential interest in the stability of South Ossetiya and Abkhaziya, one much greater than any interests the West might have there. One need only ponder the consequences for Russia if Moscow had not responded with substantial enough force to prevent a civil war or insurgency campaign in SO or Abkhaziya. The Ossetiyans' and Abkhaziyans' kin populations in Russia would have raised thousands of local volunteers who would have crossed the border to join the Ossetiyan and Abkhaz resistance, further destabilizing Russia's already jihad-plaged North Caucasus. Indeed, when Georgian forces sought to forcibly reincorporate breakaway Abkhaziya into Georgia in 1992, sparking a small civil war, Circassian volunteers flooded into Abkhazia to fight the Georgians; some were assisted by Russian military and security forces.

Medvedev and Putin had to wonder what the consequences for Moscow's international reputation, prestige and power would be if the Kremlin were to stand by and allow Georgia to slaughter members of its historical allies in the Caucasus, the Ossetiyans, just across Russia's border. In lieu of its direct military intervention, Moscow would have had two unpalatable choices. First, Moscow would have been forced to use force to restrain the local population trying to come to the defense of their compatriots across the border in Georgia, risking an internal uprising. Simultaneously, by not intervening, Moscow would have dealt a death blow to its influence across the former USSR. What country in the region or anywhere else would have been willing to rely on a partnership with Moscow against, for example, jihadi terrorism in Central Asia? The second option was to allow North Ossetiyans to enter SO and support their compatriots. This would have meant a long partisan war in the region, inevitable charges that Russia was supporting the insurgency, and the risk of a rise in Ossetiyan nationalism and separatism in Russia's North Ossetia in pursuit of a united, independent "Great Ossetia." Given all this, Moscow had no choice in August 2008 but to draw a red line at Tskhinvali when U.S.– and NATO–affiliated Georgian troops attacked SO.

IMPLICATIONS OF THE GEORGIAN-OSSETIYAN WAR

The artillery salvos on the night of August 7–8, 2008, were the first salvos in what some now call the "new cold war." To be sure, it was Saakashvili who is ultimately responsible. He took the decision to break completely the cease-fire agreement and the peace, albeit shaky, and sharply escalate the status quo of intermittent and targeted exchanges of fire to a full-scale invasion across the cease-fire line with an indiscriminate artillery assault sustained for many hours against residential Tskhinvali, killing civilians and Russian peacekeepers.

Nevertheless, it was the U.S. that trained, equipped, and conducted joint maneuvers with the Georgians as Saakashvili built up his forces for an assault on SO and likely Abkhaziya. A close partner of the U.S. and a NATO membership candidate had carried out a major ground assault and a massive, indiscriminate artillery bombardment of a population long an ally of Russia in the region. Once the Russians responded, NATO flew 2,000 Georgian forces fighting in Iraq back to Georgia to fight the Russians and Ossetiyans. These were the first bitter fruits of NATO expansion, despite at least four points of caution against doing so: (1) Moscow's opposition and resentment; (2) the post-Soviet nature of the leadership in almost the entire former USSR region; (3) the profound political complexities in the post-communist region made inherently unstable by virtue of its complex ethno-national territorial administrative legacy, histories of ethno-national animosity, and the recent collapse of the state and governmental apparatus and deficit of new viable institutional arrangements; and (4) limited space, time and energy devoted by Western governments to the region, given a slew of other, more urgent security challenges in South Asia and the Middle East.

Given the view of those who pushed NATO expansion and color revolutions that Russia was a threat to its neighbors and the West, they should have expected a military response by Moscow. If the U.S. was not prepared to defend prospective or actual new NATO members neighboring Russia from a possible, reasonably expected, even likely Russian military reaction, why risk expansion and regime-change policies? If such an expectation was valid, then NATO expansion was not enhancing these countries' security, but rather putting it at risk. Moreover, the failure to respond to any Russian military or other robust response would teach not just Moscow but the West's actual enemies that it will not stand up for its allies and interests. This could and likely did encourage them to act accordingly, further putting national and international security at risk and defeating the very ostensible purpose of NATO expansion—to strengthen international or at least Western security and stability. By sticking its nose into a regional tent fraught with complex histories, interethnic animosities, and confused and unclear sovereignty claims, the West risked getting drawn into the very kind of territorial and sovereignty entanglements the West ought to loathe getting enmeshed in. Finally, bureaucratic inertia and the Clinton administration's resulting inordinate attention to issues of NATO expansion distracted the West from undertaking a fundamental reassessment of the real security threats facing the U.S. and the West in the wake of the Cold War: Al Qa'ida and the global jihadist and Islamist revolutionary movement and Iranian and North Korean nuclear proliferation issues.

SAAKASHVILI'S DEMISE

Saakashvili's failed South Ossetiyan gambit led to a decline in his authority. He responded with an increasingly authoritarian hand when new demonstrations against him began to occur with ever greater frequency beginning in 2009. The opposition demonstrations mounted, resembling a color revolution in reverse—a color counterrevolution. Its leaders were Saakashvili's Rose "revolution" colleagues, most notably former parliament speaker Nino Burjanadze.

Western media sources close to NATO did their best to discredit the opposition for the same behavior that they routinely praised Russian opposition forces for, and in doing so threw under the bus those they formerly championed as beacons of democracy. In 2009, Eduard Lucas, editor of *The Economist*, described Burjanadze and her party this way: "The radical wing of the opposition, led by Nino Burjanadze, a former speaker of parliament, went on to block Tbilisi's railway. Ms Burjanadze, who has been one of the driving forces and financiers of the protests, is one of the country's least popular politicians. Ordinary Georgians associate her with the Soviet-era *nomenklatura*."[62] However, in 2007, after Saakashvili brutally cracked down on opposition demonstrators, Lucas wrote that Burjanadze possessed a "statesmanlike image that Mr Saakashvili has lost" because of the latter's "misuse" of power.[63] Five months after this rare critique of Saakashvili, NATO's Bucharest summit declared Georgia a NATO member-to-be. Perhaps lack of confidence in Saakashvili's stability led the bloc to put off the immediate membership offer that most new NATO members from the former Eastern Bloc sought for Georgia and Ukraine.

At the peak of the anti–Saakashvili demonstrations in early May, he appears to have ordered Georgian army units to Tbilisi, setting off a mutiny among them. The next day, the first violence occurred when demonstrators attempted to storm a police station. Fearing civil war, the Georgian Orthodox Church (GOC) appealed to all sides to refrain from violence and to compromise, but *The Economist* and Lucas suggested that the GOC addressed its appeal only to "radical opposition … leaders to be more flexible."[64] This claim was a result of cherry-picking just one of four known GOC interventions during the crisis. Other interventions clearly called on the authorities, or both the authorities and opposition, to soften their approach to the power struggle.[65]

Saakashvili survived the 2009 crisis, but his party lost the parliamentary majority in the October 2012 elections to the "Georgian Dream" coalition. Its leader, Bidzina Ivanishvili, became prime minister, opening the way for parliamentary hearings into the decisionmaking leading up to the attack on South Ossetiya, which further discredited Saakashvili. The Georgian Dream's Giorgi Margvelashvili won the October 2013 presidential elections, followed by hearings on corruption in and around the Saakashvili regime and leaked video and statements uncovering systematic beatings and torture in

Saakashvili's prison system. Saakashvili was forced to flee Georgia to avoid arrest and emigrated to the U.S., where he took up a professorship in Tufts University's School of International Politics and Diplomacy. The "beacon of democracy" had gone out all over Georgia and the former USSR. It would shine again, however, in Ukraine, where Saakashvili would be given Ukrainian citizenship by President Petro Poroshenko in violation of Ukrainian law and be appointed governor of Odessa Oblast under the new Maidan regime in early 2015. In autumn 2015, Georgia began proceedings on whether to strip Saakashvili of his Georgian citizenship, and an audiotape was published revealing Saakashvili conspiring to organize a Rose revolution 2.0 from his position as Odessa's governor, prompting a new Georgian investigation and the possibility of more criminal charges.[66]

Things seemed to come full circle when some American elites began to throw Saakashvili under the bus, and in doing so, unwittingly justified Russia's reaction to his Ossetiyan gambit. In an interview on Georgian television and Radio Liberty on November 23, 2013, the tenth anniversary of the Rose revolution, the U.S. Ambassador to Georgia during the Saakashvili era, Richard Miles, acknowledged that the former Georgian president could have and should have avoided the war and would not have started it if the U.S. and its allies had not sold him "offensive weapons, self-propelled artillery systems, heavy-armor vehicles, attack aircraft, and other equipment."[67]

Conclusion

All great powers claim interests and spheres of influence beyond their borders. The West's expansion of NATO to Russia's borders, for example, is both a claim and institutionalization of the claim that it has interests in the new member-states' region. Washington has declared—at one time or another—the entire Western Hemisphere, the Middle East, and the Persian Gulf as spheres where it has not just interests but "vital interests." Russia only claims one such sphere of influence: countries directly adjacent or near to its borders. These countries reside in only three relatively small regions of Eurasia writ large: Eastern Europe, the Caucasus, and Central Asia. The U.S. and the West respond somewhat hypocritically that they are uninterested in spheres of influence and other such "19th century thinking." It seeks to deny Russia such a sphere, but claims the entire world its sphere of vital interest. This double standard was a major cause of Russia's preparations for war, as it saw Tbilisi preparing both to enter NATO and start wars in its breakaway republics.

The geostrategic upshot of the Ossetiyan episode was that neither Georgia nor Ukraine could be brought into NATO anytime soon without igniting a major crisis in relations with Russia and risking a Russian overreaction, perhaps a military one. Russia's position vis-à-vis both countries had been strengthened. The U.S. had been shown to be unable or unwilling to protect allies in this distant region. The U.S. policy of expanding its influence in the former Soviet Union on the back of NATO seemed to have sputtered out with the Baltic states' entry. Russia's close ties to Ukraine seemed to preclude its entry into NATO. Georgia's oppression of its minority nationalities and Russia's consequent support for Abkhaziyan and South Ossetiyan independence rendered Georgia a state with a sovereignty problem of the kind that precludes NATO membership historically. Moldova and Azerbaijan are precluded for the same reason, with the Transdniestr and

Nagorno-Karabakh issues remaining unresolved. Moreover, across the former Soviet region, Russia remained the preeminent power. This was reflected in its continuing popularity across much of the region, despite its often heavy-handed and clumsy foreign policy, and the lure of Western democracy and other forms of assistance and economic largesse. According to a 2011 Gallup survey, although less popular than unpopular in Georgia, the Baltics and Belarus, majorities in eight of the other post–Soviet states polled still approved of Russia's policies in former Soviet Eurasia.[68]

Thus, the U.S. and Russia remained at odds over the entire post–Soviet region's future, complicating the new Barack Obama adminstration's "reset" and ultimately undermining its viability, along with any hopes for its long-term evolution into a closer partnership. Rather than confront and rethink the policy of NATO expansion, or even change the policy, the Obama White House chose to ignore it, at least in public and in its interactions with Russian officials—in terms of clandestine activity, matters were rather different. The issue's ugly head would rise up again, forming the geostrategic background upon which both Russia and the West would act in regard to Ukraine and its coming crisis. The Obama administration appeared to have no real strategy for U.S. policy in Eurasia, and the hard truth remains that there may have been none. This is simply a bridge too far in lieu of a partnership with Russia that recognizes Eurasia as its sphere of influence and puts an end to a broad-brushed DP-color revolution regime change strategy for furthering American interests.

However, immediately after the Rose takeover and less than a year before Ukraine's Orange "revolution," Kmara was contacted by activists from Ukraine (and at least three other post–Soviet states: Azerbaijan, Belarus, and Moldova), and Kmara student activists told the BBC they were "ready to go international" and "challenge Otpor's 'monopoly' on 'bloodless' color revolutions."[69] USAID, CANVAS and Otpor were now global operations. They were deeply involved in organizing the 2011 Egyptian revolution that temporarily removed the Arab nationalist regime and brought the extremist Muslim Brotherhood to power.[70] The handwriting for Maidan was on the wall.

5

Ukraine's "Stateness" Problem
The Tectonics of a Faultline State

Introduction

Whether geography is determinative or not on the ground, it certainly emerges as instrumental for those acting in Ukraine—both for foreigners and many natives. In Western strategic culture and for the adepts of geopolitical strategy, Ukraine was a "faultline state" (Huntington) and a "vital geopolitical pivot" (Brzezinski) at the edge of the World Island's "Pivot Area" or "Heartland"—that is, Ukraine is a window on and gateway to Russia and/or Eurasia. For many on the other side of the mirror in Moscow, Ukraine began to be viewed much the same. Neo-Eurasianists came to view Ukraine as a buffer against the West, the last line of defense against Western, especially NATO encroachment at the Eurasian steppe's western edge. Ideational constructs both led to, and were reinforced and operationalized by their institutionalization through the expansion of old, and the creation of new multinational organizations. In the bargain and in more realist terms, NATO and EU expansion eastward undermined Russian interests. Thus, Russia again must play the role of gatekeeper, preserving Ukraine as part of either Russia, a Slavic Union, or Eurasian civilization. Ukraine in reality became a faultline state, a pivot point between Western and Eurasian institutional infrastructures, vied for by NATO, the CSTO, the EU and EEU, by Washington, Brussels and Moscow.

The Ukrainian crisis would be driven by post–Soviet communalism in both Ukraine and Russia, complexities for Ukraine and Russia in discerning their national identities and in sorting out of their intermixed Slavic roots and painful histories. Complicating both of these challenges was the two countries' (especially Ukraine's) location on or near the cusp between two different civilizations—a higher level category of identity, community, and communalism. Thus, Ukraine became the object of a tussle between competing communalisms as well as interests, East and West geopolitically, and east and west internally.

The combination of a civilizational divide and exacerbating geopolitical contestation in the region helped intensify a widespread post–Soviet trend of intensifying communalism, intolerant and conflictive identity politics, and ethnic state-building rather than individualism, "secular" party politics, civic states and civil societies. International geopolitical dynamics and tectonics—the "common European home" now increasingly divided and ultimately split in two—fatally exacerbated Ukraine's several lines of schism—what Russians and Ukrainians both call "*raskol*." The new Ukrainian nationalism in the West, and the Russian nationalism and neo–Soviet patriotism in both Crimea and Donbass, would include ethno-national, religious, and regionalist elements. The external tussle for Ukraine and polarization of its domestic schisms created a perfect storm in the winter of 2013–2014, leading to the worst kind of political outcome—violent revolution and civil war.

The Tectonics of Raskol in Faultline Ukraine

As Huntington emphasized, in order to redefine its civilizational identity and simultaneously retain its stability, a torn country's political and economic elites, general public, and dominant groups all must acquiesce in the conversion.[1] As a faultline state cobbled together by a long history of conquest, reconquest, division and redivision, revolution and war, antinational Soviet state-building, and finally the Soviet collapse, post–Soviet Ukraine fulfilled none of these requirements. As history—both ancient and recent—demonstrates, Ukraine's schismatic tectonic has threatened to tear the country apart with each revolutionary earthquake. Although their common Christian and partially common Orthodox Christian heritage might suggest otherwise—as it did to Huntington—there are few societies to be found across the globe more divided than Ukrainian society.

The regional divisions within Ukraine, particularly those between eastern and western Ukraine, in electoral politics and on a host of key issues in domestic and foreign policy are well-documented—from national identity and culture to Ukraine's possible NATO membership.[2] It is precisely in the differences between western Ukraine (formerly eastern Poland) or Galicia and southeastern, and especially eastern, Ukraine—that is, at the civilization faultline—that we find the key communalist drivers of Ukraine's internal divisions, political polarization, and civil conflict. But this only scratches the surface of Ukraine's divided state and society. Ukraine was and remains divided not just by ethnic, linguistic, and religious communalist schisms but also along regional, economic, and historical-cultural lines that overlay and reinforce the former.

Ethnonational Tectonic

Although Ukraine's overall population is 77.8 percent ethnic Ukrainian, according to its most recent census conducted in 2001, its ethnic structure creates several troublesome ethno-territorial cleavages. Ethnic Russians make up 17.3 percent. All but four of pre–2014 Ukraine's 26 regions (27 if one counts Sevastopol as separate from Crimea) have greater than a 60 percent ethnic Ukrainian majority. The four regional exceptions were the only ones in pre–2014 Ukraine with a large ethnic Russian minority and therefore any realistic potential for an ethnic Russian-driven separatist movement: the Crimea Republic (24 percent Ukrainian, 58 percent Russian); Sevastopol (22 percent Ukrainian, 72 percent Russian); Donetsk Oblast' (57 percent Ukrainian, 38 percent Russian); and Luhansk Oblast' (58 percent Ukrainian, 39 percent Russian).

Only one other region has an ethnic Ukrainian majority of less than 70 percent—Odessa Oblast', with a 63 percent Ukrainian majority and a 21 percent Russian minority.[3]

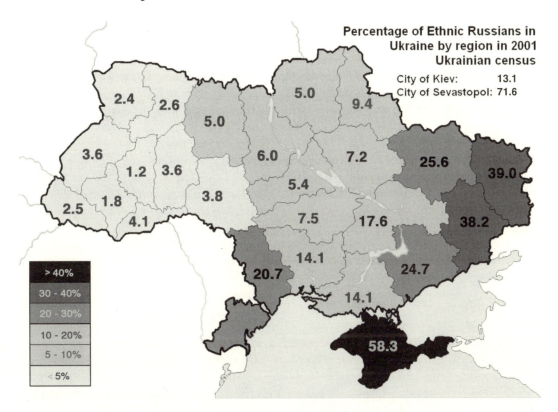

**Percentage of Ethnic Russians in
Ukraine by region in 2001
Ukrainian census**

City of Kiev: 13.1
City of Sevastopol: 71.6

> 40%
30 - 40%
20 - 30%
10 - 20%
5 - 10%
< 5%

Ethnic Russian population in Ukraine by region (2001 census data).

Lingusitic Contradictions

Linguistic divisions break down somewhat differently, but nevertheless strengthen the pro–Russian tendencies and create some separatist potential in the four aforementioned regions of Crimea (Sevastopol included) and Donbass (both Donetsk and Luhansk), as well as in several others. Thus, before the Maidan revolt, the overwhelming majority of Ukraine's citizens, up to 80 percent in some surveys, identified themselves as primarily Russian-speaking. However, the 2001 census showed Russian speakers predominant only in the Donbass (Donetsk and Luhansk Oblasts), Crimea, and some districts in six of Ukraine's other 23 regions.

However, the overwhelming majority of print and television media in pre–2014 Ukraine were in Russian, including 87 percent of books and 83 percent of journals published. This is a residual holdover from the Soviet era, when Russian was favored. In the wake of the 2004 Orange revolution and during the Yushchenko presidency, an aggressive Ukrainization policy was implemented. Contingency operationalized structure, politicizing the language issue, exacerbating inter-ethnic relations between Ukrainians and Russians, and further dividing the country.[4]

The Religious Tectonic

Just as linguistic differences within Ukraine reinforce and deepen ethnic divisions, so too do religious differences reinforce and deepen Ukraine's ethno-linguistic divide.

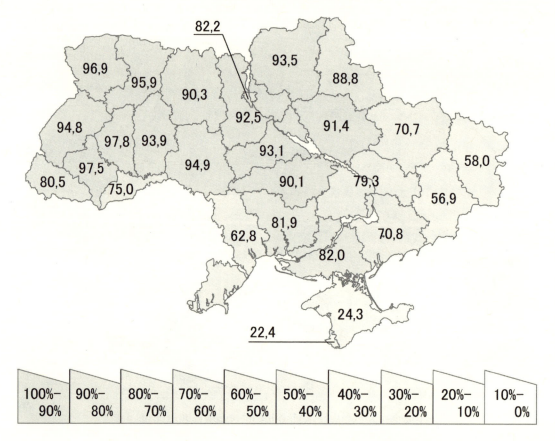

Percent of ethnic Ukrainians by region (2001 census data).

As alluded to above, over the course of centuries there was a persistent historical contest between Western Catholic and Protestant states (and indeed the Papacy itself), such as Poland and Sweden, respectively, on the one hand, and Orthodox Christian Russia, on the other hand, for control over the borderland between their respective civilizations, located precisely in Ukraine. Western Ukrainian Galicia and Volhynia became over time a largely Greek or Uniate Catholic community, while eastern and central Ukraine remained predominantly Russian Orthodox. Moreover, western and central Ukraine especially are divided between the Ukrainian Orthodox Church under the Kievan Patriarchy (40 percent of Ukraine's population) and the Ukrainian Orthodox Church of the Muscovite Patriarchy (29 percent). By contrast, the latter is predominant in eastern Ukraine and Crimea. The Ukrainian Uniate (Greek) Catholic Church is adhered to by 14 percent of Ukrainians, with almost all of them being residents of the seven or so most western Ukrainian provinces. Protestants comprise just over 2 percent (2.4) and Catholics just under 2 percent (1.7) of Ukraine's population, and almost all of these reside in western Ukraine as well. All other confessions make up under 1 percent of the population. The 0.6 percent of Ukrainians confessing Islam is confined almost in its entirety to Crimea, with the Muslim Crimean Tatars making up but 13 percent of the peninsula's population.[5]

"Secular" Regional Tectonics

Each of the cultural or civilizational differences outlined above run largely along regional lines, with Ukraine's Crimea and the Donbass provinces of Donetsk and Luhansk standing out from the rest of Ukraine. But there are other, less "secular" non-communal factors that set off Crimea and the Donbass from other regions. As noted above, contemporary Ukraine's territory was cobbled together by vicissitudes of history. None of the standard communal civilizational markers—neither ethnicity, language, nor religion—play a greater role in the present Ukrainian crisis than Ukraine's shifting and often nonexistent state and borders. Its makeshift formation, especially that contributed by Soviet power, laid the groundwork for regionalism and regional identities in addition to ethnic, linguistic, and religious ones. Regionalism is most pronounced in Donbass, Crimea, and western Ukraine or Galicia, giving them additional markers that set them off from Ukraine's other regions. All borderlands within the borderland, each adds an additional element of regional identity and regionalism that overlaps, sometimes crosscuts, but always compounds or reinforces the other divisions reviewed above.

THE DONBASS

The Donbass, or "wild steppe" (*dikoe pole*), as it has been called by locals for centuries, has been convincingly described by Kuromiya as a "particular community" in "a geographical and symbolic sense," with its own myths and identity. Kuromiya likens the Donbass to the American "wild west"—a "wild south" bearing two iconic historical realities, "freedom and terror"—"inner yearnings for freedom, wild exploitation, and everyday violence have competed for dominance" throughout Donbass's turbulent history. Located far from the political metropolises that often controlled it—Moscow and Kiev—the Donbass has been "politically unmanageable" and a refuge for those seeking not "freedom to" but rather "freedom from" various overlords—landlords, the law, urban-defined regimes.[6]

The Donbass has always exhibited a strong strain of political violence, originating in the open steppe's unfortunate locus at the crossroads of Europe and Asia. Over a millennium ago Slavs, Pechenegs, Polovtsians, and Tatars vied for military supremacy and political control. Donbass violence manifested itself in some of the ugliest episodes in Russian and Ukrainian history: Russian and Ukrainian pogroms against Jews, Russian-Ukrainian violence, revolutionary violence, the Soviet Great Terror, and genocide against the Jews in World War II (though not on the scale seen in OUN-plagued Galicia). "[A]ttracted by the freedom and opportunities this frontier region provided, all sorts of people came to settle there from all parts of the country and beyond, and harsh economic exploitation and brutal ethnic conflict were part of everyday life in the Donbass."[7]

The Cossack military tradition contributed to violence in the Donbass. Kuromiya quotes the Russian historian Georgii Vernadskii to good effect:

> … [T]he steppe held out a strong attraction to the adventurous, while repelling the weak.… In the course of the fifteenth and sixteenth centuries this no man's land became the abode of the Ukrainian and Russian Cossacks, who eventually organized themselves in strong military communes ("hosts"), of which the Zoporozhie—beyond the Dnepr cataracts—and Don hosts—latter in the lower Don region—were the most important of the two."
>
> The wild field of the Donbas [*sic*] is situated between these two historically Cosack [*sic*] areas.[8]

Cossackdom further fostered the aspiration to "freedom from" and thus independence. So too did the "highly developed underground (both literal and symbolic)," the Donbass mines, like the free-range steppe, "served as a refuge for freedom seekers." Even "at the height of Stalinism" the Donbass "continued to maintain some elements of the free steppe."[9]

Donbass's geography and economics also shaped its regional identity. Since Soviet times socioeconomic differences—separate from, but mutually reinforcing—sharpened the Donbass's ethnonational, religious and historical peculiarities in relation to central, even southern, but especially western Ukraine. The Donbass is rich in natural resources, especially coal, a large, recently discovered natural gas basin, and iron ore. Coal mining and metallurgy comprise the region's economic foundation and identity. Donbass was the backbone of these industries in Tsarist, Soviet, and post–Soviet Ukrainian times. Coal especially shaped the Donbass's rough and ready self-identity; the coal miner is no less an iconic symbol of the region than the Cossack horseman.

Donbass's industrial economy—unique regionally—generates socioeconomic differences between Donbass and much of the rest of the country. Socially, the coal miner and factory worker contrast sharply with the sophisticated white-collar worker in Kiev or the Polonized and westernized Galician shopkeeper in Lviv or Vinnitsa. Economically, differences in standard of living and contribution to Ukraine's national wealth in comparison with other regions also set the Donbass apart. After Kiev and Dnepropetrovsk, Donbass counts among the wealthiest group of regions, along with Zaprozhe, Kharkiv and Poltava. Luhansk falls into the next tier, but far ahead of western Ukraine's regions—the poorest in the country.[10] Similarly, industrial Kiev city and Dnepropetrovsk, Kiev, Poltava, and Donbass's Donetsk and Luhansk Oblasts have by far the highest GDPs per capita.[11] The financial flows to Kiev's coffers and to the pockets and banks of well-connected oligarchs with businesses located in Kiev and Dnepropetrovsk (and Donbass) created growing resentment both east and west towards the central government and the oligarchs. The burst of industrial development under Soviet rule and Donbass's growing identification of its economic self-interest with Russia, where cross-border familial relationships and trade created a network of particularistic relationships, pull Donbass farther from the rest of Ukraine.

Thus, Donbass identity is as much regional and socioeconomic as it is pro–Russian and Soviet nostalgic. It is as much "anational" or antinational as it is pro–Russian. The Donbass historically has been distinctly antinational when it comes to ethnic Ukrainian nationalism constructed to the west, in distant Galicia. Even in 1917, it rejected the nationalists. The Donbass opposed the Central Rada's anti–Bolshevik, Ukrainian national project. When the Rada declared Ukraine's independence, the Donbass effectively seceded from Ukraine as part of the Donets-Kryviy-Rih (Krivoi-Rog) Soviet Republic (DKRSR). Created largely on the initiative of the Bolshevik-infused industrial eastern Ukraine and Donbass, Kharkiv became the capital of the short-lived entity. Threatened by the independence of the steppe, Lenin opposed the DKRSR's formation, supporting unity of the front line against German forces, but locals formed it all the same.[12]

During the *perestroika* era, which began to look much like 1917 at times, with spontaneous miners' strikes in Donetsk in 1989 threatening the faltering Soviet regime, the Donbass again rejected ethnic Ukrainian nationalism. Donbass strikers' demands were purely economic. Leaders of emerging nationalist groups like "Rukh" complained as late as 1990 that the Donbass miners were "sausage people," indifferent to the national question.[13] Although neither Rukh nor any other Ukrainian nationalist party ever made inroads into the Donbass, the population evolved by December 1991 to support Ukrainian sovereignty and independence from the USSR largely because a divided Moscow seemed incapable of supplying the "sausage"—economic well-being. As discussed below, this turn away from Moscow was temporary, followed by a turn away from Kiev.

GALICIA

Galicia's self-identification contrasts with the rest of Ukraine, but most of all with the Donbass. It is European, Polonized, and Catholicized, not Russian, Russified, or Orthodox Christian. It lacks the Cossack identity of much of the rest of Ukraine. Rural countryside and bourgeois towns like Lviv look askance at industrial and Cossack Donbass. In terms of socioeconomic difference, Ukraine's rural western and central regions are the poorest, especially Galicia's Volyn and Chernihiv. The cities of Kiev and (largely supported by Moscow through the Black Sea Fleet) Sevastopol are the wealthiest regions, followed by Donbass's Donetsk and Luhansk regions. Poverty rates are highest in western and southern Ukraine, particularly in the rural areas. According to the World Bank's poverty standard of a dollar per day per capita, nearly half of western and southern Ukrainians are poor. In eastern Ukraine, only one-third of residents are poor.[14] Similarly, western Ukraine has most of the very lowest regional per capita GDPs among Ukraine's 26 regions. Galicia's oblasts of Chernovtsy, Ternopil, and Transcarpathia are the very lowest.[15] Donbass's higher standard of living creates resentment especially among western Ukrainians in Galicia, where ethnic, linguistic, religious, cultural and historical differences are preconditions for greater potential resentment.

CRIMEA

As noted earlier, Crimea had a several-hundred-year tradition of being a Russian land. Orthodox Christianity appears to have first taken root on Russian land on the peninsula. One of three contending theories on where in 988–989 Kievan Rus prince Vladimir was baptized holds it to have taken place in the then Greek city of Kherson (Hersones) on Crimea. One of the other two theories holds that he was baptized in Kiev after his successful conquest of Kherson.[16] The blood of Russian soldiers poured into the peninsula's soil in the Crimean War, World War I, and World War II. As the White Army dissolved in the south, the cream of the Tsarist elite bid farewell to their homeland on ships that embarked from Sevastopol, where first Russia and then the USSR based the Black Sea Fleet. Sevastopol is a nearly 100 percent Russian city, with most of its population made up of present or former Soviet naval and army personnel. Russia's leasing of the Black Sea Fleet naval base at Sevastopol after the Soviet collapse means that Crimea (and thus indirectly Ukraine) continues to be a beneficiary of Moscow's considerable defense expenditures. The networking that results from this and the historical connection to Russia give a major boost to Crimea's key industry—tourism. In sum, the core of Crimea's regional identity is Russian and—like that of Donbass—quasi–Soviet, with a strong strain of the Russian military ethos which Donbass largely lacks. The peninsula's Tatar and Ukrainian minorities and the Tatars' reviving Islamic tradition have little impact on Crimea's overall identity.

OTHER REGIONALISMS

Other regions mainly in the south—for example, Odessa—but also western Ukraine's Transcarpathia oblast possess their own regional identities, separate or in addition to their Ukrainian ones, though these regions are far less compact in their alternative identity as compared with Galicia, Donbass and Crimea.[17] Transcarpathia oblast possesses a significant non–Ukrainian minority population of 22 percent, including Hungarians (14 percent), Russians (6 percent), and Romanians (2 percent). Odessa's minority population is more highly fractured than Transcarpathia's, so the formation of a powerful alternative identity overshadowing its Ukrainian identity is unlikely to reach the level of potential separatism. Therefore, it is western Ukraine, the Donbass, and Crimea that produced manifestations of separatism in the revolutionary days of 2014, as I discuss in a later chapter.

Historical Tectonics: Hitler's and Stalin's Revenge

In addition to the mutually reinforcing ethnic, linguistic, religious, and socioeconomic divisions, Ukraine is broken by a great historico-cultural schism crystallized in the crucible of the 20th century's great European conflict between fascism (national socialism) and communism (international socialism). As noted earlier, western and southeastern Ukraine were divided by long histories in different states and empires after Ukraine's failure to establish its brief period of quasi-independence in the 17th century. What is today central and southeastern Ukraine found itself under Tsarist rule. Soviet power completed the destruction of the Ukrainian nationalist movement, stamping out religion, Ukrainian culture, and the Ukrainian peasantry in the late 1920s and early 1930s. The myth was developed by and among Ukrainian nationalists abroad in Galicia, the national diaspora in the West, and underground in the USSR that the famine in Ukraine during the early 1930s was intentional, an attempt at national genocide, and targeted Ukraine specifically, even alone.[18]

This myth reinforced the antagonism between western Ukraine and parts of southeastern Ukraine (especially the Donbass and Crimea) created by the fascist-communist confrontation in World War II. Many of the most politically active in western Ukraine today are the grandchildren of those who slaughtered Poles, Jews and communists during the Nazi invasion and occupation. Many of the most politically active in Donbass and Crimea are the grandchildren of Soviet Red Army and NKVD servicemen who slaughtered the Nazi-allied Ukrainian nationalists, not just in Galicia, but also elsewhere in Ukraine, where nationalist numbers were much smaller. Paraphrasing the great Russian poetess and Soviet dissident Anna Akhmatova, there were two Ukraines facing each other. Many a citizen in each Ukraine—roughly western and eastern Ukraine—hates the other for crimes against humanity commited against its grandparents by the other, and many in each Ukraine are unwilling to face up to the crimes committed by their grandparents. The historical rift between the Soviet and Nazi legacies exacerbates the ethnic, religious, regional, and social divisions between eastern and western Ukrainians.

Ukraine's Raskol' *and "Stateness" Problem*

The communalist and historicist schisms western and southeastern Ukraine are reflected in the importance Ukrainians place on local and regional identity, as opposed to Ukrainian state national identity, and the very different opinions between regions on virtually every political issue important in Ukrainian politics. VTsIOM surveys from 1992 to 2010 illustrated Ukraine's stateness problem. Though showing a small upward trend, approximately just half of Ukrainians identified themselves first as Ukrainian state nationals—45.6 percent in 1992, 51.2 percent in 2010. Approximately one-fourth (sometimes nearly a third) identified foremost as residents of a subnational territorial entity—their village, district, city, region, or several regions—with 30.8 percent in 1992 and 33.8 in 2010. Small numbers identified as citizens of the the former USSR, the world, Europe, and other identity markers.[19] As or more important than Ukrainians' weak allegiance to a national identity are the vast differences between Galician western Ukraine, on the one hand, and eastern and (somewhat less so) southern Ukraine, on the other, regarding the key issues of nation-building and statehood. Throughout its entire post–Soviet existence, eastern and western Ukrainians in one way or another have differed sharply over the fundamental issues facing the country—from the Ukrainian state's national identity, to the balance of power between Kiev and the regions, to the country's proper geopolitical orientation in foreign affairs. The country's divergent communal and historical experiences are reified into deep, contemporary political differences, producing a grave if sometimes latent stateness problem that has threatened to overwhelm the country's political stability and territorial integrity. Ukraine's stateness problem has been evidenced repeatedly in election results and opinion surveys throughout the late Soviet and post–Soviet period. The problem was often expressed in special regional efforts to carry out referenda in order to strengthen an autonomy or independence claim, amounting to a moderate form of communal separatism barely contained by Kiev from attaining full-blown secessionism.

From the *perestroika* era forward, the potential dangers of Ukraine's stateness problem were obvious. By late 1989 the Baltic states declared their independence to no avail in terms of real secession. By 1990 the 14 Soviet Union republics as well as the Russian federation began issuing declarations of sovereignty, seeking more autonomy from a Moscow split by infighting between Gorbachevite centrists, Yeltsinite radicals and revolutionaries from above, and hard-liners opposing both Gorbachev and Yeltsin. In almost each case, the sovereignty movement included or was an attempt to coopt the national issue from small but rising nationalist groups gaining popularity as a result of the historical revelations and revival of pre-communist national histories promoted by historians, writers, and linguists under Gorbachev's *"glasnost"* or openness policy.

The independence movement in Ukraine can be dated from the September 1989 inaugural congress of the Ukrainian Popular Movement (*Rukh*). *Rukh* or "the Movement" fundamentally shifted the political landscape in favor of radical reform-minded CPSU members and regime opponents in the USSR's second most populous union republic. Originally organized by a group of reformist CPSU members headed by Ivan Drach and Dmitriy Pavlichko to support Gorbachev's *perestroika*, its program confined its nationalism to a call for Ukrainian sovereignty within the USSR. As it and the population radicalized, *Rukh*'s membership soared from 280,000 in 1989 to 630,000 by early 1991.[20]

However, *Rukh* inordinately represented three western, ethnic Ukrainian-dominated, Ukrainian-speaking, and Greek Catholic–dominated Galician *oblasts*—L'viv, Ternopil,' and Ivanovo-Frankivsk. Although these three regions comprise less than 10 percent of Ukraine's population, they were home to more than 47 percent of the delegates to the second *Rukh* congress in 1990. *Rukh* enjoyed far less support in eastern "Left-Bank" Ukraine, including the Donbass, with much larger ethnic Russian populations. Ukraine's ethnic minorities—Russians, Belorussians, Poles, and Jews—all tended to reject *Rukh*. Just under 95 percent of the Second Rukh Congress's delegates were ethnic Ukrainians;

Russians and Jews represented just 3.8 and 0.3 percent, respectively. The Ukrainian nationalist movement's largely Galician and western Ukrainian constituency was also reflected in opinion polls. In a 1991 poll the NR parliamentary deputies' bloc was favored over the CPU's bloc, the "Group of 239," by a ratio of 11 to 1 nationwide. In Crimea, the only Ukrainian oblast with a strong Russian majority (68 percent according to the 1979 census), the CPU majority led by 16 to 1.[21]

The radicalization and ethno–Ukrainization of *Rukh* was clear by its second congress held in Kiev in October 1990. Its new program declared the goal of Ukraine's full state independence by gradual and peaceful means and in coalition with all democratic anti-regime forces. As a result, *Rukh* came to lead a broad coalition of nationalist and pro-democracy parties and organizations united under *Narodna Rada* (the Democratic Bloc) or NR. In the March 1991 union republic and local elections to the reformed soviets turned legislatures, *Rukh* and *Rukh*-affiliated parties won 108 seats, and the pro-democracy Democratic Rebirth of the Ukraine (PDVU) won 43 seats. *Rukh* and the PDVU formed a united opposition deputies' bloc, "*Narodna Rada*," consisting of a third (151 of 450) of the seats and led by Lviv deputy Igor Yukhnovskiy, to compete with the ruling Communist Party of Ukraine's (CPU) majority in the Ukrainian SSR's Supreme Soviet. Of 126 members of Supreme Soviet standing committees, more than half belonged to the NR bloc, and NR bloc members headed 7 of 23 standing committees. Under NR pressure and declining Communist Party discipline, Ukraine's Supreme Soviet adopted a "Declaration of State Sovereignty" on July 16, 1990, as well as a resolution calling for military service by Ukrainian SSR draftees to be fulfilled on Ukrainian territory only, and the inclusion of the "republican question" in the March 1991 all-union referendum on the USSR's preservation (see below).

As in the USSR as a whole and its constituent parts with ethnonational territorial-administrative subunits, Ukraine's stateness was under stress by 1991 from growing inter-communal tensions and the Soviet party-state's incapacitation and breakdown. As Ukrainian nationalism began to drive events in its western regions and Kiev, Ukraine's most pro–Soviet and pro–Russian Ukrainian region, Crimea, began to countermobilize, pushing for greater autonomy. On January 20, 1991, Crimea Oblast convened an oblast-wide, popular referendum on Crimean sovereignty within the Ukrainian SSR; specifically, on whether or not to reestablish the Crimean Autonomous Soviet Socialist Republic, abolished in 1945. The proposal was approved by 94 percent of the voters. Crimea had answered *Rukh*'s sovereignty movement with its own.

In the March 17, 1991 all-union referendum on preservation of the Soviet Union, 71 percent of Ukrainians voted for preserving the USSR under a new Union Treaty. Only four of Ukraine's then 27 regions voted against (under 50 percent) preservation of the USSR: Kiev city and three Galician regions—Lviv, Ivano-Frankivsk, and Ternopil.

THE 17 MARCH 1991 ALL-UNION SOVIET REFERENDUM[22]

Union Question: Do you consider necessary the preservation of the Union of Soviet Socialist Republics as a renewed federation of equal sovereign republics, in which the rights and freedoms of an individual of any nationalist will be fully guaranteed?

Republic Question: Do you agree that Ukrine should be part of the Union of Soviet Sovereign States, based on the principles of Ukraine's Declaration of State Sovereignty?

Galician Question (included only in the three Galician regions/oblasts): Do you want Ukraine to become an independent state that independently decides its domestic and foreign policies, which guarantees equal rights to all of its citizens, regardless of their national or religious allegiance?

Table 2. Referendum Results in Ukraine
Broken Down by Region

Oblast (Region)	Union Question (percent affirmative)	Republican Question (percent affirmative)	Galician Question (percent affirmative)
Cherkassy	77.3	88.8	
Chernigiv (Chernigov)	83.3	90.3	
Chernivtsy (Chernovsty)	60.7	83.2	
Crimea	87.6	84.7	
Dnepropetrovsk	77.5	85.1	
Donetsk	84.6	86.2	
Ivano-Frankivsk*	18.2	52.1	87.9
Khar'kiv (Khar'kov)	75.8	83.8	
Kherson	81.4	87.4	
Khmel'nitsk	87.9	87.9	
Kiev city	44.6	78.2	
Kiev *oblast*	66.9	84.6	
Kirovgrad	82.4	89.5	
L'viv (L'vov)*	16.4	30.1	83.3
Luhansk (Voroshilovgrad)	86.3	88.8	
Mykolayv (Nikolaev)	85.2	87.7	
Odessa	82.1	84.5	
Poltava	78.8	88.7	
Rivno (Rovno)	54.2	79.6	
Sevastopil (Sevastopol)	83.9	84.2	
Sumy	78.8	87.1	
Ternopil (Ternopol)*	19.3	35.2	85.0
Vinnitsa	81.2	89.2	
Volyn	53.7	78.0	
Zakarpat'ye	60.2	69.5	
Zaporozh'ye	79.8	86.6	
Zhitomir	81.7	88.4	

Galician oblasts

Only 5 others voted under 75 percent in favor of preservation, and four of those were western regions. The results for the western, Galician L'viv, Ivano-Frankivsk, and Ternopil' *oblasti* were particularly striking. They were the only regions among Ukraine's 27 in which less than 20 percent voted "yes" on the "union question" favoring preservation of the reformed Union under a new Union Treaty proposed by Gorbachev and being negotiated with Yeltsin and most of the other union republics' leaders. The Galician regions voted overwhelmingly "yes" on the "Galician Question," which only they proposed, entered on the ballot and voted on. It unambiguously posed the question of Ukraine's complete separation from the USSR or any successor entity and stipulated Ukraine's complete independence. The Ukrainian pro-independence parties—most notably *Rukh* and the Ukrainian Republican Party (URP)—supported a "no" vote on the "union question" regarding preservation of the Union under the Union Treaty. The "republican question," which focused on an unclear proposal for Ukrainian state sovereignty without the Union Treaty or full independence added to the referendum by the centrist Ukrainian SSR government, exposed fissures between democrats and moderate nationalists, on the one hand, and more radical nationalists, on the other. The moderate wing of *Rukh* and the Ukrainian Democratic Party (UDP) urged voting "yes" on this question, but both *Rukh* radicals and the URP urged a "no" vote.

The significance of communal identity, historical factors, and regional divergence in Ukrainians' voting behavior and Ukraine's national politics was clear also from the results in the the "Russian" eastern and southern regons and in "Hungarian" Transcarpathia (Zakapartiya). The eastern and southern regions voted in the highest percentages to preserve the Union. Of the six most pro–Union votes, five were eastern (the Donbass's Donetsk and Luhansk) or southern (Crimea, Mikolayv, and Simferopol), and only one—Khmelnitsk—was niether eastern nor southern. Transcarpathia *oblast*—with its significant Hungarian, Russian, and Romanian minority populations—approved the union question by more than 60 percent and the republican question by more than 69 percent.[23]

But eight months later, on December 1, 1991, after the failed August coup and the breakdown of treaty negotiations, Ukrainian opinion and voting behavior was completely reversed. The failed August coup and the consummation of Russia's revolution from above had fully sapped the Union's stateness. Whereas in March, 71 percent had voted for preserving the Soviet Union, in December, 90 percent of Ukrainians voted for independence. Despite the near unanimity, the communal identity factor was still evident in the regional voting results. Pro-Soviet and Russian-dominated Crimea and Sevastopol supported independence, but just barely—by 54 percent and 57 percent, respectively.[24] If one takes into account these two regions' turnouts—the lowest in the voting, which included a presidential election—then the support for an independence drops to 37 and 40 percent, respectively.[25] Six *oblasti* with large Russian minorities—all in the east or south except for Kharkiv (which voted 86 percent for independence)—were the only other regions to vote below the national tally of 90.3 percent in favor of independence: Donetsk—84 percent; Luhansk—84 percent; Odessa—85 percent; Mykolayv—89 percent; and Kherson—90.1 percent.[26]

In Ukraine's first presidential election, the results produced a similar if somewhat less pronounced pattern in regionalist and communalist voting to those in the referendum results. Centrist reform communist Supreme Soviet Chairman Leonid Kravchuk won, supported by 62 percent of voters, mostly residents in the east, south, and center. His main contender—*Rukh* candidate Vyacheslav Chernovil—won 23 percent of the vote, most of which came from Galicia and other western regions. Crimea gave Kravchuk the least support of any southeastern or eastern region (57 percent) other than the Black Sea Fleet's home of Sevastopol (55 percent). Only two other regions in which Kravchuk won gave him a fewer votes: the somewhat Russified, north-central industrial center of Dnepropetrovsk (44 percent) and Chernivtsy (43 percent) of the southwest on the Black Sea.[27] Crimea's distrust of Kravchuk helped feed the autonomy and secessionist movement on the peninsula.

This east-west regional pattern in both the 1991 Ukrainian presidential election and independence referendum would hold to one degree or another for every post–Soviet Ukrainian presidential and parliamentary election.[28] A slight waning in the salience of regionalism emerged by 1999—a period when most post–Soviet issues, such as the fate of Crimea and the Black Sea Fleet, seemed to have been resolved at least temporarily (see below).[29] Additionally, the competing interpretations of Soviet and World War II history were smoothed over throughout the 1990s and early 2000s by successive presidents, who emphasized national unity and balancing east and west. Similarly, the NATO and EU membership issues had not been stridently pursued and therefore also lacked salience.

In their opposition to the west's Ukrainian nationalism and views of Ukrainian history, the Soviet legacy, and Kiev's geopolitical orientation—what might be called the

Galician perspective—the eight most Russified regions (Donetsk and Luhansk in the east; Mykolayv, Kherson, Odessa, Crimea, and Sevastopol in the south; and Kharkiv in the central north) register throughout the *perestroika* and post–Soviet periods—most resonantly in 2014—as outliers among Ukraine's regions, whether in terms of election results, opinion surveys, or political developments and outcomes. This is especially true for Crimea, Sevastopol, Donetsk, and Luhansk. By contrast, ethnic Ukrainian L'viv, Ternopil, Ivano-Frankivsk, Volyn, and Chernivtsy in the west are outliers in their support for the Galician perspective. The rest of the country has been more evenly divided on these issues. These cleavages persisted throughout the history of post–Soviet Ukraine, and sometimes manifested themselves in conflict over relations between the center in Kiev and the outlier regions.

This schism between the west and southeast persisted through both the difficult immediate post–Soviet 1990s and the 2000s. The persistence of the tectonic was evidenced on the events of 2013–14 in the voting results in both rounds of the 2010 presidential election—the last presidential election (see Tables 3 and 4)—as well as in the 2012 parliamentary elections.

Table 3. Last Pre–Maidan Revolt Ukrainian Presidential Election First Round, Results by Region*

Region	Yanukovich	Tymoshenko	Tihipko	Yatsenyuk	Yushchenko
Total	35.3	25.0	13.1	7.0	5.5
Crimea	61.1	12.0	11.0	2.6	1.3
Vinnytsia region	15.0	46.9	11.2	9.5	2.9
Volyn region	9.6	53.8	10.2	5.4	4.5
Dnipropetrovsk region	41.7	14.8	22.5	6.5	1.2
Donetsk region	76.0	4.3	7.2	2.8	0.7
Zhytomyr region	24.3	32.6	13.5	8.4	2.8
Zakarpats'ka region	29.7	26.2	10.0	10.2	5.9
Zaporizhzhia region	50.8	12.3	17.7	5.1	1.1
Ivano-Frankivsk region	5.1	39.0	4.4	13.8	25.1
Kyiv region	15.5	42.3	15.4	8.8	3.0
Kirovohrad region	26.7	34.6	14.5	5.8	1.6
Luhansk region	71.1	6.5	9.5	2.4	0.7
Lviv region	5.7	34.7	4.8	11.0	30.8
Mykolaiv region	51.3	13.5	13.4	5.5	1.5
Odessa region	51.1	10.2	21.1	4.0	1.5
Poltava region	25.3	32.0	12.3	9.1	3.1
Rivne region	12.5	43.9	10.7	7.0	7.3
Sumy region	18.7	36.8	14.5	7.1	4.3
Ternopil region	9.8	35.7	4.8	9.9	26.4
Kharkiv region	50.2	10.7	18.8	5.9	1.5
Kherson region	40.4	19.3	15.5	5.9	1.9
Khmelnyts region	15.2	40.1	13.2	11.5	3.3
Cherkasy region	17.4	41.2	12.9	7.0	3.4
Chernivtsi region	19.1	32.3	8.9	19.3	7.9
Chernihiv region	19.5	42.7	13.4	5.5	2.1
Kyiv	15.9	35.7	19.0	8.7	3.8
Sevastopol	56.1	6.5	15.1	2.0	0.7

Includes only those candidates who succeeded in winning more than 5 percent of the votes nationwide: Viktor Yanukovich, Yulia Tymoshenko, Sergey Tihipko, Arseniy Yatsenyuk, and Viktor Yushchenko.

Source: Alex Kireyev, "Ukraine. Presidential Election 2010," *Electoral Geography 2.0*, www.electoralgeography.com/new/en/countries/u/ukraine/ukraine-presidential-election-2010.html. Retrieved November 25, 2015.

Table 4. Last Pre–Maidan Revolt Ukrainian
Presidential Election Second Round, Results by Region*

	Yanukovich	Tymoshenko	Against All
Total	48.95%	45.47%	4.36%
Crimea	78.24%	17.31%	3.23%
Vinnytsia region	24.26%	71.10%	3.32%
Volyn region	14.01%	81.85%	3.11%
Dnipropetrovsk region	62.70%	29.13%	6.75%
Donetsk region	90.44%	6.45%	2.26%
Zhytomyr region	36.70%	57.50%	4.53%
Zakarpats'ka region	41.55%	51.66%	4.46%
Zaporizhzhia region	71.50%	22.22%	5.07%
Ivano-Frankivsk region	7.02%	88.89%	2.84%
Kyiv region	23.61%	69.71%	5.10%
Kirovohrad region	39.61%	54.66%	4.46%
Luhansk region	88.96%	7.72%	2.34%
Lviv region	8.60%	86.20%	4.16%
Mykolaiv region	71.53%	22.95%	4.30%
Odessa region	74.14%	19.52%	4.61%
Poltava region	38.99%	54.20%	5.75%
Rivne region	18.91%	76.24%	3.65%
Sumy region	30.40%	62.89%	5.33%
Ternopil region	7.92%	88.39%	2.83%
Kharkiv region	71.35%	22.43%	5.12%
Kherson region	59.98%	33.73%	5.04%
Khmelnyts region	24.94%	69.74%	3.84%
Cherkasy region	28.84%	65.37%	4.48%
Chernivtsi region	27.64%	66.47%	4.11%
Chernihiv region	30.95%	63.63%	4.22%
Kyiv	25.72%	65.34%	8.05%
Sevastopol	84.35%	10.38%	4.35%

*Includes only those candidates who succeeded in winning more than 5 percent of the votes nationwide: Viktor Yanukovich, Yulia Tymoshenko, Sergey Tihipko, Arseniy Yatsenyuk, and Viktor Yushchenko.
Source: Alex Kireyev, "Ukraine. Presidential Election 2010," *Electoral Geography 2.0*, www.electoralgeography.com/new/en/countries/u/ukraine/ukraine-presidential-election-2010.html. Retrieved November 25, 2015.

The persistence of Ukraine's east-west schism is also evidenced by the results of the 2012 parliamentary election results—the last nationwide elections held before the Maidan crisis of 2013–2014 (see Table 5). The Party of the Regions or PR—like its leader, President Viktor Yanukovich—was rooted in the coal mining and industrial east and largely pro-Russian.

Table 5. Last Pre–Maidan Revolt Ukrainian
Parliamentary Election, 2012, Results by Region*

Region	Party of Regions	Fatherland	UDAR	Communist	Freedom
Ukraine	30.01	25.53	13.96	13.18	10.44
Crimea	52.34	13.09	7.16	19.41	1.04
Vinnytsia region	17.38	44.95	13.35	8.85	8.40
Volyn region	12.92	39.46	15.96	6.97	17.98
Dnipropetrovsk region	35.79	18.38	14.61	19.38	5.19
Donetsk region	65.09	5.26	4.71	18.85	1.20
Zhytomyr region	21.60	36.16	14.19	12.82	7.47
Zakarpats'ka region	30.87	27.69	20.02	5.03	8.35
Zaporizhzhia region	40.95	14.93	12.40	21.16	3.85

(Region)	(Party of Regions)	(Fatherland)	(UDAR)	(Communist)	(Freedom)
Ivano-Frankivsk region	5.19	38.21	15.25	1.78	33.79
Kyiv region	20.67	36.63	18.73	6.11	10.85
Kirovohrad region	26.25	32.16	14.87	13.46	6.21
Luhansk region	57.06	5.49	4.74	25.14	1.29
Lviv region	4.70	35.49	14.44	1.99	38.01
Kyiv	12.60	30.96	25.47	7.21	17.32
Sevastopol	46.90	5.86	5.04	29.46	1.37
Mykolaiv region	40.46	16.93	12.49	19.09	4.30
Odessa region	41.90	15.49	13.77	18.16	3.30
Poltava region	21.91	30.14	18.47	13.49	7.94
Rivne region	15.80	36.59	17.25	6.21	16.63
Sumy region	21.09	36.27	16.71	12.24	6.37
Ternopil region	6.40	39.04	14.67	1.92	31.22
Kharkiv region	40.97	15.22	12.82	20.84	3.83
Kherson region	29.34	21.78	13.63	23.34	4.71
Khmelnyts region	18.69	37.71	16.33	8.81	11.79
Cherkasy region	18.71	37.77	17.25	9.28	9.46
Chernivtsi region	20.77	39.60	19.13	5.46	8.71
Chernihiv region	20.09	30.73	12.91	13.20	5.98

Includes only those parties that received more than 5 percent of the votes nationwide.

Source: Alex Kireyev, "Ukraine. Legislative Election 2012," *Electoral Geography 2.0*, www.electoralgeography. com/new/en/countries/u/ukraine/ukraine-legislative-election-2012.html. Retrieved November 25, 2015.

Thus, it repeated its leaders' successes in the east and south but was routed in the west. For all of the historical, economic, and communal reasons feeding neo-communist nostalgia in the east, PR's only real competitor in the east was the UCP, and for the same reasons it performed miserably in the west. The Ukranian chauvinist former president Viktor Yushchenko's "Our Ukraine" party received only 1.1 of the votes nationwide, marking the final and fatal blow to Yushchenko's political career. The Ukrainian Democratic Alliance for Reform, or UDAR, which finished just ahead of the UCP for third place in the nationwide vote, was founded in April 2010 and is headed by the former boxer Vitaliy Klichko. It did poorly in the east, but did not do conversely well in the west as is usually the case, because it is not a particularly nationalist party. It was the only party that performed similarly in almost all regions. It did best in the typically divided capital of Kiev, taking 25 percent of the vote.

The nationalist wing of Ukraine's political spectrum, which was growing by this time, did quite well in the 2012 Rada elections. Fatherland or "Batkyvshchina," a Ukrainian nationalist and democratic party led by former prime minister and frequent presidential candidate Yulia Tymoshenko, performed well in Galicia and the west. Also perfoming shockingly well was the deceptively named neofascist "Svoboda" or Freedom Party (SP), which won an astonishing 10 percent of the vote countrywide. Its base of support again was in Galicia and western Ukraine and their ethnic Ukrainian population. Ukraine's schism can be seen in the breakdown of Svoboda's voters by language: two-thirds of its voters were Ukrainian-lanuguage speakers, 25 percent were bilingual (Russian and Ukrainian), and 11 percent were Russian-speaking.[30] In the 2010 and 2012 elections we see an even wider schism between east and west than was seen in the 1991 independence referendum and presidential election. This was a consequence of the polarizing Yushchenko presidency and would be reflected in other political activity that would put great stress on Ukraine's stateness problem.

The Tectonics of Ukraine's Stateness Problem
Operationalized: The First Cracks

In Crimea especially, but also in Donbass, pro–Russian feeling remained high, with a significant minority preferring exit from Ukraine, especially if their regions were to enjoy little to no autonomy and their voice would not register at the national level in the new independent Ukraine. Crimean and Donbass regionalism and communalism led to several regional referenda designed to secure greater autonomy from Kiev. The first regional referenda in post–Soviet Ukraine and the second and third in the former Soviet Union (the first occurred two years earlier in Russia's Republic of Tatarstan, approving a new republic constitution) were held in Donbass and Crimea (and Sevastopol, located on the peninsula) on March 27, 1994. They addressed regionalist and communalist issues and marked the first wave in Ukraine's post–Soviet stateness challenge.

THE DONBASS CRACK

The Donbass Inter-Movement (*Interdvizhenie Donbasa*) that pushed through the Donbass referendum emerged just three months after Ukraine's 1990 sovereignty declaration. Founded in December 1990, it began campaigning for a local referendum on whether or not Donetsk oblast should upgrade to the status of a "subject of the USSR" if Ukraine refused to sign Gorbachev's proposed Union Treaty.[31] The purpose of the upgrade—for example, to the status of an ASSR (autonomous soviet socialist republic)—was to position the region to secede from the Ukraine SSR or threaten to do so should the latter reject the treaty and pursue secession from the USSR. A series of new Union laws on the process of secession from the USSR and the equal status of SSRs and ASSRs in certain respects was passed by the USSR Supreme Soviet in April 1990, allowing for ASSRs to have the same legal status as a subject of the USSR as union republics and be a signatory to the proposed Union Treaty. Thus, an ASSR not wishing to exit the USSR that was part of an SSR (union republic) that decided to initiate the secession process could itself begin secession from the SSR and remain in the Union. The Donbass referendum was in part also an expression of dissatisfaction with the economic situation in this primarily mining and industrial region mired in the depression that plagued both post–Soviet Ukraine and Russia, the major consumer of Donbass coal. Indeed, the referendum followed a Donbass miners' strike.

Although the referendum was "consultative" and nonbinding, it potentially might affect the political agenda in the east by producing a reliable snapshot of public opinion in these two regions on questions crucial for Ukraine's stateness and statehood. Donbass voters were asked to approve or reject four propositions: (1) Ukraine's full membership in the post–Soviet CIS; (2) creation of a federative system for Ukraine; (3) establishment of Russian as Ukraine's second official state language; (4) and immediate establishment of Russian as an official language alongside Ukrainian in Donbass.[32] All four were approved by overwhelming majorities of approximately 90 percent.[33] Full membership in the CIS received the most support, with 91 percent approval in Luhansk, 89 percent in Donetsk.[34] The Donbass twice again attempted to hold a regional referendum: ten years later in backlash against the 2004 Orange revolution, and 20 years later in a last attempt to achieve autonomy in protest against the Maidan revolution.

THE CRIMEAN CRACK

As one might expect, a referendum also was held in Crimea at the time. A Crimean separatist movement favoring reunification with Russia emerged as the Soviet collapse developed in 1990–91. Some in the central CPSU apparatus in Moscow and the UCP in Kiev were encouraging separatism in the union republics as a counter to the union republics' parade of sovereignty declarations. On the other hand, some Crimeans within the independence movement were prepared to settle for broad autonomy within Ukraine, if Kiev was willing to grant it. Thus, in 1990 the Crimean Oblast's parliament, elected in spring under the reformed Soviet election system, passed a resolution convening an oblast referendum in January 1991 on whether or not to restore the oblast's status as an autonomous soviet socialist republic (ASSR), abolished in 1944 by Stalin.

As with the Donbass, the purpose of the upgrade to an ASSR was to position the peninsula to secede or threaten secession from Ukraine should the Ukraine SSR seek to secede from the USSR. The January 1991 referendum question, therefore, read: "Are you in favor of the recreation of the Crimean Autonomous Soviet Socialist Republic as a Subject of the Union of SSRs and a Participant of the Union Treaty?" The referendum saw a high turnout of 81.3 percent, with more than 93 percent voting in favor of the upgrade to ASSR status—and all it implied. Simultaneously, residents of Sevastopol, the base for Russia's Soviet Black Sea Fleet, voted on whether the city also should be granted "Union-republican" status, with 90 percent voting in favor. Both referenda were supported by president Kravchuk and the former's results ratified in the resolution "On the Renewal of the Crimean Autonomous Soviet Socialist Republic" adopted by the Ukrainian Supreme Soviet in February, restoring Crimea's ASSR status "within the borders of the Ukrainian SSR."[35]

As the Soviet collapse accelerated, Crimea began to pursue greater autonomy and even full state independence, moving to the center of world attention for neither the first nor last time. On the day Ukraine's parliament declared independence (pending a referendum) after the failed August 1991 coup in Moscow, the Republic Movement of Crimea (RDK) was founded under the leadership of Crimea's future president Yurii Meshkov. By September 4 the RDK pushed through the Crimean parliament a declaration of the peninsula's sovereignty within the Ukraine SSR, mimicking that of Ukraine issued a year earlier. It also supported Crimea's independence, an appeal to Gorbachev and the Union government to nullify the 1954 Soviet transfer of Crimea to the Ukraine SSR, repeal of a Ukraine SSR law making propaganda supporting Crimean independence a crime, and a referendum on Crimea's "independence in union with other states"—the intent being Crimea's secession from Ukraine and its joining the CIS. An RDK campaign was able within two months to collect nearly 248,000 signatures in support of the referendum; only 180,000 were needed.[36]

In response to these developments, Supreme Soviet Chairman Kravchuk held out a carrot and a stick. He supported negotiations on Crimean autonomy and a power-sharing agreement to delineate spheres of jurisdiction and dispatched a delegation to Simferopol (Crimea's capital, not to be confused with the Black Sea Fleet base Sevastopol) in February 1991. It was able to fashion a joint statement supporting Crimean autonomy and a free economic zone. In March, the two sides agreed on a draft law that would serve as the basis for a power-sharing law to be approved in succession by the Crimean and Ukrainian parliaments.[37] Kravchuk was determined not to allow Ukraine's stateness and territorial integrity to go the way of that of the USSR. But it had been Kravchuk who partnered with Yeltsin and Belarussian President Stanislav Shushkevich in putting the last nail in the Union's coffin by signing the Belovezhsk agreement abolishing the USSR and founding the CIS in December 1991.

The peninsula's status within Ukraine would be tied to an agreement between Kiev and Moscow on the fate of both the former Soviet medium-range nuclear weapons based in Ukraine and the Black Sea Fleet based in pro–Russian Sevastopol on the peninsula. According to Sergei Stankevich, then Russian President Yeltsin's liberal presidential envoy to the crumbling USSR's soon-to-be former union republics, he, together with then Russian Vice-President Aleksandr Rutskoi, began negotiating with Kravchuk and *Rukh*'s leadership in late August 1991 in the wake of the collapse of the hard-line coup. The talks intensified in September and concluded in December with a "verbal," "informal pact," suggesting Yeltsin was repeating Gorbachev's omission in failing to obtain a more legally binding signed treaty. Under the "pact," Moscow and Kiev agreed: Crimea would receive broad autonomy and remain part of Ukraine; Kiev would hand over to Moscow all of its strategic and tactical nuclear weapons; and the Black Sea Fleet would be Russia's, with Moscow to lease the Sevastopol base. According to Stankevich, Yeltsin was more interested in securing Ukraine's nuclear weapons, the fleet and the base than in winning Crimea's reunification with Russia, and therefore was willing to trade the latter for the former. The tactical nuclear weapons and Tupolev-160 strategic bombers were removed to Russia in 1992–93. The handover of its nuclear forces was not a loss for Kiev, since the entire international community strongly supported the consolidation of all the former USSR's nuclear forces under a single command. In return for the fleet, on which an agreement was indeed signed later, Ukraine retained sovereignty over Crimea, but was required to grant the peninsula broad autonomy—what was called essentially a confederative relationship—but in political science terminology was more akin to what federalism scholars refer to as a "federacy"—a state in which one region receives special, autonomous status that no other regions enjoy. Crimea would be allowed its own constitution, president, taxation powers, budget, and language and cultural rights and autonomy for both Russians and Tatars.[38] In other words, according to Stankevich, full self-determination, excluding the right of secession.[39]

Additionally, although Kravchuk sought to balance regional, communal, and economic interests in order to hold Ukraine's stateness problem at bay, his goal of political stability prompted him—as did similar considerations in Yeltsin's Russia—to pursue a centralization of power both within the central government in Kiev and between Kiev and the regions. Specifically, he requested special decree powers and the authority to appoint presidential representatives to each region, much as Yeltsin did in Russia and the CPSU had in the Soviet party-state. Kravchuk justified such powers by referencing the unaccountability of state agencies, especially those at the local level. The requisite constitutional changes were passed by the Ukrainian parliament, the Verkhovnaya Rada (Supreme Council), in February 1992. Kravchuk then announced the idea of an informal round table of "progressive" parties, groups, movements and trade unions in which, he emphasized, the predominantly ethnic and western Ukrainian "Rukh is capable … of standing now at the head."[40] In April, the Rada passed in a first reading the agreed-upon draft law on power-sharing. However, *Rukh* and its allies in the Rada watered down the document in order to limit Crimea's autonomy, treating the peninsula not as an equal partner in a bilateral treaty process but as a subject granted an autonomy that could be unilaterally abrogated. Moreover, once the RDK succeeded in gathering enough signatures to secure a referendum, Kravchuk, backed by a parliamentary majority, issued a statement condemning the referendum effort, claiming it was organized by those who wanted to destabilize Ukraine and Ukrainian-Russian relations. He emphasized that while he was willing to negotiate with the peninsula on greater autonomy, he would never negotiate on a division of Ukraine or redrawing its borders.[41]

Dissatisfaction in Crimea and other pro–Russian regions only grew, but the Crimean Soviet still hedged its steps. On May 5, 1992 the Crimean parliament—still called the Supreme Soviet, reflecting its continued allegiance to Moscow—voted 118 to 49 for conditional independence under an "Act of Independence," to be confirmed in a peninsula-wide referendum in August. A second referendum question would ask voters if they supported "an independent Crimea in union with other states." The Soviet's chairman, Nikolai Bagrov, tried to soften matters by saying a "yes" vote in the referendum did not mean secession. The Crimean Soviet reconvened the next day and approved a constitution for Crimea, but Bagrov was able to gain approval for inserting a sentence into the founding document acknowledging that Crimea "is part of the state of Ukraine and defines its relations with it on the basis of a treaty and agreements."[42]

Nevertheless, on May 14 the Ukrainian Rada annulled the Crimean declaration of independence, gave the Crimean Soviet one week to cancel the referendum, and instructed the president to take measures to restore law and order in Crimea.[43] On May 20, Crimea responded by issuing a resolution annulling a resolution on the act of independence but not annulling the act itself, suspended until June 10 the resolution proposing the August referendum, asked Kiev to repeal the diluted law on Crimean autonomy and a draft law on presidential representatives in the regions, and requested clear proposals on delineating powers. Negotiations resumed and agreement was reached on power-sharing that satisfied Simferopol. On June 30 the Ukrainian Rada passed the compromise power-sharing law, including the peninsula's status as the "Crimean Autonomous Republic" with the right to a constitution, but its coming into force was made conditional on the Crimean Soviet's canceling the referendum and bringing its constitution and laws into accordance with those of Ukraine. In July, the crisis appeared to end when the Crimean Soviet canceled the independence referendum and amended its constitution and several laws to Kiev's satisfaction.[44]

However, the threat to Ukraine's stateness remained, given: (1) its several schisms (in Crimea and elsewhere); (2) the insistence of many Crimeans, such as the RDK, on seeking closer ties to Moscow; (3) the existence of a Crimean constitution; and (4) the right in Ukraine to hold referenda. In October 1993, the Crimean Soviet again sought greater autonomy by amending its constitution to establish the office of president of Crimea. Two months later, Crimeans went to the polls to elect the peninsula's first president. In the first round, the pro–Moscow, pro-autonomy/independence vote was divided by several candidates, including UCP candidate Leonid Grach (13 percent), Russian Party candidate Sergei Shuvainykov (14 percent), and "Russia Bloc" leader Yurii Meshkov (39 percent). The pro–Moscow Meshkov won the runoff with 73 percent, defeating Kiev's candidate Mykola Bagrov, whose 18 percent came mostly from ethnic Tatars and Ukrainians.[45]

In July 1994, Leonid Kuchma was elected president of Ukraine. A power struggle then ensued between Kiev and Crimea, prompting Meshkov to initiate a referendum easily approved by Crimea's Supreme Soviet. A 1994 Crimean referendum offered three questions, and its results indicated strong support for broader autonomy from Kiev and closer ties with Russia: 78.4 percent voted for greater autonomy from Ukraine by way of developing relations with Kiev on the basis of "a treaty and agreements," 82.8 percent favored establishing dual Russian-Ukrainian citizenship, and 77.9 percent supported giving Crimean presidential decrees the force of law on the peninsula. The development of federative relations on the basis of a bilateral treaty and sub-agreements would have repeated Moscow's efforts to hold the post–Soviet Russian Federation together using precisely such instruments eventually with 46 of its regions—the first signed with Tatarstan one month before the Donbass and Crimea referenda.[46]

Thus, twenty years before the latest crisis, Ukraine had a stateness crisis, with Crimean support for broad autonomy, even secession and reunification with Russia running the risk of becoming an international crisis. From 1992, together with the growing secessionist sentiment on the peninsula, Russian resentment grew regarding the loss of Crimea—with its overwhelmingly ethnic Russian population, tens of thousands of Russian military servicemen, Black Sea Fleet naval base, military-historical resonance and mythology, and status as a popular vacation resort area. Kiev laid claim to ownership of the Black Sea Fleet and balked on surrendering the nuclear forces located on its territory, seen by some Ukrainians as a hedge against any reversion to Russian imperialism or attempts to assert sovereignty over Crimea.

The Budapest Memorandum signed in Budapest, Hungary, on December 5, 1994, seemed to resolve the crisis, codifying parts of the 1991 Russian-Ukrainian "pact" and providing security assurances from its signatories relating to Ukraine's accession to the Treaty on the Non-Proliferation of Nuclear Weapons. The Memorandum was originally signed by three nuclear powers—Russia, the U.S., and the UK. In effect, the overall set of agreements amounted to Ukraine exchanging its nuclear status and centralized control over Crimea in return for a trilateral American-British-Russian guarantee of Ukraine's national security and sovereignty over a semi-autonomous Crimea. The Budapest Memorandum and the Russian-Ukrainian agreement on Crimean autonomy within Ukraine that accompanied it, along with a lull in NATO expansion efforts, produced a temporary reduction in international tensions over, and communal dissonance within, Ukraine. By the 1999 presidential election, the regional schism over Ukraine's difficult civilizational choice had softened. An opinion survey showed that whereas in western Ukraine 69 percent were opposed to Russian economic aid, a majority (55 percent) in the east also opposed it. At the same time, 59 percent in the west opposed American assistance, a not-so-dissimilar 68 percent opposed it in the east.[47]

Domestically, however, the new comity quickly crumbled. Immediately after the Budapest Memorandum was sealed, Ukraine abandoned the 1991 informal pact with Moscow on Crimea codified under Budapest. Taking advantage of Russia's more weakened condition exacerbated by the Chechen war begun in December 1994, "Kiev broke our informal pact and took back all competencies and funding from Crimea," "an enormous mistake," in Stankevich's words.[48] Thus, the Western-sponsored Budapest Memorandum became cover for Kiev—along with the Chechen war—allowing it to violate its agreement with Moscow. As we have seen, this was only the first of several agreements broken by the West. Kiev repealed all of the agreed-upon autonomy for Crimea, emasculating its constitution and terminating its right to elect its own president, collect taxes, and form its own budget. Kiev also took control of interethnic and cultural matters, including language issues, and the Ukrainian president was empowered to appoint district heads on the peninsula.[49] On March 17, 1995 the Verkhovna Rada in Kiev unilaterally abolished Crimea's presidency and constitution. The Crimean parliament was then pressured under threat of abrogation by the Ukrainian parliament to draft a new constitution. From June through September, President Kuchma held Crimea under direct presidential administration rule until October, when the Crimean Soviet adopted a new constitution. However, Kiev's Rada refused to ratify (pursuant to Article 135 of the Ukrainian constitution stipulating Rada ratification of Crimea's constitution) until December 1998, after significant amendments had been proposed in April 1996, negotiated for two years, and finally adopted by Crimea's parliament in October 1998.

In the interim, a new Ukrainian constitution was ratified in 1996. Although Kiev rejected broad autonomy for Crimea and the formation of a federative state in favor of a unitary state, it acquiesced to some Crimean demands for autonomy by establishing formal elements of a federacy for the peninsula. Kiev's hegemony was granted by Article 136's stipulations that the appointment of the Crimean Council of Ministers chairman made by the Crimean Rada is subject to the Ukrainian president's "agreement," that the courts on the peninsula were part of a unified Ukrainian judicial system, and by Article 139's creation of a representative office or envoy of Ukraine's president to Crimea determined solely by a law of the Ukrainian parliament. Central power was further strengthened by Articles 135 and 137, which mandated that Crimean laws and governmental directives must not violate the Ukrainian constitution and laws, and that the Ukrainian president can suspend such acts by way of an appeal approved by Ukraine's Constitutional Court regarding their questionable constitutionality.[50]

Crimea's limited autonomy notwithstanding, most Crimeans continued to view Kiev's rule as lacking legitimacy. Many already looked to Moscow for a solution, according to a 1997 opinion poll carried out in Crimea. Although "only" 38 percent of the ethnic Russians and 21 percent of ethnic Ukrainians on the peninsula favored Crimea's secession from Ukraine, 72 percent and 51 of those, respectively, favored its reunification with Russia.[51] The difference is explained by the fact that many desired Crimea's reunification with Russia via Ukraine's reunification with Russia. The 2004 Orange revolt and 2014 Maidan revolution would remove the contradiction in these numbers, driving the percentage favoring secession upward.

Maidan 1.0: The 2004 Orange Revolution

Ukrainian politics in the 1990s and early 2000s significantly mimicked those of its "elder brother" Russia. Both, like almost all post–Soviet states, suffer from a variable mix of excessive corruption, criminality, lack of rule of law, overlapping of politics and business, nationalism and ultranationalism, inter-communal intolerance and violence, and authoritarian rule or democracy. In 1994, independent Ukraine's nascent democracy faced its first major test, as President Kravchuk's first term expired, requiring Ukraine's first post–Soviet presidential election. Kravchuk had shepherded Ukraine through the Soviet collapse to independent statehood, preventing violence and separatism. His reliance on *Rukh* and the ethnic Ukrainian western regions—in addition to some of the central regions—required him to adopt more nationalist rhetoric in the campaign. His more "pro–Russian" opponent, Leonid Kuchma, performed strongly in his home region of industrial Dnepropetrovsk, Kharkiv farther east, and in the south, winning the election.

As mentioned, the vote reaffirmed the country's regional schism for all future nationwide votes.

The 1990s and Kuchma's first term were a period of increasing Western, in particular American, involvement in Ukrainian politics. The key instruments were the Ukrainian diaspora, financial influence, USAID and other government and government-tied institutions' dual-use DP programs. The U.S. government instrumentalized and deployed the Ukrainian-American diaspora centered in Chicago—a hotbed of the large, strongly Russophobic and often ultranationalist Ukrainian and Polish diaspora communities.

The wife of 2004 Orange revolution president Viktor Yushchenko, Yekaterina Chumachenko, appears to be a model upon which other Ukrainian-American former officials deployed to strengthen Ukrainian-American ties and draw Kiev closer to the West. Born into a Ukrainian family in Chicago and having joined a local Ukrainian youth organization at the age of 14, Chumachenko was groomed for Ukrainian politics. Graduating Georgetown University, she developed contacts in Washington which she parlayed into a government career, working in the State and Treasury Departments and the Ronald Reagan White House.[52] She also worked at the Ukrainian National Information Center, a hotbed of Ukrainian diaspora nationalists in the U.S. In 1993, she moved to Kiev to work for KMPG Peat Marwick/Barents Group, where she immediately made contacts in the government and the Rada, and met Central Bank director Yushchenko, whom Chumachenko married in 1998. One of Chumachenko's contacts in the Rada became another Ukrainian-American turned Ukrainian citizen, Ivan Lozovoi, who simultaneously headed *Rukh*'s international department and the Pilip Orlik Center. At the latter, she conducted educational lectures for Rada deputies.[53]

As her relationship with Yushchenko became closer, the latter opened the flow of state bonds on capital markets and allowed their purchase by nonresidents in 1996—a boon for the Ukrainian diaspora seeking to deepen its influence in the home country. Eventually, the lack of regulation led to the infamous OGVZ pyramid scheme and collapse, in which foreign bond traders received privileged access to high-profit loans until the pyramid imploded, reducing the Central Bank's reserves by $3 billion. That in turn contributed to Ukraine's 1998 financial crisis along with Kiev's deeper integration into, and reliance on, American financial institutions, the troubles of which sparked the global crisis, which played a role in Ukraine's crisis as well. At this time, Chumachenko left the grant organization sector for the Ukrainian branch of Barents Group, which brought in political consultants, according to one source, and began advising Yushchenko. When Kuchma won re-election, he visited the U.S. in 1999, where U.S. Vice-President Albert Gore recommended he appoint the reformer Yushchenko as his premier. In December 1999, Kuchma backed Yushchenko for premier after his previous nominee lost the confirmation vote in the Rada by a single vote. Finally, having worked both in the State Department and U.S. embassy in Kiev on financing Ukraine's economic development, Chumachenko very likely knew Natalie Jaresko, who became a major promoter of Western interests in Ukraine in the 2000s and then finance minister, as discussed below.[54]

As Chumachenko expanded her influence and contacts in Kiev, she developed close ties with Americans and Brits of Ukrainian desecent. Three in particular were important in promoting the Western agenda in Ukraine and Yushchenko's image in the West: Marta Kolomiets, *Los Angeles Times* journalist Mary Miso, and *Financial Times* journalist Chrysta Freeland. The quartet of Chumachenko, Kolomiets, Miso, and Freeland were instrumental in bringing in Western politicians and financiers to help Yushchenko in the

Central Bank. He was visited by the likes of Brzezinski and financier-activist George Soros. Kolomiets came to Ukraine in the 1990s and was the first foreign journalist to live in Kiev on a permanent basis, inspired by the romanticism of returning to the land of her grandfather. She was proud when one Ukrainian paper called her a Ukrainian spy and President Kravchuk told a conference that such journalists needed to be stripped of their accreditation, given their anticommunist views. Kolomiets was regarded as the "brain trust" of the four ladies' quasi–think tank and led the effort begun in 1994–1995 to promote both Chumachenko and her husband internationally. Later, Kolomiets headed the Ukrainian Educational Center for Market Reform in Kiev, which instructed attendees on the ins and outs of capitalism.[55]

Mary Miso undertook the defense of journalists, including in court proceedings involving charges of violating the honor and dignity of politicians. Miso also organized a Media Club for informal meetings of journalists in her apartment. The list of attendees was compiled by Chumachenko. Freeland's journalistic work supported the idea east and west of Ukraine's Western integration. Another Ukrainian-Russian woman, Vera Nanivska, who received a doctorate from Moscow's Oriental Institute, headed Kiev's International Center for Policy Analysis funded by Soros's Open Society Fund and the World Bank. She then became rector of the Academy of State Management under the president after Yushchenko's election. The grant programs that funded these and others' centers and programs were ended once Yushchenko was elected, and were revived after Yanukovich won the presidency in 2010.[56]

More importantly, USAID, CANVAS and Otpor were very active in Ukraine during the runup to the 2004 presidential election. In 2005 the USAID-funded group "Development Associates, Inc.," or DAI, triumphantly reported on its Ukraine operations: "A USAID-supported activity known as the Strengthening Electoral Administration in Ukraine Project (SEAUP), administered by Development Associates, played a decidedly important role in facilitating Ukraine's turn to democracy in 2004." Picking up in late 2003 where a previous USAID program had left off, DAI worked "directly with NDI, IRI, Freedom House, InterNews, and ABA/CEELI." DAI expressed pride in its role in this "strategically located nation," noting: "While the Ukrainian people are clearly the ultimate owners of the Orange Revolution, the U.S. Government and its implementing partners can take pride in their role."[57] In DAI's view, "the Orange Revolution was a movement strengthened and facilitated by the democracy and governance and rule of law projects supported by Western donor agencies, including those of the United States Government." SEAUP, "funded by USAID," "succeeded because literally thousands of poll workers bought into its promise and because hundreds of local trainers delivered high-quality inputs designed by former members of the national Parliament and insightful officials from the various Ukrainian think tanks and NGOs affiliated with the project." SEAUP "owes its success to the unwavering commitment of USAID and the American Embassy in Kyiv [Kiev]."[58]

The main official use for such organizations was training in the proper conduct and monitoring of elections. However, it was also involved in helping draft election legislation, and its reach was far and wide.[59] DAI reported to USAID that in 2004, SEAUP "directly trained 7,405 individuals at the territorial election commission level (election commissioners, candidate proxies/representatives or lawyers)," "over 95,000 polling station commissioners," and at least "1,350 election judges." Training took place in each of the country's 27 administrative regions. During the build-up to November's first round of presidential voting, the training of election commissioners was in "high gear," with "over a hundred thousand individuals participating in various training events in September and October."[60] These trainees became the network of foot soldiers driving the Orange revolution.

After his reelection in 1999, Kuchma's second term was covered in corruption and scandal, culminating in the murder of *Ukrainskaya Pravda*'s investigative journalist Georgiy Gongadze, whose decapitated body was discovered in September 2000. A videotape subsequently emerged in which a voice, allegedly Kuchma's, is heard calling for Gongadze to be silenced. It was seemingly fitting that Kuchma would endorse the candidacy of his controversial prime minister, Viktor Yanukovich. The latter was surrounded in controversy, having been convicted for criminal activity twice in his youth. In 1967, at age 17 he was sentenced to three years for robbery and assault. In 1970, he received a two-year sentence for assault. Nonetheless, he was appointed Donetsk's governor in 1997 with backing from one of Ukraine's often corrupt and criminal oligarchs, the Donbass coal baron Rinat Akhmetov. Yanukovich's reign in the wild steppe combined, as Sakwa puts it, "co-optation and coercion, although not totally devoid of a rational pragmatism tempered by corruption and cronyism."[61] Kuchma appointed Yanukovich prime minister in November 2002, putting him on the national stage before endorsing him for the presidency.

The October 31 first-round vote left the southeast's Yanukovich to face the west's and radical nationalists' candidate Viktor Yushchenko in the November 21 second-round runoff. Yushchenko was Kuchma's prime minister from December 1999 to May 2001 and was backed by Kuchma's former Fuel and Energy Minister Yulia Tymoshenko and her national democratic "Bloc of Yulia Tymoshenko" (later Batkyvshina or Fatherland) or BYuT. Dubbed the "gas princess" by Ukrainians, Tymoshenko, in accordance with post–Soviet custom, enriched herself in the offices of CEO of *Yedyni Energosystemy Ukrayiny* (United Energy Systems of Ukraine, a monopoly importing Russian natural gas), Rada Budget Committee chairwoman, and Ukraine's Fuel and Energy Minister (December 1999–January 2001). In the last post, she succeeded Pavlo Lazarenko, the chairman of her first party "Hromada," after his promotion to Ukraine's premiership (1996–1997). Lazarenko was soon imprisoned in the U.S. for embezzlement.[62]

The campaign had featured not only the traditional internal east-west standoff, but internationally the two opposing campaigns were being advised by foreigners from countries with a growing interest in the electoral outcome. Russian consultants advised the Yanukovich campaign; American consultants aided the Yushchenko campaign, featuring suspiciously large numbers of orange baseball caps, orange tee-shirts, orange flags, etc. Yanukovich was declared the winner almost immediately after the polls closed, raising suspicions of a fix, especially on the background of alleged vote-buying, electoral fraud, and general massive corruption. Although no group has a monopoly on election fraud in Ukraine or in most other post–Soviet states, the incumbent always has the advantage. Allies from both the Yanukovich and Yushchenko camps (like Tymoshenko) were steeped in corruption. The Yushchenko campaign was the beneficiary of illegal "administrative resources"—the illegal support from organs of the executive branch to slant the playing field in one way or another. After the first-round voting, Ukraine's version of the FSB, the Security Service of Ukraine or SBU, as well as the Ministry of Internal Affairs (MVD), maintained regular contact with the Yushchenko's chief of staff Oleh Rybachuk, engaged in wiretapping of the Yanukovich campaign, and delivered Yanukovich campaign documents to the Yushchenko campaign and the Jamestown Foundation, an American think tank with close ties to then U.S. Vice-President Dick Cheney.[63]

For his part, Yushchenko's chief of staff Rybachuk—the conduit and likely coordinator of this illegal wire-tapping activity—had followed a widespread post–Soviet pattern of KGB operatives turning democratic, nationalistic or statist. Rybachuk's path traversed, as Ames notes, "from well-connected KGB intelligence ties, to post–Soviet neoliberal networker."[64] Although it has been repeated *ad infinitum* that Putin is former KGB, this leading operative in the Orange and Maidan revolutions also appears to have had ties to the notorious "organs." In the Soviet era, Rybachuk attended a military language program, half the graduates of which entered the KGB. He then had a shadowy overseas posting in India in the late Soviet era. This and his continuing ties to Ukraine's KGB successor organ, the SBU, suggests he might have had Soviet intelligence ties. Like many other former KBG operatives and associates, Rybachuk went into the international financial and banking sector. In 1992, he joined the newly formed Ukraine Central Bank (UCB), heading its foreign relations department under then UCB director Yushchenko. In this post, Rybachuk would establish ties with western government and financial aid institutions, as well as "proto-Omidyar figures" like color revolutionist Soros. After the Orange revolution and Yushchenko's rise to the presidency, Rybachuk was appointed deputy prime minister for the country's integration into NATO and the EU. He then moved to Yushchenko's politically divided presidential administration. With Yushchenko's election loss in 2010, Rybachuk returned to organizing revolution.[65]

The *New York Times* report on the SBU's campaign spying focused on the two security services' claim that they prevented a Kuchma crackdown on the Orange demonstrators and described them as "a clique of Ukraine's top intelligence officers, who chose not to follow the plan by President Leonid D. Kuchma's administration to pass power to Prime Minister Viktor F. Yanukovich, the president's chosen successor."[66] The *New York Times* and pro-western Ukraine, NATO-tied analysts reporting on this did not see use of Ukraine's security services to spy on the Yanukovich campaign on Yushchenko's behalf as part of the fraud they touted as fomenting and justifying the Orange revolt. Instead, such fraudulent activity was attributed by all Western governments and media solely to the Kuchma/Yanukovich camp.[67]

The ubiquitous election fraud troubled neither president Kuchma, nor the authorities in general, nor the Yanukovich camp, because the voting results favored them. Before the Central Election Commission (CEC) announced its results, exit polls were showing Yushchenko with a comfortable lead. These claims were discounted by the Commission, and on November 22, OSCE observers declared the vote fell short of democratic standards. The CEC officially declared Yanukovich the winner two days later. By November 25, the United States, Canada and the EU had officially announced that they would not recognize the second round's results.

Those for whom the hastily announced outcome was not beneficial—the clans opposed to Kuchma and Yanukovich—sprung into action with support from the few societal democratic forces networked by the U.S. DP infrastructure and network. The Orange coalition's core was led by Tymoshenko, who was promised the premiership if Yushchenko became president. The alternative count, exit polling and reports of electoral fraud that sparked the revolt were delivered by the thousands of activists trained by USAID and organizations it funded. DP's dual-use nature kicked in after the opposition's focus switched from counting and reporting the vote to protesting the official results.

These activists became the coordinators of mass demonstrations in Kiev, Lviv, and elsewhere. As was true before Georgia's Rose "revolution," former Otpor activists from CANVAS had spent months teaching its techniques for making revolution to the Ukrainian Orange Revolution's vanguard group, the youth movement "Pora!" ("It's Time" or "Enough"). Pora modeled itself, like Georgia's Khmara, on Serbia's Otpor.[68]

On the evening of November 21, Tymoshenko called on the Ukrainian people to come to the Maidan and spread the orange color. As Yushchenko was protesting irregularities at the CEC on November 23, Pora led massive protests across the country. An estimated half a million gathered in central Kiev, forming a sea of orange tents, shorts, and caps. After the first 100,000 or so protesters arrived on Maidan (Independence) Square, Yushchenko rushed to address them there, swearing an oath of loyalty to the Ukrainian people.

DAI emphasized in its report that in October "three justices of the Ukrainian Supreme Court served as SEAUP trainers—a facet of the training component that proved to be extremely fortuitous." It added: "[W]hen the scope of the fraud perpetrated around the November 21 run-off election became clear, the judges who had served as trainers felt personally assaulted. Their outrage energized them to assume leadership roles on the Court and rally colleagues in the unanimous decision on December 3 to set aside the results of the fraudulent run-off and order the re-vote of December 26."[69] The "fortuitous" nature of this USAID venture had actually become evident already on November 25, when Ukraine's Supreme Court stepped in and forbade the publication of the election results.

On the same day, Pora-led demonstrators began occupying Kiev's House of Trade Unions, Ukraine House and City Hall, and a nationwide student strike was declared, fueling demonstrations elsewhere. An orange tent city remained on Kiev's Maidan for several weeks. On November 30, protesters attempted to storm the Supreme Rada building. On December 1, the Supreme Rada declared no confidence in Yanukovich and the government, the Cabinet of Ministers and the Presidential Administration buildings in Kiev were blockaded, and Kuchma flew to Moscow to confer with Putin. Two days later, the Supreme Court fortuitously annulled the election results and set a re-vote date of December 26. Yushchenko won the re-vote with 52 percent of the vote to Yanukovich's 44 percent. Despite the alleged massive election fraud, neither Kuchma, Yanukovich, nor anyone else was arrested for their actions.

In a 2007 report, USAID emphasized: "[T]he Orange Revolution is considered irreversible. Wherever we went and no matter whom we talked with, everyone agreed that the Orange Revolution had changed the political landscape permanently. People felt the upheaval in the end was not about party or faction but rather about establishing the principle of ultimate democratic accountability of the government to the people."[70] Three years later, the Orange revolution's champion, President Yushchenko, would be voted out of power, receiving under 6 percent of the vote in the first round compared with anti-orange nemesis Yanukovich's 35 percent. Yanukovich would go on to defeat his runoff opponent, the Orange revolution's Tymoshenko, by a margin of 49 percent to 45 percent in an election recognized by the OSCE as sufficiently free and fair.

Despite the advertising, USAID, its partner organizations and subcontractors had achieved neither democracy nor any real regime change. The foreign supporters of the Orange and other color "revolutions" proved to be far off the mark in their assessments of Kiev in 2004. George Washington University's Ukrainian nationalist writer Taras Kuzio argued: "The Orange Revolution took place because many Ukrainians changed their view of Ukrainian politics from one of 'A plague on all your houses' where all politicians were viewed as corrupt. Yushchenko changed this widespread view by convincing a majority of Ukrainians that he and his political allies were different."[71] But as in Georgia, the contested election results and the Orange "revolution" had many features of an intra-elite power struggle rather than a society-led revolution from below. Elements in society, many of them primed by U.S. DP efforts, were mobilized when some of the elite clans needed their support, but they were soon demobilized and forgotten once the victorious clans took office. Orange Maidan had foiled the corruption involved in Kuchma and Yanukovich's attempt to win the electoral fraud contest, but Ukraine remained massively corrupt.

If this had been a robust, deep-rooted revolution from below, Yanukovich would not have been elected president in 2010 in a rout of Yushchenko, and another "democratic revolution" would not have been needed in 2014. The Orange revolt did not change the form of rule, just the ruling factions, and their continued infighting produced the next upheaval. There was no overturning of Ukraine's political or economic system, property relations, or socioeconomic structure. At least three scholars have questioned the appropriateness of applying the term "revolution" to the Orange days of 2004. Lane regards it as a "revolutionary coup" and refers to the persistence of structures of "oligarchic democracy" after the "revolution."[72] Indeed, a similar persistence of oligarchic power would become evident by 2015 in the aftermath of yet another complex revolt billed by its leaders and their Western backers as yet another "democratic revolution."

Orange Kiev and the Donbass

Despite or perhaps because of the shallow "revolutionary" outcome, the tremors caused by the Orange revolt reopened the fissures in Ukraine's stateness. Communal-regional schism was evident in the Orange takeover. Most of its backing came from western Ukraine; some came from central Ukraine and Kiev. As demonstrations in Kiev, Lviv, and other cities mostly in western and central Ukraine mounted, the Donbass countermobilized. On November 27–29, tens of thousands of Yanukovich supporters rallied in Donetsk threatening to seek autonomy or even secession if Yushchenko came to power. Simultaneously, pro–Yanukovich politicians convened a congress in the city of Siverodonetsk in northern Donetsk and called on Kuchma to crack down on pro–Yushchenko demonstrations. In a hint of things to come a decade later, the Donetsk Oblast Soviet moved to hold another autonomy referendum. However, after initially passing it, the soviet withdrew the referendum. One reason the tremors of 2004 did not produce a full-blown earthquake—the 2013–14 scenario—may be that on the international level, all parties took a step back to avoid confrontation. On December 9, NATO and Russia, in a rare show of compromise and unity, issued a joint appeal to Kiev for free and fair voting in the repeat election.[73] Next time, after the Orange regime (and Georgian war), matters moved in a decidedly different direction.

The Orange Regime

The Orange regime under Yushchenko's administration supported the Galician model in attempting to construct a new Ukrainian national identity. Policy was anti-eastern

142   Ukraine Over the Edge

and anti–Russian in both domestic and especially foreign policy. Western Ukraine became dominant in domestic politics, and the West moved to the forefront in foreign policy. Through its silence, the West effectively endorsed former Yushchenko's unbalanced policy, including its ultranationalist and xenophobic aspects. An emerging anti–Russian stance was disguised as an anti–Soviet one, in the hope that it would sway public opinion in favor of Ukraine's entry into NATO and the EU.

Neither Yushchenko nor his government had an explicit nationalities policy. There was no ministry for nationalities policy or interethnic relations, specific legislative bills or official policy statements addressing these issues. Instead, two domestic policy areas indirectly shaped interethnic relations, especially Russian-Ukrainian relations: (1) the proselytization of state ideology rooted in the revision and falsification of the history, and (2) language policy. The shift in favor of western Ukrainian preferences on these issues helped to revive the intercommunal and interregional schisms that shook the country's political stability and stateness during the 1990s.

World War II: Historiographical Battleground

Yushchenko succeeded in consolidating or at least further developing a Ukrainian national identity, but one that is largely ethnic and western Ukrainian rather than civic and all–Ukrainian. Consequently, it would alienate many Russians, Transcarpathian Rusyns, and even some Crimean Tatars, while it mobilized the western Ukrainians. The campaign was based on two pillars often present in the mythologies of communalist movements—a heroic myth and a victimization myth. Together, these two myths were to form the foundational myth for Ukrainian nation- and state-building, and they were particularly noxious to southeastern Ukraine, especially its pro–Russian and Soviet nostalgic elements. First, the heroic myth was the full rehabilitation of Stepan Bandera, the Organization of Ukrainian Nationalists (OUN), and the Waffen SS Galician Corps. Second, the vicitimization myth was the Great Famine or "Holodomor" ("famine-murder" or genocide), which was blamed on or at least strongly associated with Russia, rather than the internationalist communist ideology or its ethnic Georgian Soviet leader, Iosif Stalin.

Yushchenko aggressively supported the rehabilitation of Ukraine's World War II–era neofascist organizations, the OUN and UPA, as well as its leading figures. In 2007 he granted an INP request to designate Shukhevych a national hero and awarded a similarly honorific status to Stetsko. Yushchenko also used state funds to finance the building of monuments to other OUN figures at sites of the Jewish Holocaust in Ukraine, including in former Jewish ghettos and the infamous Babi Yar.[74] In addition, he was willing to engage in legal repression of those who dare question his ultranationalist false narrative on issues such as the Holodomor (see below). There were certainly moderate Ukrainian nationalist historical figures, who incidentally are more popular than Bandera and the other OUN-OPA figures. Yushchenko could have chosen to glorify the Ukrainian national liberation struggle, and in doing so would have not alienated the southeast. The revolutionary era Rada leader Mikhail Hrushevskiy and the great 19th-century poet Taras Shevchenko are the best examples.[75] Shevchenko wrote in both Russian and Ukrainian and therefore could have helped found a more inclusive civic national identity rather than the ultranationalists' preferred ethnic one.

Perhaps more problematic in terms of long-term consequences was Yushchenko's use of the state to proselytize a new, official nation-building ideology rooted in the revision and falsification of Soviet and World War II history. In particular, despite their problematic nature for a regime claiming to become European and democratic, the Orange regime rehabilitated the legacy of the neofascist OUN-UPA and held its leaders—including the infamous pro-fascists Bandera, Shukhevych and Stetsko—up as the heroes of Ukraine's national liberation struggle. This became a point of pride for many—though far from all—in the country's west, and a source of political provocation for almost all the southeast, especially in Crimea and Donbass. Yushchenko's historians depicted the OUN and UPA as pluralistic and inclusive organizations rather than the totalitarian, intolerant, and racist organizations their ideological tracts revealed. Instead of depicting an organization that deliberately sought Jews out to kill them, the Orange revolution in power claimed Jews were invited in as part of its fight not just against Stalin, but also against Hitler, with whom OUN-UPA allied.[76]

Yushchenko likely was a genuine opponent of the OUN's fascism, totalitarianism, terrorism, fuhrer principle, and ethnic cleansing, and certainly needed to appear as such in the eyes of his Western supporters. Thus, he supported the new OUN-UPA myth in a way that did not offend the Western principles of multiculturalism and intercommunal tolerance and respect. To overcome this paradox, Yushchenko's historians deployed the revised and falsified history of Ukrainian integral nationalism and Banderism contained in OUN-UPA propaganda materials dated from the post–1943 period, after its leaders decided to tone down its racist ideology in the wake of the German army's rout at Stalingrad, as it became more apparent that the Nazi experiment would collapse and the West and/or the Soviets would be deciding Ukraine's future. In addition to post–1943 propaganda materials and even revised and falsified documents from its pre–1943 period, Yushchenko's ideologists used revised and falsified histories and "scholarly" materials produced by former OUN-UPA members, their descendants, and other members of the Ukrainian diaspora in North America and Germany.[77]

Yushchenko's government used three institutions to propagandize the new myth: the Institute of National Memory (INP), founded in May 2006; the OUN-B front group or "façade structure" called the Center for the Study of the Liberation Movement (TsDVR); and the archives of Ukraine's intelligence and security organ, the SBU, with which the TsDVR cooperated closely with the Ukrainian Foreign Ministry. As the INP's director, Yushchenko appointed academician Ihor Yukhnovskyi, a supporter of the neo-Nazi Social Nationalist Party of Ukraine.[78] According to Yukhnovskyi, "[T]he basic goal of the INP is to develop activities that focus on the consolidation and growth of the state-creating patriotism of the Ukrainian people (narody) ... the resurrection of memory about the sacrifices and repressions that the Ukrainian nation (natsia) endured ... [and that] all those who fought for Ukraine, suffered, died, should be treated as national heroes of Ukraine. The policies of all government entities should be based on the Ukrainian idea."[79] All of these institutions were "interlinked"; their "directors cross-referenced and legitimized each others' existence." The SBU, according to German scholar Per Rudling, "was tasked with the most important aspects of Yushchenko's apparatus of memory management: to guard the memory, the institutions, resources, and archives of the Ukrainian security forces."[80] Speaking in 2008, historian Sofia Hrachova noted the SBU "uses this monopoly to political ends, publishing selections that represent historical events according to the current official perspective."[81]

The Yushchenko revisionists' perhaps chief ideologist was his director for both the Central State Archives of the SBU (*Archives Holovnyi Derzhavnyi Arkhiv Sluzhba Bezpeky*

Ukrainy, or HDASBU) and TsDVR, Volodomyr Vyatrovich, who devoted "particular attention" to the OUN-UPA and the Jews. Vyatrovich ignores all sources—Jewish records and memoirs, and German and Soviet archival documents—that disprove his contention that Jews were welcome and important within the OUN-UPA. Instead, he has focused on the five named Jews who served in the UPA (not OUN members), including "Stella Krentsbach/Kruetzbach," who is a fictitious person created by OUN-UPA postwar emigres. Vyatrovich's HDASBU circulated the postwar OUN forgery *Do pochatku khyha faktiv* (*The Book of Facts*) to a series of government organizations in an attempt defend the OUN, Shukhevych and his Nachtigall Battalion, which slaughtered Jews, and presented it as an authentic World War II–era document to the public.[82] In April 2008 the SBU convened a public "hearing" to focus attention on Vyatrovich's narrative that because of the UPA, the Jews and Ukrainians fought the Nazis together side-by-side. SBU director—then and again after the 2014 Maidan revolution—Valentyn Nalyvaichenko presided over this and the entire SBU portion of the Yushchenko exercise in myth-making. He noted that the goal was to replace KGB lies with "historical truth" and "liberate Ukrainian history from lies and falsifications." The SBU itself said the forgery "objectively certifies … collaboration between Ukrainians and Jews." Well-known anti–Semites and Holocaust deniers, including but not limited to Levko Lukianenko and Yurii Shukhevich, were frequent guests at Yushchenko's "research" institutes. Yushchenko's ideologists were able to popularize these falsehoods using willing popular literary figures, such as Moisei Fishbein and Oksana Zabuzhko, who repeated the government's fabrications, including the Stella Krentsbach/Kruetzbach fiction, and produced works based on Yushchenko's false narrative and OUN-fabricated documents and propaganda provided by the TsDVR.[83]

As Rudling convincingly argues, the false Semitophilic narrative of the OUN-UPA's historical revisions, proffered by its past and present supporters inside and outside Ukraine and its government, constitutes a form of Holocaust revisionism.[84] Indeed, there is much in common between Holocaust revisionism and outright denial, on the one hand, and the Ukrainian ultranationalist narrative of a benign OUN-UPA deceptively maligned by Soviet and Russian propaganda, on the other, especially as regards its discourse on OUN-UPA's relations with the Jews. Yushchenko was careful to balance his tolerance of some anti–Semitism within his ultranationalist wing by way of occasional personal demonstrations of sympathy for the Jews. Nonetheless, the Orange regime and its memory-making institutions consistently took steps to downplay and marginalize the OUN-UPA's killings of the Jews and the Jewish nature of the tragedy at Babi Yar.

Yushchenko ignored international and U.S. appeals to honor the Jewish victims of the Holocaust at Babi Yar. He appeared to take steps to ensure that none of the proposed international Holocause projects could be undertaken by transferring jurisdiction to the INP. After an international movement was formed to lobby for the building of a major memorial to the victims of the Holocaust at Babi Yar, Ukraine's Council of Ministers, on the basis of a directive issued by President Yushchenko, decreed on March 1, 2007 that the territory of Babi Yar was now designated a historical preserve and had been transferred from the authority of the Kyiv City Council to the pro–OUN-UPA INP, outraging the international Jewish community.[85] In addition, throughout the Yushchenko presidency fewer and fewer Ukrainian officials attended the Jewish commemorations at Babi Yar. By October 2008 not one Ukrainian official would attend. Rabbi Yakov Dov Bleich—who in June 2001 was accompanied by Pope John Paul II to the site to pray together—told those present: "We … do not have the right to allow what happened at Babi Yar to be forgotten. We cannot be silent, when history is being written according to someone's pleasure."[86]

Instead of commemorating the Jewish loss, Yushchenko's government allowed Babi Yar to be used by ultranationalists, many of them with anti–Semitic attitudes, such as the rising neofascist, pro–OUN Svoboda Party (SP) led by the openly anti–Semitic Oleh Tyahnybok. Their commemorations at the site in 2007, 2008, and 2009 ignored the Jewish character of the tragedy and the OUN-UPA's role in it, claiming Babi Yar was a massacre primarily of Ukrainians, especially those of the OUN-UPA ultranationalists. In February 2007 the head of SP's Kiev organization, Andriy Mokhnyk, declared at Babi Yar:

> [T]here are myths about Babyn Yar. First, Germans executed mainly non–Ukrainians at Babyn Yar [read: Jews]. Second, supposedly Ukrainian nationalists [read: OUN members] helped the Hitlerites conduct the executions.... It is a blatant lie. Babyn Yar is mainly a site of the tragedy of Ukrainians, with over 55,000 Ukrainians being murdered there. Simultaneously, Babyn Yar is a hallmark of the unbreakable Ukrainian spirit. In Babyn Yar, the Germans shot activists of the Ukrainian nationalist underground movement.... They were executed as fighters of the Ukrainian national revolution.[87]

Victim Narrative: Holodomor

The second pillar of the Orange regime's myth-making is a "victimization narrative" based on a revision and falsification of the Holodomor or Great Famine of the early 1930s. Yushchenko's wife, Yekaterina Chumachenko, was a champion of the idea of Holodomor as an attempt at genocide of the Ukrainian nation and received the Truman-Reagan Medal of Freedom award in November 2008 from the Victims of Communism Memorial Foundation for her work on the Holodomor.[88] Rather than portraying the famine as a Soviet attempt to build communism through the collectivization of all agriculture in the USSR, killing some 3 million, Yushchenko's ideologists put forward the interpretation that the famine was an attempt to commit genocide and targeted the Ukrainian nation alone. In this Ukrainian nationalist view, the Holodomor was not a consequence of the communist ideology and Stalin's practice of it, but rather part of a centuries-long Russian effort to destroy the Ukrainian nation.

While spending much time and energy attempting to revise and deny the real history of the Holocaust in Ukraine, the Yushchenko government spent even more effort endeavoring to win international recognition of the 1930s famine as a "Ukrainian Holocaust," despite the numerous other territories and peoples of the USSR who suffered from the very same famine. In April 2007, Yushchenko submitted but was unable to push through the Supreme Rada a law that would have criminalized the denial of the famine's genocidal character. Thus, those who deviated from the state ideology's current line on the intent behind Stalin's crime would have been subject to imprisonment, presumably including leading Western historians such as Robert Conquest, or those who might assert that other Soviet territories and ethnic groups also were victimized.[89]

A revolution and eight years later, the Maidain regime's own Yushchenko, President Petro Poroshenko, blamed the ethnic Georgian Stalin's Soviet famine on the Ukrainian nationalists' other favorite scapegoat—Russia. At a November 28, 2015 ceremony commemorating the Great Famine, Poroshenko transferred the blame for the tragedy from Soviet communism to Russia and by insinuation those sympathetic towards Moscow, especially ethnic Russians: "We pray for multimillion heavenly legion of the Ukrainian nation. The bright spirits with no guilt who were killed here are invisibly with us. The

Holodomor was nothing other than a manifestation of the centuries-long hybrid war that Russia has been waging against Ukraine."[90]

As I discuss in Chapter 9, Russophobia would reach dangerously racist proportions after the ultranationalist-led Maidan revolution of 2014. Ukrainian ultranationalists, such as those who came to play a major role in the Yushchenko government, are consistently careful to avoid mentioning the fact that ethnic Ukrainians played the lead role in Ukraine in carrying out the grain and seed grain confiscations and overall collectivization process. For these actions and the crimes that accompanied them, ethnic Russians and Jews are often scapegoated. The entire Soviet experiment is often referred to as the "Muscovite-Bolshevik" regime or occupation, putting the blame for the Soviets' crimes on ethnic Russia, ethnic Russians, and a mythical Russian quest to destroy Ukraine. Moreover, many Ukrainian (and Russian) ultranationalist historians quickly and frequently emphasize that there was an inordinate or disproportional number of Jews in the Bolshevik party and leadership. In this way, the term "Muscovite-Bolshevik" is a coded and discursive slur against both ethnic Russians and Jews.

Orange Anti-Semitism

The Orange regime's willful tolerance and support of ultranationalist historical revisionism and denial was the heavy price paid for national myth-making in the alleged absence of alternative models and heroes. One wonders why the far more reasonable national independence movement of the late 19th and early 20th centuries was not the Orangists' choice. The regime's choice in favor of "neo–Banderism" led to a sharp increase in explicit displays and tolerance of anti–Semitism.[91] A striking example was an article published for the Babi Yar massacre's 65th anniversary in the largest mainstream newspaper in Ukraine at the time, *Silski visti*, written by its editor-in-chief Volodomyr Bilenko. In his "appeal" to Jews, Bilenko asked them to plea to Ukrainians for forgiveness: "[I]n the name of fairness and sincere co-existence, you should apologize before the Ukrainian people for the perfidious murder of S. Petlura, for participating in mass repressions against Ukrainians, for participating in the organization of the Holodomor, and finally for the convoluted thinking used in Israel for the destruction of innocent Lebanese children. Now Israel should come and repent before Babi Yar."[92] The direction things were moving and may still move could be seen in an attempt made in not-so-veiled fashion by Yushchenko's and Nalyvaichenko's SBU to scapegoat the Jews for the horrors of Soviet rule. Thus, in July 2008 it issued a "highly selective" list of nineteen perpetrators of the Holodomor "famine-genocide." Of the nineteen, eight were designated as being of Jewish nationality by placing their Ashkenazi names next to their adopted Slavic names.[93]

Red flags should have been seen regarding the nationalist movement in Ukraine. Yushchenko in this period was repeatedly denying the existence in Ukraine of any anti–Semitism whatsoever. On September 17, 2005, Yushchenko categorically stated: "In Ukraine there is no anti–Semitism or any kind of manifestation of xenophobia." The irony was abundant, as the statement came in Philadelphia, the city of brotherly love, where America's latest "beacon of democracy" in the former USSR received the Liberty Medal award. Three years later, on September 23, 2008, Yushchenko told a conference of Jewish-American organizations: "[I]n Ukraine such a shameful phenomenon as anti–Semitism is absent."[94] None of this should have surprised. Yushchenko had long maintained a close relationship with ultranationalist elements in western Ukraine. His "Our Ukraine" coalition included several ultranationalist groups. Early on, Yushchenko was on the board of MAUP, a private university in Kiev dominated by Ukrainian nationalists, produced nearly all of Ukraine's anti–Semitic print material, and welcomed former KKK leader David Duke as a visiting scholar. Yushchenko was forced to resign from MAUP's board in 2005 after a three-year campaign by Jewish leaders in Ukraine and the U.S. demanding he do so.[95]

Overt anti–Semitism continued to plague the Ukrainian diaspora community, which strongly supported Yushchenko and bitterly opposed the contemporary Ukrainian communists, who are more akin to European socialists than Stalinist or even late Soviet communists, and who blame communism's crimes on Jews. For example, in 2011 the émigré Internet publication included a "best and worst" of 2011 written by one Oksana Bashuk Harper. She noted among her worst events of the year the following: "Ukraine's Communist Party leaders, including comrades Symonenko and Vitrenko, for saying the Holodomor, the famine orchestrated by the Soviet Communist Party, is history and no longer important, and Israel's President Shimon Peres for lecturing Ukrainians to forget their history, Holodomor included, motivated, perhaps, by the desire to protect Lazar Kaganovich, also a Jew, and a key architect of the genocide."[96]

Yushchenko, however, revealed his true leanings after his defeat in the 2010 presidential election (in which he received a mere 5.5 percent of the votes), by issuing a decree officially rehabilitating the World War II–era Ukrainian neofascist OUN leader Stepan Bandera as a national hero.[97] This provoked a sharp reaction at home and abroad. A Crimean Supreme Soviet deputy burned his passport in protest against the rehabilitation, and a lawyer from the Donbass filed a lawsuit to have Bandera's Hero of Ukraine honor annulled. Poland's President Lech Kaczynski accused Yushchenko of putting "current political interests [over] the historical truth," and warned the move had driven a wedge between the two eastern European Slavic states. In reaction to Kaczynski's remarks, ultranationalist Ukrainians marched on the Polish Embassy in Kiev.[98] In December 2010, the Kiev city council announced it would be renaming three of its streets after Bandera's associates, Shukhevych, Stetsko, and Melnyk.[99] Two years after Yushchenko's demise, Bandera, and presumably the OUN-UPA along with him, enjoyed a positive assessment among 32 percent of all Ukrainian citizens; obviously, the majority of these would be from western Ukraine and might have constituted a majority, and likely an overwhelming majority, in the west.[100]

Language Policy

In addition to his draconian historiographical policies, Yushchenko undertook the implementation of an integrated national culture based on western Ukraine's identity. Thus, he initiated an aggressive Ukrainization policy in language and education in an effort to eliminate the Ukrainian language's second-rate status created under Soviet power. In doing so, he politicized the language issue and created more fertile soil for division within the country, especially in highly Russophone regions and districts like Donbass and Crimea. Ukrainian already was instated as the only language with state status in Ukraine's constitution, several articles, including several on Crimea, posed the task of developing Ukraine's other languages as well. Moreover, during the heady days of 1991 when Ukraine was achieving its long-sought independence, a very different model was supported by the then more moderate nationalists. At that time, the Ukrainian Supreme Rada passed a Declaration of the Rights of Nationalities of Ukraine that pledged the government to grant official language status to the mother tongue of any ethnic group living compactly in any of Ukraine's regions.[101]

By contrast, the Orange regime referred to Russian as one of the minority languages, even though all data showed that far more than 50 percent and as many as 80 percent of Ukraine's mostly bilingual and even multilingual citizens were Russian-speaking. Official documents, including birth and death certificates and other legal documents, were issued only in Ukrainian. A campaign to change the names of streets, schools, and buildings was instituted. Some Russians were forced to Ukrainize their names on their passports.[102] One strategy of Ukrainian nationalists given patronage by Yushchenko's government used to strengthen a western Ukrainian ethnic state, society and identity during Yushchenko's Orange regime was to eliminate from education and dictionaries words in common usage in both the Ukrainian and Russian languages.[103]

Svoboda Rising: Rise of Ultranationalists Under Yushchenko

Not surprisingly, the Orange Revolution and Yushchenko's policies sparked a sharp rise in Ukrainian ultranationalism, anti–Semitism, and general racist xenophobia and hate crimes. On the streets, NGO monitors documented a dramatic rise in violent crimes with a suspected hate-bias motivation, in particular "a revival of anti–Jewish prejudice in the form of an increase of anti–Semitic attacks and incidents." In addition to Jews, hate crimes mostly targeted people of African and Asian origin and those from the Caucasus and the Middle East.[104] They also targeted Russians and Roma, according to a December 2011 European Commission Against Racism and Intolerance report, which noted that "tolerance towards Jews, Russians, and Romani appears to have significantly declined in Ukraine since 2000 and prejudices are also reflected in daily life against other groups, who experience problems in accessing goods and services."[105] The perpetrators of the most serious hate crimes were from loosely organized groups of skinheads "united by extreme nationalist and racist ideology."[106]

At the same time, Yushchenko's government downplayed the ultranationalists' rise and downgraded the state's capacity to combat such phenomena. In 2008, the Interior Ministry claimed there were only 500 such skinheads in Ukraine, but NGO monitors suggest that the "number … is likely to be much higher." The government also discontinued official data collection and public reporting on violent hate crimes and disbanded both the State Committee for Nationalities and Religion and the Interior Ministry's Human Rights Monitoring Department. These moves, according to *Human Rights First*, "significantly weakened the government's efforts to combat racist and bias-motivated incidents."[107]

In the corridors of power, Yushchenko's nationalist policies faciliated the rise of neofascist Oleh Tyahnybok's ultranationalist, anti–Semitic, anti–Russian and deceptively named "Svoboda" or "Freedom" Party (SP). Tyahnybok hails from Lviv. His father was a sports physician and lead physician of the Soviet National Boxing Team and was honored under the communist regime with the Hero of Sport of the USSR award. Oleh, also a physician, graduated in 1993 at the age of 23 from Lviv Medical Institute and is a certified urologist and surgeon. In October 1991, as the USSR collapsed, he and Andriy Parubiy co-founded the radical neo–Nazi Social-National Party of Ukraine (SNPU), which included Nazi insignia and anti–Semitic pronouncements. Tyahnybok was elected to the

Lviv Oblast parliament in 1994 and to Ukraine's Supreme Rada in 1998 and, as a member of Yushchenko's Our Ukraine electoral bloc, in 2002. In February 2004, the SNPU sought to rebrand itself as a more moderate nationalist party, changing its name to the All-Ukrainian Svoboda (Freedom) Union or simply the Svoboda party, discontinuing the use of the modified Nazi Wolfsangel as its symbol, disbanding its paramilitary wing, the Patriots of Ukraine, and moderating its party program and public statements. The caveat to the last change was that its neofascist ideology was to remain fully intact in reality; only its public face was being revamped.[108]

Despite the plan to soften the party's image, Tyahnybok let loose a series of inflammatory and racist remarks at a July 2004 speech in at the gravesite of a UPA commander on Yavornaya Mountain in the Carpathians. He stated the following:

> The enemy came and took their [UPA's] Ukraine. But they [UPA fighters] were not afraid; likewise we must not be afraid. They took their automatic guns on their necks and went into the woods. They got them ready and fought against the *Moskaly* [derogatory term for Russians], the Germans, *Zhydy* [derogatory term for Jews] and other scum who wanted to take away our Ukrainian state! And therefore our task—for every one of you: the grey-headed and the youthful—we must defend our native land....
>
> These young men and you, the grey-headed, are the very combination, which the *moskal'sko-zhydivs'ka* (Muscovite-Jewish) mafia ruling Ukraine fears most.[109]

The same month, Tyahnybok was expelled from Our Ukraine's parliamentary faction party for his remarks at Yavornaya. In 2012, Tyahnybok refused to renounce these words, stating to a BBC journalist: "All I said then, I can also repeat now.... Moreover, this speech is relevant even today."[110]

Tyahnybok has issued other unsavory remarks and declarations. In 2005, he and 17 others signed an open letter titled "Stop the Criminal Activities of Organized Jewry" addressed to Ukraine's leadership, including President Yushchenko. The letter listed Jewish businessmen who got rich during the 1990s, claiming they control Ukraine, and called for investigations into the activities of Jewish organisations, such as the Anti-Defamation League, which, the letter said, is led by people "suspected of serious crimes." The letter referred to Zionism as "Jewish Nazism" and asserted that "organized Jewry" spreads its influence across Ukraine through such organizations in order to commit "genocide" of the Ukrainian people through impoverishment.[111] Svoboda has called for "purging" Jews from Ukraine, damaged synagogues and Jewish cemeteries, and demonstrated against Hassidic Jews' annual pilgrimage to the grave of Rabbi Nachman of Bratslav in the southern Ukrainian town of Uman.[112] In 2012, Tyahnybok's comrade in the SP, Ihor Miroshnichenko, called actress Mila Kunis a "dirty Jewess" and not a real Ukrainian.[113]

The SP's official program begins by stating that the "state ... secures the continuous development of the Ukrainian nationality (Ukrainskaya natsiya)" rather than that of all ethnic groups comprising the population of Ukraine. The first two measures listed for achieving this goal are a "fundamental purge" of all former CPSU and KGB officials from Ukrainian state structures and their replacement by people according to their "patriotism and professionalism." Given Tyahnybok's association of Russians and Jews with the CPSU and KGB, there is little doubt who would not be considered to be in possession of sufficient "patriotism." Correspondingly, the program calls for: making "manifestations of Ukrainophobia" a crime; introducing in Ukrainian internal passports data on the holder's nationality, which would be determined by birth certificate or that of the holder's parents, and "taking into account the wishes of the Ukrainian citizen"; requiring all candidates for public office to indicate their ethnicity in their official biographical data; introducing for public discussion a legislative bill that would establish the proportional representation of Ukrainians and national minorities in the executive branch; banning dual citizenship (which would affect Russians and Jews, for the most part); "facilitation of the mass return of ethnic Ukrainians" to Ukraine; banning the adoption of Ukrainians by foreigners; creating a state committee "responsible for the defense and spread of the Ukrainian language"; requiring that no less than 78 percent of mass media communication is in Ukrainian; repealing all taxation on Ukrainian-language publishing, communications, and information; ceasing all state budget support for school textbooks and other educational materials not in Ukrainian; requiring a course on "The Culture of the Ukrainian Language" in all higher educational institutes; instituting a program for "patriotic education"; facilitating the creation of a single Ukrainian local church with its center in Kiev; acknowledgment of "the fact of the occupation of Ukraine by Bolshevik Russia in 1918–1991, as a result of which there was an unprecedented genocide of the Ukrainian people"; securing from the Verkhovna Rada, the United nations, the European Parliament, and the world's parliaments recognition of the "Ukrainian genocide in the 20th century," as "a result of which 20.5 million Ukrainians were destroyed"; opening up a "criminal case of the Holodomor to be recognized as a state crime against the Ukrainian people"; implementing a public criminal trial of communism; banning the communist ideology and establishing criminal liability for "denial of the Holodomor as a genocide of the Ukrainian people"; creating a special investigative structure to search for the criminals who destroyed the Ukrainian nation, and after uncovering them, holding them criminally responsible; recognition of the struggle of the OUN and UPA as the "national liberation struggle of the Ukrainian people," and the soldiers of the UPA and the OUN underground as participants in that struggle; awarding compensation still owed to the OUN-UPA veterans; spreading "the truth about the Liberation struggle of the Ukrainian people in the 20th century in all educational institutions"; reestablishing Ukraine's tactical nuclear potential; and repealing Crimea's autonomous status.[114]

In 2009 Svoboda joined a federation of European ultra-rightist parties called the Alliance of European Nationalist Movements which includes Belgium's National Front, Britain's National Party, Hungary's violently chauvinist "Jobbik" Party, Italy's Tricolor Flame, and Sweden's National Democrats.[115] At the time, Svoboda maintained close ties to France's National Front and honored the Front's leader Jean-Marie Le Pen at Svoboda's 2004 congress. In December 2012, the European Parliament (EP) adopted a resolution expressing "concern about the rising nationalistic sentiment in Ukraine," expressed in support for the Svoboda party, which, as a result, was one of the two new parties to enter the Verkhovna Rada. The EP resolution recalled that "racist, anti–Semitic and xenophobic views go against the EU's fundamental values and principles," and therefore appealed "to pro-democratic parties in the Verkhovna Rada not to associate, endorse, or form coalitions with this party."[116] This was just one year before the very pro-democratic parties appealed to in the resolution joined in an opposition alliance to protest President Yanukovich's decision to postpone signing the EU association agreement, and Western officials, including U.S. Assistant Secretary of State Victoria Nuland and Senator John McCain, would be meeting with Svoboda leader Tyahnybok during the opposition alliance's demonstrations on the Maidan.

The decline in Yushchenko's popularity surely played into radical parties' hands; thus, the SP's sudden rise in popularity. But the state ideology and identity played into the hands of the extremists. In March 2009, Tyahnybok's SP for the first time won a regional parliamentary election. Not surprisingly, the victory occurred in the western Galician oblast of Ternopil, with Svoboda winning 35 percent of the vote and more than doubling the vote of the second-place party's 14 percent.[117] In 2010 it won city assembly elections in the three Galician western oblasts' capitals of Lviv, Ternopil, and Ivano-Frankivsk.[118] As noted above, Svoboda then won more than 10 percent of the vote in the 2012 Ukrainian Supreme Rada elections and 30–40 percent in the same three western regions (see Table 5).

Some saw the handwriting on the wall in 2009. Academician Myroslav Popovych, director of the Philosophy Department at NANU and one of three co-chairs of the Babi Yar Community Committee, warned in March of that year: "We are suffering through a period of decline of Ukraine's national democrats.... [T]he prestige of an aggressive nationalistic course, such as that of the Svoboda Party is increasing.... [I]n place of national democrats can come [to power] an aggressive nationalistic movement and then the civil peace in Ukraine, of which we are so proud, will come to an end, and many forces for which this will be satisfactory will be found."[119] Looking back from the perspective of 2015, Popovych's words are indeed prophetic. Rabbi Andrew Baker, director of international affairs at the American Jewish Committee, summed up the results of Yushchenko's rule: "We really thought a decade ago that this sort of ultranationalism would be disappearing by now. We thought it was [a temporary] thing. We were wrong."[120]

In his last year and a half in office, not only did Ukraine collapse economically, but politically as well. In the wake of the 2008 financial meltdown in the U.S. and the ensuing global economic crisis, Ukraine suffered a major financial crisis from which it still has not recovered. Yushchenko had permanently alienated southeastern Ukraine's voters from himself—as well as from Kiev and the west—but Ukraine's declining economic fortunes and conflicts between oligarchic clans over the natural gas profits split the Orange coalition that brought Yushechnko to power. In response, he stepped up his efforts to play to the nationalist wing in the runup to the presidential election, poisoning the Ukraine political well for years to come. Yushchenko then divided the Orange movement by accusing his former Orange Revolution comrade and now main presidential rival, Yulia Tymoshenko, of "high treason" for allegedly plotting with the Kremlin to undermine Ukraine's sovereignty after she cut a new gas deal with Gazprom.

The Yanukovich Regime

Viktor Yanukovich won a narrow victory over Tymoshenko in the second round of the 2010 presidential election. For this and other reasons he was not aggressive in seeking to replace the Yushchenko legacy of Galician myths with eastern Ukrainian Soviet nostalgia or Russophilia. However, some of what western Ukraine saw as gains for its nationalist agenda—in particular, those that were most odious for the southeast—were rolled back under Yanukovich, aggravating east-west tensions. At the same time, Yanukovich's presidency was hampered by the aftermath of the 2008–2009 Ukrainian financial crisis and the perception and reality of massive corruption on the part of his administration and key oligarchs who supported it. In order to mollify public opinion, Yanukovich decided to pursue an EU association agreement, promising economic recovery and revitalization on the road to EU membership. At the same time, he did not foreclose the possibility of a deal with Moscow on joining the EEU, which began to gain new members during this period.

Historiography

Yanukovich moved to reverse Yushchenko's Galician myth-making and historical revisionism. Yushchenko's orders designating Bandera and Shukhevych as national heroes in the Ukrainian national liberation struggle were nullified by Ukrainian courts, and the orders retracted. Yushchenko's nationalistic ideologists Vyatrovych and Yukhnovskiy were dismissed from the posts, Yanukovich appointed new directors to both the SBU Archives and INP. In response, the Ukrainian diaspora in Canada and the U.S. has feted Vyatrovych with speaking engagements in which he has continued his denial of OUN-UPA involvement in the Holocaust. Among other things, he was awarded a fellowship from the diaspora-dominated Harvard Ukrainian Research Institute. The diaspora also began to inflate the number of Holodomor victims, citing a figure of 10 million, and initiated a vitriolic campaign against Yanukovich and cut off all relations with his government, regarding it an "occupation regime." A noisy demonstration was organized for Yanukovich's visit to New York for the UN General Assembly, with protesters chanting "Russian butchers, go to hell! Slava Ukrainy! Heroiam Slava!" (Glory to Ukraine! To the Heroes Glory!"). One of the demonstration's organizers and a prominent Ukrainian diaspora activist deployed openly anti–Semitic rhetoric, asserting "an ... overwhelming amount of Soviet accomplices during the Soviets' two years in Western Ukraine from 1939–1941 were Jews." He also claims Jews control the Canadian media and those who research anti–Jewish violence by the OUN and UPA are in the pay of a Jewish lobby.[121]

Language

Although Yanukovich failed to fulfill his campaign promise to officially designate Russian as Ukraine's second state language, he implemented a measure that satisfied southeastern Ukrainians' aspirations on this score. In July 2012 he pushed the Kolesnichenko-Kivalov law through the Rada, establishing the requirement that in any region of Ukraine where any ethnic minority composed more than 10 percent of the population, then the minority's language must be declared an official language in that particular region. As a result of this law, 13 of Ukraine's 27 regions established Russian as a second state language.[122] All 13 of these regions were located in the eastern half of the country.

With the Yanukovich regime's reversal of historiographical and language policies, the east-west polarization process began to peak. Much like Yushchenko's alienation of the southeastern regions through his historico-ideological and language policies, Yanukovich's policies alienated the west. Thus, with each change in power between pro-southeastern and pro-western governments, Ukraine's body politic was being bent back and forth. Like a piece of metal repeatedly bent to one side and then the other, the stress was bringing the country to a breaking point.

In addition, the high level of corruption that existed under Yushchenko and his predecessors became even more pronounced under Yanukovich. Moreover, the regional elite and oligarchs in the already far richer east, southeast, and south were the main beneficiaries of official largesse. Yanukovich, like Yushchenko, played favorites with certain regions, leaning on his support base in southern and eastern Ukraine. Reportedly, his visits across the country in 2012–2013 were most frequently made to the Donbass, Crimea, and Dnepropetrovsk, and very rarely to western Ukraine.[123]

All this fed the west's resentment of its own relatively low standard of living and the corrupt regime. The former was aggravated by the even better-off regions just over the border in EU Poland, to which Galicia had once belonged. A perfect storm would be created by additional stresses emanating from the geopolitical struggle on the international level.

6

Ukraine's "Perfect Storm"

The growing split in Ukraine was also a consequence of the stealthily intensified geopolitical struggle for Ukraine between Russia and the West. Although seemingly on the back burner, the struggle continued unabated throughout the Yushchenko and Yanukovich presidencies, despite the so-called Russian-American "reset." The "reset" policy was based on the mistaken precept that the difficult issues in the relations should be put aside, effectively neglected, and the focus limited to "lower hanging fruit." This meant ignoring the core issue of NATO's and the EU's encroachment on Russia's borders that would rise with a vengeance in Ukraine. The EU provided NATO with the Trojan horse to draw Ukraine into the full panoply of Western institutions, including NATO, and the prepared EU-Ukrainian association agreement set off an outright race for Kiev's loyalty between the Brussels and Moscow through its alternative EEU and a sharp rise in the Ukrainian public's expectations as the signing date neared. Those expectations would be crushed, removing the main barrier restraining the forces opposed to Yanukovich and his regime's corruption and well-trained in disruptive, potentially revolutionary protest activity under the West's dual-use technology of democracy promotion.

Yushchenko, Bush and NATO Expansion

Despite Yushchenko's radicalization of Ukrainian politics, the West remained fully supportive and continued its efforts to expand its institutional infrastructure to this increasingly torn country. Thus, NATO continued its march on Kiev. In November 2005, it concluded a MAP-lite—a NATO-Ukraine "Action Plan" (NUAP)—pursuant to a NATO-Ukraine Commission decision to "deepen and broaden the NATO-Ukraine relationship." The NUAP's purpose "is to identify clearly Ukraine's strategic objectives and priorities" towards its aspirations for "full integration into Euro-Atlantic security structures." Kiev was pledged to develop its democracy in view of "Ukraine's foreign policy orientation towards European and Euro-Atlantic integration, including its stated long-term goal of NATO membership." Although the document's democratization "objectives" for Ukraine included securing religious freedom, not a word was addressed to curbing ultranationalism and ethnic discrimination, intolerance and hate crimes against Jews, Russians, and other minorities. The document's section on the NUAP's "foreign and security policy "principles" began: "Full integration into Euro-Atlantic security structures is Ukraine's foreign policy priority and strategic goal. In this context, future internal developments will be based on decisions aimed at preparing Ukraine to achieve its goal of integration into Euro-Atlantic structures.... The interests of national security and the present international situation demand an essential deepening of relations between Ukraine and NATO." The first foreign and security policy objective under the NUAP should be to "update Ukraine's foreign and security policy to reflect its goal of full Euro-Atlantic integration."[1] The NUAP affirmed Ukraine's destination in NATO, while all opinion polls in Ukraine showed the majority of the population, with supermajorities in the southeast, opposed Ukraine entry into NATO. Thus, in the field of "information," NATO and Ukraine pledged in the NUAP to "improve public understanding of NATO through NATO-Ukraine cooperation in the field of information."[2] In other words, efforts would be made to change public opinion regarding Ukraine's prospective NATO membership.

Also, under Yushchenko and precisely when international Jewish leaders and some others were sounding the alarm over ideological developments in Ukraine, the Bush administration attempted at the April 2008 NATO summit to nudge NATO into offering Georgia and Ukraine MAPs, but had to settle for a summit declaration declaring that both Ukraine and Georgia would inevitably join NATO at some future juncture. It is also the period when Putin supposedly told a NATO-Russia meeting the day before the NATO summit that "Ukraine is not even a state." As noted in Chapter 4, the report of Putin's alleged statements and threats was most likely a strategic communications effort by Polish Foreign Minister Sikorski in support of Bush's position of granting MAPs to Kiev and Tbilisi.

Returning Bush's favors to Ukraine, Yushchenko strongly supported Washington's position on the August 2008 South Ossetiyan war and thereby risked dragging his divided country into the conflict by declaring solidarity with Georgia, threatening Russian warships stationed in the Crimea and, according to Moscow, sending arms to Georgia. Obviously, any Ukrainian military action on Georgia's behalf against Russia would have set off a storm of protest in southeastern Ukraine, especially in Crimea, home of Russia's Black Sea Fleet. Yushchenko and Tymoshenko whipped up further tension by claiming Moscow was seeking to destabilize Crimea, presumably as a threat to annex the peninsula. At the same time, Yushchenko's coalition split when Prime Minister Tymoshenko withdrew her party from the ruling coalition after the president criticized her for not condemning Russia's intervention in the Georgian-South Ossetiyan war.[3]

The "Reset"?—NATO's Stealth March on Ukraine

Officials in President Barack Obama's administration, such as U.S. ambassador to Russia Michael McFaul, state that NATO expansion was kept off the administration's agenda during its "reset" with Russia.[4] One Washington-based analyst wrote: "NATO had last expanded five years earlier, and further expansion of any kind was not on the alliance's agenda in 2014. No one in NATO was seriously considering inviting Ukraine to join the alliance anytime soon."[5] The operative words here are "during," "in 2014," and "anytime soon"—that is, NATO expansion was off the agenda temporarily until it would be put back on the agenda. Contrary to Washington's Russia policymakers, Russians have a long timeframe and understand that NATO expansion, once begun, would not stop on its own. For expansion to Ukraine, the country would need to be transformed and its population's views on NATO membership reshaped.

Indeed, even during President Obama's tenure, the Bush administration–era NATO 2008 Bucharest summit's statement that Georgia and Ukraine will someday join NATO would be restated numerous times. NATO reiterated no fewer than four times at no fewer than four NATO summits—2009, 2010, 2012 and 2014—that both Georgia and Ukraine will someday be NATO members; the last took place at the height of the Ukrainian crisis.[6] This insistent declaration seemed to contradict the oft-repeated claim made by proponents of NATO expansion in recent years that NATO does not seek expansion, but rather countries seek membership. This so-called "open door" policy leaves open the question of who opened or left open the door to prospective membership—that is, whether Washington or Brussels did. As Brzezinski notes in his *The Grand Chessboard*: "Washington decided, in 1996, to make NATO enlargement a central goal in America's policy of shaping a larger and more secure Euro-Atlantic community."[7] NATO's enlargement policy was clearly much more proactive than simply passively processing applications. NATO engaged in aggressive recruiting of new members through its establishment of various military-to-military aid programs, often paired with prospective or actual membership in the European Union (EU) and in the aftermath of "color revolutions," as demonstrated in previous chapters.

Thus, already in 2009—months into the Obama administration's first year—NATO deepened its "distinctive partnership" with Ukraine and the NATO-Ukraine Commission established at the 1997 Madrid NATO summit. NATO's 2009 "Declaration to Complement the Charter on a Distinctive Partnership between the North Atlantic Treaty Organization and Ukraine" announced measures to assist "Ukraine's efforts to take forward its political, economic, and defence-related reforms pertaining to its Euro-Atlantic aspirations for membership in NATO" under the NUAP and successive annual national programs.[8]

The victory of the less pro–Western Yanukovich in the 2010 presidential election put cold water on any near-term Ukrainian accession to NATO. From early in his campaign, Yanukovich asserted that Ukraine should remain a "non-aligned state" with a multidirectional foreign policy. "We will initiate a new common marker between the European Union and the CIS states. The foreign policy priority will be restoration of the full-fledged partnership with Russia, as well as the development of a mutually beneficial partnership with the United States, the EU, and all the key countries of the G20," he noted in October 2009.[9] Ukraine's cooperation with NATO had attained a level commensurate with public opinion and need not be deepened. As Yanukovich stated: "The Ukrainian people don't currently support Ukraine's entry to NATO and this corresponds to the status that we currently have. We don't want to join any military bloc."[10] On the election's eve, he reiterated this stance, saying Kiev's relations with NATO were "well-defined" and that there was "no question of Ukraine joining NATO" in the "immediate future." It could "emerge at some point," he said, but would be decided by referendum.[11] In his February 25 inaugural address, he repeated that he would pursue a strategy of a "non-aligned state."[12] In Brussels, on March 1 during his first foreign trip as president, he told the European Commission that Kiev would continue participation in NATO's "outreach programs" and pursue an EU association agreement, free trade and visa-free travel with Europe.[13]

Thus, Ukraine would continue its cooperation with NATO under the 2009 "Declaration to Complement the Charter on a Distinctive Partnership between the North Atlantic Treaty Organization and Ukraine," the NUAP, successive annual national programs, seminars, and joint tactical and strategic exercises. On June 24, 2010, Ukraine's government approved an action plan to implement its annual national program for cooperation with NATO for 2010, which included: participation of Ukrainian aviation and material in the transportation of cargo and personnel of NATO member-states' armed forces and partners operating in NATO-led peacekeeping missions; continuation of Ukraine's participation in the Kosovo peacekeeping mission; possible reinforcement of Ukrainian peacekeeping contingents in Iraq and Afghanistan; participation in a series of international NATO events organized by NATO; and training Ukrainian troops in the structures of NATO member-states.[14] Thus, in 2011 and subsequent years of Yanukovich's tenure, NATO held military exercises on Ukrainian territory.[15] In March 2012, Ukraine and NATO held joint security seminars and command-staff strategic exercises in preparing for the Euro 2012 European Football Championship in April 2012, involving five Ukrainian government ministries and agencies.[16] Ukrainian forces took part in NATO's "Ocean Shield," combating piracy off the coast of Somalia, by delegating a ship to the operation.[17] In June 2013, Yanukovich renewed the 2009 decree mandating Ukraine's annual national programs with NATO, signaling his support for continued cooperation on the eve of the 2013–2014 crisis.[18] Obviously, the West's purpose in this joint activity was to strengthen the bond between the Ukrainian military and NATO and thereby destroy any remaining bonds between the former and the Russian military, given their many years as part of the Soviet military and early post–Soviet era ties.

As the United States is a NATO member, the Obama administration can be presumed to have approved of the alliance's adoption of this declaration and subsequent measures. This would have been clear to Moscow, and consequently the Obama administration's supposed silence on NATO expansion in its dealings with the Kremlin might appear as deception. Therefore, contrary to Ambassador McFaul's assertion, Russian concerns about NATO expansion's continuation or its connection with the making of the Ukraine crisis are far from groundless.

At the same time as Yanukovich supported and even strengthened cooperation with NATO, he pushed through the Rada a law that codified Kiev's non-aligned status. The June 2010 law removed mention of Ukraine's "integration into Euro-Atlantic security and NATO membership" from the country's national security doctrine and related documents and precluded Ukraine's membership in any military alliance. The law, however, allowed for Ukraine's integration into Europe and cooperation with military blocs such as NATO and the CSTO.[19] Therefore, despite Ukraine's continuing and deepening involvement in alliance programs, NATO Assistant Secretary General for Defense Policy and Planning Jiri Sedivy seemed to sound a note of consternation with Kiev's ambiguity when he told a meeting with Ukrainian reporters in May 2010: "It is an unprecedented experience for a country, which has been working in the frames of the Annual National Program, not to want to become a NATO member."[20] There can be little doubt that this reflected growing discomfort with Yanukovich in both Washington and Brussels. Indeed, in announcing Ukraine's participation in operation "Ocean Shield" in 2013, NATO Secretary General Anders Fogh Rasmussen stated that although NATO's decision that Georgia and Ukraine will eventually join the alliance "still stands," it fully respected Kiev's non-alignment policy, adding that there was "serious concern" in about Ukraine's use of "selective justice."[21] The last was a reference to the October 2011 conviction of his former prime minister and 2010 presidential election runoff opponent, Yuliya Tymoshenko, on charges of embezzlement and abuse of power, for which she was handed a seven-year prison term and ordered to pay the state $188 million allegedly lost as a result of her 2008 gas deal with Putin. In other words, despite Yanukovich's acquiescence in, if not instigation of Tymoshenko's imprisonment, NATO was still willing to bring Ukraine into the institutions of the Western community of democracies.

Washington's and Brussels's continuing pursuit of luring Ukraine into the Western alliance notwithstanding, the country itself remained not only opposed but also bitterly divided over the issue. The Western-funded Razumkov Center's public opinion surveys show that from 2002 to 2008 the majority of Ukrainians were opposed to their country's membership in NATO, but western Ukraine supported Ukrainian membership in NATO at levels of 48–75 percent, beginning at 69 percent in 2002 and ending at 61 percent in 2008. In the east and the south, support for NATO membership was low, ranging from 42 percent in 2002 to 9 percent in 2008. In central Ukraine, support stood at 51 percent in 2002 but fell to 30 percent by 2008.[22] By contrast, despite or perhaps because of Yushchenko's pro–Western policies, pro–Russian sentiment in southeastern Ukraine remained high by the end of his presidency. In an August 2011 opinion survey carried out in the regions of Odessa, Kherson, Mikolaiv, and Crimea, respondents were asked who would be Ukraine's best ally over the next 5 years. Russia was chosen by 68.4 percent of respondents; the EU—15.9 percent; China—1.9 percent; and the U.S.—1.3 percent.[23]

Indeed, throughout the entire post–Soviet period, including both the Yushchenko and Yanukovich administrations, a majority of Ukrainians remained opposed to the country's joining NATO.[24] According to numerous independent polls conducted by various Ukrainian and foreign organizations between 2002 and 2013, Ukrainians' support for NATO membership continuously remained low. A high of 32 percent in 2002 supported membership, with only 20 percent supporting it by 2013. Thus, the level of opposition rose, with 33 percent in 2002 opposing membership, with a large undecided response, and in 2013—on the eve of the scheduled EU association agreement signing and ensuing crisis—a hefty 66 percent rejecting Ukraine's membership in NATO.[25] A 2009 Pew Research poll showed 51 percent of Ukrainians opposed NATO membership, while only 28 percent supported it.[26] Even those most in favor of Ukrainian membership in NATO, including lobbyists of the OUN-UPA diaspora such as the intensely anti–Russian Ukrainian nationalist Aleksandr Motyl, have acknowledged Ukrainian public opinion's opposition to NATO membership throughout the post–Soviet period prior to the 2013–2014 crisis.[27] NATO itself admitted in 2011 that "some" polls showed less than 20 percent support for Ukraine joining NATO: "The greatest challenge for the [sic] Ukrainian-NATO relations lies in the perception of NATO among the Ukrainian people. NATO membership is not widely supported in Ukraine, with some polls suggesting less than 20 percent of Ukrainians back membership. NATO's bombing of Belgrade was particularly unpopular in Ukraine."[28] Changing this negative attitude of the population towards Ukrainian membership in NATO was the purpose of the NATO-Ukrainian information program noted above. Only after Ukraine's loss of Crimea and control over much of Donbass, eliminating them from polling on opinion in Ukraine, did support for NATO membership exceed 50 percent, boosted in part by Russia's annexation/reunification of Crimea and the civil war in Donbass.

Moscow's Gas Weapon, or Business as Usual in Post-Sovietistan

The Russians had limited options for countering the West's creeping NATO expansion: playing the Crimea card, the Eurasian Economic Union, and economic leverage, especially natural gas prices. There was little to no effort to play the Crimean card after the 1990s, when Moscow mayor Yurii Luzhkov occasionally took steps to tie the peninsula to Russia culturally and economically and encourage separatism. The Eurasian Economic Union had made little progress in expanding beyond the Russia-Belarus-Kazakhstan Customs Union and still held no sway in Ukraine beyond the southeast. There were close business ties between Russian corporations and some of Ukraine's leading oligarchs, some of whom were not close, though not necessarily antagonistic to, Yushchenko, including coal and industrial magnate Rinat Akhmetov and Dmitrii Firtash. Other oligarchs declared their support for Yushchenko immediately after his election, including Ihor Kolomoiskiy (Privat Holdings), Viktor Pinchuk (Interpipe Steel), and Serhiy Taruta of the Industrial Union of Donbass. The last's inclusion in the latter group highlights the limits of the utility of Russia's business networks. Business interests, after all, often trump politics, even in the former Soviet Union.

Gas Wars

Russia's other leverage over Ukraine was natural gas, the purchase and transport to Europe of which Ukraine's economy was deeply dependent upon. Here again, however, there were limits to, and high costs connected with, Moscow's natural gas leverage for keeping Kiev within Moscow's orbit. Russia, after all, is just as dependent on Ukraine's purchase and consumption of Gazprom's gas, and more so on the transit of its gas through Ukraine to Europe, Gazprom's largest customer. The Russian budget (30 percent) and trade balance relies greatly on Gazprom's profits, particularly its gas exports to Europe, such that any cutoff of access to that market would be damaging in the short term and catastrophic in the long term.

In 1998, Gazprom and Naftogaz concluded a contract under which Gazprom would pay for the transit of volumes of gas and a link was established between gas prices and transit tariffs. The contract, however, did not resolve the issue of already incurred gas debts. The first Russo-Ukrainian gas dispute came in 1998, when Gazprom alleged that Ukraine had illegally diverted gas sent for export to Western European countries and briefly suspended both oil and electricity exports to Ukraine. It would be two years before Ukrainian Deputy Prime Minister Oleh Dubyna acknowledged that Kiev had illegally diverted for its own use in that year alone some 7–8 billion cubic meters of Russian natural gas from export pipelines to Europe. Kiev was also having trouble paying its bills to Gazprom, which claimed that Ukraine's gas debt had reached $2.8 billion. In October 2001, the parties resolved the debt issue by signing an intergovernmental transit agreement on "Additional Measures Regarding the Provision of Transit of Russian Natural Gas on the Territory of Ukraine."[29]

January 2006 saw the first full-blown Russian-Ukrainian gas crisis. Until 2005, Moscow sold natural gas to Ukraine and most other post–Soviet states at a fraction of the price charged to other countries. As of 2005, Ukraine enjoyed the biggest discount, which kept the otherwise anemic Ukrainian economy afloat. With the Orange regime's turn away from Moscow and growing anti–Russian policies in both domestic and foreign policy terms, Russia no longer had an interest in maintaining discounted gas prices for Kiev. In 2005 it sought to switch gas prices for Ukraine to global market prices similar to those paid by Europe. Kiev agreed with the caveat that price increases be implemented gradually and in return for increased transit fees and cash payments (rather than payment in kind) for Gazprom gas sent through Ukrainian pipelines to Europe. In negotiations over gas prices for 2006, Gazprom proposed a price of $160/tcm or per 1,000 cubic meters, up from $50/tcm. However, in May 2005, it was revealed that 7.8bcm or billion cubic meters (280 billion cubic feet) of gas deposited by Gazprom in Ukrainian storage reservoirs the previous winter were never made available to the company, though it was unclear if the gas was stolen, missing, or disappeared due to technical problems.[30] The dispute over missing gas was resolved in July, but there was no final gas supply agreement due to disagreement on a gas price. In September, one of the key Orange revolution leaders, the "gas princess" prime minister Tymoshenko, who led much of Ukraine's gas policy, was fired by Yushchenko.

By the end of the year Moscow raised its price offer to $230/tcm, but Kiev refused to pay more than $80 per 1,000 tcm. Yushchenko asked: "Why does Turkey pay $100 per thousand cubic meters, the Baltic countries pay $110, the Caucasus pays $100, and Ukraine, which is Russia's closest neighbor, must pay $230?" Putin was pushing a hard bargain and/or punishing Kiev for its westward turn. On December 31, 2005, with the 2005 contract set to expire, Putin offered a three-month delay until the onset of the market price, if Kiev signed that day a contract under the new price.[31] Kiev refused, and on New Year's Day, Moscow cut off the spigot, reducing the pressure in the pipelines from Russia to Ukraine. Although Russia cut off only Ukraine, some European countries saw supplies drop as well. After a January 4 preliminary agreement, gas supplies were resumed in full. The new five-year agreement set the $230/tcm for six months, with that price set for the Russian-Ukrainian-Swiss intermediary RosUkrEnergo, which then mixed Gazprom and Turkmenistani gas for a reduced price of $95/tcm for the gas resold to Ukraine's Naftogaz. This was essentially a scheme that allowed parties on both sides of the border and within RosUkrEnergo to skim profits off the top. This would set the stage for internal Ukrainian battles for control of gas flows and their use in the struggle for power to succeed Yushchenko. Moscow and Kiev also agreed to raise the transit tariff from U.S.$1.09/tcm to U.S.$1.60/tcm for both the transit of Russian gas to Europe and of Turkmen gas through Russia to Ukraine. On January 11, Putin and Yushchenko confirmed that the conflict had been concluded. In 2007 and 2008 there were less resonant disputes over Ukraine's debt arrears for delivered gas, with March 2008 seeing a brief, partial cutoff of gas supplies.

The most serious dispute occurred in 2009. On a background of continuing disagreement over gas and transit prices and a Ukrainian debt of $2.4 billion to Gazprom for gas already consumed, Gazprom requested full debt payment before the commencement of a new supply contract for 2009. Ukraine's Naftogaz made the last payment on its debt only on December 30, transferring $1.522 billion to Moscow, but the parties could not agree on the 2009 price. Gazprom demanded $250/tcm, but Ukraine first offered $201, and later $235.[32] Negotiations were interrupted on New Year's Eve, and on January 1, 2009, Gazprom stopped exports to Ukraine but continued exports of 300 million cubic meters per day to the EU.[33] By January 2, pipeline pressures and supplies were declining across Europe.[34] Both RosUkrEnergo and Gazprom then filed lawsuits against Ukraine and Naftogaz, respectively, with the Stockholm Tribunal of the Arbitration Institute, and Ukraine filed countersuits.[35] Ukraine ultimately would lose all the arbitration suits.[36] On January 5, 2009, Putin instructed Gazprom CEO Alexei Miller to reduce natural gas exports to Europe through Ukraine in quantities equivalent to those which Ukraine had allegedly been diverting since the January 1 cutoff.[37] Two days later, all Russian gas exports via Ukraine were stopped amid accusations by Moscow that Kiev was illegally siphoning gas. An agreement to give monitors access to pumping stations broke down when Ukraine rejected a Russian request that Russian observers be included among the monitors.[38] Thus, several countries reported a major fall in supplies of Russian gas during an unusually cold European winter.[39] After monitoring led to a brief agreement and Russia resumed gas flows on January 13, Ukraine, in the person of the same Dubyna, acknowledged it had closed hatches to stop the gas flow to Europe.[40]

On January 17, 2009, Moscow hosted an international gas conference with the EU and Ukraine's Tymoshenko, once again Ukraine's prime minister. The meeting failed to deliver an agreement, but Putin and Tymoshenko continued bilateral talks and agreed that Ukraine would start paying European prices for natural gas in 2010, with a 20 percent discount for 2009. In return for the 2009 discount, Ukraine agreed not to revise the transit fee for Russian gas in 2009. They also agreed to cease the use of intermediaries.[41] On January 19, 2009, Gazprom chief Miller and Naftogaz head Dubyna signed an agreement on supplies to Ukraine through 2019, and gas transport to Ukraine and Europe resumed.

As nationalism intensified and the 2010 presidential election approached in Ukraine, Tymoshenko's deal with Putin began to undergo sharp criticism back in Kiev. In addition, a decline in demand resulting from falling production and the 2008–2009 Ukrainian financial crisis meant Ukraine wanted to purchase considerably less gas in 2009 than originally agreed to under the January 2009 agreement. On November 20, 2009, a Tymoshenko-Putin meeting in Yalta led to revision of the January deal under which Ukraine would not be fined for buying less gas, and the annual contracted amount of gas to be supplied to Ukraine in 2010 was reduced by nearly 40 percent. In April 2010, a new Russian-Ukrainian natural gas deal was signed under which Russia agreed to a 30 percent drop in price in exchange for an extension of its lease of the Sevastopol naval base for its Black Sea Fleet for an additional 25 years with a five-year renewal option.

The history of the disputes demonstrates that Moscow's leverage was minimal and aimed at getting a fair price for its product in the new geopolitical conditions of Ukraine's Western vector, and that Ukraine no less than Moscow was responsible for the gas supply disruptions to Europe. Ukraine illegally siphoned off gas, delayed debt payments until the eve of the expiration of contracts, and lost arbitration cases in independent courts, proving its culpability. To be sure, beginning in 2005 Moscow ran a hard bargain in terms of pricing, but this was understandable given the massive discounts Ukraine had enjoyed for over a decade while moving towards NATO and the EU rather than the CSTO and the EEU. Under such circumstances Moscow had little incentive to give Kiev the same privileges in gas pricing that former Soviet states enjoyed in return for allying with Moscow. Both Moscow and Kiev lost gas purchase and transit revenues, and Ukraine lost additional revenues from the closure of chemical and steel enterprises dependent on natural gas for production energy.[42] Moreover, Russia's reputation as a reliable natural gas supplier suffered irreparable damage—as did Ukraine's—so the disputes do not appear to be part of any Russian neo-imperialist strategy, but rather were the result of Ukraine's effort to have its cake and eat it too. The EU shifted to a more aggressive pursuit of greater energy independence, which will cut into Moscow's future profits. Similar future costs hit Ukraine, as Moscow began to develop alternative customers of its natural gas and transit routes circumventing Ukraine, such as the North and South Stream projects.

In the West, the Russian-Ukrainian natural gas wars were attributed solely to Moscow's neo-imperialism—an effort to pressure Kiev to return to Moscow's fold, but it was never explained how such a strategy could have played out successfully and whether the attempt was worth the risk of lost profits and trust in both Ukraine, Europe and beyond. Ukraine was given no agency in such interpretations, despite having been proven to have amassed debts, illegally siphoned off gas intended for Europe, and lost arbitration cases. Moreover, Ukrainian domestic politics and a struggle for control over resources in the runup to the 2010 presidential campaign comprised a key driver of Ukraine's inability to make payments, agree to compromise, or conclude agreements. Tymoshenko acknowledged that the real reason the two sides were unable at one point to close the gap between a Russian offer of $250/per thousand cubic meters of gas and Ukraine's counteroffer of $235 was that elements on the Ukrainian side blocked it, seeking to preserve the role of the middleman in Russian-Ukrainian gas relations, RosUkrEnergo. Tymoshenko and Putin had agreed in a document they signed in October 2008 that RosUkrEnergo was to be written out of Russian gas sales to Ukraine in the 2009 contract. Specifically, she blamed RosUkrEnergo part-owner Dmitro Firtash and two Ukrainian opposition politicians from the Party of Regions funded by Firtash for scuttling the impending Gazprom-Naftogaz agreement.[43]

A few experts in alternative media did bother themselves to get into the weeds and pursue this line of inquiry into domestic Ukrainian politics. They observed that the reason behind a Ukrainian preference to preserve RosUkrEnergo's middleman role is that specific factions in the Ukrainian leadership benefited from the arrangement and were particularly interested in preserving their profits because of the upcoming presidential campaign in Kiev. Elements within the Ukrainian leadership have a political motive that drove its lack of enthusiasm for or inability to resolve the dispute. Tymoshenko's people control Naftogaz, and therefore Tymoshenko agreed with Putin to cut out the middleman, RosUkrEnergo, controlled by forces within the opposition Party of the Regions, so that Russian gas sales went straight to Naftogaz. Naftogaz made the counteroffer of $235/tcm that appeared to be close enough to Gazprom's offer of $250/tcm. Thus, Party of Regions leader Viktor Yanukovich (and a contender for the presidency) could have convinced Yushchenko to block the deal in order to undermine Tymoshenko. Such an interpretation (based at least in part on an internal Ukrainian political cause of the failed negotiations and ongoing dispute) is supported by the fact that on January 10 the Ukrainian president's secretariat accused Russia of artificially sparking the gas crisis in order to win political capital for the presidential ambitions of Prime Minister Tymoshenko.[44] In sum, it took two sides to make the Russian-Ukrainian gas wars, and they appeared to have much to do with Ukrainian business and domestic politics as well as geopolitics. The same would be true in the crisis of 2013–2014.

By the end of the Yushchenko administration, Russian-Ukrainian relations had hit a low point. On August 11, 2009, then Russian president Medvedev wrote a letter to Yushchenko, informing him that the Kremlin had decided to delay indefinitely sending a new Russian ambassador to Kiev. Medvedev explained his decision by reciting

Yushchenko's anti–Russian policies, including: support of Georgia in the August 2008 war by supplying weapons and interfering with Russia's Black Sea fleet based in Sevastopol; disrupting Russian natural gas deliveries to Europe; using the spectre of a Russian threat to seek NATO membership; engaging in historical revisionism and the glorification of Nazi collaborators; mistreating Russian investors; and trying to disrupt the visit of the Russian Patriarch to Ukraine. Relations would take a turn for the better under Yushchenko's successor, and Western DP responded.

Revolution-Promotion in Ukraine

From 2005 to 2010 the level of democracy-promotion activity in Ukraine declined considerably. Little or no criticism of Yushchenko's tolerance and frequent support for Holocaust revisionism and neofascist groups or Yulia Tymoshenko's and the oligarchs' kleptocratic behavior came from Western governments. After a half-decade lapse and the NATO-cold Yanukovich's election as president, the dual-use technology of democracy-promotion returned with a vengeance. Much of it focused on Yanukovich's corruption and that of the oligarchs allied with him. Although some of the structures and activists of the 2004 Orange revolution—such as Oleh Ryabchuk—remained, the new USAID-sponsored efforts led to the creation of new structures that would lay the groundwork for regime change should Yanukovich make the Russian choice rather than the European choice.

The Revolution Will Be Televised

As in Yugoslavia, Georgia and Ukraine's 2004 Orange revolution, USAID played a lead role in the dual-use democracy-promotion activities that would help spark the Maidan demonstrations leading to Yanukovich's overthrow in February 2014. The key Washington coordinators were U.S. Assistant Secretary of State for European and Eurasian Affairs Victoria Nuland and then recently appointed U.S. Ambassador to Ukraine Geoffrey Pyatt. Soon after his arrival in Kiev, Pyatt approved a $50,000 USAID grant for Ukraine's first Internet-based television channel, Hromadske TV (Hromadske.tv), which would prove essential to building and networking the Ukrainian groups behind the Euromaidan street demonstrations against Yanukovich that began in November 2013. The grant's final tranche of $4,796 was set to arrive by November 13, with Yanukovich expected to sign the EU Association Agreement (AA) on November 30 at the UE summit in Vilnius. An ethnic Afghan activist journalist, Mustafa Nayem, and a group of other activists left their jobs at companies owned by "oligarchs or political partisans" in 2013 to found Hromadske.tv. Nayem became Hromadske.tv's deputy editor-in-chief, and in an April 2014 article for Soros's Open Society Foundation on "how it all began," he focused on the channel's donations from viewers; no mention of the U.S. government grant money. He assessed Hromadske's role as follows: "The media showed everything that was happening—helping people to believe that if we all act together, we can accomplish great things."[45] Nayem would become the mythical spark of the Maidan protests in November 2013.

In fact, many of Hromadske's journalists had worked in the past with Washington-backed media organizations. Editor-in-chief Roman Skrypin was a frequent contributor to the U.S. government's public diplomacy and strategic communications organ Radio

Free Europe/Radio Liberty (RFERL) and the U.S.-funded *Ukrainskaya pravda*. Skrypin helped create Ukraine's "Channel 5" television network, which played a major role in the Orange revolution. Hromadske's biggest backer at the time was the Netherlands Embassy in Kiev, which provided a $95,168 grant. A departing U.S. envoy to the Hague acknowledged in a secret cable published by Wikileaks that "Dutch pragmatism" and "similar world-view" led the Netherlands to join in projects "others in Europe" might be reluctant to embrace. On a recommendation from Pyatt, Skrypin had already received $10,560 from George Soros's International Renaissance Foundation (IRF), which often works hand-in-hand with USAID in building color revolution infrastructure and networks; he would receive another $19,183 from the IRF.[46]

Rybachuk: The Revolution Will Be Socially Networked

In October 2008, USAID funded a nonprofit called Pact Inc. to implement the "Ukraine National Initiatives to Enhance Reforms" (UNITER). Pact had worked in Africa, Central Asia, and since 2005 in Ukraine combatting HIV/AIDS, and now would work with the Orange revolution's Oleh Rybachuk on UNITER and a series of subsequent projects. Having played a pivotal role in coordinating with the SBU as it spied on the Yanukovich campaign on behalf of the Yushchenko campaign (which he managed, as noted in Chapter 5), Rybachuk again would play a pivotal role in Orange Revolution 2.0. Rybachuk went on to serve as chief of staff in the Yushchenko administration (2005–2006) and then as deputy prime minister in charge of Ukraine's integration into NATO and the EU in the Tymoshenko government (2007–2010). With Yushchenko's unceremonious downfall and the rise of Yanukovich to the presidency, Rybachuk returned to revolutionary activity.

The new five-year UNITER project with USAID was focused on the development of civil society, democracy, and good governance. In the program's first year, Pact Inc. designated Rybachuk "a civil society activist" running his own NGO, the United Actions Center (Centre UA or Tsentr UA) or UAC. Pact and Rybachuk attracted some 60 local and national NGOs and linked them with activists and public opinion leaders under UAC's auspices and coordination. This NGO umbrella evolved into the influential New Citizen group, a "non-political" "civic platform." Simultaneously, USAID's Pact and Soros's IRF worked jointly to expand its dual-use, prerevolutionary network by giving small grants to some 80 additional local NGOs. This continued at least throughout 2010 with additional money from the East Europe Foundation.[47] In addition, Rybachuk headed the Civil Expert Council tied to the government's EU-Ukraine Cooperation Committee, which was pushing Kiev to sign the EU Association Agreement as soon as possible, declaring already in January 2012 that Ukraine was "on the brink" of doing so at a conference so titled and organized jointly by the Konrad Adenauer Institute, the Center for U.S.-Ukraine Relations, and the Institute for Euro-Atlantic Cooperation.[48]

In May 2012 Pact advised Rybachuk's New Citizen on its strategic plan for 2011, urging that the coalition "take Access to Public Information as the focus of their work for the next year." New Citizen campaigned for the new Freedom of Information Law, which passed. Pact then instructed New Citizen how to use the law to win a higher public profile, organize and train new activists, and work more closely with journalists in strategic communication efforts, helping to reduce the Yanukovich government's popularity. This included the movement to "Stop Censorship." One of its founders was Mustafa

Nayem. Although Nayem acknowledges that "[t]he press gained freedoms under Yanukovich," in the first months of the presidency of Viktor Yanukovich, they nevertheless formed "Stop Censorship!" to "protest persecution of the press."[49]

Thus, less than three months into Yanukovich's presidency, journalists already were highlighting a supposedly "growing" number of complaints against censorship. Rybachuk was quoted in a journalistic article, noting: "Censorship is re-emerging, and the opposition is not getting covered as much…. There are some similarities to what Vladimir Putin did in Russia when he started his seizure of power by first muzzling criticism in the media." The article went on to warn that if Yanukovich's alleged censorship continued, then Ukrainians would be returned to the "decade-long informational black hole" of the Kuchma era, during which Ukrainians "were bombarded by Soviet-style propaganda from leading television news programs, mostly controlled by billionaire oligarchs."[50] Somehow, the oligarchs had become inactive in the Yushchenko era, in this view.

Other Western-funded efforts further undermined Yanukovich's legitimacy. For example, the NED gave journalist Sergiy Leshchenko a Reagan Fascell Democracy Fellowship, while New Citizen distributed his exposés of Yanukovich's corruption, especially his luxurious mansion at Mezhyhirya. Rybachuk's Center UA also produced a documentary film featuring Nayem daring to ask Yanukovich about Mezhyhirya at a press conference. On another front, Pact and Rybachuk's New Citizen authored a project to monitor the implementation by politicians of their promises calling it a "Powermeter" or "Vladometer" modeled on the American Web site "Obamameter." Vladometer received funding from the U.S. Embassy's Media Development Fund under the U.S. State Department's Bureau of Democracy, Human Rights, and Labor. Other funds came from the Internews Network funded by the State Department, USAID, the United States Institute of Peace (USIP) and a series of U.S. government agencies, international organizations, and private foundations, including Soros's IRF. It is important to note that these programs began after Yushchenko's fall and during Yanukovich's administration, and, as Weismann notes, the West did not fund any anti-corruption, monitoring or other campaigns against the Ukrainian kleptocrats who favored the West during this period.[51]

An opposition network of overlapping institutions and activists and networks thereof was hence created and arrayed against the Yanukovich regime. Thus, Rybachuk's perhaps main ally in "Stop Censorship" was the journalist Sergiy Leshchenko, who had long worked with the spark of Maidan, Mustafa Nayem at *Ukrainskaya Pravda*, funded by USAID through the NED. By the eve of the Maidan protests, New Citizen and its allied organizations networked some 150 NGOs spreading across 35 cities. In 2011 these groups founded the Chesno (simultaneously connoting both the words "garlic" and "honesty") "to monitor the political integrity of the parliamentary candidates running in the 2012 elections."[52] But months before the vote, in May 2012, Rybachuk declared revolution his goal: "The Orange Revolution was a miracle, a massive peaceful protest that worked…. We want to do that again and we think we will."[53] In December 2013, the *Financial Times* highlighted the "big role" Rybachuk's "New Citizen" networking played "in getting the protest up and running."[54]

Indeed, the democracy-promotion funding to Ukraine was peaking in 2012–2013. Weissman notes that figures for the pivotal fiscal year 2013 "are more difficult to track," with Washington's foreignassistance.gov showing USAID paying Pact in Ukraine over $7 million under the general category of "Democracy, Human Rights, and Governance." According to a Pact Inc. financial audit for the Chesno campaign from October 2011 to

December 2012, Rybachuk's CUA and six associated groups received some $800,000 for Chesno, with USAID-funded PACT and the Omidyar Network, founded by eBay founder Pierre Omidyar and his wife, providing the bulk, $632,813.[55]

Although the American government in the form of USAID played a major role in funding opposition groups prior to the revolution, a large portion of the other funding to such groups came from the American billionaire Omidyar, who previously worked with U.S. government often in the furtherance of his own business interests.[56] According to White House logs, Omidyar, his wife, and Omidyar Network officials were among the most frequent visitors to the Obama White House in 2009–2013, the years leading up to the Maidan revolt.[57] According to the pro–Maidan *Kyiv Post*, Omidyar's Omidyar Network (part of the Omidyar Group) provided 36 percent of CUA's $500,000 budget in 2012, with USAID providing 54 percent and other funders, including the NED, the U.S. government-backed National Endowment for Democracy, providing the rest.[58] In March 2012 the Omidyar Network detailed its contributions to Rybachuk's CUA, New Citizen and thus the Chesno Movement, including a September 2011 two-year grant of $335,000 in order to "engage citizens on issues" so that "concerned members of society" could better "shape public policy."[59] Omidyar then gave these groups a follow-up grant of $769,000 in July 2013. Some of the funds financed the expansion of Rybachuk's Internet technology and social networking platforms and Chesno's geographical expansion into regional cities of Poltava, Vinnytsia, Zhytomyr, Chernohiv, Khmelnitskiy, Ternopil, Sumy and others, mostly in the Ukrainian west and center. New Citizen was now designated "an online platform to cooperatively advocate for social change," "a hub of social justice advocates in Kiev" that aimed "to define the nation's 'New Citizen' through digital media" including "video-advocacy campaigns," as well as "a diverse set of community initiatives."[60] Other donors to these programs besides USAID and the Omidyar Network included the USAID-funded Pact, the Swiss and British embassies, the Swedish International Development Cooperation Agency, the NED, and Soros's IRF. The Chesno Movement also received money from Canada's own USAID–the Canadian International Development Agency (CIDA).[61]

The U.S. State Department used other methods to network opposition groups, including nationalist oriented elements, in Ukraine. The case of the Maidan regime's second finance minister, Natalie Jaresko, is instructive on how the U.S. instrumentalized and deployed the Ukrainian diaspora in the U.S.[62] Similar methods were used by Canada. Jaresko was born in Chicago, and her family was deeply involved in the pro–Ukrainian diaspora's decades-long struggle to bring Kiev west. Her brother, John, had been active in Ukrainian movements and was awarded a medal in 2010 by Yushchenko. At that time, Natalie was a member of Yushchenko's Foreign Investors Advisory Council and the Advisory Board of the Ukrainian Center for Promotion of Foreign Investment, and in 2003 received the St. Olga medal from Yushchenko. Jaresko and her husband (1989–2010), Ihor Figlus, both worked in the U.S. Embassy in Kiev for a period in 1992–1995 when, according to Jaresko's resumé, she served as the First Chief of the Economic Section of the U.S. Embassy in Ukraine after serving in various economic positions at the State Department back in Washington. Figlus moved on to run the American Chamber of Commerce in Ukraine and then the Western NIS Enterprise Fund (WNISEF). Also according to the career resumé, Natalie was cofounder of Horizon Capital and served as its managing partner from March 2006, simultaneously serving as president and CEO of Figlus's WNISEF from February 2001 to 2014. Horizon Capital's other founders were two Americans with Harvard degrees and Chicago backgrounds, and a Canadian-Ukrainian.[63]

According to a recent Ukrainian community paper from Chicago, which ignored her U.S. government connections, Jaresko was described as having "worked more than 20 years in Ukraine as a venture capitalist, bringing countless foreign investments to Ukraine." Her initial fund, WNISEF, according to Jaresko herself, was "funded by the U.S. government to invest in small and medium-sized businesses in Ukraine and Moldova—in essence, to 'kick-start' the private equity industry in the region. We began investing in this region in 1995, and have invested $122 million over the past 12 years in 30 businesses in a wide variety of sectors. Based on our team's ability to successfully navigate this business environment, our track record, and Ukraine's promising economic environment, we founded Horizon Capital in 2006." That is, Jaresko received U.S. government (USAID) funding immediately after leaving her U.S. Embassy position in Kiev to begin networking a pro–American—and anti–Russian—entrepreneurial class in Ukraine in violation of revolving-door laws and U.S. government rules. According to Helmer, impact statements about its funding operations in Ukraine and Moldova between 1997 and 2005 promised by WNISEF on its Web site for disclosure are absent. WNISEF's first publicly available financial report—that for 2003—shows a USAID grant of $150 million, with a letter of credit commitment of $141.7 million. Of those funds, $113.6 million had been disbursed by the end of 2003. Despite the government support, asset value was dropping, but management salaries, business travel and other expenses were rising. The fund was $4.3 million in the red in 2002, $5.1 million in 2003. The next available report from WNISEF is for 2012. The management was still raising its own salaries and cutting business travel, but still ran a loss of $6.4 million in 2012, compared to a $401,662 gain in 2011. Horizon Capital says WNISEF was "the cornerstone limited partner" in Emerging Europe Growth Fund, L.P. (EEGF), a $132 million fund raised in 2006. Emerging Europe Growth Fund II, L.P. (EEGF II), Jaresko called a "follow-on" fund "expanding on the success" of EEGF with a similar investment strategy and investors who included European and U.S. fund-of-funds, banks, private pension funds, university endowments, family offices, and high net worth individuals. According to Jaresko, EEGF II typically invests $15–40 million in each of its portfolio companies, including expansion, buy-out and selective early stage opportunities. The alleged "success" of Horizon Capital was not reported in the loss-making years of 2003, 2004, 2005, 2006, 2008, 2009, 2010, and 2012. In the years which Jaresko managed Horizon Capital in the black, 2007 and 2011, the net gains reported were small: $1.8 million and $401,662, respectively. On the asset side, annual reports are dominated by USAID's grant of $150 million, so it appears other investors have lost their subscribed funds. When Jaresko was asked about investment performance, she said that she was "very pleased" and believed "2006 will be a very good vintage for our investors." The 2006 audit report showed a net investment loss of $5.3 million.[64]

Papers filed in the Chancery Court of Delaware in 2012 and 2013 by her now ex-husband Figlus explain Jaresko's transition from State Department officer to government-paid "asset manager" as having been made possible solely by the USAID funding, with the first investment of their own funds coming only in 2006. They also state that Jaresko arranged "improper" loans to secure her and her husband's investment commitments.[65] The impropriety, it is charged, consisted of WNISEF having been a shareholder and simultaneously a lender to the cooking oil producer Solon.[66] When Figlus tried to go to the *Kyiv Post* to expose Jaresko's conduct, she issued a reminder to her ex-husband that he had signed a nondisclosure agreement with EEGF.[67] In sum, Jaresko was not an effective asset manager and may not have been even a law-abiding one. She nevertheless succeeded in building a luxurious mansion for herself in Ukraine.[68]

Thus, it appears that Jaresko was less in the business of producing high returns on investors' outlays than in building a network of businesses and organizations tied to, and dependent on, the U.S. government and its allies in Ukraine, serving both the Orange and Maidan revolutions. The political essence of her activity was demonstrated in her and her husband's frequent attendance at the annual Yalta international conference that pushed Ukraine's Western integration.[69] As I note in Chapter 10, she would be well rewarded politically for her efforts in service of the Maidan revolution.

The above surely does not constitute a complete accounting of U.S. government and government-tied funding going to Ukraine's nascent revolutionary movement. Nor does it include the comprehensive government and government-tied public diplomacy and lobbying efforts designed to entice Ukraine away from Russia and into NATO and the EU. For example, the D.C.-based Wiley Rein legal representation group lobbied Bill and Hillary Clinton in September 2013 to attend and speak at an international conference in Yalta. Both spoke, encouraging Ukraine to bolster efforts to join the EU. Wiley Rein also lobbied Yanukovich on behalf of Yulia Tymoshenko for her release from prison, receiving $920,000 under a contract with her husband Oleksandr and funneled through a series of companies and firms. At the time, Tymoshenko's imprisonment was a major obstacle to the EU's offering Ukraine an association agreement. Jim Slattery, a Wiley Rein partner, former U.S. Democratic congressman from Kansas, and longtime Tymoshenko friend, put the political side of the firm's involvement in Ukraine in context: "I have been convinced that Ukraine is of key strategic importance, and I was surprised at how little members of Congress knew what was going on there." The parties were therefore willing to go to great lengths to secure Tymoshenko's release. In January 2013, Wiley Rein lobbyists discussed hacking the email account of Tymoshenko's daughter Eugenia with aides to Sens. Dick Durbin (D–Ill.) and James Inhofe (R–Okla.), Bill Burns of the State Department, Melanne Verveer, and "Sec. Clinton." In the immediate aftermath of Yanukovich's overthrow, Slattery said, "I would work for people who want a free, democratic Ukraine. I am not going to represent gangsters or thugs."[70]

Other American lobbyists were less picky and worked for, and profited nicely from contracts with, Yanukovich's circle. U.S. lobbyist and political consultant Paul Manafort was an adviser to Yanukovich from 2004 to 2013 and had previously worked for Ronald Reagan, George W. Bush and John McCain.[71] In 2013, the Yanukovich-tied, Brussels-based European Centre for a Modern Ukraine (ECMU) paid consulting firm Mercury $280,000 and the Podesta Group $510,000 in lobbying fees, according to disclosure records. Vin Weber, Mercury managing partner and former U.S. Republican congressman from Minnesota, disclosed Mercury had no idea where ECMU's funding came from, but knew it did not come from the government or Yanukovich's Party of the Regions, but rather from "individuals." This would mean the funds came from pro–Yanukovich Ukrainian oligarchs. Mercury acknowledged lobbying on both pro-democracy and pro–Tymoshenko resolutions in 2013. In political context, the Russia-West struggle was central; Weber said Mercury warned Congress that its pressure on Kiev "was pushing Yanukovich closer to Putin."[72] The tussle between Russia and the West would come to a head in the final failed push to get Yanukovich to sign the EU association agreement.

The Spark: EU-Ukraine Association Agreement

As noted in Chapter 4, it was during the Yushchenko presidency that the EU instituted its Eastern Partnership Program specifically set about drawing Ukraine into closer relations. Launched in 2008, the EPP endeavored to strengthen EU relationships with all the former USSR's "European" republics, including Ukraine, Belarus, Moldova, Armenia, Azerbaijan and Georgia—but excluding Russia—thereby seeking to isolate Russia's economy from those now prospective EU members and preparing the EPP partners for association agreements. By 2012, as Washington continued to nudge Kiev towards the EU, the EU began working more closely with Kiev to arrange an upgrade in its relationship with Europe—Kiev's signing of an association agreement (EU AA). As noted in the previous chapter, such agreements were followed eight years later (on average) by accession to NATO for the twelve cases of post-communist states that signed such agreements. At the end of March 2012, the EU and Ukraine initialed a preliminary EU AA for Kiev.

At the November 28–29 EU's Eastern Partnership summit in Vilnius, Lithuania approached with expectations that Ukraine would sign the EU AA, and tensions escalated between Moscow, on the one hand, and Kiev and Brussels, on the other. Moreover, the EU's unilateral approach in relation to Russia created a zero-sum game in which Moscow held the upper hand in terms of the resources it was willing to commit and certain other comparative advantages for enticing Yanukovich towards Russia's EEU or some compromise variation. In the West, the developing conflict was seen purely in terms of Aesopian fables about Russia's pursuit of the USSR's restoration and Ukraine's allegedly European roots and natural destiny. Such "subtleties" as a divided Ukraine and Huntington's "fault-line state"—and its implications for potential conflict—were forgotten. However, this was not true for Brzezinski's idea of Ukraine as a "vital geopolitical pivot" at the edge of the "heartland" of the "World Island."

Despite claims made in the West and by the Ukrainian opposition, Yanukovich was not Moscow's puppet. He signed Ukraine's 2010 law "On the Basic Directions of Domestic and Foreign Policy," which stipulated Ukraine's integration "into the European political, economic and legal area for the purpose of becoming a member of the European Union." On the other hand, he was not willing to alienate Moscow and nearly a third of his country's populace by severing Ukraine's deeply rooted ties to Russia. The issue that needed solving was how to ensure Ukraine's balanced strategic development and power-maximizing among the contending parties, and Yanukovich appeared to be playing both sides off against the other in order to extract benefits from both Russia and the West.

The conflict between Russia and the EU over Ukraine's future emerged on the basis of perceived self-interest and power-maximizing; something all states and unions of states engage in almost all of the time. One way states maximize their power (sometimes with unintended costly trade-offs, to be sure) is to join in various economic, political and/or military associations, alliances, unions, etc. Some states are powerful initiators and dominant players in such unions; others are latecomers joining out of weakness.

The formation of international organizations, regimes and unions is further driven by globalization's imperative for integration among states (coupled with some disintegration within states), including now hundreds of international organizations, as one modality for power-maximizing. Within the globe's network of networks, unions of states—like individual states—seek to maximize their influence and power, by increasing the number of their members.

Thus, Ukraine seeks to increase its economic (and even political) potential by joining such unions. Through EU membership, some Ukrainians seek markets for its products, technological development for its industries, and a role in one of the major economic, political and, one suspects, military blocs. NATO is a likely destiny after Kiev chooses the EU.

Since Russia's strategic and political cultures value its historical great-power status, Moscow is especially keen to power-maximize by creating unions around its cultural, economic, political, and military potential. Specifically, it seeks to maintain its status as the main power in Central Eurasia by constructing a series of economic unions and military alliances: the Eurasian Customs Union (with Kazakhstan, Belarus, and now Armenia); the United Economic Space (Customs Union, plus several Central Asian states); the subsequent EEU project; the CSTO; and the SCO (with China's membership containing Moscow's ambitions, in this case). The membership of Ukraine, the second most powerful of the former Soviet republics, would significantly enhance the clout of these Eurasian projects, thereby increasing Russia's own economic and political power.

Conversely, Ukraine's rejection of Eurasian structures weakens their clout and thus the attractiveness of these projects to other prospective members, confining them largely to Russia and the weakest post–Soviet economies. Without Ukraine, the EEU would be less than a robust configuration, barely enhancing Russia's power in the region and risking being more of a burden than a boost for Moscow.

Europe similarly seeks to bolster its power by bringing in Eastern Europe's largest country. Beyond increasing the common market's economic power, Ukraine's inclusion will promote Europe's energy security, assuming that Ukraine's bargaining power vis-à-vis Moscow is indeed bolstered sufficiently to preclude a gas cutoff to Europe.

For Kiev, a European choice will not be all roses. There is no guarantee that Ukraine's present leadership is capable of overcoming powerful domestic clans, corruption, and other obstacles to the domestic legal, economic and political reforms that further integration and ultimate accession to the EU requires. Moreover, Ukraine's failure to accede would drive it into Russia's arms and foster the kind of resentment of Europe that Turkey experienced after Europe spurned its entry into the EU. Although Kiev's EU choice is one in favor of more rapid democratic and free market development, it is also one in favor of Europe's socialist comprehensive cradle-to-grave government paternalism, massive welfare state, and perhaps financial insolvency. Indeed, at the onset of the crisis, Russian finances were in better shape than Europe's.

Yanukovich was still trying to have it both ways on the eve of the scheduled signing of the EU AA. Kiev was asserting it had not closed the door on its relations with Russia or even joining Russian-led organizations such as the Customs Union, and the Eurasian Economic Union. Indeed, President Yanukovich had followed this policy in other spheres, including security, by extending Kiev's treaty allowing Russia's Black Sea Fleet to continue basing in Sevastopol until 2042, as well as by signing a law making Russian an official state language along with Ukrainian in half of the country's regions. Nevertheless, Kiev would have taken several steps away from Russia and Eurasia by signing an EU association agreement. The EU had rejected the Russian preferences for Ukraine's dual membership in the EU and EEU and trilateral EU-Ukrainian-Russian trade negotiations before Kiev signed the AA. Instead, EU Enlargement and Neighborhood Commissioner Štefan Füle said at the 10th Yalta Annual Meeting on September 20 that the EU and Ukraine (but not Russia) were "working on overcoming the issue of legal incompatibility between the Association Agreement and Customs Union." It was clear that an EU AA and ultimate membership would exclude Ukraine's membership in the EEU and other Eurasian organizations.

This dynamic would have been reinforced by new economic pressures created by an EU-Ukrainian association agreement, undermining Ukrainian trade with Russia and the rest of the EEU. Yet Ukraine's economy was heavily dependent on exports of nuclear equipment, grain, chemicals, steel, coal, fuel and petroleum products to Russia and other Eurasian Economic Union member-states. Nearly two-thirds of Kiev's exports were sent to former Soviet republics, most to Russia (25 percent), Belarus and Kazakhstan. Kiev would lose some portion of this trade as its legal regime was anchored to Europe and Eurasian Economic Union and other Eurasian economic unification projects were further institutionalized.

Indeed, one Russian official warns that if, after being squeezed out by an influx of European goods on the Ukrainian market, Kiev's goods begin to flood the markets of Russia and other Eurasian Economic and Customs Unions' members, Moscow will invoke Statute 6 of the CIS Free Trade Agreement to allow blocking such dumping exportation. The Russian Customs Service banned imports of some Ukrainian goods, including those of Ukrainian chocolate goods popular across the former USSR, costing Kiev billions of dollars in trade. So part of Yanukovich's cost-benefit economic and political calculus regarding the implications of the economic trade-offs had to be whether additional trade with the EU would compensate quickly enough for the trade and other relationships lost with Customs Union member-states. For Yanukovich's political needs, this was a dubious bet, given the noncompetitiveness of Ukrainian production and the EU's financial crisis and stagnating economic performance at the time.

There also are ethno-national complications for Ukraine in joining the EU. Hungarian nationalists were threatening to scuttle the EU ratification vote should Ukraine sign the association agreement. They demanded that Kiev create a Transcarpathian enclave in Ukraine to unite a series of districts bordering Hungary where ethnic Hungarians predominate. The Crimean Tatars and the ethnic Russians of eastern Ukraine were also likely to appeal to Brussels for similar further autonomy within Ukraine.

The EU also was taking on significant risks by adopting an already fiscally strapped and sluggish Ukrainian economy with limited economic and cultural ties to Europe, as compared to its ties in the Slavic and post–Soviet east. Ukraine's debt was high and likely to get higher after signing the AA as exports to Russia would decline, Russian gas subsidies would be terminated forever, and its products failed to penetrate European markets. In June 2013, Fitch dropped Kiev's credit rating to "negative," and in September, Moody's reduced its rating, noting a very high risk of default, after Ukrainian reserves fell to $21.6 billion against an external debt service bill of $10.8 billion by the end of the year. The EU's Eastern Partnership program had already dished out 600 million Euros in the last three years to six eastern European countries. How long would German and other EU taxpayers bear such a burden, given Greek defaults and the threat of additional ones across the continent?

Although the West has been quick to note the "asymmetric" relationship between Russia and Ukraine and the former's pressure on the latter to join its favored structures, the EU is loath to acknowledge its own preponderance of power in its relationship with Ukraine. Kiev's dependence on Europe would only grow as Kiev becomes dependent on western economic assistance, just as it has on Russian implicit subsidization in the form of below-market prices for natural gas and oil since the Soviet collapse.

Europe's enticements also risked a dangerous split inside Ukraine between its Russophile east and Russophobic west. As I wrote in early November 2013, "Such a split could lead to explosive consequences, especially if NATO pursues Ukraine. Most Europeans will never acknowledge it, but EU membership is also a stepping stone to NATO membership. An attempt at that will lead to unforeseeable levels of tension and potential conflict between Russia and the West…. Tensions between Europe and Russia could place the two Slavic nations on opposite sides of the barricades. Such outcomes would be a tragedy for these deeply intertwined peoples."[73] Already, just in the runup to Ukraine's signing the association agreement, tensions ran high between Russia, on the one hand, and Ukraine and the EU, on the other. Political commentators in Ukraine had been harping on the worst aspects of Russian reality, and Prime Minister Mykola Azarov threatened to begin drastically cutting and in the future terminating Ukrainian gas imports from Russia. In turn, some Russian government and media supplied a mix of not very veiled threats and dour analyses of the consequences of Kiev's accession to the EU. Presidential advisor Sergei Glaziev offered a series of threats designed to force Kiev to think twice and thrice about turning West, including the possibility of instituting visa requirements for Ukrainians' entry to Russia. Putin later rejected such a visa policy, but this and similar actions remained in his back pocket and could be employed. Such tactical "sticks" offered Kiev little incentive to rethink its Western vector. However, a substantial material "carrot" would do the trick.

The geopolitical essence of the EU AA offer to Kiev was made clear by the EU's flaunting of the vaunted Western principles of democracy and human rights. Throughout 2012 and 2013 the EU repeatedly conditioned Ukraine's signing of the EU AA at the summit in Lithuania on the release from prison of Yuriy Lutsenko, permission for Yuliya Tymoshenko to leave prison to travel abroad for medical treatment, and tangible progress towards electoral, judiciary and constitutional reforms.[74] The December 2012 EP resolution mentioned above also addressed Ukraine's democracy deficit and warned it might affect concluding an EU association agreement by noting: "Members confirm the EU's commitment to further advancing relations with Ukraine through the signing of the association agreement as soon as the Ukrainian authorities demonstrate determined action and tangible progress, as called for above, possibly by the time of the Eastern Partnership Summit in Vilnius in November 2013. They note that progress in political association and economic integration is dependent on Ukraine's tangible commitment to democratic principles, the rule of law, the independence of the judiciary and media freedom."[75] Nevertheless, the only demand Kiev met was the release of Lutsenko in April 2013. As the November 2013 Vilnius summit approached, the remaining demands disappeared, and the EU expected the agreement to be signed.

At the same time, the EU made it clear that Ukraine could not have it both ways: close economic relations with both Russia and the EU. Yanukovich had maintained negotiations with Moscow to find the "right model" for simultaneous EU association and cooperation with the Customs Union of Belarus, Kazakhstan and Russia. Now, in February 2013, President José Manuel Barroso of the European Commission made it clear that "one country cannot at the same time be a member of a customs union and be in a deep common free-trade area with the European Union."[76]

In the end it was Ukraine, not the EU, that balked in signing the AA just days before the Vilnius summit, with all parties expecting Yanukovich would sign the agreement. Opening the autumn 2013 session of the Verkhovna Rada, Yanukovich had urged his parliament to adopt draft laws intended to meet the EU criteria for concluding the AA in November 2013, but the Tymoshenko issue was avoided.[77] Two weeks later the Ukrainian cabinet unanimously approved the draft EU AA.[78] On November 20, EU Enlargement Commissioner Fuele was expecting that the next day the Rada would pass the reform legislation necessary for signing the AA by November 29.[79] However, on November 21 the Verkhovna Rada declined six motions to allow Tymoshenko to receive medical treatment abroad.[80] In turn, Tymoshenko announced that she would request the EU drop its demand for her freedom if Yanukovich would sign the AA.[81] A November 21 Ukrainian government decree suspended preparations for signing the agreement and proposed instead the creation of a trilateral EU-Russian-Ukrainian commission for resolving trade issues between the parties. The same day, Putin's press secretary, Dmitrii Peskov, called Ukraine's decision a "strictly internal and sovereign decision" and refused to comment further on it, other than to state that Russia was prepared to have tripartite negotiations with Ukraine and the EU on trade and economic issues.[82]

However, by November 26 the Ukrainian government acknowledged that Russia had asked it to delay signing the EU association agreement, claiming it still intended to sign an EU AA but wanted "better terms." Yanukovich and Ukraine Prime Minister Mykola Azarov also reiterated that Ukraine still sought to sign an agreement, but one with "normal terms."[83] Kiev appeared to be still playing one side against the other, and the EU, despite Kiev's failure to meet its demands, maintained it still wished to continue pursuing an EU AA for Kiev.[84] At the same time, Brussels also expressed its anger over Russia's démarche. European Council President Rompuy and European Commission President Barosso declared they "strongly disapproved" of Russia's actions.[85] Barosso escalated his rhetoric during the Vilnius summit, demanding that the EU ought to "not give in to external pressure, least of all from Russia," and casting Moscow's effort to counter the West's hardball geopolitics as "a veto" and "contrary to all principles of international law."[86] Putin responded by calling for an end to the criticism of Yanukovich's decision to postpone signing the agreement and stated that the EU deal was bad for Russia's security interests.[87] It thus came as little surprise when in mid–December it was announced that Moscow and Kiev had sealed a deal whereby Moscow would purchase $15 billion in Ukrainian bonds and sell natural gas to Kiev at a discounted price.[88] With Ukraine on the verge of default, the Rada balking at passing the political reform package mandated by the EU, and Brussels offering just $3 billion in bailout aid if the EU AA was signed, Putin's offer was one Yanukovich found too difficult to refuse. Putin's offer outline was likely communicated to Yanukovich just prior to his announcement to delay signing the EU AA on or around November 21.

As the first mass demonstrations were being held on Kiev's Maidan Square, Yanukovich flew to Vilnius, not to sign the EU AA, but to make proposals in pursuit of better terms and trilateral talks with Moscow. He told the summit that Ukraine would sign an EU AA, but in light of imminent default and likely economic retaliation from Moscow, Kiev needed substantial financial aid and a more robust IMF loan, which he asked Brussels to help secure.[89] However, he also stated that Kiev wanted to sign a "strategic partnership agreement with Russia" and saw its "responsibility" to be establishing "normal relations" between the EU, Russia, and Ukraine."[90] The EU again rejected this approach and any talks with Moscow and failed to come up with enough incentives to convince Yanukovich to sign, leading to the $15-billion-plus bond and natural gas agreement between Moscow and Kiev. Putin had won a key battle, but not the final one in the greater geopolitical war by delaying Ukraine's march east and drawing it back closer to Moscow.

It seems that as the planned EU AA signing negotiations moved towards completion, the U.S. government may also have exerted some weighty pressure on Yanukovich to keep him on course to Brussels. Washington allegedly used a criminal case U.S. prosecutors opened against Yanukovich supporter and Ukrainian oligarch Dmitrii Firtash in order to force Yanukovich to agree initially to sign the EU AA. According to Firtash's testimony at his Vienna hearing on possible extradition to the U.S. which had indicted him, he claimed that the case was fabricated by U.S. prosecutors in order to use it to extract three compromises from Yanukovich: to sign the EU AA; to release Tymoshenko for medical treatment abroad; and to give the Kharkiv oil and gas field to Chevron. During her early 2013 visit to Kiev, U.S. Assistant Secretary of State Victoria Nuland issued Yanukovich an ultimatum on this score, and he therefore agreed to sign the agreement, according to Firtash.[91]

Moscow's resistance to EU expansion without Russia was motivated by several clear calculations. At a minimum, the EU's effort to bring Ukraine into the EU's orbit was intended to reduce Russia's sphere of economic influence and weaken its Eurasian Economic Union project. At a maximum, as we have seen Brzezinski and others state explicitly, EU expansion to Ukraine would have been but a prelude to Ukraine's entry into NATO. More fundamentally, even if such was unintentional, the fact is that the EU's maximizing expansion policies had the real effect in objective terms of damaging Russian interests in its effort to maximize its power. Russian officials repeatedly stated that Ukraine's entry into the AA would lead to a flood of European goods into the Ukrainian, Russian, EEU, and even CIS markets, cutting into local firms' sales and profits and thus local national budgets. This was the key issue Moscow hoped to resolve through trilateral trade talks preceding Kiev's signing an EU AA.

However, both the West's "plan maximum"—EU and NATO expansion to Ukraine—and the intended strategic goal of reducing Russian power become evident if we take a close look at the text of the draft EU-Ukraine AA, in particular some of the "non-economic" clauses in the aborted agreement. Specifically, the agreement included military and security clauses that would help Ukraine prepare for NATO membership. The agreement's Articles 5 and 10 read:

Article 5
   Fora for the conduct of political dialogue:
   (1) The Parties shall hold regular political dialogue meetings at Summit level.
   (2) At ministerial level, political dialogue shall take place within the Association Council referred to in [Article 460 of this Agreement] and within the framework of regular meetings between representatives of the Parties at Foreign Minister level by mutual agreement.
   (3) Political dialogue shall also take place in the following formats:
      (a) regular meetings at Political Directors, Political and Security Committee and expert level, including on specific regions and issues, between representatives of the European Union on the one hand, and representatives of Ukraine on the other;
      (b) taking full and timely advantage of all diplomatic and military channels between the Parties, including appropriate contacts in third countries and within the United Nations, the OSCE and other international fora;
      (c) regular meetings both at the level of high officials and of experts of the military institutions of the Parties....

Article 10

Conflict prevention, crisis management and military-technological cooperation

(1) The Parties shall enhance practical cooperation in conflict prevention and crisis management, in particular with a view to an increased participation of Ukraine in EU-led civilian and military crisis management operations as well as relevant exercises and training including those in the framework of the Common Security and Defence Policy (CSDP).

(2) The Parties shall explore the potential of military and technological cooperation. Ukraine and the European Defence Agency (EDA) will establish close contacts to discuss military capability improvement, including technological issues.[92]

According to Russian Foreign Minister Lavrov, the goal of placing before Kiev a civilizational choice and thus removing Ukrainians from Russia's economic, cultural, and geopolitical world was openly stated by EU trade officials already during the Orange revolution: "The then Belgian Foreign Minister Karel Lodewijk De Gucht, who later became the European Commissioner for Trade, said openly in the autumn of 2004 that the government and people of Ukraine should decide whether they want to stick together with the European Union or Russia. The very same calls were voiced during the Euromaidan rallies of 2013."[93]

The problem that such Western operatives failed to grasp is that Ukraine was a divided entity, and forcing the civilizational choice on it was likely to break the country apart, regardless of further Western or Russian actions. Accordingly, Donetsk and Luhansk stood out in their strong preference for Ukraine's membership in Moscow's EEU over EU membership. They held this preference as much because of regional economic considerations as ethno-communal ones. Thus, support for the EEU and opposition to the EU—the cause that sparked the Euromaidan—were often heard at anti–Maidan demonstrations in the Donbass.[94] Before the 2004 Orange revolution and Yushchenko administration further divided Ukrainian society, and perhaps because an alternative to the EU had still not appeared, Donbass was as supportive of Ukraine's joining the EU in the 1990s and early 2000s as was the west and other areas of Ukraine. From 2002 to 2005, support for EU membership in Ukraine's east fell from a high of 82 percent in 2002 to 30 percent by 2005. In the south, support for EU membership fell during the same period from 74 percent to 41 percent, and by 2007 fell to a low of 31 percent. Rarely after 2004 did support for EU membership exceed 50 percent in the east and south. By contrast, the west maintained levels of support of 79 to 93 percent from 2002 to 2008, and central Ukraine ranged from 59 to 83 percent support for the same in those years.[95] By April 2014 opinion polls showed large majorities in the Donbass (Donetsk and Luhansk regions)—72.5 percent and 64.3 percent, respectively—favored joining the EEU (then still the Customs Union) over the EU. Considerably less support (26–42 percent) was registered in other eastern regions and the south—the Novosrossiya belt.[96]

Donbass opposition to the EU likely reflected both a pro–Russian geopolitical orientation and concerns about Ukraine's and especially Donbass's economy and standard of living should they become part of the EU. Those on fixed incomes, especially the elderly, opposed the austerity measures that would accompany EU membership. The large number of industrial workers in the Donbass's major mining, metallurgy, and machine building industries knew that EEU membership would maintain key trade ties with Russia and high employment rates, whereas EU membership would break those ties and lead to a growth in unemployment in these sectors and the region as a whole, since their industries are far less competitive in European markets.[97]

Thus, while Yanukovich's postponement of the EU AA and his choice to maintain considerable ties to Moscow were enough to spark many western Ukrainians and some central Ukrainians to go into the streets and protest in late November 2013, they could not motivate any Donbassians or Crimeans, or many other southeastern Ukrainians, to do so. The West's policy of hastily drawing Ukraine towards the West and away from Russia failed to appreciate the grave risk of deep polarization and the potential for violence.

At least in his rhetoric, Putin seems to have made a similar miscalculation. In part, Putin and many other Russians are correct when they say, as Putin said in September 2013, that Russia and Ukraine are "a single nation" having "common historical roots and common fates, a common religion, a common faith, and very similar culture, languages, traditions, and mentality."[98] But where his statement is wrong, it suffers from a similar assumption of Ukrainian homogeneity that misinformed Western policy. As I have demonstrated in the previous chapters, western Ukraine is largely antagonistic towards Russia, precisely because it has fundamental historical, religious, cultural, and linguistic differences from it. These differences would manifest themselves in both constructive and destructive reactions to Yanukovich's postponement of the signing of the AA.

More crucially, the major divisions driving the general east-west *raskol* in Ukraine would be exacerbated by the pro–EU Maidan protests, leading to violence, escalation, the overthrow of Yanukovich and his southeastern-rooted Party of the Regions, radicalization east and west, and ultimately civil war.

7

Maidan

Introduction

In order to understand the unfolding of events that led to the Maidan revolutionary coup and Ukraine's civil war, it is necessary to examine the key turning points in the crisis leading up to these events. This chapter consists of analysis of several "escalation points"—coercive and violent turning points—in the making of this still ongoing Ukrainian and international crisis. Although they are not the only escalation and turning points in crisis politics, coercive and violent incidents are particularly powerful ones. Research shows that rhetoric and insult, for example, also raise the temperature in any developing or ongoing conflict. Nevertheless, it is almost always true that coercion and violence play the lead role in the development of conflictive dynamics. Coercive and violent acts sharply polarize, mobilize and radicalize actors and groups operating in the structure of strategic action attending any major political or revolutionary crisis. Therefore, I endeavor to determine here the dynamics of escalation through coercion and violence as well as which sides initiated escalations by raising the level of antagonism through coercion and violence at key moments in the Ukrainian crisis, sparked in the most immediate sense by then Ukrainian President Viktor Yanukovich's decision to delay the signing of the draft EU association agreement.

Before looking at the various violent escalation points leading to the overthrow of Yanukovich, I examine the spark for the mass "EuroMaidan" protests on the Maidan Nenadlezhnosti (Independence Square), or simply the "Maidan," and the Western-funded infrastructure's activization once the Maidan fuse was lit.

The Spark

When, on November 21, President Yanukovich reneged on signing the EU AA, deferring many Ukrainians' dreamed "European choice," Mustafa Nayem called for demonstrations on the Maidan in an 8:00 p.m. Facebook posting: "Come on guys, let's be serious. If you really want to do something, don't just 'like' this post. Write that you are ready, and we can try to start something." Within an hour, according to Nayem, there were more than 600 comments. He posted again: "Let's meet at 10:30 p.m. near the monument to independence in the middle of the Maidan." When Nayem arrived on the Maidan, there were perhaps 50 people gathered, he notes, but soon "the crowd had swelled to more than 1,000."[1] The myth would be that Nayem's FB posting set in motion the

EuroMaidan protests. In reality, he was simply part of the network of networks that USAID and other funders had been knitting together since the failure of the Orange revolution and was poised to act when opportunity rang. The delay of the EU AA's signing was the opportunity. The Maidan demonstrations had begun.

The same day, Nayem's Hromadske.tv went online. As Nayem deployed social media to summon students and other young people to rally on the Maidan, Hromadske.tv would help drive the revolution, along with other Western-funded strategic communication operations. Soros immediately stepped up to fund the "Ukrainian Crisis Media Center" to inform the international community about events on the Maidan and in Ukraine. He and other Western entities likely funded "Euromaidan PR," the Web site of the Official Public Relations Secretariat for the Headquarters of the National Resistance in Kiev.[2] The Web site's "About" page contains no information on its partners or funders.[3] These institutions became the strategic communications and propaganda infrastructure for the Maidan revolt.

Nayem described the mood and his own motivation for acting as he did in an April 2014 article published on the Web site of Soros's Open Society Foundation:

Many factors contributed to Yanukovich's downfall: his jailing of political opponents, pressure on independent journalists, and use of brutal force against peaceful protesters. But the final straw was his refusal to sign the agreement forming an alliance between Ukraine and the European Union.

The morning it happened, I was covering parliament in Kyiv. At first, I thought Yanukovich was just playing politics, holding out for more money or concessions from the EU. But soon it became clear that the agreement was truly dead. Facebook erupted with rage, people's posts dripping with venom. They were so disappointed after all the buildup. They had so little faith in their own institutions, in their ability to make their voices heard; many had come to see the EU as their chance to change everything.

It was ironic that the defeat happened on November 21—10 years after the Orange Revolution that prevented Viktor Yanukovich from becoming president. It felt cruel that hope was being dashed on the very day that had come to symbolize freedom.

The outrage needed an outlet.[4]

The outlet became the mass demonstrations on the Maidan Square—EuroMaidan—and in other major cities, most of them in western and central Ukraine.

In Nayem's view, after his spark set the pro–Western network in motion, "[t]hree acts" took place in the macabre play that over the next few months would become the Maidan: "First came the citizen protests. Then, the brutal government crackdown. And finally, after the first guy was killed on Hrushevsky Street, what I call 'the Maidan of dignity.' At that point, it had become obvious that the people would never accept Yanukovich again." This is the classic Western and pro–Maidan Ukrainian view. Initially, to be sure, the EuroMaidan protests were civil, peaceful, even joyful, as the color revolution handbooks taught. As Nayem notes, it was "a true people's movement, fueled by Ukrainian citizens' desire for a better government."[5]

To be sure, young people and middle-class families as well as grandparents graced the Maidan, but soon enough another force made its presence felt. Quite early on, in fact, some demonstrators—in particular ultranationalist and neofascist elements such as Tyahnybok's SP and a new group soon to be organized on the Maidan itself—turned to coercion and then violence. They infiltrated Kiev's central square and began to drive the violence and coercion that gradually came to dominate the tenor of the protests by deep winter. Regime violence also played an escalatory role, but that role was often played first by the protests' neofascist elements as well. The security and police forces usually responded with more violence. The regime also brought in toughs, so called "titushki," from the countryside to supplement the police and provoke the demonstrators. The pro-regime forces' coercion complemented the pro–Maidan nationalists' efforts, creating a tit-for-tat spiral of violence that escalated the crisis from a political one to a potentially regime-transformational, even a revolutionary one.

First Violence

Typically, the first violence mentioned in most media and other reports on the Maidan demonstrations is that ostensibly carried out on Yanukovich's orders by the Berkut police in the early morning dark hours of November 30. At that time, an attempt was made by the Berkut special police forces to clear the Maidan square of demonstrators during the sleeping hours when the crowd thinned down to a few hundred.

In reality, the first violent clash between police and the demonstrators occurred on the evening of November 24. Several reports in non-mainstream but far from alternative Western media report that demonstrators attacked police in the early morning hours on the evening of November 25 "for the second night running" as police "struggled to keep order." *Business News Europe* reported: "In the morning of November 25, police used tear gas and batons to disperse a crowd around the government headquarters *after numerous protesters hurled rocks and tried to tear off officers' helmets*" [my emphasis].[6] The independent and pro-democracy Russian daily *Nezavisimaya gazeta* also reported that the demonstrators initiated the violence by throwing objects at the police and that there were already numerous aggressive youths calling on the crowd to storm the presidential palace, turn over buses or engage in other such violent acts.[7] The pro–Western, pro–Maidan *Kyiv Post* reported that more clashes broke out that evening when demonstrators attacked a police van, which turned out to be a police mobile eavesdropping post. Police moved in to retaliate and more violence ensued.[8] Also, it appears that photographic evidence that would support the print reports cited above were cleansed from some Internet sites. For example, the *Kyiv Post* removed an article, which is cached on the Internet; only its accompanying photographs remain, but only 7 of the original 14 photographs. One of the seven remaining photos shows members of the Svoboda Party (SP) front and center at the demonstrations.[9] The evidence that originally there were 14 pictures and that 7 have been removed comes from a mobile phone freeze-frame still accessible on the Internet.[10] A video that briefly shows some of the violence remains on other Web sites.[11] Most Western sources did not identify which side initiated the violence, but tended to mention the police response first.[12] Therefore, the claim made by Western governments and media that the demonstrations were peaceful was already proving false. The demonstrators had escalated the situation from a political confrontation to a more tense and violent confrontation.

The likely perpetrators of this first violent episode were members of the ultranationalist, neofascist Svoboda Party and/or the Social-National Assembly. No casualty figures are available for this first violence, and it appears no one was killed, wounded, or hospitalized.

Brown Maidan: The Rise of "Right Sector"

The next data point for violent escalation was Yanukovich's November 30 late night attempt to clear the Maidan of demonstrators by deploying the "Berkut" special riot police. For the first time, Ukrainian riot police used force against the Maidan protesters when they refused to disperse, resulting in dozens of injuries and the brief detention of 35 peaceful protesters on charges of hooliganism.[13] This escalation, however, was preceded by a nonviolent escalation with implications for future violence that occurred just prior to the Berkut raid and crackdown on the Maidan's emerging tent city.

On the evening of November 29, 2013, several neofascist parties even more radical than the ultranationalist SP joined to form what they called "Right Sector" (Pravyy sektor), or RS.[14] Right Sector was to function officially as the Maidan's defense force, but its founders' real purpose was for RS to become the nucleus and shock troops for a nationalist takeover of the Maidan movement and the revolutionary overthrow of the Yanukovich government. The formation of RS meant the quasi-militarization of the Maidan and would escalate the conflict between regime and opposition, leading ultimately to the revolutionary seizure of power in February 2014. Four ultra-right and neofascist groups joined forces to found RS: Stepan Bandera's Trident, "Trizuby imeni S. Bandery," named after the head of the Ukrainian nationalist leader who allied and carried out massacres of Poles and Jews in league with the Nazis during World War II; the Ukrainian National Assembly (UNA); White Hammer; and the ultra-fascist Social National Assembly (SNA).

RS was founded by Dmitro Yarosh "on the ideological and personnel foundation" of the group, "Stepan Bandera's Trident," or simply "Trident." Born on September 30, 1971, Dmitro Anatolievich Yarosh began his political life during the *perestroika* era, becoming a member of *Rukh* in 1989. He co-founded "Trident" in 1994 and led the organization from 1996 to 1999, then becoming its "main inspector" and again heading the group until autumn 2015, when he handed the reins to his deputy and the commander of RS's military wing, Andrei Stempitskii. Like many nationalists and ideologues, Yarosh is focused on the Ukrainian language and culture, having graduated from the Ivan Franko Drogobychskii Pedagogical University's Philological Department in 2001. He then published a book putting forward his ideas of a nationalistic revolution titled *The Ukrainian Revolution in the 21st Century*. Yarosh notes the purpose of founding RS was "to state the position of rightist forces," given the EuroMaidan's limited goal of signing the EU AA, and pursue "implemention of a nationalist revolution and overthrow of the regime that we call a regime of internal occupation."[15]

The source works for Right Sector's philosophy, ideology, and propaganda are those of "integral nationalism" proselytized by Bandera, Donstov, and other inter-war and post-war Ukrainian ultranationalist luminaries.[16] Its programmatic key words are the "Ukrainian nation," "the Ukrainian national idea," "nation-centric" (*natsiotsentrichnoi*), and "nationocracy" (*natsiokratiya*).[17] The Ukrainian nationality and state—depicted as being under constant threat from alien forces: ethnic, foreign, religious and cultural—are placed above all else. The "main slogan" of RS's modified and softened electoral program is "God! Ukraine! Freedom!" The individual is subsumed to God and the "Homeland," since, according to RS, "[t]he purpose of human existence is be closer to God," and "[t]he way to God is through the Homeland." Under the main slogan "Ukraine," the program emphasizes that "the Almighty created us, the Ukrainians and the Ukrainian nation, and let His will be hallowed forever. Only in their own national state can Ukrainians, Ukrainian Christians, and Ukraine survive. So Ukraine for us—above all! By defending Ukraine and seeking to create a Ukrainian national state, we not only defend our national rights but, above all, the will of God. And so—God is with us!" Freedom is defined not in terms of individual freedom and rights but rather as the Ukrainian nation's freedom protected by its own state: "Stateless and oppressed people can not act according to the laws of God, nor its own; it is doomed to live as those who oppress it would dictate. And so the struggle for human freedom, the nation, and Ukraine is our Christian and national responsibility. Our duty is the cultivation and propagation of the Ukrainian national idea—the idea of self-assertion of state of the Ukrainian nation, and the Ukrainian national state's creation of an effective system of Ukrainian democracy."[18]

All non-ethnic Ukrainians are judged on the basis of their support for building a home for the Ukrainian ethnicity—"Ukrainian Ukraine." Thus, for RS, the "national state" is the consequence of the "natural desire" of every "developed" nation's "political self-assertion through which it becomes full and sole master of their destiny in its land." The realization of the "national state" is "a state in which citizens of other nations recognize the indigenous people of the host country and have not only the level of the [indigenous nation's] rights but also its duties, know and respect its language, laws and history." The educational system should create "nationally conscious, active, selfless and sacrificial citizens for the Ukrainian national state." Similarly, cultural policy will aim to form the "national ethical and aesthetic consciousness of society, making every Ukrainian spiritually and ideologically immune to alien cultural imperialism." In order to overcome the "religious and denominational fragmentation in Ukraine," the state will be directly involved in religion, seeking "the spiritual and ecclesiastical unity of all Christians" in "a single local national Christian Church" that will assume "responsibility before God and people for failing to lead the way and bring Christ to the people of God who entrusted that people with what he created and a people that the Lord wants to see, and not what would make it different, the invaders and their heirs—purge the servants of Satan."[19]

The program claims Ukraine is undergoing a genocide, having fallen victim to "carefully cultivated and propagated perversion, drug addiction, alcoholism, fornication, homosexuality, violence, spirituality, denationalization, political apathy and more. The anti–Ukrainian government recruited young Ukrainian obedient servants, non–Ukrainian politicians, a mindless electorate, cosmopolitan business, unpretentious mercenaries, criminals, blind artists, foreign capital, and disenfranchised and cheap slaves." Media is seen as being at present under the control of alien forces undermining the nation: "Ukraine's information space was formed by non–Ukrainian, anti–Ukrainian, cosmopolitan and pro–Russian oligarchic clans, and this is not in the interests of the Ukrainian nation, society and state. The media became a powerful and permanent factor in the de-spiritualization and ideological and political denationalization, demoralization and disorientation of Ukrainian society. Therefore, the dominance of clans in Ukraine's information space of Ukraine must be replaced by its fundamental Ukrainization."[20]

Like many nationalistic programs, RS's is fetishistic about the "village" as the purified carrier of the nation: "The Ukrainian village—formed by the millennia, an effective and unique system of full material and spiritual sustenance, nation-creating and nation-preserving—can not be 'wasted' villages. Each [village] carries a Ukrainian national share of the world and every need of the nation. [We must] revive, develop and maintain every village—not just as a production unit, but above all as a living and irreplaceable cell of the national organism."[21]

In foreign policy, RS's program proposes a nonaligned course in the current understanding of that term. Partnership with NATO, the EU, the CIS and other existing international organizations is regarded as "dangerous and destructive." Ukrainian geopolitical strategy is to be based on something like Pilsudski's "Intermarium": the creation of a "priority space" encompassing a north-south axis extending from the Baltic Sea to the Caucasus and Black Sea based on countries Ukraine has "historically cooperated with"— Sweden, Lithuania, Poland, Turkey, and Georgia.[22]

The vagueness and generalities in the program somewhat mask the true extent of the neofascist extremism that characterizes the group and its members. The extent of RS's extremism is revealed in other RS documents, public statements of RS leaders, and the program documents of its other member parties. A short course for RS members on the ideology of "nationalist revolution" and "nationocracy" states that the RS is founded on the ideas of OUN and Bandera, among other Ukrainian ultranationalists. Specifically, the polity of the "National Order" will be built not on the basis of political competition and parties, but on "orders" or brotherhoods designed not to represent various interests, but rather to unite the Ukrainian nation in a "Ukrainian Community of Independent States" (Ukrainskaya Sobornaya Samostiynoi Derzhava), or UCCD. In both Ukrainian and Russian, the concept of "sobornost" means an organic unity that presumes unity of belief and values and precludes conflict between interests within a community. Thus, quoting the nationalist philosopher Ivan Franko, the course notes assert: "Everything that goes beyond the frame of the nation is either hypocrisy or sterile sentimental fiction." The Ukrainian collective order envisaged by RS's philosophy rejects the "empires of communism, Russian great-power chauvinism, democratic liberalism and cosmopolitanism," which are inherently "hostile to the Ukrainian nation." Ukraine is seen as "caught on the edge between two worlds," and Ukrainian nationalists' "sacred mission" is to defend the West in "the ongoing struggle against the latest generation of Asian hordes" and to "create a new life."[23]

The course instructs members that "the only way to build the Nation and the State is by way of a National Revolution made by the Ukrainian people and led by the National Revolutionary Order." Thus, the RS sees the present Maidan regime as a "transitional stage between the USSR and UCCD." The "Militant Ukrainian National Revolution" will have a strong religious element and "will not distinguish between the defense of the Christian faith and the Church of the national liberation struggle." The RS views the Maidan regime, Ukraine's constitution and the law as expendable. The higher value is the nation, which supersedes the rule of law until such time as the RS is writing the laws. The course notes:

> The Constitution is a law and no more, the basic law, but only a law. Establishing the national idea should be primary in the minds of the people, not only in the Constitution. People can exist without a Constitution, but they are doomed without a national idea, which turns it into a nation. The national idea is above the law.... The national idea is the general goal of the nation; the law is just the means of implementing the national idea.... The national idea is in the category of the permanent, but the law is in the category of the transient. Change in the law—the rule in the state—that is a modification or replacement of the national idea is a national crime. Woe to the people and state authorities whose laws run contrary to the national idea. If the law is contrary to the national idea, it is not the law, but rather instructions for supervisors and rules for the conduct of slaves. Citizens do evil, if they execute laws opposed to the nation, state, or humanity.[24]

Despite the course's significant talk of Christian love, the RS rejects the idea of bloodless revolution. Yarosh's deputy Andrey Stempitskiy, who would head the RS's military wing after the Maidan's ouster of Yanukovich, warned: "Undoubtedly, completely bloodless revolution is impossible. After the revolution the intensification of hostilities is quite expected. And the one who says 'I do not want blood!' has yet to say 'I do not want the return of the occupied territories' [referring to Crimea and Donbass after March 2014] and 'I do not want Ukraine's liberation from the power of Moscow.' Freedom and greatness of a nation is something for which you pay a high price."[25]

Thus, like other extremist ideologies, the RS member is expected to sacrifice his life for the cause: "To ensure the existence of future generations of our nation, the Ukrainian nationalist revolutionary is willing to give even his life.... Death in the struggle for the freedom, power and glory of Ukraine is eternal life in the memory of the people, is the crown of eternal glory in the nation, is eternal paradise with the Lord. Each death is new proof of the holiness and justice of our ideas, its vitality and victory." In some sections of the RS short course the cult of self-sacrifice attains a level equal to that of the jihadists' cult of death and martyrdom: "This Cossack Baida, three days hanging on the hook, but did not betray his people. The woman—Olga Basarab, bloodily perished from beatings and torture without betraying the slightest confidence.... Their names have become immortal. You act in this way and when you find yourself in the most critical, hopeless situation quietly and calmly, as they killed themselves, shoot yourself in the forehead or explode a grenade—proof of your ideology, self-holiness, courage and endurance."

As in many extremist organizations there is a strain of primordial prometheanism— a harking back to the nation's ancient, eternal existence and "millennial" struggle. Its past heroes are portrayed as having attained "superhuman heroism" in their struggle against eternal and omnipresent enemies. Today's generation is obliged to emulate them for the sake of the nation's survival, encouraged to "[a]venge the deaths of the great mighty ones." "The enemies of the Ukrainian nation killed her best sons—chiefs, leaders, and political men (Grand Knights). They all perished in cruel deaths from an executioner's hand, because rightly they fought for freedom for you, your family and the entire Ukrainian people. This struggle is always a feast, and he who opposes it is a criminal and tyrant. That is why revenge for the death of our Great National Knights is infinite, reasonable, just, and holy. Their hot blood penetrated the black earth, crying for vengeance. This blood fire burns thee, that thou shouldst not forgive wrongs. This revenge was, is and shall be holy."[26] The reference to red blood sinking into the black earth invokes RS's red-over-black flag.

At the same time that RS is committed to violent national revolution, it claims to adhere to a long-term strategy focused primarily on expanding its influence in society, and secondarily on infiltrating state organs. Stempitskiy notes: "[T]o take the path of revolution does not mean to go right now and storm the Administration of the President and the Verkhovna Rada. This would mean lost opportunities in catching up rapidly in all areas—in the promotion [of the movement], the formation of structures, and winning over those social groups that understand there is no alternative to the revolutionary path and that are looking for someone to take the lead."[27] The RS short course supports an "auxiliary" strategy of the "penetration of nationalists into the camp of the authorities."[28] The strategy is clearly one of building the movement's strength before engaging the revolutionary seizure of power.

Yarosh and other RS leaders have been insistent that RS is not anti–Semitic. It would be more accurate to say that RS is not openly anti–Semitic. Thus, RS's program states anti-Semitism is an enemy ideology along with communism and several others, but it refers to "cosmopolitanism" and "cosmopolitan business"—code phrases for Jewish business.[29] Upon close questioning its members tend to reveal an anti–Jewish bias. For example, when asked in a March 2014 interview with a Western journalist whether RS was anti–Semitic, a top RS leader, Igor Mazur, said this was impossible since his son's godfather was "half Jewish." However, he also stated that all of Ukraine's hated oligarchs are Jewish and he does not like them because they "care only for their transnational business empires, for making money. They don't really care for Ukraine." When asked if all Ukrainian oligarchs are Jewish, he simply shrugged, and when asked if the unpopular Yulia Tymoshenko is Jewish, he replied: "We don't know for sure. We think she has some Jewish blood in her."[30]

Moreover, RS leaders have allied with extremists with anti–Semitic leanings. In March 2014, shortly after Yanukovich's fall, media reported that Yarosh had appealed on his social media "VKontakte" page to the amir "Abu Usman" Doku Umarov of the Caucasus Emirate, the jihadist successor group of the separatist Chechen Republic of Ichkeriya (ChRI) based in Russia's North Caucasus, for assistance in fighting the emerging Donbass separatist movement. RS rejected the charge, claiming Yarosh's account had been hacked.[31] However, RS's Igor Mazur acknowledged at the time that he along with 14 of his comrades fought against Russia for the ChRI and for Georgia against its breakaway republic of Abkhazya. He claims the ChRI separatists awarded him medals for valor in his combat role.[32]

The program of the other main RS-founding group, the SNA, also does not leave a reader sanguine. It emphasizes the very same concept of "nationocracy." It proposes banning all political parties, organizations, associations and ideological groups. The elite of the Ukrainian ethnic group or nation will hold full power: "Political power is wholly owned by the Ukrainian nation through its most talented, idealistic and altruistic national representatives who are able to ensure proper development of the nation and its competitiveness." "Supreme power (executive, legislative and judicial) of the Ukrainian state will be in the hands of the head of state, who is personally responsible to the nation's own blood and property." Capitalism is to be "dismantled" and democracy is to be "eliminated." All actions that fail "to comply with obligations to the nation and the state will entail the restriction of civil rights or deprivation of citizenship.... The ultimate goal of Ukrainian foreign policy is world domination."[33]

The SNA's leader at the time of Right Sector's formation was Andriy Biletskiy, who prior to running the SNA led the equally ultranationalist "Patriots of Ukraine," the military wing of the UNA, which was in the business of beating immigrants. In a 2010 interview he described his organization as nationalist "storm troopers."[34] A year later Biletskiy was in prison, after his organization—renamed the SNA—had been involved in a series of shootouts and fights. In 2007, Biletskiy castigated a government decision to introduce fines for racist remarks, noting: "So why the 'Negro-love' on a legislative level? They want to break everyone who has risen to defend themselves, their family, their right to be masters of their own land! They want to destroy the Nation's biological resistance to everything alien and do to us what happened to Old Europe, where the immigrant hordes are a nightmare for the French, Germans and Belgians, where cities are 'blackening' fast and crime and the drug trade are invading even the remotest corners."[35] Biletskiy has also said: "The historic mission of our nation in this critical moment is to lead the White Races of the world in a final crusade for their survival. A crusade against the Semite-led Untermenschen."[36] Following Maidan's overthrow of Yanukovich, the SNA and Patriots of Ukraine were rewarded with Biletskiy's release from prison, having regarded him as a political prisoner by the new Maidan regime. The Maidan regime's MVD would give Biletskiy command of one of the many volunteer battalions tasked with suppressing the movement for autonomy/secession in Donbass, and, as I discuss in a later chapter, his Azov Battalion would be accused of war crimes by international human rights organizations.

Throughout the early winter, RS, SNA and SP members would infiltrate the Euro-Maidan and be incorporated into the Maidan Self-Defense (MSD) units called "hundreds" (*sotnyi*), the traditional name for subdivisions of Cossack formations. Andriy Parubiy, the commander of the EuroMaidan's self-defense hundreds, was co-founder and leader of the neo–Nazi Social-Nationalist Party (SNP) along with the SP's Tyahnybok in the 1990s and later left for Tymoshenko's Fatherland Party. Parubiy coordinated the hundreds' activities in and around Maidan, aspects of the "snipers' massacre" of February 20, 2014, and ultimately the seizure of power. He would be the Maidan government's first chairman of the Defense and Security Council. Other Fatherland members would be involved in using firearms during the snipers' massacre.

Mobilization in the western provinces—wherefrom many of the radicals would come to the Maidan—began early on and strengthened the radical element on the square. On November 25, the day that saw the protesters' initial violence against the police on Kiev's Maidan, ultranationalists of the SP and other Galicians in Lviv (Lvov) called the population to the city center to mobilize for a march on Kiev. Declaring Lviv's secession from Yanukovich's Ukraine as a "free European city," the mayor hailed Galicia's European messianic mission in the east: "We have always been Europe. Today, our task is to ensure that this European spirit prevails across Ukraine."[37]

Meanwhile, Western-backed (and likely diaspora-backed) elements were lending ideological support to these more dark forces. As the Maidan violence was only just beginning to percolate in December 2013, Western-backed "pro-democracy" Ukrainian media outlets like the *Kyiv Post* were issuing apologias for Ukrainian ultranationalism:

> For someone decidedly critical of right-wing politics—in Ukraine as well as in the USA—to defend the memory of Bandera is indeed a matter of fairness and not ideological inclination. It is for me. Bandera is someone who spent most of the war in a Nazi concentration camp, where also his two brothers were murdered. He is someone who, with the OUN, openly stood up against Adolf Hitler, by declaring an independent Ukraine in Lviv on June 30, 1941, eight days after the start of German-Soviet hostilities. It promptly led to his arrest and jailing of his closest cohorts. That was when many well known personalities in western Europe, yes, cooperated with the Nazis to avoid Hitler's wrath. And he is someone who, alone among Ukraine's so-called leaders of that time, postulated an axiom saying that national liberation must rely on own [*sic*] forces, and not on foreign assistance. It was the time when the country was prostrate on its back under Stalin's boot.[38]

A November 30 crackdown would strengthen the cachet of the radical nationalists and increase the flow of radical, mainstream, and democratic Ukrainians to the Maidan.

The November 30 Berkut Crackdown

It is likely that the Berkut police or the SBU found out about RS's formation and were put on high alert beforehand, and the decision to clear the Maidan of demonstrators was likely motivated at least in part by the news of Right Sector's formation. The failed attempt to clear the square of demonstrators was executed at 4:00 a.m. on November 30 by unleashing several hundred baton-wielding Berkut and hired hands or *titushki*, who brutally beat apparently defenseless demonstrators. This was a significant escalation in violence but led to no fatalities and involved no firearms. Some 35–79 demonstrators were injured, 35 sought medical assistance, 7 were hospitalized, and 35 were arrested. Seven Berkut police were also injured, and 1,000 protesters remained on the Maidan.[39] Although President Yanukovich condemned the November 30 Berkut beatings and demanded that the General Prosecutor's office (GPO) carry out an investigation immediately, much of Kiev and all of western Ukraine and the Western media were convinced that he had ordered the crackdown.[40]

The overzealous Berkut crackdown also prompted a split within the regime ruling group's ranks, with presidential administration head Serhiy Levochkin and several leading members of Yanukovich's reigning Party of Regions resigning and as many as 30 of its deputies preparing to leave its faction in the Rada. At the same time, the incident further mobilized both democrats and nationalists in Kiev and in other parts of the country, especially in the more pro-nationalist and anti–Russian western provinces.

The December 1 March and EuroMaidan's Seizures of Government Buildings

The November 29–30 Berkut assault led directly to a sharp escalation in the number of protesters and resulted in retaliation to the resort to violence on the part of the Euro-Maidan side. Maidan's newly minted neofascist RS and its natural allies in the SP, the small "Bratstvo" group, and others were able to ride the protest wave and parlay it into a national revolution. They committed considerable violence in a multi-pronged attack on several state buildings in the Kiev city center, including an attempt to take over the presidential administration building and seize power. The opposition's aggressive reaction defied the Kiev District Administrative Court's November 30 ban on further protests in downtown Kiev until January 7. The ban included Maidan Nezalezhnosti (Independence Square); European Square, where anti–Maidan elements including so-called *titushki* thugs were beginning to assemble; and the vicinities of the presidential administration and Interior Ministry (MVD) buildings. But the EuroMaidan opposition had scheduled the rally on the 1st to take place at St. Michael's Square—another likely reason for the Berkut assault a day earlier—followed by a march to the Maidan, which would violate the new edict.

Already on November 30, a crowd of at least several thousand activists gathered on St. Michael's Square to protest the nighttime Berkut attack. This early on, Western officials were already involved in the protests, with ambassadors to Ukraine of 10 EU countries, including Poland, the Czech Republic, Finland and the EU meeting with the protesters. When the latter invited EU ambassador Yan Tombinskii to speak from the improvised stage, he refused, saying: "We are not allowed to go to demonstrations."[41] By evening, Fatherland party member Andriy Parubiy reported that the first Maidan "self-defense" (MSD) units or "sotny" (hundreds) were formed on St. Michael's Square and numbered 1,200 "activists." The first MSD hundreds were equipped with improvised protective armor and wooden sticks.[42]

At the December 1 march, radicals among the marchers smashed windows of the city council building and occupied both it and the Trade Union House, reoccupied the Maidan, and headed to the presidential administration building and the Council of Ministers building situated on adjacent streets. At the approach to the presidential administration building, "Bratstvo" and RS radical elements began to resort to extreme violence, throwing bricks and Molotov cocktails, wielding hammers and other metal objects against police, and spraying police in the face with an unidentified substance. They also seized a bulldozer and tried to smash through the police line and gate of the presidential administration building. The MVD claimed that 300 members of the well-known ultranationalist Bratstvo (Brotherhood) group led the violence at the presidential administration, while SP activists had stormed and occupied City Hall. The day's casualties saw some 100 officers wounded, according to the Kiev police, and about 50 demonstrators wounded, according to the Kiev mayor's office.[43] A day later, the Health Department reported that by the end of the day 165 protesters had been injured with 109 of them hospitalized.[44] The number of ralliers exceeded 100,000, with some claiming more than 300,000.[45] One poll found that 70 percent of the protesters attributed their participation to the violence of November 30.[46] By the end of the day, SP leader Tyahnybok called for a general strike and a "social and nationalist revolution," announcing that the SP had established a national headquarters for the revolution in the Trade Union House and that an analogous command staff was needed on the Maidan.[47]

The result of the November 30–December 1 violence was the seeming vindication of the creation of Right Sector, the radicalization and militarization of Maidan, and the greater mobilization of democratic and nationalist opposition forces in the provinces. In short, a revolutionary situation—a credible competing alternative claim to sovereignty and rule over the territory and peoples of Ukraine—had emerged. Escalation in the use of coercion and violence was coming to a new turning point that would have implications far beyond Kiev's city center, Kiev, and even Ukraine.

International and Domestic Coercive Escalation

Tension and conflict between police and Maidan demonstrators continued to gradually escalate through the first week of December, with the nationalists beginning to use sticks, bricks, and Molotov cocktails against police and the police occasionally beating demonstrators. By the second week of December, with the weather turning colder and the holidays on the horizon, the Maidan demonstrators seemed to begin to fade away. But coercion and violence on the ground in any local conflict are not the only sources of potential escalation. Foreign influences can push conflicting sides to escalate in the belief they have powerful foreign backers, the support of which can tip the scales in their favor. In mid–December, President Yanukovich was set to travel to Moscow for discussions on a possible economic rescue package and Ukraine's involvement in the Eurasian Economic Union. It was at this crucial point that Washington stepped up its backing for the protests and would-be revolution.

On Wednesday, December 12, U.S. Assistant Secretary of State Nuland and U.S. Ambassador to Kiev Geoffrey Pyatt, walking through Maidan Square and handing out cookies, encouraged the demonstrators to stay the protest course. In a press conference during her visit, Nuland said she had a "tough but realistic" conversation with President Yanukovich and believed it possible to save Ukraine's "European future" if he showed "leadership." U.S. State Department spokesperson Jen Psaki suggested the U.S. might impose sanctions on Ukraine, and the U.S. government-funded think tank Freedom House called on Yanukovich to resign immediately and declare early elections as "the only non-violent way to end the standoff with demonstrators." Like Nuland, German Foreign Minister Guido Westerwelle toured the Maidan protest camp with two Ukrainian opposition leaders and asserted that "Ukraine should be on board with Europe."[48] The Polish Foreign Ministry set up a tent on Maidan Square, according to some reports.[49]

At the same time, the U.S. government began to threaten Yanukovich with sanctions as punishment for the November 30 violence. The statements began to hold the Ukrainian administration responsible for any violence by police forces, even if it came in response to demonstrators' violence, which was increasing among the nationalists. On December 11, Sen. Ben Cardin, head of the U.S. CSCE Helsinki Commission, issued a warning: "If the Ukrainian government does not take concrete action to improve the situation, the international community should seriously consider additional measures, including targeted sanctions against Ukrainian officials responsible for violations of human rights, including the repression of peaceful protests."[50] The same day, U.S. State Department spokeswoman Jen Psaki stated that all policy options, including sanctions, were on the table.[51] At the same time, eleven U.S. senators introduced a draft Senate resolution No. 319 stipulating that "in case of further use of force against peaceful protesters, the US president and Congress may consider whether to apply targeted sanctions, including visa restrictions and the freezing of assets, on the persons responsible for the issuance of the order to commit violence."[52]

In the days that followed the cookie walk and threats of U.S. sanctions, the barricades that had been disappearing from the square were returned by the demonstrators. And on Sunday, December 15, a rally of some 200,000 supporting Ukraine's "European choice" was feted by two U.S. Senators: Sen. Christopher Murphy, a Democrat from Connecticut, and sponsor of Senate resolution No. 319 threatening sanctions against Yanukovich; and former Republican Party presidential candidate John McCain of Arizona, well-known for his anti–Russian and bitterly anti–Putin stances. McCain's words seemed calculated to whip up an anti–Russian sentiment. He declared: "We are here to support your just cause, the sovereign right of Ukraine to determine its own destiny freely and independently. And the destiny you seek lies in Europe. We … want to make it clear to Russia and Vladimir Putin that interference in the affairs of Ukraine is not acceptable to the United States. People of Ukraine, this is your moment. The free world is with you, America is with you, I am with you." Warning Putin not to interfere in Ukrainian politics from Maidan Square in central Kiev seemed blatantly hypocritical and designed to antagonize Moscow.[53] While in Kiev, McCain also met with SP leader Tyahnybok, whose followers had been and would continue to play a leading role in the violence on Maidan and the ultimate coercive seizure of power in February. Russian officials, not surprisingly, expressed their dissatisfaction with this American interference.[54]

Taken together or simply in its essential parts, the activity of Nuland, Pyatt, McCain and Smith seems to constitute a violation of the Helsinki Final Act's clauses banning the interference of member-states of the OSCE in the domestic politics of its other member-states. The Final Act's Section VI on "Non-Intervention in Internal Affairs" reads:

> The participating States will refrain from any intervention, direct or indirect, individual or collective, in the internal or external affairs falling within the domestic jurisdiction of another participating State, regardless of their mutual relations.

> They will accordingly refrain from any form of armed intervention or threat of such intervention against another participating State.
>
> They will likewise in all circumstances refrain from any other act of military, or of political, economic or other coercion designed to subordinate to their own interest the exercise by another participating State of the rights inherent in its sovereignty and thus to secure advantages of any kind.
>
> Accordingly, they will, inter alia, refrain from direct or indirect assistance to terrorist activities, or to subversive or other activities directed towards the violent overthrow of the regime of another participating State.[55]

Article VI's final clause, referring to the refraining "from direct or indirect assistance to ... subversive or other activities directed toward the violent overthrow of the regime of another participating State," is perhaps gotten around or trumped by the deniability—dubious albeit—provided by the dual-use political technologies of democracy promotion and color revolution described previously. It would seem that the politics, indeed crisis politics on the Maidan, in those days would constitute the "internal ... affairs falling within the domestic jurisdiction" of Ukraine and not that of the U.S. or its officials. Nuland, Pyatt, and McCain clearly failed to "refrain from any intervention, direct or indirect, individual or collective," in Ukraine's internal affairs. One would reasonably deem their intervention as rather direct. Democracy promotion and crisis-inducing activities in Yugoslavia, Georgia and 2004 Ukraine would also seem to fulfill the criteria of indirect if not direct subversive "activities directed towards the violent overthrow of the regime of another participating State" in the OSCE under Helsinki.

Moreover, the Budapest Memorandum much cited by Western officials and pundits after Russia annexed Crimea from Ukraine in March 2014 to prove Putin had violated international law and the "rules of the game," pledged Russia and the U.S. to a "commitment to Ukraine, in accordance with the principles of the Final Act of the Conference on Security and Cooperation in Europe, to respect the independence and sovereignty and the existing borders of Ukraine."[56]

Meanwhile, the EU seemed to be acting at cross-purposes from the Americans, simultaneously undermining its Ukraine integration efforts and Yanukovich's incentive to pursue them when it announced it was terminating all further efforts to convince Kiev to sign the agreement. As noted above, the result was that Yanukovich's trip to Moscow produced the Kremlin rescue package with the purchase of $15 billion of Ukrainian debt and a cut in the price of natural gas for Kiev.

The Road to January 21, 2014

By early January, it seemed that the American gambit had failed. Maidan had largely emptied out. The Catholic Christmas, the New Year, and the Orthodox Christmas drained the Maidan and revolutionary activity all but ceased. One pro–Maidan Western media outlet lamented "Why Did Ukraine's Eurorevolution Fail?"[57] However, this was a misimpression. Many of the EuroMaidan demonstrators had simply returned to their homes in the provinces for the holidays, though the square was filled with as many as 2 million revelers to bring in the fateful New Year. Indeed, the year began in ominous fashion with torchlight marches and demonstrations by neofascists and nationalists to commemorate Bandera's 105th birthday all across central and western Ukraine on New Year's Day, including in Kiev, Lviv, Ivano-Frankivsk, and Khmelnitsk.[58] Party of Regions Rada deputy Vadim Kolesnikov, concerned about the wave of ultranationalist demonstrations, warned of the growing neofacist presence on Maidan on New Year's Eve. He, like many others since, was ignored not on the basis of investigation of the facts but as a consequence of his political affiliation.[59]

EuroMaidan canceled the traditional "Sunday people's veche" (assembly) set for January 5, two days before Orthodox Christmas, which was celebrated on the Maidan with song and prayer and without incident. Through early January, Maidan's tent city remained relatively quiet. Some demonstrators returned to the Maidan, but they were initially few and largely limited to the ultranationalists from the RS, PS, and other radical groups. Fatherland party Rada Deputy Anatoliy Gritsenko, an opposition figure, lamented that there had been fewer protesters on Maidan in recent weeks and that many of its tents were standing empty.[60]

Simultaneously, those increasingly associated with RS and PS, such as "Commandant of the tent city" on Maidan, Fatherland party Rada Deputy Andriy Parubiy, promised Maidan would go on the offensive after Christmas on January 7.[61] Another EuroMaidan commandant, Fatherland party Rada deputy Arsen Avakov, announced at the same time that after the holidays EuroMaidan would make a decision of "beefing up security" and the heavenly hundreds, increasingly infiltrated by RS and other ultranationalists.[62] EuroMaidan's "Command of the Staff of the National Resistance" remained based in central Kiev's Trade Union House throughout the holidays, despite a dispute about whether its lease had ended.[63]

With the gathering rightist storm forming over Kiev, one of very few lulls in the crisis gave the Yanukovich regime a chance to divide the parliamentary opposition and the Maidan demonstrators and thereby secure an agreement for a peaceful resolution of the crisis. However, instead of negotiating with the troika of Fatherland (Batkyvshchina) party leader Arseniy Yatsenyuk, Udar party leader Klitchko, and Svoboda's Tyahnybok during the post-holiday lull in demonstrations, Yanukovich continued to hope that the demonstrations would peter out, and in the interim the police could maintain relative order. Talks with the opposition would come only a month later at the behest of the EU and Russia in a last ditch effort to avoid the impending catastrophe. In the absence of talks, matters escalated and spun out of control. The day after Christmas, the Maidan movement confirmed its plan for the month of January, including the formation of a strike committee, and reiterated its demands that President Yanukovich, Prime Minister Nikolai Azarov, and MVD chief Vitaliy Zakharchenko resign and extraordinary mid-term presidential and parliamentary elections be held immediately.[64]

As EuroMaidan prepared for its Sunday veche of the New Year on January 12, a clash between demonstrators and the Berkut riot police was sparked when demonstrators blocked and tried to seize a Berkut van in late evening of the 10th. Fatherland party Rada Deputy Yurii Lutsenko and three deputies from Svoboda were beaten, and Lutsenko and 17 other demonstrators were hospitalized. Some 20 Berkut were injured, according to police, and one had to be hospitalized.[65] For the first time, a Western official acknowledged that demonstrators were becoming increasingly violent, when in response to the January 10 clash the EU's deputy ambassador to Kiev called on both sides to eschew violence.[66]

As detailed further below, it was during the week of January 12 that pro–Maidan protesters seized scores of regional and city administration buildings in western Ukraine. In Kiev on January 14, demonstrators from RS and Svoboda began blocking the Supreme Rada and presidential administration buildings to prevent the parliament from beginning its winter session and passing a budget, setting off tension inside parliament and a Berkut-protest standoff on Bankovaya Street, where the presidential administration building is located.[67] On January 15, EvroMaidan's commandant Parubiy threatened that if the Berkut attempted to clear the Maidan square a second time, the self-defense "hundreds," which had increased by 500–700 fighters and now numbered some 2,500 mostly ultranationalist RS and PS fighters, would respond with force.[68]

On January 16, Yanukovich suddenly submitted a series of laws to counter the mounting protests. Passed by the Rada immediately and without debate, the new laws seriously restricted the rights to public protest and the activities of nongovernmental organizations and cracked down on independent news media. The new laws required demonstrations and the particulars of their conduct to be approved by the MVD. It was forbidden to wear masks, helmets or camouflage at demonstrations, complicating the Maidan's self-defense hundreds' and ultranationalists' tactics. A 15-day sentence was stipulated for pitching a tent.[69] Another law toughened slander laws, and another eased the circumstances for which a Rada deputy could be stripped of parliamentary immunity, both constraining freedom of speech. Although the laws were not as draconian as they were portrayed by the West and the opposition, their adoption nevertheless raised fears that another massive attempt to clear the Maidan and arrest demonstrators was imminent. This was especially so since on the morning of the 16th an influx of some 2,000 Berkut around the Maidan was being reported by the automobile movement of EuroMaidan, the so-called Auto-Maidan.[70] Therefore, the new laws breathed new life into the Maidan protest and allowed the ultranationalists to seize the initiative and become the movement's vanguard.[71]

In the evening of January 16, the parliamentary opposition troika of Udar's Klichko, Fatherland's Yatsenyuk, and the ultranationalist Svoboda's Tyahnybok took to the Maidan stage and called for a "national mobilization," a general strike, and an all-national *veche* on the Maidan for Sunday, January 19. Tyahnybok claimed that Yanukovich was taking orders from Putin, and Yatsenyuk implied the same.[72] An official opposition statement announcing a *veche* called for "full resistance" and "mass and immediate resistance by the people to stop the criminals and defend the people from mass repressions." One hundred public organizations supported the call, including the RS and SP.[73] After mid-month, the now entrenched and well-organized radicals began moving out from the square in greater numbers to storm and occupy government buildings. The ultranationalists began to systematize and intensify their use of bricks and firebombs, catapulting them with improvised devices. The numbers of demonstrators again rose to many thousands on the weekdays and tens of thousands on the weekends. The smell of an imminent explosion was in the air.

January 21, 2014: The First Fatalities and Use of Firearms

As it would turn out, the official parliamentary opposition was beginning to lose some of its luster. That luster went to the RS and SP radicals. Sensing this, perhaps, the RS and SP Maidan fighters made an attempt during a mass demonstration to seize the parliament in the first open attempt to consummate their dream of nationalist revolution. This was a tipping point, the fulcrum between peaceful protest in pursuit of a transitional regime transformation and violent, illegal revolutionary regime change.

The January 21 demonstration of at least 100,000 started peacefully enough with protesters listening to speeches from the opposition troika and other opposition figures. But as the account of American eyewitness William Risch shows, the professional politicians' rhetoric did not match the rising level of mass discontent, being whipped up by the neofascists' growing presence and violence. Nor did it meet the urgency of the moment as it had been portrayed since the January 16 laws by the opposition leaders themselves and as it was perceived by many average Ukrainians and others. The pivot point came when an unidentified member of the AutoMaidan took the stage and proposed that the opposition field a single candidate in any mid-term election agreed to by Yanukovich, but the demonstration's organizers cut off his microphone. Later Fatherland's Yatsenyuk designated anyone wanting a single opposition leader a provocateur.[74] In response, according to Risch and another Ukrainian source, thousands of protesters began to leave the Maidan, and Right Sector was able to mobilize some of them, organize attacks on the police, and thus begin to "play first fiddle" in the revolution.[75] Risch describes the scene:

> I heard two men near me arguing over the political opposition's weaknesses. I heard whistling and booing from the hill opposite the stage, and I was convinced that real provocateurs—(Yanukovich's) hired thugs, or "titushky"—had broken into the crowd and were starting a fight. Then I heard people chanting, "Lidery! Lidery!" (Leaders! Leaders!). Yatsenyuk warned that there would be provocateurs interested in starting violence with the authorities. Then I heard similar whistles and boos. The crowds started leaving. I saw hundreds of them file past me as they went up Instytuts'kyi Street, up the hill past the barricades....
>
> [T]housands of such people drifted away from the Maidan and headed in the direction of the Supreme Rada, against opposition leaders' warnings. A crowd of people stopped at the foot of Hrushevskyi Street, just beyond European Square, where a cordon of riot police and police busses and trucks blocked the road. Automaidan activists began a demonstration in front of the police barricade. When Vitaly Klychko tried to turn the crowd back to the Maidan, members of the extremist group Right Sector (Pravyi Sektor) doused him with a fire extinguisher. Then Right Sector members started a fight with the riot police. They hurled pavement stones, sticks, Molotov cocktails, and petards. The police responded by attacking them with tear gas, stun grenades, rubber bullets, and water from fire hoses. The protestors managed to burn down all of the busses blocking Hrushevskyi Street, yet police forces held firm. After 11 hours of fighting, at least 100 people were injured.[76]

Right Sector's coordinators on social networking sites like *VKontakte* had urged its activists and other protesters to openly oppose "pacifist Maidan."[77] And indeed, on the holy Day of the Epiphany, Right Sector had seized the initiative of opposition and violent revolution. RS activists set fire to the Trade Union House in central Kiev. As the violence continued through the night and the next two days, demonstrators led by Right Sector and Svoboda radicals violently seized several government buildings, including the Justice Ministry on January 19, and barricaded themselves inside, preventing access.[78] Also, RS and other radical groups tied to the self-defense hundreds escalated use of Molotov cocktails, chains, and metal bars to attack police.

From Risch's description, the Berkut and police initially conducted themselves with restraint in the face of extremely aggressive taunting by demonstrators and Right Sector "activists" before the latter attacked them. The security forces' response and the continued fighting over the next two days, January 20–21, was severe, but the pro–Maidan "Civic Maidan" group clearly exaggerated and whipped up tensions even more when it reported that the fighting led to over 30 medical workers being "shot and beaten," over 70 journalists shot, over 500 protesters injured, over 50 activists kidnapped, and over 5 protesters killed.[79] Other sources gave lower figures for protest casualties. Berkut and police casualties, according to the MVD, amounted to 235 needing medical assistance and 104 being hospitalized, with no mention of fatalities.[80]

The first deaths and use of firearms on January 21 marked another escalation in violence. Three, not five, demonstrators were killed by firearms on that day. Ukrainian Yuriy Verbytskiy became the Maidan protest's first fatality. Having been abducted, his body was later found in woods outside Kiev with signs of torture. However, no one witnessed the abduction or torture, and the perpetrators were never found. A 25-year-old Belorussian, Mikhail Zhiznevskiy, and Sergei Nigoyan from Armenia also were shot. At least one of them was reportedly killed by a police sniper, but in the chaos of the street violence no eyewitnesses could pinpoint the source of shots, much less the perpetrator.[81] The opposition contended that they were shot by police on Kiev's Hrushevskiy Street, where demonstrators had been throwing bricks torn from the pavement and improvised firebombs at riot police for several days running. The government, however, claimed the two demonstrators were killed with hunting rifles, which police do not use.[82] Video later emerged showing demonstrators from the Right Sector, Svoboda Party and other groups—including Svoboda Party parliament deputy Ruslan Koshulynsky—carrying and using hunting rifles at various periods during the unrest in January and February, including during the February sniper attacks discussed in detail below.[83]

One year later, the Maidan regime's own MVD cast doubt on the EuroMaidan's version of January 21's events, a version that itself moved the regime-opposition confrontation closer still to a revolutionary outcome. MVD deputy chief Vitaliy Sakal now reported that the first Maidan fatality, Zhiznevskiy, was shot with a pistol, and Nigoyan was shot with a hunting rifle, noting that police do not use such weapons. Sakal adds: "The investigation is also considering among other versions a killing in order to provoke an escalation of the conflict and justify the use of weapons by protestors. It is confirmed by numerous materials from public sources, where people with firearms were recorded…. It was also found that the dead bodies were removed, and the witnesses of the murder weren't found."[84] This gives credence to the Yanukovich regime's rejection of the charge that the police had committed the first killings of the Maidan revolution. A third version, which lacks any supporting evidence, is that one of the infamous *titushki*, using his own firearm or other weapons (against Nigoyan) killed one or more of the first victims of the revolutionary upheaval. The *titushki*, whether allied or paid, were mostly young thugs the regime transported to Kiev from the provinces, who participated in counterdemonstrations or engaged the Maidan demonstrators in running street battles.

With time, the Maidan myth about January 21 unraveled. According to journalist Lyubov Melnikova, for example, the leader of the White Hammer at the time, Vladislav Goranin, told her that Nigoyan and Zhiznevskiy, the first two Maidan protesters killed on January 21, were shot by Yarosh's fighters in a RS false flag operation. In January, White Hammer had broken with RS, which it helped found, because it disagreed with RS actions. The White Hammer activists went to live in the Kiev mayor's building, while RS occupied two administration buildings on Kreshchatik. Melnikova also reports that Goranin was detained several times by the authorities and met with Avakov frequently after Maidan.[85] In late 2015 a Ukrainian court decision indicated that the Prosecutor General Office was investigating a member of the ultranationalist UNA-UNSO, one of the founding members of the RS, for the January 21 killings of the three first protesters.[86] This would not be the last case in which questionable, unsubstantiated, and even false attributions of crimes would be made against the albeit corrupt and venal Yanukovich regime. Despite all of the above-mentioned contrary evidence, the Yanukovich regime was and would continue to be blamed by most in central and western Ukraine and in the Western media.

In the end, the shootings sparked an escalation of neofascist demonstrators' attacks on police, forcing the January 28 repeal of the draconian laws passed less than two weeks earlier and the resignation of Prime Minister Mikhail Azarov the same day. Sensing that the radicals, as is often so in revolutionary situations, were gaining the upper hand, in the early morning hours of January 21, Klichko reached out to Yanukovich. Klichko claimed he "appeared worried" and agreed to set up a "special commission for crisis management" with representatives of his administration, the Cabinet and the moderate opposition troika of Klichko, Yatsenyuk, and Tyahnybok.[87] This effort would help pave the way for real negotiations in February that would offer a potential exit from the crisis that ultimately would not be taken. In the mid–January bloodshed, the RS, SP and other opposition radicals played the lead role—not for the last time—in tipping the dynamic from peaceful protest to violent revolutionary action.

Escalation in the Regions: The Local Revolts

The next escalation point—the wave of regional revolts in western and central Ukraine in support of the Maidan uprising—was both violent and coercive, sometimes producing injured and wounded, sometimes not. Contrary to the now accepted view, the local revolts in the Crimea and Donbass, that seemed to spark the civil war, were not the first regional revolts with separatist undertones. Nor were the Crimean and Donbass revolts modeled simply on the seizure of power in Kiev. Rather, they took after the takeovers of local administration buildings across many of the country's pro–Maidan, nationalist regions, mostly in the west. As division, instability, and violent conflict began to grip the capital, these dynamics began to spread across the entire country. It is important to emphasize that the pro–Maidan regional takeovers in the west occurred earlier than the anti–Maidan takeovers in the east and south and held the potential for secession or latent separatism. Thus, it was western Ukraine that set in motion the tactic that would rip Ukraine apart along its eastern and southern edges.

Indeed, as early as November 25, revolutionary dual power and, more importantly, latent separatism emerged in the west. As the very first violence began on Maidan on that evening, ultranationalists of the Svoboda Party and other European-messianic Galicians in Lviv (Lvov) called the population to the city center to mobilize for a march on Kiev in support of the Maidan demonstrators. Declaring Lviv's rebirth as a "free European city," the mayor hailed Galicia's European messianic mission to transform not just the country's political practice and geopolitical orientation, but to impose western Ukraine's culture and ideology on the east: "We have always been Europe. Today, our task is to ensure that this European spirit prevails over all Ukraine."[88] This attitude, reflected in the first post-revolutionary act of repealing Russian language rights in Russian majority regions in the east, along with the threat of neofascist violence, helped to spark secessionism in Ukraine's east and south months later.

In late January, dual power and potential for secession intensified in the west. Radical, mostly ultranationalist, pro–Maidan demonstrators began storming government buildings in central Kiev housing various ministries and other government offices. Days after the neofascists in Kiev began to move out of the central square and violently seize government buildings such as the Justice Ministry and Trade Union House, pro–Maidan protesters, led by the RS and SP toughs, began seizing dozens of regional and city administration buildings across western and central Ukraine, including the regional or "oblast government administrations" (OGAs) of Lviv, Ivan-Frankivsk, Ternopil, Rovno, Khmelnitskii, Lutsk, Sumi, Chernovets, Poltava, Vinnitsa and Zhitomir. There were even attempts to do the same in the central province of Cherkassk and the mid-eastern provinces of Dnepropetrovsk and Zaporozhe.[89] Videos of some of these takeovers show just how violent these takeovers often were.[90] Some of these seizures were rolled back through talks or storming by police, and in some cases these same OGAs were retaken by the pro–Maidan forces. Thus, on February 19 in Lviv, the oblast administration, MVD, SBU, the prosecutor's and other government buildings were seized for a second time.[91] All of these seizures mimicked the Maidan demonstrators' seizures of government buildings in the country's capitol.

On February 19, 2014, Lviv went beyond its "mere" latent separatism of November, moving towards a declaration of independence from Ukraine in a decree establishing a monopoly on sovereignty in the oblast and an alternative government to Yanukovich's then crumbling regime in Kiev. The local legislature established itself as a "People's Rada" or "National Rada" and declared its full sovereignty over Lviv Oblast. The document also referred to the chairman of the Lviv Oblast Executive Committee, Petro Kolodiy, as such but also later in the document as the "chief of staff of the national (or people's) resistance" and "President of the National Rada."[92] The next step would be secession if Yanukovich were to hold on to power.

Meanwhile, in the weeks following the mid–January, pro–Maidan regional takeovers, radical demonstrators would go on to seize even more government buildings in Kiev and ultimately the presidential administration and Rada buildings in the revolutionary seizure of power on February 20. Legality had become the first casualty of the developing Maidan revolution. Revolutionary violence and illegality were spreading across the country. Consequently, the Ukrainian state began to suffer the second casualty of revolutions in multi-communal states: the breakdown of its stateness. As occurred in many previous revolutions, the societal split was leading to both constitutional and legal nihilism, administrative breakdown, and the threat of territorial division and separatist conflict. Ironically, Ukraine—the union republic that put the last nail in the coffin of the USSR in December 1991—was beginning to suffer a similar fate as a consequence of its own post–Soviet revolutionary upheaval. Once the political game moved outside legality and constitutionality, all bets were off and anything could and would happen. Ukraine would experience both the dissolution and reunification scenarios of revolutionary breakup simultaneously, albeit with some "assistance" from its eastern neighbor.

The Bulatov and Chornovol Affairs

In July 2014 Russian state television was raked over the coals for issuing a report that Ukrainians had crucified a boy in the Donbass, a report that was rapidly exposed as false.[93] But this was not the first false report of a crucifixion or torture in the Ukraine crisis. On the same day that the first casualties and use of firearms occurred, a similar atrocity allegedly carried out by Yanukovich's Berkut occurred and was reported widely in the Ukrainian, Western and even Russian media. A Maidan activist named Dmitriy Bulatov disappeared on January 22 and supposedly was kidnapped, tortured and crucified but ultimately released when thrown from a vehicle on the outskirts of Kiev by his captors on January 30. Bulatov was the leader of the AutoMaidan, which was a movement of motorcade demonstrations. The last days of January and the first days of what would be a fateful February were filled with talk of this next alleged crime of the Yanukovich regime. This further alienated many societal elements from the Yanukovich regime before an investigation could be completed.

However, beyond a few bruises, the only sign of serious injury to Bulatov came in one photograph where the very tip of his left ear appears to have been clipped off. His attempt to prove crucifixion was completely unconvincing since damage to his hands was barely visible.[94] Doctors who examined Bulatov said there had been no damage to his internal organs, and some were claiming the affair a fake.[95] The authorities suggested Bulatov's disappearance might have been a ploy to exacerbate the already highly tense crisis. The opposition spoke of death squads operating in Ukraine and demanded an international investigation.[96] Bulatov was visited in hospital by future president Poroshenko before being sent to Lithuania and Germany ostensibly for treatment.[97] One week after the Maidan's overthrow of Yanukovich, Bulatov was rewarded by his appointment as Minister of Sport and Youth.

Months later, this event appeared to have been something quite different from what had been claimed by Bulatov and other Maidan activists at the time. In November 2014 Bulatov's then deputy and now leader of AutoMaidan, Sergey Poryakov, said in a radio interview that the kidnapping was faked and those in AutoMaidan had known from the start it was so. Moreover, he described Bulatov as a "rude" person suffering from a "star complex," who had been kicked out of the group three days before his alleged kidnapping.[98]

A similar pattern occurred in the case of the alleged beating of Ukrainian journalist Tatyana Chornovol in December 2013. She was in fact beaten, but the motive remained in question. Opposition members and Western officials saw a Russian hand, but the prosecution's investigation found a simple case of road rage. Accordingly, the perpetrators claimed Chornovol, driving from Borispol to Kiev, almost caused an accident by cutting off their car. A chase ensued, and the cars bumped several times before Chornovol stopped her car and was dragged from the car and beaten.[99] In April 2015, after a long trial, a Maidan regime court upheld the apolitical version of the crime as hooliganism and aggravated assault lacking any political motive whatsoever. Chornovol is now a Rada deputy elected to parliament on the ticket of Prime Minister Yatsenyuk's National Front party.[100]

Yet U.S. Ambassador to Ukraine, Geoffrey Pyatt, had no doubts about the political nature of both the Bulatov and Chornovol cases at the time, blaming Yanukovich, an alleged "enemies list," and even a Russian "wet-job team":

> Yanukovych's guys had an enemies list. A real, honest-to-God list of "here are the journalists that we need to go after, and here are the ones that are a threat to us." There was the attack on Tatyana Chornovol; there was the attack on a guy named Dmitry Bulatov, who was the leader of the auto-Maidan and who was abducted by Russian-speaking professional interrogators, who cut part of his ear off. They tortured him. The main line of questioning: What has the American embassy told you to do? How much money have you received from the American ambassador? They put nails through his hands. Ugly, ugly stuff. You had a number of disappearances. Everyone was sure that there was some Russian wet-job team, because everybody's point of reference was the Orange revolution, which was concluded nonviolently.[101]

It is now clear that Pyatt's and the West's understanding of these two events were anything but factual. Both cases were spun to appear political for the sake of the revolution despite the lack of any and all evidence, and Bulatov may have not only spun but entirely fabricated his account from whole cloth. As is too often true in politics and would be true throughout the Ukrainian crisis, perception trumped the facts in the Bulatov and Chornovol affairs, and misperception intensified the mounting conflict.

The February Snipers' Massacre

On February 18–20 there was a major escalation of the violence, ending in a massacre on the 20th. In the center of a European capital, over one hundred police and demonstrators were shot to death and hundreds more were wounded. Despite the heavy casualties suffered by police, Western and Maidan governments and media were unanimous in reporting that the massacre was ordered by President Yanukovich and that the shooting was initiated and carried out exclusively or nearly so by snipers from the state's police and security organs using professional sniper rifles. To this day, most in Kiev believe it was more likely that Russian special forces organized and perhaps even carried out the slaughter. As discussed further below, the Maidan government's chief of the Security Service of Ukraine, Kiev's equivalent of the KGB or FSB, falsely declared in March 2015 that Russian President Vladimir Putin's advisor, Vladislav Surkov, organized and commanded the snipers. The three days of killing peaked on the 20th and ultimately scuttled an agreement to end the crisis signed on February 21 by Yanukovich and three opposition party leaders brokered by Russia and the foreign ministers of Germany, France and Poland.

Less than two weeks after the massacre and Yanukovich's ensuing removal from power, there emerged an audiotape—likely a Russian or Ukrainian government intercept—of a telephone conversation between Estonian Foreign Minister Urmas Pyatt and the EU's Catherine Ashton in which the former states that his feeling and the sense in Kiev generally was growing that someone from the new Maidan regime was behind the shooting. Although when pressed by Pyatt that there needed to be an investigation, Ashton faintheartedly agreed, neither party made any effort to push the issue again, much less demand an investigation.[102] Quite disturbingly, Ashton and Pyatt remained silent until the audiotape was leaked. The legitimacy of the new coalition government and Maidan regime depended on the snipers' massacre as their founding myth. That myth held that Yanukovich's deployment of snipers sparked his overthrow. The myth allowed Western governments to ignore the opposition's violation of an agreement between the regime and opposition that could have provided for a transitional rather than a revolutionary regime change. The martyrs of the Maidan revolution, called the "heavenly hundred" and allegedly killed by Yanukovich's forces, became the heroes and symbols of Maidan's "revolution of dignity." Thus, from the Pyatt-Ashton phone call forward, not only did Pyatt and Ashton stop discussing the shooting, but not a single Western official ever mentioned this issue or called for an investigation. Nor would any foreign government, with the exception of Russia, or any international governmental organization demand an investigation or threaten repercussions for Kiev's failure to do so.

Mounting evidence now shows that it was not police, as the Ukrainian opposition and Western governments and media assumed, but rather RS and SP fighters who had initiated the shooting on the 20th. In this view, they fired at, killed and wounded both the police and the pro–Maidan demonstrators in a false-flag operation likely intended to enrage Western governments and demonstrators, providing the pretext for Yanukovich's removal in a revolutionary takeover. The gunfire was initiated by Maidan supporters in the early morning hours, and police initially showed restraint and sought to convince Maidan leaders to find and stop the shooters so they would not have to respond. The escalation from Molotov cocktails, chains, and massive bricks was not a distant leap.

Detailed and comprehensive analysis of publicly available evidence conducted by Ottawa University professor and Ukrainian scholar Ivan Katchanovski demonstrates that the armed fighting on both February 18 and 20 was initiated by the neofascist-dominated EuroMaidan "self-defense" units, and that RS and SP fighters shot, killed, and wounded both police and EuroMaidan demonstrators. After the first version of Professor Katchanovski's research was published, his house in Vinnitsa, Ukraine, was seized by the RS- and NSA-led Azov Battalion's fighters on behalf of the Maidan regime.[103] Independent investigations by numerous organizations and a plethora of video and audio evidence support Katchanovski's findings: Germany's Frankfurter Allgemeine Zeitung, a BBC documentary film, and a documentary film by Beck-Hoffman, among several others. The following account is based on their findings and others. These include interviews with several Maidan shooters, who testify about their involvement in the killing of police.[104]

Those killed and wounded on February 18–20, 2014, in Kiev were not shot by trained police "snipers." For the most part, both police and demonstrators were shot by hunting rifles, Makarov pistols, and occasionally modified Kalashnikovs. To be sure, some videos show police aiming but rarely firing rifles with scopes. But when shooting, they were doing so long after the RS and SP fighters began the shooting and were not positioned on building roofs in order to carry out a clandestine sniping operation. The police are openly deployed on the streets during a retreat before a violent and advancing crowd, some of whom were deploying firearms as well.

February 18, "Black Tuesday," saw 17 deaths in Kiev. Most were killed in fighting around the Supreme Rada and Trade Union buildings. The day's events began when the Maidan's Self Defense (MSD) units or "hundreds" (sotniki) led by the neofascist RS attempted to storm the building of the Verkhovna Rada (for the second time—the first on January 21) and set the Party of Regions headquarters in Kiev on fire, blocking the exits, killing one worker and seven Berkut and MVD police. In response, the Yanukovich government authorized plans "Boomerang" and "Khvylia" for the seizure of the Maidan and its headquarters. An Alfa officer, who led one of the SBU groups that stormed the Trade Union Building, stated that their main task was to seize the building's 5th floor. The RS occupied the entire floor, which housed a cache of weapons and served as its headquarters and that of both the EuroMaidan and the MSD, which organized and supervised the EuroMaidan's "sotniki." The fire set by RS fighters in the Trade Union House was allegedly intended to block the advance of "spetsnaz" troops and killed at least two Maidan protesters. The Trade Union House, the Music Conservatory and especially the Hotel Ukraine would be the locus from which much of the gunfire targeting police and demonstrators would come in that day.[105]

Katchanovski's groundbreaking research on the February 18–20 violence uncovered two radio intercepts of Internal Troops units and Alfa commanders and snipers, confirming that the MSD and RS blocked their attempts to seize the Maidan headquarters and Trade Union building on February 18 by setting the building on fire and using live ammunition. Also, a radio intercept of Alfa commanders contains their report about deploying SBU snipers to counter two Maidan "snipers" or spotters located on a Maidan-controlled building.[106] The majority of February 18's deaths were reported to be the result of gunfire wounds,[107] and several policemen were wounded by gunfire on that day, at least one seriously, according to a police account.[108] This confirms the testimony of MVD National Guard antiterrorist unit Omega commander Anatoliy Strelchenko that groups of Maidan protesters had used hunting rifles and Makarov pistols as early as February 18 during the so-called "peaceful march" to shoot several of his policemen in two incidents near 22/7 Institute Street across the street from the Kiev Music Conservatory.[109]

Another protester, Ivan Uduzhov, claims that he was given a Kalashnikov rifle and shot at police from behind the shields of the protesters during the police attack shortly before police started to flee. Uduzhov's description corresponds with events on both February 18 and 20 and with both the 5.45mm AK-74 and 7.62mm caliber AKM weapons used.[110] A photograph taken by an Italian journalist shows a protester using cover from shields of other protesters and firing with an AK-74 type Kalashnikov assault rifle on advancing police during the evening of February 18.[111] On February 19 there was a relative lull, but one police report stated that they spotted demonstrators wearing RS symbols in the Music Conservatory that day.[112]

Shortly after midnight on February 20, RS leader Dmitro Yarosh announced on his Facebook page that RS would reject any agreement with the Yanukovich regime and that "the offensive of the people in revolt will continue."[113] On that day at least 49 and as many as 60 Maidan demonstrators were shot to death and more than a hundred more were wounded and 3 policemen and 17 members of special police units were killed and 196 wounded. The police and many of the demonstrators were shot from the Maidan-controlled buildings by similar types of ammunition and weapons on February 18–20.[114] Not only was the shooting on the 20th initiated by RS and PS fighters of the MDS, but many of the casualties among the protesters appear to have been shot from areas controlled by the EuroMaidan and MDS, in particular neofascist RS and SP elements. By 9:00 a.m., before any civilians were hit by gunfire, three policeman were killed and another 13 wounded. Only a few police appear to have fired at the perpetrators on February 20 and did so in self-defense and retreat after the massacre had reached its peak. The shooting of civilians and police centered on Institutska (Institute) Street in the Kiev city center, in particular from the Music Conservatory and Hotel Ukraine, and began with the shooting of Internal Troops (VV) of the Internal Affairs Ministry (MVD) and Berkut riot police in the early morning hours. Different sources contain evidence of pro–Maidan shooters or spotters in at least 12 buildings occupied by the EuroMaidan opposition or located within the general territory held by them during the February 20 massacre. This includes the Hotel Ukraine, Zhovtnevyi Palace, Kinopalats, Bank "Arkada," other buildings on both sides of Institutska Street, and several buildings on the Maidan (Independence Square) itself, such as the Music Conservatory, the Trade Union House, and the Main Post Office.[115]

On February 20 the police had been informed that neofascist elements among the demonstrators had acquired firearms. Nevertheless, for the first hour or so the VV troops and Berkut used standard crowd control techniques, including three new riot-control vehicles with water cannons just acquired from Russia, to force the crowd back to the Maidan and off Institutska Street. From Institutska the neofascists in the crowd had hoped to make it to Bankovaya (Bank) Street and storm the main government buildings of the president, government and Supreme Rada, as they would succeed in doing the next day. But in the early morning of the 20th, the police had gained their first foothold on the Maidan in weeks. Prepared to clear the square, the VV and Berkut suddenly were forced to retreat when they came under significant fire from armed protesters. All sources report that around 6:00 a.m. and as early as 5:30 a.m., gunfire coming from the demonstrators' side, specifically the Conservatory Building and the Ukraine Hotel's sixth floor, began to hit both demonstrators and police. The Ukraine Hotel, the Conservatory, and the Trade Union House were all under the Maidan's control. Right Sector fighters were located in all three buildings and controlled specifically the sixth floor of the Trade Union House.[116] One of the EuroMaidan shooters claimed he was firing at police for as long as 20 minutes and saw 10 other Maidan shooters doing the same at that time.[117] The pro–Maidan Fatherland Party's Rada deputy and former journalist Andriy Shevchenko told the BBC and other investigators that Omega commander Strelchenko, in charge of officers on Institutska, phoned him in desperation saying that his men were under fire from the Conservatory. Casualties were mounting, with 11 initially and within the hour as many as 21 wounded and three already dead, and soon he would need to return fire if the shooting did not cease.[118] Strelchenko is the same commander who reported to MSD commander Parubiy at 8:21 a.m. that casualties within his unit had grown to 21 wounded and three killed within a half an hour.[119] On the same day, pro–Maidan Rada deputy Inna Bogoslovskaya announced from the Rada's rostrum that there is a video of someone dressed in a Berkut uniform—but not of the Berkut—shooting from a window in the Ukraine Hotel at both civilians and police in the early morning.[120] Other reports, such as the BBC report, also show that the first casualties occurred in the early morning and were policemen.[121]

The first casualty among the Maidan protesters came at 9:00 a.m., which was several minutes before the Berkut arrived on the scene in force, while the Maidan protesters were firing at water cannons deployed to disperse the crowd from Institutska nonviolently.[122] Tens of other casualties among the protesters came from shots fired from territory and buildings under the direct control of EuroMaidan's MSD or "heavenly hundred" units, consisting of shooters from RS, the SP, the SNA, and the latter's military unit, the Patriots of Ukraine, throughout the day. The data supporting this include eyewitness accounts, videotapes, exit wound analyses, and markings on trees and buildings in the areas where civilians were shot. Buildings under Maidan's control included: the Hotel Ukraina, the Zhovtnevyi Palace, the Kinopalats, Muzeinyi Lane, the Arkada Building, and Horodetskoho Street. Eyewitnesses report seeing snipers shooting from buildings such as the Ukraina Hotel at both police and security forces and protesters.[123] One video shows journalists and Maidan supporters, including rank-and-file protesters as well as leaders on the stage, stating they see a sniper "coordinator" or spotter on top of the Trade Union House during the massacre.[124]

A comparable number of casualties came from police, Berkut, and Omega units' fire from the streets, but these came after the initial early morning massacre of police and Berkut and as snipers continued to fire at both sides. No evidence of police, Berkut or Omega firing from buildings has been produced. Thus, the day of mass casualties from gunfire was initiated in the early morning by the neofascist elements of the Maidan, and the same elements fired on both police and protesters later in the morning and the early afternoon. Police fired on Maidan shooters and some unarmed protesters, but in the latter case the shooting seemed to target the ground in front of demonstrators in order to drive them back as they advanced on retreating police up Institutska.[125]

Who Were the Shooters?

By midday on the 20th both sides were firing, but the government forces seemed to demonstrate some restraint. Thus, there are admissions by the official post-revolutionary investigation that Maidan protesters were killed by firearms not used by the Berkut, MVD Internal Troops or regular police. The head of the post–Maidan Rada's special parliamentary commission, Gennadii Moskal, reported that of the 76 protesters killed on February 18–20, at least 25 were shot with 7.62mm caliber bullets and at least 17 with pellets, while another was shot with a 9mm bullet from a Makarov pistol.[126] But who precisely initiated fire on the morning of the 20th is clear. Small groups of RS and SP members and fellow travelers from the MSD's heavenly hundreds were the snipers of February 20.[127]

As noted above, the buildings from which the gunfire emanated—the Trade Union House, the Music Conservatory, and the Ukraina Hotel—were under the control of Right Sector and Svoboda groups. Numerous witnesses' testimony, reports and analyses show that Maidan shooters opened fire on police as early as 5:30 a.m., wounded at least 14 Berkut police and killed at least 3 before 9:00 a.m. and before police returned fire. They were fired on mainly from three buildings: the Conservatory, Ukraina Hotel, and Trade Union Hall.[128]

BBC investigators found a Ukrainian photographer who photographed armed men in the Kiev Conservatory during the shooting. They also interviewed an ultranationalist, called Sergei, who claims he was part of an armed Maidan unit deployed in the Conservatory and was equipped with a high-velocity hunting rifle. The Conservatory directly overlooks that part of the Maidan where the police's water cannon–mounted vehicles had taken up positions. Sergei states that his unit fired on police in the early morning of February 20 at approximately 7:00 a.m., but that they did not shoot to kill, merely firing at their feet.[129] According to the German newspaper *Frankfurter Allgemeine Zeitung*, the Conservatory riflemen were under the command of 27-year-old Volodymyr Parasyuk, who was the leader of one of the MSD *sotniki* units.[130]

Although Andriy Parubiy was commander of the MSD hundreds, Parasyuk claims his group did not coordinate its joining the MSD with Parubiy, but rather with the Right Sector, speaking with representatives of opposition Udar party leader Klichko.[131] However, as Katchanovski correctly notes, it is highly unlikely that such a large unit of armed men could have been moving around on the Maidan without permission from someone in the EuroMaidan leadership—perhaps Parubiy and/or Klichko.[132] Parasyuk, a native of nationalistic Lviv in western Ukraine, states that over the years he received paramilitary training with a range of nationalist groups there and was a member of the Congress of Ukrainian Nationalists, one of the many Ukrainian organizations modeled like RS and SP on the World War II–era Nazi-allied OUN.[133] Parasyuk admitted in a *Frankfurter Allgemeine Zeitung* interview that many in his *soten* or "hundred" of some 50 men were armed with hunting rifles and fired on the police from the Music Conservatory, but supposedly only in response to initial police fire.[134] After playing this key role in the Maidan revolt, Parasyuk would serve as a company commander in the Dnepr battalion organized with the direct involvement of the Right Sector. One of Parasyuk's Maidan shooters also joined this battalion,[135] the commander of which, Semyon Semenchenko, was by February 2016 under investigation for illegally holding people, using falsified documents, and other unidentified crimes.[136] In 2015 Parasyuk would be elected to the Ukraine's Verkhovna Rada, where he would be involved in several physical attacks on his fellow parliamentarians.

Parasyuk's role in initiating the shooting on February 20 is corroborated by other sources, including RS EuroMaidan members. The aforementioned RS commander Igor Mazur, once a leader of the OUN successor organization, the Ukrainian Nationalist Army (UNA-UNSO), which was one of RS's three founding groups, stated that he saw some 50 armed protesters in Maidan's underground area and shooting at police on the Maidan on that morning.[137] Another source staying in the Ukraine Hotel overlooking the Maidan and Institutska told *Business News Europe IntelliNews* that a Maidan rifleman demanded entry to the hotel's guest rooms and then fired from the window at about that time.[138] Katchanovski and Beck-Hoffman cite and include, respectively, video showing RS and/or SP riflemen firing from the Hotel Ukraina at the same time.[139]

In an interview given a year after the events, Omega commander Strelchenko confirmed that police and security possessed prior information that some MSD hundreds were armed. He claims to have witnessed both Maidan protesters and the police being killed and wounded by shots emanating from the Hotel Ukraina on February 20. Additionally, he stated that shooters and spotters were positioned in other nearby buildings under the Maidan's control, including but not limited to the Music Conservatory, the Trade Union House, Zhovtnevyi Palace, Kinopalats, and Muzeiny Lane. At these and other places, Strelchenko and Omega troops came under fire from Maidan protesters with both hunting rifles and Kalashnikovs.[140] Strelchenko also testifies that his men were fired on twice on February 21—just after midnight and just before noon.[141] Hours later, they and all other police, MVD, and special forces pulled out of the city center in accordance with the February 20 agreement, leaving the government buildings unprotected to be stormed by the very same RS, SP and other Maidan activists who had been involved in the shootings.

One Maidan shooter was apparently a member of either the neofascist Right Sector or one of its founding neofascist parties, the Social-National Assembly (SNA), and later served in the notorious Azov Battalion fighting near Mariupol and led by SNA chairman Biletskiy. This shooter said he was recruited in January for this operation, and that on February 19 at around 6:00 p.m., he and some 20 others came forward after someone from the Maidan protest's podium requested people with shooting skills. They were offered a choice of weapons, including shotguns and Kalashnikov-based Saiga rifles, and told to take up convenient positions. The same shooter claims he saw about 10 other protesters shooting at police from the Music Conservatory building in the morning of February 20. Other Maidan protesters who witnessed these events said that organized groups from western Ukraine's Lviv and Ivano-Frankivsk regions, some with rifles, came to the Maidan and then moved to the conservatory hours after midnight on February 20.[142] Using medical emergency service reports, a Rada special commission confirmed the timeline, concluding that shooting from Maidan and neighboring streets targeting Berkut and Internal Troops on February 20 started at 6:10 a.m.[143] The BBC investigation includes photos showing Maidan shooters with hunting rifles and a Kalashnikov rifle inside the Music Conservatory shortly after 8:00 a.m.[144] Two separate "112 Ukraina" television broadcasts reported that between 8:00 a.m. and 9:00 a.m., several policeman were shot by

Maidan shooters from the Music Conservatory. At the same time, a video shows a Maidan stage speaker warning demonstrators of shooting coming from behind the stage, demonstrators pointing to a shooter on a hotel rooftop, and sounds of gunfire.[145] Numerous other reports cited by Katchanovski, including an interview with a Swedish neo–Nazi pro–Maidan protester, report Maidan shooters firing on, killing, and wounding police before 9 a.m.[146]

EuroMaidan tweeted at 8:21 a.m.—minutes after Omega commander Strelchenko informed EuroMaidan self-defense chief Parubiy about the first Berkut report of Maidan shooters firing at police—that a "sniper" was caught at the Music Conservatory, which is consistent with both BBC and Vesti interviews of the same shooter, who said that he was "captured" by Parubiy's personal security unit and driven out of Kiev.[147] This "capture" may have been an early attempt to cover up the hundreds' false-flag "sniper's massacre," since later, as Katchanovski reports, Parubiy denied his forces ever captured a sniper.[148] It is likely that the ultranationalist Parubiy played the leading role in the false-flag operation. He would be rewarded under the new Maidan regime with the post of Chairman of the Defense and Security Council of Ukraine.

Video evidence compiled by Professor Katchanovski leaves no doubt that Parasyuk and at least one of his groups of RS and SP snipers were firing from the 14th floor of the Hotel Ukraina. One video shows, beginning at 2 minutes and 37 seconds into the video, the arrival of a Parasyuk-led group with Parasyuk and Verkhovna Rada deputy speaker Ruslan Koshulynsky, who is carrying a Glock handgun. At the 2:47 mark, as the armed demonstrators are still entering, journalists attempt to photograph or film them, at which point they are confronted by people who appear to be in charge who scream, "Don't photograph [them], don't photograph [them]!"[149] Koshulynsky would chair the Verkhovna Rada emergency session in the late afternoon and evening of that same day, during which the parliament condemned the Yanukovich government for the massacre and issued a resolution ordering government forces to withdraw from downtown Kiev. In a video from Germany's ZDF television, Parasyuk can be seen removing armed comrades from a 14th-floor room of the Hotel Ukraina at 10:22 a.m., commanding the shooters to stop firing and move because "the press should not be drawn into it." The SP figure and then Koshulynsky is also seen in this video with the same group of armed shooters. The video was removed in early March 2015 from the German ZDF Web site but is available on Professor Katchanovski's Facebook page.[150] Another video shows the men inside the Hotel Ukraine room shooting out the window.[151] A Ruptly video shows another group of Maidan protesters with at least one gun and an axe breaking into the same 14th-floor hotel room, which had been occupied by journalists. Just prior to this a Ruptly reporter showed at 10:12 a.m. that he was shot in his bulletproof vest about half an hour before, and the ZDF correspondent says in the video: "They captured our room on the 14th floor of the hotel. They fired out of our window."[152] All of this, as Katchanovski points out, has been covered up or denied by the Ukrainian government investigation, avoided in both Maidan Ukrainian and Western media reporting, and ignored by Western governments.

Around the time of the second anniversary of the February massacre, yet another pro–Maidan sniper, Ivan Bubenchik, emerged to acknowledge that he shot and killed Berkut before any protesters were shot that day. In a print interview, Bubenchik previews his admission in Vladimir Tikhii's documentary film *Brantsy* that he shot and killed two Berkut commanders in the early morning hours of February 20 on the Maidan. Bubenchik hails from Lviv, having learned how to shoot in the Soviet army and undergone training at a military intelligence academy for operations planned for Afghanistan and "other hot points." He claims that he was on the Maidan from the "first day," and that he soon joined the MSD's "Ninth" *soten* tasked with guarding the subway exits onto the Maidan, so the SBU could not use them to infiltrate the square. At some point, the MVD blocked their access to the government quarters on Hrushevskii Street. The Ninth *soten* delivered a written ultimatum that if by the next day its fighters were not allowed to move freely between the Maidan and the Metro, they would attack the Internal Troops, which they did with Molotov cocktails and stones.[153]

On February 20, Bubenchik claims that the Yanukovich regime started the fire in the Trade Union House—where his and many other EuroMaidan fighters lived during the revolt—prompting the Maidan's next reaction. As noted above, however, pro–Maidan neofascists have revealed that the Right Sector started that fire. The shooters relocated to the infamous Conservatory, where Bubenchik confirms other testimony that there were pro–Maidan fighters "with hunting rifles ... shooting at the units of special troops seventy meters away." Bubenchik moved them away from windows through which they were firing at the special forces when the latter allegedly began throwing Molotov cocktails at the building in order to burn down their "last refuge." He claimed that on the morning of February 20 he had been praying for 40, then just 20 Kalashnikovs "to appear," when an unidentified person brought to them a Kalashnikov and 75 bullets in a tennis racket bag. He emphasizes that those who claim the weapons had been captured from the pro–Yanukovich *titushki* on February 18 are wrong. Bubenchik says he fired at police from a window situated behind columns farthest from the Maidan, targeting likely commanders betrayed by their "gesticulations." He expresses pride in shooting the two commanders in the back of the skull and killing them and then shooting an unspecified number of other Berkut servicemen in the legs with the intent merely to wound. Bubenchik then moved out of the Conservatory onto the street and continued to fire on police from behind the shields of other protesters, who were moved "to tears of joy." After the police began to return fire, Bubenchik ran out of ammunition and was told by "people with status" that more was on the way. He does not clarify whether it arrived, but concludes by noting that two of his comrades in the Ninth hundred were killed: Igor Serdyuk and Bogdan Vaida.[154]

Numerous videos, including those used by the BBC and other documentaries cited herein, demonstrate that by January the Maidan protests were far from peaceful. Total police casualties from gunfire for February 18–20 were at least 17 killed and 196 wounded, according to one source.[155] Another set of figures holds that there were 578 police casualties, including killed, wounded, and injured; 80 of these were victims of gunshot wounds during these three February days. Later, almost all accounts settled on the figures of 85 protesters and 18 law enforcement officials killed, with hundreds wounded on both sides.[156] For the entire history of the Maidan protests, the Ukraine MVD's official figures are 20 police killed and approximately 600 wounded in Kiev alone.[157] Some 100 civilians were killed during the protests and violence. As the Maidan revolt radicalized, it increasingly came to represent western Ukrainians. It is not accidental that residents of the ten westernmost of Ukraine's 26 regions comprise over half of the "Heavenly Hundred" martyrs—those 100 people killed on the Maidan during the revolutionary wave of November 29, 2013–February 21, 2014 (85 of them during February 18–20)—and nearly two-thirds of those who were citizens of Ukraine. Twenty percent (19 of the 99 victims with known residences and/or places of birth) were from one of Ukraine's 26 regions—the nationalist hotbed of Lviv Oblast, the heart of Galicia.[158]

Maidan Coverup?

In power, the EuroMaidan regime has stalled in investigating the February snipers' massacre and appeared to be engaged in covering up the leading role of pro–Maidan neofascist elements in shooting demonstrators. According to Katchanovski, numerous video and audio tapes used to charge the Berkut and Omega with all the casualties were edited to delete key pieces of information included in other sources cited by himself and others showing that gunfire was coming from territory and buildings controlled by the EuroMaidan and its neofascist elements. Only the footage showing the Berkut and Omega firing on the streets is advertised by the Maidan regime, the West, and supportive media.[159] Two years after the snipers' massacre, the Maidan regime had yet to develop a believable account of the massacre that could convincingly place the blame solely or even for the most part on the Yanukovich regime and the Berkut. It is ostensibly investigating the shootings of protesters and police, but in two separate investigations. No charges have been brought against anyone for shooting police, Berkut, or Omega personnel. When in autumn 2014 then Prosecutor General Oleh Makhnitskiy claimed that many of the protesters were shot with hunting rifles, as Katchanovski's research suggests, he was soon fired from his post. Later, in February 2016, Andrey Levus, leader of the command staff of the MDS, then SBU deputy head in the new Maidan government, and now Rada deputy from the nationalist People's Front, tried to lay the blame for a crucial three-month "delay" in the investigation on Makhnitskiy, claiming the SBU had handed over to him a "mass of evidence."[160]

In autumn 2015, cases were brought against three arrested Berkut police for shooting protesters, but no charges or any supporting evidence have been laid out in any detail, and what has been publicized has contradicted the GPO's indictment or has been cast in grave doubt by discrepancies with other available facts, such as those presented in this chapter. The prosecution's investigation could only place the accused in the general area where the shootings occurred and was unable to identify specific victims, match bullets with firearms, or identify precisely when or where victims were shot.[161] A Reuters investigation even found major "flaws" in the probe. For example, one of the Berkut policemen charged was missing a hand and could not have shot a weapon as prosecutors claimed.[162]

The trial's revelations, related Maidan regime General Prosecutor Office (GPO) court appeals, and resulting court decisions began to undermine the Maidan myth and support Katchanovski's version of events. The Maidan massacre trial revealed forensic ballistic reports indicating that the majority of the 39 protesters killed were shot from the same single 7.62mm AKM, its hunting versions, or other firearms of the same caliber. Forensic medical reports concerning locations and directions of entry wounds, videos showing the moments of killings of most of these 39 protesters, and testimonies of Maidan eyewitnesses show that these protesters were killed from this firearm from the Maidan-controlled Hotel Ukraina and not from the Berkut positions on the ground. According to Katchanovski's most recent research based on the trial revelations, the forensic medical reports made public during the trial confirmed that the majority of the protesters were killed from very or relatively steep angles from nearby buildings and Maidan-controlled locations. At least 12 protesters out of 21, whose cases were examined during the trial, had wounds at significant angles, three protesters were shot from nearly horizontal positions, while specific directions of the wounds had not been revealed in the cases of six protesters. The Berkut policemen were positioned at nearly horizontal levels with the slain protesters. Trial evidence also revealed that even those murdered protesters whose bullet trajectory was at nearly horizontal angles were shot by other 7.62 caliber firearms and hunting weapons from Maidan-controlled locations, such as the Bank Arkada and Muzeinyi Lane buildings. Moreover, according to Katchanovski, the investigation is denying its own findings submitted in a report to the Council of Europe. This report stated that the GPO investigation determined that at least three protesters were killed from the Hotel Ukraine and at least 10 others were killed from rooftops.[163] Nevertheless, on January 26, 2016, the GPO recharged the Berkut commander and two Berkut members with terrorism and killing not 39 but 48 out of the 49 protesters shot on February 20. The sole exclusion apparently is the death of a Georgian protester, the circumstances and location of which could not even be approximately "confirmed."[164]

Despite claims by some Maidan Ukraine officials that the Russians were behind and/or carried out the February 2014 shootings, Maidan Ukraine's legal system had begun to investigate RS fighters' involvement in the killing of at least some of the Berkut police and MVD Internal Troops by January 2016, and of at least one demonstrator. This was reflected in several Kiev court decisions, which also suggested that the GPO was beginning quietly to investigate RS members as possible suspects in the killings. Rulings by Kiev's Pecherskiy District Court in November and December 2015 appearing in Ukraine's online database of court decisions show that the investigation had determined that two wounded attackers of a separatist checkpoint near Sloviansk in Donbass on April 20, 2014, used the same weapons used to kill two MVD troopers and wound three policemen on Maidan on February 18, 2014.[165] Two members of the RS's "Viking" unit were being investigated by the GPO by the end of summer 2015 for the February 2014 killings of the police on the Maidan, following a public admission by one of these neo–Nazis.[166] Moreover, Kiev's Pecherskiy District Court decisions show that the GPO had begun investigating at least one other member of the ultranationalist UNA-UNSO, one of RS's founding groups, for murdering a protester by cutting his throat on February 18, 2014.[167] In February 2016 the Pecherskiy court had added 12 other RS members to the investigation of the Maidan shootings, tying them to the crime through matched weapons used near Sloviansk on April 20, 2014.[168]

Despite all this, Ukraine's Maidan authorities have tried to hang the snipers' massacre on Putin. In February 2015, SBU chief Nalyvaichenko claimed the SBU had evidence that Putin aide Vladislav Surkov had organized and commanded the alleged police snipers of February 20, 2014, from an SBU base. Nalyvaichenko presented none of the evidence allegedly possessed by the SBU; he simply said it had such evidence.[169] By April, a Rada deputy from President Petro Poroshenko's party (the Petro Poroshenko Bloc, or PPB) revealed that Surkov arrived in Kiev on the evening of the 20th, five hours after the shooting was over.[170] Nalyvaichenko suddenly toned down his story. Testifying at a hearing of the Anti-Corruption Committee in mid–April, he was much more circumspect, stating only that Surkov was reportedly seen in the company of then SBU chief Oleksandr Yakimenko and visited the presidential administration. Nalyvaichenko now made no mention of Surkov's coordinating the sniper attacks at the hearings.[171] When Right Sector fighters killed several police in Mukachevo in July 2015, Nalyvaichenko supported Right Sector's position.[172] This suggests he might have had strong ties to the radical group and, along with it and Parubiy, might have played a role in organizing the sniper attacks and was attempting to cover up the plot by pinning it on Surkov and the Kremlin. Nalyvaichenko would be removed from his position as SBU chief weeks later.

Only on April 29, 2015, a year and two months after the event, did prosecutors put out a public call for citizens to turn in any bullet shells they might have taken from Maidan during or after the snipers' massacre.[173] In May the Maidan-majority Rada's Anti-Corruption Committee, largely controlled by Poroshenko's PPB, assessed the investigation into the massacre of protesters as unsatisfactory, finding "sabotage and negligence," and warned that if within two months progress is not made then it would seek the removal of the leaders of the General Prosecutors Office, MVD, and SBU.[174]

The GPO has gradually and only slightly moved in the direction of Katchanovski's version of the Maidan massacre as an RS/SP-led false-flag operation under the cover of the EuroMaidan "self-defense" forces. Maidan Ukraine's first two GPs were Svoboda and Fatherland members, respectively, and they never mentioned that shots were fired from areas controlled by EuroMaidan such as the Hotel Ukraine. Its third GP appointed a new chief of the investigation, who has acknowledged that some Maidan demonstrators were wounded by shots fired from the Hotel Ukraine.[175] By October 2015, Ukraine's new GP Viktor Shokin acknowledged that there was no evidence of the Kremlin's involvement in the Maidan shootings.[176] On October 15, Shokin had the offices and homes of three SP deputies searched as part of the investigation into the shootings, and these deputies were being summoned for questioning "as witnesses."[177] However, Shokin's move seems to have been a weapon deployed in the overall power struggle between the neofascist and oligarchic wings dominating post–Maidan Ukraine's politics. The day before, the SP and RS, for the first time since Maidan, had held a joint march in Kiev ostensibly in order to honor World War II's OUN and UPA. However, their slogans condemned President Poroshenko and called for a national revolution against what they regarded as an oligarchic regime.[178] Thus, the investigation continued to bog down, and no one was fired as Poroshenko threatened. This suggests that there may be a serious split over what direction the investigation should take between the more moderate Poroshenko and his PPB, on the one hand, and the ultranationalists of Prime Minister Arseniy Yatsenyuk's National Front, Yulia Tymoshenko's Fatherland Party, RS, and SNA, among others, on the other hand. In lieu of international pressure for an objective investigation, only a final showdown between the two wings of the Maidan regime won decisively by Poroshenko can lead to an objective investigation and prosecution of both the neofascist and Yanukovich regime perpetrators of the crimes committed by the "snipers" of Maidan's February revolution.

Some Western international organizations have accused the Maidan authorities of poor progress in the investigation, or of delaying, obstructing or covering up the events of February 20. For example, the Council of Europe's (CE) International Advisory Group concluded that "serious investigative deficiencies ... have undermined the authorities' ability to establish the circumstances of the Maidan-related crimes and to identify those responsible." It regards the investigation to be hindered by numerous "failures," "obstructiveness" (in particular on the part of the MVD), a lack of will, too few investigators, and a lack of investigatory independence and transparency. The CE panel also cited efforts by prosecutors and the MVD to help Berkut officers avoid prosecution or at least interrogation.[179] In its annual report for 2015, Amnesty International concluded: "Little progress was made in investigating violations and abuses related to the 2013–14 pro–European demonstration in the capital Kyiv ('Euromaydan') and in bringing the perpetrators to justice."[180] Citing "political motives" on Kiev's part, Interpol refused to accept Kiev's request for warrants on 23 Berkut officers, whom Kiev alleges killed 39 protesters in the Maidan shootings.[181] In June 2014, SP member and the Maidan government's then acting GP Makhnitskiy claimed the GPO had given audiotapes to the FBI for enhancement in connection with the investigation, but more than 20 months later the FBI has neither confirmed receiving the tapes nor released results of their investigation.[182] But neither Washington, Brussels, Berlin, London nor Paris have ever demanded an objective investigation, mentioning the issue only when questioned by journalists, usually those from Russia.

Thus, depending on how one chooses to delineate the turning points of escalatory violence and/or coercion during the destructive phase (the weakening and overthrow of the Yanukovich regime) of the Maidan revolution from October 2013 through February 21, 2014, there were six to eight such pivotal moments:

(1) November 30: Berkut crackdown on initially peaceful Maidan demonstrators

(2) December 1: SP/RS-led assault on the presidential administration building

(3) The takeovers of regional OGAs by pro–Maidan elements

(4) January 21: shooting and violence in and around Maidan

(5) Abductions and beatings of Buratov and Chernovol

(6) February 18–19: use of firearms by both sides with no data on who fired first

(7) February 20: SP-RS false-flag shootings of demonstrators and security and police personnel, sparking that day's subsequent street regime–opposition battles with firearms

(8) The neofascists' seizure of parliament and the presidential administration and Yanukovich's flight from Kiev

Analysis of the snipers' massacre shows that the Maidan protesters initiated almost all—at least six of a possible eight—of the pivotal escalatory moments of violence and/or coercion. The only clear case of regime escalation is the November 30 Berkut crackdown on hitherto peaceful demonstrators on Maidan square. The initiating side of the February 18 shootings remains unclear. It is important to point out that the first escalation in, or rather *to* coercion, especially one to outright violence, is arguably the most important. It breaks the taboo against coercion and violence. In this regard, the regime bears some responsibility for the course of events that followed—but lesser responsibility. The opposition repeatedly escalated its use of coercion and violence thereafter, with the lone possible exception of the Buratov and Chernovol abductions, which remain shadowed in confusion, and the unknown initiation of the February 18–19 shootings. Even if one combines into a single escalation point the Berkut's November 30 attack on demonstrators with the demonstrators' attacks the next day and attributes both to the Berkut, the protesters are responsible for five of seven escalations, with one point (February 18) unattributable. If future revelations demonstrate that the Berkut or some other regime element initiated and/or carried out almost all of the violence, especially firearms use, on February 18–19 and therefore attributes blame to the regime for the pro–Maidan snipers' initiation of gunfire on February 20, then it would be reasonable to attribute approximately equal responsibility to both sides for overall escalation of violence and the revolutionary outcome. For now, the 30 November 2013 Berkut nighttime assault on the Maidan demonstrators is the only clear exception from a conclusive pattern of escalating revolutionary violence led by the Maidan's relatively small but highly motivated and well-organized neofascist element.

February 21 Agreement

As revolution and civil war broke out in Kiev, the EU and Russia belatedly joined efforts to seek a way out of the crisis. They created a framework for talks between Yanukovich and the leading opposition parties, which still maintained some influence over the more moderate Maidan demonstrators. These days would be the turning point in the balance of power between those who supported a pacted transitional outcome and those who preferred a revolutionary outcome. The West's dual-use technology had already produced a crisis, which the actions of both regime and opposition had escalated into a revolutionary situation, with EuroMaidan movement, moderates and radicals alike, constituting a "credible competing claim of sovereignty to rule." As is often the case in revolutionary situations, the radicals would hold sway and forge a revolutionary rather than evolutionary regime change.

The negotiations included President Yanukovich, on the one side, with leader of the moderate "Udar" party Vitaliy Klichko, Fatherland Party leader Arseniy Yatsenyuk, and the notorious SP's Tyahnybok, on the other. German Foreign Minister Frank-Walter Steinmeier, French Foreign Minister Laurent Fabius, and Polish Foreign Minister Radek Sikorski represented the EU, and Russia's former Ambassador to the U.S. and Presidential Ombudsman for Human Rights Vladimir P. Lukin represented Moscow. In the early morning hours of February 21, after several days of contacts and then all-night talks, President Yanukovich and representatives of the Maidan opposition signed an agreement. Steinmeier, Fabius, Sikorski, and Lukin signed as "witnesses" to the agreement (see text in box below). Under the agreement both the authorities and the opposition were obligated not only to "refrain from the use of violence" but to take steps to avoid confrontation and return Kiev to normal life. Specifically, the demonstrators were to abandon government buildings they had occupied, and the riot police were to pull out from the Kiev city center. Importantly, the parliamentary opposition parties were obliged to secure the evacuation of government and other buildings in Kiev occupied by demonstrators—mostly members of the RS, SP and other radical nationalists—as well as city parks and Maidan and Independence Squares. The Yanukovich regime was authorized under the agreement to "use law enforcement forces exclusively for the physical protection of public buildings."

In addition, Yanukovich was obligated to sign a law reinstating the 2004 "Orange Revolution" Ukrainian constitution within 48 hours, to reform the constitution by September, and to hold presidential elections by December. Investigation of the recent months' violence, in particular the "snipers' massacre," was to be organized immediately and involve the authorities, the opposition, and the Council of Europe. The stipulation requiring presidential elections by the end of the year meant that Yanukovich would become a lame duck president with reduced constitutional powers; his political career was certain to be over in no more than ten months, given his low popularity ratings. The agreement was therefore a road map from an impending and increasingly violent

Text of the 21 February 2014
"Agreement on the Settlement of Crisis in Ukraine"[183]

Concerned with the tragic loss of life in Ukraine, seeking an immediate end of bloodshed and determined to pave the way for a political resolution of the crisis, We, the signing parties, have agreed upon the following:

1. Within 48 hours of the signing of this agreement, a special law will be adopted, signed and promulgated, which will restore the Constitution of 2004 including amendments passed until now. Signatories declare their intention to create a coalition and form a national unity government within 10 days thereafter.

2. Constitutional reform, balancing the powers of the President, the government and parliament, will start immediately and be completed in September 2014.

3. Presidential elections will be held as soon as the new Constitution is adopted but no later than December 2014. New electoral laws will be passed and a new Central Election Commission will be formed on the basis of proportionality and in accordance with the OSCE & Venice commission rules.

4. Investigation into recent acts of violence will be conducted under joint monitoring from the authorities, the opposition and the Council of Europe.

5. The authorities will not impose a state of emergency. The authorities and the opposition will refrain from the use of violence. The Parliament will adopt the 3rd amnesty, covering the same range of illegal actions as the 17th February 2014 law.

Both parties will undertake serious efforts for the normalisation of life in the cities and villages by withdrawing from administrative and public buildings and unblocking streets, city parks and squares.

Illegal weapons should be handed over to the Ministry of Interior bodies within 24 hours of the special law, referred to in point 1 hereof, coming into force. After the aforementioned period, all cases of illegal carrying and storage of weapons will fall under the law of Ukraine. The forces of authorities and of the opposition will step back from confrontational posture. The Government will use law enforcement forces exclusively for the physical protection of public buildings.

6. The Foreign Ministers of France, Germany, Poland and the Special Representative of the President of the Russian Federation call for an immediate end to all violence and confrontation.

Kyiv, 21 February 2014

Signatories:
President of Ukraine: Viktor Yanukovich
For the Opposition: Vitaliy Klichko, UDAR, Oleh Tyahnybok, Svoboda, Arsenij Yatseniuk, Batkivshchyna

Witnessed by:
For the EU—Poland: foreign minister Radoslaw Sikorski; Germany: foreign minister Frank-Walter Steinmeier; France: foreign minister Laurent Fabius
For the Russian Federation—Vladimir Lukin, special envoy

revolution from below to a negotiated or "pacted" transition, with the February 21 agreement functioning as a first-order understanding towards a transition pact, in the terminology of post–Soviet "transitology."

Crucially, it was Putin who had convinced Yanukovich to sign the agreement, according to the well-known Putin critic, Polish Foreign Minister Sikorski. He reported in an interview shortly after the agreement was concluded that a telephone discussion Yanukovich had with Putin had convinced the former to sign the agreement. Discussing the February 20 talks in which he participated as the Polish representative of the EU, Sikorski says: "One of the breakthroughs was when we said, 'Well look, Mr. President, you have to declare to the opposition by when you agree for new presidential elections to be held, by when do you intend to shorten your term of office.' He was very reluctant, as you might imagine. His attitude changed after one of the conversations, we think, with President Putin."[184] As noted in earlier chapters, Sikorski is no friend of Putin; he was even caught lying about the Russian leader to discredit him on at least one and perhaps two occasions. Sikorski is so much of a Putin foe that soon after events unraveled in Kiev and Ukraine, with an ostensible "new cold war" in play, Sikorski would be touted by the American mainstream as the man to "save Europe" and force it "to stand up to Russia."[185]

The Seizure of Power

For the SP, RS and other Ukrainian radicals, the agreement was an empty piece of wood pulp. At a memorial meeting held on February 21 on the Maidan for the "heavenly hundred" killed the previous three days, Klichko called on the protesters' *veche* to support the EU-Russian sponsored peace agreement signed that day by himself, the president, Yatsenyuk, and the notorious SP leader Tyahnybok. How much Tyahnybok was involved or informed about how events would be unfolding further on the streets remains unclear. However, it seems likely that he would be involved in the actions of SP activists on the Maidan, and he certainly made no effort to call on them to stand down. As Klichko spoke, the still-unknown Parasyuk ran onto the stage, grabbed the microphone, denounced the agreement, condemned the Rada opposition parties who signed the agreement with Yanukovich, and called on the president to resign by 10:00 a.m. the next day or be overthrown. The crowd roared with approval, and the revolutionary seizure of power was all but a *fait accompli*. RS leader Dmitro Yarosh backed up Parasyuk from the Maidan stage, announcing that RS rejected the parliamentarians' agreement with Yanukovich and describing the weapons RS possessed and was putting at the disposal of the national revolution.[186] Perhaps not coincidentally, the agreement the likes of Tyahnybok, Parasyuk and Yarosh were rejecting included the noted clause requiring an investigation into the Maidan shootings or "snipers' massacre."

But the shootings of police and demonstrators and the other actions carried out by Parasyuk, his men, and other SP and RS fighters marked a tipping point, irreversible not only for the battle on Institutska but between transitional versus revolutionary regime change. The neofascist RS and SP parlayed the violence of February 18–20 into the overthrow of Yanukovich's government, seizing power in opposition to the methods of peaceful protest, limited coercion, and negotiated pacts. Demonstrators and fighters of the neofascist RS and SP led the overthrow of Yanukovich on February 21, contravening the EU-Russia sponsored regime-opposition peace agreement and transition pact. There can be little doubt that the false-flag operation's shooting of demonstrators fueled the following that the neofascists garnered on that day and later. Rather than pulling out of the city as required in the agreement, the neofascist and ultranationalist forces led the storming of the presidential administration building, Supreme Rada, and other buildings on the next day as Parasyuk had threatened. All this took place before the television cameras and international media within hours of the February 21 agreement's signing.

Yanukovich had fulfilled his first obligations under the agreement, including removing the security forces from Kiev. But this had merely facilitated the radicals' "storm of the Bastille"—the capture of the presidential administration building, parliament, and other not-yet-occupied government buildings. On February 21, as the agreement was being broken by the Maidan protesters, Obama talked to Putin by telephone, and according to a State Department spokesman: "They agreed that the agreement reached today needed to be implemented quickly, that it was very important to encourage all sides to refrain from violence, that there was a real opportunity here for a peaceful outcome."[187]

As the police pulled back, the armed neofascist and other radical elements took control of buildings, streets, and intersections, setting up roadblocks and checkpoints. Other protesters surrounded Yanukovich's residence outside the city. Now Yanukovich was forced to flee for his life. On November 22 he left Kiev for his native Kharkiv in the central northwest of the country. The same day, the Rada issued a resolution stipulating Yanukovich's *de facto* though far from *de jure* removal from power: "The president is removing himself [from power] because he is not fulfilling his obligations." The Rada also voted to hold early presidential elections on May 25. But pro–Yanukovich deputies were being beaten and threatened, so they either voted "correctly" or did not attend the Rada session on "impeachment." The Rada approved the removal and the other documents by a vote of 328–0, but it did so without a full quorum of 450 deputies required by Article 84 of the Ukrainian constitution and with only 328 of the 338 votes—the three-fourths of the Rada's 450 votes—required by Article 111 of the Ukrainian constitution for a comparable impeachment vote.[188]

The Ukrainian constitution operating at the time outlined an elaborate and rather long-term process before a vote on the Ukrainian president's removal from office by impeachment—processes that clearly were not observed in deposing Yanukovich. Article 108 stipulated that the president could be removed from carrying out the functions of the presidency before the end of his term on four bases: (1) resignation, (2) inability to perform his duties because of health conditions, (3) removal by the process of impeachment, and (4) death. Impeachment is the only process applicable to the case of February 22, 2014. The constitution's Article 111 details the impeachment process. First, impeachment can only be considered in the event that the president is determined to have committed treason or another crime. Second, the Rada must pass by a majority vote an order to initiate an impeachment investigation. The investigation must be carried out by a "special temporary investigative commission which includes a special prosecutor and special investigators." The Rada then must review the commission's findings at a full session and then charge the president by a vote of no less than 300 (two-thirds of its 450) deputies. Then Ukraine's Constitutional Court must issue a finding that confirms that all these procedures have been carried out in accordance with the constitution, and Ukraine's Supreme Court must issue a finding that the president has indeed committed treason or another crime. Only with all these procedures carried out can the Rada convene to vote to remove the president from office.[189] All the available information suggests that the Rada and other Ukrainian institutions required to carry through an impeachment carried but one step—the last step in the process. Moreover, they did so in violation of the constitutionally mandated process for that procedure, voting without a quorum and failing to garner the 338 votes needed to remove the president.

However, the Rada never claimed it had removed the president by impeachment, but that Yanukovich had "removed himself" and was "not fulfilling his obligations." Moreover, there is no constitutional basis to declare the end of a presidency and set a date for presidential elections on the basis of such a claim by the vote of 328 Rada deputies. Indeed, a legal scholar would be reasonable in analogizing the processes of impeachment or removal "because of abandonment of duties," if there were such a constitutional clause regarding the latter. Either is a weighty decision with the identical outcome, so a prospective legal adjudication would reasonably require the same extraordinary majority of 338 votes to remove a president from office, whether by impeachment for criminal actions or by removal for failure to fulfill his constitutional duties. The Rada removed the president using a shoddy, unconstitutional procedure without any concrete knowledge that he had in fact abandoned his constitutional function. One commentary claimed the fact that Yanukovich had dumped documents in a lake near his "fancy" home and packed trucks of personal property before leaving for Kharkiv legitimized the removal.[190] In fact neither action did so, as neither speaks to any of the four reasons or brings compliance with any of the procedures for removing an acting president contained in the constitution. The same commentary offers a legal argument in support of the view that in fact Yanukovich retains, or at least for some time after his flight retained, "a minimally legitimate constitutional claim to returning and claiming his office back":

> The Ukrainian Constitution (like many other constitutions) does not provide any stipulation about how to remove a president who is neither dead nor incapacitated, but is nonetheless absent or not fulfilling his duties. The lack of such provisions creates a dangerous loophole. Any leader who is about to lose power, whether because his government dissolves, or because loyal supporters abandon him, or because he is about to lose an election just as the last votes are in, could simply skip town and doom any government by declaring it as constitutionally illegitimate. Leaving the scene would undermine the constitutionality of any acts subsequently passed by whoever succeeds the missing president and would allow him to keep a minimally legitimate constitutional claim to returning and claiming his office back.[191]

Some might and some did argue that the president's removal was legitimate because he ostensibly violated the February 21 agreement, but this speaks to none of the constitutional reasons and procedures for removing the Ukrainian president—not death, not resignation, not health problems preventing him from fulfilling his duties, and not treason or criminality. Moreover, the Rada's November 22 resolution removing Yanukovich from power was passed before the expiration of the 48-hour deadline established in the February 21 agreement for him to sign the decree reverting the country back to the 2004 "Orange Revolution" constitution. Neither the Rada nor anyone else had any knowledge whether he had signed and issued the decree or not, and the extraordinary circumstances created by the violent seizure of power that forced him to take flight could certainly be exculpatory in any court adjudication of the issue. Consistent with the definition and whims of revolution, the Maidan's revolutionaries unconstitutionally and illegally had removed Yanukovich from power.

The Western Response

All along, official U.S. statements—as well as the above-mentioned actions by U.S. administration officials—encouraged revolutionary action as much if not more than they inspired negotiation and compromise. In an often ambiguous statement from Mexico on February 20, President Obama stated that the U.S. would hold Yanukovich and his government responsible most of all for avoiding violence and claimed the U.S. expected the "peaceful protesters to remain peaceful":

> [W]e hold the Ukrainian government primarily responsible for making sure that it is dealing with peaceful protesters in an appropriate way; that the Ukrainian people are able to assemble and speak freely about their interests without fear of repression.
>
> And I want to be very clear that as we work through these next several days in Ukraine that we are going to be watching very carefully and we expect the Ukrainian government to show restraint, to not resort to violence in dealing with peaceful protesters. We've said that we also expect peaceful protesters to remain peaceful. And we'll be monitoring very carefully the situation, recognizing, along with our European partners and the international community, there will be consequences if people step over the line. And that includes making sure that the Ukrainian military does not step into what should be a set of issues that can be resolved by civilians.
>
> So the United States will continue to engage with all sides in the dispute in Ukraine, and ultimately our interest is to make sure that the Ukrainian people can express their own desires. And we believe that a large majority of Ukrainians are interested in an integration with Europe, and the commerce and cultural exchanges that are possible for them to expand opportunity and prosperity.
>
> But regardless of how the Ukrainian people determine their own future, it is important that it is the people themselves that make those decisions. And that's what the United States will continue to strive to achieve.
>
> And I do think there is still the possibility of a peaceful transition within Ukraine, but it's going to require the government, in particular, to actively seek that peaceful transition, and it requires the opposition and those on the streets to recognize that violence is not going to be the path by which this issue will be resolved.[192]

President Obama's statement did not bother to condemn the opposition violence separately and referred to the protesters as "peaceful" four times, even though neofascists and some others had been acting violently for months on Maidan. Moreover, the days preceding this statement were full of protesters' engaging in outright warfare against the police on Kiev's streets, but media accounts carefully avoided any detailed descriptions of that violence, which later became accessible in numerous videos on the Internet.[193] All the violence was lumped together, with the Yanukovich government explicitly held responsible for any future outbreaks of violence. Moreover, President Obama openly backed the now increasingly violent EuroMaidan's demand for EU integration, indirectly lending the radicals legitimacy. On the issue of revolution versus transition, the president again placed ultimate responsibility for the achievement of the latter on the government. In sum, Obama's message signaled opposition radicals among the demonstrators that violence would be tolerated, even in overthrowing the regime, and signaled opposition moderates that they need not make any significant effort to rein in or counter their radicals if they pursued a revolutionary outcome.

Now with Yanukovich's fall, despite the EU's signatures and U.S. President Obama's verbal support for the Kiev talks and agreement, neither Washington nor Brussels issued a single word or undertook a single action in defense of the violated agreement. To the contrary, the U.S. and EU, like the new Maidan Ukrainian government, justified the unconstitutional removal of Yanukovich. Western capitals, especially Washington, soon began hailing the February 20–21 events as another step forward for democracy, though in the first days after Yanukovich's flight to Kharkiv, official statements appeared tentative, even noncommittal. Their omissions said more about the policy reaction than the explicit statements. On February 22, the White House statement on Ukraine welcomed the Rada's "constructive work" and urged "an end to violence by all sides and a focus on peaceful, democratic dialogue, working pursuant to Ukraine's constitution and through its institutions of government" and "the prompt formation of a broad, technocratic government of national unity" (the government eventually formed was composed entirely of people from western and western-central Ukraine). It claimed the day's "developments" moved "us closer to the goal" of "constitutional change" as well as "a de-escalation of violence, a coalition government, and early elections." But crucially, neither the words "president," "Yanukovich," "agreement of February 21," nor "agreement" appeared in the statement.[194] President Obama and the White House then maintained silence for three crucial days.

On February 26, Washington broke its silence with another statement from the White House press secretary. It declared American support for the "democratically established transitional governing structures" and the "Ukrainian leaders' ongoing work to form an inclusive, multiparty government to represent all the people of Ukraine as they prepare for May elections, and to restore order, stability, and unity to the country." It also urged "outside actors in the region"—read: Russia—"to respect Ukraine's sovereignty and territorial integrity, to end provocative rhetoric and actions, and to support democratically established transitional governing structures…."[195]

Before the ink was dry on the Rada document removing Yanukovich from office, the EU announced it was ready to restore relations with Ukraine to their pre–November 29 status. On February 23 the European Commission placed its mark of approval on the revolt by declaring its readiness to sign the scuttled EU AA with the new Ukrainian government, and the commission's economics chief Olli Rehn announced the EU was prepared to provide Kiev with immediate financial assistance in excess of the 610 million euros ($838 million) to which it originally committed.[196] Going forward, it acted as if there had never been the agreement which its representatives had signed less than 48 hours previous. On February 22, one of those EU representatives, Polish Foreign Minister Sikorski, tweeted that there had been "no coup" in Kyiv and the Verkhovna Rada's "election" of its radical nationalist speaker Oleksandr Turchynov as acting president of Ukraine that day had been done "legally."[197]

Washington soon even went further: it assisted in the scuttling of the February 21 agreement by claiming that Yanukovich had violated it first, abandoned his duties, and therefore was legally removed. The argument used to support jettisoning the agreement was that Yanukovich's flight from Kiev to Kharkiv meant he had abandoned his presidential responsibilities—an alleged constitutional cause for removal. But the Ukrainian constitution says nothing about the president's removal or impeachment because he has ostensibly abandoned his office. Nor does it stipulate a vote taken without a plenary quorum. On March 5, 2014, the U.S. State Department issued a list of Putin's alleged "10 False Claims About Ukraine." The State Department's third Putin "false claim" reads:

3. **Mr. Putin says:** *The opposition failed to implement the February 21 agreement with former Ukrainian President Viktor Yanukovich.*

The Facts: The February 21 agreement laid out a plan in which the Rada, or Parliament, would pass a bill to return Ukraine to its 2004 Constitution, thus returning the country to a constitutional system centered around its parliament. Under the terms of the agreement, Yanukovich was to sign the enacting legislation within 24 hours and bring the crisis to a peaceful conclusion. Yanukovich refused to keep his end of the bargain. Instead, he packed up his home and fled, leaving behind evidence of wide-scale corruption.[198]

By changing the 48-hour deadline to a 24-hour deadline, the State Department's list of Putin's "false claims" contained what was clearly its own false claim, though one would be foolish to rule out incompetence. Moreover, as noted in Graphic 1 above and the State Department's third "Putin false claim," the February 21 agreement required "a special law will be adopted, signed and promulgated, which will restore the Constitution of 2004 including amendments passed until now." This means that the Rada was required to pass a law, and only then was Yanukovich required to sign and promulgate it. It is important to note that the State Department's "facts" regarding Putin's "third false claim" not only falsely state the time period allotted for the reversion to the 2004 constitution—48 and not 24 hours—but do not state that the Rada passed the law it was required to pass for Yanukovich to sign and promulgate. This is because the Rada did not pass the constitutional law. Instead, it joined the neofascists in revolutionary action after their violent takeover of power.

In sum, Ukraine's duly, freely and fairly elected president had been forcefully removed from power and the February 21 agreement had been thrown to the wind. There was not a word of recognition, no less admonishment from President Obama or Washington's "democracy-promotion" community to the opposition for violating the agreement. To the contrary, they joined in defending the opposition's violation of the agreement. The official White House statements cited above and others repeatedly expressed America's support of the right of "the Ukrainian people" to decide their own future. Washington's misconceptualization of the events in Kiev, and of who had perpetrated the snipers' attacks, had reduced the "Ukrainian people" to a small group of violent neofascists and ultranationalists representing a minority even in western Ukraine. Especially to the radical nationalists, Washington's use of the phrase "Ukrainian people," rather than the "people" or "peoples of Ukraine," could be misconstrued when translated into Ukrainian and Russian to mean ethnic Ukrainians, not all the citizens of Ukraine.

In Moscow they surely had not forgotten about the agreement. The Foreign Ministry's official statement of February 27 made this clear:

> The agreement on the settlement of the Ukrainian crisis, which was signed on the 21 February and certified by the German, Polish and French Foreign Ministers, is still not being fulfilled. Militants have still not laid down arms and have not left administrative buildings, and they are declaring their intention to "establish order" in all of Ukraine's regions. There are threats of physical reprisals, as the President Viktor Yanukovich emphasized in his statement today.
>
> The agreement to jointly investigate acts of violence and the obligation to create a national unity government have been forgotten. Instead, as Maidan puts it, a "government of champions," which includes representatives of national extremists, is being created.
>
> The agreements about constitutional reform, which should precede presidential elections according to the Agreement of February 21, have been forgotten.[199]

Having convinced Yanukovich to compromise with the opposition only to have it backfire so powerfully, Putin must have been outraged. Ensconced in Sochi preparing to celebrate the close of the Winter Olympic Games, which had ended without the threatened jihadi terrorist attack and with a sweeping Russian Olympic team victory in the medal count, Putin had to feel as if he had been stabbed in the back by the Western powers. Two years later, Russian Foreign Minister Sergei Lavrov expressed Moscow's sense of betrayal:

> A day before the coup d'etat, Moscow was called up by the leaders of the United States and leading European countries, who asked us to support the agreement that the opposition signed with Ukrain-

ian President Viktor Yanukovich, although in this agreement he renounced practically all prerogatives as the head of state. Under the agreement he committed himself to use neither police nor the
army. Nonetheless, President Vladimir Putin supported this agreement, emphasising that we are
backing it because the authorities and the opposition reached this inter-Ukrainian agreement of its
own free will. When the coup was staged on the following morning, and administrative buildings,
and the presidential and government residences were seized, nobody among those who asked us to
support the agreement called Moscow—not even to apologise but at least to say, "Well, we asked you
to support it but see what happened." President Putin told them that he will back the agreement on
the condition the opposition refrain from inconsiderate steps, particularly the use of force. They said:
"Yes, yes, yes, we'll do this by all means." But nobody even called or lifted his hands in dismay at what
happened.[200]

Putin's sense of Russian honor, his code of victory, and his political reputation and legitimacy's reliance on Weberian charismatic authority demanded a firm response, and it
would come.

Conclusion

On the eve and in the aftermath of Yanukovich's fall from power, the two-tier struggle
over divided Ukraine—on both its domestic and international levels—intensified expo-
nentially. At the national level, a "revolutionary" or regime transformational situation
was ushered in certainly by December; a credible competing claim of authority to rule
over at least portions of the territory and population of Ukraine was established on Kiev's
Maidan square and in other, mostly western and some central Ukrainian cities. Many of
the elements—class, ethno-national, and ideological alike—had been created or strengthened by Western dual-use (transition or revolution) democracy-promotion political technologies and diaspora support. In February, the regime transformational mode of violent
revolution from below had won out over the paths of peaceful revolution from below
and—what was nascent, indeed inherent in the February 21 agreement—a pacted transition. The illegality of revolutionary seizures of power was compounded in the Maidan
case by the violation of the February 21 agreement by the ultranationalist/neofascist elements of the Maidan, which was backed by the western powers.

More importantly, perhaps, the reality of the violence and its perpetrators on the
Maidan sharply diverges from the picture offered by the U.S. and other Western governments and media. That picture holds that the Maidan demonstrators were exclusively
peaceful and any and all violence that occurred was attributable to the Yanukovich administration and his regime's *siloviki*. In reality, radical nationalists had hijacked a peaceful
revolution and potential pacted transition from the hands of the democrats who originally
occupied the Maidan and the practical if corrupt oligarchs who helped finance it along
with the West.

Western governments, especially the U.S. government, signed on to the Maidan
regime's false founding myth of purely democratic aspirations and innocent hundreds
martyred by Yanukovich and his henchmen. In an official statement commemorating the
revolt, the State Department noted: "Today, we join the people of Ukraine in honoring
the memory of their Revolution of Dignity and those who gave their lives to build a more
just, democratic, and European Ukraine. *They braved sniper fire* and three months in the
bitter cold, and Ukraine got a second chance for freedom, justice, and a government that
serves the people."[201] It is difficult to predict what might happen if the victims and those

who truly support a revolution of dignity discover who murdered the heavenly hundred, but as I show in Chapter 10, the Maidan regime is gravely split between oligarchic and neofascist factions, and a small group of committed democrats. For the same anniversary, one of the revolt's leading facilitators, American ambassador to Kiev Geoffrey Pyatt, played up the false narrative to the hilt: "Change has not come easily; it has come with great sacrifice. As Vice-President Biden said during his visit, to honor those who have given so much—first on the Maidan and later in Donbass—each of us has an obligation to answer the call of history and to help build a united, democratic Ukraine. The most fitting memorial to the Heavenly Hundred is a Ukraine genuinely rid of corruption, cronyism, and kleptocracy."[202]

Putting aside normative considerations, what were the causes of the violent revolutionary outcome? To be sure, as in almost any case of regime transformation, failures of the ancient regime and any structural economic, financial and/or political crises comprise the key background necessary causes. But these are neither sufficient nor necessarily immediately operational in the development of a revolutionary situation, defined, as noted in an earlier chapter and my *Russia's Revolution from Above*, as a credible competing alternative claim to sovereignty to rule over a given people and territory. Western democracy-promotion helped create the revolutionary situation, from which several possible regime transformational modes are possible, as also noted in the same. It organized a social network of civic actors, a nascent civil society and opposition movement, as noted in the previous chapter. Although USAID-funded, Soros-funded and otherwise funded Serbian, Georgian, Ukrainian, and Western NGOs' courses on peaceful resistance and democratic governance tended to oppose violent revolutionary means and nondemocratic revolutionary goals, they could not guarantee peaceful transition.

Under the cover of the democracy-promoted civil society that emerged on the Maidan after Yanukovich postponed signing the EU AA, there infiltrated an altogether different element, the ultranationalist and neofascist SP, RS, and others. This rather uncivil element within civil society tipped the balance from peaceful negotiated regime transition to violent revolutionary regime transformation. I am not one who thinks that the overthrow of Yanukovich by violent means was preferred, much less orchestrated, by Washington and Brussels. However, both bear a share in the responsibility for the violent overthrow of the regime, along with the regime itself and the radical opposition. The State Department hired and deployed to Kiev elements from the nationalist Ukrainian diaspora, educated in allegiance to the OUN-UPA and all that implies. They, in turn, naturally linked up with like-minded elements in Ukraine's civil and uncivil societies. Moreover, as we saw, there was direct support for revolutionaries during the Maidan and acceptance of their violent seizure of power, despite the February 21 agreement.

In sum, democracy-promotion created a potentially revolutionary civil society, which created a revolutionary situation on the Maidan and in numerous provincial capitals, especially across western Ukraine. Then, the revolutionary situation's inherent potential for a transitional rather than revolutionary regime transformation was confounded by the uncivil, ultranationalist element, which led the violent seizure of power. Opposition radicals, most prominently the SP and RS, instigated all of the tactical escalations, faked others (the Buratov and Chernovil "abductions"), instigated the pivotal strategic escalation on February 20–21 with their sniper shootings, and then violently overthrew the ruling regime group.

As in all regime transformations, the modalities of the transformation in Ukraine's

Maidan revolution—the key actors, their ideologies, and preferred tactics—would tell on the course of the constructive phase of the new Maidan regime. Rarely do violent revolutions from below lead to democracy. This is even truer when the violent revolution includes a strong ethnonational component.

As in any escalating regime crisis, the intensification of competition between and interference by outside parties—the Western powers and Russia—also told on the course of events. Western governments clearly violated their pledge as guarantors of the February 21 agreement between President Yanukovich and the leaders of Ukraine's opposition parties. The governments of the Polish, German, and French foreign ministers, who signed on as guarantors of the agreement, remained silent when the RS ultranationalists and neofascists illegally seized power rather than honoring the transition process the Kiev pact established. Instead of guaranteeing the agreement, in support of which Russian President Vladimir Putin personally intervened to secure Yanukovich's signature, the Western powers celebrated the illegal takeover as a democratic and legitimate revolution in pursuit of "European values." But the revolution would yield chaos; the rule of law and—in the case of multinational states—stateness were predictably the first casualties of the revolution.

Internationally, Russia had been dealt a strategic defeat and had some of its darkest suspicions confirmed. The arrival to power of a new regime in Kiev with clearly anti–Russian elements raised the spectre of a major strategic loss for Moscow. Russia's unqualified support for the corrupt and increasingly unpopular Yanukovich regime had put Moscow in a vulnerable position in a country it saw as its main bulwark against NATO. Full-scale Western civilizational or at least political and institutional expansion was occurring at the expense of Moscow's own expansive project—the EEU. With the Maidan revolt, Putin's effort to win Ukraine to Russia's orbit had seemingly failed.

From the Kremlin's perspective, the regime change in Kiev was another step in the eventual but certain entry of Ukraine into NATO. Indeed, the Russian Foreign Ministry's February 27 statement had directly raised this issue so crucial for Russia: "When NATO starts reviewing the situation in Ukraine, it sends the wrong signal. It even seemed appropriate for the NATO Secretary General to mention that 'Ukraine's membership of NATO is not an urgent priority of the Ukrainian leadership.' Does this mean that membership should be a priority, but not an urgent one? They are attempting to decide for the Ukrainian people again. We insistently recommend that everybody should refuse provocative statements and respect the out-of-bloc status of Ukraine, which is formalised in its Law on the Foundations of Domestic and Foreign Policy."[203] Worse still, Ukraine in NATO would mean the loss of the Black Sea Fleet's naval base at Sevastopol in Crimea, possible loss of suppliers of key strategic and other weapons and weapons parts for the Russian army made at plants in eastern Ukraine, and the potential threat to Russian compatriots in Ukraine with Moscow forced to helplessly stand by and unable to act.

The new Ukrainian authorities would not recognize Yanukovich's law on Ukraine's nonaligned, neutral status. Thus, Ukraine would be almost certain to renew talks on joining NATO and a Membership Action Plan. NATO clearly stated at its 2008 Bucharest Summit that both Ukraine and Georgia will become NATO members "someday." NATO would not accept the military base of a non–NATO power on the territory of a NATO member state, and the Maidan revolutionaries did not accept the Kharkiv Accord on lengthening Russia's lease of the Sevastopol naval base. This meant Russia would be forced to withdraw all of its military from Crimea by 2017 and lose its lone warm-water port. The new Ukrainian leaders' neofascist allies could oppress or engage in violence against ethnic Russians in eastern Ukraine and the Crimea, and Putin would be forced to start a war with NATO or rely on the West to protect Crimea's ethnic Russians. Given the numerous disputes over natural gas contracts between Moscow and Kiev, Ukraine's turn west would mean problems for Russia's gas exports, which go through Ukrainian pipelines to Europe and constitute 30 percent of Russia's state budget. Russia's weakened position in Ukraine compounded an overall deteriorating geostrategic situation, undermined by the "Arab Spring" and collapse of the "reset."

Until February 21, Moscow and the West seemed to be working to find a compromise in Kiev, and the West still regarded Yanukovich as the legal and even legitimate Ukrainian president. But February 20–21 would prove pivotal for Ukraine, Russia, Western-Russian relations, and European security. From the Kremlin's perspective, at the very least the West's democracy-promotion efforts had put in place a civil society and opposition organizations as the building blocks of potential revolution, and then had parlayed a crisis it had helped create into an "accidental" revolution. At the worst, the West had carried out a long- and well-planned color revolution or coup with little or no indigenous roots in Ukrainian society in an effort to create political space for NATO's expansion further east and a springboard for doing the same in Russia itself. The West's abandonment of the February 21 agreement, reflected in its embrace of Maidan's "democratic revolution," naturally raised suspicions in Moscow as to the sincerity of the negotiations and the role of Washington in the overthrow of Yanukovich.

Such perceptions were not necessarily manifestations of Russian paranoia. Aforementioned geostrategist George Friedman, President of the U.S. think tank "Stratfor" and a former CIA analyst, called the Maidan revolt/revolution the "most open coup in history."[204] One event had to have weighed on the Russian leadership's mind as it looked back on the violation of the February 21 agreement and its pre-history. On February 7 an audiotape of a phone call between U.S. Assistant Secretary of State Nuland and U.S. Ambassador to Ukraine Pyatt was leaked in which they discuss and appear to be deciding who will be Ukraine's next prime minister should the crisis play out in such a way that Azarov, Yanukovich's appointee, would be replaced. The phone call was surely accessed by either Russian and/or Ukrainian intelligence. On the tape, Nuland tells Pyatt that "Yats" (Yatsenyuk, formerly a member of a neo–Nazi party and at the time a Rada deputy for Tymoshenko's nationalistic Fatherland Party) should become the head of government rather than Udar party leader Klitchko backed by the EU, with Nuland infamously saying: "F*** the EU."[205] The clear impression was that the U.S. would have veto power or actually form part or all of the next Ukrainian cabinet. It now had leverage over the embattled Yanukovich, given his increasingly weakened position, or perhaps they were preparing for a government under a new regime they were expecting would be established soon. Putin and the rest of the leadership had reason to suspect that Washington's involvement was more than they knew, and the West's "dual-use" political technologies and other measures indeed may have been just the tip of the iceberg of Western machinations towards yet another color revolution at Russia's expense.

Finally, the West had violated not just the Helsinki Final Act but very arguably the Budapest Memorandum as well—one of the pillars of Ukraine's state sovereignty—by encouraging revolutionaries to continue their demonstrations, helping to fund those same revolutionaries, and morally backing their illegal takeover after the fact as a "democratic" development. For Moscow, this could be the green light to reunite the Crimea, the status of which Moscow agreed not to raise on the basis of the Budapest Memorandum's assurances, which consolidated both Ukraine's status as a neutral country and sovereign of Crimea.

Just two days after Yanukovich's exit from Kiev, Putin set in motion Russia's response—a countermove to mitigate the loss incurred in and potential threat from Kiev. On February 23, he gave instructions to begin preparing operations for the return of Crimea to the Russian homeland. In doing so, Putin escalated the crisis both inside Ukraine and internationally.

8

Putin's Crimea Gambit
From Revolution to Civil War

Introduction

In multi-communal states, an early if not immediate casualty of revolution, especially violent ones from below, is the country's very "stateness"—its territorial cohesiveness, even integrity. Thus, as the situation deteriorated in Kiev, other regions of Ukraine—most notably, but not surprisingly, Crimea—began to look for protection from the storm in Kiev, especially as Ukrainian ultranationalists and neofascists began to play a larger role in the increasingly violent demonstrations. Given Crimea's history, the Crimean question was in the air from the very beginning of the Ukrainian crisis. Ukrainian, Russian, and Tatar nationalists and ethnonational entrepreneurs both in Ukraine and Russia began to position themselves to take advantage of any opportunity that might arise. This was natural given the growing chaos in state institutions in Kiev and elsewhere and the undercurrent of ethnic and territorial tensions in the country. Crimea's population was dominated by ethnic Russians and Russian-speaking Ukrainians. Anti-Russian Ukrainians and Tatar nationalists were a relatively small majority and did not compose the entire Ukrainian and Tatar Crimean communities.

The EuroMaidan regime's first acts further polarized already tense relations between east and west. After Yanukovich's overthrow, the old Party of Regions plurality in parliament was blocked or intimidated from voting their preferences, and nationalists in the Rada moved to settle scores, adopting laws that sparked fears of reprisals against the Russian-dominated east and south. The Rada repealed Yanukovich-era laws that banned fascist symbols and that gave official status to minority languages in regions with large minorities, threatening Russian-speakers' hard-won language rights in eastern and southern Ukraine. Although the Rada reinstated Yanukovich's language law within days, the message had gone out and been received. Russians would be unlikely to find a warm welcome in the new western-dominated Maidan Ukraine. In addition, the RS and others made threats to send "activists" to the Crimea and elsewhere to put down growing anti–Maidan counter-demonstrations.

Meanwhile, much as violence escalated on the Maidan in February 18–20, it now escalated in the provinces. There was a pitched battle with baseball bats involving hundreds of pro–Maidan and anti–Maidan elements in Odessa. On February 20 in Talne, Cherkask, and the town of Korsun-Shenkovskiy, located on the road from Crimea to Kiev, buses loaded with alleged "*titushki*" (pro–Yanukovich provocateurs and thugs) were seized and the alleged *titushki* were beaten. In one case, some bus riders reportedly were shot by a mob that included RS activists.[1]

These actions intensified a wave of resistance to the Maidan revolutionaries that had been mounting for several weeks in eastern and southern regions with large ethnic Russian minorities, most notably in Donetsk and Luhansk Oblasts, but also in Kharkiv, Dnepropetrovsk, Zaporozhe, Kherson, Mikholayiv, and Odessa. However, the most Russian regions of all—Crimea and Sevastopol—had the greatest motivation to react to the apparent danger emanating from western Ukraine and now Kiev. When Crimeans rallied against the overthrow of Yanukovich, the spectre of a clash between the peninsula and the capital grew.

The country appeared headed to civil war. Official and/or unofficial Ukrainian elements like the SP and RS might attempt to counter the Crimeans' resistance to the Maidan, attempt to challenge the Russian Black Sea Fleet's status, or attack ethnic Russians or Russian servicemen. Civil war could break out and draw in the Russian military on the peninsula. Putin would be obliged to take military action in their defense raising the prospect of Moscow's being drawn into the civil war and a war with Kiev. Consistent with Putin's judo learning and other forms of tactical thinking, it seemed better to seize the initiative and dictate the time, place, and terms of the conflict. By protecting the Crimeans and supporting their demands for sovereignty, he could parlay the coming Crimean crisis into a play that would recoup some of the geostrategic and political-charismatic losses incurred in Kiev.

Revolution and the Operationalization of Ukraine's Stateness Problem

Indeed, as the EuroMaidan movement intensified, Crimea demanded that Yanukovich restore order. On December 2, while the leadership of Lviv Oblast was backing EuroMaidan and the leadership of Ternopol Oblast's capital, the city of Ternopol, also in western Ukraine, was urging the nation to strike in support of the Maidan protesters, the Crimean Supreme Soviet adopted by a vote of 76 "for" and 2 "against" a resolution demanding that Yanukovich declare a state of emergency in Kiev and "stop the orgy of lawlessness and anarchy" in the country and supporting "any measures" he might take to do so.[2] Six weeks later it was still demanding the same, but was now moving to consolidate the Russophilic southeast behind Yanukovich. As the neofascist-led violence in Kiev intensified in late January, Supreme Soviet chairman Konstantinov called on the leaderships of southeastern Ukraine's oblasts "to come forward in a united front against the coercive seizure of power."[3]

Not only was Crimea opposed to a EuroMaidan hijacked by radicals from western Ukraine, but, as detailed in earlier chapters, remained pro–Moscow throughout the post–Soviet era. With its strong historical Russian association, which included a powerful Russian military-patriotic component through, for example, the Crimean War, the peninsula had a strong separatist orientation. During the height of the February–March 2014 Crimean crisis, at a meeting of the National Security and Defense Council of Ukraine (*Rada national'noi bezpeki i oborony Ukraini*) or RNBOU, now controlled by the new Maidan regime and chaired by MSD hundreds commander Parubiy, the new MVD chief Arsen Avakov acknowledged Crimea's pro–Russian orientation, stating that "the majority of the population of Crimea holds a pro–Russian, anti–Ukrainian position." He also reported that even the Ukraine MVD's Internal Troops and police in the peninsula's capitol of Simferopol, though they were "for now" carrying out their duties, "would not resist the Russians," and he could not guarantee but only "hope" that the 1,000 Internal Troops "would carry out orders and, at a minimum, not surrender."[4] Thus, one of the supposedly most patriotic elements in any state apparatus, the *siloviki*, were in the case of Maidan Ukraine's forces in Crimea at best neutral and perhaps even sympathetic in regard to the population's pro–Russian aspirations. This is indeed how things played out, as the overwhelming majority of the population backed the peninsula's political leadership in moving towards independence or reunification with Russia.

As matters in Kiev worsened through the end of January and early February, the Crimean Supreme Soviet initiated plans to make changes to the autonomous republic's constitution to strengthen its autonomous status within Ukraine, including "a Crimea-wide public opinion survey on Crimea's status," and to appeal to Russia to assume the role of guarantor of that autonomy.[5] Crimea was moving in the direction fate would bring it some three weeks later. Russia's ultranationalist State Duma deputy and Liberal Democratic Party leader Vladimir Zhirinovskii seemed to presage some of the future events when on February 19 he urged the Russian leadership to use the situation in Ukraine to take back Crimea and Donbass.[6]

The day after Yanukovich's overthrow, deputies of his Party of the Regions (PR) from the regional oblast parliaments in southern and eastern Ukraine held a congress in Kharkiv. The PR held majorities in these regional parliaments, including those in Crimea and its capital, Simferopol. The Kharkiv congress of PR southeastern oblasts' deputies declared that their regional governments would "take upon themselves responsibility for guaranteeing the constitutional legal order and citizens' rights" until these were restored in Kiev. This meant that Crimea, Sevastopol and other regions in the south and east were refusing to recognize the Maidan regime in Kiev. Taking the example of Western officials' visits to Maidan, Moscow had a conspicuous presence at the PR's Kharkiv congress. The heads of the international affairs committees of the State Duma and Federation Council, Mikhail Margelov and Aleksei Pushkov, respectively, as well as the governors of four of the five Russian regions bordering Ukraine were present.[7] Indicative of the change which the events of February 21 in Kiev brought to the calculus of key actors in Ukraine is that on February 20, Crimean Supreme Soviet Chairman Vladimir Konstantinov told a delegation of Russian State Duma deputies from the pro–Kremlin Yedinaya Rossiya (United Russia) party that Crimea would "solve its problems independently."[8]

Putin's Escalation: Russia's Countermove Against the West in Crimea

With matters polarized on the ground in Ukraine, they escalated on the international level. It should have been clear that Putin would respond to the West's gambit in supporting the overthrow of Yanukovich. Putin could not let his defeat in Kiev stand. While the specifics of Putin's response in Crimea are troublesome, it was possible not only to understand Putin's decision to take some kind of action, but to foresee his countermove. Russia now had reason and perhaps even justification to respond to and utilize any appeals from Crimea for protection from Ukrainian ultranationalists—whether they were sanctioned by Kiev or not—and/or for political and other forms of support for any Crimean request for more autonomy, full independence, or reunification with Russia. After all, Crimea had become part of the Ukraine SSR on the whim of the Soviet communist regime that the Maidan demonstrators so bitterly rejected, and an overwhelming majority of the population in Crimea wanted to be Russian citizens. Moreover, the Americans' dual-use regime-change meddling, capped off by their own and their Ukrainian allies' violation of the February 21 agreement, was the straw that broke the camel's back for Putin and many Russians regarding relations with the West. The Kremlin was now bound to pursue aggressively ways to recoup its loss and exact revenge for the betrayal in Kiev.

The "camel's back" had two broken humps, as far as Putin and many Russians were concerned. One was the immediate revolutionary crisis and the geopolitical stakes that rode on the outcome of that crisis. The other was the long history of real and perceived Western broken promises that Russians have experienced since the ending of the Cold War. When the February 21 agreement was violated, Putin had visions of past broken Western promises from Washington's late Cold War promise not to expand NATO beyond reunited Germany, to the West's violation of the 2011 UN resolution on Libya not to use the legalized intervention and no-fly zone enforcement in order to support the revolt against strongman Muamar Qadhafi. The latter broken promise played a role in Putin's decision that same year to return to the Kremlin rather than let then President Dmitri Medvedev run for a second term. Medvedev had insisted against Putin's advice to refrain from vetoing the Western-backed UN resolution establishing the no-fly zone. Now, the enormous geostrategic loss that a Western-oriented and -dominated, and likely anti–Russian Maidan Ukraine represented, compounded Putin's sense of betrayal from the West's acquiescence in the violation of the February 21 agreement he had convinced Yanukovich to sign. In addition, human and political losses hung in the balance, if the writing on the wall in Kiev portended future developments across Ukraine.

Perhaps believing his own propaganda about U.S. and CIA plots to destroy Russia, Putin must have perceived the Ukrainian opposition's inability to control the Right Sector radicals as part of an elaborate Western ruse to quickly grab Ukraine. In the bargain, the West spoiled his and Russia's triumph at Sochi, where the Winter Olympic Games were completed without a terrorist attack or other problems, and Russia actually won the Sochi Games medal count. This interpretation is strengthened in light of the West's open interference in the Maidan demonstrations in the weeks leading up to Yanukovich's overthrow on the background of hypocritical Western calls for Moscow not to interfere in the crisis but rather respect Ukraine's sovereignty and "European choice." Putin's sense of betrayal was likely heightened further still by the fact that he had played a pivotal role, according to Sikorski's account, in nudging Yanukovich to sign the agreement. After the coup, this slight and subsequent betrayal must have galled Putin to no end. Putin takes neither slights nor betrayals lightly and could not and would not leave them without a response.

For Putin, the Ukrainian revolt was also deeply troubling for another reason: it suggested the possibility that the West could very well attempt to machinate a Moscow Maidan. Kiev's Maidan revolution represents a resurrection of the color revolutions that Putin had been fighting since 2004. The close ties between Russia and Ukraine and the emergence of more anti–Putin opposition in recent years, compared to the period around Ukraine's 2004 Orange Revolution 1.0, meant that Ukraine today could very well become Russia tomorrow as far as the Kremlin was concerned. Moreover, in domestic political terms the Maidan revolt meant Putin losses on two fronts. His traditionalist constituency and the radical nationalist and communist oppositions would be disappointed by the "loss of Ukraine." His democratic opposition would be encouraged and perhaps motivated to action by the example of Maidan and the likely reactionary wave that the loss of Ukraine would spark among the traditionalists, nationalists and communists.

Putting aside Putin's determination to simply exact revenge for the Western betrayal created by the neofascists' violation of the February 21 agreement, the bottom line of Putin's calculus was twofold. First, there were the domestic political implications. Putin needed to save face and avoid the defeat at the hands of the West represented by the rise of an anti–Russian regime in Kiev, something that would weaken his charismatic authority among both the elite and public. Second, he needed to undo the geopolitical strategic setback posed by such a regime in Kiev, which would lead first to resurrection of the Ukrainian EU association agreement and eventually to EU and NATO membership. This would mean Russia's loss of its Black Sea Fleet base in Sevastopol and eventually the lining of Russia's entire western border by NATO countries. Putin simply could not let stand the situation as it stood after the revolutionary seizure of power. The geostrategic situation around Ukraine had to be reset.

Thus, Putin decided to grab victory from the jaws of defeat by seizing the Crimea. This had serious plusses and minuses, and Putin's calculus contained no small degree of miscalculation. He may have overreacted to events as a result of the above-mentioned aspects of betrayal, real and perceived, in the Kiev coup/revolution, a sense of betrayal heightened by its occurrence at the peak of Russia's organizational, propaganda, and sporting triumph at Sochi Games. As Putin acknowledged in the Russian documentary film *Return to the Motherland* shown on Russian state television on the first anniversary of the March 16 referendum on Crimea's reunification with Russia, he issued orders for Crimea's return to the Russian fold on February 23, two days after the Maidan neofascists overthrew Yanukovich.[9] Putin's quick decision on such a serious gambit supports the interpretation that Putin's actions were driven at least in part by an impulse to avenge his sense of betrayal after the violation of the Kiev agreement.

Claims by certain writers that a discussed document drafted by a group outside the Kremlin and any corridors of power constituted intent on the Kremlin's part to seize Crimea before the Maidan takeover are clearly biased. A frequent presenter on Russian politics at the Heritage Foundation and elsewhere inside the D.C. beltway, former Radio Free Europe/Radio Liberty writer Paul Goble, and Catherine Fitzpatrick of the Mikhail Khodorkovskii's *The Interpreter* falsely asserted that Russian newspaper *Novaya gazeta* editor Dmitrii Muratov claimed on the *Osoboe mnenie* (Personal or Special Opinion) talk show on radio station Ekho Moskvy (Echo of Moscow) that a document in his possession "confirmed that 'the plan of war in Ukraine was developed in the administration of the president of Russia,' that is, by Putin's entourage."[10] Goble further claimed: "The 'document shows, Muratov said, that this plan was developed *in the Kremlin* [my emphasis] between February 4 and February 15 of last year, that is, before Viktor Yanukovich fled from Kyiv.'" Nowhere has Muratov ever said anything approaching the assertion that the document he says was created between February 4 and 15, and therefore before Yanukovich's overthrow, was drafted "in the Kremlin." Goble and Fitzpatrick are clearly exaggerating and indeed falsifying Muratov's much more modest claim. What Muratov did say is quite different and clearly infers that the document was not drafted in the Kremlin: "This document, which purportedly was prepared by a group of people, in which, purportedly, participated the well-known oligarch, a man who stole credit in VTB

[VneshTorgBank or the Foreign Trade Bank], who is close to AFK 'Sistema' [a major Russian holding company], a person who is the creator of his own large foundation—I have in mind that Orthodox Christian, major oligarch Konstantin Malofeev.... [interviewer interrupts] ... Someone from his circle, I think, that people [in his circle] have greater opportunity than he to go to the administration of the president, to the Kremlin, and they brought this scenario of possible events there."[11] So instead of being drafted in the Kremlin, the scenario was written by a private group headed by Malofeev. Some in the Malofeev group, in the editor's opinion, had better access to the Kremlin than Malofeev, and, in Muratov's opinion, they were in a position or could actually have taken this draft of proposed actions to the Kremlin.

Furthermore, even if the report was brought or sent to the Kremlin, it would have been one of tens of such outside reports. Much of their contents would have repeated each other or partially overlapped. The Malofeev report and others would have competed with similar reports from much more powerful entities, such as Russia's various *siloviki* departments. Many of the state-initiated reports and the proposals contained therein would have been based on previous contingency planning to annex or reunify Crimea to Russia. But contingency plans are another story. They are more general than operational plans and subject to major revisions in preparing operational plans for the myriad of potential crises, the specifics of which are not completely predictable. These are a routine, indeed obligatory practice for military or intelligence organizations. Many states have developed contingency invasion plans. An example (if it was not intended for an invasion already decided upon) is Georgian President Saakashvili's 2005 order to Defense Minister Okruashvili to draw up operational plans for an invasion of Abkhaziya and South Ossetiya.[12] Of course, the occupation and annexation/reunification would have been planned before the fact, so the Malofeev group's document is probably unimportant and certainly no "smoking gun" representing proof that Putin was realizing some long-planned operation, the timing of which followed the events in Kiev only by coincidence.

Moscow appears to have had only vague or very general contingency plans for regaining Crimea in the event of some major crisis. Indeed, an investigation of the annexation by the pro-democratic Russian Web site publication, *Gazeta.ru*, received testimony from an unnamed official in this regard, but it concluded: "[T]hese plans were akin to a strategy of action in case of nuclear war: It seems necessary to be prepared, but only an emergency can make it applicable in practice." "Moscow certainly did not act according to a clear-cut plan that had been written in advance. A great deal was decided on the go."[13] Well-known Russian liberal Aleksei Venediktov, the editor-in-chief of the pro-democratic Ekho Moskvy (Echo of Moscow) radio station, came to the same conclusion after speaking with Russian officials and seeing internal Kremlin documents.[14]

Thus, unless Putin or others in the Russian government foresaw an opportunity to parlay a change in the crisis into a play for Crimea before February 21, then Putin's February 23 order likely was the initial decision and first step in developing a specific operational plan based on standard and widely used general contingency plans. Whatever elements of such plans existed before Kiev, they could not have foreseen, much less have been adapted for the specific environment in which the operational plans would have to be carried out. Matters began to move too quickly for Moscow to have had a plan ready to be implemented when the Crimea began to unravel three days after Putin issued his order to return the peninsula to Moscow. The following description of the events demonstrates the extent to which Moscow was operating "on the go."

The Struggle for the Crimean Parliament

After the Maidan revolution/coup, different elements began to mobilize in and around the Crimean Republic rapidly. By February 26, Crimea's Supreme Soviet was set to vote on an appeal to Moscow for reunification with Russia. Given developments in Kiev and across the country in recent months and Crimea's post–Soviet record of seeking either autonomy from Kiev or reunification with Russia, this should not have been unexpected for anyone, nor in need of encouragement from Moscow. Additionally, almost any Russian contingency plan would have included mobilizing the largely ethnic Russian and pro–Russian Crimean parliament and similar public organizations. Political ties with and encouragement to seek autonomy or secession from, for example, Moscow's mayor Yurii Luzhkov in the 1990s were legend. In lieu of such schemes, the actors in Crimea would almost certainly have responded to the Maidan takeover in the way they did. Thus, in many ways, the dynamic driving the Crimean events was analogous to that which had driven events in Kiev, where Western and Ukrainian democratizers and neofascists, having already networked, then worked together towards the same goal: overthrowing Yanukovich.

Another similarity was that Moscow had no compunctions about its own direct political intervention in the Crimea crisis, acting on the model they perceived had been implemented by the West in Kiev. On February 25, when Supreme Rada Chairman and the Maidan provisional government's acting president Oleksandr Turchynov called a meeting of Ukraine's Defense and Security Council to discuss "the emergence of separatist moods and threats in connection with them" in light of signs of resistance in southeastern Ukraine to the Maidan revolt in recent weeks, officials in Moscow began to sound the alarm.[15] The same day, it was announced that Russia's upper house of parliament, the Federation Council, would dispatch a delegation to Simferopol led by its International Relations Committee Chairman Igor Morozov.[16] The next day, State Duma Committee for CIS Affairs Leonid Slutskii called on the lower house to discuss the threat of Kiev's "armed expansion to the east and southeast of Ukraine and to the Republic of Crimea."[17]

As Crimea's parliamentary deputies began to arrive at the Supreme Soviet in the center of the Crimean capital of Simferopol on February 26, ethnic Russian groups under the pro-reunification "Russian Unity" movement led by Supreme Soviet deputy Sergei Aksyonov, and ethnic Tatar groups, supporting Crimean Tatar autonomy within Ukraine, began to organize opposing rallies in close proximity to each other on the square at the parliament building. Perhaps as many as 10,000 Tatars and pro–Maidan Ukrainians and at least as many Russians and pro–Russian Ukrainians demonstrated. The latter reportedly were augmented by arrivals from Sevastopol, the home of the Black Sea Fleet and Russia's military presence on the peninsula, where thousands were demonstrating for reunification with Russia. According to participants in the Simferopol rallies, tensions were fueled further by the Tatars' breaking an "unwritten rule" not to hold a rally where the Russians already had reserved a place to hold one. This was even acknowledged by Ilmi Umerov, a member of the Tatar cultural autonomy body, the Milli Mejlis of the Crimean Tatars. Nevertheless, the Tatars, according to Umerov, had decided it was imperative to pressure the Soviet not adopt the reunification appeal: "[W]e came to defend our state. According to our information, separatist decisions were to have been adopted at the Supreme Council session—an appeal to Putin to incorporate Crimea into Russia and the scheduling of a referendum."[18]

At the same time, in the already overheated atmosphere of the revolutionary situation across the country and fears of nationalist mobilization churning in all of Ukraine's ethnic communities, the situation quickly got out of hand. On February 24, just three days after the Maidan takeover and on the day Crimea saw its first anti–Maidan demonstrations, top RS leader Ihor Mosiychuk, just freed from prison by the Rada under the new Maidan regime, declared as a "Ukrainian nationalist" on Ukrainian television Channel 112 that if Crimeans attempted to destroy Ukraine's territorial integrity, then RS would organize "friendship trains" to "harshly punish" such people and defend the "nationalist revolution," just as the ultranationalist self-declared OUN successor, "UNSO, did in 1991 when a public similar to these rats, ran away when a column of UNSO entered Sevastopol."[19] There appears to never have been a friendship train sent by RS to Crimea, despite claims in a Russian propaganda film,[20] but the threat was reported widely in Sevastopol and Crimean media, intensifying Crimeans' desire for separation from the new Ukraine.[21] The threat was made more real, as at this time RS "activists" and some other ultranationalist parties' thugs did in fact begin to fan out across the country, attempting to spread revolutionary chaos, including or perhaps especially to pro-autonomy, pro–Russian regions, as discussed in the next chapter.

At the same time, tempers were beginning to flare between the Russian and Tatar deputies. Crimean Supreme Soviet deputy and Tatar Mejlis chairman Refat Chubarov warned that Tatars would not allow the republic's fate to be decided without them,[22] and he repeatedly requested the Soviet's pro–Russian majority leader and the Soviet's speaker, Volodimir Konstantinov, to come to his office. Chubarov demanded that Konstantinov cancel the session, warning that otherwise he would be unable to control his people, according to Sergei Tsekov, then a Supreme Council deputy and after the annexation/reunification one of Crimea's two senators in Russia's upper house of the Federal Assembly, the Federation Council.[23] In an official statement, Konstantinov called a "provocation" reports claiming that the Crimean parliament would discuss secession of the autonomous region from Ukraine.[24] Tsekov says that he himself called Chubarov's people provocateurs and screamed at them.[25]

Outside on the square, Russians and pro–Russians in the crowd were chanting "Russia, Russia!" and holding the Russian tricolor and Orthodox Christian icons while Ukrainians and Tatars were yelling "Ukraine" and holding Ukrainian and Right Sector flags. Tatars could be heard yelling "Allahu Akbar." Under the press of the many-hundreds-strong and increasingly aggressive rallies, the police corridor dividing them collapsed. The ensuing clashes ended in some 30 people being hospitalized and two deaths. One Tatar was crushed under the mobs, and a Russian suffered a heart attack.[26] At the same time, several Tatar protesters burst into the Supreme Soviet building, forcing deputies and staffers to flee through a side entrance. Other deputies went onto the square to stop the rioting. Chubarov, Aksyonov, and others were able to reestablish the divide between the groups, avoiding more bloodshed. According to Galimova's investigation, a Russian politician on the scene said that the special services "were getting drunk in the bathhouse at the time," and if not for Chubanov, Aksyonov and the others who separated the mobs, anything might have happened.[27]

Regardless, the chaos disrupted the Supreme Council session, preventing a quorum and the vote, with many deputies afraid to attend the session amid the violence. Assuming the matter was won, the Tatars disbanded. Konstantinov told Umerov that no session would be held "in the immediate future," and the Tatars believed their victory would be longstanding. They were wrong.[28] Perhaps more importantly, the clash raised the spectre of civil war in Crimea that might draw in the Russian and Ukrainian troops stationed there. This risk likely pushed the pro–Russian Crimeans and Moscow to move quickly to bring the peninsula under Moscow's protection one way or the other.

Polite *Little* Green Men

Thus, after the Tatars' protests appeared to scuttle any Supreme Soviet resolution appealing to Moscow for reunification, Russian allies and Moscow operatives recently arriving in Crimea moved to secure a vote on that very point. *Gazeta.ru* journalist Galimova's investigation concludes that if not for the confrontation on February 26, there would have been neither the occupation of the Supreme Council and Council of Ministers buildings nor the vote on reunification on February 27.[29] The delay could have complicated Moscow's calculus and altered the outcome, perhaps. Instead, Russian political operatives and nationalists, who were already in Crimea or had been arriving in recent days, sprung into action, and Moscow became more convinced of the need to move rapidly.

Initially, some of the outsiders may have thought they would be joining a *fait accompli* with the resolution initiating procedures for reunification (including a referendum) already adopted. Future Donbass rebel commander Igor Girkin or the notorious "General Strelkov" appears to have been in Crimea by, and played a role on February 27. Ukraine's SBU dates Girkin-Strelkov's arrival from February 26.[30] Since the SBU would certainly have preferred to put his arrival much earlier so that his role in securing the Supreme Soviet would be heightened, this is a case in which an SBU assessment makes a good baseline. (As demonstrated below, many future SBU claims were doubtful at best and usually outright strategic communications or propaganda.) Girkin-Strelkov claims he arrived on the peninsula on February 21 and was a "commander of insurgents" who forcibly chased deputies of Crimea to vote for the resolution calling for reunification with Russia.[31] A February 21 arrival in Crimea would situate Girkin-Strelkov's arrival before the date when Putin ostensibly ordered the preparation of operational plans to reunite Crimea with Russia.

As Sergei Aksyonov told Galimova, Girkin may have led or been part of a volunteer subunit responsible for the weapons taken from the Ukrainian SBU and MVD on the peninsula. The same source also identifies him as leading only one of several groups of militia that escorted deputies to the pivotal February 27 Supreme Soviet session.[32] Girkin's prior status and earlier biography are a little unclear. Most sources indicate he was a former GRU or former FSB officer.[33] The SBU, as part of a much-falsified strategic communications campaign discussed in the next chapter, fingered Girkin as an active GRU operative.[34] Girkin says he was a career FSB officer but left the domestic intelligence service on March 31, 2013, when he was released into the reserve with the rank of colonel.[35] Various sources show that he rose to the rank of ensign to head the central apparatus of one FSB department (administration or *upravlenie*), and after serving in the Russian armed forces until 1998 in various hot spots and crises involving Russian interests and/or forces, including Bosnia, Transdniestr, Chechnya, Dagestan, he later was a journalist in Syria.[36] Since leaving the FSB and while in its service he occupied himself as a military reenactment enthusiast.[37]

There is evidence that Moscow provided some 50 to 150 "special tourists" to assist in countering the Tatar demonstration and securing the Crimean Soviet for the vote on conducting a referendum on reunification with Russia. They included military veterans, bikers, and even criminal elements organized under the auspices of veterans' organizations and branches of the pro–Kremlin United Russia party and perhaps the United People's Front. After the Crimean events—it is not known precisely when—some went on to the Donbass to add support to the pro–Russian, anti–Maidan demonstrations there.[38] It could be that Girkin-Strelkov was among these "special tourists," given the later discovered Russian practice of releasing soldiers from duty officially before sending them to fight in Donbass in summer 2014.

The evidence overall suggests that Strelkov-Girkin appears to have been a secondary player in the Crimean events rather than the leader he has tried to portray himself as. It needs to be kept in mind in regard to Girkin-Strelkov's claims about both Crimea and Donbass that he has an interest in inflating his role. He appears to have larger political ambitions and may suffer from delusions of grandeur inspired by his monarchism and life as a participant in reenactments of tsarist-era military battles. He may have been trying to bring these adventure fantasies to life when he left for Crimea and later Donbass, where indeed he would play a major role in the civil war.

A more central actor in Crimea—clearly an official Moscow operative with hitherto different functions—was Oleg Yevgenevich Belaventsev, who was on the peninsula from at least February 26. He was the general director of the Slavyanka open joint-stock company that is part of the Russian Defense Ministry's OboronServis (Defense Services), which provides various logistical and other services to the Russian military and came under scrutiny in the infamous corruption case involving Yevgeniya Vasillieva and then former Defense Minister Anatolii Serdyukov. Belaventsev was the third secretary for science and technologies in the Soviet embassy in London before being expelled from the UK for espionage in 1985. Some reports hold that he worked in Germany, meaning he might have become acquainted with Putin there, especially as his specialization coincides with reports that part of Putin's work in Dresden included technology espionage. Belaventsev is reportedly one of Russian Defense Minister Sergei Shoigu's close associates. In Crimea, Belaventsev was charged to deal with "security" issues for the Black Sea Fleet. With a large Ukrainian military contingent also stationed in Crimea, the crisis raised the risk of clashes between Black Sea Fleet and Ukrainian servicemen. But as the crisis peaked, Belaventsev appears to have shifted from logistical and security functions to military-political issues. Specifically, he became "the person chiefly responsible for the operation in Crimea, acting also as a kind of messenger between the local elites and Moscow," according to Galimova's Kremlin and Crimean sources.[39] Belaventsev seemingly was rewarded for his work. Putin appointed him the presidential plenipotentiary for the new federal district created after Crimea's reunification with Russia.

At 4:30 a.m. on February 27, the infamous unknown but armed "polite little green men" calmly but deliberately took control of the Crimean Supreme Soviet and Council of Ministers buildings and eventually tens of strategic objects on the peninsula. They began patrolling the streets of Simferopol and soon other cities on the peninsula. Putin's initial denial and later acknowledgment that the well-armed, purposeful but polite little green men were Russian special forces dealt the first blow delivered to Western trust in Putin over Crimea. When the first deputies arrived at the Supreme Soviet after speaker Kostantinov summoned them, they were met by Belaventsev before they began work. Crimean Supreme Soviet deputy Tsekov told Galimova that Belaventsev and Konstantinov "were working with Moscow."[40]

Many deputies hesitated to attend the session, fearing a backlash from Kiev or other risks given the deteriorating situation on the streets. This put gathering a quorum in doubt. Deputies were encouraged by telephone or "non-parliamentary methods," including the dispatch of groups of Cossacks or people in Cossack uniforms urging many to attend.[41] As noted above, Girkin-Strelkov confirms that the deputies had to be rounded up by groups of "guardsmen" of the kind he led in order to get them to the hall for the vote. Eventually, 53 of the soviet's 100 deputies attended and called for reunification with Russia, declared a referendum on the issue, and appointed a new prime minister.

One of the signs that Moscow was largely operating on the fly was its lack of political preparation, according to Galimova's investigation. In replacing Yanukovich's appointee as Crimean prime minister, Anatoliy Mohilov, Belaventsev first approached the pro–Russian communist leader Leonid Grach (Hrach) on February 26. Grach was the leader of the Crimean-Russian reunification movement in the 1990s and a strong defender of the Black Sea Fleet's presence on the peninsula. Thus, when Grach was offered the post, Belaventsev was accompanied by a pair of Black Sea Fleet admirals. Grach was put on a "special" telephone line—but refuses to say with whom—and told: "[W]e are going to regain Crimea." The person on the other end of the line then proposed Grach head Crimea's government. Grach replied: "Yes, I agree to everything. But will you be able [to regain Crimea]?" His interlocutor said: "Without a shadow of a doubt." According to Galimova's account, Grach's related phrase "we are going to regain Crimea" of his interlocutor preceded and matched that used by Putin in the documentary on Crimea's reunification *Return to the Motherland*, aired on the anniversary of the March 16 referendum.[42]

Contrary to Belaventsev's and presumably Moscow's preference, Konstantinov and other deputies opposed Grach's candidacy. This forced the Kremlin to switch horses in favor of Aksyonov, which suggests they "lacked a clear-cut plan prepared in advance," according to Galimova. Belaventsev was at Aksyonov's side assisting in his efforts to separate the Russians and Tatars on February 26 and, according to an unidentified Russian politician in Crimea at the time, was impressed by Aksyonov's "resolute show." Yet, according to a source of *Gazeta.ru*'s Galimova, Belaventsev and Aksyonov had been acquainted and "friendly" well before the Crimean events. The same source said that they then began to inform Moscow that it should support Aksyonov to head the council of ministers, rather than Grach. Moscow originally opposed Aksyonov, nicknamed the "Goblin," because of his rumored ties to organized crime, which had prompted the initial support for Grach. After Moscow was convinced, it then had to fight for Aksyonov's victory for some five hours, since "three or four" parliament deputies continued to oppose him, depriving him of the 51 votes necessary for approval. Eventually, 53 deputies voted for Aksyonov.[43]

Aksyonov took charge of the Ukrainian armed forces on Crimea, ordering them to ignore all orders from Kiev, and re-established the anti-riot Berkut force under his command, drawing many to Crimea, where they were treated as heroes by the local population. Simultaneously, Aksyonov issued an appeal to Putin for security assistance for maintaining order on the peninsula, and Russia began issuing Berkut officers with Russian passports, augmenting the force of special forces or "little green men."[44]

Annexation and Reunification

In moving towards secession, Crimea adopted the model which Russia's majority Tatar Muslim republic of Tatarstan used to establish broad autonomy from Moscow in

1992–2003 and which Putin gradually stripped from Tatarstan in 2003–2011.[45] An early draft of the Crimean referendum question read: "The Autonomous Republic of Crimea possesses state independence and is incorporated in Ukraine on the basis of treaties and agreements (yes/no)." A similar phrase was included in the 1992 Crimean constitution. One of Galimova's sources claims that this was done "exclusively" by Simferopol without consulting Moscow, and Konstantinov claims this was so even when the decision was taken to insert the phrase "the annexation of Crimea." But the same source also notes that at a certain point Konstantinov was connected by phone to Putin and "only after this" was the referendum issue submitted to the Crimean Supreme Soviet for approval. The Tatar model was also invoked when, instead of immediate reunification or annexation, Konstantinov envisaged an interim step after the referendum that would include first a treaty with Moscow that established Crimea's connection to the Russian state rather than Ukraine. This would have supported, in Konstantinov's words, "a soft transition to statehood, without violating international norms." In addition, deputies demanded "guarantees" from Moscow before the vote, again in fear of aggressive measures by Kiev should deployment of little green men not hold.[46]

Given the recent experience with the overthrow of the February 21 agreement in Kiev after he had convinced Yanukovich to sign and abide by it, it is unlikely that Putin would have supported such a delay—better to establish quickly a *fait accompli* and avoid the risk of revanche. Similarly, the strength of Putin's commitment to enforce Moscow's new dominion over Crimea must have been exceedingly strong, convincing the deputies. This is suggested by Putin's claim in the aforementioned documentary on the Crimean annexation that he was "ready to consider" deploying nuclear forces in the event of any foreign moves against the new order in Crimea.[47] Thus, it appears the timing and wording were subject to Putin's consideration before official action.

Galimova's investigation also suggests that Putin's resolve or support within the elite might not have been as written in stone as Putin has portrayed in the documentary film and other comments after the fact. She notes that there was a one-week delay both in the appearance of Crimea's wording about "annexation" and in the Russian Duma's approval of amendments drafted in the Kremlin to then existing Russian law in order to allow a foreign territory's unification with Russia without an agreement from the state from which it is separating or seceding if the territory's population votes in a referendum to unify with Russia. This, she suggests, shows that "Moscow was not giving a definitive signal" it was prepared to annex Crimea. Her sources also claim that there was "no unity at the top on what to do with the peninsula" and that at "one of Vice Premier Dmitrii Rogozin's closed meetings in Sevastopol" *in May*, "the supporters of annexing Crimea were in the minority." Thus, according to Galimova, the purpose of Mironov's draft bill was to show the West and Kiev what Moscow was ready to do not what it necessarily at all costs intended to do. Russia retained two options: (1) Crimea would be part of Ukraine in form but independent in practice, or (2) Russia would annex Crimea and reunify with it.[48] Perhaps more importantly, the existing requirement of a Russian agreement with the state from which a territory seeking unification with Russia is separating also enforces the view that Moscow had no intent to incorporate Crimea before the events of February 2014.

On March 1, the Federation Council backed a resolution allowing the Russian president to send a limited troop contingent into Ukraine, and polite little green men began popping up at strategic points in Crimea and patrolling Simferopol's streets. The Crimean

Supreme Soviet approved the referendum with new wording providing for Russia's annexation of Crimea on March 6. The referendum's final wording—"Do you favour the reunification of Crimea with Russia with the rights of a subject (region) of the Russian
Federation?"—was approved "at the highest level" on the night of March 5–6, and the
Russian president guaranteed the Crimean deputies, according to one of Galimova's
sources, that "there would be no Transdniester region scenario, in which a referendum
on unification with Russia was held in Moldova's Transdniester region in 2006, but Russia
never incorporated the region." According to the same source, from the moment the referendum was announced, nothing was decided in the Crimean Supreme Soviet "without
a telephone call from above." However, Konstantinov says that Russia's follow-through
on annexation was still an open question. He claims the referendum's wording was not
agreed with Moscow, and after its approval he remained uncertain whether or not Russia
would change its mind at the last moment. On March 5 he concluded that "all the risks
were being assessed up above and there would be no final decision."[49]

On March 6, the Crimean Supreme Council went ahead and officially approved the
referendum's wording and date, moving the latter forward from March 30 to March 16.[50]
Immediately following the vote, four members of the Crimean parliament's presidium—
Tsekov, Volodimir Klychnikov, Kostantin Bakharev, and chairman Konstantinov—were
flown under Mi-8 helicopter escort from Kacha Airfield near Sevastopol to Anapa,
Krasnodar, in Russia, from where a Black Sea Fleet aircraft flew them to Sochi airport
and then the Russian president's Bocharov Ruchei residence. Only Konstantinov was
granted an audience with Putin, and he showed the Russian president the Supreme Soviet's
resolution. On March 7, all four presidium members flew to Moscow, where they participated in a "People's Gathering for a Fraternal People" held under the watch of the
Kremlin walls on Vasilevskii Spusk.

The Referendum

On March 16, reunification with Russia was approved by 96.77 percent of Crimean
voters and 95.6 percent in Sevastopol, and the Crimean Supreme Soviet declared the
republic an independent state. The next day, Putin signed the treaty incorporating Crimea
and Sevastopol as the two newest subjects of the Russian Federation at a large ceremony
in the Kremlin attended by both houses of Russia's Federal Assembly and numerous other
officials and members of the Russian elite. There is some controversy surrounding the
circumstances and results of the referendum. There is no doubt that the referendum was
organized hastily and included an all-too-brief campaign period in which arguments for
and against could be assessed in a dispassionate manner by the population. However, the
circumstances of an ongoing revolution and the threat of civil war hanging over the country made anything akin to a normal campaign period risky if not impossible if the referendum was to take place. Some argue that the referendum was not held in accordance
with international standards. This is a valid point, since the number of objective international observers and their access to the electoral process was limited. The circumstances—specifically, the presence of Russian troops—is less problematic, since the
majority ethnic Russian population (59 percent) supported and supports the Russian
military. Crimean Tatars, comprising 13 percent of the population, and some among the
often Russian-speaking ethnic Ukrainian population on the peninsula (22 percent) would
have had some objection to, and therefore might be intimidated in their voting by, the

Russian military presence. However, this would have affected the voting results only at the margins, and the same could be said of elections, for example, in Iraq and Afghanistan, which were internationally recognized as free and fair. In those cases and others, the American and European occupation troops—no matter how benign—were a substantially alien force and thus must have intimidated some elements within the population.

Some have argued that the Crimean referendum's results were falsified. Political culture across the post–Soviet space, with the possible exception of the Baltic states, is such that some falsification beyond the level extant in the West is typical in almost all elections held in the former Soviet Union, including Russia as well as Ukraine. That said, almost all public opinion surveys and polling show that the overwhelming majority of Crimeans have long been pro–Russian and anti–Ukrainian and supported Crimea's secession from Ukraine and reunification with Russia. In 2008, for example, Ukraine's Razumkov Center, which in 2004 received the "Non-Governmental Organization of the Year in Central and Eastern Europe" award at an international economic forum held in Poland, found that 63.8 percent of Crimeans (75.9 percent of Russians, 55.2 percent of Ukrainians, and 13.8 percent of Crimean Tatars, respectively) preferred Crimea's secession from Ukraine and reunification with Russia.[51] In March 2011, the Razumkov Center found that public opinion in Crimea supported the Black Sea Fleet's basing at Sevastopol, with 75 percent of Crimea's residents saying the presence bolstered security in the region. Interestingly, Ukrainian experts replied nearly the mirror opposite, but at the same time placed geopolitical competition in the Black Sea region between various countries at the top of the list of security threats facing the region and Crimea.[52]

During the pro–Russian Yanukovich era, the desire for separation from Ukraine declined in Crimea. A Gallup poll from May 2013—several months before the Ukraine crisis began—found that only 23 percent preferred secession compared with 33 percent in October 2011, while a majority, 53 percent, wanted the existing autonomy within Ukraine, up from 49 percent in 2012.[53] At the same time, Crimean sentiment was distinctly pro–Russia and pro–Eurasian Economic Union, with 68 percent expressing a "warm" attitude towards Russia, 14 percent for the EU, 13 percent for Turkey, 10 percent for Poland, 6 percent for the U.S. At the same time, 53 percent expressed support for joining the Russia-Belarus-Kazakhstan Customs Union, as opposed to only 17 percent favoring the European Union.[54] Therefore, the Crimean respondents must have been satisfied with what they perceived as good relations between Kiev and Moscow at the time, with 4 percent regarding them as "friendly," 15 percent "good neighbor," 23 percent "quite warm," and 34 percent "neutral." Negative assessments had declined by slightly more than half from October 2011.[55]

The revolutionary situation across the country, the rise of anti–Russian neofascists, and the anti–Russian language amendments adopted the day after the seizure of power and then repealed under Western pressure naturally would increase the numbers among ethnic Russians and Russian-speaking Ukrainians on the peninsula from those presented above. The same dynamic has been present since the *perestroika* era and the Soviet collapse. In 1992, visits by Rada deputies from the members of Ukrainian ultranationalist groups like UNA-UNSO sparked a wave of petition-gathering by Crimeans for holding a referendum on the peninsula's status.[56]

By spring 2014, with the crisis ongoing already for months, Crimean opinion had changed radically. One week before the referendum, the Crimean Institute of Political and Social Research found that 77 percent of respondents planned to vote for reunification with Russia, and 97 percent assessed the current situation in Ukraine as negative.[57] A Pew poll conducted after the referendum showed that 88 percent of Crimeans thought Kiev should recognize the referendum's results. Only 2 percent of Crimeans thought Kiev should not recognize the referendum, and 8 percent did not know. At the same time, 54 percent favored the right of regions to secede from Ukraine, while only 12 percent opposed this and 34 percent did not know.[58] An April 2014 Gallup survey showed that an overwhelming majority of Crimeans regarded the referendum as reflecting the will of Crimean residents: 82.8 percent agreed with this assessment, and 6.7 percent disagreed. Among ethnic Russians, the figures were 93.6 and 1.7 percent; among ethnic Ukrainians, 68.4 and 14.5, respectively. The same survey also showed that 71.3 percent of Crimeans viewed Russia's role in the Ukrainian crisis as "mostly positive." Only 8.8 percent saw it as "mostly negative," and 4 percent as neutral. The figures for the U.S. were, respectively, 2.8 percent, 76. 2 percent, and 6.9 percent.[59] When one adds the likelihood that significant numbers of the anti–Russian ethnic Ukrainians and many Tatars may have sat out the referendum or were in the process of leaving the peninsula, it remains nevertheless clear that the referendum's results appear to have been falsified only very slightly, if at all, and had no bearing on the outcome.

Alternative Course?

It appears that there may have been other options available to Putin that might have been just as effective in securing Crimea for the Black Sea Fleet and protecting it from a NATO takeover and/or neofascist adventurers from Kiev. The latter was a real possibility. On February 26, as dramatic events discussed below unfolded in Crimea, the editor of a local newspaper in nationalist western Ukraine's Lviv (Lvov) feared that weapons seized by radical nationalists when they mobbed MVD and other government buildings in Lviv earlier in the month and were used in Kiev to overthrow Yanukovich might have "traveled to Crimea."[60]

One might be called the Transdniestrian option, in which Crimea held the referendum on reunification with Russia, but Russia refrained from incorporating the region and instead came forward as the region's guarantor of security from other forces. This option could have included an appeal to the international community. Under this scenario, Putin could have deployed Russian troops across the peninsula in greater numbers and depth, and then appealed to the UN to guarantee or enforce Kiev's compliance with the February 21 agreement. This would have put the three Western permanent UN Security Council members on the spot, forcing them to either pressure Kiev to restore Yanukovich and follow through on the regime transformation by pacted transition envisaged in the Kiev agreement, or openly come out as active and overt supporters for the agreement's violators and another "color revolution."

A second option was the Abkhaziyan–South Ossetiyan scenario, which in theory could have followed the Transdniestr option, should the UN and/or the West have refused to enforce the Kiev agreement. Under this option Crimea would have held a referendum on independence, which could have been recognized by Moscow. Russia would then come forward as the guarantor of Crimea's independence until such time as it was possible to roll back the decision to integrate it back into Ukraine, albeit unlikely, or reunify it with Russia. Here, a key question would have been what to do with the Ukrainian military units in Crimea. As indeed happened, they would be blockaded and, demoralized as they were, would have been given secure passage out of Crimea or the option of taking an oath to Russia, as in fact occurred.

Third, Putin could have delivered a major address to issue warnings and publicly lobbied the West, G8, the UN and the OSCE to undertake specific measures to protect all Ukrainian citizens from the radical elements within Maidan. President Putin himself has insisted repeatedly over the years that the U.S. and the West run roughshod over UN principles of the sovereignty and territorial integrity of states in the international system, pointing to Kosovo, Libya, and most recently in Syria. To back this up, he could have placed the Black Sea Fleet's troops on a heightened state of alert and issued a public warning that if radical nationalists moved to the east and south in numbers, then Russia would mobilize additional forces to the base, and if necessary take action to defend Crimeans from Ukraine's ultranationalist elements. Putting the threat to use force and deploy forces is always preferable to immediate escalation to deployment, which risks exacerbating the situation rather than containing it. In addition, he could have engaged moderate elements in the new Ukrainian regime in order to pressure them to isolate the extremists while holding back as an incentive the next tranche of the total $13 billion bailout assistance which Russia offered Ukraine before the Kiev revolt and Ukraine's bankrupt economy needed so desperately.

Putin's Calculus in Acting

Although the nature of Putin's intervention in Crimea can and should be criticized, there were solid arguments for a Russian intervention in the crisis and especially in Crimea. As Russians and pro–Russian Crimeans point out, the more complex and longer scenarios mentioned above might have allowed a conflict to develop between the Russian and Ukrainian forces or citizens on the peninsula. Russian and Russian Crimean leaders argued that quick seizure of parliament and ultimately the occupation and reunification were necessary to prevent large-scale violence either on the part of Kiev, Right Sector, and other neofascist groups to put down Crimea's Russian uprising or between Russian and Ukrainian soldiers on the peninsula. A Crimean Tatar leader also saw the risk of violence but argued naturally that it would have come from the Russian side if not for the Tatars leaving parliament square on February 26.[61]

In December 2013, Putin himself was rejecting any military intervention in Crimea. At his annual marathon press conference on December 19, in an answer to a journalist's question on whether it was appropriate to intervene militarily in Crimea as Russia had in South Ossetiya in August 2008, Putin responded:

> To compare the situation in Crimea with the situation in South Ossetiya and Abkhaziya is incorrect. There is nothing like that going on. The territories [Abkhaziya and South Ossetiya] declared their independence, and there was a large-scale, bloody interethnic conflict. And this was not the first such conflict, if you recall the situation in 1919–1921 when punitive expeditions were carried out in connection with the fact that after the collapse of the Russian Empire these territories declared they wanted to remain part of Russia and not Georgia. In Crimea there is nothing like this and, I hope, there will not be. We have a treaty on the presence of our fleet there. The presence of the Russian fleet there is a stabilizing factor of both international and regional politics.[62]

However, his description of the conditions that would perhaps justify intervention actually foreshadowed developments in Crimea: "bloody interethnic conflict" (if not "large-scale"), a declaration of independence, even a desire to be part of Russia and not another state.

The risks of the deployment of the little green men were also high, however. The tense standoff with Ukrainian troops after Russia's little green men surrounded Ukraine's Belbek air force base on March 3 seemed to risk an all-out Russian-Ukrainian war. Russian soldiers fired over the heads of several hundred unarmed Ukrainian soldiers marching towards the Russians behind their commander holding the Ukrainian and Soviet flags. The Russian commander ordered his forces to stand down, and the Ukrainian commander asked: "You wouldn't shoot the Soviet flag, would you?" Talks ensued and the Ukrainians dispersed for a soccer match on the spot before marching back to their barracks. Those two commanders perhaps did more to avert war than anyone else involved in the conflict on what could have been a very fateful day.[63] Interestingly, one Ukrainian soldier screamed out to the Russians as they drew near: "America is with us!"[64] At the February 28 National Security and Defense Council meeting mentioned previously, council chairman and Ukraine's acting president Turchynov proposed instituting martial law, mobilizing the military and moving troops to the border with Crimea, but he was the only council member to vote in favor of the decision.[65] Nevertheless, by March 8 some Ukrainian troops appeared to begin deploying in limited force towards the Crimean border to the cheers of members of Right Sector along the way.[66] To this risk one could add that of RS elements infiltrating Crimea and sparking conflict and/or potential Russian-Tatar internecine violence. So while Putin's actions risked conflict, the possibility cannot be excluded that Putin's quick response left less opportunity for escalation of the confrontation than otherwise might have been the case. Moreover, however coercive, the deployment and ultimately the entire annexation process involved little violence. One person was killed by an unknown sniper, and another was shot after attacking a Russian soldier when troops searched his house.

Putin's main motivation in moving on Crimea was political: mitigating "the loss of Ukraine" or even attempting to snatch victory from the jaws of defeat. This worked on two levels: the domestic and the international. Domestically, he could not afford to incur the damage to his authority that the "loss of Ukraine" would impart. Both conservatives and ultranationalists would have been especially outraged by the defeat at the hands of the West; many democrats and communists too. Internationally, the geostrategic blow would have been most severe. Ukraine is the most important neighboring country for Russia, given a thick web of historical, cultural, economic, and political ties supplemented by Ukraine's central geostrategic significance for Russian national security. Most fundamentally, Moscow's failure to have its say there would have exposed it as incapable of defending its interests anywhere, despite its show of force when similarly challenged on its border with Georgia six years earlier. In many ways, Putin's political-military response was similar to that at the time.

But given the deep historical, cultural, economic, political and geostrategic significance to Moscow of Ukraine compared to Georgia made some active response imperative. No Russian leader could survive and few Russian citizens would relish even the prospect of a NATO foothold in Ukraine. One of the strands in the discourse on the impending geostrategic humiliation in Ukraine perceived by Russians was the spectre of Sevastopol—fought for and won by Russia several times over the centuries—in NATO hands, with Americans and Europeans using the former Black Sea Fleet port. Here the Turkish factor was not far under the surface, which was imbedded in the NATO threat by virtue of

Ankara's membership in the alliance. Responding to a statement by Turkish Premier Tayip Erdogan's assertion that Kosovo basically was part of Turkey, State Duma International Affairs Committee Chairman Aleksei Pushkov quipped, sounding like a Western critic of Russian policy: "Kosovo is Turkey. A little more and we will hear that Crimea is also Turkey. Forward to the past? Back to the Ottoman Empire?" This was in early November 2013, before the Ukraine crisis.[67]

In an interview for the Russian-made documentary *President*, shown on the anniversary of Putin's first inauguration 15 years earlier, Putin seemed a little confused or at least driven by a series of motives. He said the most important factor in is decision-making process was whether the inhabitants wished Crimea's return to Russia, which he tied to the immediate neofascist threat posed by the radicals who led the revolutionary seizure of power in Kiev. Connected to this is reference to the "historical justice" of having Crimea return to the Russian state. He also implied the geostrategic motive—the "strategic importance in the Black Sea region," which he logically would associate with the Black Sea Fleet naval base. The entire quote reads as follows:

> The most important thing for us was to understand what the people living in Crimea wanted. What did they want? Did they want to remain in Ukraine or did they want to be with Russia? If the people want to return to Russia and do not want to be governed by neo–Nazis, radical nationalists and Banderites, we have no right to abandon them. This is an absolute matter of principle. This is what I told my partners then. I told them that for us it was an essential matter, the people. I do not know what interests you will protect, but we, as we defend ours, will go all the way. And this is an extremely important thing. Not because we want to bite something off, to snatch it. And not even because Crimea is of strategic importance in the Black Sea region. But because it is an element of historical justice. I believe that we did the right thing, and I do not regret anything.[68]

It seems reasonable to conclude that all of these factors—NATO expansion to Ukraine, loss of the Black Sea Fleet base, the threat of Ukrainian ultranationalist violence against Russians in Crimea, and an opportunity to "restore historical justice"—shaped Putin's decision.

The Escalatory Consequences of the Crimean Gambit

There can be no doubt that however unjustified Crimea's separation from Russia had been, and however nonviolent (though still coercive) Russia's occupation and annexation/reunification of Crimea was, Putin's move was a major escalation of the Ukraine crisis and the geopolitical struggle that helped create it. This is true regardless of the geopolitical and Maidan backstory. Putin argued that Maidan posed the risk of civil war and violence against ethnic Russians in Crimea and elsewhere in Ukraine, and if the latter in fact had occurred he would have had justification in acting perhaps as he did. But Putin's overly robust move into Crimea was as destabilizing as was the Maidan revolt in this regard, as elements in Donbass and elsewhere felt emboldened to attempt a repeat of the Crimean events in their regions. Thus, radical elements in eastern and western Ukraine moved to escalate from mere opposition to the new Maidan regime to efforts to openly resist and overthrow its local minions. In this way, Putin's Crimean gambit deepened Ukraine's postrevolutionary stateness crisis, contributing to the likelihood of secession, civil war, and overreaction in Kiev—all of which were already stirring as a result of the new Maidan regime's first legislative action.

By seizing Crimea, Putin also intensified the international geostrategic component of the crisis. The West's post–Cold War policy of NATO expansion without Russia is to blame in good part for the failure of Europe and Ukraine to become whole, but that cannot justify Putin's aggressive move. Putin's Crimean gambit and aspects of its implementation created a host of additional problems on the international level. It moved the conflict further into the international sphere and would have enormous consequences for international security, politics and economics in Russia, the West, and Eurasia for years to come. In addition, it marked another blow to the principles of state sovereignty in international law, which Putin traditionally trumpeted as the cornerstone of Russian domestic and foreign policy. Instead of the more carefully calibrated carrot-and-stick approaches outlined above, President Putin leapt over several interim stages of political and military escalation, choosing immediately, if stealthily, to violate the sovereignty of a neighboring state in the heart of Europe. Russia's direct involvement in forming the new government in Crimea and then annexing the peninsula amounted to no less interference in the internal affairs of another country than that the West routinely undertook in building "dual use" opposition movements and then backing their "color revolutions" in Kiev and elsewhere.

Instead of using the crisis to expose Washington's NATO overreach and domination of Europe, Putin himself overreached in Europe, and in more grave a fashion than NATO ever had. Putin's countermove in fact strengthened Washington's and to some extent also Europe's impulse to expand NATO to Ukraine, further polarizing Western-Russian relations. Putin's actions somewhat understandably raised fears, however unwarranted, and allowed speculation by self-interested parties on the theme that as-yet unclear ambitions and a geostrategic master plan lay behind his Crimean gambit. The immediate concern was that he was using the crisis not just to right a historical injustice in Crimea or take revenge for Kiev, but that he might use the crisis as an opportunity to lop off parts of eastern Ukraine and other parts of the south in order to mitigate his "loss of Ukraine" in the eyes of Russian hawks. Others made absurd claims about Moscow having its eyes on Europe, even as far as Scotland.

Putin's Crimea gambit, as such, rendered Kiev and the West even more distrustful, even paranoid regarding Putin's real intentions than otherwise might have been. Moreover, in order to cover for military and political operations, Putin made clearly false statements to the entire world community. Putin appears to have lied or gone back on his word when he said at a news conference on March 4 that Russia was not considering annexation of Crimea and "would not provoke such sentiments or such a decision." However, he qualified this by saying that "no one has yet abolished the right of nations to self-determination." Work on legalizing the peninsula's annexation already may have been underway or started right after the news conference. According to Galimova's sources—people who directly or indirectly took part in the process—the work on the new wording began roughly on March 3–4. Moreover, Putin was "personally coordinating" round-the-clock conferences, one of Galimova's sources in Russian officialdom reports, and people with legal expertise from Putin's presidential administration were assisting the Crimeans to develop a formula that would legitimize annexation under international law.[69] Regardless of whether by that date Putin had already made his final decision to move ahead with Crimea's annexation or not, when the annexation went ahead, he at a minimum had gone back on his word to the world that there would be none. Even more unsettling was Putin's claim that the "polite green men" occupying the peninsula were not Russian military. This could only deepen Ukrainian and Western fears about Putin's reliability and intentions. Was he losing control himself and did not care if he was seen as lying? In that case, how far would he go in taking revenge for the Kiev putsch?

The spiraling out of control of the Maidan revolution, and now the Russian-Western struggle over Ukraine, is the early 21st century's version of the assassination of Austria's Archduke Ferdinand by a Bosnian separatist. The latter sparked rash military responses and multiple military mobilizations that almost inadvertently but inexorably brought on World War I. Since NATO rules do not allow a country to join the alliance if it has sovereignty or self-determination disputes, Putin's occupation of Crimea and support for ethnic Russians' separatism in Donbass effectively blocks Kiev's NATO aspirations. Therefore, NATO is responding by basing more troops in Eastern Europe in violation of assurances Brussels gave Moscow under NATO-Russian agreements. Yet internal conflicts are almost never resolved when outside actors are backing opposite sides in the dispute and perceive they have a vital interest in the outcome.

For its part, the West should have foreseen such a turn of events in Crimea. It should have been obvious to any analyst, if not policymakers as well, that if the West backed the illegal seizure of power in Kiev in violation of an agreement with Moscow and cemented by Putin personally, then Putin would seek to redress the loss, and a, if not *the* most likely target would Crimea. Perhaps the signature foreign policy move undertaken throughout the course of Putin's leadership was the decision to confront Western-backed Georgia's attempts to reintegrate its breakaway regions through the use of force in August 2008. Putin had shown a willingness to stand up to such a perceived transgression and respond with robust military and political countermoves. Why would he be expected to sit by and accept a major strategic blow in Ukraine which was much more central to Moscow in its perceived strategic, security, political, economic, and cultural interests?

In rapidly annexing Crimea, Putin went a bridge too far, escalating the Ukrainian crisis. In doing so, he scuttled whatever trust in Russia that remained in the West as relations deteriorated during the Obama "reset." On the other hand, the West's hubristic post–Cold War policies in relation to Russia, Ukraine and the former USSR, the geostrategic loss that Crimea's control by an anti–Russian Maidan regime would have entailed, and the dangerous and threatening elements within the Maidan revolutionary government clearly required a prompt and robust response. Under such circumstances, good policy options are limited and rarely discovered, much less chosen.

But just as the West's major role in the making of the original crisis and its decision to back the violation of the February 21 agreement with Moscow provoked and are partially to blame for Putin's response in Crimea, then so too Putin, by his decision to annex Crimea, bears considerable responsibility for the next escalation of the crisis that would occur this time in the Donbass.

9

Terror in Donbass
Putin's War or Civil War?

Introduction

The war in Ukraine is regarded by the Maidan regime and the West as "Putin's war"—a war provoked entirely by Russian incitement and invasion. The U.S. government has played up the "Putin's war" narrative. In a statement commemorating the second anniversary of the Maidan revolt's ouster of Yanukovich, American ambassador Geoffrey Pyatt, who helped manufacture the Maidan revolt, endeavored to blame the Maidan regime's failure to rid Ukraine of oligarchy, cronyism, and kleptocracy on "Kremlin-manufactured conflict in the East."[1] In this view, the opposition to the Maidan's seizure of power was minimal and largely artificial, inspired by outside agitators, guerrilla fighters, and Russian intelligence and military personnel intervention. In this view, neither does the Donbass population support the Donbass resistance fighters and their political project, nor are those resistance fighters largely from the Donbass. In this view, the noted Girkin-Strelkov and several other Russia-dispatched acting Russian intelligence and military operatives started the war and were only able to sustain it by virtue of Moscow's direct intervention, including the supply of regular Russian troops, weapons, and ammunition.

For its part, Russia and the Donbass fighters have insisted the war was not their choice but rather Kiev's. In their view, they are freedom fighters, or at least fighters for regional autonomy and against the threat of neofascism emanating from the radicals within Maidan. In this view, Donbass's Donetsk Peoples's Republic (DNR) and Luhansk (Lugansk) People's Republic (LNR) are popularly rooted and legitimate, and any official and unofficial Russian assistance has not been crucial either for the start or continuation of the war. The evidence suggests that the Russian/Donbass view is closer to the truth, despite significant but restrained, targeted, and often belated support from both Moscow and ordinary Russians. Most fundamentally, the Russian military intervention clearly occurred after civil war was initiated by Kiev's hand.

The revolt in the Donbass emerged in January in the wake of the revolts that spread in western Ukraine as the Maidan protests in Kiev mounted in violence. These two dynamics intensified together. In a veritable reign of terror after the Maidan takeover, three sources and types of physical violence were employed by the new regime against anti–Maidan persons: (1) the "antiterrorist" operation (ATO) as carried out in Donbass by regular Ukrainian army troops using firearms and other standard military means; (2) the "antiterrorist" operation as carried out at the front by volunteer battalions dominated by ultranationalist and neofascist fighters also using firearms and many of the military means available to the regular army; and (3) "activists" or *titushki*-like thugs dispatched to the regions by the various ultranationalist and neofascist parties, especially RS, usually acting in the rear and without firearms. The latter two were the primary perpetrators of war crimes and human rights violations under the Maidan regime. The reign of intimidation, if not terror carried out across the rear was accompanied by a discourse of denigration, dehumanization, intolerance and hate encouraged by the new regime and robustly extant in society. As in Crimea, all this only intensified opposition in Donbass to the new Maidan regime and convinced many to adopt a stance of open resistance, even armed resistance, as the only way to preserve their culture, faith, family, and Russian/Soviet roots.

Kiev declared its ATO against Donbass's Donetsk and Luhanks Oblasts' resistance on April 14, 2014, and began operations the next day. Before that date there had been little organized armed violence against the Maidan regime from the Donbass, with the only serious exception the armed takeover of the MVD buildings in Slavyansk and Kramatorsk in Donetsk on April 12. But peaceful, political resistance to the Maidan revolt in eastern Ukraine began long before Grikin-Strelkov's arrival in Donetsk on that day. Now anti–Maidan elements in the Donbass moved to preempt the imminent attack from the east already signaled by Kiev's publicized plans to carry out an ATO. The only events to which Kiev's declaration of the ATO could have been a response—the peaceful anti–Maidan demonstrations followed by coercive mobs seizing several arms depots and OGAs in the region—were not legitimate *casae belli* for an all-out invasion of the region without negotiations. For comparative perspective, Chechen rebels seized the entire Republic of Chechnya in Russia's North Caucasus in the autumn of 1991, but Moscow negotiated with them for three years before undertaking its counter-terrorist operation (Kontr-Terror-isticheskaya Operatsiya, or KTO) in December 1994.

The Maidan in Power

The ultranationalists' leading role in forcing Yanukovich from power translated into key appointments in the postrevolutionary government. Five members of Tyahnybok's neofascist SP were appointed to head five ministries in the provisional government: Deputy Prime Minister Oleksandr Sych, Defense Minister Ihor Tenyukh, Prosecutor General Oleh Makhitskiy, Ecology and Natural Resources Minister Andrey Mokhnyk, and Agriculture Minister Ihor Shvayka. For his "organizational" efforts on the Maidan, radical nationalist Parubiy was given the key post of chairman of Ukraine's Security and National Defense Council. He would focus much of his activity on recruiting his "hundreds" and other ultranationalists and neofascists, like the RS and SP, into the Ukrainian army, the National Guard and volunteer battalions for the "antiterrorist" operation in the east. Another nationalist, Valentyn Nalyvaichenko, was appointed SBU director. Thus, ultranationalists and neofascists controlled the entire bloc of *siloviki* (military, security and law enforcement organs) offices. Moreover, the nationalist Arseniy Yatsenyuk was appointed prime minister. Yatsenyuk was a member of former president Yushchenko's nationalistic "Our Ukraine" bloc, which led the Orange revolution, and later joined Tymoshenko's Fatherland Party. Turchynov's cabinet was composed 90 percent of politicians from western and west-central Ukraine, disenfranchising the south and east.

Maidan Discourse: Vatniki, Kolorady, Moskaly

Residual revolutionary élan, the seemingly ubiquitous neofascists, and Putin's annexation of Crimea together created a highly charged atmosphere—a subculture of hate. It focused on ethnic Russians and pro–Russians, pro-autonomy or pro-secessionist Donbassians, or those from other regions. The Maidan's neofascist element intensified the everyday popular nationalism which infused western Ukraine and imparted to the immediate post-takeover period of the "revolution of dignity" a rather undignified tolerance of discrimination towards non–Maidan citizens. This oppressive atmosphere of intolerance and hatred aimed at the Donbass and its people manifested itself both in word and deed, the latter increasingly violent in nature. One intrepid Western journalist described this atmosphere and its pervasiveness:

> This is what I heard from respectable people in Kiev. Not from the nationalists, but from liberals, from professionals and journalists. All the bad people were in one place—why not kill them all? I asked Mishin and Bik if they'd known, when they declared independence, that it would lead to war. "If you pick up a gun, they'll come for you with guns," in the words of one anti–DNR resident of Donetsk. But Mishin and Bik, like every other DNR supporter to whom I put this question, said no. They were just trying to be heard. And they pointed out that even in early April, before Strelkov and his crew had taken Slovyansk and escalated the conflict, Ukrainian fighter jets would fly very low over the pro–Donbass protests held in Donetsk. From the very start, Kiev had been prepared to use force.[2]

Similarly, during the Maidan protests, representatives of the Ukrainian intelligentsia distributed a letter stating that southeastern Ukraine's inhabitants are "an undeveloped, lower sort of people" for whom "a kind of ghetto must be built" where they should live in accordance with their ways. Some historians specializing in the history of the Holocaust participated in the dissemination of the letter. One Ukrainian historian, Alexander Dyukov, asked them: "How can you spread such hate speeches? Hasn't the story of the Holocaust taught you anything? Because it also started with a hate speech." Dyukov received no answer, but offered another question: "How can a unified Ukraine be talked about and all of this hate speech simultaneously be spread?"[3]

Thus, the new regime, especially its ultranationalist and neofascist elements, would initiate a racist discourse to dehumanize the ethnic Russians and other pro–Russian elements in Donbass and across the country as they also proceeded to carry out a reign of intimidation in the ATO's rear and a reign of terror at the front. Usually without distinguishing between armed rebels, protesters demanding autonomy, or even the civilian population in Donbass, the Maidan regime began to characterize all these anti–Maidan elements as "potato beetles," "*vatniki*," "Moskaly," "subhumans," and "terrorists." The word "Kolorady" or potato beetles, a black and orange bug not unlike the American ladybug, was used to denigrate anti–Maidan elements, especially Donbassians, equating them with insects. It was a reaction to the widespread use of the black and orange striped St. George's ribbons (attached to some Russian military medals) that became a symbol of support for the Donbass rebels both in Ukraine and Russia. The Ukrainian journal *Korrespondent* of the popular Ukrainian newspaper and Web site *Vesti* noted: "Maidan and the ATO gave these terms as presents to Ukraine," and they were now part of the "new Ukrainian vocabulary." However, it defined the term narrowly as pertaining to the Donbass rebel fighters alone.[4]

Another derogatory term that gained broad use in public discussions and mass media was "*vatniki.*" Not directly or easily translated, it derives from the term *vatnaya kurtka*, which refers in both Ukrainian and Russian to a warm, cotton-padded jacket or short coat. The jacket came into use during the Tsarist period as warm wear for Russian soldiers and Caucasus Cossacks. A similar jacket was used in the Red Army and by prisoners in the USSR, including those of the Gulag. Thus, *vatnik* invokes the image of both the Soviet and Russian prisoners of the Gulag and connotes the idea that Russians are inherently inclined to subordination before authoritarian rule, in contrast to the ostensibly freedom-loving Galician Ukrainians. It is generally applied to those one wants to label as mindless Russian patriots and imperialists. A newspaper in the Ukrainian nationalist hotbed of Vinnitsa Oblast reviewed the ten most popular new terms which entered the vernacular in the "tense" year of 2014. Included was "*vatnik,*" which it defined as "a man with a Soviet mentality that does not understand why there is Ukraine, loves totalitarian power, hates the US and everything foreign." In this sense, the term is often applied to Donbassians and Crimeans. A derivative term, "*vyshyvatnik,*" describes Ukrainian "pseudopatriots," who "have their own opinion but blindly support the authorities." The paper added that the concept of *vatnik* "had become popular also among stars and politicians," reflecting its broad use in the state and other mass media.[5] The dehumanizing nature of the term and its use as a broad brush to desensitize Ukrainians for Kiev's use of force against those seeking autonomy or separation in the southeast, especially Crimea and Donbass, was reflected in a statement by a Ukrainian activist: "We need to raze to the ground the *vatniks*' refuge of Sevastopol.'"[6]

The term "Moskal" or "Muscovite"—a Ukrainian derogatory term for ethnic Russians and the mirror opposite of the Russians' derogatory term "*khokhol,*" meaning an ethnic Ukrainian—came into wide use as well. Use of this term originated and was especially widespread among the ultranationalists, but spread across society in the highly charged atmosphere of nationalistic revolution that was part and parcel of the Maidan takeover. Thus, the chant was organized at schools, holiday celebrations, and soccer games. During ultranationalists' and neofascists' demonstrations and marches—for example, those celebrating Bandera, the OUN and UPA—the chant "Moskaly on the knife" (*Moskaliv na nozhi*) is frequently heard.[7] Another widespread neofascist-derived demonstration and mass mobilization method is the so-called "Who Doesn't Jump Is a Moskal." Rally leaders organize a chant: "One nation, One country, One Fatherland! Hang the Muscovites! Whoever does not jump is a Moskal.'" The attendees are all then obliged to jump up and down in hysteric unison. Sometimes this method uses the "Russians on the knife" chant as well.[8] This is often used at rallies involving thousands of young people to indoctrinate them in an ideology of hate towards Russians, such as at an April 2014 "patriotic" rally for Ukrainian youth attended by several thousand teenagers in western Ukraine.[9] Some of the new terminology also began to be applied by pro–Maidan elements to ethnic Ukrainians who opposed the new order or refused to answer the military draft.

On April 29, two weeks after the beginning of the ATO, a journalist from the Ukrainian publication *Tyzhden*, Bogdan Butkevitch, during an interview on Western-funded Hromadske TV, proposed eliminating 1.5 million "extra people" in the Donetsk and Luhansk regions so the Maidan regime could make use of the regions' natural resources more easily: "The Donbass—is not just a depressed region. There's a wild amount of unwanted people there. I am absolutely and consciously talking about this. The Donetsk region has about 4 million inhabitants. At least 1.5 million are unnecessary. We do not need to understand the Donbass. We need to understand the Ukrainian national interest.

The Donbass must be used as a resource.... Concerning the Donbass—I don't have a recipe on how to do it quickly. However, there is something that must be done: there are people who just need to be killed."[10]

On the evening of June 17, prime-time television viewers in Ukraine were treated to another of the neofascist performances now part of the country's very fabric. Dmytro Korchynskiy, an ideologist of the Ukrainian far right, urged the Maidan regime to set up concentration camps for the Donbass's and Crimea's population and carry out a full ethnic cleansing and depopulation of the Donbass rebel regions and Crimea:

> Americans are our teachers of democracy. The USA is truly the most democratic country in the world today. All democratic institutions were preserved in America during WWII, such as elections, etc. Nevertheless, several million American citizens were deported to particular concentration camps—American citizens of Japanese ethnicity. In wartime they constituted a potential threat. The USA, having preserved the high level of humanism inside its own nation, carried out a nuclear strike upon Japan. They also bombed German cities. Eighty per cent of residential buildings in Germany were destroyed by Anglo-American air raids. The doctrine implied shelling of residential areas first and foremost in order to demoralize German soldiers at the front, etc. Thus, we also should have the highest level of freedom in Ukraine. We have too little freedom. We should have more freedom. Nevertheless, in the front-line zone and occupied territories we should act in the American way; that is, if we lost territories and cannot get them back, they must be lifeless. If they cannot be ours, they ought belong to no one.[11]

The dehumanizing discourse was not limited to mere opinion makers and cultural figures. On June 15, 2014, Ukraine's Prime Minister, Arsenii Yatsenyuk, referred to Donbass rebels and "those who sponsor them" as "non-humans" (*nelyudi*) prepared to come to all Ukrainians' homes and exterminate them in a statement posted on the Web site of the Ukrainian embassy in Washington and elsewhere.[12]

Of course, on the other side, Donbassians and Russians routinely referred to western Ukrainians and those who support the Maidan regime as "fascist," "Nazis," "Banderlogy" (derogatory for those who support Bandera and the OUN), and Maidowny (invoking people with Down's Syndrome). The Ukrainian conflict also gave birth to a new derogatory Russian term for Ukrainians—"ukrop," from the Russian word for "dill," which is said to deter potato beetles.[13] Putin's new Russian patriotism has sometimes encouraged a dangerous chauvinism, and those and more radical, opposition-oriented neofascists comprised a significant portion of the volunteer fighters who came from Russia to fight on the Donbass side. From the "Nashi" ("Ours") youth street gang-like pro–Kremlin youth movement of the early 2000s, to the tolerance of the Vladimir Zhirinovskii's Liberal Democratic Party, to the recent anti–American media campaigns and Putin's use of the term "national traitors" in his March 18 speech, Putinism has played a role—if inadvertent at times—in the rise of Russian ultranationalism in some circles, both in Russia and now among some in the eastern Ukrainian resistance movement. It is important to note, however, that Russian courts began to crack down severely on Russian ultranationalists beginning in 2008, and this pattern has continued in Russia during Putin's third term.

Anti-Semitism is also a factor in Donbass as it is in Maidan Ukraine. A recent article on the Russian Web site SVPress engaged in somewhat veiled anti–Semitism in reporting on an April 24, 2014, SS Waffen Galicia Corps' march in Lviv: "Yarosh gave a major press conference to local media at the 'Dnepro–Info' news agency which belongs to the present Dnepropetrovsk governor and president of the European Jewish Union, Igor Kolomoiskii. This co-founder of 'Private Bank' continues to pay $10,000 for each head of a 'separatist moskal.' Already eight Judases have been found, who sold their brothers to Kolomoiskii's mercenaries" (a reference to eight pro–Russian resistance men killed by the Ukrainian army in eastern Ukraine). In this Russian anti–Semitic response to a Ukrainian neofascist march, we see in microcosmic form how the "ultras" (ultranationalists) on both sides are feeding each other, driving events and helping to rapidly polarize Ukraine. But there should be no mistaking the greater level of xenophobic hysteria—including anti–Semitism, as I demonstrate in the next chapter—extant in Kiev and the western provinces of Galicia, as opposed to the Donbass. This rhetoric further alienated the Donbass population even before Kiev dispatched the Ukrainian army and neofascist-manned volunteer battalions to put down the rebellion it called a "Russian invasion."

The usually politically correct Western governments and media left Kiev's dehumanization campaign without criticism. To the contrary, Western politicians and pundits joined in the racist discourse. Alexander Motyl, a nationalist Ukrainian-American academic and frequent guest commentator on Ukraine for U.S. government media outlet Radio Free Europe/Radio Liberty (RFERL), called the people of the Donbass "the most retrograde part of [Ukraine's] population." Motyl made this remark in a RFERL interview on the benefits of partitioning Ukraine, and it was published just before the Maidan takeover of power.[14] This rings ironic in hindsight of the hysteria surrounding then former Polish Foreign Minister Sikorski's claims that Putin had stated "Ukraine is not a real state" and proposed to Polish President Tusk that Poland and Russia partition Ukraine. As Pietro Shkatian correctly notes, Motyl also "has attempted on more than one occasion to draw parallels between them [Donbass rebels] and white US southerners who supported Jim Crow."[15]

The Ukrainian nationalists' dehumanization campaign escalated to touch not just Russians in Ukraine but Russians and Russia as a whole, with Western political and opinion leaders driving the theme. As noted in previous chapters, the Ukraine-EU AA was characterized in quasi-, even pseudo–Huntingtonian terms by Western politicians and analysts as a "civilizational choice" for Ukrainians between a "civilized Europe" and a "barbaric, Asiatic and Mongoloid Russia." Now, as early as December 2013, Carl Bildt, Sweden's former foreign minister, former EU and UN envoy during the Yugoslav wars, and EU Eastern Partnership Program co-architect, seemed to be channeling the late Huntington. He tweeted that which many commentators were saying—that the growing conflict in Kiev was in fact "Eurasia versus Europe in the streets of Kiev."[16] In November 2014, now exiled former Georgian president Saakashvili was declaring from podiums in Kiev that Ukraine was defending Europe from a Russia that represented "a new Tatar-Mongol yoke."[17]

Maidan's "Reign of Intimidation"

With revolutionary élan still high, the three most prominent ultranationalist/neofascist parties—Svoboda, RS, and the Radical Party (RP) of the rising dark horse in Ukrainian radical politics, Oleh Lyashko—began a reign of intimidation and sometimes terror both at the front and in the rear of the ATO. They initiated this reign of terror before the Maidan government's declaration of the ATO and did so under the Maidan regime's protection. Alexander Dyukov, professor of history and coordinator for the EU-based International Group for Crimes Against the Person, gave a good overall summation of the repressive atmosphere emerging in Maidan Ukraine under the neofascists' intimidation campaign and violent attacks:

Ukraine is now consistently being transformed into an anti-democratic state. We see the pressure of censorship; an independent press de facto no longer exists. We see the consistent persecution of political opponents, both at the state level, for example, in the dissolution of the Communist Party faction in parliament and the persecution of the association "Borotba," and at the unofficial level, when the representatives of the opposition forces are subjected to attacks by various militants who burn their houses, occupy their offices, issue threats and so on. In normal countries the like is impossible. But here it is happening with the state's connivance. An atmosphere of spymania reigns in the Ukrainian society, and it even permissible to call those who protest against the deterioration of the social situation and the war in the southeast Putin's agents and send the SBU to arrest them.[18]

Indeed, beatings of former Yanukovich government officials and members and Rada deputies of the Communist Party, Socialist Party, and especially the former ruling Party of the Regions were commonplace. Humiliation was also employed, as RS and SP hooligans dumped tens of officials in garbage containers across the country. On April 7, 2014, Right Sector activists in Kiev stormed the Supreme Court building and ejected and humiliated its judges.[19]

In the immediate aftermath of the Maidan takeover, RS "activists" and some other ultranationalist parties' thugs began to fan out across the country, attempting to spread revolutionary chaos, including or perhaps especially to pro-autonomy, pro–Russian regions. This was coordinated with the new regime's *siloviki*. In mid–March the Maidan MVD sent operatives to Donetsk to meet with "civic leaders," but for the most part they met with the football ultras and "demanded that they arm themselves and prepare for battle against the pro–Russian forces in the city."[20] This strategy would lead to a terrorist pogrom in Odessa weeks later (see below). Some neofascists began an unofficial lustration of officials, forcing them to sign resignation statements under threat of violence. In March, for example, at least three Rada deputies from the Svoboda Party barged into the offices of the director of Ukrainian state television, Oleksandr Panteleimonov, beat him, forced him to resign, videotaped the entire operation, and posted the video on the Internet.[21] The same month 15 to 20 masked men—organized by the Yuschenko era governor, led by a former parliamentary deputy in the region, and supported by Fatherland Party deputies and the head of the self-defense forces of the Maidan movement in Kherson—stormed the office of governor Nikolai Kostyak of Kherson Oblast in southern Ukraine and then forced him to resign with a knife to his ribs.[22] This happened to tens of governors and mayors across the country.

The campaign of intimation targeted city councils as well. On February 27, 2014, the RS's Igor Mosiychuk, aka "Moisha," led a group of RS men wearing masks and armed with bats and hammers into a city council meeting in the town of Vasil'kov in Kiev Oblast and coerced all Party of Regions deputies in the assembly to "voluntarily" resign. The RS men warned that they had just convinced another local meeting to expel other elected members of the Party of Regions. The Party of Regions Vasil'kov council members replied that they had already done so that morning and were then forced to close the council.[23] Mosiychuk had just been released from prison under an amnesty for Yanukovich-era political prisoners, having been imprisoned to a six-year term for attempting to blow up a monument to Lenin.[24]

In late February and March, RS organized bus convoys of its activist thugs to spread the Maidan regime's reach into the Russophone-dominated regions and seize OGAs in the east, such as Donetsk, Luhansk, Kharkiv, and other regions. In many cases such expeditions failed. Locals either got wind of, or noticed the arrival of buses filled with young toughs from Lviv, Rivne, and Poltava. Many of the RS activists, some very young teenage boys led by middle-aged men, got a good beating. The entire lot was often subjected to mass shaming and chants of "Russia, Russia!" or "Berkut, Berkut!" Like the Berkut and pro–Yanukovich officials in the west, the easterners forced the RS intruders to get down on their knees, apologize to the locals, and promise never to do it again. In Kharkiv, the RS activists were discovered with primitive Maidan-style weapons—pitchforks, shovels, clubs, etc.—and the mayor claimed the city council building had been shot at, demonstrating a bullet to cameras at a mass protest against and shaming of the RS invaders, and asking Hromadskoe.TV to broadcast this bit of news.[25] In April, Gennadi Kernes, the pro–Yanukovich, pro–Russian, Jewish mayor of the city of Kharkiv, was shot in the back and nearly killed by a sniper. Prior to that, he had been accused by the new Maidan regime of separatism and organizing anti–Maidan demonstrations and kidnappings of pro–Maidan demonstrators and was detained briefly.

Lyashko and his extremist Radical Party were particularly active in waging violence. Lyashko, a deputy in Ukraine's Verkhovna Rada champions "the sacred cause—creation of a Great Kievan Empire" and the restoration of Ukraine's nuclear weapons capability.[26] One of Ukraine's youngest and most boisterous politicians, even within the ultranationalist wing, Lyashko was born on March 12, 1972, in the western region of Chernogiv. He studied law and became a journalist through the period of the Soviet collapse. In 1993 he was sentenced to six years in prison for embezzlement. His sentence was reduced to four years and he was released under a broad amnesty in honor of the 50th anniversary of the defeat of Nazi Germany. Lyashko resumed journalism and then was elected to the Verkhovna Rada on the Yulia Tymoshenko Bloc (BYT) in 2006 and again in 2010. In 2010 a video was published on the Internet of Lyashko discussing a homosexual relationship of his. He claimed the videotape was doctored, but was soon expelled from the BYT on a political pretext. In 2011 he founded the Radical Democratic Party of Ukraine, later renamed the Radical Party.

Lyashko, it is not an overstatement to say, is the most physically violent politician in the world in the direct personal sense, wont to get into fistfights and other physical dustups with political opponents, fellow parliamentarians, and security guards.[27] Thus, in the immediate post–Maidan period he and his Radical Party committed what can be characterized as terrorist attacks in the months after Yanukovich's removal. Lyashko claimed responsibility for organizing the May 23, 2014, storming of a government building in Torez by his "soldiers from the Lyashko Battalion 'Ukraine,'" who killed an unarmed pro–Russian supporter of the breakaway Donetsk People's Republic and maimed a second. Immediately after the murder, Lyashkov boasted on his Facebook page: "Soldiers from Battalion 'Lyashko Ukraine' just liquidated and released the *Kolorado* (potato beetle) from the executive committee of Torez, Donetsk Oblast. Two terrorists killed, nobody among our soldiers suffered there. Glory to Ukraine!"[28] The post received 5,000 likes in just a few hours before Lyashko deleted it. But the *Kyiv Post* retrieved a cached mobile version. One early May 2014 video shows Lyashko himself interrogating a bound, seminaked man, with cuts on his body, who under duress admits being a former defense minister in the breakaway People's Republic of Donetsk.[29] In July, with his armed militiamen backing him, Lyashko forced the mayor of Slovyansk to resign his post.[30] Promotional RP propaganda videos frequently show Lyashko berating and humiliating separatist suspects hunted down and held by his militiamen.[31]

By August 2014, Lyashko's activities earned him condemnation from Amnesty International, which called them "a terrible violation of international law and standards," adding: "Though he doesn't have the right to detain people, he abducts them and abuses them verbally and physically while the camera is rolling. His and other similar websites feature numerous video clips showing what appear to be cases of abduction and violations of the rights to fair trial, liberty and security of the person, and the right not to be subjected to torture and other ill-treatment."[32] But Lyashko boasts of his vigilante "work": "If the government and law enforcers are inactive, the patriots must act. Especially now, when Ukraine is fighting for its independence."[33] Amnesty asked Ukraine's prosecutor general to investigate Lyashko, and the latter supposedly opened an investigation, but Lyashko has refused for nearly two years to respond to a summons and has never been detained, organizing his battalions, leading his party in the Rada, and running in presidential elections. Lyashko and his party would not be the only ultranationalist elements that would be able to maraud at the front and in the rear with utter impunity.

Much of the criminal activity and many of the atrocities that would be carried out under the cover of the antiterrorist operation at the front were carried out by recruits for volunteer battalions enlisted from or through Lyashko's RP as well as Yarosh's RS and Tyahnybok's SP (see below). Lyashko was removed allegedly as a supplier of his fighters after Interior Minister Avakov claimed to discover that 12 of the first 15 Lyashko recruits had criminal issues.[34] RP members were prominent in the Shakhtyorsk Battalion, ostensibly subordinated to the MVD and Avakov, which covered Thorez, where RP members murdered an alleged "separatist" in May. Meanwhile, Lyashko was demanding that Radical Party members fighting in the antiterrorist battalions "have to immediately after the war become prosecutors, judges, etc."[35] Other volunteer battalions dominated by ultranationalist and neofascist elements also carried out vigilante abductions, arrests, beatings of alleged "separatists," coercive resignations of officials and disbandings of city councils, adding to the revolutionary disintegration in law and order, state breakdown, and democratic backsliding rather than the promised democracy-building.[36]

Whether the new regime—with its many Maidan activists and neofascists—supported these efforts to intimate former regime members and send convoys of RS thugs to the regions is unclear. What is clear is that the new regime never discouraged these actions, and Yarosh's RS, Lyashko's RP, and Tyahnybok's SP were able to act with utter impunity. The gravest crimes, however, were not carried out in the rear, but at the front, under the cover of the "antiterrorist" operation or civil war. The neofascist reign of intimidation would devolve into a reign of outright terror with the ATO's onset. As in Crimea, Donbass residents and many in other regions had good reason to distrust if not fear the new, neofascist-infested order (or disorder) and would themselves rise up against it.

The Donbass Revolt

In late January, with the Maidan revolt spreading across the country and Right Sector activists spanning out into the regions, including in Donbass's Luhansk and Donetsk Oblasts, native anti–Maidan "partisans" emerged in Luhansk and captured arms depots in Artemevsk and Slavyansk. These installations warehoused enormous caches of former Soviet weapons and ammunition and, according to some, pre–Soviet weapons of the Russian Imperial Army. This explains the appearance of ancient weaponry among the Donbass rebels in 2014.

At the same time, local oligarchs such as Rinat Akhmedov and Sergei Levochkin initially and generously began financing the Donbass opposition to Maidan, including anti–Maidan demonstrations and then the initial local resistance forces, in order to protect their assets from raids by the western Ukrainian and local ultranationalists who were beginning to grab assets on behalf of pro–Maidan and other oligarchs such as Ihor Kolomoiskii and Dmitry Firtash. Oddly, Levochkin had been demoted from his post as head of Yanukovich's presidential administration to the position of advisor of the president on January 17. The same day, the Chief of the General Staff of Ukraine's Ground Forces was fired.[37] Could Yanukovich have been pursuing the possibility of declaring martial law with deployment of the army, prompting their resignations or at least dissent and consequently Yanukovich's distrust? In conditions of crisis politics, coup politics follow close behind.

Regardless, already on the day after Yanukovich's removal, anti–Maidan forces in eastern and southern Ukraine began rejecting the Maidan's overthrow of Yanukovich and threatening separatism in earnest. The February 21 Kharkiv congress of PR southeastern oblasts' deputies declared that their regional governments would "take upon themselves responsibility for guaranteeing the constitutional legal order and citizens' rights" until these were restored in Kiev. This meant that Crimea, Sevastopol and other regions in the south and east were refusing to recognize the Maidan regime in Kiev. Soon anti–Maidan demonstrations began on squares before the oblast administration buildings across much of Donbass and in other cities in southeastern Ukraine from Kherson to Dnepropetrovsk, sometimes met with pro–Maidan protests. The urgency of the Donbass and other regions' resistance elements could only have been piqued when the pro–Maidan rump majority in the Supreme Rada—the pro–Yanukovich and pro–Russia deputies of which were under intimidation and threats from ultranationalist deputies and their allied armed revolutionaries—adopted well-known amendments to the law repealing the status of Russian as a state language in regions with large ethnic Russian and Russophone minorities or pluralities. Although the amendments were themselves repealed the next day under Western pressure, the Maidan revolution's clearly ethno-nationalistic instincts reinforced fears in the east that the revolution was ultranationalist and even fascist rather than democratic and that their rights had only just begun to be eradicated.

Anti-Maidan rallies mounted in the east and in some southern and central Ukrainian provincial capitals through March. The first seizure of a regional OGA in the east by anti–Maidan protesters occurred at the Donetsk OGA on March 2, 2014, when unarmed protesters occupied the building. Expelled by SBU forces, a larger group of protesters retook the building on March 5. On March 6, SBU forces again removed them. The demonstrators had "elected" Pavel Gubarev as Donestsk's new anti–Maidan "governor" on March 1. An unsigned article in *The Economist* misleadingly identified Gubarev as "a marginal politician previously unknown in Donetsk" and a member of Dugin's ultranationalist Eurasian Youth Movement. In fact, Gubarev was born, brought up, and went to school in Donetsk, graduated Donetsk National University, founded and led a business in Donetsk, and lived his entire life in Donetsk. Moreover, he was a member of the pro-Russian, Soviet-nostalgic Progressive Socialist Party of Ukraine active in southeastern Ukraine, historically known as Novorossiya, eponymous of the ideological and state-building project he would try to lead as Donetsk's separatist leader before being nearly assassinated in October 2014. From the beginning of the crisis in Crimea in late February, Gubarev was leading pickets and then larger demonstrations on Lenin Square in central Donetsk adjacent to the OGA.[38]

At the same time, the Maidan regime was planning its ATO against the Donbass, and in the first days of April—well before the first armed rebels moved into Slavyansk—Ukrainian fighter jets would fly low over the anti–Maidan protests in Donetsk, Luhansk, and Kharkiv.[39] Kiev was sending a message of war. On April 6, the occupation of the Donetsk OGA was repeated yet again, after 1,000–2,000 demonstrators gathered on the square in front of the building protesting "nationalism and other forms of Nazism." The protesters, unarmed, seized the OGA and would declare the "sovereign state of the People's Republic of Donetsk," or Donetsk People's Republic (DNR).[40] In an official statement, the protesters demanded an emergency session of the oblast legislative assembly for the adoption of a law declaring a referendum on the region's autonomous status within or secession from Ukraine similar to that held in Crimea. If the assembly failed to declare the referendum, the demonstrators threatened to take control of the OGA on the basis of "people's mandate" and dismiss the assembly. Those who led the storm claimed their group included representatives of 30 public associations, which had been trying by conventional means to get the assembly to vote on a referendum. During the official statement, attending protesters chanted "Donetsk is a Russian city" and appealed to Russia to "defend them." The press conference closed with the statement: "The Russian-speaking community demands autonomy."[41] The legislative assembly rejected the demand, and the protesters held their own assembly and declared their "people's republic."[42]

Protesters also broke into the OGA in Kharkiv, located in Ukraine's eponymous second largest city, but later left the building voluntarily. Some 1,000 protesters also seized the OGA buildings and SBU headquarters in Luhansk Oblast. These included former Berkut officers who had clashed with Maidan demonstrators in Kiev and now called themselves "the army of the southeast." Some reports, without photographs or video, claimed they wielded at least three machine guns and claimed to have many more weapons.[43] In response, Kiev dispatched security officials—not negotiators—to the eastern cities of Donetsk, Luhansk and Kharkiv. By nightfall in Donetsk, Ukrainian Special Forces (Spetsnaz) again had taken the SBU building back under control and soon took the OGA, and the local prosecutor's office charged the detained anti–Maidan protesters with attempting to overthrow Ukraine's constitutional order.[44] Luhansk government facilities were taken back by security forces as well.[45] The takeovers by anti–Maidan elements on April 7 in several other oblasts also were successfully overturned by special forces.[46] However, in Luhansk after the OGA was cleared, the demonstration-elected "people's governor" Aleksandr Kharitonov, who led a militia group "Luhansk Guard" (*Luganskaya gvardiya*), and other members of the Army of the Southeast were arrested. The demonstrators then reconvened on the square before the OGA building, declared a "*veche*" or "people's assembly," demanded a 'people's government" and the release of Kharitonov and other detainees as well as the rehabilitation of the Berkut. They elected Valerii Bolotov their new "people's governor" and called for either regional autonomy within Ukraine or reunification with Russia.[47] Bolotov is a near-native Luhanskian—born in Taganrog, Russia, in 1970 but having moved to Luhansk, Ukraine, in 1974. A former Soviet paratrooper, he was now leading the "Army of the Southeast" as well as the Union of Veterans of the Paratroop Forces.[48]

The next day, in response to the unrest, acting president Turchynov, who, as noted above, had supported sending troops against protesters in Crimea weeks earlier, promised the country in a televised address that an "anti-terrorist operation will be conducted" against "those who took up arms," though at this point no armed fighters had emerged in Donbass. Media organs tied to USAID such as Mustafa Nayem's *Ukrainskaya pravda* described the takeover of the Luhansk SBU headquarters as having been carried out by "armed men."[49] However, a video of the takeover shows not a single demonstrator with firearms.[50] Ignoring the role of the domestic political strife on the Maidan in Kiev, the west, and elsewhere across the country, which the takeovers in the east mimicked, Turchynov claimed the protests and OGA takeovers were "the second wave of the special operation of the Russian Federation against Ukraine," aimed at "tearing our country into pieces."[51] He was backed up by deputy head of his presidential administration, Andrei Senchenko, who warned on television the same day that not just *spetsnaz* or special troops would be deployed against the "separatists," but also "special means."[52] Hours later it was announced that Turchynov had appointed a new head of the Antiterrorist Center under the SBU, Vitaliy Tsyganko, to his new "antiterrorism" team for putting down the Donbass unrest. The remainder of the team included new National Security and Defense Council Chairman and former Maidan MSD hundreds' commander Parubiy and new SBU Director Valentin Nalyvaichenko, who were sent to Donetsk; First Vice Premier Vitaliy Yarema, who was dispatched to Donetsk; and MVD chief Arsen Avakov, who was sent to Kharkiv.[53] The Maidan leadership seemed to walk back the rhetoric days later. On April 9, MVD chief Avakov said that the Donetsk unrest would be resolved within forty-eight hours by way of either negotiations or force.[54] On the same day, acting president Turchynov signed a decree that mandated retaking the Donetsk OGA building.[55] The next day he made a vague, verbal and unreliable amnesty offer to the demonstrators that they would not suffer criminal indictment if they "laid down their arms," but the demonstrators had no firearms, adding to the latter's distrust.[56]

Like the Ukrainians, U.S. Secretary of State John Kerry publicly chimed in, asserting the events "did not appear to be spontaneous." In a great irony, Kerry also demanded in a phone call to Russian foreign minister Lavrov that Moscow "publicly disavow the activities of separatists, saboteurs and provocateurs."[57] But Washington had not disavowed the neofascists' violation of the February 21 agreement and illegal seizure of power in Kiev. These protesters were already being referred to as "separatists, saboteurs and provocateurs." With the "antiterrorist" operation begun days later, they were made out to be "terrorists" by the Maidan regime.

All this occurred before Girkin-Strelkov, not to mention non-volunteer Russian forces, had entered Donetsk and Luhansk. The West and Kiev immediately attributed the Donbass counterrevolution to Moscow and its alleged agent, the Russian monarchist Girkin-Strelkov. However, the SBU reported that Girkin had arrived in Donetsk only on April 12, having left Crimea on April 8 by the Kerch ferry and entering Ukraine through Rostov-na-Donu, Russia.[58] Girkin had entered the Donbass after the first OGA takeovers in the region. As in the Crimean case, Girkin exaggerated his role, claiming he had initiated the Donbass revolt, but this simply was an attempt to bolster his supposed credentials as a Russian national hero and leader of the Donbass resistance to the Maidan revolt. In fact, Girkin was not a player in the Crimea takeover and would only emerge as one after several weeks in Donbass. His arrival in Donbass was hardly a legitimate reason for starting a civil war against a still nonviolent, if increasingly assertive and potentially violent uprising in Donbass.

On Saturday, April 12, anti–Maidan elements in Donetsk and Luhansk deployed some armed rebels to achieve their aims. Early in the day, miners began heading to Lenin Square to join the demonstrators.[59] Then armed men, including former Berkut riot police and now Donetsk militants, seized MVD, OGA, city hall and other buildings, first in Donetsk City and then fanning out across the oblast. The first came at the Donetsk City MVD building, where they encountered no resistance. Some wore Berkut uniforms, but most had various uniforms and equipment unlike the Russian special forces' "polite little green men" in Crimea, who were outfitted uniformly with state-of-the-art Russian arms and equipment.[60] They negotiated the police chief's resignation, seized the MVD station's weapons, and then spread their control across the city and oblast. The Donetsk and Luhansk OGAs were taken again by the anti–Maidan forces on April 14, assisted this time by Russian volunteers like Girkin, not Russian forces or even recently released conscripts, as would happen later.[61] On April 16, a local activist, Aleksandr Zakharchenko, and his organization "Oplot" seized Donetsk city hall. Zakharchenko would become a leading field commander in the civil war and eventually leader of the DNR after the first ATO and exodus of Russian leaders like Girkin.[62]

After taking control of the Donetsk OGA and declaring the founding of the DNR on April 12, pro-autonomy and pro–Russian groups fanned out to seize strategic infrastructure across Donetsk Oblast and remove from power all public officials who refused to swear allegiance to the republic.[63] The same day, Girkin arrived in Donbass and led armed men also wearing unmarked camouflage uniforms as they seized MVD headquarters in Slavyansk (Slovyansk) and then Kramatorsk, using force but inflicting no casualties. In Slavyansk the takeover occurred quietly, but the police station held 20 automatic rifles and 400 pistols, giving the rebels their first arms cache. Contrary to Western, including NATO claims, the rebels, while well-equipped, were not wearing the same uniforms or using the same equipment, with wide variation in uniforms, helmets, etc.[64] This indicated that these rebels as well were not Russian servicemen or "polite green men" who occupied Crimea. In addition, Slavyansk mayor Nelly Shtepa stated that the rebels were locals, that she knew many of them, and that they were demanding a referendum on an unidentified question—likely autonomy within Ukraine or independence.[65]

Girkin's takeover in Slavyansk was not in and of itself the spark that ignited the civil war but one of many local fires to conflagrate the Donbass inferno. His men had seized a large cache of weapons in the MVD building and set up checkpoints around the city. On the morning of April 13, MVD chief Avakov declared a local ATO in the city being commanded by the SBU's central ATC and by himself from Donetsk, presumably with Turchynov's and the SNDC's approval. Avakov emphasized: "Forces are being brought in from all the country's organs of coercion (*siloviki*)." Social networks were reporting the constant buzz of helicopters flying low over the city and gunfire from machine guns and grenade launchers by mid-morning. Avakov claimed that the rebels had fired on special forces, and that one "checkpoint of the terrorists" had been destroyed and another was in the process of being so.[66]

By the end of the day on April 14, after the expiration of Turchynov's deadline of 6 p.m. that day for those occupying government buildings in the east to leave, Donetsk's anti–Maidan protesters and armed rebels had taken control of some government buildings in many cities across the oblast, including Artemevsk, Druzhkivka (Druzhkovka), Horlivka (Gorlovka), Kramatorsk, Makiivka (Makievka), Mariupol, Slovyansk (Slavyansk), Yenakiieve (Yenakieve), and Zhdanivka (Zhdanovka). By the time Donbassians awoke on the morning of the 15th, Kiev's ATO was already in operation. By the evening of April 14, the first casualties of the ATO—one SBU officer killed and five wounded in Slavyansk—had been registered when SBU special forces attempted to retake security buildings.[67] Thousands of Ukrainian army troops and largely neofascist-manned "volunteer battalions," armed with tanks and heavy artillery and supported by air power, were on the march east. On the 15th, a force of 500 Ukrainian soldiers, 20 APCs, and 2 helicopters descended on Slavyansk.[68] Ukraine's civil war had begun.

Yet the anti–Maidan takeovers of OGAs and other government buildings across Donetsk and spreading to Luhansk from April 12 to 14 came after Kiev had been discussing publicly for more than a week its intent to carry out an "antiterrorist" operation against what then were mere protesters. Moreover, the anti–Maidan takeovers in March and early April in Donbass were in response and identical to the pro–Maidan takeovers of Kiev government buildings and regional OGAs earlier. Thus, the Donbass's events were escalating in response to Kiev's actions. Certainly, Maidan Kiev's civil war or "ATO" could not have been a reaction to a Russian invasion or intervention. Even as a response to the Donbass rebels' first violence in Slavyansk, Kiev, by failing to negotiate first, was overreacting. Kiev was doing so in part precisely because of Putin's Crimean gambit.

Geneva Failure

With the situation spinning out of control on the ground, actors on the international level intervened again. Moscow had warned that any attack on Donbassians would put talks with Washington and Brussels, scheduled for Geneva later the next week, at risk.[69] Nevertheless, on April 16–17 the top foreign affairs officials of the U.S., EU, Ukraine, and Russia met in Geneva in a last-ditch, belated effort to avoid civil war in Ukraine. Unlike the talks in Kiev that produced the February 21 agreement and included the pro–Maidan opposition party leaders, neither the Donbass rebels nor any representatives from Donbass took part in Geneva. On April 17 the sides signed a vague ceasefire agreement, a "joint statement," consisting of aspirational declarations for a ceasefire, withdrawal from buildings, and the initiation of a "national dialogue" on a new constitution rather than concrete steps for implementation and support. If not for the letterhead, the entire document would have fit easily on one page. It read in full:

> The Geneva meeting on the situation in Ukraine agreed on initial concrete steps to de-escalate tensions and restore security for all citizens. All sides must refrain from any violence, intimidation or provocative actions. The participants strongly condemned and rejected all expressions of extremism, racism and religious intolerance, including anti–Semitism. All illegal armed groups must be disarmed; all illegally seized buildings must be returned to legitimate owners; all illegally occupied streets, squares and other public places in Ukrainian cities and towns must be vacated. Amnesty will be granted to protesters and to those who have left buildings and other public places and surrendered weapons, with the exception of those found guilty of capital crimes. It was agreed that the O.S.C.E. Special Monitoring Mission should play a leading role in assisting Ukrainian authorities and local communities in the immediate implementation of these de-escalation measures wherever they are needed most, beginning in the coming days. The U.S., E.U. and Russia commit to support this mission, including by providing monitors. The announced constitutional process will be inclusive, transparent and accountable. It will include the immediate establishment of a broad national dialogue, with outreach to all of Ukraine's regions and political constituencies, and allow for the consideration of public comments and proposed amendments. The participants underlined the importance of economic and financial stability in Ukraine and would be ready to discuss additional support as the above steps are implemented.[70]

At a press conference after the signing, U.S. Secretary of State Kerry put the onus for compliance with the agreement by the DNR fully on the Russian side, much as he and President Obama had with the February 21 agreement: "Responsibility [for successful implementation] will lie with those who have organized their presence, provided them with the weapons, put the uniforms on them, supported them, and have been engaged in the process of guiding them over the course of this operation."[71] But as noted above, the rebel forces were acting spontaneously, still unorganized, and poorly armed and equipped. This could not be said for Maidan Kiev.

Orthodox Easter Cease-Fire and the RS Attack at Slavyansk

The one positive that came out of the agreement was an Easter cease-fire. However, it would soon be undermined by familiar culprits. From the outset, the neofascist element within the Maidan were determined to wage war against the Donbass. Towards this end, on the very day the cease-fire agreement was signed, an RS militant in one of the volunteer battalions just moving into Donbass from the west detonated a grenade in a hazy incident, killing himself and two Donbass rebels, who allegedly attacked him at a rebel checkpoint near Slavyansk.[72] Days later, on April 20, Easter Sunday, the Easter cease-fire was undone by another Maidan-coordinated false-flag operation. RS militants carried out a coordinated attack on a Slavyansk checkpoint. The attack left three Slavyansk rebels dead and four wounded, and one RS fighter killed and two wounded. Ukraine's SBU intelligence service immediately accused Moscow and allied "saboteurs" of carrying out a "cynical provocation," while simultaneously denying that there were any Ukrainian organizations of any kind in the area: "It has been established that on that night in Slavyansk there was not one organization besides saboteurs and representatives of the criminals who the GRU of the general Staff of the Armed Forces of the Russian Federation support and arm. This was established by operational investigative activity at the site by Ukraine's law enforcement agencies."[73] The National Security and Defense Council's deputy secretary Viktoriya Sumar brushed off on her Facebook page any RS involvement as "Russian propaganda": "Reports by Russian journalists about a shootout between supposedly the 'Right Sector' and 'self-defenders' being in Slavyansk based on some 'business cards of Yarosh' and 'unknown weapons' and the number of killed which grows by the hour and some other 'details,' evidence of which no one has seen, is a typical form of Russian propaganda which not only many Russian but also many other foreign mass media circulate today." Sumar added that the event was designed by Moscow to give the appearance of a civil war and justify a Russian invasion of Ukraine.[74]

The Maidan regime's *siloviki* appeared to be coordinating the disinformation with the neofascists, since RS spokesman Artem Skoropadsky also issued a denial, saying Slavyansk was a "blasphemous provocation from Russia: blasphemous because it took place on a holy night for Christians, on Easter night. This was clearly carried out by Russian special forces."[75] In an official statement on its *VKontakte* page, RS again denied having "any relationship" to the "operation" in Slavyansk, adding: "Any attempt to tie these actions with Right Sector have only one goal—to provoke fear of RS activists among the inhabitants of Eastern Ukraine." The party, the statement claimed, had "run into an unprecedented information attack supported by falsifications, intrigues, and manipulations of the facts by Russian mass media controlled by the Kremlin." At the same time, RS acknowledged that its "activists" were "now subordinated to the state's organs of coercion" (*silovie organy*) and thus their actions were within the legal limits.[76] In this view, the ATO declared by Ukraine's government and to be carried out by its *siloviki* provided a "legal" framework for RS to carry out the "operation" it supposedly had not carried out.

The Russian Foreign Ministry expressed outrage over the killing of "innocent, peaceful citizens," regarded it as a breach of the Easter cease-fire, and blamed Right Sector, adding that the incident "testifies to a lack of desire on the part of the authorities in Kiev to rein in and disarm nationalists and extremists."[77] Ukraine's foreign ministry in turn reproached Russia for rushing to judgment and failing to fulfill its obligations under the Geneva deal: "The Russian side must be reminded about their obligations under the Geneva agreement to bring all necessary influence to bear on separatists to clear illegally held buildings, unblock roads, lay down arms and prevent any bloodshed."[78]

Despite all the official denials and charges from Maidan Kiev and the RS at the time of the incident, RS leader Yarosh acknowledged in two interviews on successive anniversaries of the incident, first in a BBC interview that he took part in combat on that day in Slavyansk, and then in a Censor.net article/interview that he led the operation, which was an attack initiated by him and his RS fighters and ordered by acting president Turchynov.[79] In addition to Turchynov, Dnepropetrovsk's deputy governor Gennadii Korban was also involved in the operation's authorization. MVD chief Avakov's assistant Anton Gerashchenko was aware of and assisting the operation. In a Censor.net interview, Yarosh claims that he and his fighters acted after being outraged by the killing of three Maidan volunteers and Gorlovka deputy mayor Volodomor Rybak.[80] Yarosh seemed to blame the murders of Rybak and the volunteers on the Donbass rebels, but the SBU blamed them on the Russian GRU.[81] Later, an RS-affiliated Web site included on its list of heroic members killed during the ATO, Mikhailo Stanislavenko, noting he was killed in Slavyansk on April 20, 2014.[82] On that day there was only one violent incident in Slavyansk.

Moreover, forensic evidence later emerged further confirming RS militants' involvement in the incident. For example, two 2016 Ukrainian court decisions show that prosecutors' investigations had determined that two RS fighters were wounded in the Easter attack and that they had used the very same firearms used on Maidan on February 18, 2014, to kill two MVD troops and wound three more. Moreover, an eyewitness reported that one of the Slavyansk separatists killed at the checkpoint was shot by a sniper, and forensics has shown the sniper used the same kind of expanding 7.62mm caliber bullets, which were recovered at the site of the attack at the checkpoint, that were used on Maidan, and with the same kind of AKM and hunting carbines based on the Kalashnikov assault rifles used on Maidan. Also, Yarosh's business card, a list with names of several other RS leaders, and an RS battalion's Security Service medallion number 20 were seized by separatists during the fight. Yet the involvement of RS in the attack was immediately denied, not just by the RS but by the SBU, the MVD, the National Security and Defense Council, and pro–Maidan media, claiming again without any evidence that the Yarosh business card and other evidence were fabrications.[83]

Thus, the data show that Maidan Ukraine's highest-ranking officials, Yarosh, and the RS stood behind the Easter attack. The coordination between the new government and RS elements reveals another Maidan-style provocation, given the history of the Maidan snipers' massacre and events to come in Odessa. Moreover, the Security and

Defense Council, the SBU, and other state organs issued what was then still at least unverifiable—and it now appears known to be false—information in designating the attack a Russian provocation and denying RS's involvement, which was later acknowledged by the RS itself and recorded in court documents. This is consistent with the Maidan Ukraine's practice of excessive and non-credible strategic communications and disinformation, usually blaming Moscow, such as was the case in the snipers' massacre and events to come in Odessa in May. With Kiev's attack at Slavyansk, the cease-fire ended. Ukraine's civil war was about to begin in earnest. This was an opportunity, lost by Kiev's aggressiveness, to prevent Luhansk's LNR from joining the mounting DNR insurgency.

Luhansk: From Oblast to Insurgency

The RS's April 20 Easter attack had an immediate effect in Luhansk. Those who in early April stormed the government buildings and others remained on the square near the OGA for weeks, and Kiev undertook no attempt to negotiate with them. Geneva offered hope, but no dialogue began, and instead the Easter attack escalated the level of violence, with the first combat casualties in Donbass. On April 21, the protesters organized a series of *veches* across the region to elect delegates to a region-wide veche held in Luhansk City the same day and attended by several thousand, chanting: "Russia! Referendum!" Some protesters appeared to support Ukraine's federalization as a path to regional autonomy within Ukraine, while others supported Ukraine's reunification with the Russian Federation. The Luhansk *veche* declared the Luhansk People's Republic (LNR) and two referenda. One referendum was scheduled for May 11 to determine whether the region should seek autonomous status within Ukraine. The second, scheduled for May 18, would determine whether the LNR should declare independence from Ukraine or join the Russian Federation should autonomy within Ukraine be rejected on the 11th.[84] The Prosecutor General's Office (GPO) deemed the rallies "separatist" in nature: "The demonstrators' speeches, insignia and federalization slogans, as well as calls to hold a local referendum, are explicitly separatist. The regional prosecutor's office sees the unrest in the Luhansk region as illegal and it entered information on them into the database of pre-trial inquiries to be controlled by the Luhansk regional prosecutor's office."[85] A week later the LNR was officially declared, and its leaders demanded that Kiev recognize the authority of Bolotov as the new governor, provide amnesty to all protesters, codify Russian as a state language, and hold a referendum on Luhansk's status. If the Maidan government leadership did not meet these demands by 2:00 p.m. on April 29, the LNR would join with the DNR in the insurgency against the ATO.[86]

The LNR's first support came from the town of Pervomaisk, which expressed its support for the rebel movement without an illegal takeover but would nevertheless see much of the fighting and be much destroyed during the war. On April 29 a demonstration of some 200 people, and then a meeting of the city council, took place in Pervomaisk. Both expressed support for the Slavyansk rebels in particular and, by implication, for resisting the establishment of Maidan regime power in Donetsk and Luhansk. A short video of the demonstration gives us a sense of the atmosphere. Some of the demonstrators seemed a bit wary of the turn of events, staying back from the stage and unsure of whether to support the resistance movement. The main speaker told the protesters that civil war was starting, that a column of the Ukrainian army was headed to Pervomaisk, and that some volunteers from Pervomaisk had gone to defend Slavyansk from the fascists and one was captured and tortured. He said the new regime would cast shame on our land freed from the Nazis, and so the referendum should be held despite the limited time for organizing it by May 11. He also noted that the city council's deputies had nothing to fear from the movement; it would support law and order and only punish criminality. He also expressed thanks to the Russian people for their support. The speaker's assistant and several old women handed out St. George's ribbons.[87]

The demonstration was followed by a city council meeting. A video shows a session convened on an emergency basis, with deputies called from the hall to attend immediately so a quorum of 25 deputies could be gathered and the decision taken "according to the law," as the chairman notes. The meeting adopted an appeal in support of the LNR and DNR and calling on the Maidan regime to call off its ATO and begin a dialogue. The speaker leading the demonstration spoke first and called for supporting the rebels with transportation and money. He repeated that a Pervomaisk volunteer had been captured and tortured by the Ukrainians and that Russia supports the Donbass. He closed calling for reunification with Russia to general applause.

With a quorum gathered, the council session voted unanimously in favor of the appeal, which included the following points:

- Kiev must withdraw the army from Slavyansk and Luhansk.
- "To send the army to start a civil war against its own people is crime."
- "The new regime calls the people of the entire southeast of the country separatists, terrorists, and saboteurs."
- In order to liberate the country from [east Ukraine's residents] the government is prepared to use the army against the people in violation of both the law and constitution.
- Ukraine's MVD and some politicians went even further, calling for the creation of an armed civilian formation to fight against its own people.
- If the regime is interested is preserving Ukraine then it must stop the military offensive and begin a dialogue. Kiev must cancel the military operation against its own people who are only fighting for their rights in a way reflecting the way people did in western Ukraine and Kiev.
- It is not right to divide the people into the title nation and a diaspora of occupiers.
- They warn that a failure to compromise will lead to the destruction of not only democracy but of the state as such.
- They demand amnesty for Berkut, MVD and army personnel, a guarantee that there will be no investigations of participants in protests, and the LNR-proposed oblast referendum.
- Ukraine must become a state where different groups treat each other with mutual respect and not one in which one group seeks to impose its values on the rest and where every citizen feels safe and comfortable regardless of the language he considers is his native tongue, the church he attends, who are his heroes, or who he votes for.

The chair opened the floor to those who wished to speak before the vote was taken, asking that those in attendance treat each other respectfully. Two speakers called for caution and appealed for preserving order in the city and salvaging Ukraine's territorial integrity. A proposal to vote on which power was legitimate in the oblast—Maidan Kiev or the LNR—was postponed. A proposal from the floor to include in the appeal or a separate document a call for a military tribunal of the Maidan Kiev authorities as "military criminals" was rejected. Another speaker stood to say that, yes, the new regime had gone outside the framework of the law, but Donbassians should not destroy Ukraine. Then the Pervomaisk appeal was approved unanimously.[88] Before, during or after the session, the Russian flag replaced the Ukrainian blue and yellow atop the Pervomaisk city hall building.[89]

There was a similarly less violent, even orderly process in many of Luhansk's towns. By mid–May government buildings in most of the larger towns in Luhansk had been seized by LNR rebels. Luhansk was taking the road paved by the DNR. By then fighting had begun in earnest in Donetsk in Kramatorsk, Slavyansk, Gorlovka and elsewhere. The first phase of the ATO/civil war began to burn. Kindling was provided by another RS operation in Odessa on May 2.

The Odessa Terrorist Pogrom

On May 2, 2014, RS and the "Odessa self-defense" hundred led a terrorist pogrom by RS and SP activists in the southern port city of Odessa. The attack grew out of fighting between pro–Maidan and anti–Maidan elements in the city center; much of it videotaped. The fighting was provoked apparently as part of the overall plan to rid the city of and intimidate "pro-separatist" elements; one RS activist was killed in the initial street fighting. The pro–Maidan RS activists then led a mob to the city's Trade Union House square. There, as numerous videotapes show, a group of anti–Maidan, pro-autonomy protesters had been occupying Kulikovo Field, the square in front of the Trade Union House, for weeks in a tent city. The RS- and OSD-led crowd stormed the square, burned the tents and then set the Trade Union House on fire after the anti–Maidan protesters fled into the building for refuge. RS and other activists threw Molotov cocktails into the building, setting it ablaze, while others shot at the windows with pistols and still others entered the building and apparently killed some of those inside. As people burned inside, pro–Maidan RS and other nationalists shouted "Glory to Ukraine!" and sang the Ukrainian national anthem. Those who decided to jump from windows to save their lives were beaten after they hit the ground, often unconscious.[90] As a result of the events at the Trade Union House at least 48 anti–Maidan protesters were killed—42 of them burned alive or dying of asphyxiation in the Trade Union House—and more than 200 were injured and wounded.

The Right Sector Web site, was effusive the about the atrocity: "May 2, 2014 is another bright page in our national history." They claimed responsibility for the Odessa pogrom, noting "about a hundred members of 'Right Sector' and patriotic-minded Odessa residents countered the rebels." Acknowledging its own losses during the early street fighting, it noted: "Yes, the men of Right Sector and other Ukrainian patriots suffered losses in killed and wounded. However, the toll of Russian terrorists were [*sic*] much higher, indeed the phenomenon of 'separatists' in Odessa disappeared as a factor. All this is to the merit of the public's united patriotic feeling." Most importantly, RS acknowledged that its leader "Dmitro Yarosh ignored the 'expedience' of the election campaign to coordinate the action against the Russian aggression."[91] RS celebrated its leading role in the terrorist attack twice around the time of the first anniversary as well. On May 1, 2015, the RS site announced a commemoration of the crime as an act of patriotic glory:

2 May at 14.00 at the Cathedral Square pro–Ukrainian forces will rally the city on the anniversary of the day when patriots defended peace in Ukrainian Odessa. May 2 last year, thanks to the bold and coordinated actions in Odessa, the plans of the occupiers and their supporters were frustrated. On that day we all fought and won! We remember our colleagues who have paid with their lives for the future of Odessa and Ukraine. Their feat will live in our hearts forever. The event will be a memorial service for the dead patriots rally commemorating the heroes [with] a minute of silence and the laying of flowers. Security will be provided by armed units of organizations that are part of the command. The perimeter is to be under the control of Right Sector activists "Automaidan," "RSL," and "Self Defense Odessa." We welcome all patriotic citizens of Odessa on May 2 at 14.00 on Cathedral Square. Total power! Eternal memory to those who gave their lives for Ukraine![92]

On the day of the anniversary, May 2, RS offered a motive to explain its terrorist pogrom a year earlier. A post on its Web site claimed that it acted after one Ivan Ivanov, said to be an RS member, was killed in the street clashes in the city center preceding the pogrom at the Trade Union building. RS proudly posted along with the anniversary statement one of the many videos showing RS and other ultranationalist Ukrainians attacking the anti–Maidan tent city on the square and then the Trade Union building.[93] On the same day, leading RS member Igor Mosiichuk praised the Odessa pogrom on his Facebook page, exclaiming: "I remember, and I am proud." He was particularly proud to have given a rebuff to "occupiers and collaborators" and said the attack "gave an impetus to the war against separatists and occupiers in Donbass."[94] In a 2016 French documentary, RS's Odessa organization leader also expresses his pride in the pogrom.[95]

The evidence shows again that this was a well-planned action undertaken by the new Maidan regime's *siloviki*, Yarosh's RS, and local RS and other neofascist elements. On April 29, three days before the pogrom, National Security and Defense Council chairman and Maidan self-defense commander-in-chief Parubiy met with the so-called "Odessa self-defense" (OSD) and its leader, Nikolai Volkov (aka Sotnik Mykola), who would be involved in the pogrom. A brief videotape of an April 29 meeting between Parubiy and Mykola Volkov shows the two discussing "coordination with the police" in organizing checkpoints in and around the city and Purubiy providing bulletproof vests to "the volunteers manning the patriotic roadblocks at the entrance to Odessa."[96] Coordination for an altogether different purpose occurred off-camera in what former Odessa MVD deputy chief Dmitrii Fuchedzhi says was nearly a four-hour meeting between Parubiy and the OSD. Pro-Maidan RS, other nationalists and soccer thugs were bused in, as were anti–Maidan soccer thugs for a soccer match to be held in Odessa that day. Parubiy coordinated the recruitment of some 500 RS and hundreds from outside the city ostensibly to man new checkpoints on roads entering the city and elsewhere, according to Fuchedzhi, who was fired after the events.[97] RS and the OSD, with the assistance of the local police, were able to parlay the violence into the pogrom.

The heavy RS and neofascist presence in the city that day is well-documented. Detailed accounts by the pro-democracy, anti–Putin *Ekho Moskvy*'s journalists in Odessa on that day state clearly that "ultras" (ultranationalists) of the RS and the Self-Defense *sotniki* from Kiev and Kharkov and Volkov's OSD led the violence on the pro–Maidan side and at the Trade Union House. They manipulated the members of the fan club of the local Odessa soccer team "Chernomorets." *Ekho*'s Ilya Azar also relays the words of one pro–Maidan activist, who came in from Vinnitsa, that 2,000 "ultras" had been brought into the city for the battle.[98] Several videos reveal the RS's leading role in the events. In one video two men discuss who the people doing the burning and killing are, and one says that they are Right Sector and adds that 3,000 people were brought into the city.[99] In one video toughs are consulting with MVD officers and talking of "killing every last one of the scum." A fighter with an Apache haircut is seen openly wearing an RS red-over-black (blood and soil) shoulder patch and a bulletproof vest.[100] Another video shows, at the 2:18 mark, a pro–Maidan *sotnik* yelling orders for his "self-defense" fighters to get moving.[101] Another shows the neofascist mob moving into the building, and as one enters he screams: "Where are you scum?"[102]

During the street fighting in the city center, one video shows a man shooting at demonstrators from behind police barricades. It emerged that 6 people were killed in the street fighting, but it has been difficult to determine on whose side most of them were fighting. The city authorities knew that large numbers of pro–Maidan activists were coming to the city to challenge a large cohort of anti–Maidan youth in the city. Yet no attempt was made to stop them at "the patriotic roadblocks at the entrance to Odessa," to make sure the two sides remained at a distance from each other, or to protect the tent city demonstrators on Kulikovo Field—most of whom were not young toughs but rather middle-aged and elderly trade union activists, communists, and pensioners. To the contrary, at noon Odessa's police chief and deputy chiefs were summoned to a meeting at the city council. The meeting lasted three hours, and they were required to turn off their mobile telephones. Thus, as the fighting broke out, the police chief was *incommunicado*.[103]

Thus, the RS, OSD and Chernomordets fighters were allowed to lead a march unhindered into the city center, with the local anti–Maidan forces in the wait. Violence quickly escalated into shooting. After the pro–Maidan mob stormed Kulikovo Field and the anti–Maidan picketers were trapped inside the burning Trade Union House, numerous videos show none other than Parubiy's Odessa contact, OSD leader and "patriotic checkpoint" organizer, the *sotnik* Mykola Volkov, wearing a black bulletproof vest and reporting on the situation and the number of wounded by walkie-talkie to an unidentifiable higher-up and later firing a pistol at the burning Trade Union House.[104] Videos show busloads of Odessa's police standing by and watching as the crowd is well into burning the building and throwing stones at the windows. Only after some six anti–Maidan protesters jump out of the burning building from windows above one of the side entrances—to the joyful cheers of pro–Maidan neofascists—do some police and others move to help the injured. When others are thinking of jumping, RS fighters scream: "Come on, jump you scum!"[105] It remains unclear where these victims ended up, but there are apparent eyewitness accounts saying that many more people were burned or killed inside the Trade Union House. One anti–Maidan activist, who was inside the building and was detained by police, stated upon his release that 116 people were killed inside the Trade Union house, that many were driven away to be buried, and that the RS and other fighters "finished off people" inside the building, including a mother with her two children.[106] When one views a video made by the perpetrators of the Odessa pogrom, as they tour the building in the aftermath, one suspects this is very likely true. Moving through the Trade Union House's corridors in the dark, they beat survivors, scream at people to state whether they are alive, and poke the charred corpses with their clubs, jokingly calling them "Negroes."[107]

It could be possible that only the clash in the city center was planned and that matters then spun out of control, leading to the Trade Union House pogrom. However, none of the RS and OSD perpetrators who celebrated the violence have made such a distinction between the two phases of the incident in claiming pride and responsibility for the act. Moreover, there has been a concerted attempt in Kiev and Odessa to delay and obstruct investigation, and thereby cover up, the Odessa pogrom. In the aftermath of the day's events, many of the anti–Maidan demonstrators, including those trapped in the Trade Union House but able to escape with their lives, were detained by police and later released. However, the later investigation would hit the anti–Maidan, pro-federalists much harder than the pro–Maidan neofascists.

In September 2014, Odessa Oblast's legislative assembly closed down its investigation and handed all evidence to the MVD and GPO of Ukraine in Kiev.[108] In November 2015, the Council of Europe's International Advisory Panel on Ukraine (CEIAPU) issued a report on Maidan Ukraine's investigations of the May 2, 2014, events in Odessa. It concluded that the investigations "failed to comply with requirements of the European Human Rights Convention" and "lacked independence" and "effectiveness" and "failed to show sufficient thoroughness and diligence." This was largely because the "fox was guarding the henhouse." In particular, the investigation was flawed because, although evidence indicated that the MVD was in cahoots with some of those who were behind the disturbances, the MVD was in charge of several of the relevant investigations. For example, the MVD-led investigation into the 40-minute delay in the arrival of the fire department was deemed flawed, as the local fire department is subordinate to the local MVD, which in turn is subordinated to the central MVD apparatus in Kiev. Moreover, the investigations have been effectively sabotaged by being divided between the MVD and GPO and reduction of investigatory personnel.[109] The panel also expressed "serious concern" over two acquittals in the case due to lack of evidence and regarded that the information provided so far was insufficient to protect the rights of the victims and next-of-kin.[110] The CEIAPU was critical of the fact that nearly 30 pro-federalist, anti–Maidan protesters had been charged with "participation in mass disorders," but only one pro–Maidan participant has been charged—this, on suspicion of committing murder. Thus, the CEIAPU's overall conclusion was that "substantial progress has not been made in the investigations into the violent events of 2 May 2014 in Odessa."[111]

In January 2016, the Ukrainian human rights group, the Kharkiv Human Rights Protection Group (KHPG) and the "2 May Group" issued statements condemning what it called efforts by the Maidan GPO to "stymie" the investigation of the Odessa terrorist pogrom. The 2 May Group has carried out its own investigation in which it has concluded that there is some evidence that the anti–Maidan, pro-autonomy forces on Kulikovo Field were also prepared for a battle, though as the evidence shows they were not the initiators of the conflict there, and that MVD deputy chief Fuchedzhi might also have coordinated with some of them. The street fighting was more evenly balanced, according to the 2 May Group, as evidenced by the fact that of the six people killed by gunfire, three were anti–Maidan and three were pro–Maidan. The group claims it has also debunked the version of events that holds that the anti–Maidan, pro-autonomy picketeers killed in the Trade House Building were overcome by asphyxiation because of toxic gases from the inflammatory materials the victims themselves supposedly used or chemicals present in the building materials. The group asserts that all the information it gathered during its investigation and presented to the MVD, GPO, and SBU authorities has been ignored. It concludes that the Kiev Maidan authorities "will never reveal the truth."[112] Odessa's new governor is former Georgian President Saakashvili, who was appointed by Maidan Ukraine's first president, Petro Poroshenko. On his first visit to Odessa after appointing Saakashvili, Poroshenko repeated the popular pro–Maidan myth that the fire was started by its victims. Saakashvili has made no attempt to revive any investigation under the control of Odessites.

The massacre at Odessa's Trade Union House changed the calculus in Donbass, strengthening the determination to resist the Maidan regime and its neofascist elements. On the day of the Odessa pogrom, the ATO's forces assaulted Slavyansk in force. There was no turning back from the Ukrainian civil war.

The Unnecessary War

The civil war in the Donbass was a thoroughly avoidable and unnecessary one. It was the consequence of a deliberate policy adopted in Kiev not to negotiate with and to deny the anti–Maidan forces the very same tactics they, the Maidan forces, had used to seize power in Kiev and much of the rest of Ukraine. Maidan Kiev preferred to reject talks, much as its radicals did on February 21. Instead, it sent regular forces and neofascist-led volunteer battalions to the southeastern Donetsk and Luhansk regions immediately after Donbass locals refused to submit to the country's new, coup-imposed authorities in lieu of talks on autonomy for their region.

Without an exhaustive attempt to avoid war through negotiations, Kiev was initiating a civil war against its native population. A very similar, indeed far more threatening situation had arisen in 1991 in Chechnya. The tradition of Caucasus-wide resistance to Russian rule meant there was a real danger that an uprising in Chechnya would spread to the Chechens' fraternal Vainakhs, the Ingush in Ingushetiya, as well as to Dagestan and perhaps elsewhere across the North Caucasus. The so-called Chechen Republic of Ichkeriya had tens of thousands of fighters, well-armed as a result of the Russian army's dissolution, followed by the sale and abandonment of equipment to the rebels. Yet Moscow negotiated for three years before starting its antiterrorist operation in December 1994. By contrast, Kiev started its ATO almost immediately, with no attempt to negotiate with the rebels directly with full Western backing.

The avoidability and unnecessary nature of the "ATO" is evident when one examines public opinion in the Donbass in April 2014 when the war kicked off. Despite the threatening nature of the events in Kiev and western and central Ukraine over the previous months, Donbassians were more preoccupied with protecting their regions' unique economic interests rather than being driven by ethnic communalism and separatism.[113] Although this balance in opinion would shift after a year of Kiev's ATO, at its outset Donbassians opposed secession.

Support in Donetsk and Luhansk for independence or reunification with Russia, though much stronger than elsewhere in Ukraine, was much weaker than in Crimea. However, as the Maidan ideology became more apparent, the ATO came on the horizon, and Ukrainian neofascists slaughtered 42 pro-autonomy activists in Odessa, support for separatism, not to mention autonomy, in the Donbass grew. At the time of the OGA takeovers, large demonstrations protesting against the Maidan regime and for autonomy or independence were the rule in both oblast capitals and several other large cities in Donbass. But overall public opinion remained tentative. According to opinion polls, approximately half of the Donetsk and Luhansk populations strongly regarded the new Maidan government and acting president Turchynov as illegitimate, compared to about a third or fewer in other southeastern regions.[114] According to a Ukrainian poll conducted

April 8–14, 2014, a minority of Donbassians—24 percent in Luhansk and 18 percent in Donetsk—supported the OGA seizures. More substantial minorities—but minorities nevertheless—supported secession from Ukraine and reunification with Moscow: 27.5 percent in Donetsk and 30.3 percent in Luhansk. A large portion of the population remained "on the fence"—17.3 percent and 12.4 percent, respectively, answered "party yes, partly no."[115]

But as Giuliano shows, although by late spring and early summer, popular support for the DNR and LNR reached approximately one-third of the population, even this limited support was not driven by a single-factor pro–Russian ethnic or linguistic sentiment. Rather, there were multiple reasons why ordinary people began to support separatism. While loyalty to Russia was a pivotal factor in the Soviet-nostalgic older generations, which rejected the USSR's collapse, more important was "a sense of betrayal by Kyiv and the rest of the country inspired by the Euromaidan events." Drivers of this sense of betrayal included: Kyiv's persecution of the Berkut special police; government failure to repudiate Ukrainian ultranationalists, which drove legitimate resentment and fear in Donbass; and the already noted attempt by Ukraine's Rada to annul the Yanukovich-era law giving the Russian language a special status in Russian-dominated areas. The Berkut hailed largely from and were a point of pride in Donbass.

The killing of many on Maidan, their humiliation by western Ukrainians, and their persecution in the wake of Yanukovich's fall created great anger. When Berkut members arrived in Crimea and Donetsk, they were hailed as heroes, rather than as enemies, and as symbols of resistance to Maidan. The divisive function performed by Ukrainian ultranationalism should be obvious by now, but suffice it to say that Giuliano's observation of Donbass demonstrators revealed a tangible fear of neofascism as a result of Maidan nationalists' "xenophobic discourses that scapegoated ethnic Russians for Ukraine's problems" and the government's appointment of Parubiy, a former leader of a neofascist party, to head the National Security and Defense Council.

According to Giuliano, although opinion polls show that fears regarding loss of language rights had not been on the list of Donbassians' top concerns recently, that changed when the Rada tried to repeal the law and then repealed its repeal days later. Still, the original lack of salience of the language issue "indicates that politicians within the Donbass faced obstacles in their attempts to draw boundaries between ethnic Russians and Ukrainians, and between Russophone and Ukrainophone populations. This suggests that ethnocultural differences among the Donbass population did not spontaneously translate into political grievances."

There also were two key economic grievances. First was alleged discriminatory redistribution from Donbass to the rest of the country, summed up in the Donbass slogan: "*Kiev maidanaet, Donbas rabotaet*" ("Kyiv protests [literally "maidans"] while the Donbass works"). Second, Donbassians feared negative effects on their economic welfare from potential EU membership in the form of likely austerity policies and loss of trade with Russia and the Eurasian Customs Union.[116] The upshot of this is that ethnic and linguistic differences did not predetermine or even determine by themselves an "inevitable," though perhaps probable interethnic conflict.

Putting aside the stresses put on Ukraine's internal politics by outsiders, there were ways for more subtle Ukrainian political leadership to co-opt portions of the Donbass population by way of several key compromises on issues of concern for Donbassians. If amnesty for the Berkut, reining in the most egregious neofascist ideological excesses, guarantees for the Russian language, and trade talks with Russia, the EU and EEU on Ukraine's accession to the EU in ways that protected jobs in Donbass, were put on the table instead of the ATO, the ground would have been pulled out from underneath the LNR's and DNR's weak support.

Similar findings on the limits of the ethnic factor's salience can be gleaned from opinion surveys conducted in Crimea. The modest strength of the ethnic factor in motivations can be seen in contradictions between Crimeans' pro–Russian views and those on relations with Kiev. According to a 1997 opinion poll carried out in Crimea, 38 percent of the ethnic Russians and 21 percent of ethnic Ukrainians on the peninsula favored secession from Ukraine and 72 percent and 51 favored Crimea's reunification with Russia.[117] This somewhat contradictory finding suggests that Ukraine's possession of Crimea—and peace in the Donbass—could have been salvaged by Kiev's accession to the EEU. Thus, as Giuliano suggests, there was reason to be "cautiously optimistic" that the grievances held most broadly in the Donbass in April 2014 were "more amenable to dialogue and policy intervention than is generally thought."[118] Unfortunately, Kiev chose to quickly abandon dialogue, and no Western power urged, much less pressured, the new Maidan regime to negotiate rather than erroneously and irresponsibly designating the Donbass separatists as terrorists.

The ATO and the Foreign Actors

It must be said that at this moment a few words threatening the withholding of badly needed Western economic assistance from President Obama or at least some authoritative source in Washington could have restrained Kiev's hand and led to a stronger cease-fire regime and concerted negotiations to prevent war. We know from the Nuland-Pyatt phone conversation leaked on February 7, 2014, that Washington had and, incidentally, continues to have enormous influence over the Ukrainian government's decisions, including appointments to the highest non-elected office in the land—the prime ministership. In April, Washington's and Brussels's sway over Kiev was even more extraordinary. The country was still bankrupt and was now facing a war in the east, where much of its wealth had been generated. The West was the only possible source of lending to keep the Ukrainian ship of state afloat. The issue of any future loans and aggression in the east without undertaking direct, serious talks could have been linked in messaging behind the scenes with Kiev. Instead, as with the violation of the February 21 agreement, there was no criticism of Kiev's actions.

Rather, Washington continued to cover for Kiev. For example, in her testimony before the U.S. House of Representatives Foreign Affairs Committee on May 8, Assistant Secretary of State Nuland did not mention Right Sector or the Odessa massacre. Moreover, when questioned by California representative Dana Rohrbacher about the presence of neofascists on Maidan, Nuland tried to avoid answering the question. After Rohrbacher raised the issue of February's Maidan snipers in the context of the neofascists, Nuland claimed that all such incidents were "subject to investigation."[119] Yet, the U.S. neither investigated the incident nor petitioned an international organization to do so. This means that along with Moscow—whose Crimea intervention surely had sown panic and potential for overreaction in Kiev, Washington and Brussels—the West, in particular the Barack Obama administration, and Kiev also bear responsibility for the war, as they do for the original crisis that brought us the Ukrainian civil war and the threat of larger conflagration in Europe for the first time in 75 years.

What were the great powers occupied with as the crisis deepened? Washington and Brussels compounded their policy foibles of NATO and EU expansion that largely caused the crisis by escalating attempts to isolate Russia economically and diplomatically—precisely the kind of policy Russians suspected the West of employing under NATO and EU expansion. Washington in particular compounded policy aggressiveness with verbal taunts of Putin and at that time still false charges of Russian military intervention in Donetsk and Luhansk. The Western, especially the U.S., government and media carried out anti–Donbass and anti–Russian propaganda that rivaled Russian state television's anti–American campaign. It portrayed the Donbass revolts, much as Russian propaganda painted Maidan, as bought and paid for by Russian intelligence.[120] The West's allies in Ukraine joined in, with the SBU producing false evidence of a Russian invasion in the east (see below), with provisional government chairman Arsenii Yatsenyuk asserting that "Russia wants to start World War III"; this and similar claims received broad circulation in Western media.[121]

In Moscow, aside from a few calls for negotiations, Putin reacted to the Donbass unrest not unlike his Western counterparts. He made no strong statement demanding restraint, disarmament or at least withdrawal from government buildings in Ukraine. Instead, having already massed some 40,000 troops on its border with Donbass, Moscow occupied itself with often equally outrageous propaganda measures to support the rebels, covering the crisis in one-sided fashion much like its Western counterpart. It organized a series of patriotic PR events highlighting the themes of the return of Crimea and Sevastopol to Russia and painting the entire Ukrainian provisional government as a fascist "junta," a word that was repeated ad infinitum in Russian media and would make it that much more difficult to engage said "junta" in talks.

Some ultranationalist elements in Russia began pushing the so-called "Novorossiya project," to be sure, but Western military and media began to grossly overstate its role in Russian policy, claiming the existence of a "Putin doctrine" aiming to recreate the USSR with the Novorossiya project. Polish Defense Minister Tomasz Siemoniak warned of the Novorossiya doctrine at a joint briefing with Defense Secretary Chuck Hagel at the Pentagon after the signing of the Geneva agreement. Hagel noted: "Russia's aggression has renewed our resolve to strengthen the NATO alliance."[122] The doctrine and project allegedly stood behind alleged Russian preparations for the annexation of not just Donbass but all of southeastern Ukraine from Kherson and Odessa in south-central Ukraine to Donbass and Kharkiv in the east—what in the 18th century St. Petersburg called "Novorossiya." Lenin had handed large swaths of "Novorossiya" to Ukraine's Bolsheviks in 1919 in order to dilute largely agrarian Ukraine with the industrial proletarian element in Novorossiya, especially Donbass with its large coal industry and miners' cohort. Novorossiya's unification with the Ukraine SSR was codified with the USSR's official formation after the civil war. However, Putin mentioned "Novorossiya" but once. That came in an off-hand comment in a 4-hour televised news conference on the same day the Polish defense minister made his comments. In hours, the mention of the word had become in the West a strategic doctrine portending Russia's recreation of the USSR by force—"Putin's New Russia."[123] Five months later, the Kremlin's Web site used the term again, this time in a headline for an entry on the site regarding a statement by Putin, but the word was never mentioned in Putin's statement itself.[124] To be sure, Russian media, including state media, began to use the term more broadly, but contrary to common belief, the Kremlin does not control everything said in Russian media, even in state media.

Russia's Military Intervention: Fiction and Fact

Moscow's military involvement in the Donbass uprising was negligible, perhaps nonexistent in spring 2014 beyond a likely strengthened GRU and Foreign Intelligence Service (SVR) presence, in addition to the usual contingent that one would expect any major power to deploy in an unstable neighboring country in which foreign competitors maintained deep involvement. Even the Maidan regime's own strategic communications and propaganda efforts rarely claimed that there was any Russian presence—volunteer or professional—in eastern Ukraine before Girkin. The first wave of the Russian volunteers in Donbass consisted of volunteers moving from Crimea after the events there, volunteers arriving directly from Russia, particularly from regions adjacent to Ukraine, and Kuban Cossacks. Nevertheless, Western governments and media joined in a rather clumsy Ukrainian strategic communications campaign to pin the Donbass uprising on Moscow, rather than acknowledge its indigenous root causes in a deeply divided and polarized Ukraine. Under the Maidan Ukraine's new SBU director Nalyvaichenko—who would be fired, as noted above, after having falsely claimed that Putin advisor Vladislav Surkov coordinated the Maidan snipers' massacre—the agency issued all sorts of false propaganda reports in 2014–15. When many of its claims were aired, they were immediately exposed as disinformation.

Fiction

In mid–April, Ukrainian and Western government and media began claiming Russia was invading Donbass and attempts were made to "prove" this claim. The West seemed on multiple occasions to either acquiesce in disseminating clear disinformation or fall prey to Kiev's falsification of data. Thus, SBU chief Valentyn Nalyvaichenko and National Security and Defense Council chairman Parubiy claimed Ukrainian intelligence had captured more than 23 Russian GRU agents.[125] They promised to produce them for public viewing, but this never happened. At the same time, acting deputy head of the Ukrainian presidential administration Andrei Senchenko claimed that its detention centers were crammed with arrested Russian spies introduced into the country four years earlier with false documents.[126] They were never produced in public, nor were there any trials of such spies. On April 16, a Ukrainian counterintelligence officer told media that Moscow planned to kill 100 to 200 Donbassians and blame it on Kiev in a false-flag operation as a pretext for invading Ukraine a half hour later.[127] The above claims came as the SBU falsely identified Girkin as an active rather than a retired Russian intelligence officer at the time of his arrival in Donbass, as noted in the previous chapter. The SBU did the same with other former Russian intelligence officers, like former GRU colonel Igor Belzer, who commanded the first rebel units in Gorlovka (Horlivka) from April. Belzer had retired from the GRU and moved to Gorlovka two years earlier, according to democratic opposition journalist Pavel Kanygin.[128] Early Maidan SBU disinformation usually included falsely identified photographs captured from social networking sites; unidentifiable audio tapes; false claims that the uniforms and equipment used by the pro–Russian groups in Donetsk and Luhansk were Russian army standard-issue; and claims that those forces must be Russian soldiers and/or special forces because of their professional demeanor.

They ignored the fact that interviews with rebels and journalists who spoke with them indicated that they were former Afghan war veterans, former Ukrainian, Russian and Soviet servicemen, former Berkut officers, local police and private security guards.

The first piece of disinformation attempted to show a significant Russian presence in Donbass already in April 2014. On April 20, 2014, a set of photos of an alleged GRU agent were provided by the SBU to NATO, Western governments, and the *New York Times*. The photos were ostensibly taken in Georgia, Russia, and eastern Ukraine, and purported to unmask a bearded GRU special forces operative who had been allegedly dispatched by Moscow to Georgia, and now six years later to eastern Ukraine. Three photographs allegedly showed one and the same Russian GRU agent in Russia, in 2008 Georgia, and in April 2014 Ukraine. NATO's Atlantic Council and the *New York Times* publicized the photographs, touting them as evidence of Russia's incursion into Donbass.[129] The SBU's "evidence" of this alleged GRU agent's presence in Ukraine was exposed immediately as a fake.[130] The *New York Times* and NATO's Atlantic Council were forced to back off their claims.[131] Simon Saradzhyan of Harvard's Belfer Center noted that the photo alleged to have been taken in Georgia shows Khamzat Gairbekov, commander of the Chechen Vostok (East) Battalion, controlled by Russia's GRU and Chechen President Ramzan Kadyrov, sent to fight in Georgia in 2008, and since disbanded.[132] Moreover, the photographer of the photo taken supposedly in Russia said that the picture was actually taken in Ukraine and was used without his permission. He said the person in the photograph taken in Ukraine was not the GRU agent Gairbekov but a private Russian citizen named Alexander Mozhaev, a Cossack who had served in the Russian army in the 1990s, was wanted for murder in Russia, and came to Donbass after participating in the Crimea events.[133]

At the same time, Ukraine's SBU claimed to have captured 20 GRU agents but never presented them to television cameras and never provided audio, pictures of them, or any identity papers. Weeks later the SBU reduced the number of its "captured" GRU agents to 10, and days after that to 3 in its falsified report to NATO's Atlantic Council. It seemed such incontrovertible proof of a significant GRU presence beyond the routine should have been paraded before television cameras. This would have been a real propaganda coup against the Kremlin, but a "perp walk" never came. If it had, then it would have been incumbent upon those seeing clear evidence to acknowledge that Putin had sent forces into Ukraine to orchestrate the east Ukrainian uprisings. Presenting conclusive evidence of a clandestine Russian incursion into eastern Ukraine therefore would have helped to mobilize support for a tougher military response than did the falsified photographs. It is perhaps for this reason that the Obama White House, U.S. State Department, NATO, its Atlantic Council, U.S. European Command chief General Phillip Breedlove, and the *New York Times* touted this as "evidence" of Russian forces in eastern Ukraine. Only the *Times* retracted the "evidence" after it was exposed as false. From the Kremlin's point of view, false reports of a Russian presence in Ukraine and Western connivance in their proselytization were added to the perfidy of the Western-backed Maidan revolt and the beginning of ground and air operations against Donbass without a word of criticism or even caution from either Washington or Brussels.

False SBU reports continued through the ATO even after there was reliable evidence that some officially sponsored Russian incursions had begun in June–July 2014. In February 2015, as the Donbass rebels, with significant Russian military support, were encircling and about to rout Ukrainian forces near Debaltsevo, Ukraine's SBU passed photographs of Russian tanks allegedly in Ukraine to a U.S. senator who showed them in a presentation on the floor of the Senate, only to have them exposed as fakes. Burned already by the SBU's sloppy stratcomm, the *New York Times* exposed the deception by showing that the photographs were from the 2008 South Ossetiya war.[134] One wonders why the SBU decided to provide falsified intelligence to its allies in Washington, since Washington and Brussels (NATO and the EU) were already issuing condemnations of Russia's "invasion of Ukraine" and were publishing satellite photos of rather small columns of armored vehicles and tanks said to be evidence of tens of thousands of troops.

Western media eagerly reprinted Kiev strategic communication pieces and totally ignored the other side of the story; for example, never reporting a word about the Odessa terrorist pogrom. The Western media's connivance with their governments and their distortions of reality were condemned by anti–Putin, opposition journalist Andrei Babitskii, who was fired from U.S. government-funded RFERL for failing to follow the Western party line: "There is a large number of foreign correspondents working here [Donbass] who do not in any way support either the DNR authorities or the population that elected them. In general, they have, let's say, a hostile attitude towards the people of Donbass. This hostility is manifested in the texts, which they publish, and in the material they film, which they remove, and no one checks them for this…. [I]t is more difficult for journalists whose views do not correspond with Kiev's official position to work here, if they let them come here at all." He described some of what was missing from the Western media's accounts about the conflict and the Donbass population: "Here they are killing the civilian population which made a different choice and does not wish to submit to a policy of Ukrainization…. They have their own interests and their own cultural identity, which the local population values, and for this the civilian population is being killed with cannons and tanks."[135]

After his June 2015 firing from his position as SBU chief, allegedly for failing to fight corruption aggressively but in reality for his department's clumsy strategic propaganda surrounding the Maidan snipers' massacre, Nalyvaichenko persisted in making allegations about the Russian incursions into Donbass. But the earliest official Russian military or intelligence presence in Ukraine he could point to was in May 2014. This was based on information gathered from two GRU agents that Kiev's forces actually did capture in April 2015 and did parade before television cameras, unlike a year earlier.[136]

In addition to the false claims, Kiev's more credible disclosures regarding an official Russian military or intelligence presence in Ukraine (outside Crimea) never claimed to show, much less did they demonstrate, such a presence existed before the April 14, 2014, start of the ATO. Thus, when the opposition Russian newspaper *Novaya gazeta* consulted the Ukrainian military on Kiev's and NATO's claims that there were 13,000 Russian troops fighting in Ukraine and that, according to Kiev, at least 4,500 had been killed as of February 2014, the earliest time for evidence of a Russian intervention, according to Ukraine's military, was August 2014, not June or July, much less April. Yet Kiev and NATO were claiming in June that Russia had "invaded" Ukraine. *Novaya gazeta* concluded that the numerical data for the number of Russian troops and Russian military casualties in Donbass trumpeted by Kiev were not realistic.[137] To this date no convincing evidence of a major Russian military intervention before August 2014 has been presented.

This reinforces the conclusion that Kiev started the war, and it is fundamentally a civil war. It is as much and, very arguably more Parubiy's war, Turchynov's war, Nalyvaichenko's war, Avakov's war, and Maidan Kiev's war than it is "Putin's war" or "Russia's war." However, what matters ultimately is not propaganda but the more concrete elements of policy. In this view, Russia deserves some of the blame for the war's escalation, its "hybrid war" or stealth occupation in Crimea having sown panic and cynical expediency among the relatively inexperienced players in Kiev.

Consequently, unrealistic strategic propaganda became a hallmark of Maidan Ukraine's secret services and media, as well as Western strategic communication both by government and media. Born of the Maidan regime's Russophobic OUN heritage, exaggerated and often absurd claims regarding Russian and Donbass intentions became the leitmotif of Ukrainian intelligence for years to come. Many were intended to reinforce the "terrorist" label the Maidan regime applied to Donbass's "*vatniki.*" For example, one of the most absurd and clumsy propaganda efforts came in August 2015, when Western and Ukrainian media—including *Newsweek*, Khlyva.net, and Euromaidan Press—began reporting that "sources in the SBU" had uncovered an ongoing Russian effort to help the Donbass rebels build a "dirty" nuclear bomb.[138] Another came in the wake of the March 2016 Islamic State terrorist attacks in Brussels, when Ukraine's SBU chief Vasyl Grytsak said Russia was possibly behind the plot as "part of Russia's hybrid war."[139]

FACT: WAR AND TERROR IN DONBASS

Contrary to Western strategic propaganda, there were never 40,000 or even tens of thousands of Russian troops in Donbass. Russia's and Russians' actual involvement occurred in two forms—volunteers and regular troops—and came in three stages. First came, as noted above, a wave of volunteers of various types. These volunteers acted separately from a very likely additional GRU and SVR penetration into Donbass for gathering intelligence towards making assessments of the two sides' relative military capabilities to inform Kremlin contingency planning and decision-making regarding any further Russian involvement on the ground in Donbass—intelligence, military, political or otherwise. Contrary to Kiev's claims, the overwhelming majority of fighters were not Russians but rather locals, as even Western journalists on the scene reported. For example, Mark Franchetti, a journalist for the British newspaper *The Sunday Times*, shocked a Ukrainian television audience when he reported on Savik Shuster's weekly live political talk show in June 2014 that after three weeks in Donbass he had found that the rebels were overwhelmingly local residents. A "small percentage" were volunteers from Russia. Most rebels had "no military experience" and were "normal, regular citizens who took up arms and are absolutely convinced they are defending their homes, as they say, from fascism."[140] The Russian volunteers included remnants of the Chechen "Vostok" (East) battalion disbanded in 2008 after the Chechen President Ramzan Kadyrov moved against the Yamadaev clan that controlled the detachment.[141] Anti-Putin opposition journalist Babitskii described the Donbass rebels as largely locals and the Russian volunteers as including a wide range of personal and ideological types, "Russian nationalists, monarchists, and pagans," as well as those who identified themselves with a broad "Russian world" or civilization.[142] Many of the local volunteers were former Berkut, MVD, SBU, and military personnel as well as veterans of these institutions who defected in opposition to the new Maidan regime.[143] In this earliest phase, much of the rebel weaponry came from stockpiles in seized government buildings such as SBU and MVD buildings, seized military bases, and weapons surrendered by Ukrainian troops.[144]

The second phase involved the Russian state's support for the mobilization of volunteers, including former and "on leave" servicemen, to Donbass in order to reinforce the volunteers and the probable deployment of some special forces teams to train and back up the rebels. The third phase involved direct military intervention, though something less than an invasion. Limited, strategic military incursions by regular forces were used to prevent major defeats, including encirclements of the rebels on the battlefield. The Russian forces deployed—some 5,000 regular forces and another several thousand "demobilized" and volunteer fighters—rarely intervened in actual combat. They did so in large numbers but twice, and in both cases they did so to prevent the encirclement and rout of Donbass rebel forces and maintain a balanced correlation of forces on the battlefield that the Kremlin and any willing partners might parlay into cease-fires and peace talks.

The Russian Armed Forces' Interventions

Ilovaisk

The first intervention in the battle of Ilovaisk in Donetsk Oblast from August 7 to 30, 2014, the DNR rebels were on the verge of being routed and expelled from the strategic town of Ilovaisk following weeks, even months of retreat after Girkin's units were forced to abandon Slavyansk. The Ukrainian Army maintained an overwhelming advantage in manpower and especially weaponry, testifying to the still limited support coming from Moscow.[145] Even by late August, unconvincing satellite photos from a private company showing a handful of Russian tanks on Ukrainian territory was NATO's best evidence of a "Russian invasion" and "Russian supplies of weapons" to the rebels. On August 28, 2014, NATO published photos showing no more than 9 alleged Russian military vehicles and 4 artillery pieces in Ukraine.[146] On the same day, the London-based International Institute for Strategic Studies found three Russian tanks in Ukraine.[147] This testifies to the limited nature of the Russian presence in Ukraine even during its first "major" incursion. Looking at the correlation of battle forces before the incursion was underway, Russian military analysts were wondering: "Is the end near" for the rebels?[148] Indeed, it seemed as though the bulk of the DNR's forces were on the verge of being destroyed. By mid–August, Kiev's forces brought the battle to the suburbs of both Donbass capitals, Donetsk and Luhansk. Seemingly miraculously the tide turned in late August, after Ukrainian army forces and neofascist-dominated volunteer battalions had taken the city center earlier in the month.

The turnaround was the result of an incursion by perhaps several thousand Russian ground forces, which reinforced—but did not spearhead—a rebel counteroffensive. On August 16, DNR leader Zakharchenko spilled the beans, announcing at a session of the DNR's parliament or Supreme Soviet that reinforcements from Russia had arrived "at the most responsible moment" and included 1,200 troops, 30 tanks, and armored personnel carriers.[149] The DNR and LNR rebels also received crucial Russian intelligence, guidance, and heavy weapons support in the form of artillery and some tanks. The Ukrainian forces were encircled inside the city and ultimately routed. Some were able to leave through a corridor of safe passage—offered by Putin demonstrating his influence among the rebels—under an agreement that, however, broke down on the ground, leading to heavy Ukrainian casualties. Large numbers of Ukrainian forces were encircled and routed, forcing Ukrainian President Petro Poroshenko, elected in May, to agree to cease-fire talks with Putin under the mediation of Germany and France. Cease-fire talks began in Minsk, Belarus, in September days after the rout, with a Russian delegation representing the Donbass rebels. On September 5 an agreement—Minsk 1—was signed on a cease-fire and steps for a full cessation of hostility and Donbass's full return under Kievan sovereignty.

That this August 2014 saw the very first incursion by regular Russian troops is confirmed by the fact that this was the period when the first casualties among Russian servicemen in Ukraine occurred. A report by the Russian news agency RosBusinessConsulting (RBK) detailed the origins of these first casualties among Russian servicemen fighting in Ukraine. It found that almost all of them came from five paratrooper units of the Russian Peacekeeping Forces stationed in Ulyanovsk, Russia, and for those for whom a time of arrival in Ukraine could be identified, they arrived in late August, having been told they were to be assigned to training maneuvers in Rostov.[150] Thus, prior to late summer 2014 at Ilovaisk, there is no evidence of any significant direct military intervention at all by Russian regular forces. The turnaround in the fortunes of the DNR forces was the result of a well-timed, limited intervention by Russian *spetsnaz* and tank and/or artillery support in accordance with the so-called "hybrid warfare" model. Poorly documented Western claims of tens of thousands of Russian troops entering Ukraine again were based on false data provided by the SBU. Indeed, a February 5, 2016, report by the International Crisis Group (ICG), an international think tank unfriendly to Moscow and the Donbass rebels, acknowledged, quoting "a senior DNR security official," that Moscow "may not have as many troops here as Ukraine says, but they can move very fast and decisively."[151]

DEBALTSEVO

Throughout autumn 2014 the Minsk cease-fire gradually weakened. By winter, Minsk 1 had collapsed completely and intense fighting resumed, culminating in the battle of Debaltsevo in January and February. Its aftermath followed a similar pattern to that of Ilovaisk. In December, Ukrainian regular and volunteer forces seized the strategic Debaltsevo railway junction and were on the verge of encircling Donbass rebels. However, by mid–February, Ukrainian forces were again being encircled in a *kotyol*, a "salient" or near-complete encirclement, after an intervention by Russian forces with heavy weapons, including from artillery located over the border inside Russia. Again Kiev's forces were routed, forcing talks on a new cease-fire agreement in which Russia again took part, this time along with a Donbass rebel delegation, the Ukrainian side, and the European intermediaries. On February 12, the Minsk 2 accord was signed, which included a cease-fire agreement and a series of 14 more detailed measures for securing both the cease-fire and a lasting peace and political agreement between Donbass and Kiev (see below).

This time, Russian journalists were able to clearly document the mechanism of hybrid military intervention. The first reliable confirmation of Russian regular forces having been deployed came in an interview published in the Russian opposition newspaper *Novaya gazeta* with twenty-year-old Russian Private Dorzhi Batomunkuev, whose tank battalion was mobilized from Russia's central republic of Buryatiya to Rostov sometime around October 26, 2014, from where they would cross the Ukrainian border in early February 2015 as the Debaltsevo *kotyol* took shape. Batomunkuev's battalion, according to his account, was deployed along with a *spetsnaz* unit from Khabarovsk that had to be cobbled together from several other units. He also witnessed the Moscow-based Kantemirskii Brigade being mobilized in a proximate echelon. Batomunkuev's battalion included 31 tanks and around 120 servicemen divided into three tank regiments with supply and communications equipment. "To every 10 tanks were joined three armored personnel carriers (APCs, in Russian BMPs), a mobile medical unit and 'Ural' trucks with ammunition." This was capped off with 300 infantrymen. All were from Buryatiya, and the majority were ethnic Buryats. The composition was a mix of conscripts and *kontraktniki* (contract servicemen). The men were not told where they were going, nor were they told they were going on maneuvers. Most seemed to understand that they were going to Ukraine. Some, including one officer, refused to go, according to Batomunkuev. They crossed the border and entered Donetsk at night. Batomunkuev had little to say about the rebels, but what he said did not impress. They are "unorganized" and "strange"; they fight intensely and then suddenly stop as though "at work." Regular Ukrainian forces suffered from a similarly low level of motivation, in contrast with the neofascist volunteer battalions. The former largely tried to sneak out of the *kotyol*, usually at night under cover of dark. He said that 2 or 3 thousand of the approximately 8 thousand encircled forces were conscripts; the rest were not, and did not have to come. He thus condemned them for killing women and children, which he apparently witnessed in some way. Batomunkuev also related an exchange with a Ukrainian soldier who admitted that his comrades were killing peaceful civilians and that he had done so himself. He also relayed a Ukrainian radio message they overheard: "Listen carefully, Moscow, Petersburg and Rostov freaks. We will kill you all. First we will kill you, your wives, children and we will get to your parents. We are fascists. We will not stop at anything. We will kill you, like your Chechen brothers, and cut off your heads. Remember this. We will send you home in zinc boxes in pieces." Apparently as a result of these experiences, despite the stealth mobilization and intervention, Batomunkuev considers that he "fought for a just cause."[152]

Four points stand out in these accounts of the civil war. First, the interventions were stealthily prepared and executed. Second, they appeared to be limited in force strength and forced by the need for key strategic interventions when a turning point on the battlefield threatening the rebels is most imminent. Third, the tendency to bring units in from the east could create a reliance on ethnic minority-dominated units like Batomunkuev's, which could exacerbate ethnic divisions within the army and the country. There is little record of poor relations between Russians and Buryats, so this approach could create a new problem for Moscow. Fourth, the nature of the mobilization, lacking in any motivational propaganda or preparation for the troops, as Batomunkuev reports, will limit the effectiveness of such interventions to some degree and could create other problems, such as defections.

These points suggest three political implications. First, Putin seems to be using these interventions not just to affect the correlation of forces on the battlefield, but also to force Kiev to the bargaining table. Second, although it does not appear to be the case with Batomunkuev, who says he supports Putin and the war, the effort to cover up the mobilization and intervention is bound to fail in the long run and could have explosive political ramifications for the Kremlin down the road. Third, Putin might or might not be engaging in effective propaganda when he taunts Kiev that its army is being defeated by "miners and factory workers," but the course of the fighting shows that the DNR and LNR forces are not able to stand on their own. At least twice—at Ilovaisk and Debaltsevo—DNR and LNR rebel forces proved incapable of defending themselves from a concerted Ukrainian offensive. That might have changed with supplies and training gaining apace, but Moscow likely still has little confidence in the rebel forces. The ICG report mentioned above notes that as of early 2016 or at least in 2015 DNR officials were saying that "units capable of responding swiftly to any sign of military emergency are now positioned around Donetsk city and other parts of the oblast" and have "almost certainly" taken part in armed clashes since the February 2015 cease-fire.[153] It also claims that Russia maintains tight control over the DNR and LNR authorities and troops, appointing "curators" (*kuratory*) to oversee civilian rebel leaders and Russian commanders from the battalion level up in the rebel military.[154]

Putin knows the West will not risk a larger war by officially supplying Kiev with lethal weapons. However, the danger grows that the most anti–Russian NATO member-states on Russia's border—Poland and the Baltic states—will learn Putin's hybrid warfare and themselves stealthily provide fighters and lethal weapons to Kiev. There are already volunteers from all over the West fighting on Kiev's side. These stresses will grow should the Minsk cease-fire and peace process break down.

The Volunteer Battalions and the Neofascists

The Maidan regime came to be based on two pillars: elements from among the previous government's state-tied oligarchs—in particular Maidan's first elected president, Petro Poroshenko, and his appointee as governor of Dnepropetrovsk, Ihor Kolomoiskii—and the ultranationalist/neofascist forces. Thus, the ideologically Ukrainian nationalist elements, with the formal exception of Right Sector, were embedded inside the Ukraine's weak state in the persons of top power ministries or *siloviki*, especially Chairman of Ukraine's National Security and Defense Council (NSDC) Parubiy, SBU Chairman Valentyn Nalyvaichenko, and Minister of Internal Affairs Arsen Avakov. Parubiy, co-founder of the neo–Nazi Social-National Party in the 1990s and commander of EuroMaidans' self-defense forces, later on joined the more moderate but still considerably national chauvinist "Fatherland" (Batkyvshina) party. Nalyvaichenko headed the SBU in 2006–2010 when the SBU archival service became the brain center for the dissemination of pro–Bandera, neofascist revisions of Ukrainian history. Avakov has been caught in repeated lies about events in Ukraine, including the Maidan snipers' massacre and the Odessa pogrom discussed below. Their appointments to the council was a reward to the far-right groups that seized power in Kiev in February in place of the more democratic elements on Maidan. Indeed, the tenor of the Maidan regime's *siloviki* was best expressed in the offer to RS leader Yarosh to take the post of deputy NSDC chief, which he turned down. Under Parubiy's oversight of the entire bloc of *siloviki* departments (military, intelligence, police, prosecutors), Avakov created a network of paramilitary groups or "volunteer battalions" loosely tied—or not, in many cases—to the Defense and Interior Ministries and the newly created National Guard.

On April 13, 2014, Avakov announced that the MVD was introducing "a number of structural innovations, answering to the challengers of today's times." Specifically, the MVD was creating "special units" for every oblast in the country from among "the patriots of the country" and would number 12,000 fighters in total. This would account for 20 percent of the some 60,000 troops sent to put down anti–Maidan revolts in Donbass. He also mentioned two battalions by name, "Dnepr" and "Vostok," and promised battalions for Donetsk, Kherson, Kharkiv, Luhansk, Nikolaev, and Odessa as well.[155] By June, Avakov listed in one social network posting some 30 such battalions, numbering already some 3,000 fighters, with a projected total cadre now of 5,660.[156] Two weeks later he indicated which volunteer battalions were subordinated to the Defense Ministry's

National Guard and which were subordinated to his MVD. Among the latter were those that would prove to be two of the most notorious battalions—Azov and Dnepr-1. Avakov also criticized the members of the volunteer battalions who a day earlier had attempted to storm the Rada in an attempt to "complete" the nationalist revolution under cover of protest against the management of the ATO—a harbinger of things to come.[157]

The volunteer battalions of "the country's patriots" were recruited largely from the ranks of the ultranationalist and neofascist organizations such as Yarosh's Right Sector, Belitskiy's Social National Assembly, Tyahnybok's SP, and other smaller such groups. For example, the MVD formed the "Sich" volunteer battalion exclusively form SP members.[158] Moreover, Avakov's list of battalions did not include the completely autonomous RS battalions under its volunteer corps DUK, which by April 2016 still had not been subordinated to state organs of coercion and enjoyed impunity when committing war crimes, terrorist attacks, and other crimes. The most prominent volunteer battalions were those of the Azov, Aidar, Donbass, and the RS DUK corps. More than Ukraine's regular army forces, these battalions or their members would be responsible for most of the atrocities, war crimes and terrorist attacks committed at the front in eastern Ukraine during the ATO's peak, as well as later in the rear in places like Odessa, Makachevo, and Kiev itself.

Right Sector's DUK Battalions

As of summer 2015 RS's DUK battalions numbered at least 2,000 fighters, with 700 permanently deployed at the front, according to Yarosh in an early 2016 interview after his departure from RS. In summer 2015, DUK's commander Andrey Skoropadskii noted there were 19 DUK battalions and 2 smaller "tactical groups." The battalions numbered sometimes fewer than 100, sometimes more than 300. The Fifth and Eighth Battalions and the two tactical groups were the only units permanently stationed at the front and therefore were probably larger. The others were based and apparently recruited from particular oblasts. In addition, each battalion had a reserve that appears to be at least as large as the active force. For example, Yarosh mentioned that the Fifth included 200 permanent fighters and 637 total. The Eighth included 317 fighters, but Yarosh does not indicate whether this figure encompasses permanent or the entire cohort of fighters. Thus, these figures suggest an overall force of some 6,000 as of summer 2015, with perhaps a smaller number at the beginning of the ATO in spring 2014. RS has four training bases, one near the front in Pesky and another in Dnepropetrovsk. Maidan-appointed governor of Dnepropetrovsk and banking and energy oligarch Ihor Kolomoiskii financed RS, its DUK battalions and other battalions, such as Dnepropetrovsk's Dnepr battalions.[159] Yarosh himself would be one of the first RS members involved in combat, beginning with his involvement in the infamous Easter attack that became Kiev's apparent pretext for abandoning the April 17, 2014, Geneva cease-fire agreement.

AZOV

The "Azov" battalion is directly subordinated to the MVD and thus to Avakov. Avakov appointed the notorious neofascist SNA leader, Andriy Biletskiy, as Azov's commander, revealing the neofascist sympathies of the Maidan regime's top law enforcement official. According to Azov's political commissar (*zampolit*) Oleg Odnorozhenko, the battalion was founded on May 4, 2014, from members of "patriotic organizations" after discussions with the MVD and Defense Ministry. However, the battalion movement had already emerged, according to Odnorozhenko, in March—that is, before the declaration of the ATO. It began from the grassroots as a movement of ultranationalists and neofascists from groups like RS and SP, calling itself the "little black men"—a counterplay on the idiom "polite little green men" used for the unmarked Russian special forces that spread out across Crimea at that time. In April, the little black men began to seek "official status" under the ATO's volunteer battalions.[160] Since the SNA was a founding group of Right Sector, it is no surprise that Azov includes many RS recruits.[161] Azov's battle insignia is the SNA's flag logo, the altered German Nazi "Wolfsangel."[162]

Azov has been the beneficiary of funding from both oligarch Igor Kolomoiskii and the ultranationalist Radical Party of Oleh Lyashko.[163] By April 2015, Azov was attempting to reach the threshold of 1,200 fighters who had undergone requisite training which would qualify it to receive heavy weaponry.[164] Azov units were dispersed in smaller groups across the Donbass front but established a base in Mariupol on the Sea of Azov adjacent to the Black Sea. Azov, along with RS and the SP, occasionally holds joint Nazi-like torchlight marches through Kiev and other cities. For example, on October 14, 2014, in the wake of the first Minsk cease-fire agreement (Minsk 1), they held a march throughout Kiev threatening the new Maidan regime with a new truly "nationalist revolution."[165]

The Azov battalion's general reputation and alleged war atrocities would prompt the U.S. Congress in June 2015 to adopt an amendment that ostensibly forbade U.S. advisors training the Ukrainian army and National Guard from training members of the Azov Battalion.[166] Anton Gerashchenko, advisor to MVD chief Avakov, responded to the U.S. Congress's move by saying there was an "anti–Ukrainian lobby" in Congress.[167] Although perhaps a good first step, this measure could not suffice either to deal with the possible training of Azov or other neo–Nazis in Ukraine or to address the Maidan regime's overall neofascist challenge. Indeed, the next month Azov sergeant Ivan Kharkiv confirmed that U.S. military advisors had been and still were training Azov fighters, and a U.S. official stated that any screening would not be for ideology but for human rights violations.[168]

AIDAR

Even the pro–Maidan *Kyiv Post* has designated Aidar "an ultranationalist organization."[169] Thus, Aidar's top commander Serhiy Melnychuk would be elected to the Rada in October 2014 from Lyashko's ultranationalist Radical Party, where he was third on the party list.[170] In September 2014 an Amnesty International report detailed war crimes committed by members of the Aidar Battalion in north Luhansk region between April and August 2014.[171] Aidar was so outside any form of control that regular army officers frequently complained about Aidar's "marauding and violence" against Luhansk locals. After being routed on June 17–18, 2014, Melnychuk claimed there were traitors inside the ATO's command structures informing the Donbass rebels of ATO battle plans.[172] Aidar's fighters—who were almost all formerly on the Maidan and hailed from Luhansk, Dometsk, Kiev, western Ukraine, and even Russia and Canada—had little training and were initially poorly armed.[173] By June 2014, there already was talk of disbanding it.[174] Yet at the same time, the EuroMaidan's media organs were publishing sympathetic pieces about Aidar.[175]

In early March 2015, Aidar was reorganized into a 'storming battalion" and more directly subordinated to the Defense Ministry, but by this time the battalion had already moved into open criminal activity, providing cover for a local organized crime group in

Luhansk.[176] In late March, Aidar's commander Melnychuk was being investigated by the GPO for kidnapping the director of the alcohol company Ukrainian Spirits (UkrSpirt).[177] On March 31, 2015, after several egregious Aidar human rights violations that month in Luhansk, Kiev's governor in the region, Gennadii Moskal, who had repeatedly reported Aidar's crimes, sent a public appeal to the Defense Ministry, forcing an investigation.[178] In July 2015, on the defensive, Aidar and RS held a joint march in Kiev protesting a cease-fire negotiated between Kiev, Donbass, Moscow, and the EU.[179]

DONBASS-1

The Donbass battalions were formed by and subordinated to the MVD. Like the Dnepr battalions, there were several. The most well-known was Donbass-1 (from here on simply Donbass), originally made up almost predominantly of Donbass residents. Its commander was an ostensible Donetsk native, Semyon Semyonchenko. Donbass closely cooperated with neofascist groups both at the front militarily and in the rear politically. Yarosh and other RS members fought alongside or under the banner of the Donbass battalion, which was based in Severodonetsk, where Aidar's filtration camp was located.[180] In December 2014, Amnesty International criticized the Donbass, Aidar and Dnepro battalions as well as RS for cooperating in blocking humanitarian aid to Donbass's war-stricken residents organized by Donbass coal oligarch Rinat Akhmetov.[181]

Although Semyonchenko was awarded the Bohdan Khmelnitskiy Medal after being wounded at the front in August 2014, he and his battalion quickly fell out of favor with the authorities. He repeatedly charged the authorities with military incompetence and expediency in relation to the lives of battalion volunteers.[182] On the eve of then newly elected President Petro Poroshenko's pivotal June 30, 2014, meeting with Parubiy, Avakov, and the powerful NSDC that would decide whether or not to extend a truce in Donbass that Poroshenko had initiated a week earlier, Semyonchenko and members of Donbass led a several-thousand-strong demonstration in Kiev backed by the Aidar and Dnepr battalions as well as RS and the SP.[183] Both Semyonchenko and RS leader Yarosh threatened to march volunteer battalions to Kiev and overthrow the oligarchic regime in favor of a truly nationalist revolution.[184] The demonstrators demanded that Poroshenko end the truce, declare martial law, and destroy the eastern rebels or they would remove the president from power "like Yanukovich." They beat up a journalist and tossed stun grenades, seriously injuring several demonstrators. One demonstrator claimed he saw MVD officers hand the stun grenades to members of Avakov's Kiev-based paramilitary group "17+ Sotny," who threw the grenades. Although Avakov condemned the violence the next day, no one was ever arrested.[185]

After the war resumed, Semyonchenko was seriously wounded on August 19, 2014, during the pivotal battle of Ilovaisk. According to his official biography, he interrupted treatment of his wounds to return to the front, helping to lead the Donbass battalion, largely decimated, out of encirclement. Famous for appearing in public always wearing a "*balaklava*," or full head mask or covering, Semyonchenko built intrigue around himself. On 1 September 2014 he unmasked in public.[186] His official autobiography, published for his successful run for parliament in October 2014 on the Self-Help (*Samopomich*) Party's slate, revealed that he was born in Sevastopol and was an ethnic Russian.[187] Although there originally were no charges about Donbass's conduct at the front of the kind leveled against Azov and Aidar, in late January 2016 Semyonchenko was stripped of his officer's rank by the National Guard, and in February prosecutors announced they had opened an investigation into Semyonchenko for illegal deprivation of freedom (abduction), exceeding his authority, and the use of falsified documents.[188] Other ultranationalist parties contributed to other battalions. For example, many members of Lyashko's Radical Party were recruited into the Shakhtersk Battalion.[189]

The oligarchs played a key role in forming and maintaining the volunteer battalions and their neofascist cohort. The crucible of war forged what would otherwise prove to be a difficult alliance of oligarchs and neofascists that predominated within the new regime. The RS, Azov, Aidar, and Donbass battalions were financed by pro–Maidan oligarch and Poroshenko-appointed Dnepropetrovsk Governor Ihor Kolomoiskii. The Dnepr 1, 2 and 3 battalions were both financed by and placed under the direct control of Kolomoiskii, as stated by his deputy governor Gennadii Korban, who was close to Yarosh and RS.[190] The neofascists' service to the Maidan regime during the ATO led to the promotion of some into high-ranking government positions. Indeed, this is precisely what Radical Party leader Lyashko demanded as the battalions were being formed, proposing offices such as judges and prosecutors for volunteers after the war.[191] Thus, RS's Yarosh, Azov's Biletskiy, Aidar's Melnychuk, and Donbass's Semyonchenko all found places on nationalist parties' lists, and/or their campaigns were funded by oligarchs like Kolomoiskii. Thus they all were elected to the Rada in October 2014. The same month Avakov appointed SNA member and Azov deputy commander Vadim Troyan as Kiev Oblast's MVD chief and in March 2016 promoted him to the post of first deputy chief of the new National Police. Troyan was captured in a photograph giving the Nazi salute with several Azov members.[192] Before the war Troyan worked in a company led by a close Avakov associate.[193]

Maidan regime officials strongly defended their use of neo–Nazis in their ATO operations. Like Avakov, his advisor Anton Gerashchenko emphasized: "The most important thing is their spirit and their desire to make Ukraine free and independent. A person who takes a weapon in his hands and goes to defend his motherland is a hero. And his political views are his own affair."[194] However, a good portion of the Maidan regime's attitude towards such "patriots" had less to do with tolerance of, and more to do with enthusiasm for, the neofascists in the battalions. Years before the SP was in power, mired in street violence and aggressive speeches, SP leader Tyahnybok's chief political advisor Yurii Mikhal'chyshyn envisioned the developing scenario. Known for praising the Holocaust as "a bright episode in European civilization" and founding the Joseph Goebbels Political Research Center, he declared in 2011: "Our Banderite army will cross the Dnipro and throw that blue-ass gang, which today usurps the power, out of Ukraine…. That will make those Asiatic dogs shut their ugly mouths."[195] Thus, the Maidan regime's use of neofascist and criminal elements in the volunteer battalions—part of the regime's founding, formative experience, along with events such as the Maidan snipers' massacre— would have a deleterious effect on Ukraine's already shaky foundations for the rule of law.

War Crimes

International monitoring organizations that have investigated the conduct of the Donbass war have concluded that both sides in equal measure have violated civil rights and committed war crimes. Since Western readers will be less familiar with the violations committed by the Ukrainian armed forces, including the volunteer battalions, I focus more on those. In this regard, it should also be borne in mind that those forces are responsible for most of the dead and wounded among Donbass's civilians, given the simple fact that Kiev's forces are the attacking force, targeting villages and cities where the rebels live, take cover, and are mounting a defensive resistance to Kiev's attempt to bring Donbass under the control of the new Maidan regime. In September 2014, after the battle of Ilovaisk and the signing of Minsk 1 marked the end of the first phase of the civil war, Amnesty International's General Secretary stated: "All sides in this conflict have shown disregard for civilian lives and are blatantly violating their international obligations."[196] The United Nations Human Rights Council's (UNHRC) 12th report on the human rights situation in Ukraine, covering the period from August 16 to November 15, 2015, concluded that the population in the areas controlled by the DNR and LNR continue to be subjected to "serious human rights violations … with new allegations of killings, torture and ill-treatment, illegal detention and forced labour" received by the UN Human Rights Monitoring Mission in Ukraine (HRMMU). Local residents "remain without any effective protection of their rights," and "[p]laces of detention maintained by the armed groups [are] virtually inaccessible for independent oversight" by international organizations, including the HRMMU. Similarly, the same report noted that the Ukrainian government's efforts in the combat zone are "accompanied by allegations of enforced disappearances, arbitrary and *incommunicado* detention as well as torture and ill treatment of people suspected of trespassing against territorial integrity or terrorism or believed to be supporters of the 'Donetsk people's republic' and 'Luhansk people's republic.'" SBU elements appeared to enjoy "a high degree of impunity, with rare investigations into allegations involving them."[197]

Examples of Donbass rebels' violations of human rights support the aforementioned reports' characterization of the types of violations occurring. Suffice it to say that Girkin-Strelkov, upon his return to Russia after being replaced as DNR rebel forces' commander, acknowledged that he had personally executed four people during his "tenure" there: "Two among the military for looting, one local for looting, and one for killing a serviceman."[198] Thus, Russia is now in a position of harboring someone who has committed a capital crime on the territory of a foreign state. Numerous Ukrainian, Russian, and Western media reports of abductions, detentions and torture by the rebels confirmed reports of the kind cited above by AI and the UN.

The July 17, 2014, shootdown of the Malaysian MH17 civilian airliner, very likely by the DNR resistance, was clearly accidental, judging by the audiotape Kiev produced and claimed proves the rebels' role.[199] The rebels mistook the plane for a military transport, of which they had shot down at least two in recent months. The accidental nature of this atrocity makes it less germane to the issue of insurgent war crimes and perniciousness. However, if the Russians supplied the rebels with the "Buk" zenith-missile air defense system that apparently shot down the plane, then Moscow would take on more culpability, not only for the escalation and sheer irresponsibility of supplying such weapons to inexperienced fighters, but for any ensuing intensification of fighting and bad blood. However, it is more likely that the Donbass rebels had seized at least one Buk system from captured Ukrainian forces. Indeed, just three days before the MH17 shootdown, the Donbass rebels shot down a Ukrainian military transport plane, which they claimed they accomplished using a captured and repaired Buk. Moreover, the resistance claimed they shot down Ukrainian air force jets on July 11 and 12.[200] Russian media reports and confirmation by

Ukraine's ATO spokesman, Aleksei Dmytrashkovskii, on June 29 indicated that in the course of seizing a Ukrainian air defense base in Donetsk that day, DNR rebels indeed captured at least one "Buk" system as well as a "Kupol" air defense system, which can locate targets up to 150 km away.[201] As a result, according to quoted DNR rebels, "an open sky over Donbass has been secured."

It is likely that the volunteer battalions were responsible for most of the war crimes committed by the pro–Maidan forces. Numerous war crimes and other violations of human rights committed by the neofascist-dominated volunteer battalions were reported by international and other human rights organizations as well as Russian, Ukrainian, and Western media. In September 2014, for example, Amnesty International (AI) reported Aidar for repeated human rights abuses in north Luhansk. It noted that battalion members "have been involved in widespread abuses, including abductions, unlawful detention, ill-treatment, theft, extortion, and possible executions." Typically, victims are accused of being "separatists" and then abducted to a filtration center in Severodonetsk, where they are beaten and otherwise abused. The Aidar commander in the area threatened researchers, warning them: "It's not Europe. It's a bit different.... There is a war here. The law has changed, procedures have been simplified.... If I choose to, I can have you arrested right now, put a bag over your head and lock you up in a cellar for 30 days on suspicion of aiding separatists." The report also noted that although Aidar was supposed to be subordinated to the Defense Ministry, there is no control over the battalion's members, who act with complete impunity.[202] The AI report was published days after Kiev-based Pravilnoe TV reported it had confirmed in part a gruesome Russian television report that two separatist fighters had been beheaded or at least had their heads sent to their mothers. Pravilnoe TV reported that it had spoken with one of the victims' mothers, who confirmed that her son was a Donetsk rebel who was captured during combat and that she had received her son's head in a wooden box by post. She blamed the nationalist volunteers for her son's death.[203]

Throughout August 2014, Aidar's human rights abuses were appearing repeatedly in the daily reports of the Organization on Security and Cooperation in Europe Special Monitoring Mission to Ukraine (OSCE SMM Ukraine). One such incident was described as follows:

> At a meeting arranged by the chief of police in Starobilsk (97 km north of Luhansk city) on 20 August, a man claimed that he had been severely beaten the previous day in Polovynkyne (88 km north of Luhansk) by members of a Ukrainian volunteer battalion. He said members of the 24th *Aidar* Battalion—already at the centre of accusations of human rights abuses in the northern Luhansk region *(see SMM daily reports of 8 August, 11 August, 14 August)*—after detaining him at a checkpoint, had accused him of separatism and had threatened to kill him, unless his wife paid over USD 10,000. She did so, whereupon he was released the same day, he said. The SMM observed that the man's head was heavily swollen, bloody and bruised and that he had bruises and smaller wounds on his arms and legs.[204]

As noted earlier, Kiev's governor in the districts of Luhansk not under rebel control, Gennadii Moskal, reported repeatedly on Aidar crimes. Two such descriptions appeared in a Ukrainian media report. The first concerned a shootout initiated by Aidar with the pro–Maidan "Ternopil" volunteer battalion in the center of the city of Lisichansk. The second was a March 16, 2015, incident when three drunken Aidar fighters broke into an apartment in Lisichansk, smashed the head of the father of the family with a rifle, and beat him repeatedly after he fell to the floor. They then went onto the street and opened fire on the building, shooting its exterior walls and windows for ten minutes and throwing the district into a panic.[205] Aidar was also involved in stealing from Russian Orthodox churches and kidnapping, extorting or otherwise terrorizing officials on the model of its closely associated Radical Party of Oleh Lyashko.[206] In July 2014, Aidar fighters abducted the deputy mayor of the town of Schastya, accusing him of financing *titushki*, who the day before had broken into his home and stolen items. His whereabouts were unknown for at least a week. The next day, they entered a city council meeting and claimed the deputy mayor had turned himself in to Aidar and that the director of a local enterprise was also wanted on suspicion of assisting the rebels.[207] In August 2015, Aidar fighters took hostage the village council of Runovshinsk in Poltava Oblast.[208]

Another notorious but lesser known battalion was "Tornado," formed by and in theory—like Azov and Aidar—subordinated to the MVD. On August 18, Ukrainian prosecutors accused members of the battalion of committing numerous and systematic beatings, rapes, murders and robberies, causing RS and other neofascist groups to come out in its support. Tornado's commander Ruslan Onischenko had several prior convictions; despite or because of this, he was put in command of Tornado's 150 men and sent to Donbass. Indeed, Radical Party leader Lyashko was urging at the time the sending of even more criminal offenders to the front, since criminals supposedly fight better.[209] In print and on television, Ukraine's chief military prosecutor Anatolii Matios detailed the crimes, including: unlawful deprivation of liberty without any legal or other grounds; torture, including but not limited to electric shock to body parts; rape of male prisoners; the murder of one after such torture; and recording videos of these crimes. Matios read the following description on Ukrainian television: "The fighters had prisoners tortured by means of an object similar to a power generator. The prisoners were held in the basement, stripped naked, placed on a concrete wall and doused with water. Then they were touched with live wires to various body parts, such as at the temple, the genitals and the testicles." According to a statement of a former prisoner, prisoners "were forced under threat of death to rape another prisoner." Two Tornado fighters were also said to have been planning to shoot Kiev Oblast's police chief.[210] Matios held MVD chief Avakov partially responsible, saying he "could have saved many lives if the Interior Ministry made the right personnel decisions." Moreover, a warning was ignored when SBU agents arrested Tornado fighters in November 2014 in Kiev, far from the front. On June 18, 2015, military police disarmed Tornado's 170 fighters, arresting several including Onishchenko.[211] Just months prior, Onishechnko was a national hero, awarded a medal by Patriarch Filaret, head of the Ukrainian Orthodox Church.[212]

Right Sector fighters also have committed atrocities. In May 2015 a RS fighter cut off the forefingers of at least one rebel fighter he caught in eastern Ukraine after battle. Internet photos posted by the RS fighters showed "prisoners," and some showed stumps of severed fingers and fresh wounds. RS commander Ilya Bogdanov claimed the perpetrator was "'working for Putin,' he wrote on Facebook." AI's Tatjana Masur stated at the time, according to *Der Spiegel*, that "there is no evidence of systematic abuse by the Ukrainian side: 'But there are such cases and they are spreading.'"[213]

It is also likely that the Ukrainian regular army has been using the neofascists' propensity for extreme violence, pushing them forward in combat as the initial shock troops against the armed rebels and civilian *vatniki*. The tactics, as described by the *New York Times*, appear to use regular army artillery in softening the target, "followed by chaotic, violent assaults" by the battalions.[214] At the same time, the Ukrainian army and even some of the more heavily armed but poorly trained neofascist battalions were using heavy weapons, including unguided Grad rockets, against civilian-populated areas for months. In July 2014, Human Rights Watch released a report condemning this Kiev practice.[215] Like many such attacks on civilians, the bloody aftermath of one of the most horrific Ukrainian air force attacks on June 2, 2014, in which at least six civilians were killed in the center of Luhansk, can be seen in a video.[216] The Ukrainian air force indiscriminately bombs from the air as well, as numerous videos demonstrate.[217]

There is also evidence that both sides have used cluster bombs and incendiary munitions, with the Ukrainian army and volunteer battalions often targeting civilians and the Donbass rebels targeting Kiev's forces. In October 2014, HRW issued a report stating: "There is particularly strong evidence that Ukrainian government forces were responsible for several cluster munition attacks on central Donetsk in early October." Although HRW also mentioned the rebels had used such weapons, a key distinction is that the Ukrainian army is accused of targeting civilians in city centers, while the "probable" use by the rebels targeted Ukrainian troops.[218] A HRW report on the use of cluster weapons in January and February 2015 found that at a minimum two of seven and likely four of seven villages hit by such weapons were targeted from areas controlled by pro–Maidan forces.[219] HRW has also detected possible use of incendiary weapons banned by international law against civilians in Donbass villages. However, it was unable to confirm which side used the weapons, but did request Germany to pressure Kiev to stop using inaccurate weapons against civilians in Donbass.[220]

Minsk 2

As noted above, Minsk 1 broke down, leading to Debaltsevo and a "Minsk 2" agreement signed by Kiev, this time with representatives of the DNR and LNR on February 12, 2015, under the auspices of Russia and the EU. As of this writing it is fifteen months since Minsk 2's signing. The cease-fire has largely held, but adherence to the agreement hangs by a thread. Both the cease-fire and the withdrawal were achieved quickly in March in compliance with the agreement. Both sides have occasionally broken the cease-fire with small-scale fighting, but it has largely held. Crucially for the lives of Donbassians, the withdrawal of troops and weapons was implemented by both sides. The parties regularly dispute which side is failing to fulfill its obligations under the agreement, with Washington and Brussels accusing Russia of failing to pressure the Donbass signatories to abide by the agreement. But in fact, Moscow has been rather rigorous in getting the DNR and LNR to abide by their obligations, which in many ways are fewer than Kiev's.

The agreement's first three points deal with the cease-fire and the withdrawal of Kiev and Donbass forces from the line of contact.[221] The already cited 2016 ICG report indeed acknowledged that as regards Moscow's enforcement of the rebels' compliance with the cease-fire, the former has "mostly done rigorously," such that: "Separatist officials and officers regularly complain that if their fighters respond to Ukrainian fire, [Russian] *kurators* threaten reduction or reduction of military supplies."[222] From Moscow's point of view, Minsk 2's text refers only to Ukrainian and rebel forces, with no mention of Russian troops. Therefore, the aforementioned ICG and others' claims of a continuous Russian military presence in Donbass, if true, would not be in violation of the letter of the relevant first three clauses in the agreement.

From the fourth clause in Minsk 2's text, a series of difficult obligations are placed on Kiev and its very divided Maidan regime (see Chapter 10). The fourth point stipulates: "On the first day following the withdrawal a dialogue [between Kiev and Donbass representatives] is to begin with respect to the modalities of the local elections in accordance with Ukrainian legislation and the Law of Ukraine 'On the temporary order of local government in certain areas of the Donetsk and the Lugansk regions,' as well as with respect to the future operation of these areas on the basis of the Law." Kiev did not fulfill this pivotal step—the first in the agreement with a specific deadline. A full year after the agreement and nearly a full year since the cease-fire and subsequent troop pullback, Kiev has refused to engage a dialogue with the Donbass rebel regions' representatives: (1) either on the modalities related to conducting elections in the Donbass, or (2) on the Ukrainian law to be adopted according to Minsk 2 "On the temporary order of local government in certain areas of the Donetsk and the Lugansk regions," or (3) "with respect to the future operation of these areas on the basis of the Law," or, for that matter, (4) on any other subject related to the crisis. Thus, Kiev was the first to violate Minsk 2's "letter" and has remained in violation of it since the second day after the implementation of the mutual troop pullbacks in March 2015.

Moreover, this means that Kiev is in violation of Minsk 2's fifth point or article, which reads: "Immediately, and not later than 30 days from the date of signing of this document, the Verkhovna Rada of Ukraine is to adopt a resolution with the specification of the territory covered by the special regime provided for in the Law of Ukraine 'On the temporary order of local government in certain areas of the Donetsk and the Lugansk regions,' [such territory] to be based on the line set out in the Minsk Memorandum of September 19, 2014." The stipulation that Kiev consult—i.e. negotiate—in dialogue with Donbass representatives on the law "On the temporary order of local government," etc., is reiterated in Minsk 2's article 12. Instead of dialogue on the temporary local government law, on March 17, 2015, the Verkhovna Rada passed unilaterally a corresponding resolution, having failed to consult with the Donbass rebels' representatives in a "dialogue.

Minsk 2's article 11 requires Kiev to adopt a new constitution "with entry into force by the end of 2015 … which shall incorporate decentralization as a key element (taking into account the characteristics of certain areas of the Donetsk and the Luhansk regions, to be agreed upon with the representatives of these areas), as well as, before the end of 2015, adoption of permanent legislation with respect to the special status of certain areas of the Donetsk and the Luhansk regions in accordance with the measures specified in the Note." Minsk 2's "Note" mandates that the new constitution and any corresponding laws for decentralization provide for: (1) "linguistic self-determination" (to allow Donbass and perhaps other regions to use minority languages such as Russian); (2) participation of local governments in appointing the heads of prosecutorial bodies and the courts in certain areas of Donbass (Donetsk and Luhansk); the possibility for the central executive authorities to conclude agreements with authorities in the Donbass on economic, social and cultural development in certain regions; the establishment of a People's Militia by order of local councils for maintaining public order in Donbass; and several other clauses. Neither a new constitution nor a law on decentralization and the other issues listed in the Note had been adopted by Kiev as of early April 2016.

Neither has Kiev lifted the blockade to the separatist Donbass regions, reopened Ukrainian banking in those regions, nor issued the across-the-board amnesty for the rebels as required by the agreement. Thus, from March 17, 2015, Kiev has been in violation of no fewer than seven articles and nine obligations it signed on to under the Minsk 2 accord. On the other side, Russia has still not handed control over the border to Kiev, but this violation followed Kiev's first violations. Again, there likely are military, intelligence and other advisors working on the Donbass side, but this issue does not fall under the scope of the agreement and remains unenforceable without the reassertion of Kiev's sovereignty over the breakaway territories.

Both Kiev and Donbass have exchanged prisoners on an equal, negotiated basis. Both Kiev and Donbass occasionally violate the ceasefire, but both have generally complied with the withdrawal of heavy weaponry to the distance from the front line imposed by the agreement. Except the timeframes mentioned above for the ceasefire and withdrawal of weapons, none of the other points in Minsk 2 were assigned time frames or deadlines, so violations of them are more difficult to identify. So, in sum, Kiev was significantly more in violation of the agreement than the Donbass rebels and/or Moscow from its early 2015 failure to enter a dialogue and begin constitutional changes with Donbass, and remained so with no constitutional reforms passed as of early April 2016.

Conclusion

Moscow did not instigate the rebellion in Donbass and did not intend to use it to annex Donbass or to destabilize Ukraine as part of some "Putin master plan" for territorial expansion. Moscow does not seek to revise the international order. Putin's decision-making—from Yanukovich's hesitation in signing the EU AA through the Donbass civil war—has been reactive and defensive in the sense of trying to take advantage of the situation to mitigate previous losses. Moscow has had less control over events than the West and Kiev, and its primary goals were to avoid the loss of Crimea's Black Sea Fleet naval base and the coercive reintegration of the Donbass under Kiev's sovereignty. Regarding the latter issue, Moscow has tried with little avail to get the Maidan government in Kiev to negotiate directly with the DNR/LNR rebels in order to cease the civil war, secure some decree of power-sharing or autonomy for the Donbass, and bring an end to Western sanctions against Russia, Crimea, and Donbass. Thus, Moscow has used its influence over the rebels and carefully deployed and calibrated military power in order to bring both parties to the negotiating table in Minsk.

Perhaps the main cause of Ukraine's failure to fulfill its obligations under Minsk 2 is the deep political paralysis in Kiev. That paralysis is driven by the ultranationalist and neofascist wings of the Ukrainian polity, which are robust and gaining strength under the stress of continued economic collapse, social dislocation, and state-supported ideological radicalization. President Poroshenko—like his forefather Viktor Yuschenko (Ukraine's president from 2004 to 2010)—would play into the hands of the ultranationalist groups like RS and the SP by rehabilitating the World War II–era neofascist OUN and UPA, hailing their members as the heroes of Maidan Ukraine's national myth along with the RS and SP. Such neofascists, who led the civil war and were responsible for so many "excesses," including war crimes and terrorism, at the front, would threaten the ceasefire, the rule of law, and the new hybrid Maidan regime itself.

10

"Revolution of Dignity" or Revolution in Vain?

Here our main focus—the causality chain of the Ukrainian crisis—ends. To sum up, what were the sources of, and parties responsible for, the crisis sparked by the ultimately violent "revolution of dignity" from below and climaxing with the Donbass civil war? Clearly, the sources were both geopolitical and Ukrainian domestic. Mackinderian geopolitics and Huntingtonian and Eurasian civilizationism created a structure for potential conflict between Russia and the West over the region separating them. These ideational factors were expressed by NATO and its goals, the transatlantic community (Atlantic Council, etc.), and the community of democracies. NATO and the EU decided to maintain and extend the institutionalization of Mackinder's World Ocean and Huntington's and the Eurasianists' "West" in creating a post–Cold War order. Thus, the engine driving the crisis was the expansion of world history's most powerful military alliance, NATO, into Russia's sphere of influence, to its very borders in violation of Western promises at the end of the Cold War that the alliance would not expand beyond reunified Germany. Russia responded by pushing the organization of the World Island and its Eurasian civilizations. These two processes would come to culminations with the color revolutions and wars in Georgia and Ukraine.

The West—the U.S. and EU combined—and Russia created a geopolitical tectonic that would tear an already divided Ukraine apart. In winter 2013–2014 the country's politics were driven over the edge, from quasi-constitutionalist to aconstitutional crisis politics and ultimately a violent quasi-revolution from below. The polarization driven by geopolitical and domestic politics confounded the potential for a pacted transition based on the February 21 agreement, producing revolutionary regime transformation. Although elite and oligarchic elements sought to control events, radical ultranationalist elements infiltrated the peaceful revolution begun on the Maidan, pushing the revolt in a direction backed by neither the original pro-democracy revolutionary element nor the political and business elite.

With the above detailed in previous chapters, I conclude examining the domestic and international consequences of the crisis and its implications and lessons for both causality and political actors' responsibility for Ukraine's present and near future. Just as the causes of the Ukrainian crisis were both domestic and international, so too are its consequences. Domestically, the crisis, revolution, state breakdown and war have not produced unity, but rather a still divided state and society. Both are split between aspects of Maidan's hybrid regime, which includes a democratic political system for the elite but lacks the rule of law and certain democratic freedoms, producing a rather uncivil society. The regime's hybridity is both democratic and authoritarian, with the latter aspect being oligarchic-ultranationalist. Many of the old oligarchs control state institutions, while ultranationalists control most of the *siloviki* and regime ideology. The oligarchs and the neofascists sometimes overlap and join forces, but the latter continue to pursue a fully "nationalist revolution," seeking to subordinate the oligarchs' business interests to their own. Internationally, the Ukrainian crisis has produced what is often called a "New Cold War." The West has sought to isolate Russia diplomatically, collapse its economy through sanctions, and expand NATO and EU influence by depicting Russia as a revisionist power pursuing territorial expansion and "the restoration of the Soviet empire" rather than acting in the context of a classic security dilemma.

The wages of the Maidan revolution and civil war were steep for the Ukrainian people—east and west. According to Maidan Ukraine officials, by the second anniversary of Yanukovich's overthrow, more than 9,000 had been killed and more than 20,000 wounded as a result of the revolt and ATO. Among these casualties, 2,600 Ukrainian servicemen were killed and 9,000 wounded. This means that approximately 6,400 Donbass civilians and rebels were killed and 11,000 were wounded. Also, two million Ukrainians—all from the Donbass—were displaced.[1] According to the UN, 800,961 Ukrainians were forced to seek asylum, residence permits or other forms of legal stay in neighboring countries; 659,143 sought asylum in Russia and an additional 81,023 did so in Belarus.[2] The country has lost territory, and its economy has been ravaged. In sum, the revolution, resistance, Russian intervention and resulting civil war cost Ukraine much. Did the price justify the purchase? Did Maidan's "revolution of dignity" bring the new European democratic political order its leaders and the West promised?

Maidan Democracy? Ukraine's Hybrid Oligarchic-Ultranationalist Regime

On its face, Maidan Ukraine's political system functions more or less democratically. Hidden behind its formal democracy, however, several oligarchic clans dominate and manipulate the political system to their benefit and to the detriment of democracy and the average Ukrainian. Corrupt courts, police and other *siloviki*, impunity for neofascist crimes, state and allied actors' repression of free speech and media, and an overall rule of law deficit continue to render Ukraine's regime more hybrid than democratic. The rise to power of Maidan's ultranationalist elements creates an oppressive atmosphere for those who do not share these groups' ideological predilections and offers impunity to ultranationalist and neofascist groups' violations of political, civil, and human rights. Galician Ukraine is thus able to impose its identity and often neo–Banderism across what is left of the country.

Political System and Elections: Democracy Deficit

Ukraine has held several more or less free and fair elections since the Maidan's coming to power. Their conduct has been certified as such by international election monitoring organizations. However, Ukraine's elections were judged to be more or less free and fair before the Maidan revolt as well. What has changed is the worsening of numerous pre–Maidan democracy deficits and the rise of ultranationalists to power in addition to the old and new oligarchs. If the overall post–Soviet experience has taught political scientists anything, it is that elections are not the be-all and end-all of democracy. In May 2015, rump Ukraine elected Petro Poroshenko as president, replacing the Maidan regime's acting president Oleksandr Turchynov. Poroshenko promptly appointed the nationalist Turchynov to head the Security and Defense Council, replacing the ultranationalist Parubiy. More importantly, the October 2014 Rada elections—the first under the Maidan government—showed nationalist, ultranationalist, and neofascist parties, many with oligarchs backing them, taking some 44.6 percent of the party list vote. Nationalist Prime Minister Arseniy Yatsenyuk's National Front won 22.2 percent of the Rada party list voting. Lyashko's Radical Party received 10.2 percent; Tymoshenko's nationalist "Fatherland" party, 5.7 percent; "Svoboda," 4.7 percent' and Right Sector, 1.8 percent of the vote in the Rada elections. In addition, there were several nationalist candidates on the winning Petro Poroshenko Bloc (PPB) ticket and Yarosh, other RS leaders, and other nationalists, like Donbass Battalion commander Semyonchenko, won seats from single-mandate districts in campaigns financed by Kolomoiskii and other oligarchs. The October 2015 Rada elections were marred by some but minimal irregularities, and again a slew of other nationalists, ultranationalists and neofascists were elected to the Rada. The infamous Parubiy—coordinator of the Odessa massacre along with Yarosh—was elected the Rada's deputy speaker.

A key problem is that the electoral playing field is shaped in the regime groups' favor before elections because of a rule of law deficit and limits on political rights like freedom of association and assembly. The rule of law is compromised not only by oligarchic corruption and criminality but by neofascists' continuing revolutionary violence and intimidation. Opposition figures and journalists are harassed, threatened, frequently attacked physically and even killed with impunity (see below). For example, the presidential election was held just 23 days after RS's terrorist pogrom in Odessa, and Yarosh was allowed to openly campaign, winning just over 1 percent of the vote. The election also was held on a somewhat tilted playing field distorted by a largely Maidan-monopolized media bias and a ban on the CPU and SPU, two parties with major support in the south and east. This contributed to lower turnout in those regions and the domination of the western Ukraine's ultranationalist orientation in the Rada.

The radical nationalists have left their mark on Maidan legislation, limiting free speech and other rights. In March 2015 the Rada passed a law allowing for the firing of bureaucrats and officials for ill-defined "separatism" or support thereof without a court decision.[3] In April, it passed a new law that, along with banning supposedly fascist as well as communist propaganda, criminalized any displays of "disrespect" for OUN veterans, who, along with its leader Stepan Bandera, are heralded as heroes by Ukraine's nationalist, ultranationalist and neofascist parties.

Maidan Oligarchy versus the Rule of Law

Behind the democratic functioning of the political system, Ukraine retains strong elements of what Wilson called "virtual" politics and Russian-style "managed democracy" like most post–Soviet states. There are elements of personalist oligarchic patrimony, with political parties and their Rada factions formed largely according to the preferences of oligarchs who bring key groups under their wing and finance or otherwise buy their way into Ukraine's political parties, parliamentary institutions, and executive branch positions, including governorships and central ministries. The main political parties in Ukraine thus remain the instruments of oligarchic power, with several major oligarchs pulling the strings from behind the scenes, sometimes from seats of state power. The persistence of oligarchy has led to the persistence of a lack of rule of law in Maidan Ukraine.

THE RETURN OF OLIGARCHIC PRESIDENCY

If, as the Russian proverb goes, the fish rots from the head, then the role of newly elected president Petro Poroshenko will determine much of the fate of the new regime's promise to cast off oligarchy and corruption and realize the "revolution of dignity." Poroshenko was an experienced oligarch with a fairly long record in post–Soviet Ukraine's oligarchic politics well before the Maidan takeover. In 1996, Poroshenko began building his chocolate empire Roshen on the foundation of several Ukrainian confectionary enterprises. Roshen now exports chocolate goods across the former USSR and much of Europe and has factories in Ukraine, Russia, Lithuania, and Hungary.[4] Dubbed the "Chocolate King," Poroshenko has holdings valued at between $1.3 and $2 billion—enormous wealth by Ukrainian standards.[5] He also owns automotive plants and importers, a bus factory, Kiev's Lenin Forge shipyard, one of Ukraine's main television channels (Channel 5), and a ship-building plant in Sevastopol.[6] Other Poroshenko assets would come to light in the wake of his becoming Maidan Ukraine's first elected president. Politically, he has associated with both the Orange Maidan camp and the Kuchma-Yanukovich camp. He began his career in the latter, switched to the Yuschenko bandwagon in 2001, and then in 2009–2012 served in government positions under Yanukovich during his premiership and presidency. Thus, Poroshenko exhibits a strong strain of oligarchic political opportunism, ambition and, some might say, lack of principle rather than a firm commitment to democracy.[7]

During his presidency as well, power and profit appear to trump principle. During Poroshenko's 2014 presidential campaign, he promised to divest all his holdings but for Channel 5 TV into a blind trust.[8] As president, Poroshenko promised an end to "oligarchy as a basis of the country's political and economic life." His chief of staff, Boris Lozhkin, outlined five priorities, including "de-shadowing," "de-monopolization," and "de-oligarchization," as key to the dignity revolution's fight against corruption and criminality.[9] Yet years into his administration, Poroshenko failed to sell or put into a trust Roshen or any of his holdings. Instead, he actively hid his assets in offshore accounts.

In April 2016, the celebrated "Panama Papers" file of the Mossack Fonseca (MF) corporation's offshore projects involving the global elite included information on Poroshenko's assets ensconced in secretive offshore accounts. The document dump revealed that in August 2014, Poroshenko became the lone shareholder of Prime Asset Partners Limited (PAPL), set up in the British Virgin Islands by MF. The Cyprus-based law firm representing PAPL described it as a "holding company of Cyprus and Ukrainian companies of the Roshen Group" established for "a person involved in politics" having "nothing to do with his political activities." In October 2014, Ukraine's International Invest Bank, in which Poroshenko holds a majority stake, recommended Poroshenko MF, claiming that his accounts "have been conducted properly up to our satisfaction."[10] Later revelations in May 2016 disclosed two more offshore operations in which Poroshenko had interests.[11]

Other Panama revelations regarding another offshore account of Poroshenko's in the Virgin Islands, Intraco Management Limited (IML), showed that Poroshenko's deputy at Roshen, Sergei Zaitsev, was involved in trading with Russia's Gazprom, despite Ukrainian sanctions on trade with the so-called "invaders." Igor Kononenko, one of Poroshenko's closest associates and deputy head of the Petro Poroshenko Bloc's group of deputies in the Verkhovna Rada before, has figured in a series of corruption allegations made by Ukrainian officials.[12] The pro–Maidan *Kyiv Post* put the "Panama Petro" scandal well: "At the least, Poroshenko is setting a poor example by sneaking around while telling the nation he will combat oligarchs, offshore firms and tax avoidance that costs the nation up to $11.6 billion a year—10 percent of its national income, 25 percent of its government budget. He promised the nation to sell his empire in 2014, but has concocted one unconvincing excuse after another...."[13] Thus, Maidan's "revolution of dignity" merely replaced the corrupt Yanukovich regime with a corrupt Poroshenko regime.

IHOR KOLOMOISKII: NEXUS OF OLIGARCHY, CORRUPTION, CRIMINALITY AND NEOFASCISM

On March 2, 2014, less than two weeks after the Maidan takeover, then acting President Turchynov appointed oligarch Ihor Kolomoiskii as the governor of Dnepropetrovsk Oblast. Like Poroshenko, Kolomoiskii had a long and equally checkered career in the rough-and-tumble business milieu in Ukraine and the former USSR. Kolomoiskii rose in Ukrainian business during the wholesale theft of state property that occurred across much of the former USSR in the 1990s, rising to head the board of directors of Privat Bank in 1997. Kolomoiskii's business holdings encompass the energy, aviation, metals, sports and media sectors, making him the third most powerful oligarch in post–Maidan Ukraine with some $1.35 billion in assets.[14] He founded the country's largest bank and banking and industrial holding company, Privat Bank, he owns stakes in Ukraine's largest oil company, "UkrNafta" (42 percent of shares); a major oil transport company UkrTransNaft (no shares but his holding manages the company); the asset management company Mansvell Enterprises Limited (MEL); the Dnipro soccer club; 1+1 Media Group; and other entities. Kolomoiskii controls Aerosvit Airlines, Dniproavia, and Donbassaero through Privat Bank, and controls the Skyways Express, City Airline, and Cimber Sterling aviation companies through MEL.[15] His 1+1 Media Group operates eight Ukrainian TV channels.[16] Kolomoiskii's activity both before and after the Maidan takeover has been a textbook case of impunity from the law in a state lacking the rule of law. In open violation of Ukrainian law, Kolomoiskii for years has maintained multiple citizenship in Ukraine, Israel, and offshore haven Cyprus.[17] In 2010 Kolomoiskii appears to have attempted to buy his way to the presidency of the European Council of Jewish Communities (ECJC).[18]

Beyond the administrative resources he wielded through his governorship in Dnepropetrovsk in 2014–15, Kolomoiskii used his business sources to establish a larger network of political, business, and military power that extends his tentacles to Kiev and the heart of Ukraine's Maidan regime in both the executive and legislative branches. Kolomoiskii's political network of clients is rooted not only in his own governorship but in the appointment (through then acting president Turchynov) of his own allies to governorships, including in Odessa with its lucrative and corrupted port and customs facilities. In the central government in Kiev, Kolomoiskii secured seats for his political clients in Ukraine's Supreme Rada in the October 2014 reelection. A primary beneficiary of his patronage was the neofascist Right Sector party, which also infiltrated candidates into several party lists, including those of the Petro Poroshenko Bloc (PPB) and the National

Front of Ukraine (NFU), the largest factions in the Rada headed by President Poroshenko and Prime Minister Arseniy Yatsenyuk, respectively. In addition to his clients in those parties' Rada factions, Kolomoiskii created his own, called "Economic Rebirth" (*Ekonomicheskoe vozrozhdenie*), or just the "Rebirth" faction.

Perhaps most importantly, Kolomoiskii has completely undermined the basic principle of state sovereignty and authority—the monopoly on the means of coercion—by essentially setting up his own private army like a warlord or Cossack chieftain. During the more active phase of the ATO, he financed the National Guard and numerous volunteer battalions, including the RS's DUK battalions, which ostensibly were subordinated to the defense and internal affairs ministries but which actually established Kolomoiskii as a de facto warlord. The armed battalions became Kolomoiskii's potential and already, in part, kinetic private army, and they could play a key role in any large-scale confrontation with Kiev. Thus, the Kolomoiskii-neofascist nexus is a curious mixture of ideologically-driven violence and criminal business activity. Kolomoiskii generously financed the RS and the political campaigns of some its leaders, including Dmitro Yarosh first as a candidate for president in May 2014, and then in his election as a deputy in the Verkhovna Rada. Right Sector's headquarters is located in Dnepropetrovsk. As noted in previous chapters, Kolomoiskii has been able in several regions to deploy RS thugs to kick governors and mayors out of office, literally, and have allies from other ultranationalist groups like Svoboda appointed in their place.

Kolomoiskii's record of impunity before the law and undermining of the state's control over the means of coercion contributed to one of several serious crises that have highlighted the instability of Ukraine's hybrid oligarchic-ultranationalist regime. In March 2015, Kolomoiskii threw down the gauntlet before the central authorities, including President Poroshenko, in response to their efforts to seize business structures and financial flows that Kolomoiskii had controlled for years. In February, deputies from Poroshenko's PPB faction in the Rada introduced a bill to amend a law on stockholder associations in order to lower the number of stockholders required for a quorum to convene a stockholders' meeting for wresting Ukraine's lucrative oil giant UkrNafta from Kolomoiskii. On March 12, the Friday evening broadcast of the popular Ukrainian television talk show *Black Mirror* (*Chernoe zerkalo*) on channel "Inter," Aleksandr Velichko, the head of the legal department of Kolomoiskii's Dnepropetrovsk Oblast administration, said that his recent alleged nine-day abduction had been organized by Kolomoiskii's deputy governor, Gennadii Korban, and Yarosh's RS, funded on and off the battlefield by Kolomoiskii. Velichko, claiming to be hiding abroad, detailed his captivity and threatened torture at the hands of the goons at RS's base, which he said was "rampant with Kolomoiskii people" and is located in Donetsk's village of Peski.[19] All this developed during a two-month period in early 2015 when no fewer than eight suspicious "suicides'" of former Yanukovich regime and PR officials, including Dnepropetrovsk city's mayor, who is said to have been tied to local Dnepropetrovsk oligarchs loyal to former Ukrainian president Viktor Yanukovich that Kolomoiskii seeks to defeat.[20] On March 19, the Rada passed the noted stockholder quorum law after a stormy morning session that forced the Rada's speaker to declare a break. Numerous Rada sessions have ended in violence, intimidation or the blocking of the podium to prevent opponents from speaking or introducing measures, as Kolomoiskii's Rada supporters did on this day.[21] With this vote, the authorities had deprived Kolomoiskii control of UkrNafta.

In response, Kolomoiskii's Privat Bank blocked the accounts of all of Poroshenko's businesses, and Kolomoiskii, with armed men in camouflage, burst into and occupied the office of UkrTransNaft, a subsidiary of UkrNafta, in order to remove from office the temporary director recently appointed by the state and reinstate Kolomoiskii's man. On March 22, men in camouflage with machine guns from the Kolomoiskii-financed "Dnepr 1" battalion, which includes neofascist elements from Right Sector, seized the office building of the majority state-owned oil company UkrNafta.[22] With his seizure of UkrNafta, Kolomoiskii openly challenged President Poroshenko and his attempts to consolidate state holdings against Kolomoiskii's business empire. In the evening of March 22, fighters, likely from RS, were removed from several volunteer battalions at the Donbass front and sent to Kiev, according to Vesti-ukr.com, and Maidan organizer and now Rada deputy Mustafa Nayem was roughed up by Kolomoiskii's armed men guarding the UkrNafta building in central Kiev when he attempted to enter the building.[23] On March 23, Kolomoiskii's Dnepropetrovsk deputy governors, Korban and Andrey Denisenko, formerly an RS and PPB member, called for a *veche* or public gathering of the population in Dnepropetrovsk on March 25 at 6:00 p.m. in order to rally public support behind their boss in his battle with Kiev; a move that harked back to the Maidan and smacked of revolt.[24]

On March 24, Poroshenko rallied the *siloviki*, issued several statements along with these departments' leaders on the *silovikis'* strict subordination to Kiev and the illegality of governors running independent armed forces, and dispatched two National Guard battalions from Kiev to Dnepropetrovsk.[25] In particular, Poroshenko went further the next day, stating that all battalions would have to be subordinated to the Defense Ministry or be liquidated, and promising he would "burn the ground under" those who go to the Donbass front to fight but instead "maraud and kill."[26] SBU chief Nalyvaichenko announced that Poroshenko had issued an order that the fighters occupying UkrNafta be disarmed and removed from the premises, and that three of Kolomoiskii's Dnepropetrovsk deputy governors—including Korban (mentioned by Velichko regarding his abduction)—had been questioned days earlier regarding their possible participation in the murder of the SBU agent investigating contraband in Volnovakha, Donetsk. Kolomoiskii soon told a foreign journalist that although he did not want it, there was a possibility that the veche would turn into an uprising.[27] As fears of violent confrontation mounted across the country, the independent news agency *Vesti Ukraina* endeavored to survey the loyalties of the volunteer battalions, finding that many neofascist fighters might support Kolomoiskii, especially those of the RS, or remain neutral in a showdown but would be willing to "restore order in Kiev."[28]

The crisis's denouement came just after midnight on March 25, when Poroshenko met with Kolomoiskii and the former granted the latter's ostensible request to be relieved of his duties in Dnepropetrovsk. Deputy governor Korban "was also resigned." This was a rather light sentence considering Kolomoiskii's behavior over the preceding 48 hours, which ranged far outside the bounds of legality. The comprehensive deal struck between the president and the oligarch was rumored to be as follows: Poroshenko agreed not to pursue Kolomoiskii for violations of the law in return for the latter's resignation, his agreement to pay all of UkrNafta's debts to the state, and his agreement that the volunteer battalions would be subordinated to the state. A source in the presidential administration, however, claimed there was no deal, and that the subordination of the volunteer battalions and the payment of UkrNafta debts were state policy and part of the administration's "plan." According to PPB Rada deputy and former journalist Sergei Leshchenko, a pivot point in the crisis was pressure exerted by U.S. Vice-President Joseph Biden on PM Yatsenyuk, who may have been leaning towards Kolomoiskii or at least remaining neutral in the conflict. As a result of that intervention, Yatsenyuk openly sided with Poroshenko, prompting Kolomoiskii to back down. To contain any reverberations from the crisis, the two oligarchs put forward a united front by holding a joint press conference on March 26 in Dnepropetrovsk, with Poroshenko noting he "valued" the oligarch for "taking on enormous responsibilities in difficult times."[29]

In early 2015, proceedings in a British court further unmasked Kolomoiskii's criminality as well as the dark underside of Ukraine's oligarchic business and politics. Ukrainian oligarch Viktor Pinchuk, who lives in Kensington, Great Britain, and is a personal friend of former UK Prime Minister Tony Blair, targeted Kolomoiskii in the lawsuit for more than $2 billion in damages for unfulfilled deals regarding iron ore mining investments. Pinchuk's lawyers and witnesses demonstrated, among much else, that Kolomoiskii had ordered several murders and attempted murders that were covered up with the help of Ukrainian prosecutors and judges.[30]

THE ULTRANATIONALIST/NEOFASCIST FACTOR

The rise to power of neofascist and ultranationalist elements with the Maidan creates an oppressive atmosphere for those who do not share these groups' ideological predilections and has facilitated impunity for the neofascists' and ultranationalist groups' political violence, terrorism, and repeated violations of others' political, civil, and human rights. The ultranationalists and neofascists are divided between those who seek to use and/or infiltrate the present Maidan regime and radicalize its nationalist policies, and those who would prefer total power and overthrow the new "order." RS has been a leader among the latter and has been engaged in a campaign of intimidation and violence—sometimes criminal, sometimes political—in an effort to destabilize and overthrow the hybrid Maidan regime and transform it into a purely ultranationalist/neofascist one. RS leader Yarosh and his successors have repeatedly called for finishing the nationalist revolution.[31] Like most extremist elements, ultranationaists and neofascists have gravitated towards the organs of coercion or *siloviki*. For example, Yarosh was offered the position of deputy chairman of the Defense and Security Council by its chairman Andriy Parubiy, who appears to have helped coordinate the neofascist snipers on Maidan. Yarosh refused the offer. A few months ago an agreement was announced that Yarosh would become an advisor to the chief of the general staff of the Ukrainian armed forces, but Yarosh never formally took up the post.[32] Simultaneously, the SBU under Nalyvaichenko and the MVD under Avakov have lent direct support to the most radical elements among the ultranationalists—the neofascists—even when the latter have violated the Ukrainian constitution and law and engaged in what can only be classified as terrorism.

THE RS AND THE RISE OF UKRAINIAN NEOFASCIST TERRORISM

On July 11, 2015, units of RS's militia in Transcarpathia attacked police in the western town of Mukachevo. In particular, RS was involved in a settling of scores between two Transcarpatian criminal "authorities" who were simultaneously deputies in the Maidan's "democratic" Rada. One of kingpin-deputies, Viktor Baloga, is said to finance RS. In the battle, RS fighters used machine guns and a grenade launcher—killing and wounding several police and several civilians, with up to 14 casualties. Security forces flooded in, but refrained from attacking and arresting the RS fighters; instead, negotiations ensued.

Some of them directly or indirectly involved Ukrainian President Petro Poroshenko him-self and his Interior Minister, Arsen Avakov, who implemented the policy of forming volunteer battalions to include a large component of neofascists, given their "patriotic enthusiasm." The RS continued to refuse to disarm its Volunteer Ukrainian Corps, DUK, and instead convened demonstrations in Kiev and some ten provincial capitals. Other neofascist groups and their battalions backed RS with moral support in the confrontation. Then recently fired SBU chief Nalyvaichenko also backed RS against the Poroshenko-led factions of the Maidan regime. For Avakov's apparent support for Poroshenko in the crisis, RS demanded the resignation of the Ukraine MVD chief as well as prosecution of Transcarpathian region MVD officials. An article on RS's Web site accused Avakov of pedophilia, economic crimes, and the repression and murder of "patriots." In the after-math of Mukachevo, the RS continues to refuse to disarm DUK.

Two days after the Mukachevo attack, RS's Lviv branch took down the European Union flag flying at the Lviv Oblast Administration's building, replaced it with RS's red and black (blood and soil) flag, and began to set up checkpoints on the outskirts of some cities, including Lviv. The next morning, two headquarters of the Ministry of Internal Affairs (MVD) in Lviv were mined and the explosions wounded two policeman. One had his foot amputated and kidney removed, and another is now blind from his wounds. RS Lviv denied any connection with the bombings but used them as a pretext for sending its goons across Lviv and setting up checkpoints. In response, RS's Lviv branch announced its intention to establish a presence and presumably act in response to any events in the city. The MVD stated it regarded the Lviv attack as being connected with the Mukachevo events, meaning it suspected RS in what the MVD correctly categorized as a terrorist attack.[33]

RS CONGRESS AND VECHE: PROBING A COUP

Despite RS's record of political violence and terrorism, Yarosh and his thugs were allowed to convene both a congress in Zhivteiny Palace in central Kiev and a people's *veche* (assembly) on the Maidan on July 21, 2015. RS delegations, many in camouflage uniforms, marched demonstratively through the city in formation to Zhivteiny. The con-gress's several hundred deputies filled Zhivteiny and heard Yarosh declare, in fact reiterate, his oft-stated goal of a "nationalist revolution" against the Maidan regime he helped bring to power. The congress decided not to take part in Ukraine's local elections to be held on October 25 and to organize a nationwide referendum on a series of questions, includ-ing the legalization of the volunteer armed battalions such as RS's DUK and a vote of confidence or no-confidence in the authorities. The decision not to participate in elections came with news that RS's popularity had grown in the wake of the trail of blood it left through Donbass, Odessa, Transcarpathia, and Lviv. A survey conducted by the Kiev International Institute of Sociology (KIIS) at the time found that Yarosh and RS had gained nearly a million new voters since the previous year's elections. The survey showed other nationalist parties making gains as well. RS's *veche*, which directly followed the congress, gathered some 3,000 attendees, who were treated to a Uniate Catholic invoca-tion from several priests, political speeches, and an appearance from Mr. Yarosh. Clearly, Yarosh was probing whether or not to complete his nationalist revolution in a "Maidan 2.0." The modest turnout for the *veche* led him to conclude that RS lacked sufficient sup-port and eventually to abandon the RS in 2016 in search of a new party project to launch him to power.[34]

SVOBODA'S FIRST TERRORIST ATTACK

Ukraine's long, hot 2015 summer of nationalist violence was punctuated on August 31. On that day, a demonstration led by the Svoboda Party and its chairman Tyahnybok against passage of constitutional amendments that ostensibly would have given the Donbass regions of Donetsk and Luhansk power-sharing with, or autonomy from, the central government in Kiev and culminated in an attempt to storm the hall of the Supreme Rada and another neofascist terrorist attack. Video shows Tyahnybok and his deputy Yurii Sirotyuk physically battled riot police in an attempt to reach the doors to the Rada building before their fighters tossed a grenade and shot firearms at police. The grenade explosion caused one policeman to lose part of his foot, and fifteen police were reported wounded and injured as a result of the battle. MVD chief Avakov reported there were 125 wounded "*siloviki*," including one in a coma, and held Tyahnybok responsible. Right Sector played a separate game that day, setting up a roadblock on a Kiev street leading to parliament in a failed attempt to prevent deputies from getting to the Rada to vote. After the violence, Right Sector and Yarosh came out in full support for Tyahnybok and Svoboda. The news from Kiev was made worse, as the more "moderate" nationalist party "Self-Help" defended Svoboda's action. Self-Help is led by the mayor of Lviv (Lvov), a hotbed of Ukrainian nationalism. However, as in the history of RS's neofascist terrorism, neither Tyahnybok, Sirotyuk, nor any SP activist was prosecuted for this attack.[35]

Thus, the rule of law is largely absent in Ukraine, with oligarchs and ultranationalists often left free to murder, rob and pillage with impunity in an organized criminal-military fashion reminiscent of warlordism and under the protection of bought-off prosecutors and judges. The Maidan regime's partially successful, Georgian-style reform of the police can neither remedy nor counterbalance the power of these thoroughly corrupted institutions. During its more than year-long record of terror, terrorism, vigilantism, and criminality, neither Yarosh nor any other RS official or ranking member has been questioned, much less arrested, for any of these crimes. After RS committed war crimes at the front, terrorist attacks in the rear, "conventional" crimes and other forms of defiance of the Maidan regime and its *siloviki*, it nevertheless was able to convene its "congress" and organize a mass demonstration in the center of the capital, without any real pressure from the regime. As demonstrated above, both national and local officials are intimidated or actively work with RS groups. Therefore, it is possible that pivotal splits could emerge within one or more of the *siloviki* departments—the MVD, SBU, the Armed Forces, and National Guard—on which Poroshenko would need to rely in the event Yarosh's RS and/or one or more of the many other armed neo-fascist volunteer battalions and civilian neofascist activists were to attempt to seize power by force. Many of these departments have been staffed in part with neofascists and/or sympathetic ultranationalists and national chauvinists.

A saving grace for the oligarchic and small democratic wings of the Maidan regime is the division among the nationalists, ultranationalists, and neofascists. If RS, SP, SNA, and other numerous extremist parties could unite forces against the oligarchs and democrats, the Maidan revoluton would indeed culminate in ultranationalism and neofascism. The regime's present impotence, therefore, is most unfortunate because this is an opportune time to move against the radical nationalists. Although this might spark other neofascist groups to rally around Yarosh's RS, the same could be true later when the regime may be more impotent and the extremists more potent if the socioeconomic situation in the country continues to deteriorate. At present it remains unclear whether any ultranationalist leaders can rally sufficient forces to infiltrate the regime mount a successful coup, and this may be dictating a "long war" strategy founded on a more broad-based "nationalist revolution." In this scenario, a coercive seizure of power could follow the Maidan model, beginning with civil disobedience, the occupation of government buildings, and then the gradual escalation of violence. Initiating this strategy now would be premature. For President Poroshenko, the Maidan regime, and the West's Ukraine policy, Kiev's acquiescence or impotence before the ultranationalist threat is bound to come home to roost. Meanwhile, broad impunity for political crimes and violence remains a key characteristic of Maidan's split regime and Ukraine's weak state. The strength of ultranationalist/neofascist elements under the Maidan regime affects not just the rule of law, the state's control over the power of coercion, and the rights of freedom of association, it also limits Ukrainians' freedoms of speech, access to information, and media.

FREEDOM OF SPEECH, INFORMATION AND MEDIA

The Maidan regime and its allied ultranationalist and neofascist actors have actively stymied freedom of speech and media, limiting Ukrainians' access to objective information and views at odds with those in power. Major media are owned in full or in part by sitting government officials or government-tied oligarchs, including President Poroshenko (Channel 5) and Ihor Kolomoiskii, who owns Channel 1+1. No less than Russian state-tied media, these Ukrainian mainstream channels sharply limit and often do not allow the on-air appearances of those opposed to the Maidan myth. Independent, "insufficiently patriotic" media are under constant threat from the authorities and its allied ultranationalist thugs. Leading Maidan revolutionaries frequently call for the closure of television stations for, among other things, criticizing Bandera and the OUN.[36] In the Maidan regime's first year the SBU had blocked more than 10,000 Web sites and searched the offices and seized the servers against two major domain registration companies.[37] An Information Ministry with the power to pressure and shut down media was established in autumn 2015. Television programs have been closed or threatened with closure for allowing "Kremlin agents" to participate. In an ironic twist, Russian television journalist Savik Shuster, whose Russian television program was taken off the air in the early years of the Putin era, had his weekly political talk show first censored and then removed from television, after which it was relegated to online broadcasting, much like Russia's channel "Dozhd." A good example of the Maidan crackdown on independent media is the coordinated attack on the independent news agency *Vesti Ukraina* (or simply *Vesti*) orchestrated by the RS, SBU and Ukraine's tax collection department, the State Tax Service, that began in April 2015. The harassment campaign included physical attacks on the offices and delivery trucks, and beatings of *Vesti* personnel by RS thugs, investigations on charges of separatism by the SBU, and charges of tax evasion by the State Tax Service. Eventually the harassment campaign forced editor-in-chief Ihor Guzhva's resignation and the takeover of the paper by elements close to the regime.[38]

One day after the SBU announced it was investigating *Vesti*, another Party of Regions deputy, Oleg Kalashnikov, was killed. Kalashnikov was an opponent of the Maidan regime and had recently organized a protest at the U.S. embassy in Kiev. The following day, the moderate anti–Maidan journalist Oles Buzina was killed. A group calling itself the Ukrainian Partisan Army (UPA), after the World War II Nazi-allied Ukrainian force responsible for atrocities committed against tens of thousands of Jews and Poles, claimed responsibility for the murder of Buzina and several of the eight recent alleged "suicides" committed by former Party of Regions deputies and Yanukovich allies. Another journalist, Sergei Sukhobok, was killed on April 13, 2015, but initial reports indicated he was likely killed by an angry neighbor. On the background of all this and other violence across Kiev and Ukraine, the creation of a new pro–Maidan government-tied project, called ironically enough Peacemaker (Mirotvorets), was uncovered. The names of both Kalashnikov and Buzina, along with their home addresses, appeared on Peacemaker's list of "enemies of the people" days before they were killed, but were later removed. The project explicitly condones and cynically suggests several methods for murdering prisoners and detainees. Anton Gerashchenko, Supreme Rada deputy from Prime Minister Arsenyi Yatsenyuk's nationalist "National Front" and secretary of the Rada's Committee on Legislative Issues Regarding the Law Enforcement Bodies, recommended "Peacemaker" on his Facebook page, touting the fact that its list includes 32 names of people who "either fought against Ukraine, subverted it from within, or betrayed their oath of loyalty to Ukraine," and said that within a matter of days tens of thousands more names would be added to the list.[39]

In April 2015, the embattled pro-democracy news agency *Vesti* issued the rather damning results of its special investigation of the Ukrainian *siloviki*. Members and leaders of several of the smaller and newer post-revolutionary ultranationalist groups, as well as sources inside the SBU, acknowledged that the SBU, under the direct leadership of its director Valentyn Nalyvaichenko, had been recruiting such groups to attack democratic opponents such as *Vesti*. *Vesti*'s interviewees also reported that the SBU was cracking down only on those radicals who threaten the leadership's economic interests, such as the group "Revansh," which has harassed and picketed companies of oligarchs like President Petro Poroshenko's Roshen chocolate company. The interviews also revealed ties between the SBU, Nalyvaichenko, several new post-revolutionary radical groups like Revansh, and Yarosh and the RS. Finally, *Vesti* found that the leader of Right Sector's division in Kiev's Svtoshinsk District with the nom de guerre "Kii" led the attacks on the news agency in recent months.[40] *Vesti*'s takeover by regime-friendly elements occurred shortly thereafter. In sum, the country has more in common with Weimar Germany and "post–Sovietistan" than a Western democracy.

Ukraine Two Years After Maidan in Western and Ukrainian Eyes

Even according to a leading Western democracy-promotion and pro–Maidan revolution institute, the Washington-based Freedom House (FH), two years after the Western-supported revolution of dignity, the level of democracy in Ukraine has seen barely marginal improvement from the late Yanukovich era's level. Ukraine's FH overall democracy rating in 2016 was 4.68, with the Yanukovich years, 2011–2014, ranging from 4.61 to 4.93. That minor improvement is due to one in a factoral category that is most intangible and difficult to measure—civil society—the rating of which improved from 2.75 in 2013 to 2.25 in 2016.[41] Moreover, left out of Freedom House's seven factoral categories is the rule of law—a category often neglected in democratization and transitological analysis and one in which, as the present study demonstrates, Maidan Ukraine is so weak that it borders on becoming a failed state, with state actors coordinating with criminal and neofascist elements to oppress political opponents. One does not, however, need to rely on the FH or other such Western rating agencies in assessing the level of democracy in Maidan Ukraine.

A December 2015 Gallup poll found that opposition to the Maidan government and regime is ubiquitous and greater than that to the Yanukovich regime on the eve of the revolution. Only 19 percent of Ukrainians say the regime is taking the country in the right direction; 65 percent think it is moving in the wrong direction. The government's approval rating is the lowest since 2007—during the Orange regime (2005–2010)—with 8 percent approval rating then as now. By contrast, under Yanukovich, public approval of the government ranged from 19 to 26 percent and was 24 percent in 2014. This pattern is evidenced in the poll's presidential approval ratings. Yanukovich's approval ratings were: 46 percent in 2010, 29 percent in 2011, 28 percent in 2012, and 28 percent in 2013. Poroshenko's ratings were 47 percent upon his arrival in office in 2014—similar to Yanukovich's 46 percent—but fell precipitously to 17 percent in 2015. Moreover, Poroshenko is unpopular in every mega-region of Ukraine—west, east, north, south, and central—with catastrophic, indeed "revolutionarily" low popularity ratings in the east and south (not including Crimea, Donetsk and Luhansk, no less) at 11 percent and 7 percent, respectively. In Ukraine's central and northern regions (the former includes Kiev), barely as many Ukrainians approve of Poroshenko (21 percent) as approved of Yanukovich (20 percent) in 2013 on the eve of the Maidan revolt.[42] The poll also found that 88 percent of Ukrainians say corruption is widespread in their government, and 81 percent say the problem is no different in the country's business circles. A mere 5 percent of respondents said the Ukrainian government is doing enough to fight corruption—lower than the 6 percent who said the same in 2013 on the eve of the Maidan "revolution."[43] It should be recalled that many Maidanists and their Western backers emphasize that the "revolution of dignity" was driven at least initially by Ukraine's rather undignified level of mass corruption.

It is important to note that the Maidan regime's poor popularity ratings come from a much more "Orange" population than that which responded to surveys during the Yanukovich era. The portion of the population that is most anti–Orange—i.e., opposed to the Maidan regime—hails from those regions that are no longer part of Ukraine as a result of the revolution: Crimea, Donetsk, and Luhansk. These regions most supported Yanukovich's politics for regional ethnic, linguistic, cultural, and economic reasons, and their populations were not included in the Gallup survey. In other words, despite having the advantage of ruling over a more politically homogeneous and otherwise more supportive pro-Orange population, the Maidan regime, government and first elected president have catastrophic ratings, worse than those of the anti–Orange president Yanukovich. Thus, Poroshenko's Maidan regime is less popular within the polity it rules than Yanukovich's was in that which he ruled. Yet the latter was overthrown in a quasi-revolution or revolt backed as democratic, and its failing regime continued to be backed by the Barack Obama administration and other Western governments.

By 2015 Ukraine was suffering from what might be termed the "Weimar syndrome," with rising ultranationalism and sociopolitical conflict being compounded by an economy near depression. Ukraine's economy ranked fourth highest on the misery index (a measure of economic dysfunction derived from the unemployment rate plus inflation rate) behind Venezuela (worst), Argentina, and South Africa.[44] In 2015 Ukraine's state debt reached approximately the size of its annual GDP, compared to 73 percent the previous year. On the verge of default, Ukraine's debt is set to nearly double by 2020, according to a new estimate by the IMF, from $58 billion today to $103 billion.[45] The same year, annual inflation was 43 percent, and unemployment had risen from 7.6 percent in June 2013 to 11 percent in the last quarter of 2014, averaging 9.7 in 2015.[46]

Maidan's Geostrategic Consequences: The "New Cold War"

The geostrategic consequences of the Ukrainian crisis, revolt and civil war are difficult to overstate. Whatever remained of the hopes for a post–Cold War common European home from Vancouver to Vladivostok was smashed on the rocks of historical legacies and contemporary ambitions. However, the commonly used nomenclature "new Cold War" is overstated as a conceptualization for the Russian-West tensions after Maidan, Crimea and Donbass. Hotheads and careerists East and West have tried to buttress the perception of a "new Cold War" by conjuring up an ideological confrontation between decadent democracies and a "new authoritarianism," respectively. In reality, "Cold War 2.0" lacks the sharp ideological foundation and global reach of the original, in which both sides worked for the collapse and ultimate destruction of the other side's system. The new confrontation is realist: great powers maximizing self-interest and coming into conflict over spheres of interest.

The present confrontation over Ukraine, democracy-promotion, color revolutions, and Russia's traditional sphere of influence is just that and is more reminiscent of the 19th century's traditional great power geopolitics Mackinder would expect and which produced the Crimean War and World War I. The Ukrainian crisis has produced a sharp deterioration in Russian-West relations and reignited the realist geopolitics of the 19th century. If the first Cold War was about the West containing Soviet communism's expansion, then the new Great Game centers around Russian efforts to contain Western influence, especially NATO expansion, into Moscow's sphere of influence: the Eurasian heartland. The Ukrainian crisis is an inevitable consequence of these conflicting interests and a pivot point over whether the parties in the "game" can manage the conflict and prevent its escalation from a proxy war in Donbass to a larger proxy or more general war.

The early signs point to increased tensions between Russia and the West and potential violent conflict between NATO and Moscow. In response to Putin's countermove in Crimea and the Kiev-Donbass civil war, Washington imposed a policy of isolating Russia diplomatically, politically, economically, financially, and militarily. Russia was expelled from the G-8 and hit with sanctions imposed by both Washington and Brussels on Russian business entities' commercial activity and access to the international banking and loan system. Arms control talks and cultural and educational exchanges have been put on hold. In response, Moscow instituted sanctions on European agricultural goods, crippling German and other European farmers. The mutual sanctions have damaged both sides' economies and put the weak recovery from the 2008 crisis at risk of regressing to another global recession.

Moreover, the military confrontation between East and West has been reignited. NATO has forward deployed a limited number of ground and air forces in Eastern Europe. In 2015 it initiated rotating military deployments of 3,500 troops to Poland and the Baltics.

In July 2016 it announced plans for 2017 to deploy another four combat battalions to the same countries, a tripling of the size of NATO's Rapid Reaction Force to 40,000, and increasing the size of its High Readiness Joint Task Force to 13,000. The NATO-Russia Founding Act obliges NATO not to deploy any "large" military contingent near Russia's borders. NATO has organized military maneuvers near Russia's borders in the Baltics and lent Kiev financial and defensive military aid and training. In turn, at the end of 2015 Moscow deployed three combined-arms divisions along its western border: at Yelnya, Smolensk; Boguchar, Voronezh, and Novocherkassk, Rostov. NATO's moves in the Baltic make it more difficult for Moscow to ensure the security of its Kaliningrad exclave, risking a countermove by deployment of its Iskander missiles. In the Black Sea region, Russia has boosted naval operations and deployed anti-access area-denial capabilities.

In addition, as during the 19th century game, the alliance system has been revived, with Moscow further strengthening previous ties with China and other greater and lesser powers in east Eurasia and backing China in its confrontation with the U.S. and its allies in and around the South China Sea. Similarly, it has been forced in the face of weakening ties with Europe to reinforce its support for its least savory allies, such as Iran and Syria. More akin to the Cold War, but also inevitable from the standpoint of geopolitics, Moscow is also stepping up efforts where and when possible to weaken Eastern Europeans' ties to the West and undermine EU and NATO solidarity.

In sum, the geopolitical upshot of the Ukrainian revolution and civil war has been a deterioration in the international relations and security that includes: a revival of the Russian-West geopolitical confrontation in Eastern Europe; a growing risk that the confrontation in Europe will lead to greater tensions and even conflict in the Asia-Pacific region involving the West, regional powers, Russia, and China; and finally a lack of global cooperation in the war against the rising global jihadi threat. Thus, the destabilization that first rocked Ukraine and then Europe is extending to the international system as a whole.

Problems of Democracy-Promotion: What Is to Be Done?

As I argued elsewhere, there is a need for greater precision in U.S. and Western democracy-promotion policies and heightened caution towards our American revolutionism.[47] Even when possessing sufficient moral superiority, democratic systems and "communities of democracies" do not have the right to risk destabilizing other states and entire regions *a priori*. Democracy-promotion funding and other assistance is too blunt an instrument at present to sufficiently minimize the risk of needless destabilization in countries, regions and even the international system as a whole, as the recent history in North Africa, the Middle East, and the former Soviet space have demonstrated. America's positive experience with revolution and the messianic vision of its Founding Fathers has transmuted into a cult of revolutionism. Almost any revolutionary against an authoritarian regime that conducts an independent foreign policy or is at all detrimental to maintaining and expanding American hegemony is greeted as pro-democratic and something deserving of U.S. backing. In future, U.S. and Western policymakers must resolve that the stakes should be very high before approving the inherently risky policy of supporting color revolutions. Several factors should condition such a decision.

First, revolutionary forms of regime change should be supported only against the most aggressive and totalitarian regimes and undertaken only after detailed intelligence and analysis of potential and kinetic revolutionary movements and the complex internal politics of revolutionary coalitions, the strength of democratic forces within such coalitions, and other factors that determine the likelihood of democratic outcomes for each of the different modes of regime transformation (violent and nonviolent, revolution from above and from below, imposed and negotiated transitions).

Western support for "color revolutions" should only be forthcoming when the cessation of large-scale, brutal regime violence or at least the gross violation of civil and human rights is at stake. Only where there is deep, countrywide support for the overthrow of a regime and that regime is particularly brutal in its authoritarianism should policymakers support peaceful (and perhaps violent) revolution from below. In terms of long-term transitional democracy-building, the Internet makes much of the direct financial and other assistance for the purposes of democracy-promotion unnecessary and superfluous, especially as the involvement of foreigners in political activity raises the suspicions of authoritarian leaders and often discredits the opposition in the eyes of some who might otherwise support their calls for democratization.

Second, in considering whether and to what degree such support should be rendered, the value of any existing regime to American and Western interests and the effect on regional or international security should be taken into account. In cases involving a regime that is both brutally authoritarian or totalitarian and a threat to U.S., Western, and/or international security interests, support for a color revolution is logical. In cases where either of these conditions is missing, decision-making is much more difficult. When only the first condition is present, the moral imperative is there, but the imperative of *realpolitik* is not, making support for a color revolution a bad bet. When only the second condition is present, the *realpolitik* urges action against the regime, but the soft nature of the authoritarian order poses grave risks for America's reputation. That is to say that in cases where rights violations are not grievous and American interests and global stability are vested in continuing survival of a particular regime, the support of "Orangism," and even the aggressive assertion of democratization, support should be reconsidered.

Finally, criteria codified in an international convention or treaty regarding foreign involvement in the domestic politics of states might be useful. By regulating democracy-promotion and/or other activities of a distinctly political nature that can be carried out by one state in relation to another, it might be possible to limit the foreign promotion of destructive revolutionary activity such that it does not devolve into interference by one state in the domestic politics and internal affairs of another. Harsh authoritarian and totalitarian regimes would be ineligible to be participants in the convention, which could perhaps be first applied to OSCE states in line with the Helsinki Final Act's prohibition against member-states' interference in other member-states' internal politics.

A Final Word on NATO Expansion

After the West's decision to expand NATO without Russia in the mid–1990s, a tectonic of mutually exclusive interests and myths increasingly divided Russia and the West again. The explicitly stated policy and myth declared by Western and Soviet leaders alike at the Cold War's end was the creation of a common European home extending from

London in the west to Vladivostok in the east. Some saw the new condominium stretching across the Pacific to encompass the entire Atlantic and Eurasian "north." Thus, Western leaders issued an unwritten promise to Moscow that NATO would not expand beyond the borders of the reunited Germany, and Moscow acquiesced to the lack of any real compensation for the full demise of the Warsaw Pact. Soon, however, the West abandoned the unwritten charter that had facilitated a peaceful end to the Cold War and a soft landing for the collapsing USSR successor states.

Emotion, like honor, cannot be ignored in all the theorizing, however; its power and impact are perhaps the ultimate contingency and unknown. The West's unwritten promise had been most important for Russia. It had agreed to abandon its empire and inherit the Soviet debt. Of the former Soviet states, only Russia lost ethnic compatriots (25 million) consigned to other union republics by Soviet fiat in drawing administrative borders, and compared to most of the former eastern bloc states, it bore a much more burdensome Soviet economic legacy. The goal of accommodating Soviet and later Russian security concerns was based on a new international community-building myth: the promise of a common European home from London to Vladivostok—indeed, one of even larger domain extending from Vancouver to Vladivostok.

The promise of a common European home was abandoned for an altogether different project. The breaking of the great unwritten post–Cold War compact by the Bill Clinton administration in the mid–1990s was not in the service of some new grand idea or even strategy. Rather, a common European home was sacrificed on the altar of far more mundane enticements such as the pressures from Eastern European diaspora lobbyists and immediate, petite and even petty political considerations ranging from wooing ethnic East European voters in key American "battleground states" to accruing campaign contributions from the defense industry lobby with its eyes on the East European weapons market. NATO expansion fit the bill. To be sure, some "strategists" had more grand designs and sought to fashion a Containment 2.0 around the Russian "black hole," but the decision-makers, in particular the former Arkansas governor turned president, were less enticed by grand strategy—whether negative or positive—in their approach towards Russia.

A real alternative strategy and myth were available to replace Cold war containment and a word split apart. The strategy would have been to bring Russia into the West in order to put an end to the centuries-long Great Game that brought the Eurasian landmass four world wars. The Napoleonic Wars saw an imperial "democracy-promotion" project ravage the Russian countryside and Moscow itself before Alexander I was able to run the little Emperor back to Paris and lead a new postwar condominium of European powers under the Congress of Vienna. The Crimean War saw Russia countered by an alliance of Western powers and the Ottoman Porte, with battles stretching from Sevastopol in the Crimea to Russia's near Arctic. A British flotilla even attacked the Solovetsky Monastery populated and defended by a handful of Orthodox monks. Readers know better what are called the First and Second World Wars, Russia's relationships to the various Western powers in those wars, and the results they brought to Russia, the USSR, and the twentieth century.

At the Cold War's end, Russia and the West had the opportunity to finally overcome the war-torn legacy of a Europe split apart. Never before in her history was Russia so psychologically prepared to jettison the pattern of arbitrary autocratic rule and state property ownership. She was poised to unleash the creativity of the Russian people, take advantage of the country's massive natural resources and other comparative advantages, and ultimately join the West. Russia's integration into the West would have precluded the possibility of shifting, unstable alliances and the risk of major conflicts in Europe. Russia's rise as a democratic global power with one foot in Asia and adjacent to most of the world's great civilizations offered the possibility of expanding the democratic capitalist model to Asia and parts of the Islamic world more easily and gradually by demonstration.

After the West's rejection of Russian President Medvedev's proposal to negotiate a new Europe-Eurasian security architecture and the August 2008 Georgian-Ossetiyan war, Zbigniew Brzezinski seemed to get some of this message. Nearly two decades too late, the former U.S. National Security Advisor reiterated the present author's idea of establishing strong NATO-Collective Security Treaty Organization (CSTO) and perhaps NATO-SCO cooperation.[48] Specifically, Brzezinski proposed negotiating a NATO-CSTO agreement on security cooperation and establishing a NATO-Shanghai Cooperation Organization council. Brzezinski's ties to the Obama administration suggested that similar "reset" policies might be in the offing, but they never came. This and Brzezinski's new thinking on Russia were long needed and too little, too late. Such a policy broached years earlier would have begun to get at the core problem in U.S. Russia policy during the Obama administration's ultimately failed "reset."

NATO expansion "in Russia's face" put an end to the potential for a brave new post–Cold War world—the common European home from Vancouver to Vladivostok. Despite the lack of any new grand strategy behind the move to expand NATO into the former Soviet bloc, a new myth did gradually emerge. It came in the form of a "community of democracies" innately attractive to, and inevitably transformative of, all countries. The promise of membership in Atlantic institutions—economic, political and, most problematically, military—would lead to smooth "transitions" to democracy and the market. The American economic juggernaut and the emerging Economic Union would integrate Atlantic and Eurasian markets, lifting all boats. NATO posed no threat and everyone was free to join. The promise of being a member of this exclusive club would incentivize Magyars, Muscovites, and Mongolians to ready their political institutions for entry into the great alliance. After the great transition, the Atlantic and Eurasian communities would fuse into one. Later, others would embark on the great transition as well, leading mankind to the final shore—the end of history.

Unfortunately, there were problems. First, there was nothing inevitable about the great transformation, and nations would have to be gently enticed rather than nudged or pushed into it. Second, the reason the transformation was not inevitable lay in the survival of alternative myths or ideologies. Communalism, whether based on ethnicity or confession, remained. Class communalism had not fully died out, and a new multifaceted gender communalism was on the rise. Third, the designers of the new strategy and its attendant myth were in a hurry. If Russia or other countries did not democratize now, they could, indeed should and would, be left out of Europe's economic and security architecture for as long as they lagged behind or "backslided." They would be excluded from the community of democracies and its NATO-based "security zone."

Thus, with NATO expansion a self-fulfilling prophecy developed in which, with every wave and attempted wave of NATO expansion, came a hardening of Russia's stance towards the West, democratization, and free-market capitalism, and a gradual but increasingly immutable reversion to its usable past of authoritarianism, nationalism, and imperialism. Perhaps most importantly, NATO expansion essentially "militarized" or "securitized" another key Western policy targeting Russia and the rest of the former Soviet Union—democracy promotion. Given the Russians' experience with Western ideological movements pairing with military aggression emanating from the states or civilizations promoting a particular ideology inside Russia, it was almost impossible that NATO expansion would not taint Russians' views of the intentions that lie behind democratization and democracy-promotion. NATO expansion made Ukraine—a historical invasion route into Russia and with deep cultural ties to, and a long biography of integration with, Russia—a military-political and proxy battleground. This international factor aggravated longstanding historical divisions and grievances as well as more recent, post–Soviet tensions within Ukraine—and between Russia and West—to the breaking point.

Chapter Notes

Chapter 1

1. George Friedman, "Geopolitical Journey Part 2—Borderlands," Stratfor, August 11, 2010 (republished June 3, 2014), w.stratfor.com/weekly/20101108_geopolitical_journey_part_2_borderlands.

2. Halford J. Mackinder, "The Geographical Pivot of History," in *Democratic Ideals and Reality: A Study in the Politics of Reconstruction*, 1996 revised edition (Washington, DC: National Defense University Press, 1942), pp. 175–193, www.scribd.com/doc/24386413/Democratic-Ideals-and-Reality.

3. Mackinder, "The Geographical Pivot of History," in *Democratic Ideals and Reality*, p. xix.

4. Nicholas J. Spykman, *The Geography of the Peace* (New York: Harcourt, Brace, 1944), p. 43.

5. Friedman, "Geopolitical Journey Part 2—Borderlands."

6. Zbigniew Brzezinski, *The Grand Chessboard: American Primacy and Its Geostrategic Imperatives*, signed first edition (Norwalk, CT: Easton Press, 1997), p. xiv.

7. Similar but less likely blows to U.S. hegemony would be dealt, according to Brzezinski, if Japan and China "were somehow to unite," or if "ejection of America by its Western partners" were to occur. Brzezinski, *The Grand Chessboard*, pp. 34–5.

8. Brzezinski, *The Grand Chessboard*, pp. 52 and 84–5.

9. Brzezinski, *The Grand Chessboard*, p. 104.

10. Mackinder, "The Geographical Pivot of History," in *Democratic Ideals and Reality*, p. xix.

11. Friedman, "Geopolitical Journey Part 2—Borderlands."

12. See Viktor Shevchuk and Vitalii Rozhdaev, "Plan Mezhdumore: Britaniya podderzhit, Frantsiya ne protiv, Ukraina i Polshe sdelayut," *Hvylya.net*, August 6, 2015, http://hvylya.net/analytics/geopolitics/plan-mezhdumore-britaniya-podderzhit-frantsiya-ne-protiv-ukraina-i-polsha-sdelayut.html.

13. Viktor Kremenchug, "Samonadeyannost' sily," *Nezavisimaya gazeta—Stsenarii*, No. 11, November 11, 1998, p. 15.

14. Kremenchug, "Samonadeyannost' sily."

15. A.S. Panarin, *Revansh Istorii: Rossiiskaya strategicheskaya initsiativa v XXI veke* (Moscow: Logos, 1998).

16. Anastasiya Mitrofanova, "Nationalizm and Paranauka," in Marlen Laruelle, ed., *Russkii natsionalizm: Sotsial'nyi i kul'turnyi kontekst* (Moscow: Novoe Literaturnoe Obozrenie, 2008), pp. 87–102, at p. 95.

17. A.S. Panarin, *Pravoslavnaya tsivilizatsiya v global'nom mire* (Moscow: Algoritm, 2002).

18. Panarin, *Revansh Istorii*.

19. Panarin, *Revansh Istorii*, pp. 364–84.

20. Panarin, *Revansh Istorii*, p. 362.

21. According to Panarin, the relevant Zarathustrian "reforms" were aimed at, on the one hand, "casting out the caste of warriors from the Indo-Iranian pantheon of ferocious gods," and, on the other, "the removal of 'consumer' cults of the agrarians." Panarin, *Revansh Istorii*, pp. 365–8.

22. Panarin, *Revansh Istorii*, pp. 369–70.

23. Panarin, *Revansh Istorii*, pp. 377–81.

24. Stephen D. Shenfield, *Russian Fascism: Traditions, Tendencies, Movements* (Armonk, N.Y.: M.E. Sharpe, 2001), p. 195. A short list of Dugin's publications includes: *Mysteries of Eurasia* (2005), *The Basics of Eurasianism* (2002), *Martin Heidegger: Philosophy of Another Beginning* (2010), *Conspirology* (2005), *Pop Culture and Signs of the Times* (2005), *The Fourth Political Theory* (2009), *The Geopolitics of the Post-Modern* (2007), and *The Basics of Geopolitics* (2000). For a complete list see *Yevraziya.tv*, www.evrazia-books.ru/index.php?option=com_virtuemart&page=shop.browse&category_id=1&Itemid=2, last accessed on August 13, 2015.

25. Mitrofanova, "Nationalizm and Paranauka," pp. 100–1.

26. Ilya Kukulin, "Reaktsiya Dissotsiatsii: Legitimatsiya ul'trapravogo diskursa v sovremennoi rossiiskoi literature," in Laruelle, ed., *Russkii natsionalizm: Sotsial'nyi i kul'turnyi kontekst*, pp. 257–338, at p. 260.

27. On false, exaggerated claims regarding Dugin's influence, see Gordon M. Hahn, "Putin Myths and Putin Ideology," *Russia: Other Points of View*, January 16, 2015, www.russiaotherpointsofview.com/2015/01/putin-myths-and-putin-ideology.html. For a good example of such exaggerations, see Robert Zubrin, "Putin Adviser Publishes Plan for Domination of Europe," *The National Review*, March 10, 2015, www.nationalreview.com/corner/373064/putin-adviser-publishes-plan-domination-europe-robert-zubrin.

28. A.G. Dugin, "Kresovyo pokhod Solntsa," in A.G. Dugin, *Konspirilogiya* (Moscow: Arktogeya, 2005), http://arcto.ru/article/1339.

29. Shenfield, *Russian Fascism*, pp. 198–9.

30. Shenfield, *Russian Fascism*, pp. 195–7.

31. A.G. Dugin, *Yevraziiskii put' kak natsional'naya ideya* (Moscow: Arktogeya Tsentr, 2002), p. 3.

32. Brzezinski, *The Grand Chessboard*, p. 111.

33. Samuel P. Huntington, "The Clash of Civilizations," *Foreign Affairs*, Vol. 72, No. 3 (Summer 1993), pp. 22–49, at p. 25.

34. Huntington, "The Clash of Civilizations," pp. 29–30.

35. Other members of the Eurasianist émigré group

were legal scholar N.N. Alekseev, theologian and philosopher G.V. Florovskii, historian L.P. Krasavin, legal scholar V.N. Il'in, geographer and economist P.N. Savitskii, historian M.M. Shakhmatov, musicologist P.P. Suvchinskii, and historian G.V. Vernadskii. Both of Trubetskoi's seminal articles on Eurasianism can be found with an excellent introduction by I.A. Isaev in *Puti Yevrazii* (Moscow: Russkaya kniga, 1992).

36. Nikolai S. Trubetskoi, "Yevraziistvo: Opyt sistematicheskogo izlozheniya" in *Puti Yevrazii*, pp. 348–415, at pp. 362 and 372.

37. Trubetskoi, "Yevraziistvo," pp. 362–5.

38. Trubetskoi, "Yevraziistvo," pp. 372–7.

39. Trubetskoi, "Yevraziistvo," pp. 378–9.

40. Trubetskoi, "Yevraziistvo," pp. 379–81.

41. Trubetskoi, "Yevraziistvo," pp. 395–7.

42. Shenfield, *Russian Fascism*, pp. 36–7.

43. Shenfield, *Russian Fascism*, p. 37.

44. Shenfield, *Russian Fascism*, pp. 37 and 43–4.

45. Lev Gumilev, *Ot Rusi do Rossii* (Moscow: Airis Press, 2004), p. 9.

46. Gumilev, *Ot Rusi do Rossii*, p. 290.

47. Gumilev, *Ot Rusi do Rossii*, pp. 286–90.

48. Gumilev, *Ot Rusi do Rossii*, pp. 291–3.

49. Panarin, *Revansh Istorii*, pp. 362.

50. Panarin, *Revansh Istorii*, p. 357.

51. Panarin, *Revansh Istorii*, pp. 371–76.

52. Panarin, *Revansh Istorii*, pp. 14–15.

53. Panarin, *Revansh Istorii*, pp. 13–15, 222–27, and 357.

54. Shenfield, *Russian Fascism*, pp. 195–7.

55. Alexander Dugin, "Yevraziya v setevoi voine: evraziiskie seti nakanune 2015 goda," *Evrazia.org*, December 8, 2014, http://evrazia.org/article/2609.

56. Dugin, *Yevraziiskii put' kak natsionalnaya ideya*, p. 85.

57. Shenfield, *Russian Fascism*, pp. 195–7.

58. Alexander Dugin, *Misterii Yevrazii* (Moscow: Arktogeia, 1996) cited in Sheffield, *Russian Fascism: Traditions, Tendencies, Movements*, pp. 196–7.

59. The emphasis in the quotation from Lavrov's speech is mine. *Vystuplenie i otvety na voprosy Ministra innostrannykh del Rossii S.V. Lavrov na Forume 'Territoriya smyslov na Klyaz'me,' Vladimirskaya oblast,' d.Dvorkin, 24 August 2015*, Mid.ru (website of the Russian Ministry of Foreign Affairs), August 24, 2015, www.mid.ru/press_service/minister_speeches/-/asset_publisher/7OvQR5KJWVmR/content/id/1680936.

60. Alexander Dugin's interview on the Ukrainian TV's "Pro Golovne" Program, "Aleksandr Dugin na ukrainskom televidenii ob aktual'nykh politicheskikh problemakh," *Evrazia.net*, March 29, 2013 www.evrazia.tv/content/aleksandr-dugin-na-ukrainskom-televidenii-ob-aktualnyh-politicheskih-problemah.

61. Hahn, "Putin Myths and Putin Ideology."

62. Vladimir Putin, "Novyi integratsionnyi proekt dlya Yevrazii—budushee, kotoroe rozhdaetsy segodnya," *Izvestiya*, October 4, 2011, http://izvestia.ru/news/502761.

63. *Vystuplenie i otvety na voprosy Ministra innostrannykh del Rossii S.V. Lavrov na Forume "Territoriya smyslov na Klyaz'me," Vladimirskaya oblast,' d.Dvorkin, 24 August 2015*.

64. I.A. Isaev, "Utopisty ili providtsy?," in Isaev, ed. *Puti Yevrazii*, pp. 3–26, at. p. 14.

65. Gumilev, *Ot Rusi do Rossii*, p. 292.

66. Gumilev, *Ot Rusi do Rossii*, p. 233.

67. A.S. Panarin, *Global'noe politicheskoe prognozirovanie* (Moscow: Algoritm, 2002), cited in Vladimir Bukarskii, "Panarin Alelsandr Sergeevich (1940–2003)—26 dekabrya velikomu russkomu filosofu sovremennosti Aleksandru Sergeevichu Panarinu ispolnilos' by 65 let," *Pravaya.ru*, December 26, 2005, http://pravaya.ru/ludi/451/6061.

68. Dugin, "Yevraziya v setevoi voine: evraziiskie seti nakanune 2015 goda."

69. "Kak by vy otneslis' k perspektive obrazovaniya 'Slavyanskogo' bloka (Rossiya-Ukraina-Belarus')," *Vserossiiskiy Tsentr Izucheniya Obschestvennogo Mneniya* (from here on cited as *VTsIOM*), March 15, 1998, http://wciom.ru/zh/print_q.php?s_id=393&q_id=32019&date=15.03.1998.

70. Denis Volkov, "Rossiiskaya sotsiologiya ukrainskogo konflikta: vmeshivat'sya ne nado, no vse pravil'no sdelali," *Moskovskii tsentr Karnegi*, August 26, 2015, http://carnegie.ru/2015/08/26/ru-61007/if5q.

71. "Ukraina: vnimanie, otnoshenie, peremirie," *Levada Center*, February 26, 2015, www.levada.ru/26-02-2015/ukraina-vnimanie-otnoshenie-peremirie.

72. "Ukrainskii krizis: uchastie Rossii i ozhidaniya," *Levada Center*, March 4, 2015, www.levada.ru/04-03-2015/ukrainskii-krizis-uchastie-rossii-i-ozhidaniya.

73. "Ukraina: vnimanie, otnoshenie, peremirie."

74. Volkov, "Rossiiskaya sotsiologiya ukrainskogo konflikta: vmeshivat'sya ne nado, no vse pravil'no sdelali."

75. Michael Stuermer, *Putin and the Rise of Russia* (London: Weidenfeld and Nicolson, 2008), pp. 43 and 50.

Chapter 2

1. Huntington, "The Clash of Civilizations," p. 43.

2. Huntington, "The Clash of Civilizations," p. 38.

3. S.F. Platonov, *Lektsii po russkoi istorii* (Moscow: Vysshaya Shkola, 1993), pp. 139–63 and Orest Subtelny, *Ukraine: A History* (Toronto, Canada: Toronto University Press, 1988), pp. 40–41.

4. Subtelny, *Ukraine: A History*, pp. 56–65.

5. Subtelny, *Ukraine: A History*, p. 102.

6. Subtelny, *Ukraine: A History*, p. 105.

7. Anton Kontenko, Olga Martynyuk, and Aleksei Miller, "Maloross," in D. Dvizhdkov and I. Shirle, eds., *Ponyatiya o Rossii: k istoricheskoi semantike iperskogo perioda II* (Moscow: Duetsches Historices Institut and Novoe Literaturnoe Obozrenie, 2012), pp. 392–443.

8. Platonov, *Lektsii po russkoi istorii*, pp. 248–333.

9. Subtelny, *Ukraine: A History*, pp. 106–22.

10. Subtelny, *Ukraine: A History*, pp. 125–30.

11. Platonov, *Lektsii po russkoi istorii*, pp. 438–9 and Subtelny, *Ukraine: A History*, pp. 130–4.

12. Platonov, *Lektsii po russkoi istorii*, p. 439.

13. Subtelny, *Ukraine: A History*, pp. 133–4.

14. Subtelny, *Ukraine: A History*, p. 134.

15. Subtelny, *Ukraine: A History*, p. 135.

16. Subtelny, *Ukraine: A History*, p. 125.

17. Subtelny argues there are five interpretations of the Pereiaslav agreement offered by scholars. In my view the only two worth serious debate are the second and third he presents. The second is that of Russian legal historian Nikolai Diakonov, who asserted that the 1654 agreement was a "real union" because Ukrainians unconditionally agreed to their land's subjugation to Russia by declaring their personal subjugation to the Russian tsar. The third is made by Ukrainian historians, in particular Mykhailo Hrushevsky. They argue that the agreement was about Ukraine's vassalage whereby Ukrainians gave the tsar tribute, military assistance, and "other considerations" in return for Russia's protection of Ukraine from foreign encroachment and Russia's own noninterference in its internal affairs. Subtelny, *Ukraine: A History*, p. 135.

18. Subtelny, *Ukraine: A History*, pp. 139–48.

19. Subtelny, *Ukraine: A History*, pp. 148–54.

20. Photocopy of material in author's archive from the Solovetskii Monastery museum acquired in Solovetsk on July 29, 2014.

21. Subtelny, *Ukraine: A History*, pp. 158–72.

22. Subtelny, *Ukraine: A History*, p. 210.

23. Ivan Lappo, "Proiskhozhdenie ukrainskoi ideologii Noveishego vremei," *Imperskoe Vozrozhdenie*, No. 7, 2007, pp. 97–107, at p. 101.

24. Richard Pipes, *The Formation of the Soviet Union: Communism and Nationalism, 1917–1923* (Cambridge, Massachusetts: Harvard University Press, 1954), pp. 29–49.

25. Pipes, *The Formation of the Soviet Union*, pp. 53–61.

26. Pipes, *The Formation of the Soviet Union*, pp. 63–5; Subtelny, *Ukraine: A History*, pp. 344–7.

27. Pipes, *The Formation of the Soviet Union*, pp. 69–73 and 115.

28. Pipes, *The Formation of the Soviet Union*, pp. 115–8; Subtelny, *Ukraine: A History*, pp. 347–8.

29. "III Universal Ukrainskoi Tsentral'noi Rady (7 noyabrya 1917)," *Likbez.ua*, http://likbez.org.ua/iii-decree-ukrainian-central-rada.html, last accessed on September 7, 2015.

30. Pipes, *The Formation of the Soviet Union*, pp. 118–9; Subtelny, *Ukraine: A History*, pp. 349–50. For a map of the territories of the nine Ukrainian Republic provinces, see "III Universal Ukrainskoi Tsentral'noi Rady (7 noyabrya 1917)" and "Administrativno-Territorial'noe delenie ukrainskikh zemel' v Rossiiskoi imperii na 1914 god," *Likbez.ua*, http://likbez.org.ua/admin-division-1914.html, last accessed on September 7, 2015.

31. Pipes, *The Formation of the Soviet Union*, pp. 123–33; Subtelny, *Ukraine: A History*, pp. 350–53.

32. Pipes, *The Formation of the Soviet Union*, pp. 133–5; Subtelny, *Ukraine: A History*, pp. 354–5.

33. Pipes, *The Formation of the Soviet Union*, pp. 137–50; Subtelny, *Ukraine: A History*, pp. 355–66.

34. Subtelny, *Ukraine: A History*, p. 354.

35. On October 16, 1925, the Presidium of the Soviet Government passed a resolution: "On the Regulation of the Borders of the Ukrainian Socialist Soviet Republic with the Russian Socialist Federative Soviet Republic and the Belorussian Socialist Soviet Republic." In accordance with the 1925 document, the Ukraine SSR transferred to the RSFSR: the city of Taganrog; five districts (*raiony*) and the eastern part of the Yekaterinov district of Taganrog Province (*okrug*); the city of Shakhty; and seven districts and part of two other districts of Shakhty Province. The RSFSR gave Ukraine: part of Novozybko county in the Gomel Governate; a settlement (*selenie*) in Pochep county; eight settlements in Sev county in the Bryansk Governate; almost all of Putivl county (including the city of Putivl, excluding Krupetsk district); a district (*volost'*) and parts of two others in the Kursk Governate; and Troitsky volost' and part of another in Valyui county in Voronezh Governate. On October 16, 1928, another Soviet government resolution mandated another set of territorial exchanges between Soviet Russia and Soviet Ukraine. Ukraine transferred to Russia the settlement in Pochep county it had received from Russia in 1925 and a village in Sev county in Bryansk Governate. Russia transferred to Ukraine: two settlements in Sev county in Bryansk Governate; three settlements from Belgorod county in Kursk Governate; and eight settlements in Graivoron county in Kursk Governate. Andrei Illarionov, "Putin i granitsy Ukrainy. I Freid," Andrei Illarionov's Live Journal Page, October 16, 2014, http://aillarionov.livejournal.com/746987.html.

36. For a simple map showing the territory ceded to the Ukraine SSR as a result of the Stalin's pre- and postwar conquests, see Subtelny, *Ukraine: A History*, p. 482.

37. Robert Conquest, *Harvest of Sorrow* (New York and Oxford: Oxford University Press, 1986), pp. 3, 189–98, and 219.

38. Subtelny, *Ukraine: A History*, pp. 425–39.

39. Subtelny, *Ukraine: A History*, pp. 442–4.

40. Subtelny, *Ukraine: A History*, pp. 441–6 and 452.

41. Subtelny, *Ukraine: A History*, pp. 459–60.

42. Aleksandra Vagner and Aleksei Dsokavitskii, "Mnogolikii Stepan Bandera," *Radio Svoboda*, December 25, 2013, www.svoboda.org/content/article/25209525.html.

43. Subtelny, *Ukraine: A History*, pp. 455–6.

44. Transcarpathia and its Ukrainian, Rusyn, and other minorities came under Hungarian occupation, which implemented a "Rusynification" policy—the ethnic Rusyns were said to be ethnic kin of Hungarians, not Slavs. Subtelny, *Ukraine: A History*, pp. 457–8.

45. Subtelny, *Ukraine: A History*, pp. 461–3.

46. Per Anders Rudling, "The OUN, the UPA and the Holocaust: A Study in the Manufacturing of Historical Myths," *Carl Beck Papers in Russian and East European Studies*, No. 2107 (Center for Russian and East European Studies, University of Pittsburgh, 2011), p. 3.

47. Fraziska Bruder, *"Dem ukrainischen Staat erkampfen oder sterben!": Die Organizatsion Ukrainischer Nationalisten (OUN), 1928–1948* (Berlin: Metropol Verlag, 2007), p. 23.

48. Rudling, "The OUN, the UPA and the Holocaust," pp. 3–5.

49. Rudling, "The OUN, the UPA and the Holocaust," p. 6.

50. Rudling, "The OUN, the UPA and the Holocaust," pp. 3–4 and 6–7.

51. Subtelny, *Ukraine: A History*, p. 463.

52. John-Paul Himka, "The Lviv Pogrom of 1941: The Germans, Ukrainian Nationalists, and the Carnival Crowd," *Canadian Slavonic Papers/Revue Canadienne des Slavistes* 53, No. 2/4 (June–Sept.–Dec. 2011): pp. 209–43; Rudling, "The OUN, the UPA and the Holocaust," p. 8.

53. Subtelny, *Ukraine: A History*, p. 472.

54. Rudling, "The OUN, the UPA and the Holocaust," pp. 8–9.

55. Subtelny, *Ukraine: A History*, pp. 464–7.

56. Rudling, "The OUN, the UPA and the Holocaust," pp. 8–9.

57. Kerel C. Berkhoff, "Dina Pronicheva's Story of Surviving the Babi Yar Massacre: German, Jewish, Soviet, Russian, and Ukrainian Records," in Ray Brandon and Wendy Lower, eds., *The Shoah in Ukraine: History, Testimony, Memorialization* (Bloomington: Indiana University Press, 2010), pp. 291–317, at pp. 303–4.

58. Dieter Pohl, "The Murder of Ukraine's Jews under German Military Administration and in the Reich Commissariat Ukraine," in Brandon and Lower, eds., *The Shoah in Ukraine*, pp. 77–113, at pp. 54–5.

59. Subtelny, *Ukraine: A History*, pp. 468 and 472–3.

60. Subtelny, *Ukraine: A History*, pp. 473–4; Rudling, "The OUN, the UPA and the Holocaust," p. 10.

61. Rudling, "The OUN, the UPA and the Holocaust," pp. 10–14.

62. Subtelny, *Ukraine: A History*, p. 475; Rudling, "The OUN, the UPA and the Holocaust," pp. 11–13.

63. Subtelny, *Ukraine: A History*, p. 476.

64. The OUN's main operative in Donbass during the war, Yevhen Stakhiv (Yevgenii Stakhov), acknowledged that the main concern of the few OUN members there was social ills, not Ukrainian independence, which was seen as one possible vehicle to correct the social order. Donbassians rejected the propaganda of Stakhiv, who was a Francoist, because they saw it as "fascist," and Stakhiv eventually discarded Dontsov's integral Ukrainian nationalism in favor of "a democratic Ukraine without discrimination against its national minorities." Hiroaki Kuromiya, *Freedom and Terror in the Donbas: A Ukrainian-Russian Borderland, 1870s–1990s* (Cambridge, UK: Cambridge University Press, 1998), pp. 277–82.

65. Kuromiya, *Freedom and Terror in the Donbas*, p. 299.

66. Subtelny, *Ukraine: A History*, pp. 488–91.

67. Subtelny, *Ukraine: A History*, pp. 488–91.

Chapter 3

1. This approximates the position of then U.S. Ambassador to Moscow Jack Matlock. See John J. Matlock, "NATO Expansion: Was There a Promise?," *JackMatlock.com*, April 3, 2014, http://jackmatlock.com/2014/04/nato-expansion-was-there-a-promise/.

2. Yevgenii Primakov, *Gody v Bolshoi Politike* (Moscow: Sovershenno Sekretno, 1999), pp. 231–32; Uwe Klussman, Matthias Schepp, and Klaus Wiegrefe, "NATO's Eastward Expansion: Did the West Break Its Promise to Moscow?" *Der Spiegel*, November 26, 2009, www.spiegel.de/international/world/nato-s-eastward-expansion-did-the-west-break-its-promise-to-moscow-a-663315.html.

3. Klussman, Schepp, and Wiegrefe, "NATO's Eastward Expansion."

4. Mikhail Gorbachev, *Zhizni i reform, Kniga 2* (Moscow: Novosti, 1995), p. 167.

5. James M. Goldgeier and Michael McFaul, *Power and Purpose: U.S. Policy Toward Russia After the Cold War* (Washington, D.C.: Brookings Institution Press, 2003), pp. 184–5.

6. "Abmachung 1990: 'Keine Osterweiterung der NATO'—Aussenminister Gensher & Baker," *Antikrieg TV*, July 6, 2014, www.youtube.com/watch?v=JXcWVTpQF3k.

7. Klussman, Schepp, and Wiegrefe, "NATO's Eastward Expansion."

8. Primakov, *Gody v Bolshoi Politike*, pp. 231–33.

9. Primakov, *Gody v Bolshoi Politike*, p. 233.

10. Georgii Shakhnazarov, *Tsena Svobody: Reformatsiya Gorbacheva glazami ego pomoshnika* (Moscow: Rissika-Zevs, 1993), p. 128.

11. Robert D. McFadden, "Strong American Voice in Diplomacy and Crisis," *New York Times*, December 13, 2010, www.nytimes.com/2010/12/14/world/14holbrooke.html?pagewanted=all&_r=0.

12. Yuli Vorontsov, "NATO Enlargement Without Russia: A Mistake on Four Counts," The NATO-Russian Charter and the Emerging Relationship, Russia and NATO International Panel, George Washington University, Washington, D.C., February 1997, http://fas.org/man/nato/ceern/gwu_conf.htm and http://fas.org/man/nato/ceern/gwu_c1.htm.

13. Brzezinski, *The Grand Chessboard*, pp. 79–80.

14. Andrei P. Tsygankov, *Russia and the West from Alexander to Putin: Honor in International Relations* (Cambridge, UK: Cambridge University Press, 2015).

15. Zoltan Barany, *The Future of NATO Expansion: Four Case Studies* (Cambridge: Cambridge University Press, 2003), pp. 16–18.

16. Kennan is quoted in Thomas L. Friedman, "Foreign Affairs: Now a Word From X," *New York Times*, May 2, 1998, www.nytimes.com/1998/05/02/opinion/foreign-affairs-now-a-word-from-x.html. For other warnings regarding the likelihood of dangerous changes occurring in Moscow's attitude towards the West as a result of NATO expansion, see Michael Mandelbaum, "NATO Expansion: Bridge to the Nineteenth Century" (Chevy Chase, Md.: Center for Political and Strategic Studies, 1997), and Gordon M. Hahn, "Russian Domestic Politics and NATO Expansion," *FOCUS*, Washington DC, Center for Political and Strategic Studies, Volume 4, Issue 6, August-September 1997, www.bu.edu/globalbeat/nato/russian.html.

17. Brzezinski, *The Grand Chessboard*, p. 101.

18. Hahn, "Russian Domestic Politics and NATO Expansion."

19. TASS, June 16, 1991.

20. See Gordon M. Hahn, *Russia's Revolution from Above: Reform, Transition, and Revolution in the Fall of the Soviet Communist Regime, 1985–2000* (New Brunswick: Transaction Publishers, 2002).

21. The preceding paragraphs summarize Hahn, *Russia's Revolution from Above*, Chapters 2–11.

22. Also, an appreciation for the duration of such a project might have suggested that foreign assistance target institution-building on behalf of the polity, the market and civil society, reforming the courts, developing small business outside of Moscow, and funding public associations rather than state structures.

23. The Group of Seven countries (G-7) put together a $30 billion aide package for Russia only in mid–1993. U.S. bilateral assistance to all the post–Soviet states, except the Baltics, was approved for fiscal year 1993 at a level of $1.6 billion, and Congress reduced that to $900 million in 1994, while shifting more of that aid from Russia to the other states of the former USSR.

24. Peter Reddaway and Dmitry Glinski, *The Tragedy of Russia's Reforms: Market Bolshevism Against Democracy* (Washington, DC: U.S. Institute of Peace Press, 2001).

25. The verbatim records of the London summits' discussions can be found at "1990 Summit: a turning point in 'East-West' relations," *NATO*, December 18, 2014, www.nato.int/cps/en/natohq/news_116133.htm.

26. Coit D. Blacker, "Russia and the West," in Michael Mandelbaum, ed., *The New Russian Foreign Policy* (Washington, D.C.: Council of Foreign Relations, 1998), pp. 167–93, at pp. 179–80.

27. *Interfax*, May 19, 1997 and Sherman W. Garnett, "Russia and the West in the New Borderlands," in Mandelbaum, *The New Russian Foreign Policy*, pp. 64–99, at p. 83.

28. *Madrid Declaration on Euro-Atlantic Security*, NATO Press Office, July 8, 1997 cited in Garnett, "Russia and the West in the New Borderlands," p. 83.

29. *Charter on a Distinctive Partnership between the North Atlantic Treaty Organization and Ukraine*, NATO, July 9, 1997, www.nato.int/cps/en/natohq/official_texts_25457.htm.

30. "Russia Offers Guarantees to Baltic States," *Jane's Defense Weekly*, September 10, 1997, vol. 28, no. 10, p. 4 cited in Garnett, "Russia and the West in the New Borderlands," p. 83.

31. Blacker, "Russia and the West," in Mandelbaum, *The New Russian Foreign Policy*, p. 174.

32. Anatolii Adamishin, "Yugoslavskaya Prelyudiya," *Rossiya v Global'noi Politike*, No. 4, July-August 2013, www.globalaffairs.ru/number/Yugoslavskaya-prelyudiya-16104.

33. Adamishin, "Yugoslavskaya Prelyudiya."

34. Adamishin, "Yugoslavskaya Prelyudiya."

35. Belgium, Canada, Denmark, France, Germany, Italy, the Netherlands, Norway, Portugal, Spain, Turkey, the United Kingdom, and the United States.

36. The use and likely the availability of precision guided munitions declined from an initial 90 percent of munitions used to 10–20 percent by mid–May.

37. "The Crisis in Kosovo," *Human Rights Watch*, 2000, www.hrw.org/reports/2000/nato/Natbm200-01.htm, last accessed October 9, 2015.

38. "54. Kak vy schitaete, imelo li NATO parvo nachinat' bombardirovki bez canktsii Soveta Bezopasnosti OON?," *VTsIOM*, February 28, 1999, http://wciom.ru/zh/print_q.php?s_id=520&q_id=37433&date=28.02.1999.

39. The remaining 6 percent were divided among several responses; all receiving just 1 percent of respondents' responses. "46. Kak vy otneslis' k bombardirovkami salami NATO Yugoslavii, predprinyatym s tsel'yu zastavit

rukovodstvo Yugoslavii predostavit' avtonomiyu dlya Kosovo?" *VTsIOM*, March 15, 1999, http://wciom.ru/zh/print_q.php?s_id=353&q_id=28615&date=15.03.1999.

40. "47. Kak vy schitaete, chto yavlyaetsya konechnoi tsel'yu SShA i NATO v etom konflikte," *VTsIOM*, March 15, 1999, http://wciom.ru/zh/print_q.php?s_id=353&q_id=28616&date=15.03.1999.

41. "Public opinion trends with regard to NATO in post–Soviet countries during the 90's—Final Report," *NATO*, 2001, www.nato.int/acad/fellow/01-03/sikharulidze.pdf, p. 3.

42. The official accession of the three Baltic states as well as Bulgaria, Romania, Slovakia and Slovenia took place at NATO's 2004 Istanbul summit.

43. "Resolution 1244 (1999)"—NATO's Role in Kosovo, *NATO*, June 30, 1999, www.nato.int/kosovo/docu/u990610a.htm.

44. "U.S. Recognizes Kosovo as Independent State," U.S. Department of State, February 18, 2008, http://2001-2009.state.gov/secretary/rm/2008/02/100973.htm, last accessed October 9, 2015.

45. "Founding Act on Mutual Relations, Cooperation and Security Between NATO and the Russian Federation, signed in Paris, France," *NATO*, May 27, 1997, www.nato.int/cps/en/natolive/official_texts_25468.htm.

46. "Confrontation over Pristina airport," BBC News, March 9, 2000, http://news.bbc.co.uk/2/hi/europe/671495.stm, last accessed October 10, 2015.

47. Jeffrey Mankoff, *Russian Foreign Policy: The Return of Great Power Politics*, second edition (New York: Council of Foreign Relations, 2012), p. 98.

48. The point in the Founding Act in its entirety reads as follows: "NATO's and Russia's respective military authorities will explore the further development of a concept for joint NATO-Russia peacekeeping operations. This initiative should build upon the positive experience of working together in Bosnia and Herzegovina, and the lessons learned there will be used in the establishment of Combined Joint Task Forces." "Founding Act on Mutual Relations, Cooperation and Security Between NATO and the Russian Federation, signed in Paris, France."

49. Adamishin, "Yugoslavskaya Prelyudiya."

50. "43. Est' li osnovaniya u Rossii opasat'sya stran Zapada, vkhodyashchikh v blok NATO?," *VTsIOM*, March 30, 1999, http://wciom.ru/zh/print_q.php?s_id=354&q_id=28693&date=30.03.1999, last accessed October 12, 2015.

51. "82_B. Kakoe znachenie immet dlya vas slovo: NATO?" *VTsIOM*, June 15, 1999, http://wciom.ru/zh/print_q.php?s_id=380&q_id=30863&date=15.06.1999, last accessed on October 15, 2015.

52. "67A. Kak vy lichno otnosites' k zayavleniyu Vladimira Putina o tom, chto Rossiya v budushem mozhet vstupit' v NATO: s odobreniem, s nedoumeniem, s osuzhdeniem, ili sravnitel'no bezrazlichno?" *VTsIOM*, June 15, 2000, http://wciom.ru/zh/print_q.php?s_id=405&q_id=32590&date=15.06.2000, last accessed on October 12, 2015.

53. Compare "36B. Est' li osnovaniya u Rossii opasat'sya stran Zapada, vkhodyashchikh v blok NATO?" *VTsIOM*, October 15, 2000, http://wciom.ru/zh/print_q.php?s_id=347&q_id=28022&date=15.10.2000, last accessed on October 12, 2015 and "43. Est' li osnovaniya u Rossii opasat'sya stran Zapada, vkhodyashchikh v blok NATO?"

54. Wade Boese, "U.S. Withdraws from ABM Treaty; Global Response Muted," *Arms Control Association*, July 8, 2002, www.armscontrol.org/act/2002_07-08/abmjul_aug02.

55. "Bucharest Summit Declaration," NATO, April 3, 2008, www.nato.int/cps/en/natohq/official_texts_8443.htm?selectedLocale=en.

56. Olga Allyonova, Yelena Geda, and Vladimir Novi-

kov, "Blok NATO razosholsya na blokpakety," *Kommersant*, April 7, 2008, www.kommersant.ru/doc/877224.

57. Gordon M. Hahn, "Did Putin Really Tell Bush 'Ukraine Is Not Even a State'?" *GordonHahn.com Russian and Eurasian Politics*, January 26, 2015, http://gordonhahn.com/2015/01/26/did-putin-really-tell-bush-ukraine-is-not-even-a-state/.

58. The relevant quote from the *Politico* article is: "Russia has attempted to involve Poland in the invasion of Ukraine, just as if it were a post-modern re-run of the historic partitions of Poland. 'He wanted us to become participants in this partition of Ukraine,' says Sikorski. 'Putin wants Poland to commit troops to Ukraine. These were the signals they sent us.... We have known how they think for years. We have known this is what they think for years. This was one of the first things that Putin said to my prime minister, Donald Tusk [soon to be president of the European Council], when he visited Moscow. He went on to say Ukraine is an artificial country and that Lwow is a Polish city and why don't we just sort it out together. Luckily Tusk didn't answer. He knew he was being recorded.'" Ben Judah, "Vladimir Putin's Coup," *Politico*, October 19, 2014, www.politico.com/magazine/story/2014/10/vladimir-putins-coup-112025_Page3.html#.ViApr36rSM8.

59. "Donald Tusk: Nie rozmawialem z Putinem o Ukrainie," *Wyborcza*, October 24, 2014, http://m.wyborcza.pl/wyborcza/1,105226,16856661,Donald_Tusk__nie_rozmawialem_z_Putinem_o_Ukrainie.html#button?__utma=70145996.203202563.1416446644.1416446644.1416446644.1&__utmb=70145996.4.9.1416446992410&__utmc=70145996&__utmx=-&__utmz=70145996.1416446644.1.1.utmcsr=(direct)|utmccn=(direct)|utmcmd=(none)&__utmv=-&__utmk=2055607.

60. *RIA Novosti*, June 7, 2006 cited in "Georgia, Ukraine NATO Accession May Cause Geopolitical Shift—FM," *Global Security*, June 7, 2006, www.globalsecurity.org/military//library/news/2006/06/mil-060607-rianovosti02.htm.

61. "Vystuplenie prezidenta Rossii Vladimira Putina na Myunkhenskoi konferentsii po voprosam politiki bezopasnosti 10 fevralya 2007 goda," *Izvestia*, February 12, 2007, http://izvestia.ru/news/321595. For a video of the speech, see "Vystuplenie V. Putina na Myunkhenskoi konferentstii (2007g.)," YouTube, February 10, 2007, www.youtube.com/watch?v=PkyjYKVYlWo.

62. "Vystuplenie prezidenta Rossii Vladimira Putina na Myunkhenskoi konferentstii po voprosam politiki bezopasnosti 10 fevralya 2007 goda," and "Vystuplenie V. Putina na Myunkhenskoi konferentstii (2007g.)."

63. "Vystuplenie prezidenta Rossii Vladimira Putina na Myunkhenskoi konferentstii po voprosam politiki bezopasnosti 10 fevralya 2007 goda," and "Vystuplenie V. Putina na Myunkhenskoi konferentstii (2007g.)."

64. "Vystuplenie prezidenta Rossii Vladimira Putina na Myunkhenskoi konferentstii po voprosam politiki bezopasnosti 10 fevralya 2007 goda," and "Vystuplenie V. Putina na Myunkhenskoi konferentstii (2007g.)."

65. Brzezinski, *The Grand Chessboard*, pp. 79–80.

66. Ronald D. Asmus and Robert C. Nurick, "NATO Enlargement and the Baltic States," *Survival* 38, No. 2 (Summer 1996): pp. 121–42.

67. The list of NATO and EU member-states are as follows (those countries in **bold**-face type in each list are not member-sates of the other organization). The 28 NATO member countries are: **Albania**, Belgium, Bulgaria, **Canada**, Croatia, Czech Republic, Denmark, Estonia, France, Germany, Greece, Hungary, Iceland, Italy, Latvia, Lithuania, Luxembourg, the Netherlands, Norway, Poland, Portugal, Romania, Slovakia, Slovenia, Spain, Turkey, United Kingdom, **United States**. The 28 EU member countries are: Austria, Belgium, Bulgaria, Croatia, **Cyprus**,

Czech Republic, Denmark, Estonia, Finland, France, Germany, Greece, Hungary, Ireland (UK), Italy, Latvia, Lithuania, Luxembourg, **Malta**, the Netherlands, Poland, Portugal, Romania, Slovakia, Slovenia, Spain, **Sweden**, the United Kingdom.

68. *Charter on a Distinctive Partnership between the North Atlantic Treaty Organization and Ukraine*, NATO, July 9, 1997, www.nato.int/cps/en/natohq/official_texts_25457.htm.

69. "Poroshenko posevetoval ne zhdat' Ukrainiu v NATO esho 8 let," *Vesti Ukraina*, November 7, 2015, http://vesti-ukr.com/strana/122612-poroshenko-posovetoval-ne-zhdat-ukrainu-v-nato-ewe-8-let and "V SShA zayavili o perekhode Ukrainy na standarty NATO do 2020 goda," *Vesti Ukraina*, November 6, 2015, http://vesti-ukr.com/strana/122485-v-ssha-zajavili-o-perehode-ukrainy-na-standarty-nato-do-2020-goda.

70. Stanislav Tkachenko, "Will the Association Agreement with the EU really help the Ukrainian economy?," *Russia Direct*, January 27, 2016, www.russia-direct.org/opinion/will-association-agreement-eu-really-help-ukrainian-economy?utm_source=Russia+Direct+free+weekly+newsletters&utm_campaign=1f10e8f23b-RD_Newsletter_jan_28_2016&utm_medium=email&utm_term=0_cd2cf54b82-1f10e8f23b-78562405.

71. Balázs Jarábik, "A Policy of Pretending," *Carnegie Moscow Center*, May 25, 2015, http://carnegie.ru/commentary/?fa=60187.

72. Sergei Lavrov, "It's not Russia that is destabilising Ukraine," *The Guardian* (UK), April 8, 2014, www.theguardian.com/commentisfree/2014/apr/07/sergei-lavrov-russia-stabilise-ukraine-west.

73. Garnett, "Russia and the West in the New Borderlands," p. 98, footnote 42.

74. Garnett, "Russia and the West in the New Borderlands," pp. 98–99, footnote 42.

75. Mitrofanova, "Nationalizm and Paranauka," p. 95.

76. Lyudmilla Saraskina, "'Spravedlivyim krik otchayaniya,'" *Literaturnaya gazeta*, No. 20–21, May 22–28, 2002, p. 4.

77. Mikhail Yur'ev, *Tret'ya Imperiya: Rossiya, kotoraya dolzhna byt'* (St. Petersburg: Limbus Press, 2006), p. 76.

78. "Rossiya: zapadniy put' dlia 'ievroaziatskoi' tsivilizatsiyi…?," Na Zapad ili v Yevraziyu: Kakim Putem idti Rossii, *VTSIOM*, No. 32, November 13, 2001, http://wciom.ru/index.php?id=236&uid=306, accessed on December 27, 2010.

79. "Kak by vy otneslis' k vstupleniyu v NATO byvshikh respublik SSSR—stran Baltii, Ukrainy i drugikh," *VTsIOM*, April 15, 1996, http://wciom.ru/zh/print_q.php?s_id=453&q_id=35325&date=15.04.1996.

80. "Kak by vy otneslis' k vstupleniyu v NATO byvshikh respublik SSSR—stran Baltii, Ukrainy i drugikh," *VTsIOM*, February 10, 1997, http://wciom.ru/zh/print_q.php?s_id=437&q_id=35005&date=10.02.1997).

81. "Kak by vy otneslis' k vstupleniyu v NATO byvshikh respublik SSSR—stran Baltii, Ukrainy i drugikh," *VTsIOM*, March 20, 1997, http://wciom.ru/zh/print_q.php?s_id=440&q_id=35061&date=20.03.1997.

82. "50. Odni schitayut, chto NATO vedet samostoyatel'nuyu politiku v interesakh vsekh stran al'yansa; drugie—chto ono yavlyaetsya v osnovnom provodnikom interesov SShA. Kakaya iz etikh dvukh tochek zreniya kazhetsya vam bolee vernoi?," *VTsIOM*, March 15, 2001, http://wciom.ru/zh/print_q.php?s_id=321&q_id=25835&date=15.03.2001.

83. The fourth option available to respondents differed in the two polls. In the 2001 survey, the fourth option was the policy of neutrality, which 32 percent chose. In the 2011 version, the fourth option was "too difficult to answer," which 23 percent chose. "46. Chto iz perechislennogo, po vashemu mneniyu, bol'she otvechaet interesam

Rossii: Vstuplenie Rossii v NATO," *VTsIOM*, November 15, 2001, http://wciom.ru/zh/print_q.php?s_id=328&q_id=26453&date=15.11.2001 and *Rossiya i NATO: Realnost' i perspektivy vzaimodeistviya* (Moscow: VTsIOM, 2011), http://wciom.ru/fileadmin/file/reports_conferences/2011/2011-11-11-nato.pdf, p. 12.

84. *Rossiya i NATO: Realnost' i perspektivy vzaimodeistviya*, p. 13.

85. *Rossiya i NATO: Realnost' i perspektivy vzaimodeistviya*, p. 9.

86. *Rossiya i NATO: Realnost' i perspektivy vzaimodeistviya*, p. 10.

87. *Rossiya i NATO: Realnost' i perspektivy vzaimodeistviya*, p. 5.

88. See Gordon M. Hahn, *The Caucasus Emirate: Global Jihadism in Russia's North Caucasus and Beyond* (Jefferson, NC: McFarland, 2014); Gordon M. Hahn, *Russia's Islamic Threat* (New Haven and London: Yale University Press, 2007).

89. *Rossiya i NATO: Realnost' i perspektivy vzaimodeistviya*, pp. 8–10 and 13.

90. *Rossiya i NATO: Realnost' i perspektivy vzaimodeistviya*, pp. 8–10 and 13.

91. Eric Shiraev and Vladislav Zubok, *Anti-Americanism in Russia: From Stalin to Putin* (New York: Palgrave, 2000), pp. 145–7.

92. Shiraev and Zubok, *Anti-Americanism in Russia*, pp. 1, 28, 38, 43.

93. *San Jose Mercury News*, May 24, 2002.

94. Shiraev and Zubok, *Anti-Americanism in Russia*, pp. 1, 28, 38, 43.

95. See *VTsIOM*, February 2013 (30 percent negative towards U.S.), http://wciom.ru/index.php?id=236&uid=113677; September 2012—32 percent, http://wciom.ru/index.php?id=236&uid=113677; September 2011—29 percent, http://wciom.ru/index.php?id=236&uid=111941; May 2010—27 percent, http://wciom.ru/index.php?id=236&uid=113326; June 2009—33 percent, http://wciom.ru/index.php?id=236&uid=13616; and September 2008—65 percent, http://wciom.ru/index.php?id=236&uid+13616.

96. "Reiting natsional'nikh ugroz," Press-vypusk No. 2351, *VTsIOM*, July 22, 2013, http://wciom.ru/index.php?id=236&uid=114302.

97. The following pages are based on Gordon M. Hahn, "Russian Domestic Politics and NATO Expansion," *FOCUS* (Washington D.C., Center for Political and Strategic Studies) 4, Issue 6 (August-September 1997), www.bu.edu/globalbeat/nato/russian.html.

98. Strobe Talbott, *The Russia Hand: A Memoir of Presidential Diplomacy* (New York: Random House, 2003), pp. 201–2.

99. Talbott, *The Russia Hand*, p. 222.

100. Talbott, *The Russia Hand*, p. 223.

101. "Kak by vy otneslis' k vstupleniyu v NATO byvshikh stran Varshavskogo Dogovora—Polsh'i, Chekhii, Vengrii, i drugikh?" *VTsIOM*, April 15, 1996, http://wciom.ru/zh/print_q.php?s_id=453&q_id=35324&date=15.04.1996 and "Kak by vy otneslis' k vstupleniyu v NATO byvshikh stran Varshavskogo Dogovora—Polsh'i, Chekhii, Vengrii, i drugikh?" *VTsIOM*, February 10, 1997, http://wciom.ru/zh/print_q.php?s_id=437&q_id=35004&date=10.02.1997.

102. Mitrofanov added that the former "will be obliged to return immediately all German and Belorussian lands," "encouraged" by "missiles and other types of arms returned to the territory of a Belarus unified with Russia." A second Molotov-Ribbentrop pact with Germany should be negotiated, according to Mitrofanov, on an "agreed approach regarding the Baltics and Ukraine and regarding German lands in France and the Czech Republic." The Russo-German alliance in Europe will form part of a

Berlin-Moscow-Tokyo military-political "axis" for "a partition of spheres of influence in Europe, Southeast Asia, Africa and Latin America." A second, southern axis, a "Russia-China-India bloc" (a premonition of BRICS), should be formed in order to "deliver a last blow to the Anglo-Saxon principles of divide-and-rule and unrestrained robbery of Asia," "open a path to China for territorial expansion to the West through southern Kazakstan, Iran and Turkey and strengthen India's leading role on the Indian subcontinent." This will facilitate "Turkey's liquidation as Russia's opponent in the Middle East" and northern Kazakstan's reunification with Russia. Hahn, "Russian Domestic Politics and NATO Expansion."

103. Hahn, "Russian Domestic Politics and NATO Expansion."

104. Hearing on "United States Policy Regarding NATO Expansion," U.S. House of Representatives, Committee on National Security, Washington, D.C., July 17, 1997, http://commdocs.house.gov/committees/security/has198000.000/has198000_1.HTM, last accessed October 8, 2015.

105. Hahn, "Russian Domestic Politics and NATO Expansion."

106. *Krasnaya zvezda*, July 22, 1997, p. 2.

107. Alexei Arbatov, "As NATO Grows, Start 2 Shudders," *New York Times*, August 26, 1997, p. A 12, cited in Hahn, "Russian Domestic Politics and NATO Expansion."

108. Hahn, *Russia's Islamic Threat*, pp. 179–98.

109. "Putin: UN Libya resolution defective, reminds of Medieval call for Crusade," *YouTube*, March 21, 2011, www.youtube.com/watch?v=BvP3BW21VWU.

110. "Statement by Dmitry Medvedev on the situation in Libya," *Kremlin.ru*, March 21, 2011, http://en.kremlin.ru/events/president/news/10701.

111. See Gordon M. Hahn, "Tandemology 2.0: Putin's Return, Medvedev's Decline, and Tandem Spats," *Russia—Other Points of View*, October 7, 2012, www.russiaotherpointsofview.com/2012/10/tandemology-20-putins-return-medvedevs-decline-and-tandem-spats.html; Gordon M. Hahn, "Perestroika 2.0: Towards Non-Revolutionary Regime Transformation in Russia?" *Post-Soviet Affairs* 28, No. 4 (October-December 2012): pp. 472–515; and Gordon M. Hahn, "The Russian Federation in 2012: From 'Thaw' and 'Reset' to 'Freeze,'" *Asian Survey* 53, No. 1 (Winter 2013): pp. 214–223.

112. "Muammar Gaddafi Dead: Mansour Iddhow, Former Servant, Recounts Colonel's Final Days," *The World Post*, February 21, 2012, www.huffingtonpost.com/2012/02/21/muammar-gaddafi-dead-mansour-iddhow_n_1290789.html. The first video of Qadhafi's capture appeared on October 20, 2011. See, for example, " Muammar Gaddafi Killed, Captured in Sirte (GRAPHIC VIDEO)," *The World Post*, October 20, 2011, www.huffingtonpost.com/2011/10/20/muammar-gaddafi-killed_n_1021462.html.

113. "Dmitrii Petrov, Medvedev ne isklyuchaet, chto budet ballotirovatsya na novyi srok," *Vesti.ru*, July 13, 2011, www.vesti.ru/doc.html?id=444571 and Matvei Ganapolskii, "V perevode s kitaiskogo," *Moskovskii komsomolets*, April 13, 2011, www.mk.ru/politics/2011/04/13/580794-v-perevode-s-kitayskogo.html.

114. See the interview with Aleksei Venediktov, "Sut' sobytii" Program, *Radio Ekho Moskvy*, September 28, 2012, http://echo.msk.ru/programs/sut/934598-echo/.

115. See the interview with Dimitri Simes, "Why Russia Won't Yield on Syria," *Council on Foreign Relations*, July 17, 2012, www.cfr.org.

116. "How America Switched Sides in the War on Terror," Interim Report by the Citizens' Commission on Benghazi, *Accuracy in Media*, April 22, 2014, www.aim.org/benghazi/wp-content/uploads/2014/04/CCB-Interim-Report-4-22-2014.pdf.

117. See Hahn, *The Caucasus Emirate*; Gordon M.

Hahn, "REPORT: An Anatomy of North Caucasus-Tied Jihadi Groups in Syria and Iraq," *Gordonhahn.com Russian and Eurasian Politics*, October 20, 2015, https://gordonhahn.com/2015/10/20/report-an-anatomy-of-north-caucasus-tied-jihadi-groups-in-syria-and-iraq/; and Gordon M. Hahn, WHITE PAPER: "The Caucasus Emirate and Other North Caucasus Mujahedin in Syria and the Implications for Russia, Eurasia, and the Global Jihadi Revolutionary Movement," *Gordonhahn.com Russian and Eurasian Politics*, April 1, 2014, https://gordonhahn.com/2014/04/01/the-caucasus-emirate-and-other-north-caucasus-mujahedin-in-syria-implications-for-russia-eurasia-and-the-global-jihadi-revolutionary-movement/.

118. The fourth option available to respondents differed in the two polls. In the 2001 survey the fourth option was the policy of neutrality, which 32 percent chose. In the 2011 version, the fourth option was "too difficult to answer," which 23 percent chose. "46. Chto iz perechislennogo, po vashemu mneniyu, bol'she otvechaet interesam Rossii: Vstuplenie Rossii v NATO," *VTsIOM*, November 15, 2001, http://wciom.ru/zh/print_q.php?s_id=328&q_id=26453&date=15.11.2001 and *Rossiya i NATO: Realnost' i perspektivy vzaimodeistviya* (Moscow: VTsIOM, 2011), http://wciom.ru/fileadmin/file/reports_conferences/2011/2011-11-11-nato.pdf, p. 12.

119. *Rossiya i NATO: Realnost' i perspektivy vzaimodeistviya*, p. 13.

120. Thus, 51 percent were in favor, 23 percent were not, and 26 percent were undecided. "34. A kak vy schitatet, nuzhno ili ne nuzhno Rossii segodnya sozdat' mezhdunarodnyi voenno-politicheskii blok, podobnyi Varshavskomu Dogovoru ili NATO?," *VTsIOM*, June 19, 2011, http://wciom.ru/zh/print_q.php?s_id=729&q_id=52695&date=19.06.2011.

121. Primakov, *Gody v Bolshoi Politike*, pp. 230–31.

122. Michael R. Gordon, "Russia-China Theme: Contain the West," *New York Times*, April 24, 1997, p. A3.

123. By October 2015, China, Turkey, and Syria had expressed interest in talks on forming a FTZ with the EEU. In April 2015, Prime Minister Dmitry Medvedev offered Thailand a FTZ with the EEC. In May, Vietnam became the first country to sign a FTZ agreement with the EEC. At the EEC summit on July 6, Russian presidential aide foreign policy Yuri Ushakov announced that India and the EEC had agreed to create a working group for exploring an India-EEC FTZ. A recent Kazakhstani report indicates that more than 30 countries—including Zimbabwe, Jordan, Mongolia and Albania—have applied to the Eurasian Economic Commission for a FTZ with the EEU. Assel Satubaldina, "Over 30 countries interested in signing free trade agreement with EEU," *Tengrinews.kz*, July 21, 2015, http://en.tengrinews.kz/politics_sub/Over-30-countries-interested-in-signing-free-trade-agreement-261289/.

124. SCO emerged from the "Shanghai Five" based on the April 1996 "Treaty on Deepening Military Trust in Border Regions" signed in Shanghai by Russia, China, Kazakhstan, Kyrgyzstan, and Tajikistan—part of Sino-Russian efforts to normalize relations and resolve their longstanding border disputes.

125. Bates Gill, "Shanghai Five: An Attempt to Counter U.S. Influence in Asia?" *Brookings Institute*, May 4, 2001, www.brookings.edu/research/opinions/2001/05/04china-gill.

126. This included: building two more Russian nuclear power plants in China; joint development of commercial aircraft and helicopters; setting up a $4 billion investment fund; and increased cooperation in the electricity, tourism and energy sectors.

127. "Hu, Putin pledge to boost China-Russia ties," *China Daily*, June 6, 2012, 02:03, www.chinadaily.com.cn/china/2012–06/06/content_15476799.htm.

128. "Kontseptsiya uchastiya Rossiiskoi Federatsii v

ob"edinnenii BRIKS, *Kremlin.ru*, March 21, 2013, www.
kremlin.ru/events/president/news/17715 and http://news.
kremlin.ru/media/events/files/41d452a8a232b2f6f8a5.pdf.

129. "Kontseptsiya uchastiya Rossiiskoi Federatsii v
ob"edinnenii BRIKS." For Russia's most recent Foreign Policy Concept, see "Kontseptsiya vneshnei politiki Rossiiskoi
Federatsii," MID.ru, February 18, 1013, http://archive.mid.
ru/bdomp/ns-osndoc.nsf/e2f289bea62097f9c325787a0034
c255/c32577ca0017434944257b160051bf7f!OpenDocument.

130. "Kontseptsiya uchastiya Rossiiskoi Federatsii v
ob"edinnenii BRIKS."

131. "Kontseptsiya uchastiya Rossiiskoi Federatsii v
ob"edinnenii BRIKS."

132. "Kontseptsiya uchastiya Rossiiskoi Federatsii v
ob"edinnenii BRIKS."

133. Future projects might soon extend to non-EU European countries such as Serbia and Macedonia, and later
to projects in the Southern Hemisphere that will facilitate
member-states' trade in those regions. The bank's president, Kundapur Vaman Kamath, suggested that it might
assist in the reconstruction of Syria.

134. The Chinese-Russian-Indian economic axis anchored by these powers' common membership in SCO
and BRICS is already spurring economic and transport
infrastructure development across the New Silk Road. A
few examples of present and future projects include: the
Bangladesh-China-India-Myanmar economic corridor,
including a multilane highway between India and China;
the Russo-Iranian-Azerbaijani, north-south Persian Gulf-
Gulf of Oman-Caspian Sea-Volga River water transportation corridor; the Indian-Iranian-Russian maritime corridor to extend from Mumbai to Iran's Bandar Abbas port
to Russia's north Caspian Sea port at Astrakhan; and the
Chinese-built railway from Urumqi, Xinjiang Province,
to Almaty, Kazakhstan, that some claim might be extended
to Iran and the Persian Gulf.

135. See Gordon M. Hahn, "Special Report: China and
Central Asia After Afghanistan's Kabulization," *Islam, Islamism and Politics in Eurasia Report*, No. 67, October 14,
2013, http://gordonhahn.com/2013/10/14/islam-islamism-
and-politics-in-eurasia-report-no-67-oct-2013-special-re
port-china-and-central-asia-after-afghanistans-kabulization/.

136. Except for Brazil and South Africa, BRICS also
meets the geographical expectations of neo–Eurasianist
and Mackinderian geopolitics and encompasses the core
countries of three of Huntington's seven civilizations.

Chapter 4

1. Philippe C. Schmitter and Imco Brouwer, *Concep-
tualizing, Researching, and Evaluating Democracy Promotion and Protection* (Florence, Italy: European University
Institute, 1999), p. 14.

2. See Alessandra Pinna, "The International Dimension of Democratization: Actors, Motivations, and Strategies," *Marine Corps University Journal* 5, No. 1 (Spring
2014): pp. 27–57, at pp. 49–50.

3. Pinna, "The International Dimension of Democratization," pp. 54–6.

4. Pinna, "The International Dimension of Democratization," p. 55.

5. For a more detailed discussion of the various
modes of regime transformation, see Hahn, *Russia's Revolution From Above: Reform, Transition, and Revolution
in the Fall of the Soviet Communist Regime, 1985–2000*,
Chapter 1.

6. Reform, transitions, and revolutions all begin with
some crisis or pre-crisis disequilibrium, often economic
or financial in nature. On revolution and macro-structural
contradictions, international pressures, disequilibrium
and crisis, see respectively Theda Skocpol, *States and So-

cial Revolutions: A Comparative Analysis of France, Russia
and China* (Cambridge: Cambridge University Press,
1979); Chalmers Johnson, *Revolutionary Change*, second
edition (Stanford: Stanford University Press, 1982); and
Crane Brinton, *The Anatomy of Revolution*, revised edition
(New York: Vintage Books, 1965). On "great reforms," see
Michael Oksenberg and Bruce J. Dickson, "The Origins,
Processes, and Outcomes of Great Political Reform: A
Framework of Analysis," in Dankwart A. Rustow and Kenneth Paul Erikson, eds., *Comparative Political Dynamics:
Global Research Perspectives* (New York: HarperCollins,
1991), pp. 235–61. As was the case in the Soviet revolution
from above, about 75 percent of transition cases followed
economic downturns. Haggard and Kaufman, *The Political
Economy of Democratic Transitions*, p. 33. On transition,
see also Guillermo O'Donnell and Philippe Schmitter,
"Tentative Conclusions About Uncertain Democracies,"
in Guillermo O'Donnell, Philippe Schmitter and Laurence
Whitehead, eds., *Transitions from Authoritarian Rule*, part
4 (Baltimore: Johns Hopkins University Press, 1986). From
here forward cited as "Tentative Conclusions."

7. James March and Johan Olsen, *Rediscovering Institutions: The Organized Basis of Politics* (New York: The
Free Press, 1989), pp. 64–5.

8. A "radical shock," or deliberate, fundamental reorganization of institutions undertaken in the hope that it
"will destabilize political arrangements and force a permanent realignment of the existing system," is a blunt instrument, because "the same factors of institutional autonomy and stability that make shock strategies possible
also make them difficult to implement and to control. Formal changes in structure are resisted or corrupted, and efforts to make radical changes are often frustrated." March
and Olsen, *Rediscovering Institutions*, pp. 64–65.

9. Theda Skocpol, "Bringing the State Back In: Current Research," in Peter B. Evans, Dietrich Rueschemeyer
and Theda Skocpol, *Bringing the State Back In* (Cambridge: Cambridge University Press, 1985), pp. 14 and 28.
Institutionalists point toward a research agenda focused
on "watershed periods in which state apparati are constructed or reconstructed," on the "effects on policy-mak-
ing capacities and the patterned relationships of state organizations and actors to social groups," and on "episodes
when deliberate attempts at reform or reorganization are
made within solidly established state structures," not only
for their successes, "but for their failures and unintended
consequences as well." Peter B. Evans, Dietrich Rueschemeyer and Theda Skocpol, "On the Road toward a
More Adequate Understanding of the State," in Evans,
Rueschemeyer and Skocpol, *Bringing the State Back In*,
pp. 360–1.

10. Skocpol stresses the dissolution of state structures
resulting from state executives' competing to control them
as the state loses capacity in revolutionary situations.
Skocpol, *States and Social Revolutions*.

11. O'Donnell and Schmitter, "Tentative Conclusions,"
pp. 37–47.

12. While transitions do not require pacts, they are
seen as facilitating both transition and democratic consolidation under the new regime in several ways. O'Donnell and Schmitter, "Tentative Conclusions," p. 38.

13. The most important task in any democratic transition is to "institutionalize uncertainty"—to form a broad
consensus among the main political actors and groups on
the setting up of procedures to ensure that the right to
rule is founded in free and fair electoral contestation, and
"a real possibility of partisan alternation in office" is institutionalized. Adam Przeworski, *Democracy and the
Market: Political and Economic Reforms in Eastern Europe
and Latin America* (Cambridge: Cambridge University
Press, 1991), p. 60.

14. Youssef Cohen, *Radicals, Reformers, and Reactionaries: The Prisoners' Dilemma and the Collapse of Democracy in Latin America* (Chicago: Chicago University Press, 1994), Chapter 5.

15. Hahn, *Russia's Revolution From Above: Reform, Transition, and Revolution in the Fall of the Soviet Communist Regime, 1985–2000*, Chapters 5 and 8.

16. Imposed transitions are least in need of strong democratic opposition movements, at least during the outset of the transformation process, since a core group of regime softliners is committed to a democratic regime transformation and needs little or no pressure to stay the course. However, as the process moves from declaration of intent and institutional design to implementation, a strong, united democratic movement must be nurtured in society or culled from one or more of the ruling groups into one or more parties agreeing to the uncertainty of the democratic process and prepared to be out of power for some period of time as elections are held.

17. See Gordon M. Hahn, "*Perestroika* 2.0: Towards Non-Revolutionary Regime Transformation in Russia?" *Post-Soviet Affairs* 28, No. 4 (October–December 2012): pp. 472–515. See also Gordon M. Hahn, "Medvedev, Putin, and Perestroika 2.0," *Demokratizatsiya* 18, No. 3 (Summer 2010): pp. 228–259, www.gwu.edu/~ieresgwu/assets/docs/demokratizatsiya%20archive/GWASHU_DEMO_18_3/C6RV2N817P0572R3/C6RV2N817P0572R3.pdf and Gordon M. Hahn, "The Russian Federation in 2012: From 'Thaw' and 'Reset' to 'Freeze,'" *Asian Survey* 53, No. 1 (Winter 2013): pp. 214–223.

18. Czechoslovakia's peaceful "velvet" revolution from below led to the partitioning of the country into two. In Yugoslavia, the demise of communism led to the rise of several nationalisms, civil wars, and successor states.

19. It was natural for Germans to rejoin in a single state after the removal of the ideological divide and Soviet occupation that drew the artificial border between them.

20. Hahn, *The Caucasus Emirate*; Hahn, *Russia's Islamic Threat*.

21. Ethno-national communalism and separatism have emerged strongly not only in Yugoslavia but also in West Europe in Scotland and Catalonia. The European Union's increasing difficulties have seen the rise of ultranationalism in eastern and southern Europe, both at the state and communal group level, most notably in Hungary, Greece, the Netherlands, France, and even Germany. Regarding non-ethnic, religious communalism, the global Islamist and jihadist revolutionary movements, represented by Al Qaʻida and the Islamic State, are the most obvious examples and extend across the globe.

22. USAID planned to build a subscriber base through noncontroversial content such as sports news and music. When a critical mass of perhaps hundreds of thousands of subscribers was reached (the project drew in more than 40,000 Cubans at its peak), political content would be included aimed at inspiring and organizing "smart mobs" that at a moment's notice could trigger a Cuban Spring, or, as a USAID document phrased it, "renegotiate the balance of power between the state and society." Desmond Butler, Jack Gillum, and Alberto Arce, "U.S. secretly created 'Cuban Twitter' to stir unrest," Associated Press, April 4, 2014, http://news.yahoo.com/us-secretly-created-cuban-twitter-stir-unrest-063637846.html. See also Desmond Butler, Jack Gillum, Alberto Arce, and Andrea Rodriguez, "U.S. sent Latin youth undercover in anti–Cuba ploy," Associated Press, August 4, 2014, http://bigstory.ap.org/article/us-sent-latin-youth-undercover-anti-cuba-ploy and "When Is Foreign Aid Meddling?" *New York Times,*

April 15, 2014, www.nytimes.com/roomfordebate/2014/04/15/when-is-foreign-aid-meddling.

23. Roger Cohen, "Just Who Brought Down Milosevic?" *New York Times Magazine*, November 26, 2000, www.nytimes.com/library/magazine/home/20001126magserbia.html.

24. "Prospects for Democracy in Yugoslavia," Hearing of the European Affairs Subcommittee of the Senate Foreign Affairs Committee, United States Senate, July 29, 1999, http://emperors-clothes.com/analysis/hearin.htm, last accessed on October 22, 2015.

25. Tom Gallagher, *The Balkans in the New Millennium: In the Shadow of War and Peace* (London: Routledge, 2005), p. 112.

26. Cohen, "Just Who Brought Down Milosevic?"

27. Michael Dobbs, "U.S. Advice Guided Milosevic Opposition," *Washington Post*, December 11, 2000, p. A1, https://groups.yahoo.com/neo/groups/decani/conversations/topics/41337.

28. Otpor already had 20,000 active members and a reputation, but its leaders did not see how they could translate membership growth into the overthrow of Milosevic. Helvey explained Sharp's idea that a regime's power to rule rests in the obedience of the ruled. A democracy movement must persuade people to disobey the regime. The law enforcement organs need to be neutralized or won over to the opposition. From the outset, Otpor had treated the police not as enemies but as potential allies. For instance, instead of jeering at police, Otpor members cheered them or delivered cookies to police, sometimes with a TV camera in tow. Tina Rosenberg, "Revolution U," *Foreign Policy*, February 17, 2011, http://foreignpolicy.com/2011/02/17/revolution-u-2/.

29. Dobbs, "U.S. Advice Guided Milosevic Opposition."

30. Rosenberg, "Revolution U."

31. Large actions are risky to the movement's reputation and well-being of its cadres. They risk people getting arrested, beaten or shot, and poor turnout damages credibility. Rosenberg, "Revolution U."

32. The last, funerals, are sometimes the only place where people can meet in large numbers without bringing down the organs of coercion on activists. Thus, mass attendance at the funeral of anyone related to the movement can be a pivot point. Rosenberg, "Revolution U."

33. Rosenberg, "Revolution U."

34. On CANVAS's activities, see its library of printed and video materials at Library, *CANVAS*, www.canvasopedia.org/index.php/library, last accessed on November 10, 2015. On CANVAS's financing, see "Who We Are," *CANVAS*, www.canvasopedia.org/index.php/who-we-are, last accessed November 10, 2015.

35. Rosenberg, "Revolution U."

36. Natalia Antelava, "How to stage a revolution," *BBC*, December 4, 2003, http://news.bbc.co.uk/2/hi/europe/3288547.stm.

37. Rosenberg, "Revolution U."

38. See Robert English, "Georgia: The Ignored History," *The New York Review of Books* 55, Number 17 (November 6, 2009), www.nybooks.com/articles/archives/2008/nov/06/georgia-the-ignored-history/.

39. "The Georgian Commander-in-Chief on TV threatens the Abkhazian nation with genocide," *YouTube*, October 28, 2008, www.youtube.com/watch?v=XzvtaZIMy98, last accessed October 14, 2015.

40. *Le Monde Diplomatique*, April 1993.

41. "A history erased: Abkhazia's archive: fire of war, ashes of history," *Abkhaz World*, March 17, 2009, http://abkhazworld.com/aw/conflict/690-a-history-erased.

42. "Georgia's Iron Fist of Independence," *The Economist*, June 1, 1991, www.encyclopedia.com/doc/1G1-10822281.html.

43. Brian Rohan, "Saakashvili 'planned S. Ossetian invasion': ex-minister," *Reuters*, September 14, 2008, 4:54, www.reuters.com/article/2008/09/14/us-georgia-russia-opposition-idUSLD12378020080914.

44. Ironically, the program would end up training one of the world's leading jihadi terrorists, "Umar al-Shishani" (Umar the Chechen), born Tarkhan Batirashvili, the amir of the Islamic State's (IS) Northern Front and mastermind of IS's march through Anbar Province to Mosul, where Abubakr al-Baghdadi was able to declare the so-called "Caliphate" in 2013. Will Cathcart, Vazha Tavberidze, and Nino Murchuladze, "The Secret Life of an ISIS Warlord," *The Daily Beast*, October 27, 2014, www.thedailybeast.com/articles/2014/10/27/the-secret-life-of-an-isis-warlord.html.

45. Tea Gularidze, "U.S. Boosts Successful Military Cooperation with Georgia," *Civil.ge*, August 5, 2004, www.civil.ge/eng/article.php?id=7556.

46. Yelena Milashina, "Roman s vlast'yu zakonchilsya na ulitse," *Novaya gazeta*, May 21, 2008, www.novayagazeta.ru/articles/2008/05/22/37950-roman-s-vlastyu-zakonchilsya-na-ulitse.

47. "Georgia: Parliamentary Elections, May 21, 2008," OSCE/ODHIR Election Observer Mission Final Report (Warsaw: OSCE Office for Democratic Elections and Human Rights, September 9, 2008, www.osce.org/odihr/elections/georgia/33301?download=true, p. 24.

48. "Georgia: Presidential Elections, 5 January 2008," OSCE/ODHIR Election Observer Mission Final Report (Warsaw: OSCE Office for Democratic Elections and Human Rights, March 4, 2008, www.osce.org/odihr/elections/georgia/30959?download=true, p. 1.

49. Condoleezza Rice, *No Higher Honor: A Memoir of My Years in Washington* (New York: Crown Publishers, 2011), cited in Joshua Kucera, "Condoleezza Rice Warned Georgian Leader on War with Russia," *The Atlantic*, November 16, 2011, www.theatlantic.com/international/archive/2011/11/condoleezza-rice-warned-georgian-leader-on-war-with-russia/248560/.

50. Gordon M. Hahn, "The Making of the Georgian-Russia Five-Day August War, June–August 8, 2008," *Russia—Other Points of View*, September 22, 2008, www.russiaotherpointsofview.com/files/Georgia_Russian_War_TIMELINE.doc; Rice, *No Higher Honor*, cited in Kucera, "Condoleezza Rice Warned Georgian Leader on War with Russia."

51. Hahn, "The Making of the Georgian-Russia Five-Day August War."

52. See the report on the liberal-oriented, human rights Russian website *Kavak uzel* at "V Yuzhnoi Osetii zayavlyayut, chto Gruzia razmestila artilleriyu bliz zony konflikta," *Kavkaz uzel*, August 4, 2008, www.kavkaz-uzel.ru/newstext.newsid/1226489.html.

53. Hahn, "The Making of the Georgian-Russia Five-Day August War, June–August 8, 2008"; Rice, *No Higher Honor*, cited in Kucera, "Condoleezza Rice Warned Georgian Leader on War with Russia"; Larisa Sotieva, "Eyewitnesses: Carnage in Tskhinvali," *Caucasus Reporting Service*, Institute of War and Peace Reporting, August 12, 2008, www.iwpr.net; and Sara Rainsford, "S. Ossetia's Ruins Seethe with Anger," *BBC News*, August 13, 2008.

54. Ronald D. Asmus, *A Little War That Shook the World: Georgia, Russia, and the Future of the West* (New York: St. Martin's Press, 2010), pp. 186–7.

55. See "Sakashvili's Televised Address on S. Ossetia," *Civil Georgia*, August 7, 2008, 21:45, www.civil.ge.

56. Gordon M. Hahn, "Georgia's Propaganda War (Long Version)," *Russia—Other Points of View*, September 5, 2008, www.russiaotherpointsofview.com/files/Georgia_Propaganda_War_Long_Version.doc.

57. Report of the European Union Independent International Fact-Finding Mission on the Conflict in Georgia, Vol. I, http://91.121.127.28/ceiig/pdf/IIFFMCG_Volume_I.pdf and Report of the European Union Independent International Fact-Finding Mission on the Conflict in Georgia, Vol. II, http://91.121.127.28/ceiig/pdf/IIFFMCG_Volume_II.pdf.

58. Report of the European Union Independent International Fact-Finding Mission on the Conflict in Georgia, Vol. I, pp. 31–32.

59. Report of the European Union Independent International Fact-Finding Mission on the Conflict in Georgia, Vol. I and Report of the European Union Independent International Fact-Finding Mission on the Conflict in Georgia, Vol. II.

60. Report of the European Union Independent International Fact-Finding Mission on the Conflict in Georgia, Vol. II.

61. The only difference here is that Abkhaziya, unlike South Ossetiya, was not subjected to Georgian aggression in August 2008 but much earlier—in 2004 (a Georgia-backed coup attempt) and in the early 1990s. Incidentally, in both cases there was greater temporal proximity between the aggression and the declaration of independence than there was in the case of Kosovo.

62. Eduard Lucas, "The opposition locks itself up, and out," *The Economist*, May 28, 2009, www.economist.com/node/13745838.

63. Lucas wrote in full: "Georgia's friends should also urge Mr. Saakashvili to postpone the presidential vote, and instead hold a fair, internationally supervised parliamentary election in the spring. The speaker of parliament, Nino Burjanadze, who retains the statesmanlike image that Mr. Saakashvili has lost, should convene talks between all political forces, at first to reach agreement on election rules, then to discuss constitutional changes. A new parliament should take back some of the powers that the presidency has recently misused. Until that happens, Mr. Saakashvili should be in political quarantine." Edward Lucas, "Misha's mess," *The Economist*, November 15, 2007, http://edwardlucas.blogspot.com/2007/11/leader-from-economist.html. In January 2008, the well-respected Estonian president Toomas Hendrik Ilves noted: "I've known Nino Burjanadze for years and years. She's very impressive…. She's someone that's very impressive. For a woman to be in that position and to have that kind of authority in a post–Soviet, macho, troglodyte world—she's a real asset for Georgia." "Interview: Toomas Hendrik Ilves," *The Messenger* (Tbilisi), January 25, 2008, www.messenger.com.ge/issues/1532_january_25_2008/1532_ilves_interview.html.

64. Lucas, "The opposition locks itself up, and out."

65. On April 26, seventeen days after the demonstrations had begun, the church called on all of Georgia's leaders to repent and pray together. "Church Leader Calls on Politicians for Repentance Prayer," *Civil Georgia*, April 26, 2009, www.civil.ge/eng/article.php?id=20797&search=Orhtodox%20Church%20urges. In a May 26 communiqué consisting of comments by Patriarch Ilya II to opposition demonstrators, it is not always clear that he was directing his comments to the opposition alone. See "Church Leader: Give Up Categorical Thinking," *Civil Georgia*, May 26, 2009, 20:51, www.civil.ge/eng/article.php?id=20996&search=Orhtodox%20Church%20urges. On May 7, the church requested that the authorities release those arrested in an apparent attempt to ambush Georgian television. "Church Calls on Authorities to Release Opposition Activists," *Civil Georgia*, May 7, 2009, 01:10, www.civil.ge/eng/article.php?id=20865&search=Orthodox%20Church%20urges. On May 28, the Orthodox Church released an official statement calling on the authorities to take steps to defuse the crisis. "Defuse Tensions—Church Leader to

Authorities," *Civil Georgia*, May 28, 2009, 17:07, www.civil.ge/eng/article.php?id=21008&search=Orhtodox%20Church%20urges.

66. "Wiretapped Recordings of Saakashvili Discussing Rustavi 2 TV Leaked," *Civil.ge*, October 30, 2015, www.civil.ge/eng/article.php?id=28713.

67. Georgi Dvali, "SShA dali Mikhailu Saakashvili simmetrichnyi otvet," *Kommersant*, November 26, 2013, www.kommersant.ru/doc/2352493.

68. The percentages of approval were as follows: Tajikistan (94 percent), Kyrgyzstan (84 percent), Uzbekistan (81 percent), Armenia (75 percent), Kazakhstan (73 percent), Ukraine (61 percent), Moldova (56 percent), and Azerbaidzhan (54 percent). Only Belarus disapproved more than approved of Russia's leadership and Russian policy in the CIS. Turkmenistan was not included in the poll. Julie Ray, "Russia's Leadership Not Popular Worldwide," *Gallup*, August 5, 2011, www.gallup.com/poll/148862/Russia-Leadership-Not-Popular-Worldwide.aspx.

69. Antelava, "How to stage a revolution."

70. Rosenberg, "Revolution U."

Chapter 5

1. Huntington, *The Clash of Civilizations*, pp. 44–45.

2. Ralph S. Clem and Peter R. Craumer, "Shades of Orange: The Electoral Geography of Ukraine's 2004 Presidential Elections," *Eurasian Geography and Economics* 46, 2005, pp. 364–385; Ivan Katchanovski, "Regional Political Divisions in Ukraine in 1991–2006," *Nationalities Papers* 34, 2006, pp. 507–532; Stephen Shulman, "Cultural comparisons and their consequences for nationhood in Ukraine," *Communist and Post-Communist Studies* 39, 2006, pp. 247–263; Ralph S. Clem and Peter R. Craumer, "Orange, Blue and White, and Blonde: The Electoral Geography of Ukraine's 2006 and 2007 Rada Elections," *Eurasian Geography and Economics* 49, 2008, pp. 127–151; and Lowell Barrington and Regina Faranda, "Reexamining Region, Ethnicity, and Language in Ukraine," *Post-Soviet Affairs* 25, 2009, pp. 232–256.

3. Only four of the remaining regions of pre-2014 Ukraine have less than an 80 percent ethnic Ukrainian majority: Chernovtsy in southwestern Ukraine (75 percent ethnic Ukrainian) and three oblasts in central-eastern Ukraine: Kharkiv/Kharkov (71 percent), Dnepropetrovsk (79.3 percent), and Zaporozhe (71 percent). See 2001 Ukrainian census data in "Russians In Ukraine," *Wikipedia*, https://en.wikipedia.org/wiki/Russians_in_Ukraine, last accessed September 1, 2015.

4. Richard Sakwa, *Frontline Ukraine: Crisis in the Borderlands* (London: I.B. Tauris, 2015), p. 59. A map showing the native languages spoken according to the 2001 census is available online at https://en.wikipedia.org/wiki/Demographics_of_Ukraine.

5. Jews make up just one 0.2 percent of Ukraine's population, composing a much smaller percentage of the population than historically typical in this part of the world since medieval times and during Tsarist times. This decline is the result of World War II's Nazi occupation and Polish, Ukrainian and Russian nationalists' strong anti-Semitism. "Viruyuchim yakoi tserkvi, konfesii Vi sebe vvazhaet," *Razumkov Center*, May 2006, http://razumkov.org.ua/ukr/poll.php?poll_id=300, last accessed September 11, 2015.

6. Kuromiya, *Freedom and Terror in the Donbas: A Ukrainian-Russian Borderland, 1870s–1990s*, pp. 2, 4–5 and 11.

7. Kuromiya, *Freedom and Terror in the Donbas*, p. 2.

8. Kuromiya, *Freedom and Terror in the Donbas*, p. 12.

9. Kuromiya, *Freedom and Terror in the Donbas*, pp. 2–3.

10. "Poverty in Ukraine," Institute for Economic Research and Policy Consulting in Ukraine and the German Advisory Group on Economic Reform, 2003, http://pdc.ceu.hu/archive/00001784/01/t25_en.pdf, p. 3; State Statistics Committee of Ukraine, October 2010, www.ukrstat.gov.ua/operativ/operativ2010/gdn/reg_zp_m/reg_zpm10_u.htm; and Jacques Sapir, "Ukraine at the Turn," *RussEurope*, December 3, 2015, http://russeurope.hypotheses.org/4521. All last accessed December 4, 2015.

11. "Valoviy regionalniy product, 2004–2013," State Committee of Statistics of Ukraine, *Ukrstat.gov.ua*, 2013, www.ukrstat.gov.ua/operativ/operativ2008/vvp/vrp/vrp2008_u.htm, last accessed January 20, 2014.

12. The DKRSR was dissolved by the brief German occupation, and its territories incorporated into Soviet Ukraine after the Bolshevik takeover in Kiev. Later, there was much resistance to Soviet rule, reflected in the infamous Shakhty miners' tribunal. Kuromiya, *Freedom and Terror in the Donbas*, pp. 71, 98–9, and 109.

13. Kuromiya, *Freedom and Terror in the Donbas*, pp. 332–33.

14. "Poverty in Ukraine" and State Statistics Committee of Ukraine, October 2010, www.ukrstat.gov.ua/operativ/operativ2010/gdn/reg_zp_m/reg_zpm10_u.htm, both last accessed December 14, 2013.

15. "Valoviy regionalniy product, 2004–2013."

16. Platonov, *Lektsii po russkoi istorii*, pp. 108–9.

17. Kharkiv might also be said to have a separate tone, given its historical industrial and thus limited cultural ties to German capitalists in the late 19th and early 20th centuries.

18. As noted in Chapter 3, neither Soviet collectivization, nor Stalin's grain confiscation, nor the resulting famine, nor other repressive Soviet policies targeted or alone impacted Ukraine or Ukrainians. Thus, the famine had its greatest impact in Ukraine simply because of the region's large agricultural sector.

19. Other first allegiances of respondents included: citizen of the former Soviet Union—12.7 percent in 1992, 6.9 percent in 2010; citizen of the world—6.4 percent in 1992, 3.1 percent in 2010; citizen of Europe—3.8 in 1992, 0.9 in 2010; representative of an ethnic group or nation—3.0 in 2002, 3.1 in 2010. A.A. Kislaya, "Etnicheskaya identifikatsiya v Ukraine: paradoks 'without the dynamics,'" in *Yezhegodnaya nauchno-prakticheskaya sotsiologicheskaya konferentsiya 'Prodolzhaya Grushina'* (Moscow: VTsIOM, 2012), pp. 157–8, http://wciom.ru/fileadmin/file/nauka/grusha_2012/tezisy/soc/kislaja.pdf.

20. Gene Fishel, "Radicalization of Independence in Ukraine," Institute for the Study of Conflict, Ideology, and Policy at Boston University, *Perspective* 1, No. 4 (April 1991): www.bu.edu/iscip/vol1/Fishel.html.

21. Fishel, "Radicalization of Independence in Ukraine," p. 5.

22. Fishel, "Radicalization of Independence in Ukraine," p. 5.

23. Fishel, "Radicalization of Independence in Ukraine," p. 6.

24. Chrystyna Lalpychak, "Independence—Over 90 percent vote 'yes' in referendum, Kravchuk elected president of Ukraine," *The Ukrainian Weekly* 59, No. 49 (December 8, 1991), www.ukrweekly.com/old/archive/1991/499101.shtml.

25. Pal Kolsto, *Russians in the Former Soviet Republics* (Bloomington: Indiana University Press, 1995), p. 191; Serhiy Plokhy, *Ukraine and Russia: Representations of the Past* (Toronto: Toronto University Press, 2008), p. 184.

26. Lalpychak, "Independence—Over 90 percent vote 'yes' in referendum."

27. Alex Kireev, "Ukraine. Presidential Election in 1991," *Electoral Geography 2.0*, www.electoralgeography.

com/new/en/countries/u/ukraine/ukraine-presidential-
election-1991.htm.

28. The persistence of regionalist impact in all post–
Soviet Ukrainian national elections is also noted in Sakwa,
Frontline Ukraine: Crisis in the Borderlands, p. 51.

29. See Thomas F. Klobucar, Arthur H. Miller, and
Gwyn Erb, "The 1999 Ukrainian Presidential Election:
Personalities, Ideology, Partisanship, and the Economy,"
Slavic Review 61, No. 2 (Summer 2002): pp. 315–44 (see
especially pp. 328–9, and 338).

30. I.E. Bekeshkin, "Parlamentskie vybory v Ukraine:
predvidimoe in nepredvidimoe," in *Yezhegodnaya
nauchno-prakticheskaya sotsiologicheskaya konferentsiya
'Prodolzhaya Grushina'* (Moscow: VTsIOM, 2012), http://
wciom.ru/fileadmin/file/nauka/grusha_2013/7.pdf, pp.
413–15, at p. 414. Retrieved November 28, 2015.

31. Bohdan Lupiy, *Ukraine and European Security—International Mechanisms as Non-Military Options for National Security of Ukraine*, North Atlantic Treaty Organization Individual Democratic Institutions Research
Fellowships 1994–1996 (Brussels: NATO, 1996), www.nato.
int/acad/fellow/94-96/lupiy/01-02.htm. Retrieved November 23, 2015.

32. Kataryna Wolczuk, *The Moulding of Ukraine: The
Constitutional Politics of State Formation* (Budapest: Central European University Press, 2001), pp. 129–188, at p.
183, fn 11.

33. Lupiy, *Ukraine and European Security*.

34. Elise Giuliano, "The Origins of Separatism: Popular
Grievances in Donetsk and Luhansk," *PONARS Policy
Memo 396*, October 2014, www.ponarseurasia.org/memo/
origins-separatism-popular-grievances-donetsk-and-
luhansk.

35. Roman Solchanyk, *Ukraine and Russia: The Post-
Soviet Transition* (Lanham, Md.: Rowman and Littlefield,
2000), pp. 187–8 and Viktor Lyashchenko, "Krymskaya
Avtonomiya 23 goda spustya: kak sberegli mir i ne pustili
v dom voinu," *Krymskoe informatsionnoe agentsvo*, January 20, 2014, www.kianews.com.ua/page/krymskaya-avto
nomiya-23-goda-spustya-kak-sberegli-mir-i-ne-pustili-v-
dom-voynu.

36. Solchanyk, *Ukraine and Russia*, p. 188.

37. Solchanyk, *Ukraine and Russia*, p. 189.

38. Interview with Sergei Stankevich, Program 'Arena
Sobytii,' *Online TV*, November 20, 2014, www.onlinetv.ru/
video/1982/?autostart=1; author's email interview with
Sergei Stankevich, November 23, 2015; and author's email
interview with Sergei Stankevich, December 16, 2015.

39. Interview with Sergei Stankevich, Program "Arena
Sobytii," *Online TV*.

40. *Radio Free Europe/Radio Liberty (RFERL) Research
Report* 1, No. 21 (May 22, 1992): pp. 2–3.

41. Solchanyk, *Ukraine and Russia*, p. 189.

42. Solchanyk, *Ukraine and Russia*, pp. 189–90;
"Postanovlenie Verkhovogo Soveta Kryma 'Ob Akte ob
provozglashenii gosudarstvennoi samostoyatel/nosti Re-
spubliki Krim," *Vedomosti Verkhovonogo Soveta Kryma
1991–1992*, No. 6, pp. 240–44, http://sevkrimrus.narod.ru/
ZAKON/1992ref.htm; and Serge Schmemann, "Crimea
Parliament Votes to Back Independence From Ukraine,"
New York Times, May 6, 1992, p. A8.

43. Solchanyk, *Ukraine and Russia*, p. 190; Kolsto, *Russians in the Former Soviet Republics*, p. 194.

44. Solchanyk, *Ukraine and Russia*, pp. 190–1.

45. Solchanyk, *Ukraine and Russia*, pp. 190–2.

46. Hahn, *Russia's Islamic Threat*, pp. 181–2.

47. Klobucar, Miller, and Erb, "The 1999 Ukrainian
Presidential Election: Personalities, Ideology, Partisanship,
and the Economy," p. 325.

48. Author's email interview with Sergei Stankevich,
December 16, 2015.

49. Interview with Sergei Stankevich, Program "Arena
Sobytii," *Online TV*, November 20, 2014, www.onlinetv.ru/
video/1982/?autostart=1; author's email interview with
Sergei Stankevich, November 23, 2015; and author's email
interview with Sergei Stankevich, December 16, 2015.

50. Article 132 stipulated the "unity and indivisibility"
of the state territory, combining centralization and decentralization," balanced development of the regions "taking
into account their historical, economic, ecological, geographic and demographic specifics and ethnic and cultural
traditions." Article 133 created 24 regions, two city-regions
(Kiev and Crimea's Sevastopol), and the "Autonomous Republic of Crimea," or ARC. The quasi-federacy with
Crimea was codified in Chapter X (Articles 134–139). Articles 134–136 allowed Crimea its own parliament (the
Supreme Rada of Crimea), governmental Council of Ministers, and a constitution to be confirmed by a majority of
deputies in Ukraine's Supreme Rada. Article 138 gave
Crimea the power to: schedule its parliamentary elections;
hold referenda; manage ARC properties; develop, implement, and monitor spending under an ARC budget; develop and administer Crimean socioeconomic, cultural,
and environmental programs; establish and manage re-
sorts; participate in securing the rights and freedoms of
citizens, national harmony, and assist in the securing law
and order and public safety; guarantee the use and development of the national languages and cultures of Crimea;
participate in carrying out functions under programs for
the return of deported peoples; and establish emergency
ecological zones. Article 137 gave the Crimea jurisdiction
over "regulation" in nine spheres, including: agriculture;
social work and philanthropy; city planning and housing;
tourism and hotels; festivals; museums, libraries, theaters,
historical and cultural sites, and other cultural institutions;
public transport, roads, and water utilities; fishing and
game; and sanitary and health services. "Kontstitutsiya
Ukrainy," *Nezavisimay gazeta-Stsenarii*, August 29, 1996,
pp. 3–5, at p. 5.

51. Contradictorily, only 38 percent of the ethnic Russians and 21 percent of ethnic Ukrainians on the peninsula
favored secession from Ukraine. Solchanyk, *Ukraine and
Russia*, p. 117. Perhaps the others responding in favor of
reunification with Russia thought that Kiev's accession to
the EEU would obviate the need for secession from
Ukraine, or perhaps they favored Ukraine's reunification
with Russia.

52. At State, she worked as a special assistant to the Assistant Secretary for Human Rights and Humanitarian Affairs. Subsequently, she moved to the White House in the
Office of Public Liaison during the Reagan administration.
During the George H. W. Bush administration she worked
in the Treasury Department's office of the executive secretary.

53. "Tainy zhen i zhenshin Viktora Yushchenko. Yekaterina Kler i eyo podrugi," *Vlasti.net*, November 8, 2009,
http://vlasti.net/news/66390.

54. "Tainy zhen i zhenshin Viktora Yushchenko. Yekaterina Kler i eyo podrugi."

55. "Tainy zhen i zhenshin Viktora Yushchenko. Yekaterina Kler i eyo podrugi."

56. "Tainy zhen i zhenshin Viktora Yushchenko. Yekaterina Kler i eyo podrugi."

57. Jeffrey Clarke and Jason Stout, "Elections, Revolution and Democracy in Ukraine: Reflections on a Country's Turn to Democracy, Free Elections, and the Modern
World," *USAID*, October 2005, http://pdf.usaid.gov/pdf_
docs/PNADE309.pdf, first and last sentences in the 'Pre-
face' and p. 2, retrieved on December 2, 2015.

58. Clarke and Stout, "Elections," p. 5.

59. Clarke and Stout, "Elections," p. 7.

60. Clarke and Stout, "Elections," pp. 11 and 17.

61. Sakwa, *Frontline Ukraine*, p. 51.

62. In February 1999, Lazarenko fled to the U.S. to avoid embezzlement charges only to be arrested and convicted for money laundering, wire fraud, extortion, and embezzlement of some $200 million during his premiership. Sentenced to nine years in prison in 2006, he was released in November 2012.

63. C.J. Chivers, "How Top Spies in Ukraine Changed the Nation's Path," *New York Times*, January 17, 2005, www.nytimes.com/2005/01/17/world/europe/how-top-spies-in-ukraine-changed-the-nations-path.html?_r=0; Taras Kuzio, "Did Ukraine's Secret Service Really Prevent Bloodshed During the Orange Revolution?" *Jamestown's Foundation Eurasia Daily Monitor*, Volume 2, Issue 16, January 24, 2005, www.taraskuzio.net/media14_files/37. pdf.

64. Mark Ames, "Pierre Omidlyar co-funded Ukraine revolution groups with U.S. government, documents show," *Pando.com*, February 28, 2014, http://pando.com/2014/02/28/pierre-omidyar-co-funded-ukraine-revolution-groups-with-us-government-documents-show/.

65. Ames, "Pierre Omidlyar."

66. It is possible that the SBU's illegal activities were carried out in service of both campaigns, hedging its bets on the outcome and in the bargain gathering compromising materials with which it could manipulate officials later on. But there is no evidence that either the SBU or MVD was working for the Yanukovich campaign as well. Chivers, "How Top Spies in Ukraine Changed the Nation's Path."

67. Chivers, "How Top Spies in Ukraine Changed the Nation's Path"; Kuzio, "Did Ukraine's Secret Service Really Prevent Bloodshed During the Orange Revolution?"; and Adrian Karatnycky, "Ukraine's Orange Revolution," *Foreign Affairs*, March-April 2005, www.foreignaffairs.com/articles/russia-fsu/2005-03-01/ukraines-orange-revolution.

68. Rosenberg, "Revolution U."

69. Clarke and Stout, "Elections," p. 18.

70. *Ukraine Local Government Assessment*, USAID, February 19, 2007, http://pdf.usaid.gov/pdf_docs/PNADK461.pdf, p. 5.

71. Clarke and Stout, "Elections," p. 12.

72. Sakwa, *Frontline Ukraine*, p. 52; David Lane, "The Orange Revolution: 'People's revolution or revolutionary coup?'," *British Journal of Politics and International Relations* 10, No. 4 (November 2008): pp. 525–49; Gordon M. Hahn, "Color Revolutions Darken," *Russia—Other Points of View*, April 18, 2008, www.russiaotherpointsofview.com/2008/04/the-darkening-o.html#more; Gordon M. Hahn, "The Color Revolution Disease Hits Moldova," *Russia—Other Points of View*, April 8, 2009, www.russiaotherpointsofview.com/2009/04/the-colored-revolution-disease-hits-moldova.html; and Gordon M. Hahn, "Mainstream Media Backtracks on Tulip and Color Revolutions," *Russia—Other Points of View*, June 17, 2010, www.russiaotherpointsofview.com/2010/06/mainstream-media-backtracking-on-tulip-and-colored-revolutions.html.

73. "Ukraine poll call by Russia-NATO," *BBC*, December 9, 2004, http://news.bbc.co.uk/2/hi/europe/4082155.stm.

74. Rudling, "The OUN, the UPA and the Holocaust," pp. 28.

75. Volodomyr Kulyk, "One Nation, Two Languages? National Identity and Language Policy in Post-Euromaidan Ukraine," *PONARS*, Policy Memo 389, September 2015,www.ponarseurasia.org/memo/one-nation-two-languages-national-identity-and-language-policy-post-euromaidan-ukraine.

76. Rudling, "The OUN, the UPA and the Holocaust," pp. 26–38.

77. Rudling, "The OUN, the UPA and the Holocaust," pp. 10–11 and 14–26.

78. Rudling, "The OUN, the UPA and the Holocaust," pp. 26–7.

79. Aleksandr Burakovskiy, "Holocaust remembrance in Ukraine: memorialization of the Jewish tragedy at Babi Yar," *Nationalities Papers*, Volume 39, Number 3, May 2011, pp. 371–89, at p. 382, www.pendleton.k12.ky.us/userfiles/119/Classes/401/Holocaust%20remembrance%20in%20Ukraine.pdf. Last retrieved December 5, 2015.

80. Rudling, "The OUN, the UPA and the Holocaust," p. 27.

81. Sofia Hrachova, "Unknown Victims: Ethnic-Based Violence of the World War II Era in Ukrainian Politics of History after 2004," paper presented at the Fourth Annual Danyliv Research Seminar in Contemporary Ukrainian Studies, Chair of Ukrainian Studies, University of Ottawa, October 23–25, 2008, p. 9. Cited in Rudling, "The OUN, the UPA and the Holocaust," pp. 27 and 65, footnote 275.

82. Rudling, "The OUN, the UPA and the Holocaust," pp. 15, 25 and 28–9.

83. Rudling, "The OUN, the UPA and the Holocaust," pp. 29–33.

84. Rudling, "The OUN, the UPA and the Holocaust," p. 35.

85. Burakovskiy, "Holocaust remembrance in Ukraine," pp. 382–3.

86. Burakovskiy, "Holocaust remembrance in Ukraine," p. 385.

87. Burakovskiy, "Holocaust remembrance in Ukraine," pp. 384–5.

88. Truman-Reagan Medal of Freedom, Victims of Communism Memorial Foundation, http://victimsofcommunism.org/initiative/truman-reagan/, last accessed on January 7, 2016.

89. Rudling, "The OUN, the UPA and the Holocaust," pp. 35 and 70, footnote 329.

90. "Poroshenko: Golodomor—proyavlenie gibridnoi voiny," *Korrespondent*, November 28, 2015, http://korrespondent.net/ukraine/3596061-poroshenko-holodomor-proiavlenye-hybrydnoi-voiny.

91. Aleksandr Burakovskiy, "Key Characteristics and Transformation of Jewish-Ukrainian Relations during the Period of Ukraine's Independence: 1991–2008," *Nationalism and Ethnic Politics* 15, Number 1 (January 2009): pp. 109–32.

92. Burakovskiy, "Key Characteristics," p. 120; Burakovskiy, "Holocaust remembrance in Ukraine," p. 384.

93. Rudling, "The OUN, the UPA and the Holocaust," pp. 29–31.

94. Burakovskiy, "Key Characteristics," p. 120.

95. Nadine Epstein, "The Mysterious Tale of a Ukrainian University's Anti-Semitic Crusade," *Scholars for Peace in the Middle East*, October 31, 2009, http://spme.org/campus-news-climate/civil-discourse-and-academic-freedom/the-mysterious-tale-of-a-ukrainian-universitys-anti-semitic-crusade/7572/.

96. Oksana Bashuk Hepburn, "The 2011 Ukrainian Best & Worst (UBaWL)," *Eposhta.com* 13, Number 1 (January 2, 2012), www.eposhta.com/newsmagazine/ePOSHTA_120102_World_Eng.html.

97. Rudling, "The OUN, the UPA and the Holocaust," p. 36.

98. Mark Ames, "Hero of the Orange Revolution Poisons Ukraine," *The Nation*, February 12, 2010, www.thenation.com/article/hero-orange-revolution-poisons-ukraine/.

99. Rudling, "The OUN, the UPA and the Holocaust," p. 65, footnote 278.

100. Kulyk, "One Nation, Two Languages?"

101. Bohdan Nahaylo, "Toward the Rule of Law—Ukraine," *RFE/RL Research Report* 1, Number 27 (July 3, 1992): pp. 50–6, at p. 54.

102. Sakwa, *Frontline Ukraine*, pp. 58–9.

103. L.I. Romashenko, "Yazyk kak otrazhenie sovre-mennykh sotiokul'turnykh protsessov (na primere Ukrainy)," in *Yezhegodnaya nauchno-prakticheskaya sotsiologich-eskaya konferentsiya 'Prodolzhaya Grushina'* (Moscow: VTsIOM, 2012), pp. 180–82, http://wciom.ru/fileadmin/file/nauka/grusha_2012/tezisy/soc/romawenko.pdf.

104. "Violent Hate Crime in Ukraine," *Human Rights First*, 2012, http://lib.ohchr.org/HRBodies/UPR/Documents/Session14/UA/HRF_UPR_UKR_S14_2012_HumanRights First_E.pdf, pp. 2–3. Last accessed on December 11, 2015.

105. *European Commission against Racism and Intol-erance (ECRI) Report on Ukraine (fourth cycle)*, Council of Europe, December 8, 2011, www.coe.int/t/moni toring/ecri/Country-by-country/Ukraine/UKR-CbC-IV-2012-006-ENG.pdf, p. 8. Last accessed on December 11, 2015.

106. "Violent Hate Crime in Ukraine," p. 2.

107. "Violent Hate Crime in Ukraine," p. 4.

108. Anton Shekovtsov, "The Creeping Resurgence of the Ukrainian Radical Right?: The Case of the Freedom Party," *Europe-Asia Studies* 63, Number 2 (March 2011): pp. 203–28, at p. 215.

109. Shekovtsov, "The Creeping Resurgence," p. 216.

110. David Stern, "Svoboda: The rise of Ukraine's ultra-nationalists," BBC, December 26, 2012, www.bbc.com/news/magazine-20824693.

111. Stern, "Svoboda: The rise of Ukraine's ultra-na-tionalists."

112. "The anti-Semitic Svoboda Union wins represen-tation in the Ukrainian parliament," *The Coordinating Forum for Countering Antisemitism*, November 6, 2012, http://antisemitism.org.il/article/75709/antisemitic-svo boda-all-ukrainian-union-wins-representation-ukrainian-parliament.

113. Jill Heller, "Mila Kunis Targeted in Anti-Semitic Facebook Rant by Ukrainian Politician, Simon Weisenthal Center Expresses 'Outrage,'" *International Business Times*, December 21, 2012, www.ibtimes.com/mila-kunis-tar geted-anti-semitic-facebook-rant-ukrainian-politician-simon-wiesenthal-center-958530.

114. "Programma partii 'Svoboda,'" *Kiev1.org*, Decem-ber 15, 2013, http://kiev1.org/programma-partii-svoboda.html.

115. "Vybory: total'ne domirovannya Partiy regioniv," BBC, November 6, 2010, www.bbc.com/ukrainian/news/2010/11/101104_svoboda_analysis_it.shtml.

116. "European Parliament Resolution 2012/2889 (RSP) on the Situation in Ukraine," European Parliament/Leg-islative Observatory, December 13, 2012, www.europarl.europa.eu/oeil/popups/summary.do?id=1239823&t=e&l=en.

117. Svitlana Michko, "Generalnaya repetitsiya prezi-dentskikh vyboriv: na Ternopolshchiny stavsya prgnozo-vaniya triumfa natsionalistiv i krakh Tymoshenko," *Ukraina moloda*, November 2010, www.umoloda.kiev.ua/number/1369/180/48272/.

118. "Vybory: total'ne domirovannya Partiy regioniv"; Natalia Fedyuschak, "Nationalist Svoboda scores election victories in western Ukraine," *Kyiv Post*, November 11, 2010, www.kyivpost.com/content/politics/nationalist-svo boda-scores-election-victories-in-w-89664.html. For comparison, in 2006 Svoboda won 6 percent in the Lviv Oblast council elections, 7 percent in the Lviv city council election and 4 percent in the Ternopil city council election. Shekovtsov, "The Creeping Resurgence," p. 218. At the na-tional level, in 1998, the SP's predecessor, the SNPU, par-ticipated in the election bloc "Less Words" and won 0.16 percent of the votes. In the 2006 parliamentary elections the SP won 0.36 percent, and in the 2007 special parlia-mentary vote, 0.76 percent. Bekeshkin, "Parlamentskie vy-bory v Ukraine: predvidimoe in nepredvidimoe."

119. Iryna Kyrychenko, "Popovych: V Ukraini lamaiut-sya zasady hormodianskogo myru," *Dzerkalo tyzhnia*, March 28, 2009, http://www.dt.ua/3000/3050/65794/.

120. Ames, "Hero of the Orange Revolution Poisons Ukraine."

121. Rudling, "The OUN, the UPA and the Holocaust," pp. 36–7.

122. Sakwa, *Frontline Ukraine*, p. 59.

123. "Yanukovych v 2013 godu ne posetil 11 oblastei, odnako trizhdy pobyval na Donbasse," *Ukrainskaya pravda*, January 5, 2014, www.pravda.com.ua/rus/news/2014/01/5/7009069/.

Chapter 6

1. NATO-Ukraine Action Plan, NATO, November 22, 2005, www.nato.int/cps/en/natohq/official_texts_217 35.htm?selectedLocale=en.

2. NATO-Ukraine Action Plan, NATO.

3. "Ukraine Prez: Russia Wants to Destabilize Ukraine," Associated Press as cited in *Kiev Ukraine News Blog*, September 16, 2008, http://news.kievukraine.info/2008/09/ukraine-prez-russia-wants-to.html.

4. Kathryn Stoner and Michael McFaul, "Who Lost Russia (This Time)? Vladimir Putin," *The Washington Quarterly*, Summer 2015, http://twq.elliott.gwu.edu/who-lost-russia-time-vladimir-putin.

5. Kimberly Marten, "Putin's Choices: Explaining Russian Foreign Policy and Intervention in Ukraine," *The Washington Quarterly*, Summer 2015, http://twq.elliott.gwu.edu.

6. "NATO's Relations with Georgia," NATO, Septem-ber 7, 2015, www.nato.int/cps/en/natohq/topics_38988.htm?selectedLocale=en.

7. Brzezinski, *The Grand Chessboard*, p. 101.

8. "Declaration to Complement the Charter on a Distinctive Partnership between the North Atlantic Treaty Organization and Ukraine, as signed on 9 July 1997," NATO, August 21, 2009, www.nato.int/cps/en/natohq/offi cial_texts_57045.htm?selectedLocale=en.

9. "Yanukovych: Ukraine will be a non-aligned state," *Kyiv Post*, October 23, 2009, http://www.kyivpost.com/con tent/ukraine/yanukovych-ukraine-will-be-non-aligned-state-51207.html.

10. "Yanukovych describes current level of Ukraine's cooperation with NATO as sufficient," *Inerfax-Ukraine*, January 12, 2010, http://en.interfax.com.ua/news/general/29568.html.

11. "Yanukovych opens door to Russian navy keeping base in Ukraine," *Global Security*, February 13, 2010, www.globalsecurity.org/wmd/library/news/ukraine/2010/ukraine-100213-rianovosti02.htm citing *RIA Novosti*.

12. "Yanukovych Says Ukraine Seeks 'Non-Aligned' UE ties (Update 2)," *Bloomberg*, February 25, 2010, http://www.bloomberg.com/apps/news?pid=newsarchive&sid=a89SZz9MfVt0.

13. "Ukraine's Yanukovych: EU ties a 'key priority,'" *Kyiv Post*, March 1, 2010, http://www.kyivpost.com/con tent/ukraine/ukraines-yanukovych-eu-ties-a-key-prior ity-60720.html.

14. "Cabinet approves action plan for annual national program of cooperation with NATO in 2012," *Kyiv Post*, June 24, 2010, www.kyivpost.com/content/politics/cabinet-app roves-action-plan-for-annual-national-p-70823.html.

15. "Military Maneuvers in Ukraine," *Euronews*, Au-gust 4, 2011, www.euronews.com/nocomment/2011/08/04/military-manoeuvres-in-ukraine/.

16. "Ukraine, NATO to hold security exercises during Euro 2012," *Kyiv Post*, March 26, 2012, www.kyivpost.com/content/ukraine/ukraine-nato-to-hold-security-exercises-during-eur-124954.html?flavour=ful.

17. John Thys, "Ukraine Joins NATO's Counter-Piracy Operation," *RIA Novosti (Sputnik)*, February 22, 2013, http://sputniknews.com/military/20130222/179631923/Ukraine-Joins-NATOs-Counter-Piracy-Operation.html.

18. "Yanukovych signs decree on Ukraine-NATO annual cooperation programs," *Interfax-Ukraine*, June 12, 2013, www.kyivpost.com/content/politics/yanukovych-signs-decree-on-ukraine-nato-annual-cooperation-programs-325558.html.

19. "Ukraine's parliament votes to abandon NATO ambitions," *BBC News*, June 3, 2010, http://www.bbc.com/news/10229626.

20. "NATO considers Ukraine's behavior 'unprecedented,'" *Kyiv Post*, May 25, 2010, www.kyivpost.com/content/ukraine/nato-considers-ukraines-behavior-unprecedented-67634.html.

21. Thys, "Ukraine Joins NATO's Counter-Piracy Operation."

22. Ivan Katchanovski, "Political Regionalism in 'Orange' Ukraine," Working paper, www.academia.edu/454776/Political_Regionalism_in_Orange_Ukraine, at p. 38 (last accessed on December 19, 2015) as calculated from "Informatsiina skladova evropeiskoi ta evroatlantychnoi integratsii: gromadska dumka," *Natzionalna bezpeka i oborona* 1 (2008): pp. 42–60; "Sotsiologichne opituvannya: Yakbi nastupnoi nedili vidbuvavsya referendum shchodo vstupu Ukrayni do NATO, yak bi Vi progolosovali? (dinamika, regional'nii rozpodil, 2002–2008)," *Razumkov Center*, 2009, www.uceps.org/ukr/poll.php?poll_id=116, last accessed on December 19, 2015.

23. Ye. V. Knyazeva, "20 let nezavisimosti: mneneie ekspertov i naseleniya yuga Ukrainy," in *Yezhegodnaya nauchno-prakticheskaya sotsiologicheskaya konferentsiya 'Prodolzhaya Grushina,'* p. 156, http://wciom.ru/fileadmin/file/nauka/grusha_2012/tezisy/soc/knjazeva.pdf.

24. See, for example, Lowell Barrington, "The Geographic Component of Mass Attitudes in Ukraine," *Post-Soviet Geography* 38 (1997): pp. 601–614; Vicki Hesli, William Reisinger, and Arthur Miller, "Political Party Development in Divided Societies: The Case of Ukraine," *Electoral Studies* 17 (1998): pp. 235–256; Stephen Shulman, "Asymmetrical International Integration and Ukrainian National Disunity," *Political Geography* 18 (1999): pp. 913–939; Sarah Birch, "Interpreting the Regional Effect in Ukrainian Politics," *Europe-Asia Studies* 52 (2000): pp. 1017–1042; Paul Kubicek, "Regional Polarisation in Ukraine: Public Opinion, Voting and Legislative Behaviour," *Europe-Asia Studies* 52 (2000): pp. 272–293; Lowell Barrington and Erick Herron, "One Ukraine or Many?: Regionalism in Ukraine and its political consequences," *Nationalities Papers* 32 (2004): pp. 53–86; Dominique Arel, "The Orange Revolution's hidden face: Ukraine and the denial of its regional problem," *Revue Detudes Comparatives Est-Ouest* 37 (2006): pp. 11–48.

25. For the results of 12 opinion surveys conducted between 2002 and 2013, see "Ukrainian-NATO Relations," *Wikipedia.org*, http://en.wikipedia.org/wiki/Ukraine%E2%80%93NATO_relations, last accessed December 19, 2015.

26. "End of Communism Cheered But Now With More Reservations—Chapter 9. Rating the EU and NATO," *Pew Global Research*, November 2, 2009, www.pewglobal.org/2009/11/02/chapter-9-rating-the-eu-and-nato/; Simon Shuster, "NATO Too Wary of Russian Threats to Let Ukraine Join," *Time*, September 4, 2014, http://time.com/3271057/nato-ukraine-membership/.

27. Motyl admitted in a November 2014 discussion that in the past opinion polls showed 15–20 percent of Ukrainians maximum supported NATO membership. Just before 2012, support hovered around 25–35 percent. It fell to approximately 15–20 percent in favor of NATO membership in 2013, he noted. "Podcast: A Year of Living Dangerously," *RFERL*, November 21, 2014, www.rferl.org/content/podcast-a-year-of-living-dangerously/26703995.html, last accessed on December 19, 2015.

28. "'Post-Orange' Ukraine: Internal Dynamics and Foreign Policy Priorities," *NATO Parliamentary Assembly*, 2011, www.nato-pa.int/default.Asp?SHORTCUT=2439, last accessed December 19, 2015.

29. *Ukraine: Energy Policy Review 2006*, International Energy Agency/Organization for Economic Cooperation and Development, 2006, www.iea.org/publications/freepublications/publication/ukraine2006.pdf (last accessed December 16, 2015); Simon Pirani, "Ukraine's Gas Sector," *Oxford Institute for Energy Studies*, June 2007, www.oxfordenergy.org/wpcms/wp-content/uploads/2010/11/NG21-UkrainesGasSector-SimonPirani-2007.pdf, pp. 204 and 220, last accessed December 17, 2015.

30. Jonathan Stern, "The Russian-Ukrainian gas crisis of January 2006," *Oxford Institute for Energy Studies*, January 16, 2006, www.oxfordenergy.org/wpcms/wp-content/uploads/2011/01/Jan2006-RussiaUkraineGasCrisis-JonathanStern.pdf.

31. "Ukraine Rejects Putin's Eleventh-Hour Natural Gas Price Offer," Associated Press, December 31, 2005, http://blog.kievukraine.info/2005_12_01_kievukrainenewsblog_archive.html.

32. Dmitrii Zhdannikov, "Ukraine says repaid gas debt, Russia says not yet," *Reuters*, December 30, 2008, http://uk.reuters.com/article/russia-ukraine-gas-idUKLU15776220081230?sp=true, last accessed December 18, 2015; Andrew Osborn, "Russian Firm Cuts Gas to Ukraine, But EU Hit Is Cushioned," *Wall Street Journal*, January 2, 2009, www.wsj.com/articles/SB123080339916446769, last accessed on December 18, 2015.

33. Pavel Polityuk, Sabina Zawadzki, and Dmitry Zhdannikov, "Russia: gas talks fail, will cut off Ukraine," *Reuters*, December 31, 2008, http://uk.reuters.com/article/russia-ukraine-gas-idUKLV43959420081231?sp=true; "Russia fully cuts gas to Ukraine, ups supplies to Europe," *RIA Novosti*, January 1, 2009, http://sputniknews.com/world/20090101/119302144.html, last accessed on December 18, 2015.

34. "Ukraine warns EU of gas 'problem,'" BBC, January 2, 2009, http://news.bbc.co.uk/2/hi/europe/7809450.stm, last accessed on December 18, 2015.

35. Yuri Kulikov and Tanya Mosolova, "Russia gas disruption spreads to Czechs, Turks," Reuters, January 4, 2009, www.reuters.com/article/us-russia-ukraine-gas-idUSTRE4BN32B20090108, last accessed on December 18, 2015; "Naftohaz Ukraine: Intermediary RosUkrEnergo owes $40 million for gas transit," *Kyiv Post*, January 3, 2009.

36. In March 2010, the Stockholm tribunal ordered Naftogaz to pay RosUkrEnergo $200 million for breaches of supply, transit, and storage contracts. In June 2010, the tribunal ordered Naftogaz to return 11 billion cubic meters (bcm) of natural gas to RosUkrEnergo and another 1.1 bcm in lieu of its paying RosUkrEnergo for damages from contract breach. "Stockholm court obliges Naftogaz to return 12.1 billion cubic meters of gas to RosUkrEnergo," *Kyiv Post*, June 8, 2010, www.kyivpost.com/content/business/stockholm-court-obliges-naftogaz-to-return-121-bil-69022.html and "BYuT publishes documents on sales of disputed 11 billion cubic meters of gas by Gazprom to Naftogaz," *Kyiv Post*, June 25, 2010, www.kyivpost.com/content/business/byut-publishes-documents-on-sales-of-disputed-11-b-70879.html, last accessed on December 18, 2015.

37. "Russia to cut Ukraine gas supply," *BBC News*, January 5, 2009, http://news.bbc.co.uk/2/hi/europe/7812368.stm, last accessed on December 18, 2015.

38. David Jolly, "Deal Struck to End Gas Cutoff," *New York Times*, January 8, 2009, www.nytimes.com/2009/01/09/world/europe/09gazprom.html?_r=4&partner=rss&emc=rss.

39. "Ukraine has stolen 86 mln cu m of gas in 2009—Gazprom," *RIA Novosti*, January 7, 2009, http://sputniknews.com/world/20090107/119390033.html, last accessed on December 18, 2015; "Kremlin wants Ukraine to stop diverting Russian gas, reopen transit," *Interfax-Ukraine*, January 7, 2009, http://en.interfax.com.ua/news/general/4433.html, last accessed on December 18, 2015; and "Russia says will restore gas when monitors in place," Reuters, January 8, 2009, www.reuters.com/article/us-russia-ukraine-gas-idUSTRE5062Q520090120, last accessed on December 18, 2015.

40. "Exec Admits Naftogaz Did Not Remove Hatch On Way Of Russian Gas To Europe," *Itar-Tass*, January 13, 2009.

41. "EU wary as Russia and Ukraine reach gas deal," *Reuters*, January 18, 2009, www.reuters.com/article/us-russia-ukraine-gas-idUSTRE5062Q520090120, last accessed on December 18, 2015.

42. Andrei Nesterov, "Russia-Ukraine 'Gas war' Damages Both Economies," *Worldpress.org*, February 20, 2009, www.worldpress.org/Europe/3307.cfm, last accessed on December 18, 2015.

43. "Yu. Timoshenko: Peregovory s RF sorvali ukrainskie politiki," *RBK*, January 14, 2009, http://top.rbc.ru/politics/14/01/2009/273991.shtml; "Swiss-based firm fuels intrigue in Russia gas conflict," *AFP*, January 14, 2009.

44. See Jérôme Guillet, "Ukraine-Russia gas spat: some background and context," *The Oil Drum -Europe*, January 3, 2009, http://europe.theoildrum.com in *Johnson's Russia List*, No. 2, January 5, 2009, #30; Jérôme Guillet and John Evans, "The battle of the oligarchs behind the gas dispute," *Financial Times*, January 6, 2009; "Gas Situation Is Way To Fight For Independence, Sovereignty—Yushchenko," *Itar-Tass*, January 13, 2009. On this scenario see Vladimir Frolov, "The Pipe is Blocked in Kiev—Russia and Europe are hostages to Ukraine's politics," *Russia Profile*, January 13, 2009, www.russiaprofile.ru.

45. Mustafa Nayem, "Uprising in Ukraine: How It All Began," *Open Society Foundation*, April 4, 2014, www.opensocietyfoundations.org/voices/uprising-ukraine-how-it-all-began.

46. Steve Weissman, "Meet the Americans Who Put Together the Coup in Kiev," *Ron Paul Institute*, March 25, 2014, http://ronpaulinstitute.org/archives/featured-articles/2014/march/25/meet-the-americans-who-put-together-the-coup-in-kiev.aspx.

47. Weissman, "Meet the Americans."

48. Weissman, "Meet the Americans"; "Ukraine and the EU on the Brink of the New Association Agreement: Free Trade, Energy Security, and Democracy," Konrad Adenauer Stiftung, January 2012, www.kas.de/ukraine/en/events/46752/.

49. Nayem, "Uprising in Ukraine."

50. Yuriy Onishkiv, "Media expert: Only two TV stations still give viewers fair news coverage," *Kyiv Post*, May 13, 2010, www.kyivpost.com/content/ukraine/media-expert-only-two-tv-stations-still-give-viewe-66674.html.

51. Weissman, "Meet the Americans."

52. Weissman, "Meet the Americans."

53. Diane Francis, "In Ukraine, 'how little has changed' even after Orange Revolution," *Financial Post*, March 10, 2012, http://business.financialpost.com/diane-francis/in-ukraine-how-little-has-changed-even-after-orange-revolution.

54. Roman Olearchyk, "Ukraine: Inside the pro–EU protest camp," *Financial Times*, December 14, 2013, http://blogs.ft.com/beyond-brics/2013/12/14/ukraine-inside-the-pro-eu-protest-camp/.

55. Weissman, "Meet the Americans."

56. Ames, "Pierre Omidyar."

57. Together they made at least 13 visits to the White House in 2009–2013. Moreover, the logs indicate that, on several occasions, Omidyar visited the White House several times in one day, and Carr removed the "same-day duplicates" from the totals. Putting these numbers in perspective, Carr notes that Omidyar's six visits alone compare to four visits during the same period by NBC Universal chief Stephen Burke, two by Fox News boss Roger Ailes, two by MSNBC's Phil Griffin, one by *New York Times* owner Arthur O. Sulzberger, and one each by Dow Jones's Robert Thompson, Gannett/*USA Today*'s Gracia Martore and Omidyar's fellow tech billionaire and media owner, Jeff Bezos. Paul Carr, "Pierre and Pamela Omidyar's Cozy White House Ties," *Pando.com*, March 23, 2014, https://pando.com/2014/03/23/revealed-visitor-logs-show-full-extent-of-pierre-and-pamela-omidyars-cozy-white-house-ties/.

58. Mark Rachkevych, "Rybachuk: Democracy-promoting nongovernmental organization faces 'ridiculous' investigation," *Kyiv Post*, February 10, 2014, www.kyivpost.com/content/politics/rybachuk-democracy-promoting-nongovernmental-organization-faces-ridiculous-investigation-336583.html?flavour=mobile.

59. See Ames, "Pierre Omidlyar," and "New Citizen Centre (UA)," *Omidlyar Network*, https://web.archive.org/web/20120310103804/http://www.omidyar.com/portfolio/new-citizen-centre-ua, last accessed January 5, 2015.

60. Weissman, "Meet the Americans," and Ames, "Pierre Omidlyar."

61. Weissman, "Meet the Americans."

62. The following paragraphs are based on John Helmer's superb journalistic investigation. See John Helmer, "Meet and Greet Natalie Jaresko, U.S. Government Employee, Ukraine Finance Minister," *Dances with Bears*, December 3, 2014, http://johnhelmer.net/?p=12317.

63. Helmer, "Meet and Greet Natalie Jaresko."

64. Helmer, "Meet and Greet Natalie Jaresko."

65. Helmer, "Meet and Greet Natalie Jaresko."

66. "Tainy zhen i zhenshin Viktora Yushchenko. Yekaterina Kler i eyo podrugi."

67. Helmer, "Meet and Greet Natalie Jaresko."

68. For a photograph of her home, see "Opublikovany pervyie foto shikarnogo osobnyaka Yaresko," *Vesti Ukraina*, December 10, 2014, http://vesti-ukr.com/svetskie-vesti/81018-opublikovany-pervye-foto-shikarnogo-osobnjaka-jaresko.

69. Helmer, "Meet and Greet Natalie Jaresko."

70. Kevin Bogardus, "Who lobbyists for Ukraine leader courted," *The Hill*, February 25, 2014, http://thehill.com/business-a-lobbying/business-a-lobbying/199114-lobbyists-for-jailed-ukraine-leader-courted-the.

71. Alexander Burns and Maggie Haberman, "Mystery man: Ukraine's U.S. political fixer," *Politico.com*, March 5, 2014. www.politico.com.

72. Bogardus, "Who lobbyists for Ukraine leader courted."

73. Gordon M. Hahn, "Russia-Ukraine-EU," *Russia—Other Points of View*, November 4, 2013, www.russiaotherpointsofview.com/2013/11/russia-ukraine-eu.html.

74. "EU leaders: Ratification of Association Agreement and DCFTA depends on settlement of Tymoshenko-Lutsenko issue," *Kyiv Post*, July 20, 2012, www.kyivpost.com/content/politics/eu-leaders-ratification-of-association-agreement-a-310272.html; "Ukraine's Lutsenko jailed for 4 years (updated)," *Kyiv Post*, February 27, 2012, www.kyivpost.com/content/politics/ukraines-lutsenko-jailed-for-4-years-updated-123206.html; and Daryna Krasnolutska and James G. Nueger, "Ukraine Faces EU Reform Deadline as Key to Association Pact," *Bloomberg*, February 25, 2013,

www.bloomberg.com/news/articles/2013-02-25/ukraine-faces-eu-reform-deadline-as-key-to-association-pact-1-.

75. "European Parliament Resolution 2012/2889 (RSP) on the Situation in Ukraine."

76. "EU to Ukraine: Reforms necessary for trade pact," *Kyiv Post*, February 25, 2013, www.kyivpost.com/content/ukraine/eu-to-ukraine-reforms-necessary-for-trade-pact-320910.html.

77. Richard Balmforth, "Ukraine leader urges pro–Eu rope drive despite Kremlin pressure," *Reuters*, September 3, 2013, www.reuters.com/article/us-ukraine-russia-yanukovich-idUSBRE9820HG20130903.

78. "Ukraine's Cabinet Backs EU Association Agreement," RFERL, September 18, 2013, www.rferl.org/content/ukraine-eu-membership-association-agreement-government-approve/25109791.html.

79. "EU Commissioner Fule expects Rada to pass European integration bills on November 21," *Interfax Ukraine*, November 20, 2013, http://en.interfax.com.ua/news/general/175853.html.

80. "Cox-Kwasniewski mission to continue until Eastern Partnership Summit," *Interfax Ukraine*, November 21, 2013, http://en.interfax.com.ua/news/general/176135.html.

81. "Jailed Tymoshenko on hunger strike over EU U-turn by Ukraine," *Euronews.com*, November 25, 2013, www.euronews.com/2013/11/25/jailed-tymoshenko-begins-hunger-strike-over-ukraines-eu-u-turn/.

82. "Russia ready for tripartite talks with Ukraine, EU—Peskov," *Interfax-Ukraine*, November 21, 2013, http://en.interfax.com.ua/news/general/176159.html.

83. "Cox-Kwasniewski mission to continue until Eastern Partnership Summit"; "Ukraine has no alternative but European integration—Yanukovych," *Interfax-Ukraine*, November 21, 2013, http://en.interfax.com.ua/news/general/176156.html; and "Ukraine Still Wants Historic Pact with EU," *Oman Observer*, November 27, 2013, http://omanobserver.om/ukraine-still-wants-historic-pact-with-eu/.

84. "Cox-Kwasniewski mission to continue until Eastern Partnership Summit."

85. "Putin says Ukraine-EU deal a threat to Russia," Al Jazeera, November 27, 2013, www.aljazeera.com/news/europe/2013/11/putin-says-ukraine-eu-deal-threat-russia-20131126235224640384.html.

86. "EU rejects Russia 'veto' on Ukraine agreement," BBC, November 29, 2013, www.bbc.com/news/world-europe-25154618.

87. "Putin says Ukraine-EU deal a threat to Russia."

88. Vladimir Isachenkov and Maria Danilov, "Putin: Russia to buy $15 billion in Ukrainian binds," Associated Press, December 17, 2013, http://finance.yahoo.com/news/putin-russia-buy-15-billion-153000779.html.

89. "Putin says Ukraine-EU deal a threat to Russia."

90. "Yanukovich says Ukraine-EU Deal is Suspended not Cancelled," *Euronews.com*, November 29, 2013, www.euronews.com/2013/11/29/yanukovich-says-ukraine-eu-deal-is-suspended-not-cancelled/Yanukovych.

91. "5 Glavnykh politicheskii sensatssii ot Firtasha," *Vesti Ukraina*, April 30, 2015, http://vesti-ukr.com/strana/98500-5-glavnyh-politicheskih-sensacij-ot-firtasha.

92. "Association Agreement Between the European Union and its Member States, of the One Part, and Ukraine, of the Other Part," *Bilaterals.org*, 2012, www.bilaterals.org/IMG/pdf/eu-ukraine-association-agreement-english.pdf. Last accessed December 9, 2015.

93. The emphasis in the quotation from Lavrov's speech is mine. *Vystuplenie i otvety na voprosy Ministra innostrannykh del Rossii S.V. Lavrov na Forume 'Territoriya smyslov na Klyaz'me,' Vladimirskaya oblast,'* d. Dvorkin, August 24, 2015.

94. Giuliano, "The Origins of Separatism."

95. Katchanovski, "Political Regionalism in 'Orange' Ukraine," p. 39, as calculated from "Spivrobitnytstvo Ukrainy z ES: Otsinky hromadian," *Natzionalnabezpeka i oborona* 6 (2008): pp. 37–56.

96. "Dumki da poglyadi xhiteliv pivdenno-skhidnikh oblastei Ukraini: kviten' 2014," *Kievskii Mezhdunarodnyi Institut Sotsiologii* (Kiev International Institute of Sociology or KIIS), April 20, 2014, www.kiis.com.ua/?lang=rus&cat=reports&id=302&y=2014&m=4&page=1.

97. Giuliano, "The Origins of Separatism."

98. "Putin: Wherever Ukraine Goes but we will meet," *Inforos.ru*, September 4, 2013, http://inforos.ru/en/?module=news&action=view&id=35427.

Chapter 7

1. Nayem, "Uprising in Ukraine."
2. Weissman, "Meet the Americans."
3. "About" page, *EuromaidanPR.com*, https://euromaidanpr.wordpress.com/about/, last accessed on January 4, 2016.
4. Nayem, "Uprising in Ukraine."
5. Nayem, "Uprising in Ukraine."
6. "Ukraine's president tries to calm tensions as clashes continue," *Business New Europe*, November 26, 2013 and *Kyiv Post*, www.kyivpost.com/multimedia/photo/maidan-tonight-332445.html.
7. Tatyana Izhvenko, "Yevrointegratsiyu v Kieve travili gazom," *Nezavisimaya gazeta*, November 26, 2013, www.ng.ru/cis/2013–11–26/1_ukraina.html.
8. Brian Bonner, "EuroMaidan rallies in Ukraine—Nov. 25 coverage," *Kyiv Post*, November 27, 2013, www.kyivpost.com/content/ukraine/euromaidan-rallies-in-ukraine-nov-25-coverage-332512.html.
9. Kostyantyn Chernychkin, "Police, demonstrators clash in Nov. 25 evening rally," *Kyiv Post*, November 26, 2013, www.kyivpost.com/multimedia/photo/maidan-tonight-332445.html.
10. See *Kyiv Post*, www.kyivpost.com/multimedia/photo/maidan-tonight-332445.html?flavour=mobile.
11. See "Yevromaidan v Kieve, den chetvortyi: Khronika," *Liga.net*, November 25, 2013, http://news.liga.net/articles/politics/928623-bolshe_100_tys_chelovek_na_evromaydane_trebuyut_assotsiatsii_s_es.htm.
12. See, for example, Luke Baker and Richard Balmforth, "Police, pro–Europe protesters clash in Ukraine, EU condemns Russia," Reuters, November 25, 2013.
13. Amnesty International Annual Report 2014/15—Ukraine, www.amnesty.org/countries/europe-and-central-asia/ukraine/report-ukraine/.
14. "Privitannya Dmitra Yarosha z richnetseyu 'Pravogo sektora,'" *Pravyysektor.info*, November 29, 2015, http://old.pravyysektor.info/appeals/pryvitannya-dmytra-yarosha-z-richnytseyu-pravoho-sektora/.
15. "Dmitrii Yarosh," *112.ua*, http://112.ua/profiles/dmytryi-yarosh-145.html, last accessed on January 27, 2016.
16. "Ideologichni osnovi Ukrainskoi derzhavnosti: Problema Vybori," *Pravyysector.info*, June 11, 2015, http://pravyysektor.info/news/chogo-pragnemo/57/ideologichni-osnovi-ukrayinskoyi-derzhavnosti-problema-viboru.html, last accessed on January 31, 2016.
17. "Ideologichni osnovi Ukrainskoi derzhavnosti: Problema Vybori"; "Programa Pravogo Sektora," *Pravyysektor.info*, http://pravyysektor.info/programa.html, last accessed on January 30, 2016; and "Korotkiy ideolohichno vyhovniy kurs dlya vo tryzub im s Bandery ta pravoho sektora," *Pravyysektor.info*, November 27, 2015, http://old.pravyysektor.info/articles/korotkyj-ideolohichno-vyhovnyj-kurs-dlya-vo-tryzub-im-s-bandery-ta-pravoho-sektora/, last accessed on January 15, 2016.
18. Programa Pravogo Sektora.
19. Programa Pravogo Sektora.

20. Programa Pravogo Sektora.

21. Programa Pravogo Sektora.

22. Programa Pravogo Sektora.

23. "Korotokiy ideolohichno vyhovniy kurs dlya vo tryzub im s Bandery ta pravoho sektora."

24. "Korotokiy ideolohichno vyhovniy kurs dlya vo tryzub im s Bandery ta pravoho sektora."

25. "Doroga na Donbas i Krym lezhit cherez Kyiv," *Pravyysektor.info*, November 11, 2015, http://pravyysektor.info/news/1155/doroga-na-donbas-i-krim-lezhit-cherez-kiyiv.html.

26. "Korotokiy ideolohichno vyhovniy kurs dlya vo tryzub im s Bandery ta pravoho sektora."

27. "Doroga na Donbas i Krym lezhit cherez Kyiv."

28. "Korotokiy ideolohichno vyhovniy kurs dlya vo tryzub im s Bandery ta pravoho sektora."

29. Programa Pravogo Sektora.

30. Matthew Schofield, "Leader of Ukraine's revolution rails against Putin, Russian military and Jewish oligarchs," *Miami Herald*, March 15, 2014, www.miamiherald.com/latest-news/article1961440.html.

31. "Dmitrii Yarosh." On the Caucasus Emirate, see Hahn, *The Caucasus Emirate Mujahedin*.

32. Schofield, "Leader of Ukraine's revolution rails against Putin."

33. Programa, Sotsialno-Natsionalna Assembleya, Snaua.info, http://snaua.info/programa/, last accessed September 15, 2014. See also Gordon M. Hahn, "Maidan Ukraine's Neo-Fascist Problem," *Fair Observer*, September 23, 2014, www.fairobserver.com/region/europe/the-ukrainian-revolutions-neo-fascist-problem-14785/.

34. "Andrei Biletskii | Sotsial-natsionalizm—zolotoi vek Ukrainy," *YouTube*, December 7, 2014, www.youtube.com/watch?v=0KfqYT6U6xc; Leonid Bershidskiy, "Ukraine's Neo-Nazis Won't Get U.S. Money," *Bloomberg*, June 12, 2015, www.bloombergview.com/articles/2015-06-12/ukraine-s-neo-nazis-won-t-get-u-s-money; and Robert Parry, "U.S. House Admits Nazi Role in Ukraine," Consortium News, June 13, 2015, http://readersupportednews.org/opinion2/277-75/30719-us-house-admits-nazi-role-in-ukraine.

35. "Slovo bilogo vozhdya.pdf," *VKontakte*, http://vk.com/doc29866988_319980052?hash=14c0a1bebe416193ef&dl=a33eceb6cbe50c4daf, last accessed on January 29, 2016; Bershidskiy, "Ukraine's Neo-Nazis Won't Get U.S. Money"; and Parry, "U.S. House Admits Nazi Role in Ukraine."

36. Tom Parfitt, "Ukraine crisis: The neo–Nazi brigade fighting pro–Russian separatists," *Telegraph* (UK), August 11, 2014, www.telegraph.co.uk/news/worldnews/europe/ukraine/11025137/Ukraine-crisis-the-neo-Nazi-brigade-fighting-pro-Russian-separatists.html.

37. Maryana Petsukh, "Lvovskii Yevromaidan: messianstvo v raskolotom vide," *Ukrainskaya pravda*, November 25, 2013, www.pravda.com.ua/rus/articles/2013/11/25/7002990/.

38. Boris Danik, "The Science of Bandera Bashing," *Kyiv Post*, December 30, 2013, www.kyivpost.com/opinion/op-ed/boris-danik-the-science-of-bandera-bashing-334483.html.

39. "75 were injured during Nov. 30 dispersal of Euro-Maidan," *Kyiv Post*, December 5, 2013 www.kyivpost.com/article/content/ukraine/75-were-injured-during-nov-30-dispersal-of-euromaidan-333103.html; "Na Mikhailovskoi ploshchadi formiruyut otryady samooborony," *Ukrainskaya pravda*, November 30, 2013, www.pravda.com.ua/rus/news/2013/11/30/7003906/.

40. "Ukraine leader 'outraged,' slams violence in Kiev as police disperse protesters," *RT*, November 30, 2013, https://web.archive.org/web/20131201100025/http://rt.com/news/ukraine-yanukovich-violence-protests-534/.

41. "Na Mikhailovskoi ploshchadi—tysyachi nedovol nykh kievlyan. 10 poslov YeS takzhe na mitinge," *Ukrainskaya pravda*, November 30, 2013, www.pravda.com.ua/rus/news/2013/11/30/7003797/.

42. "Na Mikhailovskoi ploshchadi formiruyut otryady samooborony."

43. "Clashes rage as 100,000 Ukrainians demand EU pact," *Global Post*, December 1, 2013, www.globalpost.com/dispatch/news/afp/131201/clashes-rage-100000-ukrainians-demand-eu-pact-0; "Ukrainian Protesters Occupy Kiev after Violent Clashes," I24news, https://web.archive.org/web/20140204190151/http://www.i24news.tv/en/news/international/europe/131202-ukrainian-protesters-occupy-kiev-square-after-violent-clashes; "'Revolution!' Thousands pour in for pro EU rally in Ukraine, storm govt buildings," *RT*, December 1, 2013, http://rt.com/news/ukraine-protests-court-ban-538/; and "Police say over 300 radicals led attack on president's office," *Kyiv Post*, December 2, 2013, www.kyivpost.com/content/ukraine/police-say-over-300-radicals-led-attack-on-presidents-office-332786.html.

44. "Postradalikh vid sutichok y Kyevi stae vsei bilshe," *Ukrainskaya pravda*, December 2, 2013, www.pravda.com.ua/news/2013/12/2/7004210/.

45. Timothy Ash, "The Orange Revolution MKII," *Kyiv Post*, December 1, 2013, www.kyivpost.com/opinion/op-ed/the-orange-revolution-mkii-332761.html.

46. Andrey Slivka, "Rage in Kiev," *The New Yorker*, December 11, 2013, http://www.newyorker.com/news/news-desk/rage-in-kiev.

47. "Oleh Tiahnibok: The time has come for total social and national revolution," *Svoboda*, December 1, 2013, http://en.svoboda.org.ua/news/comments/00008465/.

48. Fred Weir, "Russia cries foul over Western embrace of Ukraine's demonstrators," *Christian Science Monitor*, December 13, 2013.

49. "KYIV BLOG: Yanukovych backed into corner as EU suspends talks," *Business New Europe*, December 16, 2013.

50. News release, "Cardin Urges Immediate Action by Ukrainian Officials to Respect Human Rights," Commission on Security and Cooperation in Europe, December 11, 2013, www.csce.gov/index.cfm?FuseAction=Content Records.ViewDetail& ContentRecord_id=1116&Content RecordType=P&ContentType=P&CFID=2039749&CFTO KEN=dc1d5da2b924f61b-F019953C-9E0D-566C-6B2EE9 A222F6A826, last accessed on December 11, 2013.

51. "Jen Psaki, Spokesperson, Daily Press Briefing, Washington, DC, 11 December 2013," U.S. Department of State, December 11, 2013, www.state.gov/r/pa/prs/dpb/2013/12/218597.htm.

52. "S.Res.319—A resolution expressing support for the Ukrainian people in light of President Yanukovych's decision not to sign an Association Agreement with the European Union.113th Congress (2013–2014), Congress.gov, December 12, 2013, www.congress.gov/bill/113th-congress/senate-resolution/319/text.

53. *The Guardian*, www.theguardian.com/world/2013/dec/15/ukraine-protesters-return-central-kiev-eu-campaign; *Fox News*, www.foxnews.com/politics/2013/12/15/senators-mccain-murphy-join-massive-ukraine-anti-government-protest-threaten/; *Reuters*, and www.reuters.com/article/2013/12/15/ukraine-idUSL6N0JU0BV20131215.

54. Weir, "Russia cries foul over Western embrace of Ukraine's demonstrators."

55. "Helsinki Final Act, Conference on Security and Cooperation in Europe, Helsinki, 1975," Osce.org, www.osce.org/mc/39501?download=true, p. 5, last accessed February 4, 2016.

56. "Budapest Memorandums on Security Assurances," *Council on Foreign Relations*, December 5, 1994, www.cfr.org/arms-control-disarmament-and-nonproliferation/budapest-memorandums-security-assurances-1994/p32484.

57. Vijai Maheshwari, "Why Did Ukraine's Eurolution Fail?" *The Daily Beast*, January 5, 2014, www.thedailybeast.com.

58. "Po Ukraine prokhodyat mitingi v chesti dnya rozhdeniya Bandery," *Ukrainskaya pravda*, January 1, 2014, www.pravda.com.ua/rus/news/2014/01/1/7008936/.

59. "Kolesnichenko uvidel na Maidane 'peshernyi natsionalizm i element natsizma," *Ukrainskaya pravda*, January 2, 2014, www.pravda.com.ua/rus/news/2014/01/2/7008955/.

60. "Gritsenko: lyudei na Maidane vse men'she , chast palatok pustuyut," *Ukrainskaya pravda*, January 13, 2014, www.pravda.com.ua/rus/news/2014/01/13/7009385/.

61. "Oppozitsiya gotovitsya k novomu razgonu Yevromaidana," *Ukrainskaya pravda*, January 4, 2014, www.pravda.com.ua/rus/news/2014/01/4/7009015/.

62. "Avakov: Maidan primet reshenie po usileniyu bezopasnst posle prazdnikov," *Ukrainskaya pravda*, January 6, 2014, www.pravda.com.ua/rus/news/2014/01/6/7009114/.

63. "Yevromaidan ostanetsya v dome profsoyuzov, potomu chto 'de-fakto dogovor deistvitelen," *Ukrainskaya pravda*, January 6, 2014, www.pravda.com.ua/rus/news/2014/01/6/7009100/.

64. "Maidan sozdaet stachkom i utverdil plan deistvii na yanvar," *Ukrainskaya pravda*, January 8, 2014, www.pravda.com.ua/rus/news/2014/01/8/7009185/.

65. "Byvzshie podchinennyie izbili Lutsenko i aktivistov Yevromaidana," *Ukrainskaya pravda*, January 11, 2015, www.pravda.com.ua/rus/photo-video/2014/01/11/7009328/.

66. "V YeS prizvali aktivistov i silovikov vozderzhat'sya ot nasiliya," *Ukrainskaya pravda*, January 11, 2015, www.pravda.com.ua/rus/news/2014/01/11/7009335/.

67. "Oppozitsiya blokiruet Radu. Benyuk zasevaet. Pod AP miting," *Ukrainskaya pravda*, January 14, 2014, www.pravda.com.ua/rus/news/2014/01/14/7009484/.

68. Valeriya Kondratova, "Parubiy: Vlast' gotova rasognat' Maidan, est' dva stsenarii," *Liga.net*, January 15, 2014, http://news.liga.net/interview/politics/959704-parubiy_vlast_gotova_razognat_maydan_est_dva_stsenariya.htm.

69. "Vlasti vybrali repressii. Ot strakha," *Ukrainskaya pravda*, January 16, 2014, www.pravda.com.ua/rus/columns/2014/01/16/7009750/ and "Rada prinyla zakony, otkryvayushchie put' k massovym repressiyam, fond 'Vozrozhdeni," *Ukrainskaya pravda*, January 16, 2014, www.pravda.com.ua/rus/news/2014/01/16/7009773/.

70. "Yevromaidan ne shturmirovali, no v tsentr Kieva styagivayut silovikov," *Ukrainskaya pravda*, January 16, 2014, www.pravda.com.ua/rus/news/2014/01/16/7009678/.

71. "SShA vzvolnovany 'zakonami po diktatury," *Ukrainskaya pravda*, January 16, 2014, www.pravda.com.ua/rus/news/2014/01/16/7009779/.

72. "Oppozitsiya sozyvaet novoe veche i gotovitsya k zabastovke," *Ukrainskaya pravda*, January 17, 2014, www.pravda.com.ua/rus/news/2014/01/17/7009841/.

73. "V Ukraine ob"yavlena vseobshchaya mobilizatsiya," *Ukrainskaya pravda*, January 17, 2014, www.pravda.com.ua/rus/news/2014/01/17/7009841/.

74. William Risch, "Maidan Chronicle—January 19–20, 2014—The Day Kyiv Blew Up (In Lieu of a Conclusion)," *Maidan Chronicle*, January 20, 2014, https://williamrisch.wordpress.com/2014/01/29/maidan-chronicle-january-19-20-2014-the-day-kyiv-blew-up-in-lieu-of-a-conclusion/.

75. Risch, "Maidan Chronicle—January 19–20, 2014"; and Pyotr Shuklynov, "Praviy Sektor. Yak i chomu vibukhnuv Maidan," *Liga novosti*, January 20, 2014, http://news.liga.net/ua/articles/politics/962721-praviy_sektor_yak_chomu_vibukhnuv_maydan.htm.

76. Risch, "Maidan Chronicle—January 19–20, 2014;" and Shuklynov, "Praviy Sektor. Yak i chomu vibukhnuv Maidan."

77. Shuklynov, "Praviy Sektor. Yak i chomu vibukhnuv Maidan."

78. *CBS News*, www.cbsnews.com/news/as-ukraine-protests-grow-slain-demonstrators-mourned/.

79. Risch, "Maidan Chronicle—January 19–20, 2014."

80. "Kolichestvo postradavshikh na Hrusheskogo aktivistov dostiglo 160 chelovek—KGGA," *Ukrainskaya pravda*, January 23, 2014, www.pravda.com.ua/news/2014/01/23/7010891/.

81. Maidan Translations, http://maidantranslations.com/2014/01/22/english-translations-jan-22/.

82. *CBS News*, www.cbsnews.com/news/as-ukraine-protests-grow-slain-demonstrators-mourned/.

83. *YouTube*, https://www.youtube.com/watch?v=n2PTeUBCPAQ; and www.youtube.com/watch?v=0YUDbQ4r6w.

84. "Maidan activists Nihoian and Zhiznevskiy 'not killed by police," *Unian.info*, January 26, 2015, www.unian.info/society/1036260-maidan-activists-nihoian-and-zhiznevskiy-not-killed-by-police.html.

85. Lyubov Melnikova, *Facebook*, November 18, 2015, www.facebook.com/mlnkv/posts/1002533856477859?fref=nf and cited by Ivan Katchanovski, *Facebook*, January 22, 2016.

86. "Ukhvala imenem Ukraini—Sprava No. 757/37009/15-k," Pecherskiy raionniy sudy mista Kiev, *Yediniy Derzhavniy reestr sudovikh rishen,'* October 7, 2015, http://reyestr.court.gov.ua/Review/52580547 and "Ukhvala imenem Ukraini—Sprava No. 757/37002/15-k," Pecherskiy raionniy sudy mista Kiev, *Yediniy Derzhavniy reestr sudovikh rishen,'* October 7, 2015, http://reyestr.court.gov.ua/Review/52580748.

87. Shuklynov, "Praviy Sektor. Yak i chomu vibukhnuv Maidan."

88. "Protestnaya Ukraina—region strany okhvatili masshtabnyie bunty (obnovleno)," *Segodnya Ukraina*, January 24, 2014, www.segodnya.ua/hot/maidan2013/protestnaya-ukraina-regiony-strany-ohvatili-masshtabnye-putchi-491015.html and "Militsiya zaderzhala 58 chelovek," *RBC*, January 24, 2014, http://top.rbc.ru/politics/24/01/2014/901392.shtml and *Lb.ua*, January 24, 2014, http://society.lb.ua/accidents/2014/01/24/252921_militsiya_zaderzhala_58_chelovek_shturm.html.

89. "Protestnaya Ukraina—region strany okhvatili masshtabnyie bunty (obnovleno)," *Segodnya Ukraina*, 24 January 2014, www.segodnya.ua/hot/maidan2013/protestnaya-ukraina-regiony-strany-ohvatili-masshtabnye-putchi-491015.html; "Militsiya zaderzhala 58 chelovek," *RBC*, January 24, 2014, http://top.rbc.ru/politics/24/01/2014/901392.shtml and http://society.lb.ua/accidents/2014/01/24/252921_militsiya_zaderzhala_58_chelovek_shturm.html.

90. See, for example, the violent seizure of the Vinnitsa OGA at "Vinnitsa. Zakhvat oblastnoi gosudarstbennoi administratsii, 25.01.2014," *YouTube*, January 26, 2014, www.youtube.com/watch?v=-qoRDfyZNCg and "V semi oblastyakh Ukrainy razgoraetsya narodnoe vosstanie: aktivisty shtormiruyut OGA i vozvodyat barrikady," *Censor.net*, January 24, 2014, http://censor.net.ua/video_news/267817/v_semi_oblastyah_ukrainy_razgoraetsya_na rodnoe_vosstanie_aktivisty_shturmuyut_oga_i_vozvodya t_barrikady.

91. "Vo L'vove zakhvatyvali OGA, SBU, prokuraturu, militsiyu i nalogovuyu," *Fakty.ua*, February 19, 2014, http://fakty.ua/177020-vo-lvove-zahvatili-oga-sbu-prokuraturu-miliciyu-i-nalogovuyu-foto.

92. Gianluca Mezzofiore, "Ukraine Facing Civil War: Lvov Declares Independence from Yanukovich Rule," *International Business Times*, February 19, 2014, http://www.ibtimes.co.uk/ukraine-facing-civil-war-lviv-declares-independence-yanukovich-rule-1437092. For the view that

this declaration had little or nothing to do to with secession, see "Did Lviv Just Declare Independence?" *Ukrainian Policy*, February 19, 2014, http://ukrainianpolicy.com/did-lviv-just-declare-independence/.

93. "State-Run News Station Accused of Making Up Child Crucifixion," *The Moscow Times*, July 14, 2014, www.themoscowtimes.com/news/article/state-run-news-station-accused-of-making-up-child-crucifixion/503397.html.

94. "Bulatova nikto ne pokhishal—lider Avtomaidana," *Korrespondent*, November 20, 2014, http://korre spondent.net/ukraine/politics/3446285-bulatova-nyktone-pokhyschal-lyder-avtomaidana and "Bulatov—feikovaya figura i ego nikto ne pokhishal," *Podrobnosti.ua*, November 20, 2014, http://podrobnosti.ua/1003884-lider-av tomajdana-bulatov-fejkovaja-figura-i-ego-nikto-ne-pohis chal.html.

95. "One of Maidan leaders kidnapped, tortured and crucified," *Pravda*, January 31, 2014, http://english.pravda.ru/news/hotspots/31-01-2014/126732-maidan_leader_cru cified-0/.

96. "Ukraine Government Says 'Tortured' Activist Dmytro Bulatov Is Both Victim and Suspect," *Kiev Ukraine News Blog*, February 2, 2014, http://news.kievukraine.info/2014/02/ukraine-government-says-tortured.html.

97. "Ukraine Government Says 'Tortured' Activist Dmytro Bulatov Is Both Victim and Suspect."

98. "Bulatova nikto ne pokhishal—lider Avtomaidana."

99. "Na Chornovol napali iz khuliganskikh pobuzhdenii—itogi sledstvii," *Korrespondent*, February 6, 2014, http://korrespondent.net/ukraine/politics/3302182-na-ch ornovol-napaly-yz-khulyhanskykh-pobuzhdenyi-ytohysledstvyia.

100. "Sud osvobodil obvinyaemykh v izbienii Chornovol," *Korrespondent*, April 7, 2015, http://korrespondent.net/ukraine/3500556-sud-osvobodyl-obvyniaemykh-v-yzbyenyy-chornovol.

101. Julia Ioffe and Frank Foer, "Ambassador to Ukraine: The Russian Strategy was Intended to Create Chaos," *New Republic*, May 20, 2014, http://www.newrepublic.com/article/117821/ukraine-conversation-us-ambasador-geoffrey-pyatt.

102. "Breaking: Estonian Foreign Minister Urmas Paet and Catherine Ashton discuss Ukraine over the phone," *You Tube*, March 5, 2014, www.youtube.com/watch?v=ZEgJ0oo3OA8.

103. Katchanovski's initial and revised reports are based on evidence that includes publicly available but largely unreported and misrepresented videos and photos of suspected shooters, statements by the Maidan announcers and leaders, radio intercepts of shooters, "snipers" and commanders of the SBU's special Alfa unit, analysis of ballistic trajectories, eyewitness reports by both Maidan protesters and government special unit commanders, public statements by the government officials, similar ammunition and weapons used against the police and the protesters, and similar types of wounds among both protesters and the police. Ivan Katchanovski, "The 'Snipers' Massacre' on the Maidan in Ukraine," Academia.edu, Paper presented at the Chair of Ukrainian Studies Seminar at the University of Ottawa, Ottawa, October 1, 2014, www.academia.edu/8776021/The_Snipers_Massacre_on_the_Maidan_in_Ukraine, p. 55; and Ivan Katchanovski, "The 'Snipers' Massacre' on the Maidan in Ukraine (Revised and Updated Version)," *Academia.edu*, February 20, 2015, www.academia.edu/8776021/The_Snipers_Massacre_on_the_Maidan_in_Ukraine, p. 55; or *Johnson's Russia List*, #33, February 21, 2015, Institute for European, Russian and Eurasian Studies at George Washington University's Elliott School of International Affairs, http://archive.constant contact.com/fs053/11 02820649387/archive/11029116942 93.html.

104. Konrad Schuller, "Wie kam es zum Blutbad auf dem Majdan?," February 8, 2015, *Frankfurter Allgemeine Zeitung*, www.faz.net/aktuell/politik/ausland/europa/uk raine-die-hundertschaften-und-die-dritte-kraft-134140 18.html; Gabriel Gatehouse, "The untold story of the Maidan massacre," *BBC News Magazine*, February 12, 2015, www.bbc.com/news/magazine-31359021; *Maidan Massacre*, documentary film by John Beck-Hofmann, *You Tube*, February 14, 2015, www.youtube.com/watch?v=Ary_l4vn5ZA; and Vyacheslav Khrypun, "Obshee mnenie boitsov bylo takim, chto nas prosto predali," *Apostrophe.com*, February 20, 2015, http://apostrophe.com.ua/article/society/2015-02-20/obschee-mnenie-boytsovbyilo-takim-chto-nas-prosto predali/1284. For a brief summary of the evidence in the *Frankfurter Allgemeine Zeitung* and BBC investigations, see Graham Stack, "KYIV BLOG: What triggered the Maidan massacre?" *Business News Europe*, February 13, 2015, http://bne.eu/content/story/kyiv-blog-what-triggered-maidan-massacre.

105. Margarita Chimiris, "Kto i kak skryvaet pravdu o rasstrelakh na Maidane," *Vesti Ukraine*, November 20, 2014, http://vesti-ukr.com/strana/78265-kto-i-kak-skry vaet-pravdu-o-rasstrelakh-na-majdane, cited in Katchanovski, "The 'Snipers' Massacre' on the Maidan in Ukraine," p. 15.

106. Katchanovski, "The 'Snipers' Massacre' on the Maidan in Ukraine (Revised and Updated Version)," p. 55.

107. Margarita Chimiris, "Kto i kak skryvaet pravdu o rasstrelakh na Maidane."

108. Vyacheslav Khrypun, "Obshee mnenie boitsov bylo takim, chto nas prosto predali," *Apostrophe.com*, February 20, 2015, http://apostrophe.com.ua/article/society/2015-02-20/obschee-mnenie-boytsov-byilo-takim-chtonas-prosto-predali/1284.

109. Khrypun, "Obshee mnenie boitsov bylo takim, chto nas prosto predali."

110. "Na Maidany strilyav til'ki odin Avtomat AK-74," *YouTube*, November 24, 2014, www.youtube.com/watch ?v=cZz_VOa9REA, cited in Ivan Katchanovski, "The 'Snipers' Massacre' on the Maidan in Ukraine," APSA paper delivered to the American Political Science Association annual conference (from here on identified as "APSA paper"), San Francisco, California, September 3–6, 2015, http://papers.ssrn.com/sol3/papers.cfm?abstract_id=2658 245, p. 14.

111. See the photograph shot in evening with a series of pro–Maidan demonstrators wearing helmets and holding shields with one demonstrator in the foreground whose helmet bears a white letter "V" in a white circle at "Ukraine. 2014. Kiev, February 18th. Maidan square clashes," *Cesura.it*, www.cesura.it/projectGallery.php?pagineCod=2205416.

112. *Maidan Massacre*, documentary film by Beck-Hofmann.

113. "'Pravyi sektor' otvetil SBU: 'ob"yavil 'aktsiyu prinuzhdeniya k miru," *Ukrainskaya pravda*, February 20, 2014, www.pravda.com.ua/rus/news/2014/02/20/7014989/.

114. Katchanovski, "The 'Snipers' Massacre' on the Maidan in Ukraine (Revised and Updated Version)."

115. Katchanovski, "The 'Snipers' Massacre' on the Maidan in Ukraine (Revised and Updated Version)," and *Maidan Massacre*, documentary film by Beck-Hoffman.

116. Katchanovski, "The 'Snipers' Massacre' on the Maidan in Ukraine," pp. 14–15; Schuller, "Wie kam es zum Blutbad auf dem Majdan?"; Gatehouse, "The untold story of the Maidan massacre"; *Maidan Massacre*, documentary film by John Beck-Hofmann; Khrypun, "Obshee mnenie boitsov bylo takim, chto nas prosto predali"; and Sonya Koshkina, "Vozrozhdenie Rady," *Lb.ua*, February 22, 2014, http://lb.ua/news/2014/02/22/256600_vozrozhdenie_radi.html.

117. Chimiris, "Kto i kak skryvaet pravdu o rasstrelakh na Maidane," cited in Katchanovski, "The 'Snipers' Massacre' on the Maidan in Ukraine," p. 15.

118. Chimiris, "Kto i kak skryvaet pravdu o rasstrelakh na Maidane"; Koshkina, "Vozrozhdenie Rady"; Katchanovski, "The 'Snipers' Massacre' on the Maidan in Ukraine," p. 15; Gatehouse, "The untold story of the Maidan massacre"; *Maidan Massacre*, documentary film by John Beck-Hofmann; and Koshkina, "Vozrozhdenie Rady."

119. "Zvit TCK shodo podii 18–20 lyutogo v Kievi," *Offitsialnyi sait Gennaddiy Moskal*," May 7, 2014, www.moskal.in.ua/?categoty=news&news_id=1099.

120. "Bogoslovskaya: est' video, gde muzhchina v forme 'Berkut' strelyaet po Maidanu i silovikam," *Lb.ua*, February 21, 2014, http://lb.ua/news/2014/02/21/256446_bogoslovskaya_video_gde.html.

121. Gatehouse, "The untold story of the Maidan massacre."

122. Katchanovski, "The 'Snipers' Massacre' on the Maidan in Ukraine," p. 21.

123. Katchanovski, "The 'Snipers' Massacre' on the Maidan in Ukraine," p. 32, Map 1, and pp. 33–52.

124. "Maidan—February 20, 2014 (3)," *YouTube*, February 20, 2014, www.youtube.com/watch?v=PXwLuDlhfIE, last accessed May 7, 2015.

125. Katchanovski, "The 'Snipers' Massacre' on the Maidan in Ukraine," p. 32, Map 1, and pp. 33–52. See also the numerous sources cited by Katchanovski, in particular the BBC documentary—Gatehouse, "The untold story of the Maidan massacre"—and the UkrLife documentary—"Dvadtsyat' svidchen' pro perelamnii den' protistoyan' na Maidani (English subtitles)."

126. Zvit TSK shodo podii 18–20 lyutogo v Kyevi."

127. At the time a group identifying itself as the "Ukrainian Insurgent Army" or UPA—apparently named after the World War II Nazi-allied Ukrainian organization responsible for mass murders of Jews and Poles—claimed responsibility for the February 20 massacre. This could have been a RS and/or SP subunit. A group calling itself UPA also claimed responsibility for the murder of five Opposition Bloc and former Party of Regions deputies and a journalist in 2015. Danil Yevtukhov, "Ubiitsy Buziny iz 'UPA' vpervyie zasvetilis' vo vremya Yevromaidana," *Podrobnosti*, April 17, 2015, http://podrobnosti.ua/2029175-vpervye-upa-zasvetilas-v-ubijstve-militsionera-vo-vremja-evromajdana.html. On the claim for the 2015 murders, see "'Oppozitsionyi Blok' zayavil ob ugrozakh ot 'Ukrainskoi povstancheskoi armii,'" *Korrespondent*, April 17, 2015, http://korrespondent.net/ukraine/3504818-oppozytsyonnyi-blok-zaiavyl-ob-uhrozakh-ot-ukraynskoi-povstanch eskoi-armyy?hc_location=ufi.

128. Katchanovski, "The 'Snipers' Massacre' on the Maidan in Ukraine"; *Maidan Massacre*, documentary film by John Beck-Hofmann; and Khrypun, "Obshee mnenie boitsov bylo takim, chto nas prosto predali." It should be emphasized that in coming to conclusions in his study, Katchanovski crosschecks data from numerous sources and reports including those from the BBC and *Frankfurter Allgemeine Zeitung*.

129. Gatehouse, "The untold story of the Maidan massacre."

130. Schuller, "Wie kam es zum Blutbad auf dem Majdan?"

131. Oksana Kovalenko, "Sotnik, yakii perelomiv khid istorii: Treba bulo dotiskati," *Ukrainskaya Pravda*, February 24, 2014, www.pravda.com.ua/articles/2014/02/24/7016048/.

132. Katchanovski, "The 'Snipers' Massacre' on the Maidan in Ukraine," APSA paper, p. 20.

133. Kovalenko, "Sotnik, yakii perelomiv khid istorii: Treba bulo dotiskati."

134. Schuller, "Wie kam es zum Blutbad auf dem Majdan?"

135. Katchanovski, "The 'Snipers' Massacre' on the Maidan in Ukraine," APSA paper, p. 20.

136. "Protiv Semenchenko vozbudili ryad ugolovnykh del," *Vesti Ukraina*, February 11, 2016, http://vesti-ukr.com/strana/135685-protiv-semenchenko-vozbudili-rjad-ugolovnyh-del.

137. Yevgenii Shvets, "Igor Mazur: Na Maidani buli lyudi, yaki strilyali po 'Berkutu.' Ya—ne zmig," *LB.ua*, April 4, 2014, http://lb.ua/news/2014/04/04/261907_igor_mazur_bilogo_%20odnoznachno.html.

138. Stack, "KYIV BLOG: What triggered the Maidan massacre?"

139. Katchanovski, "The 'Snipers' Massacre' on the Maidan in Ukraine," p. 19; *Maidan Massacre*, documentary film by John Beck-Hofmann.

140. Khrypun, "Obshee mnenie boitsov bylo takim, chto nas prosto predali."

141. Khrypun, "Obshee mnenie boitsov bylo takim, chto nas prosto predali."

142. "Dvadtsyat' svidchen' pro perelamnii den' protistoyan' na Maidani (English subtitles)," *UkrLife*, May 27, 2014, www.youtube.com/watch?v=vs_4skLIqns.

143. Margarita Chimiris, "Kto i kak skryvaet pravdu o rasstrelakh na Maidane," cited by Katchanovski, "The 'Snipers' Massacre' on the Maidan in Ukraine, "APSA paper.

144. Gatehouse, "The untold story of the Maidan massacre," and Katchanovski, "The 'Snipers' Massacre' on the Maidan in Ukraine," APSA paper, p. 15.

145. Katchanovski, "The 'Snipers' Massacre' on the Maidan in Ukraine," APSA paper, p. 15. For the sources for the two "112 Ukraina" broadcast videos and the other video showing the warning from the stage and so on, see Katchanovski, "The 'Snipers' Massacre' on the Maidan in Ukraine," APSA paper, p. 68, fns 48, 49, and 50.

146. Katchanovski, "The 'Snipers' Massacre' on the Maidan in Ukraine," APSA paper, p. 17. Katchanovski's sources, see APSA paper, p. 69, fn 55.

147. Katchanovski, "The 'Snipers' Massacre' on the Maidan in Ukraine"; Chimiris, "Kto i kak skryvaet pravdu o rasstrelakh na Maidane"; and Gatehouse, "The untold story of the Maidan massacre."

148. "Spetsnazovets Asavelyuk rasskazal kak ego rasstrelivali maidanshiki," *YouTube*, February 25, 2014, www.youtube.com/watch?v=FlhoUCQVODQ.

149. "200214," *YouTube*, March 17, 2014, www.youtube.com/watch?v=0YUDbQ-4r6w, last accessed on 16 February 2016.

150. ZDF Special, Professor Ivan Katchanovski's Facebook Page, Facebook.com, March 13, 2015, www.facebook.com/video.php?v=989716864391533&pnref=story.

151. "Ukraine: Snipers target police in Independence Square," *YouTube*, February 20, 2014, www.youtube.com/watch?v=n2PTeUBCPAQ, last accessed on 16 February 2016.

152. "Ukraine: Ruptly reporter shot by Maidan sniper," *YouTube*, February 20, 2014, www.youtube.com/watch?v=wzqlxUGnzIs, last accessed February 16, 2016.

153. Ivan Siyak, "Ivan Bubenchik: 'Ya ubil ikh v zatylok. Eto pravda," *Bird in Flight*, February 19, 2016, https://birdinflight.com/ru/mir/ivan-bubenchik-ya-ubil-ih-v-zatylok-eto-pravda.html.

154. Siyak, "Ivan Bubenchik: 'Ya ubil ikh v zatylok. Eto Pravda."

155. "Zvit TCK shodo podii 18–20 lyutogo v Kievi."

156. "Amnesty International konstantirovala otsutsvii progressa v rassledovanii ubiistv na Maidane i v Odesse," *Vesti Ukraina*, February 24, 2016, http://vesti-ukr.com/kiev/137366-amnesty-international-konstratirovala-otsut

stvii-progressa-v-rassledovanii-ubijstv-na-majdane-i-v-odesse.

157. Vladimir Ivakhchenko and Andrei Sharii, "V Protsesse raskritiya," *Radio Svoboda*, May 8, 2015, www.svoboda.org/content/article/26963387.html.

158. A total of 57 were from the ten westernmost regions in and around Galicia, and 36 were from Ukraine's 16 other regions. There were six foreigners: three from Georgia, two from Belarus, and one from Russia. One victim's residence and place of birth were not indicated. Calculated from "Nebesnaya sotna," http://nebesnasotnya.com.ua/ru/, last accessed February 25, 2016.

159. Katchanovski, "The 'Snipers' Massacre' on the Maidan in Ukraine," pp. 29, 47–48.

160. "Kolossalnoi oshibkoi byla poterya trekh mesyatsev rassledovaniya," *112.ua*, January 25, 2016, http://112.ua/interview/kolossalnoy-oshibkoy-byla-poterya-pervyh-treh-mesyacev-rassledovaniya-sobytiy-maydana-287156.html.

161. Katchanovski, "The 'Snipers' Massacre' on the Maidan in Ukraine," APSA paper, p. 5, and Mariya Zhartov'ska, "Sdichiy u spravi Maidanu: V 'Berkuta' faktichno vubulasya lishe zmina nazvi," *Ukrainskaya pravda*, January 23, 2015, www.pravda.com.ua/rus/articles/2015/01/23/7056061/.

162. Steve Stecklow and Oleksandr Akymenko, "Special Report: Flaws found in Ukraine's probe of Maidan massacre," Reuters, October 10, 2014, www.reuters.com/article/2014/10/10/us-ukraine-killings-probe-special-report-idUSKCN0HZ0UH20141010.

163. Ivan Katchanovski, "January 28 at 9:35 P.M.," Facebook, January 28, 2016, www.facebook.com/ivan.katchanovski/posts/1167164089980142?pnref=story and Ivan Katchanovski, "February 6 at 4:37 P.M.," Facebook, February 6, 2016, https://www.facebook.com/ivan.katchanovski/posts/1172375942792290.

164. "Sud pochav rpzglyad spravi she tr'okh eks-berkutivtsiv," *YouTube*, January 26, 2016, www.youtube.com/watch?v=RgBoTKewzVQ.

165. "Ukhvala imenem Ukraini—Sprava No. 757/42824/15-k," Pecherskiy raionniy sudy mista Kiev, *Yediniy Derzhavniy reestr sudovikh rishen*,' November 20, 2015, http://reyestr.court.gov.ua/Review/54278484; "Ukhvala imenem Ukraini—Sprava No. 757/47700/15-k," Pecherskiy raionniy sudy mista Kiev, *Yediniy Derzhavniy reestr sudovikh rishen*,' December 23, 2015, http://reyestr.court.gov.ua/Review/54672972; "Ukhvala imenem Ukraini—Sprava No. 757/13417/15-k," Pecherskiy raionniy sudy mista Kiev, *Yediniy Derzhavniy reestr sudovikh rishen*,' April 23, 2015, http://reyestr.court.gov.ua/Review/52100569; and "Ukhvala imenem Ukraini—Sprava No. 757/39038/15-k," Pecherskiy raionniy sudy mista Kiev, *Yediniy Derzhavniy reestr sudovikh rishen*,' October 30, 2015, http://reyestr.court.gov.ua/Review/53868110. In addition, there is an investigation of involvement in the Maidan massacre of two robbers of a jewelry store arrested in Kremenchuk in May 2015. The registration number of one of the robbers' Makarov pistol matches one taken during the seizure of the SBU headquarters in Ivano-Frankivsk on February 18, 2014 by the Maidan protesters and, according to the GPO, was used possibly to shoot police on the Maidan on February 20, 2014. "Ukhvala imenem Ukraini—Sprava No. 757/40033/15-k," Pecherskiy raionniy sudy mista Kiev, *Yediniy Derzhavniy reestr sudovikh rishen*,' October 29, 2015, http://reyestr.court.gov.ua/Review/53416626. The names of the two Kremenchuk robbery suspects were not made public, but were reported to have stated during the robbery that they fought in unidentified units during the civil war in Donbas. "Strilyanina u Kremenchutsi: v misti lovili garbizhnikiv, yaki stverdzhuvali, scho vony—z ATO, Hromadskoe TV," *YouTube*, May 19, 2015, https://www.you

tube.com/watch?v=OqC9SfQZQcw. Hennadii Moskal, the governor of the Transcarpathian Region, stated in January 2016 that a handgun confiscated from one RS activist during a recent attack on a ski resort in the region was also taken during the seizure of the SBU offices in Ivano-Frankivsk on February 18, 2014. "Odin iz pistoletiv, viluchenikh vid predstavnikiv 'Pravogo sektora' na 'Dragobaty,' buv vikradenii y lyutomu 2014 roku pid chas zakhlopennya upravlinnya SBU v Ivano-Frankiviskiy oblasti," *Zakarpat'ska oblasna derzhanva administratsiya*, January 16, 2016, www.carpathia.gov.ua/ua/publication/content/12885.htm. All that is cited in this footnote is based on Ivan Katchanovski, "January 26 at 2:43," Facebook, January 26, 2016, www.facebook.com/ivan.katchanovski/posts/1165670110129540.

166. "Ukhvala imenem Ukraini—Sprava No. 757/26405/15-k," Pecherskiy raionniy sudy mista Kiev, *Yediniy Derzhavniy reestr sudovikh rishen*,' August 5, 2015, http://reyestr.court.gov.ua/Review/48107496 and Katchanovski, "January 26 at 2:43."

167. "Ukhvala imenem Ukraini—Sprava No. 757/37009/15-k," Pecherskiy raionniy sudy mista Kiev, *Yediniy Derzhavniy reestr sudovikh rishen*,' October 7, 2015, http://reyestr.court.gov.ua/Review/52580547 and "Ukhvala imenem Ukraini—Sprava No. 757/37002/15-k," Pecherskiy raionniy sudy mista Kiev, *Yediniy Derzhavniy reestr sudovikh rishen*,' October 7, 2015, http://reyestr.court.gov.ua/Review/52580748.

168. "Roku slidchiy suddya Pechers'kogo raionnogo sudu m. Kieva Karaban' V.M., pri sekretari Maiorenko Ya.M., za uchastyu storoni kriminal'nogo provadzhennya slidchogo Nechitalyuka M.M.," Ukhvala Imenem Ukrainiy, Sprava No. 757/5885/16-k, Pecherskiy Raionniy Sud Mista Kieva," Ediniy derzhavniy ryeestr sudovikh rishen,' *Reyestr.court.gov.ua*, February 12, 2016, http://reyestr.court.gov.ua/Review/55966993. See also Ivan Katchanovski, "Maidan Shootings," Facebook, March 6, 2016, 11.29 a.m., https://www.facebook.com/ivan.katchanovski?fref=ts and Ivan Katchanovski, "Maidan Shootings," Facebook, March 6, 2016 in *Johnson's Russia List*, #39, Issue 46, March 7, 2016, Institute for European, Russian, and Eurasian Studies at The George Washington University's Elliott School of International Affairs, http://archive.constantcontact.com/fs053/1102820649387/archive/1102911694293.html.

169. "Nalyvaichenko obvinil sovetnika Putina v organizatsii rasstrelov na Maidane," *Vesti Ukraina*, February 20, 2015, http://vesti-ukr.com/kiev/89706-nalivajchenko-obvinil-sovetnika-putina-v-organizacii-rasstrelov-na-majdane and "Nalyvaichenko: Surkov keruvav snaiperami—inozemtsyami na Maidani," *Ukrainskaya pravda*, February 19, 2015, www.pravda.com.ua/news/2015/02/19/7059184/.

170. "Pochemu possorilis' Poroshenko i Nalyvaichenko," *Vesti Ukraina*, June 15, 2015, http://vesti-ukr.com/strana/103514-pochemu-possorilis-poroshenko-i-nalivajchenko.

171. Serhiy Leschenko, "Nalyvaichenko protiv Surkova—stsenariy dlya Medvedchuka," *Ukrainskaya pravda*, April 16, 2015, http://blogs.pravda.com.ua/authors/leschenko/552ee534b5a10/.

172. "Valentin Nalyvaichenko podderzhal rebyat iz 'Pravogo sektora' Zarkapat'ya," *Anons Zakarpat'ya*, July 12, 2015, http://anons.uz.ua/news/politics/21855-valentin-nalivaychenko-podderzhal-rebyat-iz-pravogo-sektora-zakarpatya.html.

173. "GPU sobiraet u naseleniya gilzy i shlemy s Maidana," *Vesti Ukraine*, April 29, 2015, http://video.vesti-ukr.com/strana/3837-gpu-sobiraet-u-naselenija-gilzy-i-shlemy-s-majdana.

174. Ivakhchenko and Sharii, "V Protsesse raskritiya."

175. Katchanovski, "The 'Snipers' Massacre' on the

Maidan in Ukraine," APSA paper, p. 5; Mariya Zhartov'ska, "Sdichiy u spravi Maidanu: V 'Berkuta' faktichno vubulasya lishe zmina nazvi," *Ukrainskaya pravda*, January 23, 2015, www.pravda.com.ua/rus/articles/2015/01/23/7056061/.

176. "Shokin: V rasstrele nebesnoi sotni rossiiskiy sled ne obnaruzhen," *Vesti Ukraina*, October 16, 2015, http://vesti-ukr.com/kiev/119327-shokin-v-rasstrele-nebesnoj-sotni-rossijskij-sled-ne-obnaruzhen.

177. "Troe zamestitelei Tyahniboka pribyli na dopros v Genprokuraturu," *Liga.net*, October 16, 2015, http://news.liga.net/news/politics/6870914-troe_zamestiteley_tyagniboka_pribyli_na_dopros_v_genkprokuraturu.htm.

178. "Marsh geroiv u stol'nomu gradi," *Pravyysektor.info*, October 14, 2015, http://pravyysektor.info/news/news/999/marsh-geroyiv-u-stolici.html; Alina Bondareva, "Marsh natsionalistov v Kieve: v aktsii uvideli nachalo protivostoyaniya s vlast'yu," *Vesti Ukraina*, October 15, 2015, http://vesti-ukr.com/kiev/119107-marsh-nacionalistov-v-kieve-v-akcii-uvideli-nachalo-protivostojanija-s-vlastju.

179. "Report of the International Advisory Panel on its review of the Maidan Investigations," Council of Europe International Advisory Council, March 31, 2015, https://rm.coe.int/CoERMPublicCommonSearchServices/DisplayDCTMContent?documentId=09000016802f038b and Allison Quinn "International report finds numerous failures in Maidan murders investigation," *Kyiv Post*, March 31, 2015, http://www.kyivpost.com/content/kyiv-postplus/international-report-findsnumerous-failure-in-investigation-into-maidan-shootings-384957.html.

180. Amnesty International Report 2015/16: The State of the World's Human Rights, *Amnesty.org*, February 23, 2016, www.amnesty.org/en/documents/pol10/2552/2016/en/, p. 378.

181. "Interpol vidmovivsya rozshukuvati bepkutivt-siv—GPU," *Ukrinform*, April 15, 2015, www.ukrinform.ua/ukr/news/interpol_vidmovivsya_rozshukuvati_berkutivt siv___gpu_2043451.

182. "GPU peredala FBR video s mest rasstrelov na Maidane," *LB.ua*, June 13, 2014, http://lb.ua/news/2014/06/13/269720_gpu_peredala_fbr_video_mest.html.

183. For an English translation of the agreement, see the German Foreign Ministry's website text at "Agreement on the Settlement of Crisis in Ukraine—full text," Website of the German Foreign Ministry, February 21, 2014, www.auswaertiges-amt.de/cae/servlet/contentblob/671350/publicationFile/190051/140221-UKR_Erklaerung.pdf or "Agreement on the Settlement of Crisis in Ukraine—full text," *The Guardian*, February 21, 2014, www.theguardian.com/world/2014/feb/21/agreement-on-the-settlement-of-crisis-in-ukraine-full-text.

184. Mick Krever, "Putin phone call convinced Yanukovych to change attitude, says Polish foreign minister," *Amanpour Blog, CNN.com*, February 26, 2014, http://amanpour.blogs.cnn.com/2014/02/26/vladimir-putin-viktor-yanukovych-radoslaw-sikorski-ukraine-poland-russia/.

185. Michael Weiss, "Can Radek Sikorski Save Europe?" *Foreign Policy*, May 2, 2014, www.foreignpolicy.com/articles/2014/04/30/can_radek_sikorski_save_europe_poland_russia_ukraine.

186. Katchanovski, "The 'Snipers' Massacre' on the Maidan in Ukraine," p. 21.

187. Lesley Wroughton and Roberta Rampton, "Obama, Putin agree on need to ensure Ukraine deal works," *Reuters*, February 22, 2014, www.reuters.com/article/2014/02/22/us-ukraine-crisis-obama-idUSBREA1K1FF20140222.

188. Sam Frizell, "Ukraine Proesters Seize Kiev as President Flees," *Time*, February 22, 2014, updated 11:06am EST, http://world.time.com/2014/02/22/ukraines-president-flees-protestors-capture-kiev/.

189. "Konstitutsiya Ukrainy," *Nezavisimaya gazeta-Stsenarii*, August 29, 1996, pp. 3–5, at pp. 4–5. The 1996 Ukrainian constitution was amended in 2004 and 2010, but the articles on impeachment were never changed.

190. Maria Popova, "Was Yanukovych's Removal Constitutional?," *Ponars*, March 20, 2014, www.ponarseurasia.org/article/was-yanukovych%E2%80%99s-removal-constitutional.

191. Popova, "Was Yanukovych's Removal Constitutional?"

192. "Remarks by President Obama before Restricted Bilateral Meeting," *White House*, February 20, 2014, www.whitehouse.gov/the-press-office/2014/02/19/remarks-president-obama-restricted-bilateral-meeting.

193. For one of the clearest examples of Maidan protesters' warfare, see the video of the Kiev street fighting on February 18, 2014. "18 lyutogo 2014r., biy na rozy Kryposnogo provulku ta Instituts'koy," *YouTube*, June 24, 2014, www.youtube.com/watch?v=Osb8oC4gm20&ebc=ANyPx Kq0mZmQ4PHsP3Rdo6kGY2zwPxay2ATNsAZib5_Qh pmdGPamTSf9pfOM7Q8nTU6iengGm0yE2XO1c-2I6lB vQMbfIrpXtA, last accessed on March 17, 2016.

194. "Statement by the Press Secretary on Ukraine," *White House*, February 22, 2014 www.whitehouse.gov/the-press-office/2014/02/22/statement-press-secretary-ukraine.

195. "Statement by the Press Secretary on Ukraine," *White House*, February 26, 2014, www.whitehouse.gov/the-press-office/2014/02/26/statement-press-secretary-ukraine.

196. "Ukraine MPs appoint interim president as Yanukovych allies dismissed—February 23 as it happened," *The Guardian*, February 23, 2014, www.theguardian.com/world/2014/feb/23/ukraine-crisis-yanukovych-tymoshenko-live-updates.

197. Daisy Sindelar, "Was Yanukovych's Ouster Constitutional?" *RFERL*, February 23, 2014, www.rferl.org/content/was-yanukovychs-ouster-constitutional/25274346.html.

198. "President Putin's Fiction: 10 False Claims About Ukraine," U.S. State Department 'Diplomacy in Action,' March 5, 2014, www.state.gov/r/pa/prs/ps/2014/03/222988.htm.

199. "Zayavlenie MID Rossii po situatsiyam na Ukraine," Ministry of Foreign Affairs of the Russian Federation, Mid.ru, February 27, 2014, www.mid.ru/press_service/spokesman/official_statement/-/asset_publisher/t2G CdmD8RNIr/content/id/73254.

200. *Vystuplenie i otvety na voprosy Ministra innostrannykh del Rossii S. V. Lavrov na Forume 'Territoriya smyslov na Klyaz'me,' Vladimirskaya oblast,' d.Dvorkin, 24 August 2015.*

201. "Second Anniversary of Ukraine's Revolution of Dignity"—Press Statement, U.S. Department of State, February 20, 2016, www.state.gov/r/pa/prs/ps/2016/02/2530 92.htm.

202. U.S. Ambassador Geoffrey Pyatt, "Making Good on the Promise of the Maidan," U.S. Embassy Kyiv Blog, February 19, 2016, https://usembassykyiv.wordpress.com.

203. "Zayavlenie MID Rossii po situatsiyam na Ukraine."

204. "'Interesy RF and SShA v otnoshenii Ukrainy nesovmestimy drug s drugom,'" *Kommersant*, December 19, 2014, www.kommersant.ru/doc/2636177.

205. "Ukraine crisis: Transcript of leaked Nuland-Pyatt call," *BBC*, February 7, 2014, www.bbc.com/news/world-europe-26079957.

Chapter 8

1. For Talne, Cherkasy, see "18+ Shturm. Titushek vytashili c avtobusov/STORM bus with TITUSHKAMI,"

YouTube, February 23, 2014, www.youtube.com/watch?v=KIAYDSZPD-Q, last accessed 27 February 2016; "TAL'NE Zlovili tik sho tikali," *YouTube*, February 20, 2014, www.youtube.com/watch?v=aFXfG66TckE, last accessed January 15, 2016; and "TAL'NE koridor gan'by dlya titushok," *YouTube*, February 20, 2014, www.youtube.com/watch?v=qkd4G0lJYOU, last accessed January 15, 2016. For the RS activist, see the PS patch on one of the members of the mob seizing the bus near the end of the video at "Tal'noe Cherkassy perekhvat avtobusa titushek," *YouTube*, February 20, 2014, www.youtube.com/watch?v=nJ8T-5CPUmg. For Korsun-Shenkovskiy, see, "Izbienie titushek," *YouTube*, February 20, 2014, www.youtube.com/watch?v=jcCRP8Fchxc, last accessed on September 18, 2015.

2. "Krym trebuet ot Yanukovicha vvesti chrezvychainoe polozhenie," *Segodnya.ua*, December 2, 2013, www.segodnya.ua/regions/krym/parlament-kryma-prosit-yanukovicha-vvesti-v-strane-chrezvychaynoe-polozhenie-479304.html and "Krym trebuet ot Yanukovicha vvesti chrezvychainoe polozhenie v Kieve, Galichina—bastuet," *Regnum.ru*, December 2, 2013, www.regnum.ru/news/polit/1739759.html.

3. "Krym prizyvaet rukovodstvo oblastei Yugo-Vostoka Ukrainy 'vystupit' edinym frontom protiv silovogo zakhvata vlasti," *Regnum.ru*, January 24, 2014, www.regnum.ru/news/polit/1758533.html.

4. "Stenograma zasedannya Rady natsional'noi bezpeki i oborony Ukrainy, vid 28 lyutogo 2014 roku shodo sitsuatsii, yaka skalalsya v derzhavi kyntsy lyutogoberozni 2014 roky (pitanyaya aneksii Avtonomnoi Respubliki Krym," *Rady natsional'noi bezpeki i oborony Ukrainy*, February 22, 2016, www.rnbo.gov.ua/files/2016/stenogr.pdf, pp. 8–9.

5. "'Krym—eto russkaya avtonomiya': vlasti Kryma khotyat poprosit' Rossiyu o zashite i pomoshi," *Regnum.ru*, February 4, 2014, www.regnum.ru/news/polit/1762771.html.

6. "Rossiya dolzhna vospol'zovat'sya situatsiei i vernut' sebe Donbass i Krym—Vladimir Zhirinovskii," *Regnum.ru*, February 19, 2014, www.regnum.ru/news/polit/1769071.html.

7. "V Kharkove S'ezd deputatov vzyal na sebe obespechenie konstitutsionnogo poryadka," *TV Dozhd,'* February 22, 2014, http://tvrain.ru/teleshow/here_and_now/v_harkove_sezd_deputatov_vzjal_na_sebja_obespechenie_konstitutsionnogo_porjadka-363559/ and "Yugovostochnyie oblasti Ukrainy, Krym i Sevastopol' ob'yavili o samoupravlenii do navedeniya poryadka v Kieve," *Regnum.ru*, February 22, 2014, www.regnum.ru/news/polit/1770240.html.

8. "Krym budet reshat' problemy samostoyatel'no, bez pomoshi' Rossii—spiker Verkhovnogo Soveta," *Regnum.ru*, February 20, 2014, www.regnum.ru/news/polit/1769502.html.

9. "Krym. Put' na Rodinu," *Rossiya 1 TV*, March 16, 2015, http://russia.tv/video/show/brand_id/59195/episode_id/1180834/video_id/1147633/.

10. The quote in my text is from Paul Goble, "Putin Aide Linked to Maidan Killings," Window on Eurasia posted in *Johnson's Russia List*, No. 32, February 20, 2015, http://russialist.org/putin-aide-linked-to-maidan-killings/. Catherine Fitzpatrick concurred weeks later in Catherine Fitzpatrick, "Putin's Usual Suspects: The Bullshit Chechen Charlie Hebdo Connection," *The Daily Beast*, March 9, 2015, www.thedailybeast.com/articles/2015/03/09/putin-s-usual-suspects-the-bullshit-chechen-charlie-hebdo-connection.html.

11. See Dmitrii Muratov Interview, "Osobie mnenie," *Ekho Moskvy*, February 18, 2015, echo.msk.ru/programs/personalno/1494328-echo/.

12. Rohan, "Saakashvili 'planned S. Ossetian invasion': ex-minister."

13. Natalya Galimova, "My idyom v Rossiyu. Kak—ne znayu," *Gazeta.ru*, March 12, 2015, www.gazeta.ru/politics/2015/03/11_a_6503589.shtml.

14. Interview with Aleksei Venediktov, Program *Bez Obid*, LTV7 (Latvia), May 4, 2015, www.youtube.com/watch?v=9RdrcCI6TtQ.

15. "Turchinov provodit zasedanie SNBO po ugroze separatizma v Ukraine," *Ukraine Online*, February 25, 2014, http://ukr-online.com/politic/2321-turchinov-provodit-zasedanie-snbo-po-ugroze-separatizma-v-ukraine.html.

16. "Delegatsiya Soveta Federatsii posetit Krym," *Regnum.ru*, February 25, 2014, www.regnum.ru/news/polit/1771389.html.

17. "GosDuma dolzhna obsudit' vooruzhennuyu ekspansiyu Kieva v Krym—glava komiteta," *Regnum.ru*, February 26, 2014, www.regnum.ru/news/polit/1771541.html.

18. Galimova, "My idyom v Rossiyu. Kak—ne znayu."

19. "Pravyi sector grozit Krymu, UPA, poezd druzhby," *YouTube*, March 19, 2014, www.youtube.com/watch?v=6BXUFCDmvG0; "'Pravyi sektor' grozit Krymu prislat' poezd druzhby," *YouTube*, March 21, 2014, www.youtube.com/watch?v=o4–81TScFvY.

20. "Crimea. Way Back Home. Episode 6—Greeting Right Sector's Train of Friendship. Simferopol Airport," LiveLeak, March 19, 2015, www.liveleak.com/view?i=1df_1426815885. For the entire film in Russian, see "Krym—put' na Rodinu," *Rossiya TV*, March 2015, https://russia.tv/brand/show/brand_id/59195.

21. "'Pravyi sector' poobeshal otpravit' v Sevastopol 'poezd druzhby," *Novosti Sevastopolya*, February 25, 2014, www.sevnews.info/rus/view-news/Pravyj-sektor-hochet-otpravit-v-Sevastopol-poezd-druzhby/13543; and "'Pravyi sector' prigrozil otpravit v nedovolnyi Sevastopol' karatel'nyui 'poezd druzhby," *Sevas*, February 26, 2014, http://news.sevas.com/politics/pravyj_sektor_grozit_sevastopolyu_karatelnymi_otryadami_i_poezdami_druzhby.

22. "Stones, bottles thrown as pro–, anti–Russian protesters clash in Crimea," *Russia Today*, February 26, 2014, http://rt.com/news/crimea-ukraine-protest-clashes-840/.

23. Galimova, "My idyom v Rossiyu. Kak—ne znayu."

24. "Stones, bottles thrown as pro–, anti–Russian protesters clash in Crimea."

25. Galimova, "My idyom v Rossiyu. Kak—ne znayu."

26. "Stones, bottles thrown as pro–, anti–Russian protesters clash in Crimea" and "Video: Stones, bottles & shoes thrown as pro– & anti–Russian protesters clash in Ukraine's Crimea," *YouTube*, February 26, 2014, https://youtu.be/QuZohqW3aBE, last accessed May 26, 2015.

27. Galimova, "My idyom v Rossiyu. Kak—ne znayu."

28. Galimova, "My idyom v Rossiyu. Kak—ne znayu."

29. Galimova, "My idyom v Rossiyu. Kak—ne znayu."

30. "SBU ustanovila lichnost' rossiiskogo diversanta Strelka," *Liga.net*, April 28, 2014, http://news.liga.net/news/politics/1534120-sbu_ustanovila_lichnost_rossiyskogo_diversanta_strelka.htm.

31. "Girkin: My nasil'no sgonyali deputatov Kryma golosovat za otdelenie ot Ukrainy," *YouTube*, January 24, 2015, www.youtube.com/watch?v=QVb6iJb1c48, last accessed May 28, 2015.

32. Galimova, "My idyom v Rossiyu. Kak—ne znayu."

33. Galimova, "My idyom v Rossiyu. Kak—ne znayu."

34. "SBU ustanovila prichastnost' rossiiskogo razvedchika k diversiyam v Slavyanske," *LB.ua*, April 15, 2014, http://lb.ua/news/2014/04/15/263196_sbu_ustanovila_prichastnost.html.

35. See Girkin-Strelkov's July 2014 press conference in Donetsk at "Igor' Strelkov o sebe," *Youtube.com*, July 10,

2014, www.youtube.com/watch?v=oz2tUtWQpx0, last accessed June 1, 2015. See his See also Dmitrii Vinogradov, "Boevyie zaslugy: Kto nauchil voevat' Igorya Strelkova," *Svobodnaya pressa*, June 5, 2014, http://svpressa.ru/soci ety/article/89194/?twrss=1&utm_source=svpressa&utm_ medium=twitter and Ostap Zhukov, "Strelkov rasskazal, kak sluzhil v FSB i gde voeval," *Moskovskii komsomolets*, July 12, 2014, www.mk.ru/politics/2014/07/12/strelkov-rass kazal-kak-sluzhil-v-fsb-i-gde-voeval.html.

36. Vinogradov, "Boevyie zaslugy: Kto nauchil voevat' Igorya Strelkova"; Zhukov, "Strelkov rasskazal, kak sluzhil v FSB i gde voeval"; and "Komandir Donetskikh terroristov sluzhit v FSB, lubit rekonstruktsii i druzhit s geyami, FOTOreportazh," *Censor.net.ua*, April 29, 2014, http://cen sor.net.ua/photo_news/283194/komandir_donetskih_ter roristov_girkin_slujit_v_fsb_lyubit_rekonstruktsii_i_dru jit_s_geyami_fotoreportaj.

37. "Komandir Donetskikh terroristov sluzhit v FSB, lubit rekonstruktsii i druzhit s geyami, FOTOreportazh."

38. "Geroi pod grifom 'Sekretnoi,'" *Novaya gazeta*, No. 64, June 16, 2014, www.novayagazeta.ru/inquests/64030. html and "Spetsturisty," *Novaya gazeta*, No. 71, July 2, 2014, www.novayagazeta.ru/inquests/64242.html.

39. Galimova, "My idyom v Rossiyu. Kak—ne znayu."

40. Galimova, "My idyom v Rossiyu. Kak—ne znayu."

41. Galimova, "My idyom v Rossiyu. Kak—ne znayu."

42. Galimova, "My idyom v Rossiyu. Kak—ne znayu."

43. Galimova, "My idyom v Rossiyu. Kak—ne znayu."

44. Galimova, "My idyom v Rossiyu. Kak—ne znayu."

45. Hahn, *Russia's Islamic Threat*, pp. 179–98.

46. Galimova, "My idyom v Rossiyu. Kak—ne znayu."

47. "Krym. Put' na Rodinu."

48. Galimova, "My idyom v Rossiyu. Kak—ne znayu."

49. Galimova, "My idyom v Rossiyu. Kak—ne znayu."

50. In February the referendum was originally scheduled to coincide with the Ukrainian presidential election, May 25.

51. "Prospects of Crimea: Regional Status," *National Security and Defence*, No. 10, 2008, www.razumkov.org. ua/eng/files/category_journal/NSD104_eng_2.pdf, p. 19.

52. "Security Problems of the Black Sea Region and the Crimea in Experts' Assessments," *National Security and Defence*, Nos. 4–5, 2011, www.razumkov.org.ua/eng/files/ category_journal/NSD122-123_eng.pdf, pp. 21–6, at pp. 21 and 24.

53. Public Opinion Survey Residents of the Autonomous Republic of Crimea—May 16–30, 2013, International Republican Institute and the United States Agency for International Development, May 2013, www.iri.org/ sites/default/files/2013%20October%207%20Survey%20of %20Crimean%20Public%20Opinion,%20May%2016– 30,%202013.pdf, p. 17.

54. Public Opinion Survey Residents of the Autonomous Republic of Crimea—May 16–30, 2013, pp. 14–15.

55. Public Opinion Survey Residents of the Autonomous Republic of Crimea—May 16–30, 2013, p. 16.

56. "The Crimea on the Political Map of Ukraine," *National Security and Defence*, No. 4, 2001, www.razumkov. org.ua/eng/files/category_journal/NSD16_eng.pdf, pp. 2– 39, at p. 3.

57. "Dannyie oprosa v Krymu podtverdyatsya na refereendume, schitayut eksperty," *RIA Novosti*, March 11, 2014, http://ria.ru/world/20140311/999032876.html.

58. "Despite Concerns about Governance, Ukrainians Want to Remain One Country," Global Attitudes, *Pew Research Center*, May 8, 2014, www.pewglobal.org/2014/05/ 08/despite-concerns-about-governance-ukrainians-want-to-remain-one-country/.

59. "Newsgathering and Policy Perceptions in Ukraine," *Gallup*, April 2014, http://www.bbg.gov/wp-content/me dia/2014/06/Ukraine-slide-deck.pdf, p. 25–27.

60. "L'vov predupredil Krym o vooruzhennikh boevikakh," *Regnum.ru*, February 26, 2014, www.regnum.ru/ news/polit/1771928.html.

61. Galimova, "My idiom v Rossiyu. Kak—ne znayu."

62. "Putin: Sravnivat' Krym s Yuzhnoi Osetiei i Abkhaziei nel'zya," *Regnum.ru*, December 19, 2013, www.reg num.ru/news/polit/1747547.html.

63. "Russia keeps pressure on Ukraine with Crimea Standoff," BBC, March 4, 2014, www.bbc.com/news/ world-europe-26430846 and "Tense Standoff between Russian, Ukrainian Soldiers in Crimea Ends," Reuters on *YouTube.com*, March 4, 2014, www.youtube.com/watch?v =H_TmpjMA2x4

64. See the 54–55 second mark in the video at "From Bullets to Footballs: Ukraine Belbek Airforce Base Standoff Defused," *Euronews*, March 4, 2014, www.euronews. com/2014/03/04/stop-or-we-ll-shoot-standoff-at-ukraine-s-belbek-base/.

65. "Stenograma zasedannya Rady natsional'noi bezpeki i oborony Ukrainy, vid 28 lyutogo 2014 roku shodo sitsuatsii, yaka skalalsya v derzhavi kyntsy lyutogo-berozni 2014 roky," p. 34.

66. "Ukrainian Troops Move Toward Crimean Peninsula Border," *YouTube.com*, March 9, 2014, www.youtube. com/watch?v=DpkLVt9aWEU.

67. "Pushkov: 'Esho nemnogo, i my ushlishim, chto Krym—eto tozhe Turtsiya,'" *Regnum.ru*, November 4, 2013, www.regnum.ru/news/polit/1727831.html.

68. Documentary film "Prezident," *Rossiya 1 TV*, April 26, 2015, http://russia.tv/video/show/brand_id/59329/ episode_id/1193264/video_id/1165983/viewtype/picture.

69. Galimova, "My idiom v Rossiyu. Kak—ne znayu."

Chapter 9

1. Pyatt, "Making Good on the Promise of the Maidan."

2. Keith Gessen, "Why not kill them all?" *London Review of Books*, September 11, 2014, www.lrb.co.uk/v36/n17/ keith-gessen/why-not-kill-them-all.

3. Alexander Dyukov, "There is no Intolerance for Nazism in Ukraine," *Grupa Informatsii za zlochinami proti osobi*, August 4, 2014, http://igcp.eu/publikacii/alexander-dyukov-there-no-intolerance-nazism-ukraine?language =en and Marina Baltacheva, "'Ukraina postratdala ot fashizma chuzhogo, seichas on svoi," *Delovaya gazeta*, August 1, 2014, www.vz.ru/politics/2014/8/1/698299.html.

4. "Kolorady vs Ukropy: Kakie slova podarili Ukraine Maidan i voina," *Korrespondent*, June 6, 2014, http://kor respondent.net/ukraine/politics/3374179-koloradу-vs-ukropy-kakye-slova-podaryly-ukrayne-maidan-y-voina.

5. Tatyana Shcherbatchyuk, "10 sliv i fraz, scho uviyshly do vzhitku Vinnichan 2014-ogo roku," *Vlasno.info*, January 10, 2015, http://vlasno.info/suspilstvo/7/tochka-zoru/item/ 1073-10-sliv-i-fraz-shcho-uviishly-do-vzhytku-vinnychan-2014-ho-roku.

6. See the video at "Oplot vatnikov Sevastopol' nado sravnyat' so zemlei—Krymskaya aktivistka," *Odnoklassniki.ru*, February 21, 2015, http://ok.ru/video/6937118113, last accessed on March 8, 2016.

7. See, for example, "Kiev. 'Moskaliv na nozhi' Marsh v chest' dlya rozhdeniya S. Bandery," *YouTube*, January 1, 2015, www.youtube.com/watch?v=epwfd5P8u9I, last accessed on March 8, 2016; "Kherson fakelnoe shestvie 21 02 15 (Moskaly na nozhi)," *Bing Videos*, February 21, 2015, www.bing.com/videos/search?q=%D0%9C%D0%BE %D1%81%D0%BA%D0%B0%D0%BB%D1%96%D0%B2+ %D0%BD%D0%B0+%D0%BD%D0%BE%D0%B6%D1% 96!+youtube&qpvt=%D0%9C%D0%BE%D1%81%D0%B A%D0%B0%D0%BB%D1%96%D0%B2+%D0%BD%D0% B0+%D0%BD%D0%BE%D0%B6%D1%96!+youtube&vie w=detail&mid=3D72F5E3CAFFF2BD49103D72F5E3CAF

FF2BD4910&rvsmid=5CAB554CE540E71148B35CAB554 CE540E71148B3&FORM=VDMCNR&fsscr=0; "Shturm Rady nazvaly repetitsiei budushikh bubntov," *Vesti Ukraina*, October 15, 2014, http://vesti-ukr.com/strana/73361-shturm-rady-nazvali-repeticiej-buduwih-buntov. Follow this search string link for a series of demonstrations in Ukraine using the "Russians on the knife" chant: www.bing.com/videos/search?q=%D0 %9C%D0%BE%D1%81%D0%BA%D0%B0%D0%BB%D1%96%D0%B2+%D0%BD%D0%B0%D0%B6%D1%96!+youtube&qpvt=%D0%9C%D0%BE%D1%81%D0%BA%D0%B0%D0%BB%D1%96%D0%B2+%D0%BD%D0%B0+%D0%BD%D0%BE%D0%B6%D1%96!+youtube&view=detail&mid=2D11E4667548C5B2CDB52D11E4667548C5B2CDB5&rvsmid=5CAB554CE540E71148B35CAB554CE540E71148B3&FORM=VDQVAP&fsscr=0. Such manifestations were prevalent before 2014 but less so. See for example, "RUSSIA & UKRAINE. 'Get' moskaliv na nozhi," *YouTube*, September 29, 2011, www.youtube.com/watch?v=lSGqlV65TwI, last accessed on March 8, 2016.

8. See, for example, "Vatnik. Otkuda vzaylos' Kto ne skachet, tot Moskal," *Krasview*, March 1, 2016, http://krasview.ru/video/655732-Vatnik-otkuda_vzyalos_Kto_ne_skachet_tot_Moskal, last accessed on March 8, 2016 and "Studgorodok KNY im. Shevchenko 09.04.14 Khto ne skache, toi moskal.' Moskaliv na nozhi," *YouTube*, April 8, 2014, www.youtube.com/watch?v=oBrgaFH02UE, last accessed on March 8, 2016.

9. "Moskaly na nozhi," *YouTube*, April 20, 2014, www.youtube.com/watch?v=tyXToXTNDpc, last accessed on May 17, 2014.

10. Dyukov, "There is no Intolerance for Nazism in Ukraine," and "Ukrainskii zhurnalist predlozhil ubit' 1,5 mln zhitelei Donbassa," *Delovaya gazeta*, August 1, 2014, www.vz.ru/news/2014/8/1/698288.html.

11. Dmytro Korchinskiy's comments on Ukraine's channel "112," June 17, 2015 at "Na ukrainskom TV prizvali k sozdaniyu kontslagerei dlya zhitelei Donbassa," *YouTube*, June 17, 2015, www.youtube.com/watch?v=HSv3fixJPc4, last accessed April 5, 2016.

12. The complete relevant sections read: "We will commemorate the heroes by cleaning our land from the evil." "We bow our heads to the heroes who lost their lives for the sake of their country, to prevent the war from coming into the house of each of us." "They lost their lives because they defended men and women, children and the elderly who found themselves in a situation facing a threat to be killed by invaders and sponsored by the inhumans. First, we will commemorate the heroes by wiping out those who killed them and then by cleaning our land from the evil." See "My uvichnimo pam'yat geroiv, ochistivshi nashu zemlyu vid nichisti, Arsenii Yatsenyuku spyvchutti ridnim i bliz'kim zagiblikh voiniv u Lugans'ku," *Ukrainian Embassy in the United States of America*, June 15, 2014 http://usa.mfa.gov.ua/ua/press-center/news/24185-mi-uvichnimo-pamjaty-gerojiv-ochistivshi-nashu-zemlyu-vid-nechis tiarsenij-jacenyuk-u-spivchutti-ridnim-i-blizykim-zagib lih-vojiniv-u-lugansyku and "Rosiyski ZMI pidozryuyut' Yatsenyuka v natsists'kikh vislovlyuvannyakh," *Rakurs*, June 18, 2014, http://ua.racurs.ua/news/29502-rosiyski-zmi-pidozruut-yacenuka-v-nacystskyh-vyslovluvannyah.

13. Shcherbatchyuk, "10 sliv i fraz, scho uviyshly do vzhitku Vinnichan 2014-ogo roku."

14. "Interview: The Benefits of a Partitioned Ukraine," *RFERL*, February 20, 2014, www.rferl.org/content/ukraine-split-partition-/25270988.html.

15. Pietro Sarkisian, "Equalization and Dehumanization in Eastern Ukraine," *Reconsidering Russia*, March 7, 2015, http://reconsideringrussia.org/2015/03/07/equalization-and-dehumanization-in-eastern-ukraine/. For an attempt by Motyl to equate the Donbass with American

Southern racists, see Alexander Motyl, "Ukraine's Donbas is Like America's Deep South," *Huffington Post*, January 5, 2015, www.huffingtonpost.com/alexander-motyl/alexan der-motyl_b_6414802.html.

16. Carl Bildt, "Eurasia versus Europe in the streets of Kiev. Tonight…," *Twitter*, December 10, 2013, https://twitter.com/carlbildt/status/410661410599751680.

17. "Saakashvili: Ukraina zashishaet Yevropu ot tataro-mongolskogo iga," *Novyi region*, November 15, 2014, http://nr2.com.ua/News/Kiev_and_regions/Saakashvili-Uk raina-zashchishchaet-Evropu-ot-tataro-mongolskogo-iga-84741.html.

18. Dyukov, "There is no Intolerance for Nazism in Ukraine," and Baltacheva, "'Ukraina postradala ot fash-izma chuzhogo, seichas on svoi.'"

19. "Pravyi Sektor vzyal shturmom Verkhovnyi Sud Ukrainy—Chrezvychainyie novosti—07.04," *YouTube*, April 7, 2014, www.youtube.com/watch?v=jitMYO-xCc8, last accessed on March 7, 2016.

20. Gessen, "Why not kill them all?"

21. "Violent video: Ukraine TV boss beaten up by far right Svoboda MPs," *Euronews*, March 19, 2014, www.youtube.com/watch?v=F5GeBpZ5VHY, last accessed on March 10, 2014.

22. "Gubernator Khersonskoi oblasti zayavil ob ot-stavke pod ugrozoi nozha," *From-ua.com*, March 4, 2014, http://from-ua.com/news/302378-gubernator-hersonskoi -oblasti-zayavil-ob-otstavke-pod-ugrozoi-nozha.html.

23. "Pravyi Sektor na sessii v Vasil'kove. Regionaly otkazasilis' pet' gimn Ukrainy???" *YouTube*, February 25, 2014, www.youtube.com/watch?v=9fKIq8fE1CE.

24. "Hammer-wielding nationalists storm town council meeting in Kiev suburbs (VIDEOS)," *Russia Today*, March 4, 2014, www.rt.com/news/nationalists-storm-council-meeting-701/.

25. For Donetsk, see "Massovaya boinya v Donetske slabonervnym ne smotret," *YouTube*, March 2014, www.youtube.com/watch?v=kMY-9PjwS28, last accessed on March 14, 2016. For Kharkiv, see "Boitsy 'Pravogo Sektora' na kolenyakh prosyat prosheniya pered kharkovchanami," *YouTube*, March 2, 2014, www.youtube.com/watch?v=VJNJOtEbmR0, last accessed on March 14, 2016.

26. Svetlana Gamova, "V Tiraspole zhdut napadeniya s yuga Ukrainy," *Nezavisimaya gazeta*, August 7, 2014, www.ng.ru/cis/2014-08-07/1_tiraspol.html.

27. See, for example, Lyasho attacking pro–Yanukovych Kharkiv Governor at "Lyashko nabil mordu Dobkinu," *YouTube*, May 24, 2014, https://www.youtube.com/watch?v=CaHT78OQbpo, last accessed on March 10, 2016. See Lyashko pushing a security guard around at "Lyashko ustroil potasovku s okhrannikom na Bankovoi. Polnaya versiya (04-04-2013)," *YouTube*, April 5, 2013, www.youtube.com/watch?v=XlPfht-Cpqk, last accessed on March 10, 2016.

28. Oleg Lyashko, *Facebook*, May 23, 2014, https://m.facebook.com/story.php?story_fbid=646486682086599&id=100001758206922.

29. The pro–Maidan Kiev Post later removed the incriminating video. See "Militia backed by presidential candidate Lyashko takes credit for assassination of Russian-backed separatist (VIDEO)," *Kyiv Post*, May 23, 2014, www.kyivpost.com/content/ukraine/militia-backed-by-presidential-candidate-lyashko-takes-credit-for-murder-of-russian-backed-separatists-349093.html. See also Richard Balmforth and Natalia Zinets, "Ukraine's 'pitchfork' populist could be wild card in new line-up," *Reuters*, October 19, 2014, www.reuters.com/article/us-ukraine-cri sis-idUSKCN0I80A520141019 and Charles McPhedran, "Thug Politics," *ForeignPolicy.com*, October 9, 2014, www.foreignpolicy.com/articles/2014/10/09/thug_politics_kiev _oleh_lyashko_radical_ukraine. For the video, see "Lyashko

Mocks Detained Defense Chief Donetsk. 07.05.2014," *You Tube*, May 8, 2014, www.youtube.com/watch?v=LLI-KDt zOLw.

30. See the video at "Lyashko segodnya v Slavyanske: Zhestkie razborki s merom Slavtanska!!!," *YouTube*, July 9, 2014. www.youtube.com/watch?v=gdr6M--9SZM.

31. Balmforth and Zinets, "Ukraine's 'pitchfork' populist could be wild card in new line-up."

32. Christopher J. Miller, "'Vigilante' Ukrainian lawmaker Lyashko gets slammed by Amnesty International report," *Kyiv Post*, August 6, 2014, www.kyivpost.com/article/content/ukraine/amnesty-international-criticizes-vigilante-ukrainian-lawmaker-lyashko-359586.html.

33. Miller, "'Vigilante' Ukrainian lawmaker Lyashko."

34. Arsen Avakov, "Lozh' i pravda," *Ekho Moskvy*, June 17, 2014, http://echo.msk.ru/blog/echomsk/1342014-echo/.

35. Miller, "'Vigilante' Ukrainian lawmaker Lyashko."

36. See, for example, "Pravyi Sektor na sessii v Vasil'kove. Regionaly otkazasilis' pet' gimn Ukrainy???" *You Tube*, February 25, 2014, www.youtube.com/watch?v= 9fK Iq8fE1CE, last accessed on March 12, 2016 and "Arest separatista DNR. Batal'on Dnepr | 05.08.14," *YouTube*, August 5, 2014, www.youtube.com/watch?v=UXnNDbJ7r0k &feature=youtu.be, last accessed on March 12, 2016.

37. "Yanukovich uvolil konaduyshchego Sukhoputnymi voiskami," *Ukrainskaya pravda*, January 17, 2014, www.pravda.com.ua/rus/news/2014/01/17/7009861/.

38. Jan Cienski, "Oligarch tries to stamp Kiev authority on restive east," *Financial Times*, March 6, 2014," www.ft.com/cms/s/c427c7dc-a558-11e3-8070-00144feab7de.html; "The End of the Beginning?" *The Economist*, March 8, 2014, www.economist.com/news/briefing/21598744-having-occupied-crimea-russia-stirring-up-trouble-eastern-ukraine-end.

39. "SMI: Nad 'bespokoinymi' regionami letayut ukrainskie istrebiteli," *Ukrainskaya pravda*, April 7, 2014, www.pravda.com.ua/rus/news/2014/04/7/7021640/ and Gessen, "Why not kill them all?"

40. "Kak v Donetske, zakhvatyvali OGA—Chrezvychainyie novosti, 07.04," *YouTube*, April 7, 2014, www.youtube.com/watch?v=C12ewZOQxAM; "Kak prorossiiskie separatisty segodnya zakhvatyvali zdanie Donetskoi OGA (VIDEO)," *Munitsipal'naya gazeta*, April 6, 2014, http://mungaz.net/main/l1622-kak-prorossiyskie-separatisty-segodnya-zahvatyvali-zdanie-donetskoy-oga-video.htm; and "Spetsnaz osvobodil zakhvachennoe separatistami zdanie SBU v Donetske," *Ukrainskaya pravda*, April 16, 2014, www.pravda.com.ua/rus/news/2014/04/7/7021678/; "Voskresnyi shturm DonOGA v fotografiyakh," *Novosti Donbassa*, April 6, 2014, http://novosti.dn.ua/details/22 1959/; "Separatisty vystavali ultimatum: referendum o vkhozhdenii Donetsloi oblasti v sostav RF," *Novosti Donbassa*, April 6, 2014, http://novosti.dn.ua/details/221964/; "Ukraine: Pro-Russians storm offices in Donetsk, Luhansk, Kharkiv," BBC, April 7, 2014, www.bbc.com/news/world-europe-26910210; "Ukraine Crisis: Protesters declare Donetsk 'republic,'" BBC, April 7, 2014, www.bbc.com/news/world-europe-26919928.

41. "Voskresnyi shturm DonOGA v fotografiyakh."

42. "Ukraine: Pro-Russians storm offices in Donetsk, Luhansk, Kharkiv"; "Ukraine Crisis: Protesters declare Donetsk 'republic'"; "Kak v Donetske, zakhvatyvali OGA—Chrezvychainyie novosti, 07.04"; "Kak prorossiiskie separatisty segodnya zakhvatyvali zdanie Donetskoi OGA (VIDEO)"; and "Spetsnaz osvobodil zakhvachennoe separatistami zdanie SBU v Donetske."

43. Alec Luhn, "Pro-Russian occupiers of Ukrainian security service building voice defiance," *The Guardian*, April 10, 2014, www.theguardian.com/world/2014/apr/10/luhansk-protesters-occupy-security-headquarters.

44. "Ukraine: Pro-Russians storm offices in Donetsk,

Luhansk, Kharkiv"; "Ukraine Crisis: Protesters declare Donetsk 'republic'"; "Kak v Donetske, zakhvatyvali OGA—Chrezvychainyie novosti, 07.04"; "Kak prorossiiskie separatisty segodnya zakhvatyvali zdanie Donetskoi OGA (VIDEO)"; and "Spetsnaz osvobodil zakhvachennoe separatistami zdanie SBU v Donetske."

45. "Lugansk vo vlasti separatistov: kak zakhvatyvaly OGA, militsiyu, prokuraturu i sud," *BigMir.net*, April 29, 2014, http://news.bigmir.net/ukraine/812829-Lugansk-vo-vlasti-separatistov--kak-zahvatyvali-OGA--miliciju--prokuraturu-i-sud.

46. For Kharkiv (Kharkov), see "V Khar'kove osvobodili OGA, no popytalis' zakhvatit televyshku," *Ukrainskaya pravda*, April 7, 2014, www.pravda.com.ua/rus/news/2014/04/7/7021681/. For Nikolaev, see "V Nikolaev stolknulis' storonniki Maidana i separtisty. Lyubitelei Putina zastavili uiti," *Ukrainskaya pravda*, April 7, 2014, www.pravda.com.ua/rus/news/2014/04/7/7021682/.

47. "Trebovaniya Luganskikh boevikov pochti takie, kak u Rossii," *Ukrainskaya pravda*, April 7, 2014, www.pravda.com.ua/rus/news/2014/04/7/7021654/; Alan Yuhas and Tom McCarthy, "Crisis in east Ukraine: a city-by-city guide to the spreading conflict," *The Guardian*, April 16, 2014, www.theguardian.com/world/2014/apr/16/crisis-east-ukraine-city-by-city-guide-map.

48. "Kto oni, 'narodnyie gubernatory': Khar'kov vozglavil avtoslesar', Luhansk—desantnik," *Komsomolskaya pravda*, April 23, 2014, www.kp.by/daily/26224.3/3106364/.

49. "Trebovaniya Luganskikh boevikov pochti takie, kak u Rossii."

50. The crowd of several thousand surrounds the SBU building, later chanting "Russia! Russia!" Those closest to the building simply push their way past the several- deep police line without even the use of sticks, clubs or other implements, and some climb to the roof of the entrance vestibule and break windows to enter on the second floor. Some break windows by throwing bricks, tiles and stones; others appear to have started the fire which engulfs the entrance. The whole affair looks like winter 2013–14 in Kiev, minus the firearms. See "06.04.2014 Zakhvat zdaniya SBU v Luganske," *YouTube*, April 6, 2014, www.youtube.com/watch?v=a1bTEa4SSbY, last accessed on March 25, 2016.

51. "Turchynov: Protiv vooruzhenykh separatistov provedut antiterroristicheskie operatsii," *Ukrainskaya pravda*, April 7, 2014, www.pravda.com.ua/rus/news/2014/04/7/7021616/.

52. "Protiv separatistov mogut primenit' spetssredstva i spetsnaz," *Ukrainskaya pravda*, April 7, 2014, www.pravda.com.ua/rus/news/2014/04/7/7021674/.

53. "Turchinov nazval rukovoditelya antiterroristicheskogo tsentra," *Ukrainskaya pravda*, April 7, 2014, www.pravda.com.ua/rus/news/2014/04/7/7021653/ and "Turchynov: Protiv vooruzhenykh separatistov provedut antiterroristicheskie operatsii."

54. Laura Smith-Spark and Kellie Morgan, "Ukraine unrest will be resolved by force or talks within 48 hours, minister says," CNN, April 10, 2014, http://edition.cnn.com/2014/04/09/world/europe/ukraine-crisis/index.html.

55. "Turchynov prikazal vzyat pod gosokhranu zdanie Donetsloi OGA," *Ukrainskaya pravda*, April 9, 2014, pravda.com.ua/rus/news/2014/04/9/7021915/.

56. "Turchynov gotov osvobodit' separtistov, bez kriminala, esli oni slozhat oruzhie," *Ukrainskaya pravda*, April 10, 2014, www.pravda.com.ua/rus/news/2014/04/10/7021944/.

57. "Ukraine Crisis: Protesters declare Donetsk 'republic.'"

58. "SBU: Yanukovicha kontroliruet rossiiskaya voennaya razvedka," *Ukrainskaya pravda*, April 16, 2014, www.pravda.com.ua/rus/news/2014/04/16/7022681/.

59. Alec Luhn, "East Ukraine protesters joined by miners on the barricades," *The Guardian*, April 12, 2014, www.theguardian.com/world/2014/apr/12/east-ukraine-protesters-miners-donetsk-russia.

60. Roland Oliphant, "Fears of full-scale Russian invasion as eastern Ukraine cities toppled," *Telegraph* (UK), April 12, 2014, www.telegraph.co.uk/news/worldnews/europe/ukraine/10763008/Fears-of-full-scale-Russian-invasion-as-eastern-Ukraine-cities-toppled.html; "Donetsskii 'Berkut' pereshel na storonu mitinguyushikh," *LifeNews*, April 12, 2014, http://lifenews.ru/news/131113; and "Armed pro–Russian extremists launch coordinated attacks in Donetsk Oblast, Seize regional police headquarters, set up checkpoints (UPDATE)," *Kyiv Post*, April 12, 2014, www.kyivpost.com/article/content/ukraine/armed-pro-russian-extremists-seize-police-stations-in-donetsks-slavyansk-shaktarysk-fail-to-take-donetsk-prosecutors-office-343195.html.

61. "Kak zakhvatyvali OGA i prokuraturu v Luganske," *BBC Russian Service*, April 14, 2014, www.bbc.com/ukrainian/multimedia_russian/2014/04/140430_ru_gallery_lugansk.

62. "Zdanie Donetskogo gorsovetazakhvatili aktivisty Kharkovskoi organizatsii 'Oplot,'" *TASS*, April 16, 2014, http://tass.ru/mezhdunarodnaya-panorama/1125050.

63. Gabriel Baczynska, "Separatists in Ukraine's Donetsk vow to take full control of region," *Reuters*, April 14, 2014, www.reuters.com/article/us-ukraine-crisis-donetsk-idUSBREA3D1A320140414.

64. See the photos at "Mesyats okkupatsii. Slavyansk," *LB.ua*, May 12, 2014, http://lb.ua/news/2014/05/12/266103_dim_donbassa.html.

65. "Mesyats okkupatsii. Slavyansk."

66. "V Slavyanske nachalas' Antiterroristicheskaya operatsiya—Avakov," *Ukrainskaya pravda*, April 13, 2014, www.pravda.com.ua/rus/news/2014/04/13/7022234/.

67. "Mesyats okkupatsii. Slavyansk" and "Ukraine Army Launches 'Anti-Terror' Operation," *Sky News*, April 14, 2014, http://news.sky.com/story/1241376/ukraine-army-launches-anti-terror-operation.

68. "Mesyats okkupatsii. Slavyansk."

69. "Ukraine Army Launches 'Anti-Terror' Operation."

70. "Geneva Statement on Ukraine," *EU External Action Service*, April 17, 2014, www.eeas.europa.eu/statements/docs/2014/140417_01_en.pdf.

71. Julian Borger and Alec Luhn, "Ukraine crisis: Geneva talks agreement on defusing conflict," *The Guardian*, April 17, 2014, www.theguardian.com/world/2014/apr/17/ukraine-crisis-agreement-us-russia-eu.

72. Yekaterina Stulen,' "Boets 'Pravogo sektora' vzorval sebya i dvukh 'zelenikh chelovechkov,'" *Vesti Ukraina*, April 17, 2014, http://vesti-ukr.com/donbass/48168-boec-pravogo-sektora-vzorval-sebja-i-dvuh-zelenyh-chelovechkov.

73. See the SBU statement at "Shchodo zbroinoi provokatsii u Paskhal'nu nich bilya m. Slov'yansk," *Sluzhba bezopeki Ukrainy*, April 20, 2014, www.sbu.gov.ua/sbu/control/uk/publish/article?art_id=124389&cat_id=39574. See also "SBU: Separatisty s rossiiskimy diversantami instsenirovali napadenie na blokpost Slavyanska," *Gordonua.com*, April 20, 2014, http://gordonua.com/news/separatism/sbu-separatisty-s-rossiyskimi-diversantami-inscenirovali-vneshnee-napadenie-na-blokpost-slavyanska-19184.html.

74. "V SNBO raskritikovali lzhivyie soobshcheniya Rossiiskoi pressy o perestrelke v Slavyanske," *TSN.ru*, April 20, 2014, http://ru.tsn.ua/politika/v-snbo-raskritikovali-lzhivye-soobscheniya-rossiyskoy-pressy-o-perestrelke-v-slavyanske-361755.html.

75. Aleksandr Vasovic and Alissa De Carbonnell, "Deadly gun attack in eastern Ukraine shakes fragile Geneva accord," Reuters, April 20, 2014, www.reuters.com/article/us-ukraine-crisis-idUSBREA3A1B520140420.

76. "Pravyi sector otritsaet svoyu prichastnost' k perestrelke v Slavyanske," *Korrespondent*, April 20, 2014, http://korrespondent.net/ukraine/politics/3352145-pravyi-sektor-otrytsaet-svoui-prychastnost-k-perestrelke-v-slavianske.

77. "Pravyi sector otritsaet svoyu prichastnost' k perestrelke v Slavyanske."

78. Vasovic and De Carbonnell, "Deadly gun attack in eastern Ukraine shakes fragile Geneva accord."

79. "Dmitro Yarosh: nam she Krim povertati," BBC (Ukrainian), February 11, 2015, www.bbc.com/ukrainian/politics/2015/02/150211_yarosh_interview_vs and Yurii Butusov, "Dmitro Yarosh: Pershii nastupatel'nyi biy viyny vibuvsya 20 kvytnya 2014-go—dobrovoltsy atakovali blokpost pid Slovyans'kom," *Censor.net*, April 22, 2016, http://censor.net.ua/resonance/385673/dmitro_yarosh_pershiyi_nastupalniyi_byi_vyini_vdbuvsya_20_kvtnya_2014go_dobrovolts_atakovali_blokpost.

80. Butusov, "Dmitro Yarosh: Pershii nastupatel'nyi biy viyny vibuvsya 20 kvytnya 2014-go—dobrovoltsy atakovali blokpost pid Slovyans'kom."

81. "Drugim zagiblim, znaidenim razom iz deputatom Gorlivskoi mis'kradi Ribakom, buv stident KPI—rektor," *Interfaks*, April 25, 2014, http://ua.interfax.com.ua/news/general/202342.html.

82. "DUK 5-I Okremii Batal'ion," *VKontakte*, October 12, 2014, http://archive.is/4a5bM, cited in Ivan Katchanovski, "January 26 at 2:43," *Facebook*, January 26, 2016, www.facebook.com/ivan.katchanovski/posts/1165670110129540.

83. "Ukhvala imenem Ukraini—Sprava No. 757/428 24/15-k"; "Ukhvala imenem Ukraini—Sprava No. 757/47700/15-k"; and "V Slavyanske Pravyi sektor atakoval blokpost, pogibli troe zhitelei," *YouTube*, April 8, 2015, www.youtube.com/watch?v= 9J3bp6Ml4ag; all cited in Katchanovski, "January 26 at 2:43."

84. "Luhansk prosecutors launch probes into federalization support rallies," *Interfax-Ukraine*, April 21, 2014, http://en.interfax.com.ua/news/general/201534.html and "V Luganske separatisty reshili provesti dva referenduma," *Ukrainskaya pravda*, April 21, 2014, www.pravda.com.ua/rus/news/2014/04/21/7023176/.

85. "Luhansk prosecutors launch probes into federalization support rallies."

86. "Latest from the Special Monitoring Mission to Ukraine—based on information received up until 28 April 2014, 19:00 (Kyiv time)," *Organization on Security and Co-operation in Europe*, April 28, 2014, www.osce.org/ukraine-smm/118153 and "Federalization supporters in Luhansk proclaim people's republic," *Tass*, 28 April 2014, http://tass.ru/en/world/729768.

87. "29/04/2014 Pervomaisk Luganskaya oblast,'" *YouTube*, posted by Aleksandr Anikin, April 29, 2014, www.youtube.com/watch?v=NYnQKnwwcwE, last accessed on March 25, 2016.

88. "Srochno! Sessiya Pervomaisk Liganskaya Oblast' 29.04.2014," *YouTube*, posted by Aleksandr Anikin, April 29, 2014, www.youtube.com/watch?v=NYnQKnwwcwE, last accessed March 26, 2016.

89. "29.04.14 Lugansk Pervomaisk pod Rossiiskom flagom," *YouTube*, posted by InfoVoina, April 29, 2014, www.youtube.com/watch?v=jcUiH_Mi6y4, last accessed on March 25, 2016.

90. Perhaps the most comprehensive compilation, more than four hours of raw footage beginning from the street fighting in the city center, can be found at "Odessa. Tragediya 2-ogo maya 2014 goda. Ot nachal i do … kontsa," *YouTube*, December 19, 2014, www.youtube.com/watch?v=vRXHVSjV1IM, last accessed on March 27, 2016.

For a similarly long, raw video beginning after the city street fighting from the storm of Kulikovo Field, see "Odessa dom profsoyuzov POLNOE VIDEO," *YouTube*, May 2, 2014, www.youtube.com/watch?v=s9AMjLBIliw, last accessed on March 28, 2016. A good collection of links to videos and other material can be found at "Ne 46, a 189 chelovek unichtozheno v Odesse 2 maya…," *Stikhi.ru*, May 5, 2014, www.stihi.ru/2014/05/05/5404, last accessed on March 27, 2016. An early journalistic account with photographs and video is available at "Massovyie besporyadki v Odesse. Khronika sobytii," *Ekho Moskvy*, May 2, 2014, http://echo.msk.ru/blog/echomsk/1312248-echo/, last accessed on March 28, 2016. For an eyewitness account just after the events by one of the people trapped in the building, see "04.05.2014, Odessa Osvobozhdennyi iz GorUVD activist antimaidana," *YouTube*, May 4, 2014, www.youtube.com/watch?v=w7DLMvs HmcI, last accessed on May 28, 2016. Several documentary films seek to sort out the facts and contain much of the same footage. See Ulrich Heyden, German documentary film "Lauffleuer," at "lauffleuer—Rassledovanie zlodeyanii Odesse 2 maya 2014 (Nemetskii s subtitrami na russkom yazyke)," *YouTube*, March 13, 2015, https://www.youtube.com/watch?v=WZ6WDfAx1LM&feature= youtu.be, last accessed on March 27, 2016, and Paul Moreira, French documentary film *Ukraine—Les Masques De La Revolution*, at *The Daily Motion*, February 2, 2016, www.dailymotion.com/video/x3pxmfe_ukraine-les-masques-de-la-revolution_tv, last accessed on March 27, 2016.

91. Eugene Trofymenko, "ATO Po-narodnomu, Abo chomu ne Vladimir Putin ne vviv viyska," *Pravyisektor.info*, May 2, 2014, http://pravyysektor.info/articles/ato-po-narodnomu-abo-chomu-ne-vladimir-putin-ne-vviv-vijska/, archived at http://archive.is/y12mT, last accessed on March 27, 2016.

92. "Anons richnytsi 2 travnya v Odesi," *Pravyysektor.info*, May 1, 2015, http://pravyysektor.info/news/anons-richnytsi-2-travnya-v-odesi/.

93. "Odesa, 2 travnya 2014, ho roku zhadaymo—video," *Pravyysektor.info*, May 2, 2015, http://pravyysektor.info/news/odesa-2-travnya-2014-ho-roku-zhadajmo-video/.

94. Aleksandr Garmatenko, "Na traurnom mitinge v Odesse skandirovali 'Ne zabudem, ne prostim'," *Vesti Ukraina*, May 2, 2015 http://vesti-ukr.com/odessa/98618-na-kulikovom-pole-proshel-traurnyj-miting.

95. Paul Moreira, *Ukraine—Les Masques De La Revolution*.

96. "Andrei Parubiy podaril dobrovol'tsam odesskoi samoborony sovremennyie bronezhilety," *YouTube*, April 29, 2014, www.youtube.com/watch?v=8tVITa8wegQ.

97. See the interview with Fuchedzhi at "Byvshii zamnachalnik odesskoi militsii Dmitrii Fechudzhi rasskazal o sobytiyakh v Odesse 2 maya," *1TV* (Russia), May 22, 2014, www.1tv.ru/news/world/259433.

98. Il'ya Azar, "Zdes' polmaidana, chego esho zhdat'?" *Ekho Moskvy*, May 5, 2014, http://echo.msk.ru/blog/azar_i/1313892-echo/. See also "Massovyie besporyadki v Odesse. Khronika sobytii."

99. "Eto moi narod?" *YouTube*, May 2, 2014, www.youtube.com/watch?v=IVXm9nnY-AQ#t=412, last accessed on March 28, 2016.

100. "Odessa, 02.05.2014, 'Kill Them All!!!'" *YouTube*, May 4, 2014, www.youtube.com/watch?v=5E12kkFM3nQ, last accessed on March 28, 2016.

101. "Odessa beginning pravy sector flags inside," *YouTube*, May 7, 2014, www.youtube.com/watch?v=5HOfLxp8961&feature=youtu.be, last accessed on March 28, 2016.

102. "Odessa pravy sector inside the customs house," *YouTube*, May 7, 2014, www.youtube.com/watch?v=VaCV xP_QApk&feature=youtu.be, last accessed on March 28, 2016.

103. Marina Perevozkina, "Ubiistva c Dome Profsoyuzov planirovali zaranee: sensatsionnoe rassledovanie," *Moskovskii komsomolets*, April 8, 2015, www.mk.ru/politics/2015/04/08/pervoe-chto-ya-uznal-o-russkikh-oni-za puskayut-sobak-v-kosmos.html.

104. "Sotnik Mykola strelyavshii po ltydyam 2 maya v Odesse umer v bol'nitse," *YouTube*, May 6, 2014, www.youtube.com/watch?v=97CnI006jwc, last accessed on March 28, 2016. See also "Eto moi narod?," *YouTube*, May 2, 2014, www.youtube.com/watch?v=IVXm9nnY-AQ#t= 412, last accessed on March 28, 2016.

105. Odessa police stand by and watch, see from 15:53 into the previously cited YouTube video "Eto moi narod?"

106. "04.05.2014, Odessa Osvobozhdennyi iz GorUVD activist antimaidana."

107. "#Odessa 2 maya. Polnaya khronologiya (ch. 1–6)+bloger+ubiitsa #Odessa holocaust chronology (18+)," *YouTube*, May 21, 2014, www.youtube.com/watch?v=n2s H8IqEGR4, last accessed on March 28, 2016.

108. "Odesskie deputaty raspustili kommissiyu po rassledovaniyu tragedii v Dome profsoyuzov," *Ekho Moskvy*, September 5, 2014, http://echo.msk.ru/news/1393878-echo.html.

109. See the press release at "Investigation of May 2014 events in Odesa failed to comply with requirements of European Human Right Convention, says International Advisory Panel's report," Council of Europe Press Release—DC155(2015), Council of Europe, November 4, 2015, https://wcd.coe.int/ViewDoc.jsp?Ref=DC-PR155(2015)&Language=lanEnglish&Ver=original&Site=DC&BackColorInternet=F5CA75&BackColorIntranet=F5CA75&BackColorLogged=A9BACE. For the CEIAPU report, see *Briefing on the Events in Odessa, Ukraine on 2 May 2014*, Council of Europe International Advisory Panel, November 4, 2015, www.coe.int/en/web/portal/international-advisory-panel/-/asset_publisher/EPeqGGDr0yBr/content/the-iap-and-the-events-in-odessa-on-2-may-2014 and http://coe.kiev.ua/iap/news/2014/09/12-09-2014-en.html, pp. 46–51.

110. *Briefing on the Events in Odessa*, pp. 55 and 62.

111. *Briefing on the Events in Odessa*, pp. 63–64.

112. "Odesskaya tragediya: Po itogam 20 mesyatsev rassledovaniya," *2 May Group Blogspot*, January 14, 2016, http://2maygroup.blogspot.ca/2016/01/20.html#more; "Pidsumki slidstva shodo masovikh zavorushen' v Odesi 2 travnya 2014 roku. YKMTs, 14-01-2016," *YouTube*, January 14, 2016, www.youtube.com/watch?v=miCCGaepGFw; and Halya Coynash, "'Clear Signs of Sabotage' in Odessa 2 May Investigation," *Kharkiv Human Rights Protection Group*, January 16, 2016, http://khpg.org/en/index.php?id=1452811753.

113. Giuliano, "The Origins of Separatism: Popular Grievances in Donetsk and Luhansk," and "Dumki da poglyadi xhiteliv pivdenno-skhidnikh oblastei Ukraini: kviten' 2014."

114. "Mneniya i vzglyadi zhitelei yugo-vostoka Ukrainy: Aprel' 2014," *Zn.ua*, April 18, 2014, http://zn.ua/UKRAINE/mneniya-i-vzglyady-zhiteley-yugo-vostoka-ukrainy-aprel-2014-143598_.html.

115. "The Views and Opinion of South-Eastern Regions Residents of Ukraine, April 2014," *KIIS*, April 20, 2014, www.kiis.com.ua/?lang=eng&cat=reports&id=302&page=1&y=2014&m=4.

116. Giuliano, "The Origins of Separatism: Popular Grievances in Donetsk and Luhansk."

117. Solchanyk, *Ukraine and Russia: The Post-Soviet Transition*, p. 117.

118. Giuliano, "The Origins of Separatism: Popular Grievances in Donetsk and Luhansk."

119. "Hearing: Russia's Destabilization of Ukraine," United States House of Representatives Committee on Foreign Affairs, May 8, 2014, http://foreignaffairs.house.gov/hearing/hearing-russia-s-destabilization-ukraine. For the relevant excerpt, see www.youtube.com/watch?v=6TpZa4OMFVk. See also http://nsnbc.me/2014/05/09/house-grilled-nuland-us-cooperation-neo-nazis-ukraine/.

120. Smith-Spark and Morgan, "Ukraine unrest will be resolved by force or talks within 48 hours, minister says."

121. "Russia 'Wants to Start World War III: Ukrainian PM Yatsenyuk," *NBC News*, April 25, 2014, www.nbcnews.com/storyline/ukraine-crisis/russia-wants-start-world-war-iii-ukrainian-pm-yatsenyuk-n89481.

122. Ben Watson, "Poland Fears Russia's 'New Russia' Doctrine," *DefenseOne.com*, April 17, 2014, www.defenseone.com/threats/2014/04/poland-fears-putins-new-russia-doctrine/82750/?oref=d-skybox.

123. Putin said: "The question is to ensure the rights and interests of the Russian southeast. It's New Russia. Kharkiv, Luhansk, Donetsk, Odessa were not part of Ukraine in czarist times; they were transferred in 1920. Why? God knows. Then, for various reasons, these areas were gone, and the people stayed there. We need to encourage them to find a solution." David M. Herszenhorn, "What Is Putin's 'New Russia'?," *New York Times*, April 19, 2014, www.nytimes.com/2014/04/19/world/europe/what-is-putins-new-russia.html?_r=0.

124. "Prezident Rossii Vladimir Putin obratilsya k opolcheniyu Novorossii," *Kremlin.ru*, August 29, 2014, www.kremlin.ru/events/president/news/46506.

125. "V Ukraine zaderzhany 23 rossiiskikh shpiona—SMI," *Ukrainskaya pravda*, April 16, 2014, www.pravda.com.ua/rus/news/2014/04/16/7022677/.

126. "Senchenko utverzhdaet, chto SIZO 'zabity' rossiiskoi agenturoi," *Ukrainskaya pravda*, April 14, 2014, www.pravda.com.ua/rus/news/2014/04/14/7022433/.

127. "Kontrrazvedka: Rossiya sobiraetsya ubit 100–200 lyudei v vvesti v Ukrainu voiska," *Ukrainskaya pravda*, April 16, 2014, www.pravda.com.ua/rus/news/2014/04/16/7022667/.

128. "Igry Stelkov," Makeeva, *TV Dozhd*,' April 30, 2014, https://tvrain.ru/teleshow/makeeva/makeeva_igry_strelkov-367809/.

129. Andrew Higgins, Michael R. Gordon, and Andrew E. Kramer, "Photos Link Masked Men in East Ukraine to Russia," *New York Times*, April 20, 2014, www.nytimes.com/2014/04/21/world/europe/photos-link-masked-men-in-east-ukraine-to-russia.html?_r=1.

130. From the photos it was immediately clear that they were anything but; they were hazy and could very well be showing two different men. Moreover, it seemed strange that a special forces agent would consistently wear a tell-tale beard in a clandestine operation rather than shave it off or shorten it so as to avoid detection, given the ubiquity of mobile phone cameras and CCTV nowadays. See my post and another by Harvard University Kennedy School of Government scholar Sergei Saradzhyan in *Johnson's Russia List*, No. 94, April 24, 2014, http://russialist.org/russia-ukraine-jrl-2014-94-contents-with-links-thursday-24-april-2014/.

131. Michael R. Gordon and Andrew E. Kramer, "Scrutiny of Photos Said to Tie Russian Units to Ukraine," *New York Times*, April 22, 2014, www.nytimes.com/2014/04/23/world/europe/scrutiny-over-photos-said-to-tie-russia-units-to-ukraine.html?action=click&contentCollection=Europe&module=RelatedCoverage&region=Marginalia&pgtype=article.

132. Sergei Saradzhyan, "No Smoking Spetsnaz Gun in E. Ukraine or Why Khamzat of GRU's Vostok Wouldn't Pose As Donetsk Native," *Saradzhyan: From the Global Tank—Live Journal*, April 22, 2014, http://saradzhyan.livejournal.com/34407.html.

133. Simon Shuster, "Exclusive: Meet the Pro-Russian Separatists of Eastern Ukraine," *Time*, April 23, 2014, http://time.com/74405/exclusive-pro-russian-separatists-eastern-ukraine/.

134. Robert Mackey, "Shifting Ukrainian Fact from Ukrainian Fiction," *New York Times*, February 13, 2015, http://mobile.nytimes.com/2015/02/14/world/europe/sifting-ukrainian-fact-from-ukrainian-fiction.html?referrer&_r=1.

135. Babitskii made his name during the Chechen wars exposing the brutality and war crimes committed by Russian troops and was hailed in the West for doing so. He was kidnapped by Russian intelligence and "exchanged" for Russian soldiers, after which time he left Russia and eventually ended up working for RFERL. Andrei Babitskii, "Andrei Babitskii: 'Ni odnu iz storon konflikta ne priemlyu," *Slon.ru*, July 20, 2015, https://slon.ru/posts/54216.

136. Mark Snowiss, "Ex-Ukrainian Spy Chief: Russian Camps Spreading Chaos," *Voice of America*, July 24, 2015, www.voanews.com/content/ex-ukrainian-spy-chief-russian-camps-spreading-chaos/2877981.html.

137. The article "War. Feedback" consists of a response from the Ukrainian Defense Ministry to *Novaya gazeta* queries on this and other issues the paper sent to the ministry. The paper then subjected the Ukrainian Defense Ministry's claims to analysis by a Russian General Staff expert and one of its own military experts. Ivan Zhilin, "Voina. Obratnaya svyaz,'" *Novaya gazeta*, No. 21, March 2, 2015, www.novayagazeta.ru/politics/67467.html.

138. See Maxim Tucker, "Ukraine Says Pro-Russia Rebels Are Building a Dirty Bomb," *Newsweek*, July 31, 2015, www.newsweek.com/2015/08/14/ukraine-says-rebels-are-building-dirty-bomb-358885.html; Maxim Tucker, "Ukraine Rebels Building 'Dirty Bomb' with Russian Scientists," *The Times*, August 1, 2015, www.thetimes.co.uk/tto/news/world/europe/article4514313.ece; Paul Goble, "Moscow mulling 'nuclear provocation' against Ukraine, Kyiv analyst says," *Window on Eurasia*, August 4, 2015, http://russialist.org/moscow-mulling-nuclear-provocation-against-ukraine-kyiv-analyst-says/; *Euromaidan Press*, August 4, 2015 http://euromaidanpress.com in *Johnson's Russia List*, Issue No. 150, August 5, 2015, Item #28, http://russialist.org/moscow-mulling-nuclear-provocation-against-ukraine-kyiv-analyst-says/; and Sergei Kilmenko, "Pochemu ugrozu yadernogo udara so storony Rossii nuzhno rassmatrivat' ser'tzno," *Khlyva.net*, August 3, 2015, http://hvylya.net/analytics/geopolitics/pochemu-ugrozu-yadernogo-udara-so-storonyi-rossii-po-ukraine-nuzhno-rassmatrivat-serezno.html.

139. "Gritsak ob'yasnil, chto on imel v vidu pod 'rossiiskim sledom' v teraktakh," *Ukrainskaya pravda*, March 23, 2016, www.pravda.com.ua/rus/news/2016/03/23/7103081/ and "Glava SBU: Ne udivlyus,' esli vzryvy v Bryussele—element gibridnoi voiny RF," *Ukrainskaya Pravda*, March 22, 2016, www.pravda.com.ua/rus/news/2016/03/22/7102893/.

140. See "Die Wahrheit uber den Krieg in Donbass/Ukraine—Mark Franchetti—Sunday Times—Deutsch," *YouTube*, June 17, 2014, www.youtube.com/watch?v=W1x7xmsYArs. For a rough English translation of some of Franchetti's remarks on the broadcast taken from a Russian news report on the Ukrainian talk show's proceedings, see "British journalist Mark Franchetti describes reality in Ukraine," *YouTube*, June 17, 2014, www.youtube.com/watch?v=4BVPtiwdrlI, last accessed on April 1, 2016.

141. Alice Speri, "Yes, There Are Chechen Fighters in Ukraine, and Nobody Knows Who Sent Them There," *Vice News*, May 28, 2014, https://news.vice.com/article/yes-there-are-chechen-fighters-in-ukraine-and-nobody-knows-who-sent-them-there.

142. Babitskii, "Andreii Babitskii: 'Ni odnu iz storon konflikta ne priemlyu."

143. For examples of defections, in addition to those from the Berkut mentioned previously, see "Peskov uveryaet: Nikakikh rossiiskikh voisk na vostoke Ukrainy net," *Ukrainskaya pravda*, April 15, 2014, www.pravda.com.ua/rus/news/2014/04/15/7022542/; "'Podpolkovnik RF' v Gorlovke okazalsya mestnym kriminal'nym avtoritetom—SMI," *Ukrainskaya pravda*, April 15, 2014, www.pravda.com.ua/rus/news/2014/04/15/7022553/; and "Oborets: Na Donetchine neizvestbyie ubili okolo 10 separatistov," *Ukrainskaya pravda*, April 15, 2014, www.pravda.com.ua/rus/news/2014/04/15/7022442/.

144. See, for example, "Minoborony priznalo, chto separatisty zakhvatili shest' BMD," *Ukrainskaya pravda*, April 16, 2014, www.pravda.com.ua/rus/news/2014/04/16/7022679/; "Kramators'k: separatisty vidpustily zablokovanikh vyis'kovyikh, ale zmusili rozzbroitisya," *Radio Svoboda*, April 16, 2014, www.radiosvoboda.org/content/article/25351998.html; "Ukrainskie boennyie sdali separatistam oruzhie v Kramatorske," *Ukrainskaya pravda*, April 16, 2014, www.pravda.com.ua/rus/news/2014/04/16/7022729/.

145. For a detailed account of the imbalance in the correlation of forces in Kiev's favor, especially in weaponry, see Yevgenii Pozhidaev, "Voina i oruzheinyi disbalans v Novorossii—konets blizok?," *Regnum.ru*, July 31, 2014, http://regnum.ru/news/polit/1831327.html.

146. "New Satellite Imagery Exposes Russian Combat Troops Inside Ukraine," The U.S. Mission to NATO, August 28, 2014, http://usnato.tumblr.com/post/96003086125/new-satellite-imagery-exposes-russian-combat.

147. See Shena Shankar, "UK Institute Says There Is Proof Russia Is Sending Battle Tanks Into Eastern Ukraine," *International Business Times*, August 28, 2014, www.ibtimes.com/uk-institute-says-there-proof-russia-sending-battle-tanks-eastern-ukraine-1671906.

148. Pozhidaev, "Voina i oruzheinyi disbalans v Novorossii—konets blizok?"

149. Maksim Sokolov, "Rassledovanie RBK: otkuda na Ukraine rossiiskie soldaty," *RBC.ru*, October 2, 2014, www.rbc.ru/politics/02/10/2014/542c0dcfcbb20f5d06c1d87a.

150. According to a Ukrainian volunteer battalion commander interviewed for the RBK report, several of some 20 Russian servicemen taken prisoner were killed by "friendly" artillery fire during some of the Ukrainians' hectic escape from encirclement. Sokolov, "Rassledovanie RBK: otkuda na Ukraine rossiiskie soldaty."

151. "Russia and the Separatists of Eastern Ukraine," *International Crisis Group*, No. 79, February 5, 2016, crisisgroup.org/~/media/Files/europe/ukraine/b079-russia-and-the-separatists-in-eastern-ukraine.pdf, p. 8.

152. Batomunkuev's group did not fare well. On February 19 he was severely burned when his tank was hit by an artillery shell fired from a Ukrainian tank. His commander was similarly wounded some time around February 12–14. Yelena Kostyuchenko, "'My vse znali, na chto idem i chto mozhet byt,'" *Novaya gazeta*, No. 22, March 4, 2015, www.novayagazeta.ru/society/67490.html.

153. "Russia and the Separatists of Eastern Ukraine," p. 8.

154. "Russia and the Separatists of Eastern Ukraine," pp. 3–4, 6, 9, 12 and 15.

155. "MVD sobiraetsya organizovat' spetspodrazdeleniya iz patriotov v vostochnyk oblastyakh," *LB.ua*, April 13, 2014, http://lb.ua/news/2014/04/13/262987_mvd_sobiraetsya_organizovat.html.

156. Avakov, "Lozh' i pravda."

157. "Avakov rasskazal o spetsrazdeleniyakh-uchastnikakh ATO," *Vesti Ukraina*, July 2, 2014, http://vesti.ua/kiev/59203-avakov-rasskazal-o-specpodrazdelenijah-uchastnikah-ato.

158. "Avakov sozdal batal'on iz aktivistov 'Svobody,'" *Vesti Ukraina*, June 13, 2014, http://vesti-ukr.com/don

bass/56407-avakov-sozdal-batalon-iz-aktivistov-svobody#.

159. Roman Chernyshov, "Yarosh: Ya pereotsenil organizatsionnye vozmozhnosti Pravogo sektora," *Liga.net*, February 1, 2016, http://news.liga.net/interview/politics/8764969-yarosh_ya_pereotsenil_organizatsionnye_vozmozhnosti_pravogo_sektora.htm and Valeriya Kondratova, "Skol'ko battalionov u Pravogo sektora," *Liga.net*, July 14, 2015, http://news.liga.net/articles/politics/6174219-skolko_batalonov_u_pravogo_sektora.htm.

160. "Donets'kii dialog na Gromads'komu 19 serpnya," *YouTube*, August 19, 2014, posted by Gromads'ke Tellbachennya, www.youtube.com/watch?v=tfRFT6vVaEI&list=UU2oGvjIJwxn1KeZR3JtE-uQ, last accessed April 4, 2016.

161. "Ukraine segodnya|Chto proiskhodit?," Program *Arena sobytii*, *Online TV*, June 26, 2014, www.onlinetv.ru/video/1670/?autostart=1.

162. See the Nazi insignia being used by Azov at "Andriy Biletskiy pro zvil'nennya Mariupolya," *You Tube*, June 13, 2015, www.youtube.com/watch?v=1lu3HanEJ78, last accessed April 4, 2016; "Shestvia Azova i Pravogo sektora po Kievu," *YouTube*, October 14, 2014, uploaded by Pavel Sheremet, www.youtube.com/watch?v=AJjBrgxWF8M&ebc=ANyPxKpXOG CNqrTf38UgQ4S7BiH5rQc UoXvwzuplFHT3LEbn8STOELJ3awAK1mojqrSpneaX uDEK9ToxMoFje9EYDudWnQc0NA, last accessed on April 4, 2016.

163. Taras Kozub, "Lyashko otkazalsya idti pod krylo Kolomoisogo," *Vesti Ukraina*, August 4, 2014, http://vesti.ua/strana/63937-ljashko-otkazalsja-idti-pod-krylo-kolomojskogo.

164. Nolan Peterson, "A Ukrainian national Guard Unit Trains to 'Fight to the Death,'" *Newsweek*, April 21, 2015, www.newsweek.com/ukrainian-national-guard-unit-trains-fight-death-323891.

165. See a brief video of the march at "Shestvia Azova i Pravogo sektora po Kievu."

166. Parry, "U.S. House Admits Nazi Role in Ukraine."

167. "Pochemu SShA Otkryli Front Protiv Bataliona Azov," *Vesti Ukraina*, June 15, 2015, http://vesti-ukr.com/strana/103513-pochemu-ssha-otkryli-front-protiv-batalona-azov.

168. "Is America Training Neonazis in Ukraine?" *The Daily Beast*, July 4, 2015, www.thedailybeast.com/articles/2015/07/04/is-the-u-s-training-neo-nazis-in-ukraine.html. There are many more neo-fascist elements in the Ukrainian army and National Guard than those of the Azov Battalion. Some ultranationalists or neo-fascists never served in the Azov or other volunteer battalions and may never serve in either those or regular units. Some are former members of those battalions, and identifying who is a former, present or future member will be impossible to determine. Thus, Congress's measure could be a measure to cover up the training of neo-fascists in the Ukrainian army and National Guard. Akin to our training "moderate" revolutionaries and "moderate jihadists" in Syria, this policy would lead to a similarly sad result: more violence in Ukraine. Moreover, the Congress's move seemed at odds with the claims of Deputy Secretary of State Victoria Nuland, the D.C. think tank community, academia, and mass media that there are no neo-fascists in Ukraine.

169. Anastasia Vlasova, "Volunteer Aidar Battalion Fights on Front Lines," *Kyiv Post*, July 21, 2014, www.kyivpost.com/multimedia/photo/volunteer-aidar-battalion-fights-on-front-lines-in-luhansk-oblast-357129.html.

170. "Povniy Spisok Novoobranikh Narodnikh Deputativ," *TSN*, November 12, 2014, http://tsn.ua/vybory-v-rady2014/povniy-spisok-novoobranih-narodnih-deputativ-391270.html and "Ukraine Votes on Oct. 26 To Elect

New Parliament," *Kyiv Post*, October 24, 2014, www.kyiv post.com/article/content/ukraine/ukraine-votes-on-oct-26-to-elect-new-parliament-369193.html.

171. "Ukraine: Abuses and War Crimes by the Aidar Volunteer Battalion in North Luhansk Region," *Amnesty International*, September 8, 2014, www.amnesty.org/en/documents/EUR50/040/2014/en/.

172. "Komandir 'Aidara' zayavil ob izmene rukovod-stva," *Vesti Ukraina*, June 24, 2014, http://video.vesti-ukr.com/donbass/1675-komandir-ajdara-obvinil-rukovod stvo-ato-v-izmene.

173. Vlasova, "Volunteer Aidar Battalion Fights on Front Lines"; Anastasia Stanko, "Batal'on 'Aidar' zhdet prikaz, chtoby nachat' osvobozhdenie Ukrainy," *Ukrain-skaya pravda*, June 15, 2014, www.pravda.com.ua/rus/photo-video/2014/06/15/7029129/; and Mark Mackinnon, "Bypassing official channels, Canada's Ukrainian diaspora finances and fights a war against Russia," *The Globe and Mail*, February 26 and 28, 2015, www.theglobeandmail.com/news/world/ukraine-canadas-unofficial-war/article 23208129/.

174. "Kombat zayavil o rasformirovanii batal'ona 'Aidar,'" *Vesti Ukraina*, June 23, 2014, http://vesti-ukr.com/donbass/57948-kombat-zajavil-o-rasformirovanii-bata lona-ajdar and Taras Kozub, "'Aidar' ne rasformiruyut," *Vesti Ukraina*, August 6, 2014, http://vesti.ua/donbass/64394-ajdar-ne-rasformirujut.

175. Galina Titish and Dmitro Laryn, "Aidar, Poperedu inshikh," *Ukrainskaya pravda*, July 22, 2014, www.pravda.com.ua/articles/2014/07/22/7032645/ and "Aidar Battal-ion: On the front lines," *Euromaidan Press*, July 24, 2014, http://euromaidanpress.com/2014/07/24/aidar-battalion-in-the-front-lines/.

176. "Minoborony pereformirovalo 'Aidar' v shtur-movoi batal'on," *Vesti Ukraina*, March 2, 2015, http://vesti-ukr.com/donbass/90843-minoborony-pereformirovalo-ajdar-v-24-j-shturmovoj-batalon.

177. "GPU otkryla delo protiv kombata 'Adaira' Mel'ny-chuk," *Vesti Ukraina*, March 30, 2015, http://vesti-ukr.com/strana/94354-gpu-otkryla-delo-protiv-kombata-ajdara-melnichuka.

178. "Minoborony naznachilo rassledovanie v otno-shenii 'Aidar,'" *Vesti Ukraina*, March 31, 2015, http://vesti-ukr.com/donbass/94544-minoborony-naznachilo-rassle dovanie-v-otnoshenii-ajdara.

179. "Ukraine: Aidar Battalion and Right Sector de-mand end to ceasefire in E. Ukraine," *YouTube*, July 3, 2015, www.youtube.com/watch?v=fI5NLekWP_4.

180. "Praviy sector—rozvidka boem pid Karlivkoyu 10.07.2014," *YouTube*, July 11. 2014, uploaded by Olena Biloz-erska, www.youtube.com/watch?v=SadSxC-zgdc#t=177, last accessed on April 5, 2016.

181. "Eastern Ukraine: Humanitarian disaster looms as food aid blocked," *Amnesty International*, December 24, 2014, www.amnesty.org/en/latest/news/2014/12/eastern-ukraine-humanitarian-disaster-looms-food-aid-blocked/.

182. "Kombat Donbassa—Geleteiyu: 'Nuzhen nemed-lennyi udar rezervami na Ilovaisk," *Censor.net*, August 25, 2014, http://censor.net.ua/news/299601/kombat_don bassa_geleteyu_nujen_nemedlennyyi_udar_rezervami_n a_ilovayisk.

183. Tat'yana Stanovaya, "Pyat prichin neizbezhnosti voiny, ili Chto Poroshenko delal proshlym vecherom," *Slon.ru*, July 4, 2014, http://slon.ru/russia/pyat_prichin_ neizbezhnosti_voyny_ili_chto_poroshenko_delal_proshl ym_vecherom-1121407.xhtml?utm_source=slon&utm_ medium=email&utm_campaign=20140704.

184. "Marsh Svyatoslava u stolnomu gradi—anons," *Praviy sektor*, July 1, 2014, http://pravyysektor.info/news/marsh-svyatoslava-u-stolnomu-hradi-anons/.

185. Olga Omelyanchuk, "Pod Kabminom nachali vzryvat' granaty," *Vesti Ukraina*, July 1, 2014, http://vesti.ua/kiev/59088-pod-kabminom-vzorvali-granaty.

186. "Kombat 'Donbassa' Semenchenko snyal balak-lavu," *Korrespondent*, September 1, 2014, http://korrespon dent.net/ukraine/3412892-kombat-donbassa-semen chenko-snial-balaklavu.

187. Semen Semenchenko, "Biografiya," *Samopomich.ua*, September 2, 2014, http://samopomich.ua/wp-con tent/uploads/2014/09/02_Semenchenko.pdf.

188. "Semenchenko kommetrioval lishenie ego ofitser-skogo zvaniya," *Vesti Ukraina*, January 29, 2016, http://vesti-ukr.com/strana/134017-semenchenko-prokommen tiroval-lishenie-ego-oficerskogo-zvanija and "," *Vesti Uk-raina*, February 2016.

189. Miller, "'Vigilante' Ukrainian lawmaker Lyashko gets slammed by Amnesty International report."

190. "V Depropetrovske formiruyut iz patriotov elitnyi battalion spetsnaznacheniya," *Ukraine Inform*, April 14, 2014, www.ukrinform.ru/rubric-lastnews/1647927-v_dne propetrovske_formiruyut_iz_patriotov_elitniy_batalon_s petsnaznacheniya_1623696.html, "Kolomoiskii sozdaet spetznaz," *LB.ua*, April 14, 2014, http://lb.ua/news/2014/04/14/263031_kolomoyskiy_sozdaet_spetsnaz.html; and "Yarosh: Ya pereotsenil organizatsionnye vozmozhnosti Pravogo sektora."

191. Miller, "'Vigilante' Ukrainian lawmaker Lyashko gets slammed by Amnesty International report."

192. "Pochemu SShA Otkryli Front Protiv Bataliona Azov" and "SMI: Troyan soglasilsya stat' pervym zamom Dekanoidze," *Ukrainskaya pravda*, March 2, 2016, www.pravda.com.ua/rus/news/2016/03/2/7100934/.

193. Oleg Bazar and Yevgenii Shvets, "Vadim Troyan: 'My ponimali: sdadim Mariupol'—proigraem voinu," *LB.ua*, December 2, 2014, http://society.lb.ua/life/2014/12/02/287807_vadim_troyan_mi_ponimali_sdadim.html.

194. Tom Parfitt, "Ukraine crisis: the neo–Nazi brigade fighting pro–Russian separatists," *The Daily Telegraph* (London), August 11, 2014.

195. Pers Anders Rudling, "The Return of the Ukrain-ian Far Right. The Case of VO Svoboda," in Ruth Wodak and John E. Richardson, eds., *Analysing Fascist Discourse: European Fascism in Talk and Text* (New York and Lon-don: Routledge, 2013), pp. 228–55, at p. 241, http://defend inghistory.com/wp-content/uploads/2013/01/PA-Rudling-on-Return-of-Ukrainian-Far-Right-2013.pdf.

196. "Ukraine: Mounting evidence of war crimes and Russian involvement," Amnesty International, September 7, 2014, www.amnesty.org/en/latest/news/2014/09/-uk raine-mounting-evidence-war-crimes-and-russian-in volvement/.

197. "UN Human Rights Council: Human Rights situ-ation in Ukraine," Human Rights Council, December 9, 2015, www.hrw.org/news/2015/12/09/un-human-rights-council-human-rights-situation-ukraine and "Report on the Human Rights Situation in Ukraine, August 16 to No-vember 15, 2015," UN Office of the High Commissioner on Human Rights, December 2015, www.ohchr.org/Doc uments/Countries/UA/12thOHCHRreportUkraine.pdf.

198. "Former Commander of Pro-Russian Separatists Says He Executed People Based on Stalin-Era Laws," *RFERL*, January 19, 2016, www.rferl.mobi/a/ukraine-gir kin-strelkov-executions-stalin-era/27497491.html.

199. The audio tape makes clear that those speaking are not happy about the incident, calling it "*blin.*" "AUDIO RECORDING of Malaysian MH-17 SHOOTDOWN of Russian Rebel Forces in Ukraine," *YouTube*, July 17, 2014, www.youtube.com/watch?v=ZJnD1wgofYM, last accessed on April 6, 2016.

200. "Opolchentsy soobshili, iz chego sbili ukrainskii An-26," *Vzglad.ru*, July 14, 2014, http://vz.ru/news/2014/7/14/695525.html.

201. "V chastichno zakhvacennoi v/ch v Donetske nakhiditsya ZRK 'Buk,'" *Vesti Ukraina*, June 29, 2014, http://vesti-ukr.com/donbass/58829-v-chastichno-zahvachennoj-v-ch-v-donecke-nahoditsja-zrk-buk and "MOLNIYA: chistoe nebo nad Donetskom—spetsnaz DNR zakhvatil garnison raketnykh voisk PVO," *Russkaya vesna*, June 29, 2014, http://rusvesna.su/news/1404041521. Interviewed by *Ukrainskaya pravda*, Dmytrashkovskii said the several Buk systems on the captured base were not in working order, but when asked if they could be repaired, he said: "I don't think they need them." "Boeviki chastichno zakhvatili voennuyu chast PVO," *Ukrainskaya pravda*, June 29, 2014, www.pravda.com.ua/rus/news/2014/06/29/7030482/.

202. "Ukraine: Abuses and War Crimes by the Aidar Volunteer Battalion in North Luhansk Region."

203. Damien Sharkov, "Ukrainian Nationalist Volunteers Committing 'ISIS-Style' War Crimes," *Newsweek*, September 10, 2014, www.newsweek.com/evidence-war-crimes-committed-ukrainian-nationalist-volunteers-grows-269604?rx=us.

204. See "Latest from OSCE Special Monitoring Mission (SMM) to Ukraine based on information received as of 18:00 (Kyiv time), August 21, 2014," OSCE, August 22, 2014, http://www.osce.org/node/122920.

205. "Minoborony naznachilo rassledovanie v otnoshenii 'Aidar.'"

206. In December 2014, for example, Aidar fighters posed as Ukrainian counter-intelligence and confiscated from a church 50,000 griven, a monitoring camera, and a cell phone. "Moskal' rasskazal podrobnosti ogrableniya tserkvi 'boitsom' 'Aidara,'" *Vesti Ukraina*, March 4, 2014, http://vesti-ukr.com/donbass/91253-moskal-rasskazal-po drobnosti-ograblenija-cerkvi-bojcom-ajdara.

207. Tatyana Dibovaya, "'Aidarovtsy' obvinyayut zaderzhannogo zammera Schastya v finansirovanie titushek," *Vesti Ukraina*, July 15, 2014, http://vesti-ukr.com/don bass/61180-zaderzhannogo-zammjera-schastja-ajdarovcy-obvinjajut-v-finansirovanii-titushek.

208. "Boitsy 'Aidara' zakhvatili sel'sovet v Poltavskoi oblasti," *Vesti Ukraina*, August 13, 2015, http://vesti-ukr.com/strana/110910-bojcy-ajdara-zahvatili-selsovet-v-poltavskoj-oblasti.

209. Bidder, "Kampf gegen separatisten: Ukrainische Freischarler sollen Graueltaten begangen haben" and Hahn, "One Day in the Life of Ukrainian Democracy," *Gordonhahn.com Russian and Eurasian Politics*, June 21, 2015, http://gordonhahn.com/2015/06/21/one-day-in-the-life-of-ukrainian-democracy/

210. Anatolii Matios, "Prestupleniya 'Tornado': Privyazali cheloveka k sportivnomu snaryadu i isnasilovali," *Vesti Ukraina*, June 19, 2015, http://112.ua/mnenie/prestupleniya-tornado-privyazali-cheloveka-k-sportivnomu-snaryadu-i-iznasilovali-18-238616.html; "Matios v prymom efire rasskazal uzhasy o zverstvakh batal'ona 'Tornado,'" *Vesti Ukraina*, June 20, 2015, http://vesti-ukr.com/donbass/104244-matios-v-prjamom-jefire-rasskazal-uzhasy-o-zverstvah-batalona-tornado; and Benjamin Bidder, "Kampf gegen separatisten: Ukrainische Freischarler sollen Graueltaten begangen haben," *Der Spiegel*, July 29, 2015, www.spiegel.de/politik/ausland/ukraine-prozess-gegen-pro-ukrainischer-kaempfer-a-1045801.html. For a partial English translation of *Der Spiegel*'s account, see Hahn, "One Day in the Life of Ukrainian Democracy."

211. "Boitsy 'Tornado' zaderzhany za pytki i gruppovoe iznasilovanie—Matios," *112.ua*, June 17, 2015, http://112.ua/ato/boycy-tornado-zaderzhany-za-pytki-i-gruppovoe-iznasilovanie-matios-238141.html; "Ukrainian military commander arrested over torture, rape—and unit disbanded," *Russia Today*, June 18, 2015, https://www.rt.com/news/268105-ukraine-tornado-torture-rape/.

212. Bidder, "Kampf gegen separatisten: Ukrainische Freischarler sollen Graueltaten begangen haben"; Hahn, "One Day in the Life of Ukrainian Democracy."

213. Bidder, "Kampf gegen separatisten"; and Hahn, "One Day in the Life of Ukrainian Democracy."

214. Andrew E. Kramer, "Ukraine Strategy Bets on Restraint by Russia," *New York Times*, August 9, 2014, http://www.nytimes.com/2014/08/10/world/europe/ukraine.html?_r=0.

215. "Ukraine: Unguided Rockets Killing Civilians," *Human Rights Watch*, July 24, 2014, https://www.hrw.org/news/2014/07/24/ukraine-unguided-rockets-killing-civilians.

216. "Bombing of the city of Lugansk the Ukrainian jet on June 2, 2014," *YouTube*, June 4, 2014, www.youtube.com/watch?v=T8IG_xm6Gbo, last accessed on April 5, 2016.

217. "'Why?' Entire E. Ukraine village bombed by air-strike, 5 yr-old among dead," *YouTube*, July 3, 2014, www.youtube.com/watch?v=fxAdc9JRAo0.

218. "Ukraine: Widespread Use of Cluster Munitions," *Human Rights Watch*, October 20, 2014, www.hrw.org/news/2014/10/20/ukraine-widespread-use-of-cluster-muni tions; Andrew Roth, "Ukraine Used Cluster Bombs, Evidence Indicates," *New York Times*, October 21, 2014, www.nytimes.com/2014/10/21/world/ukraine-used-cluster-bombs-report-charges.html?google_editors_picks=true; and Nicolas Miletitch, "Surgeons in Ukraine's rebel Donetsk confirm cluster bomb usage," *AFP*, October 21, 2014.

219. "Ukraine: More Civilians Killed in Cluster Munition Attacks," *Human Rights Watch*, March 19, 2015, www.hrw.org/news/2015/03/19/ukraine-more-civilians-killed-cluster-munition-attacks.

220. "HRW Calls on Germany to Pressure Ukraine on Civilian Casualties," *Voice of America*, January 6, 2015, www.voanews.com/content/hrw-calls-on-germany-to-pressure-ukraine-on-civilian-casualties/2587203.html and "Incendiary Weapons: Recent use and Growing Opposition," *Human Rights Watch*, November 2014, www.hrw.org/sites/default/files/supporting_resources/incendi ary_weapons_recent_use_and_growing_opposition_nov2 014_final.pdf, pp. 6–7.

221. "Minsk agreement on Ukraine crisis: text in full," *The Guardian*, February 12, 2015, www.telegraph.co.uk/news/worldnews/europe/ukraine/11408266/Minsk-agree ment-on-Ukraine-crisis-text-in-full.html.

222. "Russia and the Separatists of Eastern Ukraine," *International Crisis Group*, p. 9.

Chapter 10

1. "Klimkin: 'Iz-za rossiiskoi agressii Ukraina poteryala 9 tyc., chelovek," *Ukainskaya pravda*, March 2, 2016, www.pravda.com.ua/rus/news/2016/03/2/7100830/; "MID: Bolee 2,500 ukrainskikh voennykh pogibli v techenie 2 let," *Ukrainskaya pravda*, February 29, 2016, www.pravda.com.ua/rus/news/2016/02/29/7100705/; Nick Cumming-Bruce, "Death Toll in Ukraine Conflict Hits 9,160, U.N. Says," *New York Times*, March 3, 2016, www.nytimes.com/2016/03/04/world/europe/ukraine-death-toll-civilians.html?_r=1; and "UN: 9,000 Killed in Ukraine Conflict, but Now Violence Eases," *Associated Press*, December 9, 2015.

2. "UN: 9,000 Killed in Ukraine Conflict, but Now Violence Eases."

3. "Uvol'nyat' chinovnikov za separatizm sobirayutsya bez resheniya suda," *Vesti Ukraina*, March 12, 2015, http://vesti-ukr.com/strana/92160-uvolnjat-chinovnikov-za-separatizm-sobirajutsja-bez-reshenija-suda.

4. Tatyana Ivzhenko, "U 'Pravogo sektora' poyavilas' smena," *Nezavisimaya gazeta*, January 22, 2015, www.ng.ru/cis/2015–01–22/6_pravsek.html.

5. Maxim Tucker, "Explosive Court Case Puts Ukraine's Chocolate King in Dock," *Newsweek.com*, February 19, 2015, www.newsweek.com/2015/02/27/explosive-court-case-puts-chocolate-king-dock-307920.html; Tadeusz A. Olszanski and Agata Weirzbowska-Miazga, "Poroshenko, President of Ukraine," *Osrodek Studiow Wschodnich im. Marka Kapiya*, May 28, 2014, www.osw.waw.pl/en/publik acje/analyses/2014-05-28/poroshenko-president-ukraine; and Ivzhenko, "U 'Pravogo sektora' poyavilas' smena."

6. Anastasiya Rafal, Yulia Gutova, and Vitalii Leibin, "Porokh," *Russkii reporter*, May 29, 2014, http://rusrep.ru/article/2014/05/29/poroh and Olszanski and Agata Weirzbowska-Miazga, "Poroshenko, President of Ukraine."

7. Poroshenko's political career began in the pro–Kuchma Social Democratic Party of Ukraine (United). In 2000 he formed his own center-left party, the Solidarity Party of Ukraine, which later the same year merged with the Party for the Regional Renaissance Solidarity of Labour Ukraine to form what would be renamed the Party of Regions (PR) of Yanukovych-era infamy. In 2001, however, Poroshenko left the PR, reestablished his own party in 2001, and became chief of staff and main sponsor for Yushchenko's "Our Ukraine" electoral bloc. In 2004, Poroshenko was the Yuschenko presidential campaign's deputy chief and a key sponsor of the Orange revolution protests. Poroshenko's closeness to the Orange camp did not prevent him from serving in government positions under Yanukovych before and after the latter's election as president in 2010. In 2009–2010 he was then Prime Minister Yanukovych's Minister of Foreign Affairs. Poroshenko remained a board member of the National Bank of Ukraine, becoming its chairman in 2012. In March–December 2012 he was the Azarov government's Economic Development and Trade Minister, before running for and winning a Rada seat in 2012. Olszanski and Agata Weirzbowska-Miazga, "Poroshenko, President of Ukraine," and Rafal, Gutova, and Leibin, "Porokh."

8. Olszanski and Agata Weirzbowska-Miazga, "Poroshenko, President of Ukraine."

9. David Herszenhorn, "In Ukraine, Corruption Concerns Linger a Year After a Revolution," *New York Times*, May 17, 2015, www.nytimes.com/2015/05/18/world/eu rope/in-ukraine-corruption-concerns-linger-a-year-after-a-revolution.html?emc=edit_th_20150518&nl=todays headlines&nlid=17170127&_r=0.

10. "Petro Poroshenko—The Power Players," *Panama Papers*, The International Consortium of Investigative Journalists, April 2016, https://panamapapers.icij.org/the_power_players/ and "Panama and Poroshenko," *Wall Street Journal*, April 5, 2016, www.wsj.com/articles/pan ama-and-poroshenko-1459900665.

11. In the first, Poroshenko's Prime Assets Capital purchased on March 25, 2016, nearly 4 million Euros' worth of stock in a Cyprus-based company, contradicting Poroshenko's claims that his holdings were stagnant since his election in preparation for their deposit into a trust, which has yet to occur more than two years after his election. "Poroshenko okazalsya v epicenter novogo ofshornogo skandala," *Vesti-Ukraina*, May 18, 2016, http://business.vesti-ukr.com/149138-poroshenko-okazalsja-v-jepicentre-novogo-ofshornogo-skandala. In the second, *Deutsch Welle*'s Ukrainian service uncovered another offshore scheme through which Poroshenko and Zaitsev garnered ownership of a factory in Germany in such a way so as to maintain anonymity and reduce tax exposure. Yevgenii Teize, "Rassledovanie DW: ofshorniye skhemy okruzheniya Poroshenko v FRG," *Deutsche Welle*, May 19, 2016, www.dw.com/ru/%D1 %80%D0%B0%D1%81%D1%81D0%BB%D0%B5%D0%B4%D0%BE%D0%B2%D0%B0%D0%BD%D0%B8%D0%B5-dw-%D0%BE%D1%84%D1%88%D0%BE%D1% 80%D0%BD%D1%8B%D0%B5-

%D1%81%D1%85%D0%B5%D0%BC%D1%8B-%D0%BE%D0%BA%D1%80%D1%83%D0%B6%D0%B5%D0%BD%D0%B8%D1%8F-%D0%BF%D0%BE%D1%80%D0%BE%D1%88%D0%B5%D0%BD%D0%BA%D0%BE-%D0%B2-%D1%84%D1%80%D0%B3/a-1926797 0#nomobile and "U Poroshenko nashli zavod v Germanii s oborotom v shest' millionov ecro," *Vesti Ukraina*, May 19, 2016, http://business.vesti-ukr.com/149328-u-poroshe nko-nashli-zavod-v-germanii-s-oborotom-v-shest-mil lionov-evro. There is also evidence that Poroshenko benefited from, and quashed investigations into damage of a protected historic site in central Kiev from a shady deal amounting to "the biggest and most important free-appropriation land scheme in Kyiv." Maksym Savchuk and Daisy Sindelar, "Questions Raised Over Poroshenko's Role in Valuable Kyiv Land Deal," RFERL, May 13, 2015, www.rferl.org/content/ukraine-poroshenko-land-deal-ques tions-tsars-village/27013945.html.

12. "Poroshenko taki prichasten k offshore, torguyushemu s 'Gaspromom,'" *Ukrainskaya pravda*, May 10, 2016, www.pravda.com.ua/rus/news/2016/05/10/7107945/; "Abromavichyus zayavlyal ob ostavke. Odna iz prichin—Kononenko," *Ukrainskaya Pravda*, February 3, 2016, www.pravda.com.ua/rus/news/2016/02/3/7097676/; and "Shokin treboval vypolnyat' instruktsii Kononenka—Kas'ko," *Ukrainskaya pravda*, February 26, 2016, www.pravda.com.ua/rus/news/2016/02/26/7100344/.

13. "Panama Petro," *Kyiv Post*, April 8, 2016, www.kyiv post.com/article/opinion/editorial/panama-petro-411570.html.

14. "The World's Billionaires: #1367 Ihor Kolomoyskyy," *Forbes*, 2016, www.forbes.com/profile/ihor-kolomo yskyy/.

15. Tom Zaitsev, "Three Ukrainian carriers seek tie-up approval," *Flightglobal.com*, February 12, 2010, http://beta.flightglobal.com/news/articles/three-ukrainian-carriers-seek-tie-up-approval-338364/ and Metet Fraende, "Cimber Sterling gets 165 mln DKK lifeline," *Reuters*, July 7, 2011, www.reuters.com/article/cimbersterling-mansvell-idUSLDE6BL15L20110707.

16. "President v oligarch," *The Economist*, March 28, 2015, www.economist.com/news/europe/21647355-build ing-nation-means-putting-plutocrats-their-place-presi dent-v-oligarch.

17. "Ukraine's tycoon and governor Kolomoysky confesses to holding 3 passports," *Itar-Tass*, October 3, 2014, http://tass.ru/en/world/752691.

18. Toby Axelrod, "European Jewish Parliament off to a semi-comic start," *Jweekly.com*, November 3, 2011, www.jweekly.com/article/full/63331/european-jewish-parlia ment-off-to-a-semi-comedic-start/; Ben Hartman, "A necessary putsch," *Jerusalem Post*, October 29, 2010, www.jpost.com/Features/Front-Lines/A-necessary-putsch; and Uriel Heilman, "Like NBA's Nets, European Jewish group gets an oligarch, but some see Soviet-style takeover," *Jewish Telegraphic Agency*, November 2, 2010, www.jta.org/2010/11/02/news-opinion/world/like-nbas-nets-european-jewish-group-gets-an-oligarch-but-some-see-soviet-style-take over.

19. Program "Chernoe zerkalo," *Inter TV*, March 12, 2015, www.youtube.com/user/podrobnosti.

20. Tatyana Izhvenko, "V Ukraine razgoraetsya voina oligarkhov," *Nezavisimaya gazeta*, March 16, 2015, www.ng.ru/cis/2015–03–16/1_ukraina.html.

21. "Deputaty ot BPP ustroili demarsh v Rade," *Vesti Ukraina*, March 19, 2015, http://vesti-ukr.com/strana/93 052-deputaty-ot-bpp-ustroili-demarsh-v-rade.

22. "V tsentre Kieva lyudi v kamuflyazhe i s avtomatami blokirovali zdanie neftyanoi kompanii 'UkrNafta,'" *Ekho Moskvy*, March 22, 2015, www.echo.msk.ru/news/1516388-echo.html; "Poroshenko vs Kolomoiskii: Khro-

nika sobytii," *Vesti Ukraina*, March 22, 2015, http://busi ness.vesti-ukr.com/93481-poroshenko-vs-kolomojskij-hronika-sobytij; and "Vkhod v Ukrnaftu blokiruyut avtomatchiki, podekhala militsiya," *Korrespondent*, March 22, 2015, http://korrespondent.net/ukraine/3494140-vkhod-v-ukrnaftu-blokyruuit-avtomatchyky-podekhala-mylyt syia.

23. Yaroslav Markin, "V Dnepr otpravili dva batal'ona Natsgvardii," *Vesti Ukraina*, March 23, 2015, http://vesti-ukr.com/pridneprove/93459-v-dnepr-otpravili-dva-bat alona-nacgvardii and "Batal'ona Natsgvardii napravlena v Kiev," *YouTube*, March 23, 2015, www.youtube.com/watch?v=t8a_zT0SClc&t=81.

24. "Nardepy Dnepra eeevyshli iz partii Poroshenko i zovut na novoe veche," *Vesti Ukraina*, March 25, 2015, http://vesti-ukr.com/pridneprove/93505-naredpy-dnepra-vyshli-iz-partii-poroshenko-i-zovut-na-novoe-veche and "Poroshenko v Kolomoiskii: Khronika Sobytii," *Vesti Ukraina*, March 23, 2015, http://business.vesti-ukr.com/93481-poroshenko-vs-kolomojskij-hronika-sobytij.

25. "Poroshenko prigrozil otobrat' u Kolomoiskogo batal'on 'Dnepr,'" *Vesti Ukraina*, March 25, 2015, http://vesti-ukr.com/strana/93499-poroshenko-prigrozil-oto brat-u-kolomojskogo-batalon-dnepr; "Poroshenko v Kolomoiskii: Khronika Sobytii"; and Markin, "V Dnepr otpravili dva batal'ona Natsgvardii."

26. "Poroshenko vydvinul dobrovol'cheskim batal'onam ultimatum," *Vesti Ukraina*, March 24, 2015, http://vesti-ukr.com/strana/93991-poroshenko-vydvinul-dobrovolch eskim-batalonam-ultimatum.

27. "Poroshenko prigrozil otobrat' u Kolomoiskogo batal'on 'Dnepr'" and "Poroshenko v Kolomoiskii: Khronika Sobytii."

28. "'Dnepr-1': 'My svoikh ne sdaem chast' nashikh uzhe v Kieve,'" *Vesti Ukraina*, March 24, 2015, http://vesti-ukr.com/pridneprove/93563-dnepr-1-my-svoih-ne-sdaem-chast-nashih-uzhe-v-kieve.

29. "Kolomoiskii i Poroshenko ni o chem ne dogovorilis," *Vesti Ukraina*, March 27, 2015, http://vesti-ukr.com/strana/94036-kolomojskij-i-poroshenko-ni-o-chem-ne-dogovorilis and "Leshchenko rasskazal o davlenii Baidena na Yatsenyuka iz-za Kolomoiskogo," *Vesti Ukraina*, March 27, 2015, http://business.vesti-ukr.com/94125-lewenko-rasskazal-o-davlenii-bajdena-na-jacenjuka-iz-za-kolomo jskogo.

30. Jim Armitrage, "Oligarchs at war: Claims of murder among Ukrainian billionaires in High Court case," *The Independent*, March 13, 2015, www.independent.co.uk/news/uk/home-news/oligarchs-at-war-claims-of-murder-among-ukrainian-billionaires-in-high-court-case-10107612.html.

31. "'Pravyi sektor' za zakrytoi dver'yu prigrozil 'menyat' rezhim putem revolyutsii," *Vesti Ukraina*, July 21, 2015, http://vesti-ukr.com/kiev/108102-smenit-rezhim-my-mozhem-tolko-putem-revoljucii-v-kieve-proshel-sezd-ps; "Z'izd 'Pravogo Sektora' v tsentri stolitsy," *Pravyi Sektor*, July 21, 2015, http://pravyjsektor.info/news/news/3451/zy izd-pravogo-sektora-v-centri-stolici.html; and "Na veche 'Pravogo Sektora' v Kieve prishli tri tysyachi chelovek," *RBC.ru*, July 21, 2015, http://top.rbc.ru/politics/21/07/2015/55ae7de79a79473857deec29).

32. "Geraschenko zayavil o nalichii vakansii dlya Yarosha v Minoborony," *Vesti Ukraina*, March 26, 2015, http://vesti-ukr.com/strana/94012-gerawenko-zajavil-o-nalichii-vakansii-dlja-jarosha-v-minoborony and Gordon M. Hahn, "NeoFascist Yarosh Appointed to Ukraine's Defense Ministry," *Gordonhahn.com Russian and Eurasian Politics*, April 6, 2015, https://gordonhahn.com/2015/04/06/neo-fascist-yarosh-appointed-to-ukraine-defense-ministry/.

33. For details and sources on Mukachevo and the Lviv bombings, see Gordon M. Hahn, "Saving Maidan Ukraine From Itself: Mukachevo's Implications," *Gordonhahn.com*

Russian and Eurasian Politics, July 13, 2015, https://gordon hahn.com/2015/07/13/saving-maidan-ukraine-from-itself-mukachevos-implications/ and Gordon M. Hahn, "Right Sector and the Impotence of Ukraine's Weimar Maidan Regime," *Gordonhahn.com Russian and Eurasian Politics*, July 22, 2015, https://gordonhahn.com/2015/07/22/right-sector-and-the-impotence-of-ukraines-weimar-maidan-regime/.

34. For details and sources on the congress, *veche* and KIIS poll, see Gordon M. Hahn, "Ukraine's Neo-Fascist Right Sector: Preparing a Revolt?," *Gordonhahn.com Russian and Eurasian Politics*, August 5, 2015, https://gordon hahn.com/2015/07/14/ukraines-neo-fascist-right-sector-preparing-a-revolt/.

35. For details and sources, see Gordon M. Hahn, "Ukraine's Neo-Fascist 'Tea Party' Throws Grenades, Shoots at Police," *Gordonhahn.com Russian and Eurasian Politics*, August 31, 2015, https://gordonhahn.com/2015/08/31/uk raines-neo-fascist-tea-party-throws-grenades-shoots-at-police-attempts-storm-of-rada/ and Gordon M. Hahn, "Europe's New Terrorist Threat," *Gordonhahn.com Russian and Eurasian Politics*, November 5, 2015, http://gordon-hahn.com/2015/11/05/europes-new-terrorist-threat/.

36. "Turchynov potreboval zapretit' veshchanie telekanalu–Inter,'" *Vesti Ukraina*, January 1, 2015, http://vesti-ukr.com/politika/83684-turchinov-potreboval-zapretit-vewanie-telekanalu-inter and "V Rade predlozhili nakazat' '1+1' za unizhenie Bandery," *Vesti Ukraina*, January 3, 2015, http://vesti-ukr.com/strana/83767-v-rade-predlozhili-nakazat-1-1-za-unizhenie-bandery.

37. "SBU zablokirovala bolee 10 tysyach saitov," *Vesti Ukraina*, April 9, 2015, http://business.vesti-ukr.com/95 702-sbu-zablokirovala-bolee-10-tysjach-sajtov.

38. For details and sources, see Gordon M. Hahn, "The Maidan Regime's Growing Democracy Deficit," *Gordon-hahn.com Russian and Eurasian Politics*, April 12, 2015, https://gordonhahn.com/2015/04/12/the-maidan-re gimes-growing-democracy-deficit/ and Gordon M. Hahn, "Maidan Ukraine's Authoritarianism Surplus: Update on Maidan Ukraine's Democracy Deficit," *Gordonhahn.com Russian and Eurasian Politics*, April 21, 2015, https://gor donhahn.com/2015/04/21/maidan-ukraines-authoritari anism-surplus-update-on-maidan-ukraines-democracy-deficit/; Hahn, "One Day in the Life of 'Ukrainian Democracy'"; "How Kiev Silenced Ukraine's Biggest Opposition Newspaper," *Off-Guardian*, October 22, 2015, https://off-guardian.org/2015/10/22/how-kiev-silenced-ukraines-biggest-opposition-newspaper/; and "Gazeta 'Vesti' i svoboda slova v epokhu Poroshenko," *Vesti Ukraina*, June 2015, http://vesti-ukr.com/strana/104230-gazeta-vesti-i-svoboda-slova-v-jepohu-poroshenko.

39. For details and sources, see Hahn, "Maidan Ukraine's Authoritarianism Surplus: Update on Maidan Ukraine's Democracy Deficit" and Hahn, "One Day in the Life of 'Ukrainian Democracy.'"

40. "Ukrainskie spetssluzhby sozdayut armii iz radikalov—foto," *Vesti Ukraine*, April 20, 2015, http://vesti-ukr.com/kiev/96547-ukrainskie-specsluzhby-sozdajut-armii-iz-radikalov.

41. "Ukraine," *Nations in Transit 2016* (Washington, D.C: Freedom House, 2016), https://freedomhouse.org/re port/nations-transit/2016/Ukraine.

42. Julie Ray, "Ukrainians Disillusioned With Leadership," Gallup, December 23, 2015, www.gallup.com/poll/187931/ukrainians-disillusioned-leadership.aspx.

43. Ray, "Ukrainians Disillusioned With Leadership."

44. Michelle Jamrisko, "Most Miserable Economies in the World," Bloomberg, March 2, 2015, www.bloomberg.com/news/articles/2015-03-02/the-15-most-miserable-economies-in-the-world. For more data, see Gordon M. Hahn, "Ukraine's Crisis Economy in Ten New Stats," *Gor-*

donhahn.com Russian and Eurasian Politics, 17 March 2015, https://gordonhahn.com/2015/03/17/ukraines-crisis-economy-in-10-new-stats/.

45. "MVF uviel uvelichenie gosdloga Ukrainy do $100 dollarov," *Vesti Ukraina*, March 13, 2015, http://business.vesti-ukr.com/92294-mvf-uvidel-uvelichenie-gosdolga-ukrainy-do-100-mlrd.

46. "The Inflation Rate in Ukraine," *StatBureau*, www.statbureau.org/en/ukraine/inflation, last accessed on September 27, 2016 and "Ukraine Unemployment Rate," *Trading Economics*, September 22, 2016, www.tradingeconomics.com/ukraine/unemployment-rate, last accessed on September 27, 2016.

47. See Gordon M. Hahn, "Dirty-Dealing Democratizers, the 'War of Values' with Russia, and Problems of Democracy Promotion," *Gordonhahn.com Russian and Eurasian Politics,* April 24, 2015, https://gordonhahn.com/2015/04/29/dirty-deal-democratizers-the-war-of-values-with-russia-and-problems-of-democracy-promotion/.

48. See Zbigniew Brzezinski, "NATO and World Security," *New York Times*, August 20, 2009, www.nytimes.com/2009/08/20/opinion/20iht-edbrzezinski.html?_r=0 and Gordon M. Hahn, "U.S.-Russian Relations and the War Against Jihadism," Century Foundation, Hart-Matlock Russia Working Group Paper, May 2009, pp. 20, 21 and 24.

Bibliography

Primary Sources

"06.04.2014 Zakhvat zdaniya SBU v Luganske," *You Tube*, 6 April 2014, www.youtube.com/watch?v=a1bTEa4SSbY.

"1990 Summit: a turning point in 'East-West' relations," *NATO*, 18 December 2014, www.nato.int/cps/en/natohq/news_116133.htm.

"III Universal Ukrainskoi Tsentral'noi Rady (7 noyabrya 1917)," *Likbez.ua*, http://likbez.org.ua/iii-decree-ukrainian-central-rada.html, last accessed on 7 September 2015.

"18 lyutogo 2014r., biy na rozy Kryposnogo provulku ta Instituts'koy," *YouTube*, 24 June 2014, www.youtube.com/watch?v=Osb8oC4gm20&ebc=ANyPxKq0mZmQ4PHsP3Rdo6kGY2zwPxay2ATNsAZib5_QhpmdGPamTSf9pfOM7Q8nTU6iengGm0yE2XO1c-2I6lBvQMbf1rpXtA.

"29.04.14 Lugansk Pervomaisk pod Rossiiskom flagom," *YouTube*, 29 April 2014, www.youtube.com/watch?v=jcUiH_Mi6y4.

"29/04/2014 Pervomaisk Luganskaya oblast'," *YouTube*, 29 April 2014, www.youtube.com/watch?v=NYnQKnwwcwE.

"36B. Est' li osnovaniya u Rossii opasat'sya stran Zapada, vkhodyashchikh v blok NATO?" *VTsIOM*, 15 October 2000, http://wciom.ru/zh/print_q.php?s_id=347&q_id=28022&date=15.10.2000, last accessed on 12 October 2015.

"43. Est' li osnovaniya u Rossii opasat'sya stran Zapada, vkhodyashchikh v blok NATO?" *VTsIOM*, 30 March 1999, http://wciom.ru/zh/print_q.php?s_id=354&q_id=28693&date=30.03.1999, last accessed 12 October 2015.

"46. Chto iz perechislennogo, po vashemu mneniyu, bol'she otvechaet interesam Rossii: Vstuplenie Rossii v NATO," *VTsIOM*, 15 November 2001, http://wciom.ru/zh/print_q.php?s_id=328&q_id=26453&date=15.11.2001.

"46. Kak vy otneslis' k bombardirovkami salami NATO Yugoslavii, predprinyatym s tsel'yu zastavit rukovodstvo Yugoslavii predostavit' avtonomiyu dlya Kosovo?" *VTsIOM*, 15 March 1999, http://wciom.ru/zh/print_q.php?s_id=353&q_id=28615&date=15.03.1999.

"47. Kak vy schitaete, chto yavlyaetsya konechnoi tsel'yu SShA i NATO v etom konflikte," *VTsIOM*, 15 March 1999, http://wciom.ru/zh/print_q.php?s_id=353&q_id=28616&date=15.03.1999.

"50. Odni schitayut, chto NATO vedet samstoyatel'nuyu politiku v interesakh vsekh stran al'yansa; drugie—chto ono yavlyaetsya v osnovnom provodnikom interesov SShA. Kakaya iz etikh dvukh tochek zreniya kazhetsya vam bolee vernoi?" *VTsIOM*, 15 March 2001, http://wciom.ru/zh/print_q.php?s_id=321&q_id=25835&date=15.03.2001.

"54. Kak vy schitaete, imelo li NATO parvo nachinat' bombardirovki bez canktsii Soveta Bezopasnosti OON?" *VTsIOM*, 28 February 1999, http://wciom.ru/zh/print_q.php?s_id=520&q_id=37433&date=28.02.1999.

"67A. Kak vy lichno otnosites' k zayavleniyu Vladimira Putina o tom, chto Rossiya v budushem mozhet vstupit' v NATO: s odobreniem, s nedoumeniem, s osuzhdeniem, ili sravnitelmno bezrazlichno?" *VTsIOM*, 15 June 2000, http://wciom.ru/zh/print_q.php?s_id=405&q_id=32590&date=15.06.2000, last accessed on 12 October 2015.

"82_B. Kakoe znachenie immet dlya vas slovo: NATO?," *VTsIOM*, 15 June 1999, http://wciom.ru/zh/print_q.php?s_id=380&q_id=30863&date=15.06.1999, last accessed on 15 October 2015.

"Abmachung 1990: 'Keine Osterweiterung der NATO'—Aussenminister Gensher & Baker," *Antikrieg TV*, 6 July 2014, www.youtube.com/watch?v=JXcWVTpQF3k.

"About" page, EuromaidanPRwww, https://euromaidanpr.wordpress.com/about/.

"Administrativno-Territorial'noe delenie ukrainskikh zemel" v Rossiiskoi imperii na 1914 god," *Likbez.ua*, http://likbez.org.ua/admin-division-1914.html, last accessed on 7 September 2015.

"Agreement on the Settlement of Crisis in Ukraine—full text," *Website of the German Foreign Ministry Auswaertiges-amt.de*, 21 February 2014," www.auswaertiges-amt.de/cae/servlet/contentblob/671350/publicationFile/190051/140221-UKR_Erklaerung.pdf.

Amnesty International Report 2015/16: The State of the World's Human Rights, *Amnesty.org*, 23 February 2016, www.amnesty.org/en/documents/pol10/2552/2016/en/.

"Andrei Biletskii | Sotsial-natsionalizm—zolotoi vek Ukrainy," *YouTube*, 7 December 2014, www.youtube.com/watch?v=0KfqYT6U6xc.

"Andrei Parubiy podaril dobrovol'tsam odesskoi samoborony sovremennyie bronezhilety," *YouTube*, 29 April 2014, www.youtube.com/watch?v=8tVITa8wegQ.

"Andriy Biletskiy pro zvil'nennya Mariupolya," *You Tube*, 13 June 2015, www.youtube.com/watch?v=1lu3HanEJ78.

"Anons richnytsi 2 travnya v Odesi," *Pravyysektor.info*, 1 May 2015, http://pravyysektor.info/news/anons-richnytsi-2-travnya-v-odesi/.

"Association Agreement Between the European Union and its Member States, of the One Part, and Ukraine, of the Other Part," *Bilaterals.org*, 2012, www.bilaterals.org/IMG/pdf/eu-ukraine-association-agreement-english.pdf.

"AUDIO RECORDING of Malaysian MH-17 SHOOT-DOWN of Russian Rebel Forces in Ukraine," *You Tube*, 17 July 2014, www.youtube.com/watch?v=ZJnD1wgofYM.

Avakov, Arsen. "Lozh' i pravda," *Ekho Moskvy*, 17 June 2014, http://echo.msk.ru/blog/echomsk/1342014-echo/.

"Bombing of the city of Lugansk the Ukrainian jet on June 2, 2014," *YouTube*, 4 June 2014, www.youtube.com/watch?v=T8IG_xm6Gbo, last accessed on 5 April 2016.

"Breaking: Estonian Foreign Minister Urmas Paet and Catherine Ashton discuss Ukraine over the phone," *You Tube*, 5 March 2014, www.youtube.com/watch?v=ZEgJ0oo3OA8.

"*Briefing on the Events in Odessa, Ukraine on 2 May 2014*," Council of Europe International Advisory Panel, 4 November 2015, www.coe.int/en/web/portal/international-advisory-panel/-/asset_publisher/EPeqGGDr0yBr/content/the-iap-and-the-events-in-odessa-on-2-may-2014 and http://coe.kiev.ua/iap/news/2014/09/12–09-2014-en.html.

"Budapest Memorandums on Security Assurances," *Council on Foreign Relations*, 5 December 1994, www.cfr.org/arms-control-disarmament-and-nonproliferation/budapest-memorandums-security-assurances-1994/p32484.

"Bucharest Summit Declaration," NATO, 3 April 2008, www.nato.int/cps/en/natohq/official_texts_8443.htm?selectedLocale=en.

Charter on a Distinctive Partnership between the North Atlantic Treaty Organization and Ukraine, NATO, 9 July 1997, www.nato.int/cps/en/natohq/official_texts_25457.htm.

"The Crisis in Kosovo," *Human Rights Watch*, 2000, www.hrw.org/reports/2000/nato/Natbm200-01.htm, last accessed 9 October 2015.

"Declaration to Complement the Charter on a Distinctive Partnership between the North Atlantic Treaty Organization and Ukraine, as signed on 9 July 1997," *NATO*, 21 August 2009, www.nato.int/cps/en/natohq/official_texts_57045.htm?selectedLocale=en.

"Despite Concerns about Governance, Ukrainians Want to Remain One Country," Global Attitudes, *Pew Research Center*, 8 May 2014, www.pewglobal.org/2014/05/08/despite-concerns-about-governance-ukrainians-want-to-remain-one-country/.

"Dvadtsyat' svidchen' pro perelamnii den' protistoyan' na Maidani (English subtitles)," *UkrLife*, 27 May 2014, www.youtube.com/watch?v=vs_4skLIqns.

"Eastern Ukraine: Humanitarian disaster looms as food aid blocked," *Amnesty International*, 24 December 2014, www.amnesty.org/en/latest/news/2014/12/eastern-ukraine-humanitarian-disaster-looms-food-aid-blocked/.

European Commission against Racism and Intolerance

(ECRI) Report on Ukraine (fourth cycle), Council of Europe, 8 December 2011, www.coe.int/t/dghl/monitoring/ecri/Country-by-country/Ukraine/UKR-CbC-IV-2012-006-ENG.pdf.

European Parliament Resolution 2012/2889 (RSP) on the Situation in Ukraine, European Parliament/Legislative Observatory, 13 December 2012, www.europarl.europa.eu/oeil/popups/summary.do?id=1239823&t=e&l=en.

"Founding Act on Mutual Relations, Cooperation and Security Between NATO and the Russian Federation, signed in Paris, France," *NATO*, 27 May 1997, www.nato.int/cps/en/natolive/official_texts_25468.htm.

"Geneva Statement on Ukraine," *EU External Action Service*, 17 April 2014, www.eeas.europa.eu/statements/docs/2014/140417_01_en.pdf.

"Georgia: Parliamentary Elections, 21 May 2008," OSCE/ODHIR Election Observer Mission Final Report (Warsaw: OSCE Office for Democratic Elections and Human Rights, 9 September 2008, www.osce.org/odihr/elections/georgia/33301?download=true.

"Georgia: Presidential Elections, 5 January 2008," OSCE/ODHIR Election Observer Mission Final Report (Warsaw: OSCE Office for Democratic Elections and Human Rights, 4 March 2008, www.osce.org/odihr/elections/georgia/30959?download=true.

"Hammer-wielding nationalists storm town council meeting in Kiev suburbs (VIDEOS)," *Russia Today*, 4 March 2014, www.rt.com/news/nationalists-storm-council-meeting-701/.

"Hearing: Russia's Destabilization of Ukraine," United States House of Representatives Committee on Foreign Affairs, 8 May 2014, http://foreignaffairs.house.gov/hearing/hearing-russia-s-destabilization-ukraine.

"Helsinki Final Act, Conference on Security and Cooperation in Europe, Helsinki, 1975," Osce.org, www.osce.org/mc/39501?download=true.

"HRW Calls on Germany to Pressure Ukraine on Civilian Casualties," *Voice of America*, 6 January 2015, www.voanews.com/content/hrw-calls-on-germany-to-pressure-ukraine-on-civilian-casualties/2587203.html.

"Ideologichni osnovi Ukrainskoi derzhavnosti: Problema Vybori," *Pravyysector.info*, 11 June 2015, http://pravyysektor.info/news/chogo-pragnemo/57/ideologichni-osnovi-ukrayinskoyi-derzhavnosti-problema-viboru.html.

"Igor' Strelkov o sebe," Youtubewww, 10 July 2014, www.youtube.com/watch?v=oz2tUtWQpx0.

"Incendiary Weapons: Recent Use and Growing Opposition," *Human Rights Watch*, November 2014, www.hrw.org/sites/default/files/supporting_resources/incendiary_weapons_recent_use_and_growing_opposition_nov2014_final.pdf.

"The Inflation Rate in Ukraine," *StatBuraeau*, www.statbureau.org/en/ukraine/inflation.

"Interview: Toomas Hendrik Ilves," *The Messenger* (Tbilisi), 25 January 2008, www.messenger.com.ge/issues/1532_january_25_2008/1532_ilves_interview.html.

"Investigation of May 2014 events in Odesa failed to comply with requirements of European Human Right Convention, says International Advisory Panel's report," Council of Europe Press Release—

DC155(2015), Council of Europe, 4 November 2015, https://wcd.coe.int/ViewDoc.jsp?Ref=DC-PR155 (2015)&Language=lanEnglish&Ver=original&Site= DC&BackColorInternet=F5CA75&BackColorIn tranet=F5CA75&BackColorLogged=A9BACE.

"Jen Psaki, Spokesperson, Daily Press Briefing, Washington, D.C., 11 December 2013," U.S. Department of State, 11 December 2013, www.state.gov/r/pa/prs/dpb/2013/12/218597.htm.

"Kak by vy otneslis' k perspektive obrazovaniya 'Slavyanskogo' bloka (Rossiya-Ukraina-Belarus')," *VTsIOM*, 15 March 1998, http://wciom.ru/zh/print_q.php?s_id=393&q_id=32019&date=15.03.1998.

"Kak by vy otneslis' k vstupleniyu v NATO byvshikh respublik SSSR—stran Baltii, Ukrainy i drugikh," *VTsIOM*, 15 April 1996, http://wciom.ru/zh/print_q.php?s_id=453&q_id=35325&date=15.04.1996.

"Kak by vy otneslis' k vstupleniyu v NATO byvshikh respublik SSSR—stran Baltii, Ukrainy i drugikh," *VTsIOM*, 10 February 1997, http://wciom.ru/zh/print_q.php?s_id=437&q_id=35005&date=10.02.1997).

"Kak by vy otneslis' k vstupleniyu v NATO byvshikh respublik SSSR—stran Baltii, Ukrainy i drugikh," *VTsIOM*, 20 March 1997, http://wciom.ru/zh/print_q.php?s_id=440&q_id=35061&date=20.03.1997.

"Kak by vy otneslis' k vstupleniyu v NATO byvshikh stran Varshavskogo Dogovora—Polsh'i, Chekhii, Vengrii, i drugikh?," *VTsIOM*, 15 April 1996, http://wciom.ru/zh/print_q.php?s_id=453&q_id=35324&date=15.04.1996.

"Kak by vy otneslis' k vstupleniyu v NATO byvshikh stran Varshavskogo Dogovora—Polsh'i, Chekhii, Vengrii, i drugikh?, *VTsIOM*, 10 February 1997, http://wciom.ru/zh/print_q.php?s_id=437&q_id=35004&date=10.02.1997.

"Kak prorossiiskie separatisty segodnya zakhvatyvali zdanie Donetskoi OGA (VIDEO)," *Munitsipal'naya gazeta*, 6 April 2014, http://mungaz.net/main/11622-kak-prorossiyskie-separatisty-segodnya-zahvatyvali-zdanie-doneckoy-oga-video.htm.

"Kak v Donetske, zakhvatyvali OGA—Chrezvychainyie novosti, 07.04," *YouTube*, 7 April 2014, www.youtube.com/watch?v=C12ewZOQxAM.

"Kontseptsiya uchastiya Rossiiskoi Federatsii v ob"edinnenii BRIKS, *Kremlin.ru*, 21 March 2013, www.kremlin.ru/events/president/news/17715 and http://news.kremlin.ru/media/events/files/41d452a8a232b 2f6f8a5.pdf.

"Kontstitutsiya Ukrainy," *Nezavisimay gazeta-Stsenarii*, 29 August 1996: 3–5.

"Korotokiy ideolohichno vyhovniy kurs dlya vo tryzub im s Bandery ta pravoho sektora," *Pravyysektor.info*, 27 November 2015, http://old.pravyysektor.info/articles/korotkyj-ideolohichno-vyhovnyj-kurs-dlya-vo-tryzub-im-s-bandery-ta-pravoho-sektora/.

"Latest from OSCE Special Monitoring Mission (SMM) to Ukraine based on information received as of 18:00 (Kyiv time), 21 August 2014," *OSCE*, 22 August 2014, http://www.osce.org/node/122920.

"Latest from the Special Monitoring Mission to Ukraine—based on information received up until 28 April 2014, 19:00 (Kyiv time)," *OSCE*, 28 April 2014, www.osce.org/ukraine-smm/118153.

Library, *CANVAS*, www.canvasopedia.org/index.php/library.

"Lyashko nabil mordu Dobkinu," *YouTube*, 24 May 2014, https://www.youtube.com/watch?v=CaHT78 OQbpo.

Lyashko, Oleg. *Facebook*, 23 May 2014, https://m.facebook.com/story.php?story_fbid=646486682086599&id=100001758206922.

"Lyashko ustroil potasovku s okhrannikom na Bankovoi. Polnaya versiya (04-04-2013)," *YouTube*, 5 April 2013, www.youtube.com/watch?v=XlPfht-Cpqk.

"Maidan—February 20, 2014 (3)," *You Tube*, 20 February 2014, www.youtube.com/watch?v=PXwLuDlhf1E.

"Minsk agreement on Ukraine crisis: text in full," *The Guardian*, 12 February 2015, www.telegraph.co.uk/news/worldnews/europe/ukraine/11408266/Minsk-agreement-on-Ukraine-crisis-text-in-full.html.

"Moskaly na nozhi," *YouTube*, 20 April 2014, www.youtube.com/watch?v=tyXToXTNDpc.

"My uvichnimo pam'yat geroiv, ochistivshi nashu zemlyu vid nichisti, Arsenii Yatsenyuku spyvchutti rodnim i bliz'kim zagiblikh voiniv u Lugans'ku," *Ukrainian Embassy in the United States of America*, 15 June 2014 http://usa.mfa.gov.ua/ua/press-center/news/24185-mi-uvichnimo-pamjaty-gerojiv-ochistivshi-nashu-zemlyu-vid-nechistiarsenij-jacenyuk-u-spivchutti-ridnim-i-blizykim-zagiblih-vojiniv-u-lugansyku.

"Na Maidany strilyav til'ki odin Avtomat AK-74," *YouTube*, 24 November 2014, www.youtube.com/watch?v=cZz_VOa9REA.

"NATO's Relations with Georgia," *NATO*, 7 September 2015, www.nato.int/cps/en/natohq/topics_38988.htm?selectedLocale=en.

NATO-Ukraine Action Plan, *NATO*, 22 November 2005, www.nato.int/cps/en/natohq/official_texts_21735.htm?selectedLocale=en.

"Ne 46, a 189 chelovek unichtozheno v Odesse 2 maya…," *Stikhi.ru*, 5 May 2014, www.stihi.ru/2014/05/05/5404, last accessed on 27 March 2016.

"Nebesnaya sotna," http://nebesnasotnya.com.ua/ru/.

"New Citizen Centre (UA)," *Omidlyar Network*, https://web.archive.org/web/20120310103804/http://www.omidyar.com/portfolio/new-citizen-centre-ua, last accessed 5 January 2015.

"New Satellite Imagery Exposes Russian Combat Troops Inside Ukraine," The U.S. Mission to NATO, 28 August 2014, http://usnato.tumblr.com/post/9600308 6125/new-satellite-imagery-exposes-russian-combat.

News release, "Cardin Urges Immediate Action by Ukrainian Officials to Respect Human Rights," Commission on Security and Cooperation in Europe, December 11, 2013, www.csce.gov/index.cfm?FuseAction=ContentRecords.ViewDetail&ContentRecord_id=1116&ContentRecordType=P&ContentType=P&CFID=2039749&CFTOKEN=dc1d5da2b9 24f61b-F019953C-9E0D-566C-6B2EE9A222F6A826.

"Newsgathering and Policy Perceptions in Ukraine," *Gallup*, April 2014, www.bbg.gov/wp-content/media/2014/06/Ukraine-slide-deck.pdf.

"Odessa, 02.05.2014, 'Kill Them All!!!'" *YouTube*, 4 May 2014, www.youtube.com/watch?v=5E12kkFM3nQ.

"Odessa 2 maya. Polnaya khronologiya (ch. 1–6)+ bloger+ubiitsa #Odessa holocaust chronology (18+)," *YouTube*, 21 May 2014, www.youtube.com/watch?v=n2sH8IqEGR4.

"Odessa, 2 travnya 2014, ho roku zhadaymo—video," *Pravyysektor.info*, 2 May 2015, http://pravyysektor.info/news/odesa-2-travyna-2014-ho-roku-zhadajmo-video/.

"Odessa beginning pravy sector flags inside," *YouTube*, 7 May 2014, www.youtube.com/watch?v=5HOfLxp896I&feature=youtu.be, last accessed on 28 March 2016.

"Odessa dom profsoyuzov POLNOE VIDEO," *You Tube*, 2 May 2014, www.youtube.com/watch?v=s9AMjLBIliw.

"Odessa pravy sector inside the customs house," *You Tube*, 7 May 2014, www.youtube.com/watch?v=VaCVxP_QApk&feature=youtu.be.

"Odessa. Tragediya 2-ogo maya 2014 goda. Ot nachal i do...kontsa," *YouTube*, 19 December 2014, www.youtube.com/watch?v=vRXHVSjV1IM.

"Odesskaya tragediya: Po itogam 20 mesyatsev rassledovaniya," *2 May Group BlogSpot*, 14 January 2016, http://2maygroup.blogspot.ca/2016/01/20.html#more.

"Odin iz pistoletiv, viluchenikh vid predstavnikiv 'Pravogo sektora' na 'Dragobaty,' buv vikradenii y lyutomu 2014 roku pid chas zakhlopennya upravlinnya SBU v Ivano-Frankiviskiy oblasti," *Zakarpat'ska oblasna derzhanva administratsiya*, 16 January 2016, www.carpathia.gov.ua/ua/publication/content/12885.htm.

"Oleh Tiahnibok: The time has come for total social and national revolution," *Svoboda*, 1 December 2013, http://en.svoboda.org.ua/news/comments/00008465/.

"Pidsumki slidstva shodo masovikh zavorushen' v Odesi 2 travnya 2014 roku. YKMTs, 14-01-2016," *You Tube*, 14 January 2016, www.youtube.com/watch?v=miCCGaepGFw.

"Postanovlenie Verkhovogo Soveta Kryma 'Ob Akte ob provozglashenii gosudarstvennoi samostoyatel'nosti Respubliki Krim," *Vedomosti Verkhovonogo Soveta Kryma 1991–1992*, No. 6, pp. 240–44, http://sevkrimrus.narod.ru/ZAKON/1992ref.htm.

"'Post-Orange' Ukraine: Internal Dynamics and Foreign Policy Priorities," *NATO Parliamentary Assembly*, 2011, www.nato-pa.int/default.Asp?SHORTCUT=2439.

"Pravyi Sektor vzyal shturmom Verkhovnyi Sud Ukrainy—Chrezvychainyie novosti—07.04," *YouTube*, 7 April 2014, www.youtube.com/watch?v=jitMYOxCc8.

"Pravyi sector—rozvidka boem pid Karlivkoyu 10.07.2014," *YouTube*, 11 July 2014, uploaded by Olena Bilozerska, www.youtube.com/watch?v=SadSxCzgdc#t=177.

"Pravyi Sektor na sessii v Vasil'kove. Regionaly otkazasilis' pet' gimn Ukrainy???" *YouTube*, 25 February 2014, www.youtube.com/watch?v=9fKIq8fE1CE.

"President Putin's Fiction: 10 False Claims About Ukraine," U.S. State Department "Diplomacy in Action," 5 March 2014, www.state.gov/r/pa/prs/ps/2014/03/222988.htm.

"Prezident Rossii Vladimir Putin obratilsya k opolcheniyu Novorossii," *Kremlin.ru*, 29 August 2014, www.kremlin.ru/events/president/news/46506.

"Programa Pravogo Sektora," *Pravyysektor.info*, http://pravyysektor.info/programa.html.

"Programa, Sotsialno-Natsionalna Assembleya," *Snaua.info*, http://snaua.info/programa/.

"Programma partii 'Svoboda,'" *Kievl.org*, 15 December 2013, http://kievl.org/programma-partii-svoboda.html.

"Prospects for Democracy in Yugoslavia," Hearing of the European Affairs Subcommittee of the Senate Foreign Affairs Committee, United States Senate, 29 July 1999, http://emperors-clothes.com/analysis/hearin.htm, last accessed on 22 October 2015.

Public Opinion Survey Residents of the Autonomous Republic of Crimea—May 16–30, 2013, International Republican Institute and the United States Agency for International Development, May 2013, www.iri.org/sites/default/files/2013%20October%207%20Survey%20of%20Crimean %20Public%20Opinion,%20May%2016-30,%202013.pdf.

"Public opinion trends with regard to NATO in post–Soviet countries during the 90's—Final Report," *NATO*, 2001, www.nato.int/acad/fellow/01-03/sikharulidze.pdf.

"Putin: UN Libya resolution defective, reminds of Medieval call for Crusade," *YouTube*, 21 March 2011, www.youtube.com/watch?v=BvP3BW21VWU.

Putin, Vladimir. "Novyi integratsionnyi proekt dlya Yevrazii—budushee, kotoroe rozhdaetsy segodnya," *Izvestiya*, 4 October 2011, http://izvestia.ru/news/502761.

"Remarks by President Obama before Restricted Bilateral Meeting," *White House*, 20 February 2014, www.whitehouse.gov/the-press-office/2014/02/19/remarks-president-obama-restricted-bilateral-meeting.

Report of the European Union Independent International Fact-Finding Mission on the Conflict in Georgia, Volume I, http://91.121.127.28/ceiig/pdf/IIFFMCG_Volume_I.pdf.

Report of the European Union Independent International Fact-Finding Mission on the Conflict in Georgia, Volume II, http://91.121.127.28/ceiig/pdf/IIFFMCG_Volume_II.pdf.

"Report of the International Advisory Panel on its review of the Maidan Investigations," Council of Europe International Advisory Council, 31 March 2015, https://rm.coe.int/CoERMPublic CommonSearch Services/DisplayDCTMContent?documentId=09000016802f038b.

"Report on the Human Rights Situation in Ukraine, 16 August to 15 November 2015," UN Office of the High Commissioner on Human Rights, December 2015, www.ohchr.org/Documents/Countries/UA/12thOHCHRreportUkraine.pdf.

"Resolution 1244 (1999)"—NATO's Role in Kosovo, *NATO*, 30 June 1999, www.nato.int/kosovo/ docu/u990610a.htm.

"Roku slidchiy suddya Pechers'kogo raionnogo sudu m. Kieva Karaban' V.M., pri sekretari Maiorenko Ya.M., za uchastyu storoni kriminal'nogo provadzhennnya slidchogo Nechitalyuka M.M.," Ukhvala Imenem Ukrainiy, Sprava No. 757/5885/16-k, Pecherskiy Raionniy Sud Mista Kieva," Ediniy derzhavniy ryeestr sudovikh rishen', *Reyestr.court.gov.ua*, 12 February 2016, http://reyestr.court.gov.ua/Review/55966993.

Roth, Andrew. "Ukraine Used Cluster Bombs, Evidence Indicates," *New York Times*, 21 October 2014, www.nytimes.com/2014/10/21/world/ukraine-used-cluster-bombs-report-charges.html?google_editors_picks=true.

"RUSSIA & UKRAINE. 'Get' moskaliv na nozhi," *You Tube*, 29 September 2011, www.youtube.com/watch?v=lSGqlV65TwI.

"Sakashvili's Televised Address on S. Ossetia," *Civil Georgia*, 7 August 2008, 21:45, www.civil.ge.

"Shchodo zbroinoi provokatsii u Paskhal'nu nich bilya m. Slov'yansk," *Sluzhba bezopeki Ukrainy*, 20 April 2014, www.sbu.gov.ua/sbu/control/uk/publish/art icle?art_id=124389&cat_id=39574.

"Second Anniversary of Ukraine's Revolution of Dignity"—Press Statement, U.S. Department of State, 20 February 2016, www.state.gov/r/pa/prs/ps/2016/02/253092.htm.

Semen Semenchenko, "Biografiya," *Samopomich.ua*, 2 September 2014, http://samopomich.ua/wp-con tent/uploads/2014/09/02_Semenchenko.pdf.

"S. Res. 319 - A resolution expressing support for the Ukrainian people in light of President Yanukovych's decision not to sign an Association Agreement with the European Union.113th Congress (2013–2014), Congress.gov, 12 December 2013, www.congress. gov/bill/113th-congress/senate-resolution/319/text.

"Separatisty vystavali ultimatum: referendum o vkho-zhdenii Donetsloi oblasti v sostav RF," *Novosti Donbassa*, 6 April 2014, http://novosti.dn.ua/details/221 964/.

"Shestvia Azova i Pravogo sektora po Kievu," *YouTube*, 14 October 2014, uploaded by Pavel Sheremet, www. youtube.com/watch?v=LcTHHuqAf10&feature= youtu.be and www.youtube.com/watch?v=AJjBrgx WF8M&ebc=ANyPxKpXOGCNqrTf38UgQ4S7BiH 5rQcUoXvwzuplFHT3LEbn8STOELJ3awAKlmojqr SpneaXuDEK9ToxMoFje9EYDudWnQc0NA.

"Slovo bilogo vozhdya.pdf," *VKontakte*, http://vk.com/doc29866988_319980052?hash=14c0a1bebe416193ef &dl=a33eceb6cbe50c4daf.

"Sotnik Mykola strelyavshii po ltydyam 2 maya v Odesse umer v bol'nitse," *YouTube*, 6 May 2014, www.youtube.com/watch?v=97CnI006jwc.

"Spetsnaz osvobodil zakhvachennoe separatistami zdanie SBU v Donetske," *Ukrainskaya pravda*, 16 April 2014, www.pravda.com.ua/rus/news/2014/04/7/7021678/.

"Srochno! Sessiya Pervomaisk Liganskaya Oblast' 29. 04.2014," *YouTube*, posted by Aleksandr Anikin, 29 April 2014, www.youtube.com/watch?v=NYnQKnw wcwE.

State Statistics Committee of Ukraine, October 2010, www.ukrstat.gov.ua/operativ/operativ2010/gdn/reg_zp_m/reg_zpm10_u.htm.

"Statement by Dmitry Medvedev on the situation in Libya," *Kremlin.ru*, 21 March 2011, http://en.kremlin.ru/events/president/news/10701.

"Statement by the Press Secretary on Ukraine," *White House*, 22 February 2014, www.whitehouse.gov/the-press-office/2014/02/22/statement-press-secretary-ukraine.

"Statement by the Press Secretary on Ukraine," *White House*, 26 February 2014, www.whitehouse.gov/the-press-office/2014/02/26/statement-press-secretary-ukraine.

"Stenograma zasedannya Rady natsional'noi bezpeki i oborony Ukrainy, vid 28 lyutogo 2014 roku shodo sitsuatsii, yaka skalalsya v derzhavi kyntsy lyutogo-berozni 2014 roky (pitanyaya aneksii Avtonomnoi Respubliki Krym," *Rady natsional'noi bezpeki i oborony Ukrainy*, 22 February 2016, www.rnbo.gov. ua/files/2016/stenogr.pdf.

"Strilyanina u Kremenchutsi: v misti lovili garbizhnikiv, yaki stverdzhuvali, scho vony—z ATO, Hromadskoe TV," *YouTube*, 19 May 2015, www.youtube.com/watch?v=OqC9SfQZQcw.

"Studgorodok KNY im. Shevchenko 09.04.14 Khto ne skache, toi moskal.' Moskaliv na nozhi," *YouTube*, 8 April 2014, www.youtube.com/watch?v=oBrgaFH 02UE.

"Sud pochav rpzglyad spravi she tr'okh eks-berku-tivtsiv," *YouTube*, 26 January 2016, www.youtube.com/watch?v=RgBoTKewzVQ.

Trofymenko, Eugene. "ATO Po-narodnomu, Abo chomu ne Vladimir Putin ne vviv viyska," *Pravyisektor.info*, 2 May 2014, http://pravyysektor.info/art icles/ato-po-narodnomu-abo-chomu-ne-vladimir-putin-ne-vviv-vijska/, archived at http://archive.is/ y12mT.

"Ukhvala imenem Ukraini—Sprava No. 757/13417/15-k," Pecherskiy raionniy sudy mista Kiev, *Yediniy Derzhavniy reestr sudovikh rishen*,' 23 April 2015, http://reyestr.court.gov.ua/Review/52100569.

"Ukhvala imenem Ukraini—Sprava No. 757/37002/15-k," Pecherskiy raionniy sudy mista Kiev, *Yediniy Derzhavniy reestr sudovikh rishen*,' 7 October 2015, http://reyestr.court.gov.ua/Review/52580748.

"Ukhvala imenem Ukraini—Sprava No. 757/37009/15-k," Pecherskiy raionniy sudy mista Kiev, *Yediniy Derzhavniy reestr sudovikh rishen*,' 7 October 2015, http://reyestr.court.gov.ua/Review/52580547.

"Ukhvala imenem Ukraini—Sprava No. 757/39038/15-k," Pecherskiy raionniy sudy mista Kiev, *Yediniy Derzhavniy reestr sudovikh rishen*,' 30 October 2015, http://reyestr.court.gov.ua/Review/53868110.

"Ukhvala imenem Ukraini—Sprava No. 757/40033/15-k," Pecherskiy raionniy sudy mista Kiev, *Yediniy Derzhavniy reestr sudovikh rishen*,' 29 October 2015, http://reyestr.court.gov.ua/Review/53416626.

"Ukhvala imenem Ukraini—Sprava No. 757/42824/15-k," Pecherskiy raionniy sudy mista Kiev, *Yediniy Derzhavniy reestr sudovikh rishen*,' 20 November 2015, http://reyestr.court.gov.ua/Review/54278484.

"Ukhvala imenem Ukraini—Sprava No. 757/47700/ 15-k," Pecherskiy raionniy sudy mista Kiev, *Yediniy Derzhavniy reestr sudovikh rishen*,' 23 December 2015, http://reyestr.court.gov.ua/Review/54672972.

"Ukraina: vnimanie, otnoshenie, peremirie," *Levada Center*, 26 February 2015, www.levada.ru/26-02-2015/ukraina-vnimanie-otnoshenie-peremirie.

"Ukraine. 2014. Kiev, February 18th. Maidan square clashes," *Cesura.it*, www.cesura.it/projectGallery. php?pagineCod=2205416.

"Ukraine: Abuses and War Crimes by the Aidar Volunteer Battalion in North Luhansk Region," *Amnesty International*, 8 September 2014, www.amnesty.org/en/documents/EUR50/040/2014/en/.

"Ukraine: Aidar Battalion and Right Sector demand end to ceasefire in E. Ukraine," *YouTube*, 3 July 2015, www.youtube.com/watch?v=fI5NLekWP_4.

Ukraine Local Government Assessment, USAID, 19 February 2007, http://pdf.usaid.gov/pdf_docs/PNADK 461.pdf.

"Ukraine: More Civilians Killed in Cluster Munition Attacks," *Human Rights Watch*, 19 March 2015, www. hrw.org/news/2015/03/19/ukraine-more-civilians-killed-cluster-munition-attacks.

"Ukraine: Mounting evidence of war crimes and Russian involvement," Amnesty International, 7 September 2014, www.amnesty.org/en/latest/news/2014/09/ukraine-mounting-evidence-war-crimes-and-russian-involvement/.

"Ukraine: Ruptly reporter shot by Maidan sniper," *You*

Tube, 20 February 2014, www.youtube.com/watch?v=wzq1xUGnzIs.

"Ukraine: Snipers target police in Independence Square," *YouTube*, 20 February 2014, www.youtube.com/watch?v=n2PTeUBCPAQ.

"Ukraine Unemployment Rate," *Trading Economics*, 22 September 2016, www.tradingeconomics.com/ukraine/unemployment-rate.

"Ukraine: Unguided Rockets Killing Civilians," *Human Rights Watch*, 24 July 2014, https://www.hrw.org/news/2014/07/24/ukraine-unguided-rockets-killing-civilians.

"Ukraine: Widespread Use of Cluster Munitions," *Human Rights Watch*, 20 October 2014, www.hrw.org/news/2014/10/20/ukraine-widespread-use-cluster-munitions.

"Ukrainian Troops Move Toward Crimean Peninsula Border," YouTubewww, 9 March 2014, www.youtube.com/watch?v=DpkLVt9aWEU.

"Ukrainskii krizis: uchastie Rossii i ozhidaniya," *Levada Center*, 4 March 2015, www.levada.ru/04-03-2015/ukrainskii-krizis-uchastie-rossii-i-ozhidaniya.

"UN Human Rights Council: Human Rights situation in Ukraine," Human Rights Watch, 9 December 2015, www.hrw.org/news/2015/12/09/un-human-rights-council-human-rights-situation-ukraine.

"United States Policy Regarding NATO Expansion," U.S. House of Representatives, Committee on National Security, Washington, D.C., July 17, 1997, http://commdocs.house.gov/committees/security/has198000.000/has198000_1.HTM, last accessed 8 October 2015.

U.S. Ambassador Geoffrey Pyatt, "Making Good on the Promise of the Maidan," U.S. Embassy Kyiv Blog, 19 February 2016, https://usembassykyiv.wordpress.com.

"US Recognizes Kosovo as Independent State," U.S. Department of State, 18 February 2008, http://2001-2009.state.gov/secretary/rm/2008/02/100973.htm.

"V semi oblastyakh Ukrainy razgoraetsya narodnoe vosstanie: aktivisty shtormiruyut OGA i vozvodyat barrikady," *Censor.net*, 24 January 2014, http://censor.net.ua/video_news/267817/v_semi_oblastyah_ukrainy_razgoraetsya_narodnoe_vosstanie_aktivisty_shturmuyut_oga_i_vozvodyat_barrikady.

"Valoviy regionalniy product, 2004–2013," State Committee of Statistics of Ukraine, *Ukrstat.gov.ua*, 2013, www.ukrstat.gov.ua/operativ/operativ2008/vvp/vrp/vrp2008_u.htm.

"Vatnik. Otkuda vzaylos' Kto ne skachet, tot Moskal," *Krasview*, 1 March 2016, http://krasview.ru/video/655732-Vatnik-otkuda_vzyalos_Kto_ne_skachet_tot_Moskal.

"The Views and Opinion of South-Eastern Regions Residents of Ukraine, April 2014," *KIIS*, 20 April 2014, www.kiis.com.ua/?lang=eng&cat=reports&id=302&page=1&y=2014&m=4.

"Vinnitsa. Zakhvat oblastnoi gosudarstbennoi administratsii, 25.01.2014," *YouTube*, 26 January 2014, www.youtube.com/watch?v=-qoRDfyZNCg.

"Violent video: Ukraine TV boss beaten up by far-right Svoboda MPs," *Euronews*, 19 March 2014, www.youtube.com/watch?v=F5GeBpZ5VHY.

Vystuplenie i otvety na voprosy Ministra innostrannykh del Rossii S.V. Lavrov na Forume 'Territoriya smyslov na Klyaz'me,' Vladimirskaya oblast,' d.Dvorkin, 24 August 2015, Mid.ru (website of the Russian Ministry of Foreign Affairs), 24 August 2015, www.mid.ru/press_service/minister_speeches/-/asset_publisher/7OvQR5KJWVmR/content/id/1680936.

"Vystuplenie prezidenta Rossii Vladimira Putina na Myunkhenskoi konferentstii po voprosam politiki bezopasnosti 10 fevralya 2007 goda," *Izvestia*, 12 February 2007, http://izvestia.ru/news/321595.

"Vystuplenie V. Putina na Myunkhenskoi konferentstii (2007g.)," *YouTube*, 10 February 2007, www.youtube.com/watch?v=PkyjYKVYlWo.

"Who We Are," *CANVAS*, www.canvasopedia.org/index.php/who-we-are, last accessed 10 November 2015.

"'Why?' Entire E. Ukraine village bombed by airstrike, 5 yr-old among dead," *YouTube*, 3 July 2014, www.youtube.com/watch?v=fxAdc9JRAo0.

"Zayavlenie MID Rossii po situatsiyam na Ukraine," Ministry of Foreign Affairs of the Russian Federation, Mid.ru, 27 February 2014, www.mid.ru/press_service/spokesman/official_statement/-/asset_publisher/t2GCdmD8RNIr/content/id/73254.

Secondary Sources

Adamishin, Anatolii. "Yugoslavskaya Prelyudiya." *Rossiya v Global'noi Politike*, No. 4, July–August 2013, www.globalaffairs.ru/number/Yugoslavskaya-prelyudiya-16104.

Ames, Mark. "Hero of the Orange Revolution Poisons Ukraine." *The Nation*, 12 February 2010, www.thenation.com/article/hero-orange-revolution-poisons-ukraine/.

_____. "Pierre Omidlyar co-funded Ukraine revolution groups with US government, documents show." Pandowww, 28 February 2014, http://pando.com/2014/02/28/pierre-omidyar-co-funded-ukraine-revolution-groups-with-us-government-documents-show/.

"The anti–Semitic Svoboda Union wins representation in the Ukrainian parliament." *The Coordinating Forum for Countering Antisemitism*, 6 November 2012, http://antisemitism.org.il/article/75709/antisemitic-svoboda-all-ukrainian-union-wins-representation-ukrainian-parliament.

Arel, Dominique. "The Orange Revolution's hidden face: Ukraine and the denial of its regional problem," *Revue Detudes Comparatives Est-Ouest*, Volume 37, 2006: 11–48.

Asmus, Ronald D. *A Little War That Shook the World: Georgia, Russia, and the Future of the West.* New York: St. Martin's Press, 2010.

Asmus, Ronald D., and Robert C. Nurick. "NATO Enlargement and the Baltic States." *Survival* 38, Number 2 (Summer 1996): 121–42.

Axelrod, Toby. "European Jewish Parliament off to a semi-comic start." Jweeklywww, 3 November 2011, www.jweekly.com/article/full/63331/european-jewish-parliament-off-to-a-semi-comedic-start/.

Babitskii, Andrei. "Andreii Babitskii: 'Ni odnu iz storon konflikta ne priemlyu," *Slon.ru*, 20 July 2015, https://slon.ru/posts/54216.

Barany, Zoltan. *The Future of NATO Expansion: Four Case Studies.* Cambridge: Cambridge University Press, 2003.

Barrington, Lowell. "The Geographic Component of Mass Attitudes in Ukraine." *Post-Soviet Geography* 38 (1997): 601–614.

Barrington, Lowell, and Erick Herron. "One Ukraine

or Many? Regionalism in Ukraine and its political consequences." *Nationalities Papers* 32 (2004): 53–86.

Barrington, Lowell, and Regina Faranda. "Reexamining Region, Ethnicity, and Language in Ukraine." *Post-Soviet Affairs* 25 (2009): 232–256.

Bekeshkin, I.E. "Parlamentskie vybory v Ukraine: predvidimoe in nepredvidimoe," in *Yezhegodnaya nauchno-prakticheskaya sotsiologicheskaya konferentsiya 'Prodolzhaya Grushina,'* Moscow: VTsIOM, 2012, http://wciom.ru/fileadmin/file/nauka/grusha_2013/7.pdf.

Berkhoff, Kerel C. "Dina Pronicheva's Story of Surviving the Babi Yar Massacre: German, Jewish, Soviet, Russian, and Ukrainian Records." In Ray Brandon and Wendy Lower, eds., *The Shoah in Ukraine: History, Testimony, Memorialization.* Bloomington: Indiana University Press, 2010: 291–317.

Bidder, Benjamin. "Kampf gegen separatisten: Ukrainische Freischarler sollen Graueltaten begangen haben." *Der Spiegel*, 29 July 2015, www.spiegel.de/politik/ausland/ukraine-prozess-gegen-pro-ukrainischer-kaempfer-a-1045801.html.

Birch, Sarah. "Interpreting the Regional Effect in Ukrainian Politics." *Europe-Asia Studies* 52 (2000): 1017–1042.

Blacker, Coit D. "Russia and the West." In Michael Mandelbaum, ed., *The New Russian Foreign Policy.* Washington, D.C.: Council of Foreign Relations, 1998: 167–93.

Boese, Wade. "US Withdraws from ABM Treaty; Global Response Muted." *Arms Control Association*, 8 July 2002, www.armscontrol.org/act/2002_07-08/abmjul_aug02.

Brandon, Ray, and Wendy Lower, eds. *The Shoah in Ukraine: History, Testimony, Memorialization.* Bloomington: Indiana University Press, 2010: 291–317.

Brinton, Crane. *The Anatomy of Revolution*, revised edition. New York: Vintage Books, 1965.

Bruder, Fraziska. *"Dem ukrainischen Staat erkampfen oder sterben!": Die Organizatsion Ukrainischer Nationalisten (OUN), 1928–1948.* Berlin: Metropol Verlag, 2007.

Brzezinski, Zbigniew. *The Grand Chessboard: American Primacy and Its Geostrategic Imperatives.* Signed first edition. Norwalk, CT: Easton Press, 1997.

_____. "NATO and World Security." *New York Times*, 20 August 2009, www.nytimes.com/2009/08/20/opinion/20iht-edbrzezinski.html?_r=0.

Bukarskii, Vladimir. "Panarin Alelsandr Sergeevich (1940_2003)—26 dekabrya velikomu russkomu filosofu sovremennosti Aleksandru Sergeevichu Panarinu ispolnilos' by 65 let." *Pravaya.ru*, 26 December 2005, http://pravaya.ru/ludi/451/6061.

Burakovskiy, Aleksandr. "Holocaust remembrance in Ukraine: memorialization of the Jewish tragedy at Babi Yar." *Nationalities Papers* 39, Number 3 (May 2011): 371–89, www.pendleton.k12.ky.us/userfiles/119/Classes/401/Holocaust%20remembrance%20in%20Ukraine.pdf.

_____. "Key Characteristics and Transformation of Jewish-Ukrainian Relations during the Period of Ukraine's Independence: 1991–2008." *Nationalism and Ethnic Politics* 15, Number 1 (January 2009): 109–32.

Butusov, Yurii. "Dmitro Yarosh: Pershii nastupatel'nyi biy viyny vibuvsya 20 kvytnya 2014-go—dobrovoltsy atakovali blokpost pid Slovyans'kom." *Censor.net*, 22 April 2016, http://censor.net.ua/resonance/385673/dmitro_yarosh_pershiyi_nastupalniyi_byi_vyini_vdbuvsya_20_kvtnya_2014go_dobrovolts_atakovali_blokpost.

Carr, Paul. "Pierre and Pamela Omidlar's Cozy White House Ties." Pandowww, 23 March 2014, https://pando.com/2014/03/23/revealed-visitor-logs-show-full-extent-of-pierre-and-pamela-omidyars-cozy-white-house-ties/.

Cathcart, Will, Vazha Tavberidze, and Nino Murchuladze. "The Secret Life of an ISIS Warlord." *The Daily Beast*, 27 October 2014, www.thedailybeast.com/articles/2014/10/27/the-secret-life-of-an-isis-warlord.html.

Chivers, C.J. "How Top Spies in Ukraine Changed the Nation's Path." *New York Times*, 17 January 2005, www.nytimes.com/2005/01/17/world/europe/how-top-spies-in-ukraine-changed-the-nations-path.html?_r=0.

Clarke, Jeffrey, and Jason Stout. "Elections, Revolution and Democracy in Ukraine: Reflections on a Country's Turn to Democracy, Free Elections, and the Modern World." *USAID*, October 2005, http://pdf.usaid.gov/pdf_docs/PNADE309.pdf.

Clem, Ralph S. and Peter R. Craumer. "Orange, Blue and White, and Blonde: The Electoral Geography of Ukraine's 2006 and 2007 Rada Elections." *Eurasian Geography and Economics* 49 (2008): 127–151.

_____. "Shades of Orange: The Electoral Geography of Ukraine's 2004 Presidential Elections." *Eurasian Geography and Economics* 46 (2005): 364–385.

Cohen, Roger. "Just Who Brought Down Milosevic?" *New York Times Magazine*, 26 November 2000, www.nytimes.com/library/magazine/home/20001126mag-serbia.html.

Cohen, Youssef. *Radicals, Reformers, and Reactionaries: The Prisoners' Dilemma and the Collapse of Democracy in Latin America.* Chicago, IL: Chicago University Press, 1994.

Conquest, Robert. *Harvest of Sorrow.* New York and Oxford: Oxford University Press, 1986.

Coynash, Halya. "Clear Signs of Sabotage' in Odesa 2 May Investigation." *Kharkiv Human Rights Protection Group*, 16 January 2016, http://khpg.org/en/index.php?id=1452811753.

Dugin, A.G. "Kresovyo pokhod Solntsa." In A.G. Dugin, *Konspirilogiya.* Moscow: Arktogeya, 2005, http://arcto.ru/article/1339.

_____. *Yevraziiskii put' kak natsional'naya ideya.* Moscow: Arktogeya Tsentr, 2002.

_____. "Yevraziya v setevoi voine: evraziiskie seti nakanune 2015 goda." *Evrazia.org*, 8 December 2014, http://evrazia.org/article/2609.

Dvizhdkov, D., and I. Shirle, eds. *Ponyatiya o Rossii: k istoricheskoi semantike iperskogo perioda II.* Moscow: Duetsches Historices Institut and Novoe Literaturnoe Obozrenie, 2012.

Dyukov, Alexander. "There is no Intolerance for Nazism in Ukraine." *Grupa Informatsii za zlochinami proti osobi*, 4 August 2014, http://igcp.eu/publikacii/alexander-dyukov-there-no-intolerance-nazism-ukraine?language=en.

"End of Communism Cheered But Now With More Reservations—Chapter 9. Rating the EU and NATO." *Pew Global Research*, 2 November 2009, www.pewglobal.org/2009/11/02/chapter-9-rating-the-eu-and-nato/

English, Robert. "Georgia: The Ignored History." *New York Review of Books* 55, Number 17 (6 November 2009): www.nybooks.com/articles/archives/2008/nov/06/georgia-the-ignored-history/.

Epstein, Nadine. "The Mysterious Tale of a Ukrainian University's Anti-Semitic Crusade." *Scholars for Peace in the Middle East*, 31 October 2009, http://spme.org/campus-news-climate/civil-discourse-and-academic-freedom/the-mysterious-tale-of-a-ukrainian-universitys-anti-semitic-crusade/7572/.

Evans, Peter B., Dietrich Rueschemeyer, and Theda Skocpol. *Bringing the State Back In.* Cambridge: Cambridge University Press, 1985.

Fishel, Gene. "Radicalization of Independence in Ukraine." Institute for the Study of Conflict, Ideology, and Policy at Boston University, *Perspective* 1, Number 4 (April 1991): www.bu.edu/iscip/vol1/Fishel.html.

Friedman, George. "Geopolitical Journey Part 2—Borderlands." *Stratfor*, 11 August 2010 (republished 3 June 2014), www.stratfor.com/weekly/20101108_geopolitical_journey_part_2_borderlands.

Friedman, Thomas L. "Foreign Affairs; Now a Word From X." *New York Times*, 2 May 1998, www.nytimes.com/1998/05/02/opinion/foreign-affairs-now-a-word-from-x.html.

Gallagher, Tom. *The Balkans in the New Millennium: In the Shadow of War and Peace.* London: Routledge, 2005.

Garnett, Sherman W. "Russia and the West in the New Borderlands." In Michael Mandelbaum, ed., *The New Russian Foreign Policy.* Washington, D.C.: Council of Foreign Relations, 1998: 64–99.

Gatehouse, Gabriel. "The untold story of the Maidan massacre." *BBC News Magazine*, 12 February 2015, www.bbc.com/news/magazine-31359021.

"Geroi pod grifom 'Sekretnoi.'" *Novaya gazeta*, No. 64, 16 June 2014, www.novayagazeta.ru/inquests/64030.html.

Gessen, Keith. "Why not kill them all?" *London Review of Books*, 11 September 2014, www.lrb.co.uk/v36/n17/keith-gessen/why-not-kill-them-all.

Gill, Bates. "Shanghai Five: An Attempt to Counter U.S. Influence in Asia?" *Brookings Institute*, 4 May 2001, www.brookings.edu/research/opinions/2001/05/04china-gill.

Giuliano, Elise. "The Origins of Separatism: Popular Grievances in Donetsk and Luhansk." *PONARS Policy Memo 396*, October 2014, www.ponarseurasia.org/memo/origins-separatism-popular-grievances-donetsk-and-luhansk.

Goldgeier, James M., and Michael McFaul. *Power and Purpose: U.S. Policy Toward Russia After the Cold War.* Washington, D.C.: Brookings Institution Press, 2003.

Gorbachev, Mikhail. *Zhizni i reform, Kniga 2.* Moscow: Novosti, 1995.

Gumilev, Lev. *Ot Rusi do Rossii.* Moscow: Airis Press, 2004.

Haggard, Stephen, and Robert R. Kaufman. *The Political Economy of Democratic Transitions.* Princeton, NJ: Princeton University Press, 1995.

Hahn, Gordon M. "An Anatomy of North Caucasus-Tied Jihadi Groups in Syria and Iraq." *Gordonhahn.com Russian and Eurasian Politics Report*, 20 October 2015, https://gordonhahn.com/2015/10/20/report-an-anatomy-of-north-caucasus-tied-jihadi-groups-in-syria-and-iraq/.

_____. "The Caucasus Emirate and Other North Caucasus Mujahedin in Syria and the Implications for Russia, Eurasia, and the Global Jihadi Revolutionary Movement." *Gordonhahn.com Russian and Eurasian Politics White Paper*, 1 April 2014, https://gordonhahn.com/2014/04/01/the-caucasus-emirate-and-other-north-caucasus-mujahedin-in-syria-implications-for-russia-eurasia-and-the-global-jihadi-revolutionary-movement/.

_____. *The Caucasus Emirate Mujahedin: Global Jihadism in Russia's North Caucasus and Beyond.* Jefferson, NC: McFarland, 2014.

_____. "China and Central Asia After Afghanistan's Kabulization." *Islam, Islamism and Politics in Eurasia Report*, No. 67, 14 October 2013, http://gordonhahn.com/2013/10/14/islam-islamism-and-politics-in-eurasia-report-no-67-oct-2013-special-report-china-and-central-asia-after-afghanistans-kabulization/.

_____. "The Color Revolution Disease Hits Moldova." *Russia—Other Points of View*, 8 April 2009, www.russiaotherpointsofview.com/2009/04/the-colored-revolution-disease-hits-moldova.html.

_____. "Color Revolutions Darken." *Russia: Other Points of View*, 18 April 2008, www.russiaotherpointsofview.com/2008/04/the-darkening-o.html#more.

_____. "Did Putin Really Tell Bush 'Ukraine Is Not Even a State'?" *GordonHahn.com Russian and Eurasian Politics*, 26 January 2015, http://gordonhahn.com/2015/01/26/did-putin-really-tell-bush-ukraine-is-not-even-a-state/.

_____. "Dirty-Dealing Democratizers, the 'War of Values' with Russia, and Problems of Democracy Promotion." *Gordonhahn.com Russian and Eurasian Politics*, 24 April 2015, https://gordonhahn.com/2015/04/29/dirty-deal-democratizers-the-war-of-values-with-russia-and-problems-of-democracy-promotion/.

_____. "Europe's New Terrorist Threat." *Gordonhahn.com Russian and Eurasian Politics*, 5 November 2015, http://gordonhahn.com/2015/11/05/europes-new-terrorist-threat/.

_____. "Georgia's Propaganda War (Long Version)." *Russia—Other Points of View*, 5 September 2008, www.russiaotherpointsofview.com/files/Georgia_Propaganda_War_Long_Version.doc.

_____. "The Maidan Regime's Growing Democracy Deficit." *Gordonhahn.com Russian and Eurasian Politics*, 12 April 2015, https://gordonhahn.com/2015/04/12/the-maidan-regimes-growing-democracy-deficit/.

_____. "Maidan Ukraine's Authoritarianism Surplus: Update on Maidan Ukraine's Democracy Deficit." *Gordonhahn.com Russian and Eurasian Politics*, 21 April 2015, https://gordonhahn.com/2015/04/21/maidan-ukraines-authoritarianism-surplus-update-on-maidan-ukraines-democracy-deficit/.

_____. "Maidan Ukraine's Neo-Fascist Problem." *Fair Observer*, 23 September 2014, www.fairobserver.com/region/europe/the-ukrainian-revolutions-neo-fascist-problem-14785/.

_____. "Mainstream Media Backtracks on Tulip and Color Revolutions." *Russia—Other Points of View*, 17 June 2010, www.russiaotherpointsofview.com/2010/06/mainstream-media-backtracking-on-tulip-and-colored-revolutions.html.

_____. "The Making of the Georgian-Russia Five-Day August War, June–August 8, 2008." *Russia—Other*

Points of View, 22 September 2008, www.russiaother pointsofview.com/files/Georgia_Russian_War_ TIMELINE.doc.

_____. "Medvedev, Putin, and Perestroika 2.0." *Demokratizatsiya* 18, Number 3 (Summer 2010): 228–259.

_____. "NeoFascist Yarosh Appointed to Ukraine's Defense Ministry." *Gordonhahn.com Russian and Eurasian Politics*, 6 April 2015, https://gordonhahn.com/2015/04/06/neo-fascist-yarosh-appointed-to-ukraine-defense-ministry/.

_____. "One Day in the Life of 'Ukrainian Democracy.'" *Gordonhahn.com Russian and Eurasian Politics*, 21 June 2015, https://gordonhahn.com/2015/06/21/one-day-in-the-life-of-ukrainian-democracy/.

_____. "*Perestroika* 2.0: Towards Non-Revolutionary Regime Transformation in Russia?" *Post-Soviet Affairs* 28, Number 4 (October–December 2012): 472–515.

_____. "Putin Myths and Putin Ideology." *Russia—Other Points of View*, 16 January 2015, www.russiaotherpointsofview.com/2015/01/putin-myths-and-putin-ideology.html.

_____. "Right Sector and the Impotence of Ukraine's Weimar Maidan Regime." *Gordonhahn.com Russian and Eurasian Politics*, 22 July 2015, https://gordonhahn.com/2015/07/22/right-sector-and-the-impotence-of-ukraines-weimar-maidan-regime/.

_____. "Russian Domestic Politics and NATO Expansion." Washington, D.C., Center for Political and Strategic Studies, *FOCUS* 4, Issue 6 (August–September 1997): www.bu.edu/globalbeat/nato/russian.html.

_____. "The Russian Federation in 2012: From 'Thaw' and 'Reset' to 'Freeze.'" *Asian Survey* 53, Number 1 (Winter 2013): 214–223.

_____. *Russia's Islamic Threat*. New Haven and London: Yale University Press, 2007.

_____. *Russia's Revolution from Above: Reform, Transition, and Revolution in the Fall of the Soviet Communist Regime, 1985–2000*. New Brunswick, NJ: Transaction Publishers, 2002.

_____. "Saving Maidan Ukraine From Itself: Mukachevo's Implications." *Gordonhahn.com Russian and Eurasian Politics*, 13 July 2015, https://gordonhahn.com/2015/07/13/saving-maidan-ukraine-from-itself-mukachevos-implications/.

_____. "Tandemology 2.0: Putin's Return, Medvedev's Decline, and Tandem Spats." *Russia—Other Points of View*, 7 October 2012, www.russiaotherpointsofview.com/2012/10/tandemology-20-putins-return-medvedevs-decline-and-tandem-spats.html.

_____. "Ukraine's Neo-Fascist Right Sector: Preparing a Revolt?" *Gordonhahn.com Russian and Eurasian Politics*, 5 August 2015, https://gordonhahn.com/2015/07/14/ukraines-neo-fascist-right-sector-preparing-a-revolt/.

_____."Ukraine's Neo-Fascist 'Tea Party' Throws Grenades, Shoots at Police." *Gordonhahn.com Russian and Eurasian Politics*, 31 August 2015, https://gordonhahn.com/2015/08/31/ukraines-neo-fascist-tea-party-throws-grenades-shoots-at-police-attempts-storm-of-rada/.

_____. "U.S.-Russian Relations and the War Against Jihadism." Century Foundation, Hart-Matlock Russia Working Group Paper, May 2009, https://gordonhahn.com/2015/11/17/report-2009-u-s-russian-relations-and-the-war-against-jihadism/

Hartman, Ben. "A necessary putsch." *Jerusalem Post*, 29 October 2010, www.jpost.com/Features/Front-Lines/A-necessary-putsch.

Heilman, Uriel. "Like NBA's Nets, European Jewish group gets an oligarch, but some see Soviet-style takeover." *Jewish Telegraphic Agency*, 2 November 2010, www.jta.org/2010/11/02/news-opinion/world/like-nbas-nets-european-jewish-group-gets-an-oligarch-but-some-see-soviet-style-takeover.

Helmer, John. "Meet and Greet Natalie Jaresko, US Government Employee, Ukraine Finance Minister." *Dances with Bears*, 3 December 2014, http://john helmer.net/?p=12317.

Hepburn, Oksana Bashuk. "The 2011 Ukrainian Best & Worst (UBaWL)." Eposhtawww 13, Number 1 (2 January 2012): www.eposhta.com/newsmagazine/ePOSHTA_120102_World_Eng.html.

Hesli, Vicki, William Reisinger, and Arthur Miller, "Political Party Development in Divided Societies: The Case of Ukraine." *Electoral Studies* 17 (1998): 235–256.

Heyden, Ulrich. German documentary film *Lauffleuer*, at "Lauffleuer—Rassledovanie zlodeyanii Odesse 2 maya 2014 (Nemetskii s subtitrami na russkom yazyke)," *YouTube*, 13 March 2015, www.youtube.com/watch?v=WZ6WDfAx1LM&feature=youtu.be.

Himka, John-Paul. "The Lviv Pogrom of 1941: The Germans, Ukrainian Nationalists, and the Carnival Crowd." *Canadian Slavonic Papers/Revue Canadienne des Slavistes* 53, No. 2/4 (June–Sept.–Dec. 2011): 209–43.

"A history erased: Abkhazia's archive: fire of war, ashes of history." *Abkhaz World*, 17 March 2009, http://abkhazworld.com/aw/conflict/690-a-history-erased.

"How America Switched Sides in the War on Terror." Interim Report by the Citizens' Commission on Benghazi, *Accuracy in Media*, 22 April 2014, www.aim.org/benghazi/wp-content/uploads/2014/04/CCB-Interim-Report-4-22-2014.pdf.

"How Kiev Silenced Ukraine's Biggest Opposition Newspaper." *Off-Guardian*, 22 October 2015, https://off-guardian.org/2015/10/22/how-kiev-silenced-ukraines-biggest-opposition-newspaper/.

Huntington, Samuel P. "The Clash of Civilizations." *Foreign Affairs* 72, Number 3 (Summer 1993): 22–49.

Illarionov, Andrei. "Putin i granitsy Ukrainy. I Freid," Andrei Illarionov's *Live Journal* Page, 16 October 2014, http://aillarionov.livejournal.com/746987.html.

Interview with Aleksei Venediktov, Program "Bez Obid," LTV7 (Latvia), 4 May 2015, www.youtube.com/watch?v=9RdrcCI6TtQ.

Interview with Sergei Stankevich, Program "Arena Sobytii," *Online TV*, 20 November 2014, www.onlinetv.ru/video/1982/?autostart=1.

Isaev, I.A., ed. *Puti Yevrazii*. Moscow: Russkaya kniga, 1992.

_____. "Utopisty ili providtsy?" In I.A. Isaev, ed., *Puti Yevrazii*. Moscow: Russkaya kniga, 1992: 3–26.

Jarábik, Balázs. "A Policy of Pretending." *Carnegie Moscow Center*, 25 May 2015, http://carnegie.ru/commentary/?fa=60187.

Johnson, Chalmers. *Revolutionary Change*, second edition. Stanford: Stanford University Press, 1982.

Karatnycky, Adrian. "Ukraine's Orange Revolution." *Foreign Affairs*, March–April 2005, www.foreignaffairs.com/articles/russia-fsu/2005-03-01/ukraines-orange-revolution.

Katchanovski, Ivan. "Political Regionalism in 'Orange' Ukraine." Working paper, www.academia.edu/4547 76/Political_Regionalism_in_Orange_Ukraine.

_____. "Regional Political Divisions in Ukraine in 1991–2006." *Nationalities Papers* 34 (2006): 507–532.

_____. "The 'Snipers' Massacre' on Maidan in Ukraine." Paper delivered to the American Political Science Association Annual Conference, San Francisco, California, 3–6 September 2015, http://papers.ssrn.com/sol3/papers.cfm?abstract_id=2658245.

_____. "The Snipers' Massacre on the Maidan in Ukraine." *Academia.edu*, paper presented at the Chair of Ukrainian Studies Seminar at the University of Ottawa, Ottawa, October 1, 2014, www.academia.edu/8776021/The_Snipers_Massacre_on_the_Maidan_in_Ukraine.

_____. "The 'Snipers' Massacre' on the Maidan in Ukraine (Revised and Updated Version)." *Academia.edu*, 20 February 2015. www.academia.edu/8776021/The_Snipers_Massacre_on_the_Maidan_in_Ukraine (or *Johnson's Russia List*), #33, 21 February 2015, Institute for European, Russian and Eurasian Studies at George Washington University's Elliott School of International Affairs, http://archive.constantcontact.com/fs053/11 02820649387/archive/1102911694293.html.

Kireev, Alex. "Ukraine. Presidential Election in 1991." *Electoral Geography 2.0*, www.electoralgeography.com/new/en/countries/u/ukraine/ukraine-presidential-election-1991.htm.

Kislaya, A.A. "Etnicheskaya identifikatsiya v Ukraine: paradoks 'without the dynamics.'" In *Yezhegodnaya nauchno-prakticheskaya sotsiologicheskaya konferentsiya 'Prodolzhaya Grushina.'* Moscow: VTsIOM, 2012, pp. 157–8, http://wciom.ru/fileadmin/file/nauka/grusha_2012/tezisy/soc/kislaja.pdf.

Klobucar, Thomas F., Arthur H. Miller, and Gwyn Erb. "The 1999 Ukrainian Presidential Election: Personalities, Ideology, Partisanship, and the Economy." *Slavic Review* 61, Number 2 (Summer 2002): 315–44.

Klussman, Uwe, Matthias Schepp, and Klaus Wiegrefe. "NATO's Eastward Expansion: Did the West Break Its Promise to Moscow?" *Der Spiegel*, 26 November 2009, www.spiegel.de/international/world/nato-s-eastward-expansion-did-the-west-break-its-promise-to-moscow-a-663315.html.

Knyazeva, Ye.V. "20 let nezavisimosti: mneneie ekspertov i naseleniya yuga Ukrainy." In *Yezhegodnaya nauchno-prakticheskaya sotsiologicheskaya konferentsiya 'Prodolzhaya Grushina,'* http://wciom.ru/fileadmin/file/nauka/grusha_2012/tezisy/soc/knjazeva.pdf.

Kolsto, Pal. *Russians in the Former Soviet Republics.* Bloomington: Indiana University Press, 1995.

"Komandir Donetskikh terroristov sluzhit v FSB, lubit rekonstruktsii i druzhit s geyami, FOTOreportazh." *Censor.net.ua*, 29 April 2014, http://censor.net.ua/photo_news/283194/komandir_donetskih_terroristov_girkin_slujit_v_fsb_lyubit_rekonstruktsii_i_drujit_s_geyami_fotoreportaj.

Kontenko, Anton, Olga Martynyuk, and Aleksei Miller. "Maloross." In D. Dvizhdkov and I. Shirle, eds., *Ponyatiya o Rossii: k istoricheskoi semantike iperskogo perioda II.* Moscow: Duetsches Historices Institut and Novoe Literaturnoe Obozrenie, 2012: 392–443.

Kostyuchenko, Yelena. "'My vse znali, na chto idem i chto mozhet byt.'" *Novaya gazeta*, No. 22, 4 March 2015, www.novayagazeta.ru/society/67490.html.

"Krym. Put' na Rodinu." *Rossiya 1 TV*, 16 March 2015. http://russia.tv/video/show/brand_id/59195/episode_id/1180834/video_id/1147633/.

Kubicek, Paul. "Regional Polarisation in Ukraine: Public Opinion, Voting and Legislative Behaviour." *Europe-Asia Studies* 52 (2000): 272–293.

Kucera, Joshua. "Condoleezza Rice Warned Georgian Leader on War with Russia." *The Atlantic*, 16 November 2011, www.theatlantic.com/international/archive/2011/11/condoleezza-rice-warned-georgian-leader-on-war-with-russia/248560/.

Kukulin, Ilya. "Reaktsiya Dissotsiatsii: Legitimatsiya ul'trapravoogo diskursa v sovremennoi rossiiskoi literature." In Marlen Laruelle, ed., *Russkii natsionalizm: Sotsial'nyi i kul'turnyi kontekst.* Moscow: Novoe Literaturnoe Obozrenie, 2008: 257–338.

Kulyk, Volodymyr. "One Nation, Two Languages? National Identity and Language Policy in Post-Euromaidan Ukraine." *PONARS Policy Memo 389*, September 2015, www.ponarseurasia.org/memo/one-nation-two-languages-national-identity-and-language-policy-post-euromaidan-ukraine.

Kuromiya, Hiroaki. *Freedom and Terror in the Donbas: A Ukrainian-Russian Borderland, 1870s–1990s.* Cambridge, UK: Cambridge University Press, 1998.

Kuzio, Taras. "Did Ukraine's Secret Service Really Prevent Bloodshed During the Orange Revolution?" *Jamestown's Foundation Eurasia Daily Monitor* 2, Issue 16 (24 January 2005): www.taraskuzio.net/media14_files/37.pdf.

Lalpychak, Chrystyna. "Independence—Over 90 percent vote 'yes' in referendum, Kravchuk elected president of Ukraine." *Ukrainian Weekly* 59, Number 49 (8 December 1991): www.ukrweekly.com/old/archive/1991/499101.shtml.

Lane, David. "The Orange Revolution: 'People's revolution or revolutionary coup?'" *British Journal of Politics and International Relations* 10, Number 4 (November 2008): 525–49.

Lappo, Ivan. "Proiskhozhdenie ukrainskoi ideologii Noveishego vremei." *Imperskoe Vozrozhdenie*, No. 7, 2007: 97–107.

Lavrov, Sergei. "It's not Russia that is destabilising Ukraine." *The Guardian* (UK), 8 April 2014, www.theguardian.com/commentisfree/2014/apr/07/sergei-lavrov-russia-stabilise-ukraine-west.

"Lugansk vo vlasti separatistov: kak zakhvatyvaly OGA, militsiyu, prokuraturu i sud." *BigMir.net*, 29 April 2014, http://news.bigmir.net/ukraine/812829-Lugansk-vo-vlasti-separatistov--kak-zahvatyvali-OGA--miliciju--prokuraturu-i-sud.

Lupiy, Bohdan. *Ukraine and European Security—International Mechanisms as Non-Military Options for National Security of Ukraine.* North Atlantic Treaty Organization Individual Democratic Institutions Research Fellowships 1994–1996. Brussels: NATO, 1996. www.nato.int/acad/fellow/94-96/lupiy/01-02.htm. Retrieved 23 November 2015.

Lyashchenko, Viktor. "Krymskaya Avtonomiya 23 goda spustya: kak sberegli mir i ne pustili v dom voinu." *Krymskoe informatsionnoe agentsvo*, 20 January 2014, www.kianews.com.ua/page/krymskaya-avtonomiya-23-goda-spustya-kak-sberegli-mir-i-ne-pustili-v-dom-voynu.

Mackinder, Halford J. "The Geographical Pivot of History." In *Democratic Ideals and Reality: A Study in the Politics of Reconstruction*, 1996 revised edition. Washington, D.C.: National Defense University Press, 1942, www.scribd.com/doc/24386413/Democratic-Ideals-and-Reality.

Maidan Massacre. Documentary film by John Beck-Hofmann. *YouTube*, 14 February 2015, www.youtube.com/watch?v=Ary_l4vn5ZA.

Mandelbaum, Michael. "NATO Expansion: Bridge to the Nineteenth Century." Chevy Chase, MD: Center for Political and Strategic Studies, 1997.

Mandelbaum, Michael, ed. *The New Russian Foreign Policy*. Washington, D.C.: Council of Foreign Relations, 1998.

Mankoff, Jeffrey. *Russian Foreign Policy: The Return of Great Power Politics*, second edition. New York: Council of Foreign Relations, 2012.

March, James, and Johan Olsen. *Rediscovering Institutions: The Organized Basis of Politics*. New York: The Free Press, 1989.

Marten, Kimberly. "Putin's Choices: Explaining Russian Foreign Policy and Intervention in Ukraine." *The Washington Quarterly*, Summer 2015, http://twq.elliott.gwu.edu.

"Massovyie besporyadki v Odesse. Khronika sobytii." *Ekho Moskvy*, 2 May 2014, http://echo.msk.ru/blog/echomsk/1312248-echo/, last accessed on 28 March 2016.

Matlock, John J. "NATO Expansion: Was There a Promise?" JackMatlockwww, 3 April 2014, http://jackmatlock.com/2014/04/nato-expansion-was-there-a-promise/.

McFadden, Robert D. "Strong American Voice in Diplomacy and Crisis." *New York Times*, 13 December 2010, www.nytimes.com/2010/12/14/world/14holbrooke.html?pagewanted=all&_r=0.

Miller, Christopher J. "'Vigilante' Ukrainian lawmaker Lyashko gets slammed by Amnesty International report." *Kyiv Post*, 6 August 2014, www.kyivpost.com/article/content/ukraine/amnesty-international-criticizes-vigilante-ukrainian-lawmaker-lyashko-359586.html.

Mitrofanova, Anastasiya. "Nationalizm and Paranauka." In Marlen Laruelle, ed., *Russkii natsionalizm: Sotsial'nyi i kul'turnyi kontekst*. Moscow: Novoe Literaturnoe Obozrenie, 2008: 87–102.

Moreira, Paul. French documentary film *Ukraine—Les Masques De La Revolution*. *The Daily Motion*, 2 February 2016, www.dailymotion.com/video/x3pxmfe_ukraine-les-masques-de-la-revolution_tv.

Motyl, Alexander. "Ukraine's Donbas is Like America's Deep South." *Huffington Post*, 5 January 2015, www.huffingtonpost.com/alexander-motyl/alexander-motyl_b_6414802.html.

Nahaylo, Bohdan. "Toward the Rule of Law—Ukraine." *RFE/RL Research Report* 1, Number 27 (3 July 1992): 50–6.

Nayem, Mustafa. "Uprising in Ukraine: How It All Began." *Open Society Foundation*, 4 April 2014, www.opensocietyfoundations.org/voices/uprising-ukraine-how-it-all-began.

O'Donnell, Guillermo, and Philippe Schmitter. "Tentative Conclusions About Uncertain Democracies." In Guillermo O'Donnell, Philippe Schmitter and Laurence Whitehead, eds., *Transitions from Authoritarian Rule*, part 4. Baltimore, MD: Johns Hopkins University Press, 1986.

O'Donnell, Guillermo, Philippe Schmitter and Laurence Whitehead, eds. *Transitions from Authoritarian Rule*, part 4. Baltimore, MD: Johns Hopkins University Press, 1986.

Oksenberg, Michael, and Bruce J. Dickson. "The Origins, Processes, and Outcomes of Great Political Reform: A Framework of Analysis." In Dankwart A. Rustow and Kenneth Paul Erikson, eds., *Comparative Political Dynamics: Global Research Perspectives*. New York: HarperCollins, 1991: 235–61.

Olszanski, Tadeusz A., and Agata Weirzbowska-Miazga. "Poroshenko, President of Ukraine." *Osrodek Studiow Wschodnich im. Marka Kapiya*, 28 May 2014, www.osw.waw.pl/en/publikacje/analyses/2014-05-28/poroshenko-president-ukraine.

"'Oppozitsionyi Blok' zayavil ob ugrozakh ot 'Ukrainskoi povstancheskoi armii," *Korrespondent*, 17 April 2015. http://korrespondent.net/ukraine/3504818-oppozytsyonnyi-blok-zaiavyl-ob-uhrozakh-ot-ukraynskoi-povstancheskoi-armyy?hc_location=ufi.

"Panama and Poroshenko." *Wall Street Journal*, 5 April 2016, www.wsj.com/articles/panama-and-poroshenko-1459900665.

Panarin, A.S. *Pravoslavnaya tsivilizatsiya v global'nom mire*. Moscow: Algoritm, 2002.

_____. *Revansh Istorii: Rossiiskaya strategicheskaya initsiativa v XXI veke*. Moscow: Logos, 1998.

"Petro Poroshenko—The Power Players." *Panama Papers*. The International Consortium of Investigative Journalists, April 2016, https://panamapapers.icij.org/the_power_players/.

Pinna, Alessandra. "The International Dimension of Democratization: Actors, Motivations, and Strategies." *Marine Corps University Journal* 5, Number 1 (Spring 2014): 27–57.

Pipes, Richard. *The Formation of the Soviet Union: Communism and Nationalism, 1917–1923*. Cambridge, MA: Harvard University Press, 1954.

Pirani, Simon. *Ukraine's Gas Sector*. Oxford, UK: Oxford Institute for Energy Studies, June 2007, www.oxfordenergy.org/wpcms/wp-content/uploads/2010/11/NG21-UkrainesGasSector-SimonPirani-2007.pdf.

Platonov, S.F. *Lektsii po russkoi istorii*. Moscow: Vysshaya Shkola, 1993.

Plokhy, Serhiy. *Ukraine and Russia: Representations of the Past*. Toronto: Toronto University Press, 2008.

Pohl, Dieter. "The Murder of Ukraine's Jews under German Military Administration and in the Reich Commissariat Ukraine." In Ray Brandon and Wendy Lower, eds., *The Shoah in Ukraine: History, Testimony, Memorialization*. Bloomington: Indiana University Press, 2010: 77–113.

Popova, Maria "Was Yanukovych's Removal Constitutional?" *Ponars*, 20 March 2014, www.ponarseurasia.org/article/was-yanukovych%E2%80%99s-removal-constitutional.

"Poroshenko: Golodomor—proyavlenie gibridnoi voiny." *Korrespondent*, 28 November 2015, http://korrespondent.net/ukraine/3596061-poroshenko-holodomor-proiavlenye-hybrydnoi-voiny.

"Poverty in Ukraine." Institute for Economic Research and Policy Consulting in Ukraine and the German Advisory Group on Economic Reform, 2003, http://pdc.ceu.hu/archive/00001784/01/t25_en.pdf.

Prezident (documentary film). *Rossiya 1 TV*, 26 April 2015, http://russia.tv/video/show/brand_id/59329/

episode_id/1193264/video_id/1165983/viewtype/pic
ture.

Primakov, Yevgenii. *Gody v Bolshoi Politike*. Moscow:
Sovershenno Sekretno, 1999.

Przeworski, Adam. *Democracy and the Market: Polit-
ical and Economic Reforms in Eastern Europe and
Latin America*. Cambridge: Cambridge University
Press, 1991.

Rafal, Anastasiya, Yulia Gutova, and Vitalii Leibin.
"Porokh." *Russkii reporter*, 29 May 2014, http://rus
rep.ru/article/2014/05/29/poroh.

Ray, Julie. "Russia's Leadership Not Popular Worldwide." *Gallup*, 5 August 2011, www.gallup.com/poll/
148862/Russia-Leadership-Not-Popular-Worldwide.
aspx.

_____. "Ukrainians Disillusioned with Leadership."
Gallup, 23 December 2015, www.gallup.com/poll/
187931/ukrainians-disillusioned-leadership.aspx.

Reddaway, Peter, and Dmitry Glinski. *The Tragedy of
Russia's Reforms: Market Bolshevism Against Democracy*. Washington, D.C.: U.S. Institute of Peace Press,
2001.

Risch, William. "Maidan Chronicle—January 19–20,
2014—The Day Kyiv Blew Up (In Lieu of a Conclusion)." *Maidan Chronicle*, 20 January 2014, https://
williamrisch.wordpress.com/2014/01/29/maidan-
chronicle-january-19-20-2014-the-day-kyiv-blew-
up-in-lieu-of-a-conclusion/.

Romashenko, L.I. "Yazyk kak otrazhenie sovremen-
nykh sotiokul'turnykh protsessov (na primere
Ukrainy)." In *Yezhegodnaya nauchno-prakticheskaya
sotsiologicheskaya konferentsiya 'Prodolzhaya Grushina,'* Moscow: VTsIOM, 2012: 180–82, http://wci
om.ru/fileadmin/file/nauka/grusha_2012/tezisy/
soc/romawenko.pdf.

Rosenberg, Tina. "Revolution U." *Foreign Policy*, 17
February 2011, http://foreignpolicy.com/2011/02/17/
revolution-u-2/.

*Rossiya i NATO: Realnost' i perspektivy vzaimodeis-
tviya*. Moscow: VTsIOM, 2011, http://wciom.ru/file
admin/file/reports_conferences/2011/2011-11-11-
nato.pdf.

"Rossiya: zapadniy put' dlia 'ievroaziatskoi' tsivilizatsiyi…?" *Na Zapad ili v Yevraziyu: Kakim Putem idti
Rossii*, *VTSIOM*, No. 32, 13 November 2001, http://
wciom.ru/index.php?id=236&uid=306, accessed on
December 27, 2010.

Rudling, Per Anders. "The OUN, the UPA and the
Holocaust: A Study in the Manufacturing of Histor-
ical Myths." *Carl Beck Papers in Russian and East
European Studies*, No. 2107, University of Pittsburgh,
Center for Russian and East European Studies, 2011.

_____. "The Return of the Ukrainian Far Right. The
Case of VO Svoboda." In Ruth Wodak and John E.
Richardson, eds., *Analysing Fascist Discourse: European Fascism in Talk and Text*. New York and London: Routledge, 2013: 228–55, http://defendinghis
tory.com/wp-content/uploads/2013/01/PA-Rudling-
on-Return-of-Ukrainian-Far-Right-2013.pdf.

"Russia and the Separatists of Eastern Ukraine." *International Crisis Group*, No. 79, 5 February 2016, www.
crisisgroup.org/~/media/Files/europe/ukraine/
b079-russia-and-the-separatists-in-eastern-ukraine.
pdf.

"Russians in Ukraine." *Wikipedia*, https://en.wikipedia.
org/wiki/Russians_in_Ukraine, last accessed 1 September 2015.

Rustow, Dankwart A., and Kenneth Paul Erikson, eds.
*Comparative Political Dynamics: Global Research
Perspectives*. New York: HarperCollins, 1991.

Sakwa, Richard. *Frontline Ukraine: Crisis in the Borderlands*. London: I.B. Tauris, 2015.

Sapir, Jacques. "Ukraine at the Turn." *RussEurope*, 3
December 2015, http://russeurope.hypotheses.org/
4521. All last accessed 4 December 2015.

Saradzhyan, Sergei. "No Smoking Spetsnaz Gun in E.
Ukraine or Why Khamzat of GRU's Vostok Wouldn't
Pose As Donetsk Native." *Saradzhyan: From the
Global Tank—Live Journal*, 22 April 2014, http://
saradzhyan.livejournal.com/34407.html.

Sarkisian, Pietro. "Equalization and Dehumanization
in Eastern Ukraine." *Reconsidering Russia*, 7 March
2015, http://reconsideringrussia.org/2015/03/07/
equalization-and-dehumanization-in-eastern-
ukraine/.

Satubaldina, Assel. "Over 30 countries interested in
signing free trade agreement with EEU." *Tengri-
news.kz*, 21 July 2015, http://en.tengrinews.kz/poli
tics_sub/Over-30-countries-interested-in-signing-
free-trade-agreement-261289/.

Savchuk, Maksym, and Daisy Sindelar. "Questions
Raised Over Poroshenko's Role In Valuable Kyiv
Land Deal." RFERL, 13 May 2015, www.rferl.org/
content/ukraine-poroshenko-land-deal-questions-
tsars-village/27013945.html.

Schmitter, Phillippe C., and Imco Brouwer. *Conceptu-
alizing, Researching, and Evaluating Democracy Promotion and Protection*. Florence, Italy: European
University Institute, 1999.

Schuller, Konrad. "Wie kam es zum Blutbad auf dem
Majdan?" 8 February 2015, *Frankfurter Allgemeine
Zeitung*, www.faz.net/aktuell/politik/ausland/eur
opa/ukraine-die-hundertschaften-und-die-dritte-
kraft-13414018.html.

Shakhnazarov, Georgii. *Tsena Svobody: Reformatsiya
Gorbacheva glazami ego pomoshnika*. Moscow: Rissika-Zevs, 1993.

Shekovtsov, Anton. "The Creeping Resurgence of the
Ukrainian Radical Right?: The Case of the Freedom
Party." *Europe-Asia Studies* 63, Number 2 (March
2011): 203–28.

Shenfield, Stephen. *Russian Fascism: Traditions, Tendencies, Movements*. Armonk, NY: M.E. Sharpe, 2001.

Shiraev, Eric, and Vladislav Zubok. *Anti-Americanism
in Russia: From Stalin to Putin*. New York: Palgrave,
2000.

Shulman, Stephen. "Asymmetrical International Integration and Ukrainian National Disunity." *Political
Geography* 18 (1999): 913–939.

Simes, Dmitri. "Why Russia Won't Yield on Syria."
Council on Foreign Relations, 17 July 2012, www.cfr.
org.

Shulman, Stephen. "Cultural comparisons and their
consequences for nationhood in Ukraine." *Communist and Post-Communist Studies* 39 (2006): 247–263.

Siyak, Ivan. "Ivan Bubenchik: 'Ya ubil ikh v zatylok.
Eto Pravda." *Bird in Flight*, 19 February 2016, https://
birdinflight.com/ru/mir/ivan-bubenchik-ya-ubil-
ih-v-zatylok-eto-pravda.html.

Skocpol, Theda. "Bringing the State Back In: Current
Research." In Peter B. Evans, Dietrich Rueche-
meyer, and Theda Skocpol, eds., *Bringing the State
Back In*. Cambridge: Cambridge University Press,
1985: 1–32.

_____. *States and Social Revolutions: A Comparative Analysis of France, Russia and China.* Cambridge: Cambridge University Press, 1979.

Slivka, Andrey. "Rage in Kiev." *The New Yorker,* 11 December 2013, www.newyorker.com/news/newsdesk/rage-in-kiev.

Solchanyk, Roman. *Ukraine and Russia: The Post-Soviet Transition.* Lanham, MD: Rowman and Littlefield, 2000.

Sotieva, Larisa. "Eyewitnesses: Carnage in Tskhinvali." *Caucasus Reporting Service,* Institute of War and Peace Reporting, 12 August 2008, www.iwpr.net.

Speri, Alice. "Yes, There are Chechen Fighters in Ukraine, and Nobody Knows Who Sent Them There." *Vice News,* 28 May 2014, https://news.vice.com/article/yes-there-are-chechen-fighters-in-ukraine-and-nobody-knows-who-sent-them-there.

"Spetsturisty." *Novaya gazeta,* No. 71, 2 July 2014, www.novayagazeta.ru/inquests/64242.html.

Spykman, Nicholas J. *The Geography of the Peace.* New York: Harcourt, Brace, 1944.

Stecklow, Steve, and Oleksandr Akymenko. "Special Report: Flaws found in Ukraine's probe of Maidan massacre." *Reuters,* 10 October 2014, www.reuters.com/article/2014/10/10/us-ukraine-killings-probe-special-report-idUSKCN0HZ0UH20141010.

Stern, Jonathan. "The Russian-Ukrainian gas crisis of January 2006." *Oxford Institute for Energy Studies,* 16 January 2006, www.oxfordenergy.org/wpcms/wp-content/uploads/2011/01/Jan2006-RussiaUkraineGasCrisis-JonathanStern.pdf.

Stoner, Kathryn, and Michael McFaul, "Who Lost Russia (This Time)? Vladimir Putin." *The Washington Quarterly,* Summer 2015, http://twq.elliott.gwu.edu/who-lost-russia-time-vladimir-putin.

Stuermer, Michael. *Putin and the Rise of Russia.* London: Weidenfeld and Nicolson, 2008.

Subtelny, Orest. *Ukraine: A History.* Toronto, Canada: Toronto University Press, 1988.

"Tainy zhen i zhenshin Viktora Yushchenko. Yekaterina Kler i eyo podrugi." *Vlasti.net,* 8 November 2009, http://vlasti.net/news/66390.

Talbott, Strobe. *The Russia Hand: A Memoir of Presidential Diplomacy.* New York: Random House, 2003.

Teize, Yevgenii. "Rassledovanie DW: ofshorniye skhemy okruzheniya Poroshenko v FRG." *Duetsche Welle,* 19 May 2016, www.dw.com.

Tilly, Charles. *European Revolutions, 1492–1992.* Oxford, UK: Blackwell, 1993.

Trimberger, Ellen Kay. *Revolution from Above: Military Bureaucrats and Development in Japan, Turkey, Egypt, and Peru.* New Brunswick, NJ: Transaction Books, 1978.

Trubetskoi, Nikolai S. "Yevraziistvo: Opyt sistematicheskogo izlozheniya." In *Puti Yevrazii,* Moscow: Russkaya kniga, 1992: 348–415.

Truman-Reagan Medal of Freedom, Victims of Communism Memorial Foundation, http://victimsofcommunism.org/initiative/truman-reagan/, last accessed on 7 January 2016.

Tsygankov, Andrei P. *Russia and the West from Alexander to Putin: Honor in International Relations.* Cambridge, UK: Cambridge University Press, 2015.

Ukraine: Energy Policy Review 2006, International Energy Agency/Organization for Economic Cooperation and Development, 2006, www.iea.org/publications/freepublications/publication/ukraine2006.pdf.

"Ukraine." *Nations in Transit 2016.* Washington, D.C.: Freedom House, 2016, https://freedomhouse.org/report/nations-transit/2016/Ukraine.

"Ukraine segodnya|Chto proiskhodit?" Program 'Arena sobytii,' *Online TV,* 26 June 2014, www.onlinetv.ru/video/1670/?autostart=1.

Vagner, Aleksandra, and Aleksei Dsokavitskii. "Mnogolikii Stepan Bandera." *Radio Svoboda,* 25 December 2013, www.svoboda.org/content/article/25209525.html.

"Valentin Nalyvaichenko podderzhal rebyat iz 'Pravogo sektora' Zarkapat'ya." *Anons Zakarpat'ya,* 12 July 2015, http://anons.uz.ua/news/politics/21855-valentin-nalivaychenko-podderzhal-rebyat-iz-pravogo-sektora-zakarpatya.html.

Vinogradov, Dmitrii. "Boevyie zaslugy: Kto nauchil voevat' Igorya Strelkova." *Svobodnaya pressa,* 5 June 2014, http://svpressa.ru/society/article/89194/?twrss=1&utm_source=svpressa&utm_medium=twitter.

"Violent Hate Crime in Ukraine." *Human Rights First,* 2012, http://lib.ohchr.org/HRBodies/UPR/Documents/Session14/UA/HRF_UPR_UKR_S14_2012_HumanRightsFirst_E.pdf

"Viruyuchim yakoi tserkvi, konfesii Vi sebe vvazhaet." *Razumkov Center,* May 2006, http://razumkov.org.ua/ukr/poll.php?poll_id=300, last accessed 11 September 2015.

Volkov, Denis. "Rossiiskaya sotsiologiya ukrainskogo konflikta: vmeshivat'sya ne nado, no vse pravil'no sdelali." *Moskovskii tsentr Karnegi,* 26 August 2015, http://carnegie.ru/2015/08/26/ru-61007/if5q.

Vorontsov, Yuli. "NATO Enlargement Without Russia: A Mistake on Four Counts." The NATO-Russian Charter and the Emerging Relationship, Russia and NATO International Panel, George Washington University, Washington, D.C., February 1997, http://fas.org/man/nato/ceern/gwu_conf.htm and http://fas.org/man/nato/ceern/gwu_cl.htm.

Weissman, Steve. "Meet the Americans Who Put Together the Coup in Kiev." *Ron Paul Institute,* 25 March 2014, http://ronpaulinstitute.org/archives/featured-articles/2014/march/25/meet-the-americans-who-put-together-the-coup-in-kiev.aspx.

"Wiretapped Recordings of Saakashvili Discussing Rustavi 2 TV Leaked." *Civil.ge,* 30 October 2015, www.civil.ge/eng/article.php?id=28713.

Wolczuk, Kataryna. *The Moulding of Ukraine: The Constitutional Politics of State Formation.* Budapest: Central European University Press, 2001.

"The World's Billionaires: #1367 Ihor Kolomoyskyy." *Forbes,* 2016, www.forbes.com/profile/ihor-kolomoyskyy/.

Yevtukhov, Danil. "Ubiitsy Buziny iz 'UPA' vpervyie zasvetilis' vo vremya Yevromaidana." *Podrobnosti,* 17 April 2015, http://podrobnosti.ua/2029175-vpervye-upa-zasvetilas-v-ubijstve-militsionera-vo-vremja-evromajdana.html.

Yezhegodnaya nauchno-prakticheskaya sotsiologicheskaya konferentsiya "Prodolzhaya Grushina." Moscow: VTsIOM, 2012, http://wciom.ru/fileadmin/file/nauka/grusha_2012/tezisy/soc/kislaja.pdf.

Yezhegodnaya nauchno-prakticheskaya sotsiologicheskaya konferentsiya "Prodolzhaya Grushina." Moscow: VTsIOM, 2013, http://wciom.ru/fileadmin/file/nauka/grusha_2013/7.pdf.

Yur'ev, Mikhail. *Tret'ya Imperiya: Rossiya, kotoraya dolzhna byt'.* St. Petersburg: Limbus Press, 2006.

"V Yuzhnoi Osetii zayavlyayut, chto Gruzia razmestila artilleriyu bliz zony konflikta." *Kavkaz uzel*, 4 August 2008, www.kavkaz-uzel.ru/newstext.newsid/1226489.html.

Zaitsev, Tom. "Three Ukrainian carriers seek tie-up approval." Flightglobalwww, 12 February 2010, http://beta.flightglobal.com/news/articles/three-ukrainian-carriers-seek-tie-up-approval-338364/.

Zhilin, Ivan. "Voina. Obratnaya svyaz." *Novaya gazeta*, No. 21, 2 March 2015, www.novayagazeta.ru/politics/67467.html.

Zhukov, Ostap. "Strelkov rasskazal, kak sluzhil v FSB i gde voeval." *Moskovskii komsomolets*, 12 July 2014, www.mk.ru/politics/2014/07/12/strelkov-rasskazal-kak-sluzhil-v-fsb-i-gde-voeval.html.

Zubrin, Robert. "Putin Adviser Publishes Plan for Domination of Europe." *The National Review*, 10 March 2015, www.nationalreview.com/corner/373064/putin-adviser-publishes-plan-domination-europe-robert-zubrin.

"Zvit TCK shodo podii 18–20 lyutogo v Kievi." *Offitsialnyi sait Gennaddiy Moskal,'* 7 May 2014, www.moskal.in.ua/?categoty=news&news_id=1099.

Independent Ukrainian Media Sources

112.ua, http://112.ua.
Anons Zakarpat'ya, http://anons.uz.ua.
Apostrophe.com, http://apostrophe.com.ua.
Censor.net, http://censor.net.ua.
Dzerkalo tyzhnia, http://www.dt.ua.
Euromaidan Press, http://euromaidanpress.com.
Fakty.ua, http://fakty.ua.
Gordonua.com, http://gordonua.com.
Hvylya.net.
Interfax Ukraine.
Kiev Ukraine News Blog, http://news.kievukraine.info.
Kyiv Post, www.kyivpost.com.
Korrespondent, http://korrespondent.net.
Lb.ua, http://lb.ua.
Liga novosti, www.liga.net.
Novosti Donbassa, http://novosti.dn.ua.
Novosti Sevastopolya, www.sevnews.info.
Novyi region, http://nr2.com.ua.
Podrobnosti.ua, http://podrobnosti.ua.
Pravyysektor.info.
Rakurs, http://ua.racurs.ua.
Segodnya Ukraina, www.segodnya.ua.
Sevas, http://news.sevas.com.
TSN.ru, http://ru.tsn.ua.
Ukraina moloda, www.umoloda.kiev.ua.
Ukraine Online, http://ukr-online.com.
Ukrainform, www.ukrinform.ua.
Ukrainskaya Pravda.
Unian.info, www.unian.info.
Vesti-Ukraina, vesti-ukr.ua.
Zn.ua, http://zn.ua.

Ukrainian Websites and Think Tanks

Kievskii Mezhdunarodnyi Institut Sotsiologii (KIIS), www.kiis.com.ua.
Razumkov Center.

Official Ukrainian Government Sources

Rady natsional'noi bezpeki i oborony Ukrainy, www.rnbo.gov.ua.
State Statistics Committee of Ukraine, www.ukrstat.gov.ua.
Yediniy Derzhavniy reestr sudovikh rishen,' http://reyestr.court.gov.ua.
Zakarpat'ska oblasna derzhanva administratsiya, www.carpathia.gov.ua.

Western Newspapers, Magazines, and News Agencies

Associated Press.
Bloomberg, www.bloomberg.com.
BBC (British Broadcasting Corporation, UK).
CBS News, www.cbsnews.com.
Christian Science Monitor.
CNN (www.cnn.com).
The Daily Telegraph (UK).
DefenseOne.com, www.defenseone.com.
Der Spiegel (Germany).
Deutsche Welte (Germany), www.dw.com
The Economist (UK).
Euronews, www.euronews.com.
Financial Post, http://business.financialpost.com.
Financial Times.
Forbes, www.forbes.com.
Fox News.
Globe and Mail (UK).
The Guardian (UK).
The Hill.
The Independent (UK).
International Business Times.
Le Monde Diplomatique (France).
Miami Herald.
Moscow Times.
The Nation.
The National Review.
The New Republic.
The New York Times.
New York Times Magazine.
Newsweek Russia.
Politico.
Reuters.
San Jose Mercury News.
Sky News, http://news.sky.com.
Telegraph (UK).
Time.
The Wall Street Journal.
The Washington Post.
Worldpress.org, www.worldpress.org.
Wyborcza (Poland).

Western Websites and Think Tanks

Amnesty International.
Business New Europe, www.bne.com.
Cesura, http://cesura.it.
The Daily Beast, www.dailybeast.com.
EU External Action Service, www.eeas.europa.eu.
Foreign Policy, www.foreignpolicy.com.
Gallup.
Global Post, www.globalpost.com.

Global Security, www.gobalsecurity.org.
Huffington Post, www.huffingtonpost.com.
Human Rights First, http://lib.ohchr.org.
Human Rights Watch.
Institute of War and Peace Reporting, www.iwpr.net.
International Crisis Group, www.crisisgroup.org.
Jamestown Foundation Eurasia Daily Monitor.
Konrad Adenauer Stiftung.
New Citizen Centre (Ukraine).
Omidlyar Network.
Open Society Foundation.
Pando.com.
Pew Global Research, www.pewglobal.org.
Professor Ivan Katchanovski's Facebook Page, www.facebook.com/ivan.katchanovski.
Ron Paul Institute.
Russia—Other Points of View, www.russiaotherpointsofview.com.
Stratfor, www.stratfor.com.
Window on Eurasia, http://windowoneurasia.blogspot.com.
YouTube, www.youtube.com.

Official U.S. Government Sources

Radio Free Europe/Radio Liberty.
Radio Svoboda.
U.S. State Department website, www.state.gov.
White House website, www.whitehouse.gov.
United States Agency for International Development (USAID), http://pdf.usaid.gov.
Voice of America, www.voanews.com.

Independent Russian Newspapers and News Agencies

Izvestiya.
Kommersant.
Komsomolskaya Pravda.
Literaturnaya gazeta.
Moskovskii komsomolets.
Nezavisimaya gazeta.
Nezavisimaya gazeta—Stsenarii.
Novaya gazeta.
Radio Ekho Moskvy, http://echo.msk.ru.
Russia Direct.
Russkaya vesna, 29 June 2014, http://rusvesna.su.
Vedomosti.

Official Russian Government Sources

Itar-Tass.
Krasnaya Zvezda.
RIA Novosti.
Rossiiskaya gazeta.
Russia Today International Television Channel.

Russian Federation President's Office, www.kremlin.ru.
Russian Ministry of Foreign Affairs website, www.mid.ru.
Sputnik, http://sputniknews.com.
State Statistics Committee of the Russian Federation (GosKomStat), www.gks.ru.

Non-State Russian Websites and Think Tanks

Delovaya gazeta, www.vz.ru.
Gazeta, www.gazeta.ru.
Inforos.ru.
LifeNews.ru, www.lifenews.ru.
Moskovskii tsentr Karnegi, http://carnegie.ru.
Novyi region, http://www.nr2.ru.
Online TV, www.onlinetv.ru.
Pravda, http://english.pravda.ru.
RBC, www.rbc.ru.
Regnum, www.regnum.ru.
Russia Profile, www.russiaprofile.ru.
Slon.ru, http://slon.ru.
Svobodnaya pressa, http://svpressa.ru.
Tsentr Levady (Levada Center), www.levada.ru.
TV Dozhd,' http://tvrain.ru.
VKontakte, http://vk.com.
Vserossiiskii tsentr issledovaniya obshchestvennogo mneniya (VTsIOM), http://wciom.ru.
Vzglad.ru, http://vz.ru.
Yevraziya.tv, www.evrazia-books.ru/.

International Governmental Organizations

Council of Europe, www.coe.int.
European Parliament, www.europarl.europa.eu.
International Energy Agency, www.iea.org.
North Atlantic Treaty Organization (NATO) official website, www.nato.int.
Organization on Security and Cooperation in Europe (OSCE), www.osce.org.

Interviews

Author's email interview with Sergei Stankevich, 23 November 2015.
Author's email interview with Sergei Stankevich, 16 December 2015.

Other Sources

Civil Georgia, www.civil.ge.
Johnson's Russia List.
The Messenger (Tbilisi).
Wikipedia.org, http://en.wikipedia.org.

Index